Deploying QoS for Cisco IP and Next-Generation Networks

Deploying QoS for Cisco IP and Next-Generation Networks

The Definitive Guide

Vinod Joseph

Brett Chapman

AMSTERDAM • BOSTON • HEIDELBERG • LONDON
NEW YORK • OXFORD • PARIS • SAN DIEGO
SAN FRANCISCO • SINGAPORE • SYDNEY • TOKYO
Morgan Kaufmann Publishers is an imprint of Elsevier

Morgan Kaufmann Publishers is an imprint of Elsevier
30 Corporate Drive, Suite 400, Burlington, MA 01803, USA

Library of Congress Cataloging-in-Publication Data
Joseph, Vinod.
Deploying QoS for Cisco IP and next generation networks : the definitive guide / Vinod Joseph, Brett Chapman.
p. cm.
Includes bibliographical references and index.
ISBN 978-0-12-374461-6 (hardcover)
1. Computer networks–Quality control. 2. Network performance (Telecommunication) 3. Cisco Systems, Inc. I. Chapman, Brett. II. Title.
TK5105.5956.J67 2009
004.6–dc22

2009003603

For information on all Morgan Kaufmann publications,
visit our Web site at: *www.mkp.com* or *www.books.elsevier.com*

Printed and bound by CPI Group (UK) Ltd, Croydon, CR0 4YY

Transferred to Digital Print 2011

Contents

Preface

Rationale

Next-generation networks, or NGNs, have emerged through several key drivers:

- Industry drive toward IP as the converged network layer protocol for applications
- IP network technology evolving toward multiservice, carrier-class, and high-bandwidth capabilities
- The opportunity for consolidation of disparate network infrastructures and operational teams

The emergence of the Internet and IP has fueled unprecedented growth in IP-capable desktop and laptop computers. This trend has quickly been embraced by the enterprise sector in terms of productivity tools for workers. Desktop applications such as word processors, spreadsheets, and electronic mail have revolutionized the workplace, allowing much greater efficiency and cost effectiveness in companies of every size. Vendors realized the potential to disrupt entrenched communication technologies, such as voice and video, driving cheaper, more feature-rich IP products into these markets. This revolution heralded IP as the converged protocol for communications. The modern mobile phone, based on 3G or 4G, uses IP exclusively for communication of voice, signaling, and data, giving a reference for the extensive penetration of IP into application transport.

The Internet was originally a best-effort infrastructure in terms of traffic treatment and, often, availability and operational excellence. Network equipment was relatively simple, with modest features focused on availability and differentiated services. Internet service provider networks typically grew rapidly and organically with poor management and little or no change control or meaningful documentation. As applications with varying traffic requirements, such as voice, have been carried on IP networks, the need for network equipment to be more efficient, available, and priority aware has increased. Voice and associated signaling are clear examples of traffic for which best effort for packet transport and equipment availability is simply not adequate. IP communications equipment, network design, and operational practices have evolved to meet these new requirements.

Large telecommunications providers found that they were installing, operating, and maintaining multiple IP networks for Internet, enterprise VPN, mobile 3G, and internal enterprise applications. With the continuing maturity of IP communications networks toward scalable, multiservice, carrier-class-capable infrastructures, network providers are seizing the opportunity to consolidate costly equipment, transmission trunks, and operational teams.

Effective quality of service (QoS) is the cornerstone of network efficiency. Bandwidth on communications trunks, particularly overseas links, can be a large component of network provider budgets. Efficient use of these assets is essential for network providers to manage costs and, ultimately, business profits. QoS implementation, coupled with sound capacity planning processes, forms the basis for successfully meeting the traffic requirements of various services on the network in the most cost-effective manner.

The topics covered in this book provide a comprehensive guide to implementation of quality of service in a multiservice Cisco IP network.

Organization and Approach

The chapters in this book focus on building the fundamentals of QoS and developing the specific configurations for network deployment on selected platforms and line-card types.

Chapter 1 gives an overview of the evolution of communications systems toward the highly complex, multiservice IP networks of the modern era. Chapter 2 introduces the QoS framework and standards as applied to NGNs. Chapter 3 reviews the requirements for QoS in a "Quad-Play" network running voice, video, data, and mobility. Chapter 4 covers the QoS framework and configuration for customer edge routers in a Cisco IP NGN.

Chapter 5 gives technical background on the evolution of mobile networks toward the Third Generation and a framework for QoS implementation. Chapter 6 explores the concept of service assurance and service-level agreements (SLAs) in the context of IP NGN infrastructures. Chapter 7 reviews the architectural basics for the premier routing platforms from Cisco Systems: the CRS, the 12000, the ASR1000, and the 7600.

Chapter 8 investigates implementation models and device configurations for enterprise Layer 3 virtual private network (VPN) services in a service provider network. Chapter 9 covers Layer 2 VPNs. Chapter 10 reviews the implementation of QoS for Internet services. Chapter 11 covers QoS for multicast services. Chapter 12 explores testing recommendations for proving QoS is functioning as required and expected. Chapter 13 investigates the concept of performance monitoring and evaluates technical options available to NGN operators. Finally, Chapter 14 gives a summary and reviews the possible direction IP networks will take in the future.

Audience

This book is intended for solution architects and network engineers who are designing and implementing QoS on multiservice IP network infrastructures. Although the information in this book is more appropriate for service provider infrastructures, large enterprise network operators will find the details useful, since often they adopt a service provider business model.

Background information provided in this text, including fundamentals of 3G mobile and performance management frameworks, will be useful for solution architects who require an understanding of design in the context of the end-to-end technology. Chapters specific to device configuration will be relevant to network engineers responsible for network design and implementation.

Acknowledgments

Writing a book of this complexity while working full-time requires support both professionally and personally.

A special thanks to the document technical reviewer, Jeff Apcar, for his guidance and tireless effort in reviewing and refining each chapter and for his amazing attention to detail. His assistance has ensured an accurate, concise outcome.

I want to dedicate this book to my dear wife Vinitha and my loving daughter Rochelle, who had to sacrifice so much of their time with me. My wife constantly provided me with all the support and motivation needed to ensure that this dream became a reality. This book is also dedicated to my mother Tanis (who gave me the foundation in life) and Grandparents Hylda James and Harold James (who taught me to dream), all of whom gave me the values in life that helped me attain this level.

Vinod Joseph, United Kingdom

Further thanks to my manager, John Bateman, for his understanding and flexible approach to work commitments, allowing me to keep the book on schedule. Finally, a special thanks to my family and friends for their support and understanding while I worked on this book.

Brett Chapman, Singapore

About the Authors

Vinod Joseph is a Service Provider Solution Architect for Cisco Systems Asia Pacific and has over 15 years of industry experience. Vinod provides architectural design, advisory services, and service support to a number of large carriers and operators in the Asia Pacific, Europe, Middle East, and Emerging Markets regions. These organizations include Telekom Malaysia, BSNL India, Beijing Communications Corporation (a subsidiary of China Netcom), Vodafone Middle East, Telekomsel Indonesia, and Tata VSNL India. The network deployment in Tata VSNL India is the largest metro Ethernet triple-play network in the world; this deployment, for which Vinod was the technical leader, involved one of the largest network integration projects ever undertaken.

Vinod's responsibility includes the planning and design of large network architectures, together with guiding deployment and providing operational advice. At Cisco Vinod has overseen the deployment of MPLS-IP in both enterprise and service provider environments. He has also been largely instrumental in helping carriers migrate quad-play applications to IP NGN infrastructures.

Prior to joining Cisco, Vinod worked with a large consulting and professional services partner of Juniper Networks, helping to build some of the largest service provider and carrier networks in Asia.

Vinod holds dual Master's degrees in business management and computer engineering from the United States.

Brett Chapman is a Service Provider Solution Architect for Cisco Systems Singapore. Brett is responsible for the design and implementation of large, multiservice IP networks in the Asia Pacific region. Previously Brett worked as a senior network consultant for Pacific Bell in California. Brett holds a Bachelor's degree in electronics and communication engineering from the University of Canberra, Australia.

CHAPTER 1

The Evolution of Communication Systems

From the traditional telecommunications point of view, the network is a way to link two end devices from different locations for short periods of time. Network users generally pay for access to the telecom network as well as paying per-connection charges.

Contrast this scenario with the traditional data networking ideology, whereby the media are shared by groups of people all working at the same time. Data represented the important aspect of the system; the network was merely a resource allowing users to execute applications, such as browsing Websites, sending email, printing documents, and transferring files. Whether it took 2 seconds or 20 for the transfer of data was not the issue in general; the priority was that the data were received uncorrupted.

Both the telecom and the data networking industries have changed over time, particularly with the convergence of user requirements and expectations. The need for real-time media formats such as audio, video, and gaming has certainly increased the bandwidth requirements, as has applications development, embedding more media-rich functionality in basic desktop programs such as word processing and yielding larger files. Real-time audio- and videoconferencing over data networks have created a need for the same real-time quality-of-service (QoS) guarantees that the telecom industry has enjoyed since the inception of digital telephony. Even within nonreal-time data communications, there has been a drive for differentiated delivery based on premium paying customers and the expectation for service-level agreement contracts between service providers and enterprises.

This chapter gives a brief overview of QoS definitions and the evolution toward converged, IP-based next-generation networks (NGNs). Both the underlying transmission infrastructure and the overlayed transport networks are discussed.

1.1 Quality-of-Service Definition

There is no true formal definition of QoS. Protocol frameworks such as asynchronous transfer mode, or ATM (discussed in a later section), started the concept of QoS in response to networks converging to carry data with varying requirements. ATM can provide QoS guarantees on bandwidth and delay for the transfer of real-time and nonreal-time data.

In seeking a definition, the following sources give insight into what QoS means:

- The International Telecommunication Union (ITU) standard X.902, Information Technology/Open Distributed Processing Reference Model, defines QoS as "A set of quality requirements on the collective behavior of one or more objects." QoS parameters are listed as the speed and reliability of data transmission, that is, throughput, transit delay, and error rate.

- The ATM Lexicon defines QoS as "A term which refers to the set of ATM performance parameters that characterize the traffic over a given virtual connection." These parameters include cell loss ratio, cell error rate, cell misinsertion rate, cell delay variation, cell transfer delay, and average cell transfer delay.
- The IEEE paper *Distributed Multimedia and Quality of Service: A Survey* provides a general definition of QoS for real-time applications: "The set of those quantitative and qualitative characteristics of a distributed multimedia system, which are necessary in order to achieve the required functionality of an application."

A starting point for the definition for QoS comes from the Internet Engineering Task Force (IETF). RFC-1946, Native ATM Support for ST2+, states: "As the demand for networked real time services grows, so does the need for shared networks to provide deterministic delivery services. Such deterministic delivery services demand that both the source application and the network infrastructure have capabilities to request, setup, and enforce the delivery of the data."

Ultimately the goal of a QoS framework is to ensure that data are transferred in a deterministic manner that at least meets the performance requirements of each service being delivered.

1.2 Transmission Infrastructure Evolution

In the late 1800s, signals were analog and were allocated a single channel per physical line for transmission—technology called *circuit switching*. Development of the vacuum tube led to analog systems employing Frequency-Division Multiplexing (FDM) in 1925, allowing multiple circuits across a single physical line. Coaxial cable infrastructure started deployment in the 1930s, allowing greater bandwidth (and resulting in more circuits) to the telecom provider and yielding a more efficient infrastructure.

In the early 1970s the invention of transistors and the concept of Pulse Code Modulation (PCM) led to the first digital channel bank featuring toll-quality transmission. Soon after, a high-bit-rate digital system employing Time-Division Multiplexing (TDM) was realized, allowing digital multiplexing of circuits and giving further efficiency in the use of physical communications infrastructure.

Advances in FDM and TDM allowed greater efficiency in physical infrastructure utilization. TDM communicates the bits from multiple signals alternatively in timeslots at regular intervals. A timeslot is allocated to a connection and remains for the duration of the session, which can be permanent, depending on the application and configuration. The timeslot is repeated with a fixed period to give an effective throughput.

Multirate circuit switching was the next step away from basic circuit switching. This is an enhancement to the synchronous TDM approach used initially in circuit switching. In circuit switching, a station must operate at a fixed data rate regardless of application requirements. In multirate switching, multiplexing of a base bandwidth is introduced. A station attaches to the network by means of a single physical link, which carries multiple fixed data-rate channels (for example, in the case of ISDN, B-channel at 64 kbps). The user has a number of data-rate choices through multiplexing basic channels. This allows for services of different rates to be accommodated, whereby the number of channels allocated is greater than or equal to the service bandwidth.

The next evolutionary step from pure circuit switching is fast circuit switching (FCS). This transfer mode attempts to address the problem of handling sources with a fluctuating natural information rate. FCS only allocates resources and establishes a circuit when data need to be sent. However, the rapid allocation and deallocation of resources required to achieve this goal proved complex and required high signaling overhead. Ultimately and quickly, FCS became infeasible as more high data-rate services emerged with the dominance of data over voice transport.

It was not until the advent of optical transmission systems that the very high-bandwidth systems we know today emerged. Optical transmission is accomplished by modulating transmitted information by a laser light-emitting diode, or LED, passing the information signal over optical fiber and reconstructing the information at the receiving end. This technology yielded 45 Mbps optical communications systems, which have developed to 1.2, 1.7, and 2.4 Gbps. The emergence of Dense Wave-Division Multiplexing (DWDM) technology has seen the potential bandwidth over a single fiber reach 400 Gbps and beyond.

In the mid-1980s the most common digital hierarchy in use was plesiosynchronous digital hierarchy (PDH). A *digital hierarchy* is a system of multiplexing numerous individual base-rate channels into higher-level channels. PDH is called *plesio* (Greek for *almost*) because the transmission is neither wholly synchronous nor asynchronous. PDH was superseded by synchronous digital hierarchy (SDH) and synchronous optical network (SONET), which took the PDH signals and multiplexed them into a synchronous time-division multiplexing (STM) of basic signals. So, development went from asynchronous multiplexing used in PDH to synchronous multiplexing in SDH/SONET.

In contemporary NGN systems with the emergence of IP-based networks, many service providers are using simple underlying DWDM optical switch physical infrastructure or even driving dark fiber directly from the IP routing and switching equipment.

DWDM works by combining and transmitting multiple signals simultaneously at different wavelengths on the same fiber. In effect, one fiber is transformed into multiple virtual fibers. So, if you were to multiplex eight 2.5 Gbps signals into one fiber, you would increase the carrying capacity of that fiber from 2.5 Gbps to 20 Gbps. DWDM technology can drive single fibers to transmit data at speeds up to 400 Gbps.

A key advantage to DWDM is that it is protocol and bit-rate independent. DWDM-based networks can transmit data in IP, ATM, SDH/SONET, and Ethernet and handle bit rates between 100 Mbps and multiples of 2.5 Gbps.

1.3 The First Global Communications Network: PSTN

Communications networks began with the telegraph system in the 1800s. The first recorded telegraph line was connected in 1844 from Washington, D.C., to Baltimore. In 1858 the first transatlantic cable was commissioned. By 1860 the telegraph system covered the majority of the United States.

The start of the 19th century saw the establishment of the analog public switched telephone network, or PSTN. Users were connected using temporary circuits through switches. This revolutionary approach was known as *circuit switching* as mentioned earlier. Alexander Graham Bell actually envisaged the telephone network as a one-way communications system for broadcasting music. As others became aware of the existence of Bell's invention, they realized the potential for two-way communication—hence the birth of Morse code messages and ultimately the existence of the PSTN.

As previously discussed, circuit switching allocates a dedicated line on the network path between the communicating parties. Channel capacity has to be available and reserved between each pair of nodes on the path, and each node has to have a switching capability to ensure that the next hop is correct.

For various applications, utilization of the line can vary enormously and can be very inefficient, even for voice applications during periods in which neither party is speaking. However, there is little delay and effective transparency for the users transferring information, whether that is voice or data, once the circuit is established.

TDM provides a fixed bit rate for transmission, which leads to problems in handling services of vastly different bit rates or fluctuating information rates, as was the case for data applications. TDM-based networks also tend to be inefficient because the bandwidth is dedicated to a communications circuit and if the end users are not active within the session, the bandwidth cannot be utilized for other users.

Through the 1970s and 1980s, data transfer through interconnection of computer systems rapidly became a requirement in parallel with the explosive growth of voice communications. This greatly influenced the direction of network development. The following section discusses the Computer Age and the advent of data internetworking.

1.4 The Internet and TCP/IP History

Much of the available Internet history literature suggests that the Internet began with some military computers in the Pentagon in a network called the Advanced Research Projects Agency Network (or Arpanet) in 1969. One theory is that the network was designed to survive a nuclear attack. This project led to the development of the Internet protocols sometime during the 1970s.

In reality, Bob Taylor, the Pentagon official in charge of the Arpanet, suggests that the purpose was not military but scientific. According to Taylor, there was no consideration of surviving a nuclear attack. In fact, Larry Roberts, who was employed to build the Arpanet, has stated that Arpanet was not even intended to be a communications infrastructure.

The Arpanet was invented to make it possible for research institutions to use the processing power of other institutions' computers when they had large calculations to do that required more power or when other agencies' computers were better suited for a given task.

The most notable contribution of the Arpanet project was to evolve packet-switching communications techniques. In 1965, before the Arpanet came into existence, a British engineer named Donald Davies developed the concept of packet switching, a means by which discrete messages can travel from point to point across a network. There was concurrent work across the United States on technologies that could be considered packet switching; however, it was Davies' brainchild that first powered the Arpanet.

The Arpanet therefore made some significant discoveries that were to result in the creation of the first Internet. These include electronic mail, data packet-switching implementations, and development of the Transport Control Protocol/Internet Protocol (TCP/IP).

TCP/IP, the communications protocol used as the basis for the Internet, was developed in the 1970s in California by Vinton Cerf, Bob Kahn, Bob Braden, Jon Postel, and other members of the Networking Group headed by Steve Crocker. TCP/IP was developed to enhance earlier communication between computers in the Arpanet.

In 1972 the Arpanet was demonstrated at the International Computer Communications Conference in Washington, D.C. Subsequently, an international networking group chaired by Vinton Cerf was established.

Although it is not clear who first used the word *Internet*, the term actually referred to *internetworking* rather than any reference to IP. By 1975 the first prototype protocols were being tested, and in 1978 TCP/IPv4 was released. TCP/IP was officially added to the Arpanet in 1983.

1.5 The Computer Age

The first notable roots of the modern computer were developed during World War II by the U.K. government (the Colossus project) and the U.S. government (the ENIAC project). The invention of the transistor in 1947 was an enormous step in the acceleration of computing power.

In the 1960s, Texas Instruments, Fairchild Computing, and IBM truly embraced the computing age with revolutionary and, for the time, extraordinarily powerful computing mainframes. The Arpanet and the other research networks adopted these platforms for use by scientists to explore the obvious potential of these computers.

The first true personal computer, the Altair 8800, was delivered to customers in 1975. In 1977 the Radio Shack TRS 80, the Apple II, and the Commodore PET were added to the personal computer market. IBM certainly raised the technology bar in this space with the release of the first IBM PC in the early 1980s.

Apple Computer, founded by Steve Jobs and Steve Wozniak, dominated the personal computing market through the 1980s, at one stage holding more than three quarters of the global PC market. The original Apple operating system was AppleDOS, evolving into the CP/M operating system in the 1980s. At the same time, a little-known engineer named Bill Gates released a new version of his operating system, called MS-DOS ("MS" standing for Microsoft).

1.6 Computer Internetworking

Personal computers, and indeed the first-generation mainframes, were initially designed as standalone processing powerhouses with no consideration given to communications. The possibilities of connecting these computers quickly became apparent—hence the concept of networks. Two connection methods were quickly developed: the modem and Ethernet.

Ethernet, the invention of an Arpanet contractor, Robert Metcalfe, was a protocol developed for *local area networks* (LANs), originally intended to connect devices within the same room. Ethernet was an extension of the packet-switching and Internet protocols being developed for the Arpanet, adapted for use on short-reach cabled networks. After the Arpanet research, Metcalfe founded a company called 3Com, which pioneered Ethernet products for networking mainframes and minicomputers in 1981. 3Com expanded the product line the following year to include personal computer local area networking.

The requirement to communicate over distances beyond the reach of Ethernet was driven by applications such as electronic mail. Technologists sought to leverage the existing, extensive PSTN communication network for point-to-point data communications; hence the invention of the modem. Modems could generate analog signals compatible with the PSTN from the digital computer data.

Modems became commercially available in the 1970s and allowed communications at 75 bps. In 1994, modems using highly effective compression techniques could communicate at 28.8 kbps, which was considered the limit of the technology. But along came the 56 k modem and a new set of standards, so the speeds continued to push the envelope of the capacity of the telephone system.

Although the geographical expanse was an advantage, the analog PSTN was unsuitable for data communications in terms of bandwidth and channel noise. The high noise on the PSTN forced modems to negotiate lower throughput rates and to implement error-correcting protocols; hence there was dramatically reduced throughput of data.

With these data communications developments in place, technology was readily available to connect both within a short distance and over long distances by leveraging the PSTN. As networks grew, companies such as Novell and Cisco drove the communications industry from this point. By the mid-1980s, the tools required for an explosion in internetworking and the Internet were in place.

X.25 and Frame Relay are the most common examples of packet switching. These technologies are discussed in the following sections.

1.7 X.25 Packet Switching

Circuit switching was proving inadequate in the face of emerging data communications internetworking through the 1970s. Data communications typically comprises short bursts of information followed by little or no traffic. The ability to dynamically assign resources with the flexibility required to satisfy data requirements could not be adequately addressed with circuit-based communication systems.

The packet-switching transfer mode is a significant step away from circuit switching. Packet switching uses only resources required by the application by transferring packets as data are available. Trunk connections are statistically multiplexed rather than circuit based, with obvious benefits to packet-switch network providers. These attributes of the mode make it flexible and efficient in terms of bandwidth allocation for both end users and service providers.

X.25 emerged globally from the 1970s as a standards-based packet-switched network protocol. X.25 and associated protocols were complex, statistically multiplexed, virtual circuit-based technology. They use virtual circuits in the sense that the underlying technology is packet switched; however, the connection to the end devices appears as a circuit for the duration of a session.

The X.25 packet-switching protocol was intended to operate on low quality and subsequently high bit-error-rate channels. The X.25 protocol suite was therefore highly complex, with significant overhead. An X.25 system performs error correction functions at every transmission hop, from the edges of the network through intermediate switches, therefore introducing significant time delays in the transfer end to end. These inherent delays prevent X.25 from transferring at high speeds required by emerging applications or latency- and jitter-sensitive real-time data.

X.25 was more bandwidth effective for data communications than circuit switching by virtue of the packet-switching technology. This inherent advantage gave a cheaper data network alternative compared to leased lines because communications service providers could more efficiently use expensive global bandwidth across many customers. X.25 also allowed more granular bandwidth access speeds to more closely match user requirements.

X.25 was also very flexible because it was a globally and uniquely addressed network protocol, deliberately mimicking the PSTN and allowing dynamic connection from a given point to any other compatible network terminal for data transfer.

Private global network enterprises would operate separate networks for voice and data when they utilized X.25 for digital data. The capital savings typically far outweighed the inconvenience of managing two communications systems.

1.8 The Evolution of Packet Switching: Frame Relay

The advantages of packet switching to end users and network operators for data communications were becoming clear through the proliferation of X.25. Further advances in computer technology drove the requirement for networks to provide higher-speed data transfer. The physical communications infrastructure was also evolving into a faster, more reliable transport medium (fewer bit errors) through the 1980s. These forces led to the more streamlined data transfer protocol known as Frame Relay.

Frame Relay (FR) drastically reduces complexity and delays by moving the error correction functions to the edge of the network only. Each switch inside a Frame Relay network simply switches the data frame to the next node with a simple cyclic redundancy check (CRC) rather than the overhead of error detection and correction. Given that X.25 performs error correction on a per-hop basis, FR was clearly positioned as a new-generation, faster technology for data transfer. Frame Relay was implemented by network operators as an upgrade to X.25 and typically provides an enhanced throughput of up to 140 Mbps.

The FR protocol implementation is similar to that of an X.25 network except that all virtual circuits are permanently assigned. This made dimensioning of networks and provisioning of customers easier for providers. X.25 circuits are generally initiated and ended from the end-user access terminals as required.

1.9 Asynchronous Transfer Mode

Asynchronous Transfer Mode (ATM) was designed as a single unified networking standard that could support both circuit-switched networking and packet-based networking.

ATM was a significant step in the convergence of real-time and nonreal-time applications on a single communications infrastructure. ATM was the first protocol suite to enable true differentiation of traffic classes and certainly set the standards by which subsequent technologies are measured. In fact, the ATM approach to QoS is the foundation for much of the mechanisms and terminology used in IP-based, QoS-aware networks of the modern era.

ATM is a virtual circuit-based technology through which a connection is established between the two endpoints before the data exchange begins. The term *asynchronous* refers to the switching of cells, whereas the bit stream that carries the cell is actually synchronous. Asynchronous, in the context of ATM, means that sources are not limited to sending data (or cells) during a set timeslot, which is the case with circuit switching, a truly synchronous technology.

ATM was conceived as the transport technology for the Broadband Integrated Services Digital Network (B-ISDN) that was intended to be the new-generation communications standard. The ATM standard was defined to cater to the telecommunications community and the computer internetworking community.

ATM attempted to carry all forms of traffic and hence proved a highly complex technology. ATM supported applications from global telecommunications networks to local area computer networks. ATM has been a partial success as a holistic technology, but the intended goal of providing a single integrated technology for LANs, public networks, and user services was never truly realized.

The ATM cell concept is streamlined to allow very high-speed switching. The fixed length of the ATM cell simplifies the transmission and reception of the cell compared with the variable-length packets of Frame Relay and Ethernet.

The fundamental design goal of the ATM protocol suite was to efficiently provide bandwidth to both time- and delay-sensitive, real-time services such as voice and video and to loss-sensitive, nonreal-time services such as computer data. This design brief led to the birth of the QoS concept as we know it today.

ATM defined five distinct QoS classes: Constant Bit Rate (CBR), Variable Bit Rate–Real Time (VBR-RT), Variable Bit Rate–Non-Real Time (VBR-nRT), Unspecified Bit Rate (UBR), and Available Bit Rate (ABR).

The CBR service class is intended for real-time applications—those applications sensitive to delay and jitter. Applications reliant on TDM, such as "raw" voice or video, are the perfect candidates for CBR QoS.

The real-time VBR service class is intended for real-time applications that are sensitive to delay and jitter. Sources are assumed to transmit at a rate that varies with time. Examples are compressed voice or video.

The nonreal-time VBR service class is intended for nonreal-time applications that have bursty traffic. These applications are less sensitive to delay and jitter parameters. Examples are video playback, video training, and other types of download-then-play-back applications.

The UBR service class is intended for applications that are not sensitive to delay and jitter. Sources are expected to transmit in short bursts. The UBR service is often referred to as a *best-effort service* that does not specify bit rate or traffic parameters. An example of UBR is basic computer communications such as Internet browsing or storing files on servers.

ABR, like UBR, is a best-effort service, with allowances made for some guarantee of cell delivery.

The failure of ATM as a true converged protocol suite partly lies in its complexity. This complexity resulted in high cost of devices, which certainly limited adoption in LANs. Ethernet rapidly overtook ATM in terms of speed at a much lower cost point for both device access and switch internetworking.

As discussed in the following section, TCP/IP emerged as a unified network layer for any data link, so the complexity and expense of ATM were no longer warranted. With various driving forces at work, TCP/IP also acted as a converged network layer for voice, video, and data. IP-based network equipment vendors quickly recognized and embraced the QoS inherent in the ATM protocol suite, obviating the need for a separate ATM network. With the mechanisms for QoS in place and using ATM as the benchmark, IP gave a more flexible and simple solution.

1.10 Ethernet Beyond the LAN

Ethernet is well defined and understood, has an outstanding track record of service in LANs, and is very simple and cost effective to implement. Most important, few network-enabled appliances, from personal computers to the most complex control systems, are not equipped with an Ethernet connector. The Ethernet specification is extremely flexible in its application, from the variety of speeds at which it can operate to the services that can be offered and simple

Internet access to more complex offerings such as integrated voice, video, and data, widely referred to as *triple-play services.*

Over the years the continuous advancement of Ethernet technology has allowed it to move beyond its original LAN origins of a half-duplex shared medium. Ethernet today is a full-duplex, switched technology that not only rivals competing legacy wide area network (WAN) technologies such as ATM and Frame Relay but meets the requirements of metropolitan area networks (MANs) such as long-range transport, bandwidth capacity, and resiliency. The result is a combination of speed, scalability, operational simplicity, and economics that is driving Ethernet into both the WAN and the MAN.

The original Ethernet V1.0 specification emerged in 1980 and delivered a shared 10 Mbps half-duplex transport over 500 meters. This was eventually defined as a standard in ANSI/IEEE Standard 802.3-1985. Over the years a number of supplements to the standard have been defined to take advantage of improvements in the technologies, support additional network media, and provide higher data rates to meet the demands of bandwidth-intensive applications. One of the great enhancements in Ethernet efficiency came with the introduction of IEEE Standard 802.3x, allowing full-duplex operation. This enhancement allowed the transmit and receive signals to operate simultaneously, thereby doubling the available bandwidth. However, this type of operation only allows Ethernet devices to be connected at each end (usually PC/host to switch).

The IEEE standards of 802.3z (gigabit Ethernet over fiber) and 802.3ab (gigabit Ethernet over twisted pair, released in 1998) and 802.3ae (released in 2002) have allowed Ethernet to move into the gigabit range, providing abundant bandwidth for high-end networked applications. These gigabit Ethernet standards have resulted in a technological evolution in response to demands of the industry for greater bandwidth capabilities. The gigabit Ethernet standards allow operation over various physical layers such as multimode fiber (MMF), single-mode fiber (SMF), and shielded or unshielded twisted pair at distances of up to 40 Km for 10 gigabit Ethernet and 80 Km for 1 gigabit Ethernet. This long-range capability makes Ethernet an ideal transport mechanism in WANs and MANs.

One of the primary enablers for the use of Ethernet in the WAN and MAN space has been its evolution into a gigabit transport technology over long distances. As discussed, there has been an exponential growth in Ethernet bandwidth capability from half-duplex 10 Mbps to 100 Mbps Fast Ethernet over copper and fiber interfaces to the 10 Gbps full-duplex Ethernet of today.

1.11 IP as the Converged Protocol

As previously mentioned, the TCP/IP communications revolution gained added momentum through the extraordinary growth of the Internet. The Internet allowed any-to-any connection as well as access to vast amounts of information.

Businesses soon realized that the Internet could be leveraged to dramatically multiply potential buyers and hence the birth of electronic commerce, encompassing everything from banking to buying movie tickets to bidding for items in virtual auction houses. Internet-based business models allowed genuine globalization to flourish and fuelled further growth in the infrastructure.

With Ethernet-connected PCs using IP communication suites dominating the enterprise desktop business by the mid-1990s, vendors started to leverage this network infrastructure for other applications such as voice and video. Traditional purpose-built private automatic branch exchange (PABX) voice systems were replaced with feature-rich IP-enabled phones and server-based communication gateways using the same Ethernet network infrastructure as desktop computers.

Not only were the applications converging on the Ethernet infrastructure, they were also converging to the desktop PCs. As the PCs became more powerful, with ever-increasing processing power, disk capacity, and network access bandwidth, applications such as real-time videoconferencing and voice were soon running on the desktop. Inevitably these desktops used IP to communicate.

Cellular network phones started adopting computer technology to enhance functionality that required data applications, including basic Web access. As these devices became more powerful, even the cellular networks were carrying more and more data. Eventually standards were released for third-generation mobile handheld device networks, which were completely IP centric (3GPP Release 5). IP communicating devices were now clearly infringing on traditional telecommunications voice transmission boundaries across fixed and mobile line businesses.

1.12 The Emergence of Service-Level Agreements

Large enterprises were becoming increasingly reliant on their network infrastructure from the 1990s onward. Network downtime could not be tolerated because it carried all the applications critical to the heart of business execution. All forms of communications, from voice and video to mission-critical data for manufacturing and financial sectors, were carried on the network infrastructure. Downtime of mere minutes could potentially cost a business hundreds of thousands of dollars.

These private network operators were realizing that running these infrastructures was becoming a complex and expensive exercise. Building and maintaining networks capable of meeting application demands was extremely challenging. Highly skilled individuals were needed to run these networks in a market where technical engineering skills were in huge demand and therefore expensive. Coupled with the infrastructure itself, comprising expensive routers, switches, management platforms, and transport bandwidth, there were compelling reasons to seek the assistance of specialist providers.

Service providers (SPs) could support multiple customers over the same infrastructure operated by the same technical teams, allowing economies of scale that private operators could never hope to achieve. These SPs were specialists in operating such networks, giving enterprise customers the reasonable expectation of superior communications performance and uptime.

Customers who were previously using simple communications channels from the SPs, such as Frame Relay, ATM, or leased lines, now sought for SP involvement deeper into their networks. Given the emergence of IP as the *de facto* converged communication standard, the majority, if not all, of the communications customers were already using IP including data, voice, and video. Service providers implementing Multiprotocol Label Switching (MPLS) gave enterprises a virtual private network to carry IP applications with the security advantages of FR or ATM.

Enabling the outsourcing process required contracts outlining strict expectations on the service providers. These service-level agreements (SLAs) generally outlined performance parameters such as bandwidth, delay, jitter, packet loss, and network uptime that the customer required from the network infrastructure to successfully execute its business goals. How the service provider met these SLA parameters was of no concern to the customer, but failing to meet clauses would lead to repayment of part or even all of the service fees.

The required new network profile was now evident. Private network operators required varying degrees of priority across multiple real-time applications such as voice and video and nonreal-time data applications such as email, desktop, and mission-critical applications. The private network operators no longer wanted the headache of managing the infrastructure and maintaining the technical expertise required to meet stringent business demands.

1.13 The Service Provider Virtual Private Network

With enterprise customers seeking alternatives to operating their own network infrastructure, SPs sought to position themselves for this potential business offering.

The technical requirements to support this service generally included the following:

- Ability to connect the enterprise regionally and possibly globally with security at least equivalent to Layer 2 technologies such as Frame Relay and ATM.
- Ability to support different traffic types. The majority is IP traffic, including unicast and multicast, with some Layer 2 protocols such as Ethernet, ATM, and Frame Relay.
- Ability to support multiple applications with varying SLAs, such as voice, video, and data.
- The ability to support multiple classes of service within data, such as mission-critical applications, email, and Internet.
- The ability to provide high availability for mission-critical applications such as financial transactions.
- The ability to facilitate secured Internet access.
- The ability to connect remote users back to enterprise networks securely through the Internet.
- The ability to securely connect enterprises together with controlled access, referred to as *extranets*.

- The ability to support enterprises with very high security requirements dictating the use of encryption technology.
- The ability to introduce new services in a flexible, seamless, and timely manner.

Typically the service providers had a vast IP network for the Internet. However, as discussed in the following section, operational, technical, and security concerns led providers to roll out purpose-built IP networks using MPLS technology for enterprise customers.

These networks were generally highly complex, redundant, well managed, and controlled networks with the ability to support services portfolios and provision, enforce, and measure SLAs expected by the enterprise customer base. Interfaces to the Internet service provider (ISP) network was firewalled and tightly secured to minimize the impact to the risk-averse enterprise customers.

1.14 Evolution of the Telecommunications Industry

Providers now face an interesting trend in their network profiles. They typically have multiple independent networks to operate, which could include:

- A legacy ATM/FR network for data
- A dedicated corporate MPLS/IP-based network for enterprise customers
- A traditional voice network for fixed line
- A mobile voice network with some data-enabled gateways for GPRS
- An emerging, third-generation (3G) mobile network based on IP
- A best-effort Internet network
- A broadband data network that could be one or more of the following: digital subscriber line (DSL), cable, wireless, metro-Ethernet, or passive optical network (PON)-based technology

The ATM/FR networks were carrying less enterprise customer traffic because these customers moved to more efficient MPLS/IP-based networks. Instead, the ATM networks tended to backhaul broadband data in the form of DSL, from digital subscriber line access multiplexer (DSLAM) to some form of IP aggregator. The majority operators also leveraged the ATM network for mobile network base station connectivity.

The new generation of mobile network standards for the third generation (originating from 3GPP and 3GPP2) are completely IP based for signaling, voice, and data. This will ultimately render the existing mobile networks obsolete, requiring massive investment by telecom providers to remain competitive in this space.

Even the traditional voice business based on voice switches is being replaced with IP communicating devices. New emerging services such as IP-based TV and video on demand have recently emerged as services options leveraging the broadband access already deployed by SPs.

Effectively, the vast majority of existing and planned revenue-creating services streams in the telecommunications business were communicating using IP. IP had now genuinely evolved into the converged communications protocol.

The Internet was initially considered the "poorer cousin" of the huge telecom providers. As the Internet started to double in size every two to three months during the late 1990s, these telecom operators quickly realized its potential for revenue streams and started to either purchase or establish ISPs and invest heavily in these infrastructures. Some ISPs literally could not increase trunk bandwidth fast enough to meet demand. Having the telecom providers operating the ISPs allowed more streamlined provisioning of bandwidth to track the explosive demand because they generally controlled the physical infrastructure. The Internet networks now dominated the providers' network portfolios, having vast geographical penetration and bandwidth.

1.15 The Next-Generation Network Vision

Given the clear direction of IP as the converged network protocol, SPs sought to converge their IP services onto a single network infrastructure to streamline operation and capital expenditure. These services currently span at least four networks:

- A dedicated corporate MPLS/IP-based network for enterprise customers
- A 3G mobile network based on IP
- A vast, best-effort Internet network
- A broadband data network, which could be one or more of DSL, cable, wireless, metro-Ethernet, or PON-based technology

Owning and operating these networks multiply equipment and operational expenses. The convergence of these multiple infrastructures and services was the key to streamlined cost and superior operational efficiency.

As previously discussed, a successful converged infrastructure must deliver the following service categories:

- *Video services*. Video services, traditionally carried on terrestrial lines or air, satellite, or dedicated cable-based infrastructures, are moving to IP platforms capable of delivery over any broadband access technology.
- *Broadband networking*. Broadband access technologies are rapidly expanding. The transition from being used as simple Internet access to providing for networked home environments capable of multiple services is a clear direction for SPs.
- *Legacy wireline data services*. Many business data services are still being delivered through Frame Relay or ATM for technical reasons (possibly non-IP protocols) or perception reasons (e.g., customers feel that "new age" IPVPN networks are not secure).

- *Enterprise IP networking*. Recent times have seen the SP implementing MPLS/IP networks for enterprise customer connectivity.
- *Telephony services*. Traditional carrier telephony has moved toward packet technology as traditional circuit-switching vendors are shipping packet-based solutions. In addition, the convergence between fixed and mobile voice services is under way.
- *Wireless and mobile services*. As mobile services converge with fixed voice services, the mobile handset is becoming a multimedia window into the converged voice, video, and data world, with real-time video and online gaming all potential services.
- *Internet access*. Internet access is the cornerstone service for the IP network. Internet access will be a requirement across other services categories such as enterprise IP networking, wireless and mobile services, and broadband networking.

SP applications such as voice and Layer 2 ATM/FR are required to be "carrier class" at the service delivery level. These requirements must be carried into a packet network, so the IP infrastructure must be able to meet or exceed the same carrier-class requirement in delivery of the services.

The converged IP network will effectively replace multiple service delivery infrastructures used for various applications and services. In the case of the core devices particularly, many or all of the services may be carried through a single device. Concurrently, all service-specific requirements imposed by each individual service must be honored.

With IP as the common denominator, service- and feature-specific platforms will form the multicapable edge, converging around a common IP/optical core. Each different application and technology will place its own unique set of requirements on each layer of the IP infrastructure.

1.16 The Cisco Next-Generation Network Framework

Cisco Systems has developed a framework architecture to achieve the NGN vision. As depicted in Figure 1.1, central to the Cisco IP NGN framework are three fundamental areas of convergence:

- *Application convergence*. Carriers integrate new IP data, voice, and video applications to customer devices, including PCs, personal digital assistants (PDAs), or tablets over a single infrastructure for increased profitability.
- *Service convergence*. The Cisco IP NGN makes a service available to end users across any access technology. For example, a service available in the office can be available over a wireless LAN, a broadband connection, or a cellular network.
- *Network convergence*. As discussed, a converged network will eliminate multiple service-specific networks. Embracing a network model in which a single network can support all existing and new services will dramatically reduce the total cost of ownership for service providers.

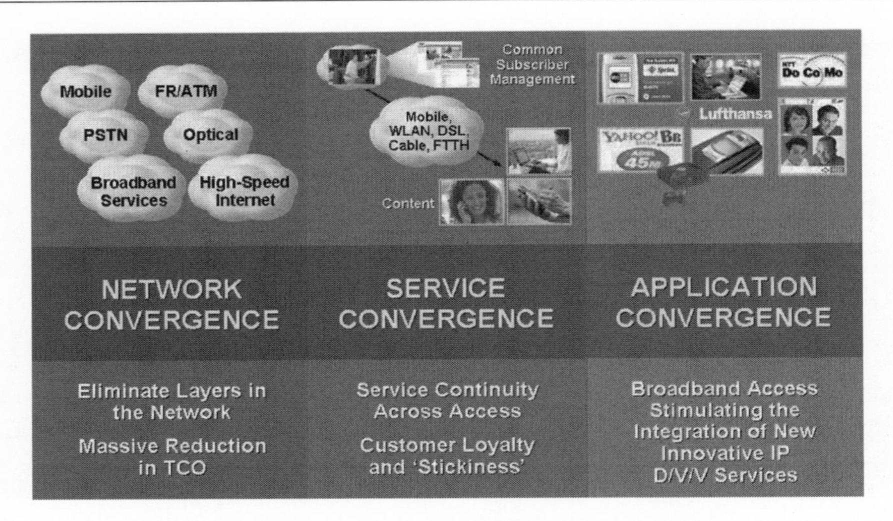

Figure 1.1: Cisco IP NGN Architectural Overview

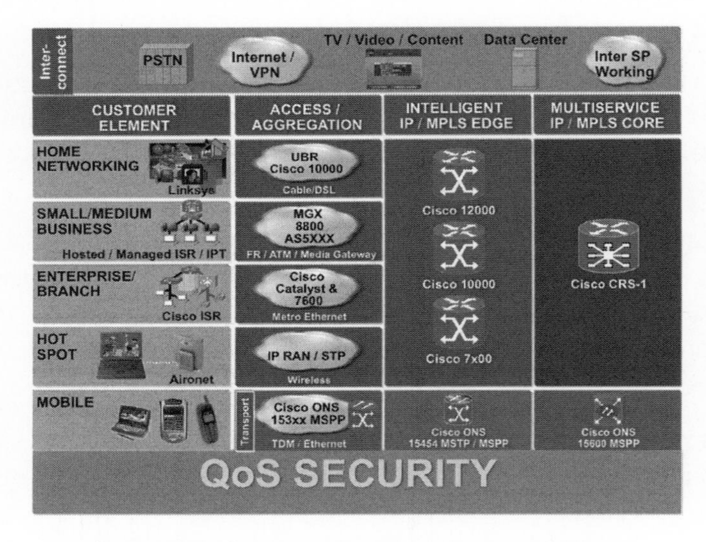

Figure 1.2: Cisco IP NGN Secure Network Layer

At the foundation of an IP NGN is a secure, QoS-capable network layer composed of a customer element, access and aggregation, intelligent edge, and multiservice core components, with transport and interconnect elements layered below and above.

As shown in Figure 1.2, the IP/MPLS core network forms the basis of the IP NGN architecture. Given that all services are built on this IP/MPLS core, this layer must meet the carrier-class requirement for this architecture to be viable.

Traditional services, such as PSTN voice, now being migrated to IP are perceived to have nearly perfect service quality on existing infrastructure, and the networks currently used to deliver them are designed with equipment that defines carrier class in every aspect. The converged IP infrastructure must likewise be carrier class if it is truly to be an alternative to the legacy infrastructure.

The requirements the IP NGN must meet to adequately carry services fall into five categories:

- *Service requirements*. These requirements are placed on the infrastructure for transparent delivery of services. Service requirements may differ between service providers and even between different tiers of the same service (for example, multiple classes of service within enterprise VPNs).
- *Network requirements*. These requirements are network specific, filtering down from specific services requirements, or they may be based on the overall performance requirements of the IP NGN infrastructure.
- *Security requirements*. With a converged network come much more stringent security requirements. Specific requirements for limiting access to services or service nodes should be deliverables as part of a security infrastructure and policy.
- *Operational requirements*. Services previously offered on TDM or traditional Layer 2-based architectures such as FR and ATM have existing operational requirements for tracking, troubleshooting, health monitoring, and proactive performance monitoring. These requirements must be adequately met by the new NGN infrastructure.
- *Network design*. The design of the network must ensure that the requirements of all previously listed categories are met. Most design decisions are made based on a cost-benefit analysis. What is important is that these decisions are made with the understanding of the tradeoffs involved.

1.17 The Network Requirements

To meet the strict requirements of services such as telephony and video, the IP NGN must have network attributes that might not be in place in current IP networks, with the possible exception of the modern enterprise VPN infrastructure.

The network-level requirements can be divided into three broad categories:

- *Network availability*. This is a prerequisite for service availability, ensuring that services remain available under changing conditions such as failure.
- *QoS*. The network elements in the service path must enforce a reliable QoS in accordance with the service requirements.
- *Predictable performance*. While providing the features necessary for a new service, the performance of existing services and subscribers must not be adversely impacted.

Modern IP networks are implemented with redundancy and features to ensure that stringent network availability goals are met in line with services such as mission-critical applications for enterprise customers. Unfortunately, this does not necessarily mean they are currently designed to deliver requirements of converged services such as toll-quality voice or video over cable. The basic requirement is that the NGN should meet the delay, jitter, and packet-loss requirements during reasonable network conditions, including peak load, unexpected stress, and failure.

Subsecond service restoration is often considered a fundamental criterion for a carrier-class infrastructure. This must be considered in selecting IP equipment, designing the network, and deciding on a protection and restoration strategy.

In a circuit-switched telephony environment, a resource conflict results in calls not being established, so if the appropriate resources cannot be reserved from end to end, the call is rejected. Resource conflicts in an IP environment are handled differently, and the consequences can affect not only the call about to be established but also established calls.

In a multiservice environment it is critical to ensure that certain traffic is treated with priority to ensure successful service delivery. Traffic types such as telephony and video do not generate bursts of traffic; however, these services must not suffer from the congestion caused by other traffic types that might be bursty in nature. Consistent and strict QoS and low-latency treatment, through every network element across the network, are prerequisites for predictable service performance.

Security is a fundamental consideration in the execution of an NGN strategy. Threats such as worms, viruses, denial-of-service (DoS) attacks, and other malicious activities commonplace on the Internet must not degrade service delivery. To ensure stability in the network, strategies that cover several different areas need to be in place:

- *Network element security*. Providing strong security starts at the node level. Every network element must provide sufficient protection of its own resources and services.
- *Network and IP-spoofing protection*. Providing infrastructure security includes blocking access to internally used addresses, IP spoofing protection and blocking, DoS protection and tracking, and more.
- *Control-plane protection*. Protected control-plane operation is imperative to ensure stable operation of the network. This protection includes both internal and external protection policies, since attacks may originate from either.
- *Service protection*. Enabling service-specific security policies can be an effective threat mitigation strategy.

Network design is the cornerstone to meeting carrier-class requirements. The design phase must take input from the entire scope of requirements across service, network, security, and operations. Without all these elements taken into account, the NGN's ability to successfully meet expectations will be compromised.

The fundamental design goal for a carrier-class IP network is to enable deterministic network behavior during any reasonable operating conditions. For example, the IP NGN infrastructure must be able to meet services SLAs in the event of transport and device outages. Ideally, the

NGN should be capable of converging and rerouting without the service users even being aware that an outage has occurred. Achieving this goal is a matter of balancing infrastructure investment against reasonable assumptions around failure scenarios.

The IP NGN framework is fundamentally changing the way that service providers build networks. Service-level requirements inherited from previous services and networks, including non-IP, must be honored. This makes the NGN the first true carrier-class IP-based network framework encompassing strict requirements from traditional PSTN voice to evolving services such as Internet Protocol television (IPTV) with arguably even harsher SLAs. QoS is the key to building this NGN network efficiently.

1.18 The Path to the Next-Generation Network

With the NGN vision understood, service providers now must formulate the best possible path toward realizing the NGN dream. To meet the goal of a converged infrastructure, the SP has various options. The three approaches most worthy of consideration are as follows:

- Upgrade the existing ISP network.
- Upgrade the existing enterprise VPN infrastructure.
- A completely new core network.

The ultimate choice relies on a variety of factors, sometimes competing:

- Optimal reuse of existing equipment
- Minimum disruption to existing services
- Minimum complexity and risk in the migration process
- Ensuring that the new infrastructure is flexible, scalable, and manageable well beyond the capacity and baseline services required from Day 1

1.19 Upgrade the Existing ISP Network

As discussed, SPs generally had substantial ISP networks installed on dedicated IP infrastructure. The broadband access technologies already deployed for Internet connectivity were viewed as the fastest way to implement services across residential users, the majority of the SPs' customer base. This same technology could also be leveraged to connect small/medium-sized business customers for value-added services beyond Internet access.

These ISP networks had evolved over more than a decade, with operational equipment often spanning this entire period. Many ISPs started with dialup remote access servers and low-bandwidth links for applications such as email.

The roots of the ISP networks were best effort, with no regard for class of service enforcement, and in fact much of the existing equipment lacked the technical ability to support any form of QoS. These networks had endured unprecedented explosive growth, resulting in organic, uncontrolled network growth.

The ISP often lacked any change control or accurate documentation for the infrastructure, with necessary knowledge held by a select few engineers. There were also few overlaying management systems with day-to-day operations relying on network engineers who preferred manual telnet to provision connections and troubleshoot infrastructure issues.

There are also substantial security concerns related to the Internet globally. The infrastructure typically included primitive mechanisms such as access lists and reverse-path forwarding checks for security. More modern features allowing rate limiting of traffic types that may be attacks evolved over time; however, these cannot hope to match purpose-built appliances such as firewalls and intrusion detection systems for effectiveness. The majority of Internet autonomous system infrastructure devices are publicly addressed to facilitate troubleshooting, leaving critical router and switch devices open to attack unless complex access lists are employed.

Basically the Internet is an open, global network that places the onus for security on end users. In the worst case, an infrastructure DoS attack can impact any traffic transiting the router device.

Considering these limitations, the prospect of upgrading the Internet infrastructure to support an NGN's requirements was daunting, to say the least.

1.20 Upgrade the Existing Enterprise VPN Infrastructure

The enterprise MPLS/IP network operated by SPs was the next candidate for the NGN nucleus. This network typically has the technology, availability, and operational mechanisms to meet NGN requirements encompassing availability, class-of-service differentiation, and security.

However, the enterprise service network was typically not designed to meet the bandwidth requirements for broadband services such as Internet and video without forklift upgrades of core equipment. In some cases, providers had chosen adequate equipment that could simply be upgraded to NGN bandwidth; however, this is certainly the exception rather than the rule.

1.21 A Completely New Core Network

The third option has proved to be the most popular among large providers contemplating the NGN concept. These providers are preferring to install dedicated NGN core infrastructure with very large routers, such as the CRS-1, and migrating services in a controlled fashion across to the new infrastructure. This ensures scalability and the features required for services across traditional networks such as Internet, enterprise, ATM/FR, and 3G as well as emerging services such as voice and video over IP (VoIP).

1.22 What's in This Book

QoS is arguably the most important aspect of these NGN infrastructures if expensive network resources such as bandwidth and routers are to be efficiently utilized. Effective, scalable execution of an end-to-end QoS framework is discussed later in this book.

The chapters in this book are as follows:

Chapter 2: Introduction to Cisco's Quality-of-Service Architecture for IP Networks. This chapter introduces concepts such as the QoS framework using Cisco Modular QoS CLI; QoS mechanisms including congestion avoidance, congestion management, and scheduler modes; the QoS functional flow; the trust boundary in managed vs. unmanaged CE scenarios; QoS transparency with DiffServ tunneling modes; and the enterprise-to-SP-class mapping models.

Chapter 3: Class-of-Service Requirements for Quad-Play Networks. This chapter introduces concepts such as service-level agreements; budgeting for traffic classes; guidelines and requirements for data, voice, and video traffic; call admission control for voice and video traffic; QoS design for data, voice, and video traffic; guidelines and requirements for control and signaling traffic; classifying and grouping applications into QoS categories; Cisco's QoS baseline; RFC-4594 configuration; guidelines for DiffServ classes; in-contract traffic, out-of-contract traffic, and QoS and network perimeter security.

Chapter 4: Carrier CE Services in Cisco IP NGN Networks. This chapter covers the configuration options for Customer Equipment (CE) connectivity to IP NGN networks in both managed and unmanaged options.

Chapter 5: Quality of Service for IP Mobile Networks. This chapter discusses topics such as the transition of mobile networks to IP, mobile applications and QoS requirements, grouping mobile applications within the DiffServ framework, Cisco's QoS solution suite for mobile operators, and recommendations for QoS deployment in mobile networks.

Chapter 6: QoS Service Assurance. This chapter covers service-level agreements and metrics for measurement, trends in service provider networks, creating baseline information for QoS measurement, tools for creating baseline information, and creating a meaningful index of baseline information for MQC and PFC-based QoS.

Chapter 7: Cisco CRS-1, 12000, 7600, and ASR1000 Router Architecture. This chapter introduces the hardware architectures for the four prominent Service Provider routing platforms in the Cisco product range.

Chapter 8: Cisco IOS and IOS-XR Quality-of-Service Implementation for MPLS Layer 3 VPN Services. This chapter includes implementation of edge and core devices for CRS-1, 12000, 7200, and 7600 series routers and implementation template for SP-managed CE devices using Cisco IOS.

Chapter 9: Cisco IOS and IOS-XR Quality-of-Service Implementation for Carrier Ethernet and Virtual Leased-Line Services. This chapter covers implementation of edge and core devices for CRS-1, 12000, 7200, and 7600 series routers.

Chapter 10: Cisco IOS and IOS-XR Quality-of-Service Implementation for IP Internet Services. This chapter includes implementation of edge and core devices for CRS-1, 12000, 7200, and 7600 series routers; implementation template for SP-managed CE devices using Cisco IPS, and implementation templates on using QoS for securing the network perimeter.

Chapter 11: Cisco IOS and IOS-XR Quality-of-Service Implementation for Multicast Services. This chapter covers an overview of IP multicast and multicast VPN deployments, multicast deployment models for IP video services, and implementation of edge and core devices for CRS-1, 12000, 7200, and 7600 series routers.

Chapter 12: Proof of Concept for Verifying QoS Behavior in Cisco IP NGN Networks. This chapter includes the test bed and topology, behavior of traffic classes on a network without congestion, behavior of traffic classes on a network with congestion using traffic simulators, and verifying and validating traffic behavior in line with industry best practices.

Chapter 13: QoS Performance Monitoring and Measurement. This chapter focuses on IP network performance measurement and monitoring options. Technologies such as IP SLA NetFlow, SNMP and NBAR are described.

Chapter 14: This chapter gives a possible direction for the evolution of IP networks beyond the current NGN trend.

1.23 Summary

The NGN infrastructure will carry real-time traffic in the form of voice and video. Voice would be from traditional fixed-line business, mobile users for 3G, and VoIP, all with high packet loss, delay, and jitter sensitivity. Signaling for the voice services would also be carried across the converged infrastructure, requiring priority. The network will also be carrying data with varying tolerance to SLA parameters. Premium paying customers would also expect their data to be differentiated based on the additional fees they are charged.

Video in real time introduces extreme packet-loss sensitivity previously unheard of in the IP world. Losses greater than one packet in 1 million are often considered unacceptable. High-definition streams can reach 10 Mbps each depending on the compression technology, placing a huge demand on bandwidth with the deployment of video on demand across broadband.

If the NGN infrastructure does not honor the requirements of each of the services adequately, the costs can be very high. Aside from obvious costs such as liquidated damages and lost call minutes, there is the ever-present, less tangible impact on customer satisfaction and experience and, subsequently, brand erosion.

CHAPTER 2

Introduction to Cisco's Quality-of-Service Architecture for IP Networks

2.1 Building Blocks of the IP NGN QoS Framework

This section presents details of the various components that fit into the overall QoS framework, for deployment in a service provider IP NGN infrastructure. Even though this section focuses on providing architectural details that are central to SP IP/MPLS networks, most or all of the components discussed here can be considered relevant to enterprise IP networks (for that matter, any IP network) as well.

To facilitate true end-to-end QoS in an IP network, the Internet Engineering Task Force (IETF) has defined two QoS models: Integrated Services (IntServ) and Differentiated Services (DiffServ). IntServ follows the signaled QoS model, in which the end hosts signal their QoS needs to the network using Resource Reservation Protocol (RSVP), whereas DiffServ works on the provisioned QoS model, whereby network elements are set up to service multiple classes of traffic with varying QoS requirements. IntServ provides an end-to-end QoS solution by way of end-to-end signaling, state maintenance (for each RSVP flow and reservation), and admission control at each network element. DiffServ, on the other hand, addresses the clear need for relatively simple and coarse methods of categorizing traffic into various classes, also called *class of service* (CoS), and applying QoS parameters to those classes. In summary, IntServ uses per-flow QoS, whereas DiffServ, on the other hand, uses aggregated QoS.

To accomplish this task, packets are first divided into classes by marking the Type of Service (ToS) field in the IP header.

2.2 IP Precedence

The ToS field describes 1 entire byte (8 bits) of an IP packet. *IP precedence* refers to the three most significant bits of the ToS field—that is, *[XXX]XXXXX*. There could be some occasional usage confusion because the term ToS is also used to refer to the next 3 bits: *XXX[XXX]XX*. To be consistent with the original RFC-791 specification, this document uses the term ToS to refer to the entire 8 bits.

The three most significant bits of the ToS field, the *precedence bits*, define the IP packet priority under RFC-791. The precedence portion of the ToS field—*[XXX]XXXXX*—defines the

Table 2.1: IP ToS Field

0-2	3	4	5	6	7
Precedence	Delay	Throughput	Reliability	Reserved = 0	Reserved = 0
111 = Network Control = Precedence 7; 110 = Internetwork Control = Precedence 6; 101 = Critical = Precedence 5; 100 = Flash Override = Precedence 4; 011 = Flash = Precedence 3; 010 = Immediate = Precedence 2; 001 = Priority = Precedence 1; 000 = Routine = Precedence 0; 000XXX00 Bits 3, 4, 5: Bit 3 = Delay [D] (0 = Normal; 1 = Low); Bit 4 = Throughput [T] (0 = Normal; 1 = High); Bit 5 = Reliability [R] (0 = Normal; 1 = High); 000000XX Bits 6,7: Reserved for future use					

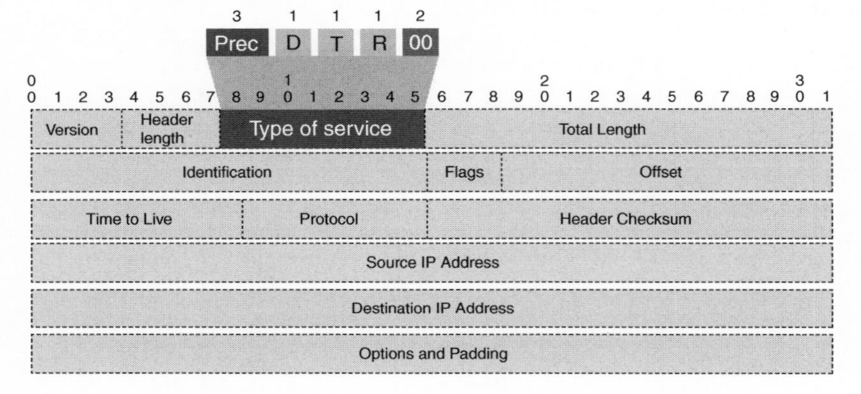

Figure 2.1: Complete Structure of the IP ToS Field

priority or importance of the field. Table 2.1 illustrates the method used to interpret this 8-bit portion of the IP packet.

The keyword values for IP precedence are Critical, Flash, Flash Override, Immediate, Internet, Network, Priority, and Routine, as indicated in the table. These values correspond to numeric values 7 to 0, respectively. The complete structure of the IP ToS field in the IP header is illustrated in Figure 2.1.

2.3 IP DSCP

The DiffServ standard proposes a way of interpreting a field that has always been part of an IP packet. In the DiffServ standard, the ToS field will be renamed to Differentiated Services Code Point (referred to as the *DSCP field*) and will have new meaning. This redefined header field is intended to supersede the existing definitions of the IPv4 TOS octet (RFC-791) and the IPv6 Traffic Class octet (IPv6). The IP DSCP field is illustrated in Figure 2.2.

A redefined header field, called the *DS field*, is defined; it is intended to supersede the existing definitions of the IPv4 TOS octet (RFC-791) and the IPv6 Traffic Class octet (IPv6). Six bits of the DS field are used as a code point (DSCP) to select the treatment/preference a packet

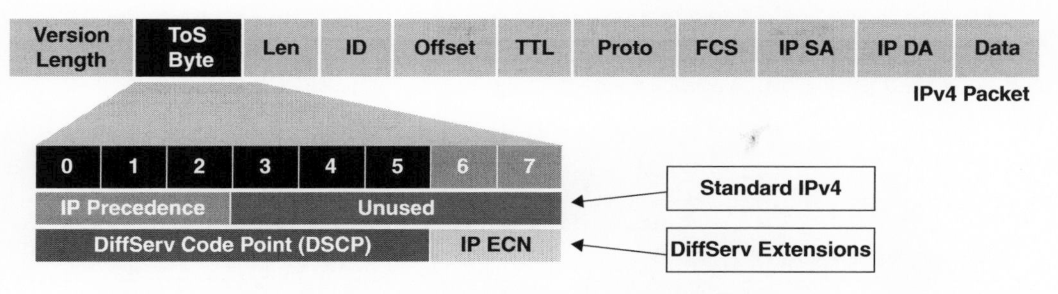

- DiffServ: First 6 bits of ToS byte are called DiffServ Code Point (DSCP)—remaining 2 bits used for flow control.
- DSCP is backward-compatible with IP precedence.
- A value of 0 in bits 3 and 4 indicates the first 3 bits as Class Selector.
- Nonzero value in bits 3 and 4 indicates a DSCP class such as an AF or EF PHB.

Figure 2.2: IP DSCP Field

experiences at each node in the network. A 2-bit currently unused ECN field, described in RFC-3168, is reserved and is currently unused in the context of DSCP. The values of the ECN bits are ignored by differentiated services-compliant nodes in the network when determining the preferential treatment to apply to a received packet. In a DSCP value notation *xxxxxx* (where *x* can equal 0 or 1), the leftmost bit signifies bit 0 of the DS field, and the rightmost bit signifies bit 5.

The following rules apply to IP packets marked with DSCP values:

- The DSCP field is 6 bits wide. DS-compliant nodes in the network choose the preferential treatment to the IP packet by matching against the entire 6-bit DSCP field.
- The value of the ECN field is completely ignored.
- Packets with an unrecognized code point are treated as though they were marked for default behavior (explained in detail in the following sections).

Once the traffic has been identified for their respective classes, specific forwarding treatments, formally called *per-hop behavior* (PHB), are applied on each network element, providing the packet the appropriate delay-bound, jitter-bound, bandwidth, and so on. This combination of packet classification and marking and well-defined PHBs results in a scalable QoS solution for any given packet and therefore any application. (Packet classification, marking, class selectors, and PHBs are detailed in the following sections.) Thus, in DiffServ, signaling for QoS is eliminated, and the number of states required to be kept at each network element is drastically reduced, resulting in an aggregated, scalable, and end-to-end QoS solution.

The use of the ToS byte by both IP precedence and IP DSCP for offering preferential treatment to IP traffic is illustrated in Figure 2.3.

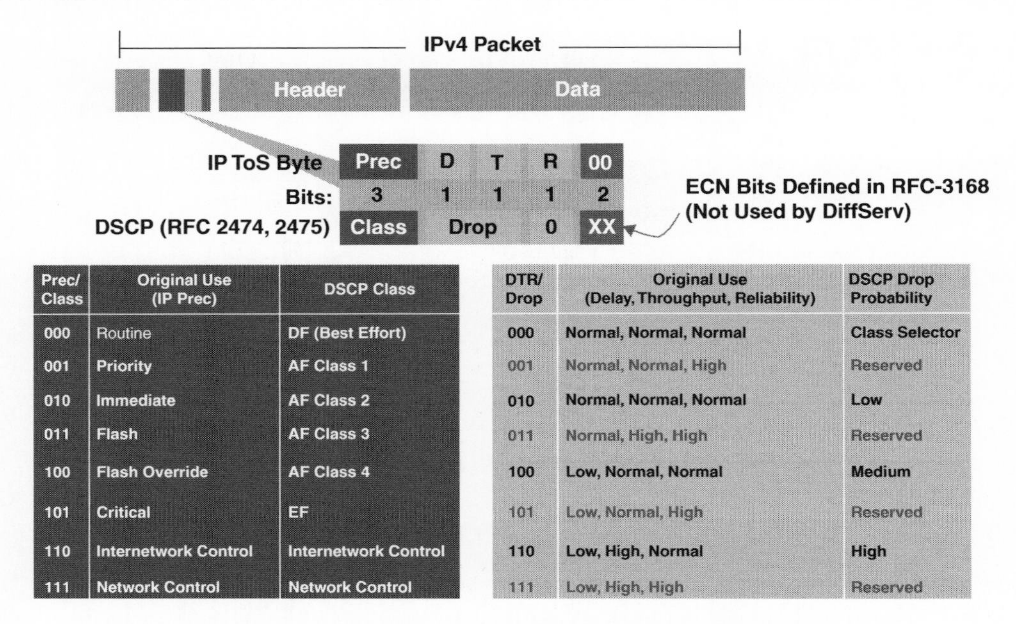

Prec/ Class	Original Use (IP Prec)	DSCP Class
000	Routine	DF (Best Effort)
001	Priority	AF Class 1
010	Immediate	AF Class 2
011	Flash	AF Class 3
100	Flash Override	AF Class 4
101	Critical	EF
110	Internetwork Control	Internetwork Control
111	Network Control	Network Control

DTR/ Drop	Original Use (Delay, Throughput, Reliability)	DSCP Drop Probability
000	Normal, Normal, Normal	Class Selector
001	Normal, Normal, High	Reserved
010	Normal, Normal, Normal	Low
011	Normal, High, High	Reserved
100	Low, Normal, Normal	Medium
101	Low, Normal, High	Reserved
110	Low, High, Normal	High
111	Low, High, High	Reserved

Figure 2.3: IP Precedence vs. IP DSCP and ToS Byte Usage

2.4 IntServ Strengths and Shortcomings

The IETF defined models, IntServ and DiffServ, are simply two ways of considering the fundamental problem of providing QoS for a given IP packet. The IntServ model relies on RSVP to signal and reserve the desired QoS for each flow in the network. A *flow* is defined as an individual, unidirectional data stream between two applications and is uniquely identified by the five tuples (source IP address, source port number, destination IP address, destination port number, and the Transport Protocol). Two types of service can be requested via RSVP, assuming all network devices support RSVP along the path from the source to the destination:

- The first type is a very strict guaranteed service that provides for firm bounds on end-to-end delay and assured bandwidth for traffic that conforms to the reserved specifications.
- The second type is a controlled load service that provides for a better-than-best effort and low-delay service under light to moderate network loads.

Thus, it is possible to provide the requisite QoS for every flow in the network, provided it is signaled using RSVP and the resources are available. However, there are several drawbacks to this approach:

- Every device along a packet's path, including the end systems such as servers and PCs, need to be fully aware of RSVP and should be capable of signaling the required QoS.
- Reservations in each device along the path are "soft," which means that they need to be refreshed periodically, thereby adding to the traffic on the network and increasing

the chance that the reservation may time out if refresh packets are lost. Though some mechanisms alleviate this problem, it adds to the complexity of the RSVP solution.

- Maintaining soft states in each router, combined with admission control at each hop, adds to the complexity of each network node along the path, along with increased memory requirements, to support a large number of reservations.
- Since state information for each reservation needs to be maintained at every router along the path, scalability with hundreds of thousands of flows through a network core becomes an issue. This would be a particularly significant problem if the IntServ method was used in an SP core, due to millions of flows that could exist at any given point of time.

DiffServ, on the other hand, is considered a more scalable approach, especially for deployment in the SP network core. Hence this chapter and the subsequent chapters in this book focus only on the architectural and deployment-specific nuances of the DiffServ model.

2.5 The Differentiated Services (DiffServ) Architecture

DiffServ was ratified as a series of IETF standards (RFCs) toward the end of 1998. The differentiated service approach to providing quality of service in networks employs a small, well-defined set of building blocks from which a variety of aggregate behaviors may be built. DSCP values are used to mark a packet to receive a particular forwarding treatment, or per-hop behavior, at each network node. A common understanding of the use and interpretation of this bit pattern is required for interdomain use, multivendor interoperability, and consistent reasoning about expected aggregate behaviors in a network. RFC-2474 and RFC-2475 define the architecture and the general use of bits within the DS field. A detailed discussion on the key components of the DiffServ architecture is provided in the following sections.

2.5.1 Per-Hop Behaviors

Now that packets can be marked using the DSCP, how do we provide meaningful classification on flows (CoS) and provide the QoS that is needed? First, the collection of packets that have the same DSCP value (also called a *code point*) in them and crossing in a particular direction is called a *behavior aggregate* (BA). Thus, packets from multiple applications/sources could belong to the same BA. Formally, RFC-2475 defines a PHB as the externally observable forwarding behavior applied at a DS-compliant node (a network node that complies to all the core DiffServ requirements) to a DS behavior aggregate. In more concrete terms, a PHB refers to the packet-scheduling, queuing, policing, drop probability, or shaping behavior of a node on any given packet belonging to a BA and as configured by an SLA or policy. To date, four standard PHBs are available to construct a DiffServ-enabled network and achieve aggregate end-to-end CoS and QoS. Figure 2.4 visits the relationship between BAs, PHBs, and their alignment into queues for forwarding over the network links.

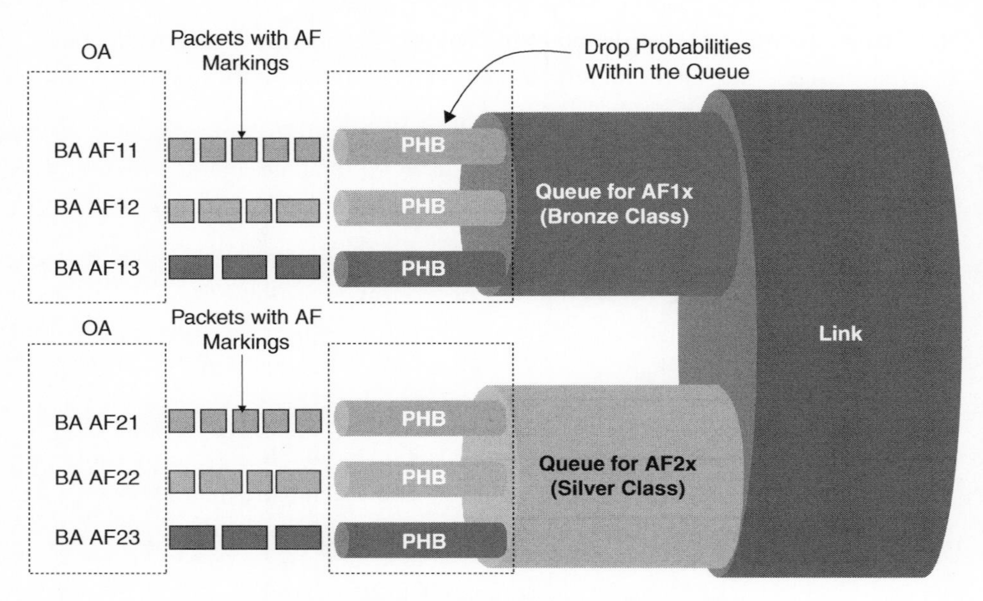

Figure 2.4: DiffServ Terminology and How They Fit

Class Selector Provides Support for IP Prec Using DSCP Terminology

	Type	Class Selector Code Point
Prec 0	Routine	000000 (0)
Prec 1	Priority	001000 (8)
Prec 2	Immediate	010000 (16)
Prec 3	Flash	011000 (24)
Prec 4	Override	100000 (32)
Prec 5	Critical	101000 (40)
Prec 6	Internet	110000 (48)
Prec 7	Net Control	111000 (56)

Low
Priority Classes
High

match ip dscp 24
is the same as
match ip prec 3

Figure 2.5: Class Selector Code Point

Figure 2.5 illustrates the various DiffServ PHBs in more detail.

2.5.2 The Default PHB (Defined in RFC-2474)

Essentially, the default PHB specifies that a packet marked with a DSCP value of 000000 gets the traditional best-effort service from a DS-compliant node. Also, if a packet arrives at a DS-compliant node and its DSCP value is not mapped to any of the other PHBs, it will get mapped to the default PHB.

2.5.3 Class-Selector PHBs (Defined in RFC-2474)

To preserve backward compatibility with the IP precedence scheme, DSCP values of the form *xxx*000, where *x* is either 0 or 1 are defined. These code points are called *class selector* code points. Note that the default code point is also known as a class-selector code point (000000). The PHB associated with a class selector code point is a *class selector PHB*. These PHBs retain almost the same forwarding behavior as nodes that implement IP precedence-based classification and forwarding. As an example, packets with a DSCP value of 110000 (IP precedence 110) have a preferential forwarding treatment (scheduling, queuing, and so on) compared to packets with a DSCP value of 100000 (IP precedence 100). These PHBs ensure that DS-compliant nodes can coexist with IP precedence-aware nodes, with the exception of the DTS bits. Figure 2.5 provides an illustration on the use of class selector PHBs.

2.5.4 Expedited Forwarding (EF) PHB (Defined in RFC-2598)

Just as RSVP, via the IntServ model, provides for a guaranteed bandwidth service, the Expedited Forwarding (EF) PHB is the key ingredient in DiffServ for providing a low-loss, low-latency, low-jitter, and assured bandwidth service. Applications such as Voice over IP (VoIP), video, and online trading programs require such a robust network treatment. EF can be implemented using priority queuing, along with rate limiting on the class (formally, a BA). Although EF PHB, when implemented in a DiffServ network, provides a premium service, it should be specifically targeted toward the most critical applications because, if congestion exists, it is not possible to treat all or most traffic as high priority. EF PHB is especially suitable for applications (such as VoIP) that require strict service-level guarantees with very low packet loss, guaranteed bandwidth, low delay, and low jitter. The recommended DSCP value for EF is 101110 (RFC-2474).

2.5.5 Assured Forwarding (AFxy) PHB (Defined in RFC-2597)

Assured Forwarding (AFxy) defines a method by which BA can be given different forwarding assurances. For example, traffic can be divided into gold, silver, and bronze classes, with gold being allocated 50 percent of the available link bandwidth, silver 30 percent, and bronze 20 percent. The AFxy PHB defines four AFx classes; namely, AF1, AF2, AF3, and AF4. Each class is assigned a certain amount of buffer space and interface bandwidth, dependent on the SLA with the SP policy. Within each AFx class, it is possible to specify three drop precedence values. Thus, if there is congestion in a DS node on a specific link and packets of a particular AFx class (say, AF1) need to be dropped, packets in AFxy will be dropped such that $dP(AFx1) <= dP(AFx2) <= dp(AFx3)$, where $dP(AFxy)$ is the probability that packets of the AFxy class will be dropped. Thus, the subscript *y* in AFxy denotes the drop precedence within an AFx class. In our example, packets in AF13 will get dropped before packets in AF12 and before packets in AF11. This concept of drop precedence is useful, for example, to penalize flows within a BA that exceed the assigned bandwidth. Packets of these flows could be remarked by a policer to higher drop precedence. Figure 2.6 illustrates the DSCP values and associated PHBs in more detail.

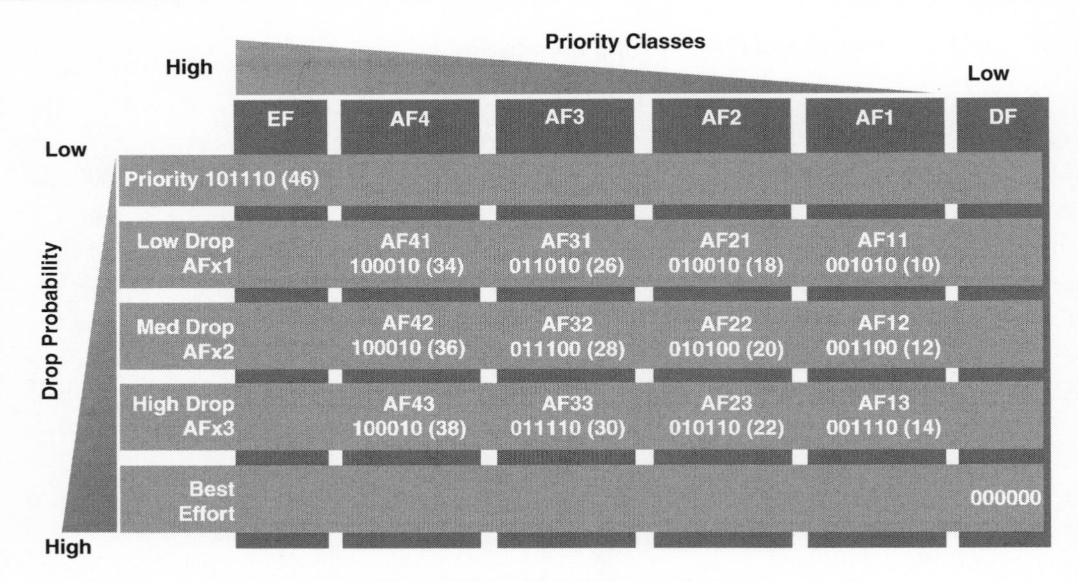

Figure 2.6: DiffServ Behavior Aggregates

NOTE 2.1: PHB Enforcement

When the packet leaves the ingress router and goes into the network core, PHBs are enforced, depending on the packet marking. In Cisco IOS software, EF can be implemented using low-latency queuing (LLQ). AFxy PHBs can be implemented using a combination of class-based weighted fair queuing (CBWFQ) and weighted random early detect (WRED). More on CBWFQ and WRED follows in the subsequent sections.

2.6 DiffServ in Cisco Software

An important aspect to note is that, even though DiffServ is an architecture built for IP networks, it has been extended as a reference for building IP/MPLS-based networks as well. MPLS DiffServ is defined in RFC-3270. Today the DiffServ model only defines the use of the DSCP and the four PHBs. The PHBs simply describe the forwarding behavior of a DS-compliant node. The model does not specify how these PHBs may be implemented. A variety of queuing, policing, metering, and shaping techniques may be used to affect the desired traffic conditioning and PHB.

An SP IP/MPLS network can use several features in the Cisco IOS to deliver class/quality of service based on the DiffServ model. These are:

- CLI Match using IP Precedence, IP DSCP, 802.1p, and MPLS EXP fields to identify packet priorities. Other methods used for traffic classification include Network-Based Application Recognition (NBAR) and Access Control Lists (ACLs).
- Policing for rate limiting and classifying packets.

- Weighted Random Early Detection for congestion avoidance.
- CBWFQ and Modified Deficit Round Robin for congestion management.
- Modular QoS Command Line Interface (CLI) for device configurations.

2.7 Classification and Marking

Classification is the process of categorizing traffic into predefined classes in the network. These classes are basically buckets that map to specific traffic properties such as priority and latency for the traffic involved. Traffic is normally classified as it enters the network, where it is marked for appropriate treatment. Once the traffic has been classified and marked at the edge of the network, the network must be set up to provide differential service to the various traffic flows. Common methods to differentiate traffic in an SP network core include Layer 2 CoS or 802.1p, IP precedence, Layer 3 DSCP, or MPLS experimental bits, which are described in detail in subsequent sections. The method chosen for providing differentiated services could be based on the following:

- Network type
- Traffic type

Packet classification features allow traffic to be partitioned into multiple priority levels, or classes of service. Packets can be classified in a variety of ways, ranging from input interface or NBAR for applications that are difficult to classify to arbitrary ACLs. Choosing the appropriate and correct method to differentiate traffic is an essential part of building a successful QoS model.

You can mark classified packets to indicate their traffic class. You can color packets by marking the IP precedence or DSCP field in the packets IP header or the Experimental field in the MPLS label header.

2.7.1 Network Type

The network type influences the method used for differentiating between traffic classes and providing differentiated services for each class. An IP network can choose to differentiate traffic based on either IP precedence or IP DSCP values. On the other hand, an MPLS-based core infrastructure would use the EXP values to differentiate between the various classes. Similarly, a Layer 2-based core such as an Ethernet-switched network may use the 802.1p bits for the same purpose. Hence it becomes very important for the SP to mark traffic at the network edge using the appropriate scheme that is being used in the network core.

2.7.2 Traffic Type

The traffic type has a bearing on the method used for providing differentiated services. Certain traffic types might not support a given method if used for the purpose of differentiating classes.

A good example is using MPLS EXP as a scheme for providing differentiation for VoIP traffic that is not labeled (and placed in the global routing table) in an MPLS-based core. Since this traffic is not label switched and instead is carried as pure IP (unlabeled) traffic, the scheme for providing differentiated services would indeed fail. Hence it is imperative to clearly identify the various traffic types to be transported in the network and appropriately choose the correct scheme for deployment. In certain cases, more than one method can be used for this purpose. For instance, it is common to deploy an EXP and IP precedence plus DSCP-based scheme in the core, for supporting the various traffic types in a given environment.

2.7.3 Classification and Marking Using the MPLS Experimental Field

The MPLS header consists of several fields. One of them is the 3-bit-long Experimental field, as illustrated in Figure 2.7. The EXP field was originally called the CoS field when Cisco developed tag switching. When MPLS became a formal standard, the CoS field was renamed the Experimental, or EXP, field as its use was not clearly defined. However, the EXP field is still used to carry CoS bits. The network core uses the EXP markings to apply the necessary priorities for traffic.

2.7.4 Classification and Marking Using the 802.1p Field in 802.1Q

802.1p, part of the IEEE 802.1Q standard, allows for the marking of Layer 2 frames with a user-priority value. The 802.1p field is 3 bits wide and thus provides for easy mapping with the IP precedence and MPLS EXP fields. An 802.1Q frame is created from an Ethernet frame by changing the ether type of the frame to 0 × 8100 (indicating 802.1Q) and inserting a 4-byte 802.1Q tag, as illustrated in Figure 2.8.

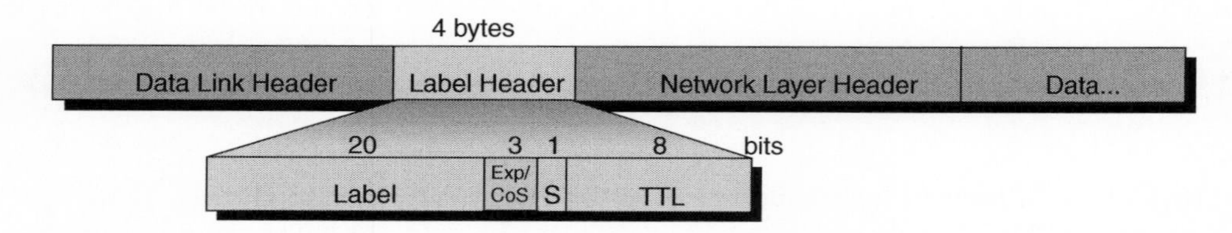

Figure 2.7: MPLS EXP Field

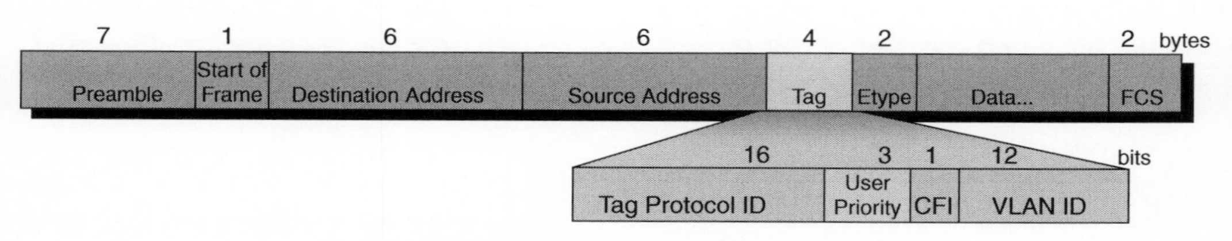

Figure 2.8: 802.1Q Tag Showing 802.1p Field

2.7.5 Classification Using Network-Based Application Recognition

Network-Based Application Recognition (NBAR), a feature first available in Cisco IOS Software Release 12.0(5)XE2, provides intelligent network classification for network infrastructure. NBAR is a classification engine that can recognize a wide variety of applications, including Web-based applications and client/server applications that dynamically assign TCP or User Datagram Protocol (UDP) port numbers.

After the application is recognized, the network can invoke specific services for that particular application. NBAR currently works with QoS features to help ensure that the network bandwidth is best used to fulfill the objectives. This feature includes the ability to mark packets appropriately so that the network and the SP's network can provide QoS from end to end—for example, if the network requires a fast response when the user passes a query for an order status in the corporate data warehouse hosted on an Oracle database server. Unfortunately, if others on the network are using high-bandwidth applications such as VDOLive or viewing large GIF files, the SQL*NET transaction to the Oracle database could be delayed. NBAR addresses this problem by properly classifying the applications and then invoking other QoS features that provide guaranteed bandwidth services, such as CBWFQ (described later in this section), to ensure guaranteed bandwidth to SQL*NET queries. Figure 2.9 illustrates NBAR in more detail.

NBAR intelligently classifies and allows you to enforce QoS policy on today's mission-critical applications. NBAR supports a wide range of network protocols, including some of these stateful protocols that were difficult to classify before NBAR:

- HTTP classification by URL, host, and Multipurpose Internet Mail Extensions (MIME) type

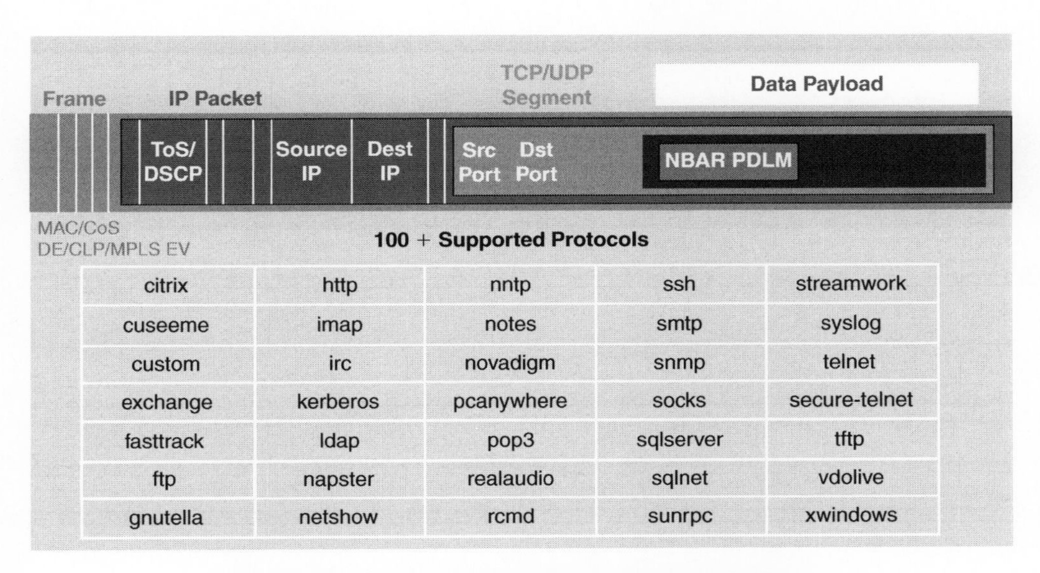

Figure 2.9: Network-Based Application Recognition

```
class-map match-all Voice
 match protocol rtp audio
!
policy-map Voice-Traffic
 class Voice
 set mpls experimental imposition 5
!
end
```

Figure 2.10: Classification Using NBAR

- Oracle SQL*Net
- Sun RPC
- Microsoft Exchange
- UNIX r commands
- VDOLive
- RealAudio
- Microsoft NetShow
- File Transfer Protocol (FTP)
- StreamWorks
- Trivial File Transfer Protocol (TFTP)

The class map in Figure 2.10 uses the protocol name for classifying traffic. In this case, the keyword *RTP* is used to indicate VoIP traffic. As mentioned earlier, NBAR simplifies the classification process by identifying numerous application types, which would have otherwise required complex ACLs to match traffic based on application port numbers.

NOTE 2.2: MPLS EXP Marking

The use of the keyword *imposition* indicates the EXP marking during MPLS imposition—that is, to indicate that the packet is in the IP2MPLS path. Use of the command *set mpls experimental <exp>* without the *imposition* keyword will still configure the command with the *imposition* keyword automatically.

2.7.6 Traffic Classification and Marking at the Service Provider Edge

Now that we have discussed various components that are used for classifying traffic to define various PHBs, let's discuss the points in the network at which this process is performed.

Classification is always performed at the network edge, also known as the *point of demarcation* between the SP and end user or customer domain (we refer to the customer domain as the *enterprise network* for the rest of this chapter). The edge devices are responsible for examining IP packets arriving from customer-edge (CE) devices for various characteristics

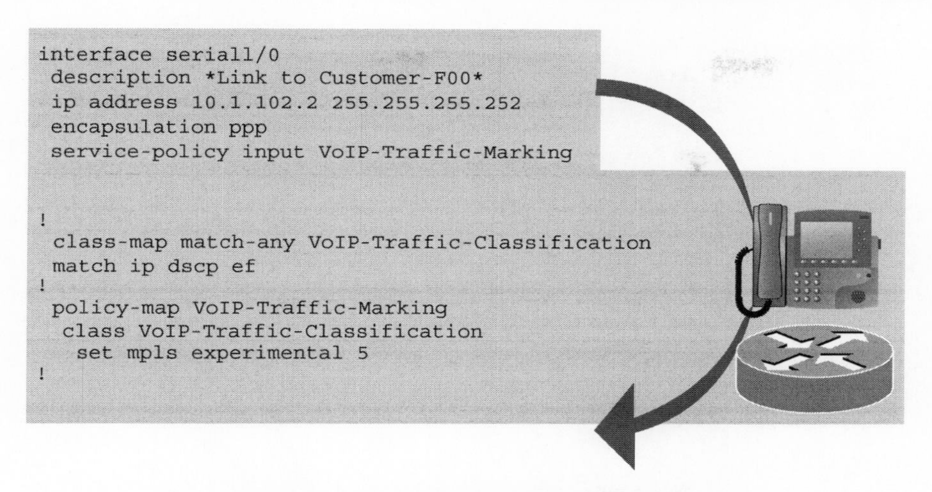

Figure 2.11: Classification Using DSCP bits

such as application type (Telnet, SMTP, FTP) and traffic destinations. The packets can then be classified, using for example, IP DSCP according to the SLA with the customer. For instance, all traffic from a given customer in the SP IP/MPLS network could be given a certain classification, which could mean higher priority over all other traffic of lesser priorities.

Figure 2.11 illustrates the process of classifying traffic for differential treatment in the SP network core. In this illustration the classifier (a class map named VoIP Traffic Classification) matches all incoming traffic with a DSCP value of *expedited forwarding*. Furthermore, it is assumed that either the end device (which could be a Cisco VoIP phone) or the CE router has premarked the traffic with the specified DSCP value (EF, in this case). The policy map is used to mark MPLS EXP Value 5 during label imposition, based on classifier.

Another illustration (Figure 2.12) provides an insight into using ACLs as the classification criteria. Extended ACLs are used to identify traffic based on subnets and port numbers prior to marking them. Once classified, the traffic is marked using MPLS EXP Value 3. Finally, the packaged policy is attached to an ingress interface (Serial 2/0).

2.8 Traffic Policing

Traffic policing involves monitoring network traffic for conformity with a traffic contract and, if required, marking down or even dropping the excess traffic to enforce compliance with the contract. A contract here could be the committed information rate (CIR), committed burst, and excess burst rate offered on a given interface. Traffic exceeding a traffic contract may be tagged as noncompliant. The actions taken for noncompliant traffic may vary based on the configuration. The most common configuration using policing is to drop traffic exceeding the contract offered. Other possible tasks include marking of traffic with the appropriate CoS, IP DSCP/precedence, or EXP values. For instance, traffic that adheres to the specified contract may be allowed to pass through and also get marked with the respective code points. Another

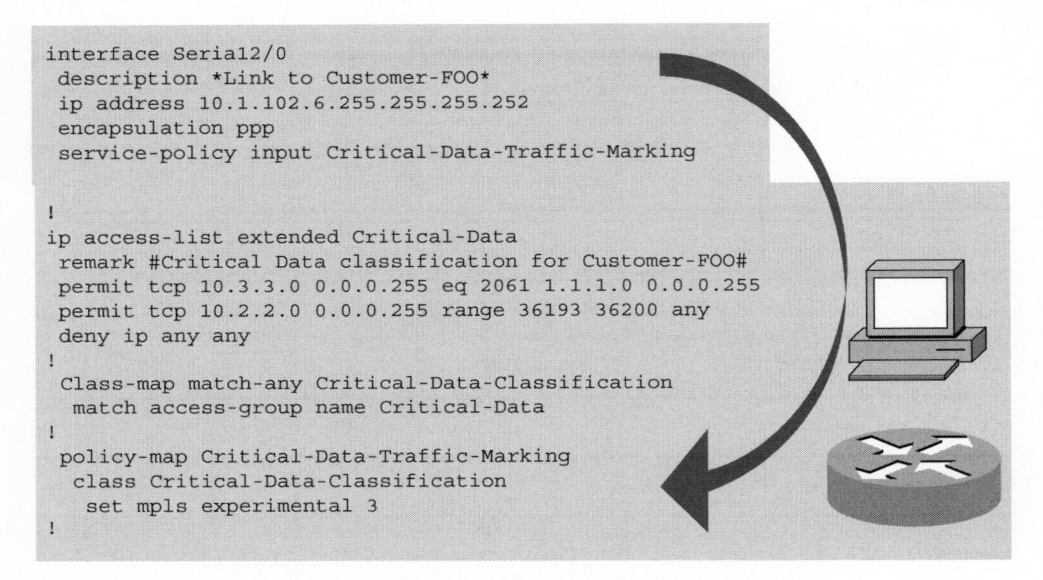

```
interface Serial2/0
 description *Link to Customer-FOO*
 ip address 10.1.102.6.255.255.255.252
 encapsulation ppp
 service-policy input Critical-Data-Traffic-Marking

!
ip access-list extended Critical-Data
 remark #Critical Data classification for Customer-FOO#
 permit tcp 10.3.3.0 0.0.0.255 eq 2061 1.1.1.0 0.0.0.255
 permit tcp 10.2.2.0 0.0.0.255 range 36193 36200 any
 deny ip any any
!
 Class-map match-any Critical-Data-Classification
  match access-group name Critical-Data
!
 policy-map Critical-Data-Traffic-Marking
  class Critical-Data-Classification
   set mpls experimental 3
!
```

Figure 2.12: Classification Using ACL

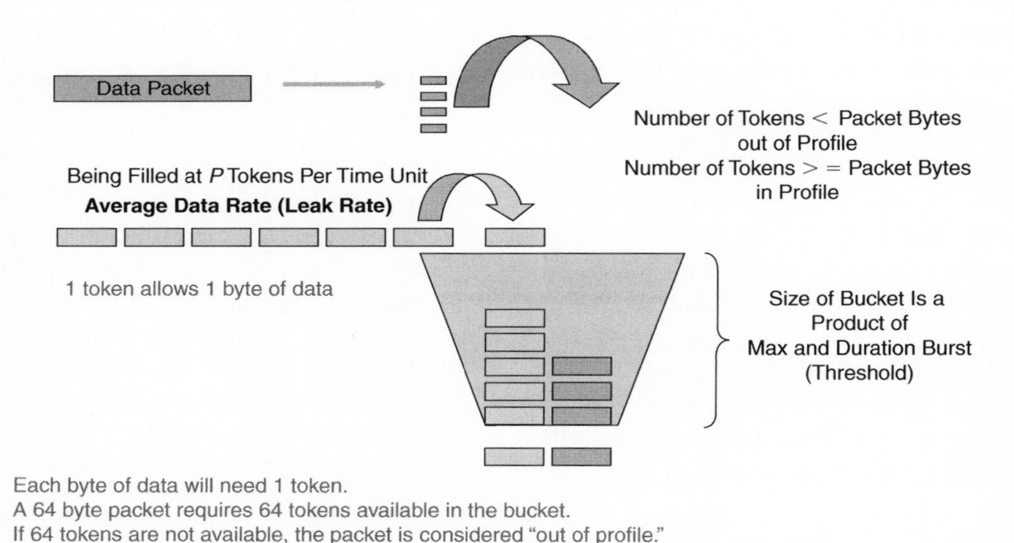

Figure 2.13: Conceptual View of a Policer

possibility is remarked or mark-down traffic that exceeds or violates the contract. *Remarking* is the process of permitting excess traffic to pass through but with a lesser priority in the network core, as against traffic that adheres to the contract. Policing can be used in various locations of a network to rate-limit the quantity of traffic permitted onto a link. It is most useful at the network edge to enforce some agreed traffic rate from a network user and mark the appropriate QoS values. Figure 2.13 illustrates a conceptual view of a policer.

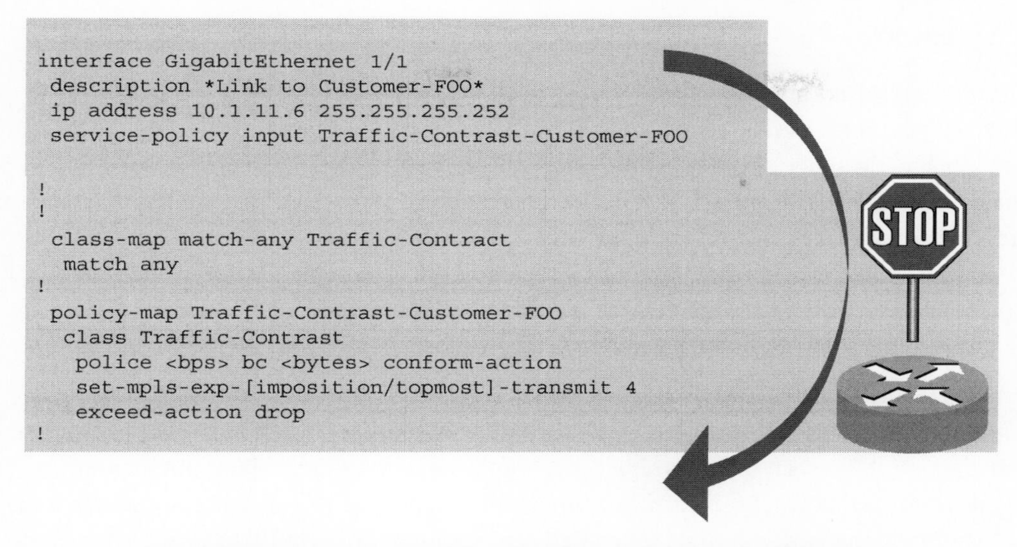

Figure 2.14: Policing to Enforce Service Contracts and Marking

The recipient of traffic that has been policed will observe packet loss distributed throughout periods that exceeded the contract. If the source does not respond to this (for example, through a feedback mechanism), this process will continue and might appear to the recipient as though link errors or some other disruptions are causing random packet loss. The received traffic will typically comply with the contract, give or take jitter introduced by elements in the network downstream of the policer. Sources with feedback-based congestion control mechanisms (for example, TCP) typically adapt rapidly to static policing, converging on a rate just below the policed sustained rate.

Figure 2.14 illustrates the use of a policer to enforce a contract for traffic entering an interface. In this illustration the policer is used to enforce a service contract at the network edge for all incoming traffic. A CIR (defined in bits per second) and committed burst (Bc, defined in bytes) are defined. As per the policy, all traffic that adheres to the CIR and Bc would be allowed to pass through and have its EXP bits marked to a value of 4. Excess traffic in this example would be merely dropped, indicating a violation in the contract. Contracts and service-level agreements are discussed in more detail in Chapter 3, "Class-of-Service Requirements for Quad-Play Networks."

2.8.1 Policing Rate and Burst Calculation

The policer burst size should be sufficient to accommodate expected traffic bursts. For instance, if a policer is used for enforcing a contract for voice traffic, the following is applicable: Burst in bytes = N * VoIP (or Avg Real Time) packet size, where N = max number of (VoIP/REALTIME) packets that could be arriving at the same time. For VoIP traffic, an upper bound could be the maximum number of simultaneous calls.

2.9 Shaping

Traffic shaping (also known as *packet shaping*) is primarily used to control traffic so as to optimize or guarantee performance, low latency, and/or bandwidth by delaying packets. More specifically, traffic shaping is any action on a set of packets (often called a *stream* or a *flow*) that imposes additional delay on those packets such that they conform to some predetermined constraint (for example, a contract). It provides a means to control the volume of traffic being sent into a network during a specific period (also known as *bandwidth throttling*). However, it is to be noted that traffic shaping is always applied by delaying packets.

A traffic shaper works by delaying metered traffic such that each packet complies with the relevant traffic contract. Metering may be implemented with, for example, the token bucket algorithms. Metered packets are then stored in a first-in/first-out (FIFO) buffer for each separately shaped class until they can be transmitted in compliance with the prevailing traffic contract. This could occur immediately (if the traffic arriving at the shaper is already compliant), after some delay (waiting in the buffer until its scheduled release time), or never (in case of buffer overflow).

All traffic shaper implementations have a finite buffer and must cope with the case where the buffer is full. A simple and common approach is to drop traffic arriving while the buffer is full (tail drop), thus resulting in traffic policing as well as shaping. A more sophisticated implementation could apply a dropping algorithm such as Weighted Random Early Discard (WRED); a crude alternative would be to allow overflowing traffic through unshaped.

A common question is, how do shapers and policers differ? Shaping implies the existence of a queue and of sufficient memory to buffer delayed packets, whereas policing does not. In addition, shaping requires a scheduling function for later transmission of any delayed packets. This scheduling function allows you to organize the shaping queue into different queues. Examples of scheduling functions are class-based weighted fair queuing (CBWFQ) and low-latency queuing (LLQ), described later in this chapter. Figure 2.15 provides an illustration of the differences between policers and shapers.

2.10 Fitting the Components Together

To reflect on the various aspects discussed to this point: Classification is the process of identifying traffic profiles, policing is the task of metering traffic to ensure that contracts are not violated, marking is a way to differentiate and define PHBs in the SP network core, and, finally, shaping delays traffic so as to adhere to service contracts without dropping traffic. Figure 2.16 fits all the components together, providing insight into the complete picture of the aspects discussed thus far.

2.11 Congestion Avoidance Using Weighted Random Early Detection

Weighted Random Early Detection (WRED) provides congestion avoidance. This technique monitors network traffic load in an effort to anticipate and avoid congestion at common network bottlenecks as opposed to congestion management techniques that operate to control congestion once it occurs. WRED is designed to avoid congestion in networks before it

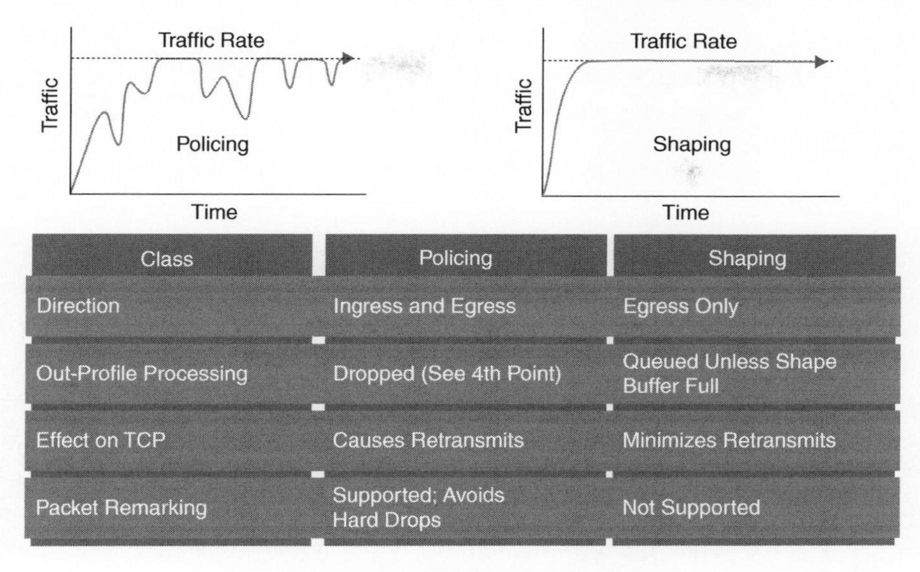

Class	Policing	Shaping
Direction	Ingress and Egress	Egress Only
Out-Profile Processing	Dropped (See 4th Point)	Queued Unless Shape Buffer Full
Effect on TCP	Causes Retransmits	Minimizes Retransmits
Packet Remarking	Supported; Avoids Hard Drops	Not Supported

Figure 2.15: Policing vs. Shaping

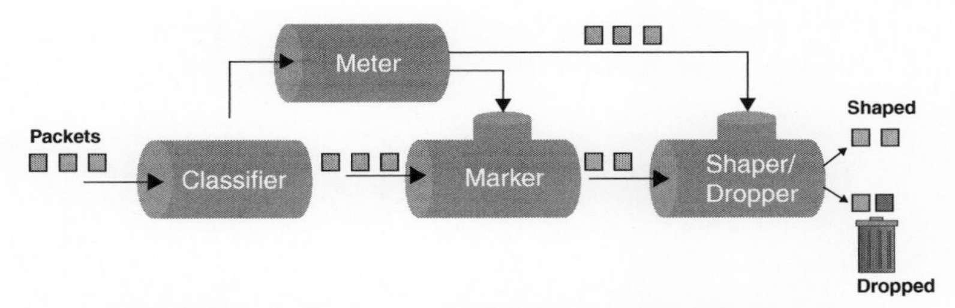

- Classifier: Selects a packet in a traffic stream based on the content of some portion of the packet header.
- Meter: Checks compliance to traffic parameters (e.g., Token Bucket) and passes result to the marker and shaper/dropper to trigger a particular action for in/out-of-profile packets.
- Marker: Writes/rewrites DSCP.
- Shaper: Delays some packets to be compliant with a profile.

Figure 2.16: Reflections on the Various Components

becomes a problem. It leverages the flow-monitoring capabilities of TCP. WRED monitors traffic load at points in the network and discards packets if the congestion begins to increase. The result is that the source detects the dropped traffic and slows its transmission. WRED interacts with other QoS mechanisms to identify class of service in packet flows. It selectively drops packets from low-priority flows first, ensuring that high-priority traffic gets through. When a packet arrives, WRED applies the following process:

- The average queue size is calculated.
- If the average is less than the minimum queue threshold, the arriving packet is queued.

- If the average is between the minimum queue threshold for that type of traffic and the maximum threshold for the interface, the packet is either dropped or queued, depending on the packet drop probability for that type of traffic.
- If the average queue size is greater than the maximum threshold, the packet is dropped.

2.11.1 WRED Metrics

WRED provides drop probabilities for each class; the higher the class, the less the probability of a packet being dropped. The *random-detect* command defines the precedence value, minimum threshold in packets, maximum threshold in packets, and mark probability denominator. These values determine the behavior of WRED in each queue. When the weighted queue average is below the minimum threshold, no packets will be dropped. When the weighted queue average is above the maximum queue threshold, all packets will be dropped. When the average is between the minimum and the maximum thresholds, the probability that a packet is going to be dropped can be calculated by a straight line from the minimum threshold (probability 0) to the maximum threshold (probability is equal to 1/mark probability denominator). The drop probability defines whether all or only a fraction of the packets are dropped when the maximum threshold is reached. Figure 2.17 illustrates this behavior wherein AF13 traffic gets dropped before AF12 and AF12 traffic is dropped before AF11 traffic.

TIP 2.1: Max-Probability Denominator

It is found that setting a max-probability denominator of 1 suits all network deployments and is considered an optimal value for all traffic types.

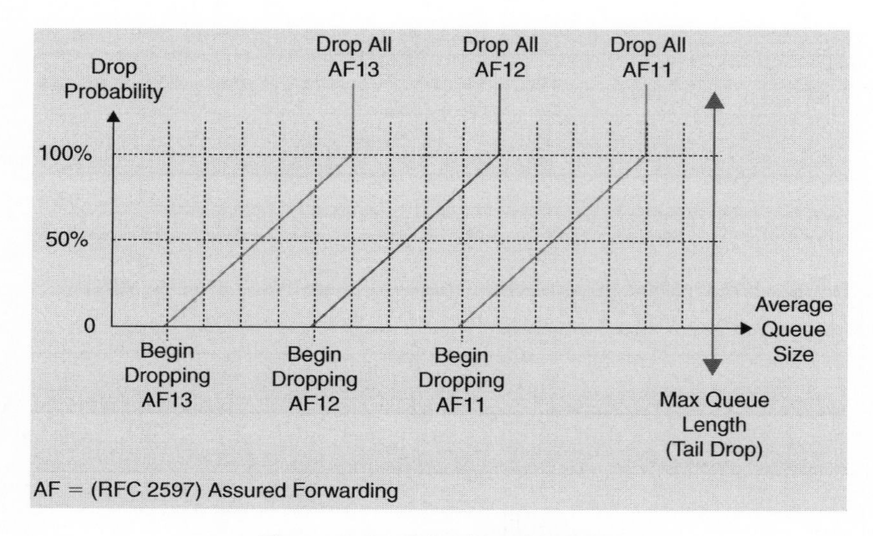

Figure 2.17: Behavior of WRED

2.11.2 Exponential Weighting Constant

All WRED calculations are based on an average queue depth. The exponential weighting constant command defines the weight used in calculating the average queue depth. The weight configures how fast the average queue depth tracks the instantaneous queue depth. All WRED drop calculations are done on the weighted average queue depth. Controlling the exponential weighting constant essentially defines how much burst traffic can be accommodated before random dropping takes effect. Figure 2.18 provides the WRED configuration values for the various interface speeds.

Cisco platforms that perform QoS in hardware (ASICs), such as the Cisco 12000, do not accept any user-configurable values for the exponential weighting constant, because these values are automatically adjusted in hardware based on the queue depth. The same applies to current-generation line cards such as the Ethernet Services Module (ESM 20G) on the Cisco 7600 series hardware. These values are considered optimal for an IP/MPLS service provider environment. On the other hand, platforms that perform QoS processing in software, such as the 7200, allow the user to configure these values manually. In such cases, the guidelines provided in Figure 2.18 can be used for the appropriate configurations.

Figure 2.19 illustrates the effect of various exponential constants on the average queue size. The instantaneous queue depth is shown as the thicker blue line. The lower the exponential weighted constant, the more immediately the average queue depth will reflect the instantaneous queue depth. For example, the queue using an exponential weighted constant of 1 (graph line Exp 1) changes more quickly than the queue that uses a constant of 10 (graph line Exp 10).

Line Speed Mbps	Designator	Exponential Weighting Constant
2.048	E1	4
8.192	4xE1	6
10	10BaseX	6
16.384	8 x E1	7
34.368	E3	8
44.736	DS3	8
51.840	HSSI	8
100.00	100BaseX	9
155.52	OC3/STM-1	10
622.08	OC12/STM-4	12
1000	GigE	13
2488.32	OC48/STM-16	14

Figure 2.18: WRED Configuration Values

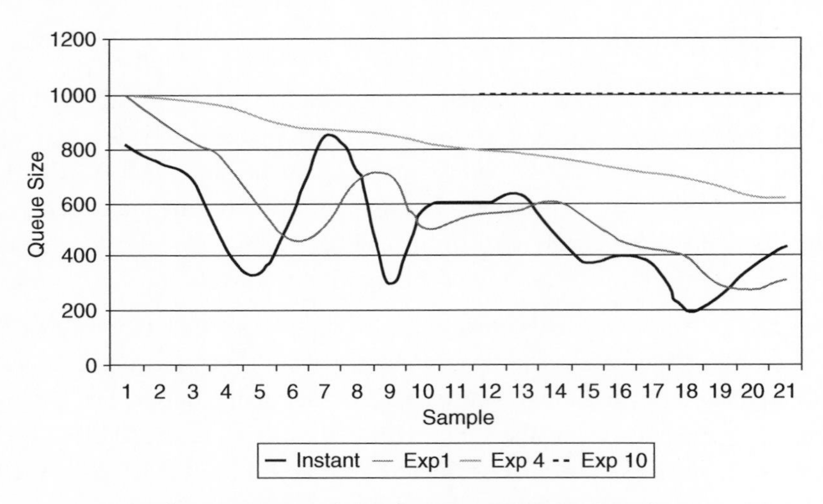

Figure 2.19: Weighted Average Queue Depths

2.11.3 Choosing Min and Max Values Based on Latency and Round-Trip Time

Many early recommendations for WRED value tuning were based on a function of round-trip time (RTT), which would guarantee that the TCP sender had enough time to react to the congestion notification before the queue filled. Though optimal in a purely academic sense, this solution considered neither the case where multiple TCP flows were sharing a queue nor the practical issues of providing sufficient buffering for high-speed links over long geographical distances. (Example: A trans-Pacific OC48 circuit would require over 300 Mbits of buffering to support a 1xRTT buffer for a single flow.) Based on early theoretical work and lab tests using both real and emulated TCP stacks, a general recommendation was to set the minimum threshold to approximately 30 ms of buffering (based on the dequeue rate) and the maximum threshold to approximately 100 ms. Recent academic work has shown that for high-speed interfaces that carry large numbers of unique flows, using smaller min and max threshold values works better than sticking strictly to the 30 ms/100 ms rule, because in general these flows will at some later point be separated and queued individually. Figure 2.20 illustrates that very low-speed links have more buffering relative to their link speed than do the high-speed interfaces. This is to accommodate the much lower number of unique flows for low-speed interfaces and provide high-speed interfaces with more aggressive drop behaviors.

2.11.4 Optimal Values for Min/Max Threshold Configurations

Based on both historical and recent academic work as well as a great number of deployments, Figure 2.20 illustrates a guideline for setting optimal min/max threshold values for WRED on Cisco platforms. The figure illustrates details for configuring min/max settings in terms of both bytes and packets, since specific hardware platforms can have specific requirements as to what terms are used to configure WRED values. In the general case, a 256 B/packet can be assumed,

Link Speed (bps)		Min (Packets)	Max (Packets)	Min (Bytes)	Max (Bytes)
64,000	64k	4	12	1,024	3,072
128,000	128k	6	15	1,536	3,840
256,000	256k	8	20	2,048	5,120
384,000	384k	10	30	2,560	7,680
512,000	512k	15	40	3,840	10,240
1024,000	1024k	24	64	6,144	16,384
1540,000	T1	32	96	8,192	24,576
3080,000	2xT1	64	150	16,384	38,400
6160,000	4xT1	128	300	32,768	76,800
12,320,000	8xT1	256	600	65,536	153,600
10,000,000	Ethernet (10M)	256	600	65,536	153,600
34,000,000	E3	300	900	76,800	230,400
44,700,000	T3	300	900	76,800	230,400
100,000,000	FastEthernet (100M)	500	1,500	128,000	384,000
155,000,000	OC3/STM1	750	2,000	192,000	512,000
622,000,000	OC12/STM4	3,000	15,000	768,000	3,840,000
1,000,000,000	GigabitEthernet	5,000	20,000	1,280,000	5,120,000
2,400,000,000	OC48/STM16	10,000	30,000	2,560,000	7,680,000
9,600,000,000	OC192/STM64	15,000	45,000	3,840,000	11,520,000
10,000,000,000	TenGigabitEthernet	15,000	45,000	3,840,000	11,520,000
38,400,000,000	OC768/STM192	15,000	45,000	3,840,000	11,520,000

Figure 2.20: Guidelines for Min/Max Threshold Values

which is also the conversion rate that the Cisco MQC software uses when converting from byte units to packet units and hence applies to all platforms that support MQC.

2.11.5 A Word About Hardware

Although these recommendations are platform-independent and fairly generic, it should be noted that in many cases there are specific requirements for min/max threshold values based on a particular hardware implementation. One very common observation is that on most of the Cisco 12000 Series Linecards, the difference between min and max must be an even power of 2. Otherwise this results in an internal "rounding error" within the system, whereby the system maintains the configured max value and adjusts the min value such that (*max–min*) is an integer power of 2. (This rounding has virtually no impact on the effectiveness of the WRED configuration, and generic values can be used to simplify their operations and allow particular implementations to alter the values internally as needed.)

Hardware-specific WRED/queue-limit implementations may measure the current queue depths in terms of bytes or in terms of packets. In cases where the software allows for either "time-based" or byte-based configurations, an internal conversion is applied before programming the hardware. The conversion rate for this operation is 256 B/packet.

2.11.6 Queue Limit vs. WRED

Queue limit is the terminology used to describe a depth at which we begin tail-dropping all traffic. In general, WRED is preferred over queue limit because it provides an increasing drop function instead of an all-or-nothing approach. But this certainly depends on the type of traffic and the bearing WRED will have over certain types of traffic. Using WRED with video applications will have a bearing on the overall quality and has the potential to disrupt numerous sessions, even if a few packets are dropped in anticipation of network congestion. This is especially true in the case of IPTV deployments and hence is best avoided in such deployments. However, it is very common to have WRED and queue limits used together in a network, each serving its own set of traffic that has its own unique characteristics and requirements.

Queue limits are still effective in preventing congestion and are generally simpler to configure, so many deployments prefer this approach. In trying to select queue-limit sizes, the value from the max threshold column for the given interface speed on Figure 2.13 can be used.

2.11.7 Time-Based WRED

Time-based thresholds for WRED and queue limit are features that allow an operator to specify the WRED minimum and maximum thresholds and the queue limit thresholds in milliseconds (ms) or in microseconds (μs). After the threshold limits are configured, the same can be applied to the various network interfaces. Time-based WRED helps in simplifying the process of configuring the various thresholds because it gives the user an idea of how much delay would be caused by virtue of configuring WRED and queue limit ranges, and the system would automatically do the conversion from time into packets/bytes for the actual internal processing.

2.11.8 Understanding WRED Values

It is essential at times to understand the conversion done internally when using time-based WRED for defining WRED and queue limit thresholds. When values are entered in units of time (let's say ms), it is interesting to understand how many bytes/packets a given unit corresponds to. The same applies when entering thresholds in terms of number of packets, which would raise a question as to how much of a delay (in terms of units of time) is being caused. This section illustrates the formula used for calculating these values, as follows. Figures 2.21–2.23 provide insight into the WRED conversion, along with an example providing the output.

Figures 2.22 and 2.23 provide a snapshot of a WRED configuration and help in understanding the conversion of WRED to packets, specified in units of time.

2.12 Congestion Management

As the term implies, *congestion management* enables you to manage the congestion that is experienced by packets at a given point in the network. Congestion management involves three main steps:

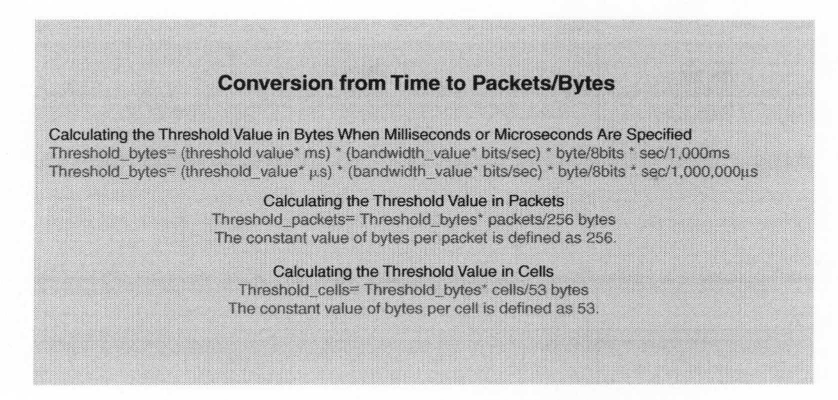

Figure 2.21: Time-Based WRED Conversion

```
!
 class class-default
  random-detect
  random-detect precedence 0 50 ms 100 ms
  random-detect precedence 1 50 ms 100 ms
  random-detect precedence 2 50 ms 100 ms
  random-detect precedence 3 50 ms 100 ms
  random-detect precedence 4 50 ms 100 ms
  random-detect precedence 5 50 ms 100 ms
!
#When converting maximum threshold to packets on a GigabitEthernet Link:
         1G/(256byte*8bits))*100ms/1000=48828 packets
```

Figure 2.22: Time-Based WRED Configuration

```
Router#show policy-map interface gigabitethernet1/2
  Class-map: class-default (match-any) (8052769/0)
       3184489694 packets, 815229361664 bytes
            Class of service queue: 12
        Queue-limit: 65536 packets (default)
          Random-detect: precedence-based
  Precedence   RED Label  Minimum      Maximum     Mark
                          threshold  threshold probability
   0               1          32444        48828      1
   1               1          32444        48828      1
```

Figure 2.23: Validating WRED Output

1. Queues are created at the interface where QoS is required. Depending on the specific feature or mechanism being used to provide QoS and the platform on which the QoS is being configured, multiple queues could be created.
2. Packets (which could also be frames, but for the sake of simplicity we use the word packets) are then assigned to these queues based on classification such as DSCP, IP TOS, or 802.P bits. It is even common to use extended ACLs to classify traffic based

on port numbers. The classification of packets by characteristic is user defined, and packets are placed into queues by these predetermined characteristics.

3. Packets are then scheduled for transmission. Determining the scheduling of packets is specific to the congestion management scheme used, but generally there will be a way to provide for the transmission of more packets out of some queues compared to others. That is, you will be able to give some packets better treatment/higher priority than others with regard to the amount of bandwidth that those packets receive.

2.12.1 Queuing

Whenever packets enter a device faster than they can exit it, as is the case with interface speed mismatches (for example, Gigabit Ethernet traffic heading to a Fast Ethernet interface), a point of potential congestion, or a bottleneck, occurs. Devices have buffers that allow for temporary storage of these backed-up packets in a process known as *queuing*. In short, queuing is the logic of ordering packets in linked output buffers. It is important to recognize that queuing processes are engaged only when the interface is experiencing congestion and are deactivated shortly after the interface congestion clears.

2.12.2 Scheduling

Scheduling is the process of deciding which packet to transmit next. Scheduling occurs when the interface is experiencing congestion but also (unlike queuing) when the interface is not experiencing congestion (that is, there is still a decision, albeit a simple one, of which packet should be transmitted next, even if there is no congestion on the interface). If there is no congestion on the interface, packets are transmitted as they arrive. If the interface is experiencing congestion, queuing algorithms are engaged. However, the scheduler still has to decide which QoS queue to service next.

2.12.3 Class-Based Weighted Fair Queuing

Weighted fair queuing (WFQ) is a dynamic process that divides bandwidth among queues based on weights. The process is designed to be fair, such that WFQ ensures that all traffic is treated fairly with regard to its weight. Class-Based Weighted Fair Queuing, or CBWFQ, a form of WFQ, provides the ability to reorder packets and control latency at the edge and in the core. By assigning different weights to different service classes, a switch or router can manage buffering and bandwidth for each service class. Because weights are relative and not absolute, underutilized resources can be shared between service classes for optimal bandwidth efficiency. CBWFQ allows application service classes to be mapped to a portion of network link. For example, a QoS class can be configured to occupy, at most, 25 percent of a link. Figure 2.24 provides an example of three service classes provisioned using CBWFQ with the following characteristics:

- Class 1, with guaranteed latency and delivery
- Class 2, with guaranteed delivery
- Class 3, a best-effort service

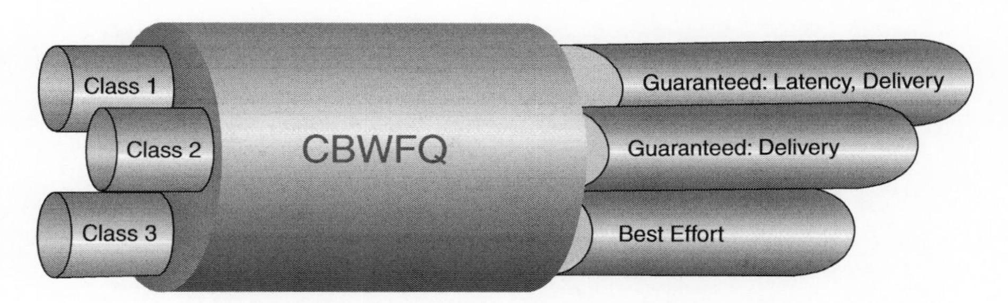

Figure 2.24: Illustration of CBWFQ

By separately allocating bandwidth and buffering space, a given class of traffic can have its own characteristics that will result in diverse behaviors between the various traffic classes. Since the shares are relative weights, allocating a large share to Class 1 means that a minimum is guaranteed. If Class 1 is underutilized, the bandwidth will be shared by the remaining classes in proportion to their weights. For CBWFQ, the weight of a packet belonging to a specific class is derived from the bandwidth that is assigned to the class. Therefore, the bandwidth assigned to the packets of a given class determines the order in which packets are sent. All packets are serviced fairly based on weight, and no class of packets may be granted absolute and strict priority. This scheme poses problems for voice traffic, which is largely intolerant to delay, especially variation in delay. For voice traffic, variations in delay introduce irregularities of transmission manifesting as jitter in the heard conversation.

2.12.4 Low-Latency Queuing

Low-latency queuing (LLQ) is CBWFQ in combination with a strict priority queue (PQ). Traffic is typically assigned to the LLQ using the IOS *Priority* command and gets serviced with exhaustive priority up to its assigned bandwidth (that is, traffic is sent out first until no more traffic is present or the bandwidth assigned is exceeded) and before all the other queues are serviced. Two components are of interest. First, the LLQ is serviced using a strict priority algorithm and ideal for servicing voice traffic because it offers both latency and bandwidth guarantees. Second is the CBWFQ mechanism, which is a class-based complex of queues and is an effective algorithm in serving data applications because it provides bandwidth guarantees but does not guarantee latency. Figure 2.25 illustrates the LLQ operation.

The threat posed by the strict priority scheduling algorithm is that it could starve lower-priority traffic. To prevent this, the LLQ mechanism has a built-in policer. The policer engages only when the interface is facing congestion. Therefore it is important to provision adequate bandwidth for the LLQ. If the total amount of provisioned priority-class bandwidth is less than the total amount of voice traffic being offered to the priority queue, the excess traffic will be tail-dropped by the LLQ policer under periods of congestion. The policer in the LLQ will start dropping excess traffic indiscriminately, which could affect all the voice calls, not just the last one passing through. Cisco software supports two types of LLQ policing algorithms, known as congestion-aware/conditional policing and always-on/hard policing. Each of these is described next.

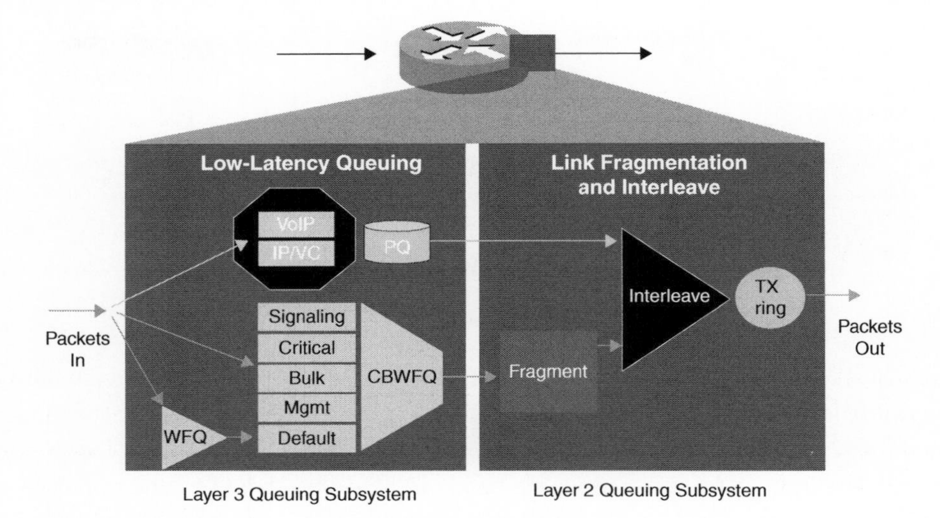

Figure 2.25: LLQ Operation

```
!
policy-map network-core
 class voice
 priority percent 30 ------------→ Congestion Aware Policer
class mission-critical-data
 bandwidth percent 20
class best-effort-data
!bandwidth percent 10
```

Figure 2.26: Congestion-Aware Policer

2.12.5 Congestion-Aware Policing

In the case of *congestion-aware* or *conditional policing*, the LLQ is allowed to use more than its configured bandwidth if bandwidth is available and not being used by the other classes. However, when there is contention for bandwidth, the LLQ is reduced to its actual size, thus providing the available bandwidth for use by other queues. This is to ensure fair play among the various classes. Figure 2.26 illustrates the configuration.

2.12.6 Always-On Policer

In the case of the *always-on* or *hard policer*, the LLQ is allowed only to use only the subscribed amount of bandwidth, even in times when the network has more bandwidth (noncongestion). The LLQ will never exceed the configured percentage of bandwidth (configured via the policer), even if the other queues are not using the wire or utilizing the maximum of their reserved bandwidth percentages. Figure 2.27 illustrates this configuration.

2.12.7 Always-On Policer vs. Congestion-Aware Policing

To understand the impact of using either of the policing approaches, a short illustration using congestion-aware policing is provided here: Let's imagine that nonpriority queues are empty

```
!
policy-map network-core
 class voice
  police priority <bps> ---------→ Always on Policer
class mission-critical-data
 bandwidth percent 20
class best-effort-data
 bandwidth percent 10
!
```

Figure 2.27: Always-On Policer

at t0 (first instance of a unit of time), and LLQ traffic could utilize up to link speed. At t1 the non-LLQ traffic starts to build up, which would essentially affect some or more of the existing voice calls. Then at t2 (the second instance of a unit of time), non-LLQ traffic reduces, so again there's more room for voice, and at t3 (the third instance of a unit of time), assuming that the traffic load increases, the LLQ drops might start again. The congestion-aware (conditional) policer may impact voice calls due to nondeterministic behavior and potential SLA and RFC-2598 violations (packet loss in EF class due to changes in non-LLQ traffic streams). Hence the use of the always-on policer has gained more popularity in recent network deployments. Platforms that perform QoS functionality in software such as the 7200 series routers only support congestion-aware policing, whereas platforms such as the CRS-1, 12000, and 7600, which process QoS in ASICs, support the use of the always-on policer.

2.12.8 Dual-Priority Queues

In Cisco IOS software, the existing LLQ functionality has been enhanced with the introduction of *multilevel priority queuing* (MPQ). This extension brings a second priority queue for latency-sensitive traffic. MPQ enables differentiation between two types of traffic with strict latency requirements. For example, a QoS policy using MPQ can provide isolation between real-time voice and real-time video traffic while still meeting their latency targets. At this writing, the Cisco 7600 SIP-400 line cards support the use of dual-priority queues in the egress direction.

2.12.9 Low-Latency Queuing Bandwidth Provisioning

It is important to understand the goal of convergence: to allow voice, video, and data to coexist transparently on a single network. If real-time applications dominate a network, as in the case of a dominantly provisioned LLQ (in which the priority classes have the majority of the bandwidth), data applications might fluctuate significantly in their network response times when voice (which is hosted in the LLQ) calls are made. This destroys the transparency of the converged network. User feedback has consistently reflected that most users prefer consistent (even if moderately slower) application response times over varying response times (as would occur if the LLQ dominates the network links). Testing has revealed a conservative rule of thumb for priority-class provisioning, which is to limit the sum of all priority-class traffic to not more than 33 percent of the network link capacity. This includes the sum of traffic used, even in the case of dual-priority queues. This will ensure that only minimal delays are introduced into the LLQ and ensure that other traffic classes get an adequate share of the network bandwidth.

It is vitally important, however, to understand that this strict priority queuing rule is simply a best-practice design recommendation, not a mandate. There might be cases in which specific business objectives cannot be met while holding to this recommendation. In such cases, enterprises and SPs must provision according to their detailed requirements and constraints. However, it is important to recognize the tradeoffs involved with overprovisioning strict priority traffic and its negative performance impact on nonreal-time application response times. It is also worth noting that the 33 percent rule only applies to converged networks. In cases where an enterprise or SP network hosts only VoIP traffic, for instance, the 33 percent rule does not apply, since voice (and perhaps some nominal amount of management and signaling traffic) is the only traffic on the circuit. In these cases, the network is free to use up to 98 percent of the link capacity for voice (reserving 2 percent for routing protocols, network management traffic such as SSH and SNMP, and signaling).

2.12.10 Modified Deficit Round Robin

The Cisco 12000 series of routers implements a queuing mechanism referred to as *Modified Deficit Round Robin* (MDRR) on line-card engines (such as Engines 2, 3, 4, 5, and above). On the engine 0 line card, the queuing mechanism is *Deficit Round Robin* (DRR). The difference between DRR and MDRR is the absence of an LLQ on the DRR line cards (explained later in this section). DRR/MDRR essentially has a similar effect as CBWFQ, discussed in the previous section. Each queue within MDRR is defined by two variables:

- *Quantum value.* This is the average number of bytes served in each round.
- *Deficit counter.* This counter is used to track how many bytes a queue has transmitted in each round. It is initialized to the quantum value.

Each non-empty queue is served in a round-robin fashion. Packets in a queue are served as long as the deficit counter is greater than zero. Each packet served decreases the deficit counter by a value equal to its length in bytes. A queue can no longer be served after the deficit counter becomes zero or negative. In each new round, each non-empty queue's deficit counter is incremented by its quantum value. In general, the quantum size for a queue should not be smaller than the maximum transmission unit (MTU) of the interface. This ensures that the scheduler always serves at least one packet from each non-empty queue. Each queue in MDRR/DRR has a relative weight assigned to it. The weights assign relative bandwidth for each queue when the interface is congested.

In DRR/MDRR, packets are mapped to queues based on the EXP bits set in the MPLS label header or the IP ToS/DSCP field in the IP header. The MDRR algorithm dequeues data from each queue in a round-robin fashion if there are data in the queue to be sent. With MDRR, one of these queues is called the *high-priority queue* and is treated differently from the other queues. It is processed using either strict priority or alternate priority mode. This provides a feature much like the LLQ found in CBWFQ.

2.12.11 Strict-Priority Mode

In strict priority mode, the high-priority (low-latency) queue is serviced immediately whenever the queue is not empty. In other words, it is serviced first and before all other queues. Only when all the high-priority traffic is cleared will other queues be considered. This system ensures the lowest possible delay for this traffic type. However, it can detrimentally affect all other queues if the traffic destined for the high-priority queue uses a large amount of bandwidth. Figure 2.28 shows the topmost queue as the LLQ that gets immediately serviced; the other queues are served by DRR.

2.12.12 Alternate Priority Mode

In alternate priority mode, the queues are serviced, alternating between the high-priority queue and each of the other queues. The LLQ has a weight assigned to it and can send only a certain amount of traffic, but because the time between its turns is much shorter, it will provide low latency. The weight is the only variable parameter in DRR/MDRR. It influences two things: the relative amount of bandwidth a traffic class can use and how much traffic is sent in one turn. Using larger weights means that the overall cycle takes longer and possibly increases latency. In addition, we should note that the LLQ in alternate priority mode is serviced more than once per cycle and thus takes more bandwidth than other queues with the same nominal weight. How much more is a function of how many queues are defined—for example, with three queues in total, the LLQ is serviced twice as often as the other queues and sends twice its weight per cycle. If eight queues are defined, the LLQ is serviced seven times more often and the "effective" weight is seven times higher.

In alternating priority mode, the LLQ is serviced after each individual regular DRR queue is serviced, as shown in this example: Suppose we have defined four queues, 0, 1, 2, and the low-latency queue. If all queues were congested, they would be serviced as such: 0, LLQ, 1, LLQ,

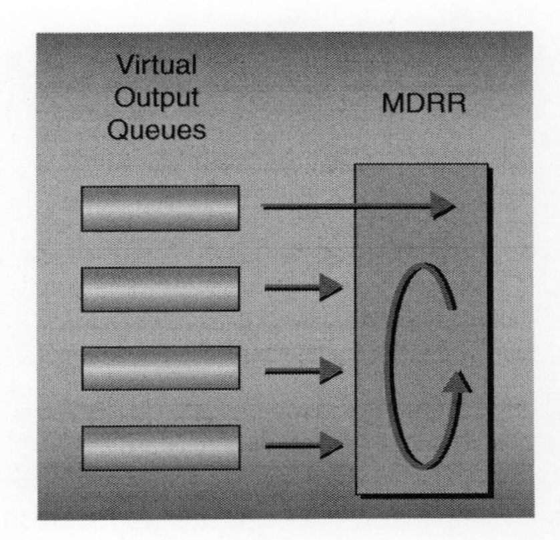

Figure 2.28: Strict Priority Mode in MDRR

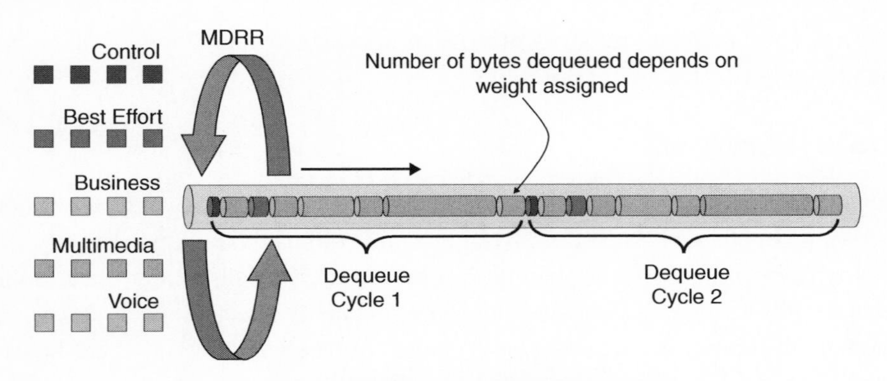

Figure 2.29: Alternate Priority Mode

2, LLQ, 0, LLQ, 1, and so on. In effect, the scheduler alternates, in a given cycle, between the LLQ and each normal queue defined in the network. Figure 2.29 illustrates this behavior.

2.12.13 A Word About the MDRR Implementation and MQC

MQC support on the Cisco 12000 Series does not imply that the same QoS feature set available on another platform, such as the Cisco 7600 Series, is now available on the Cisco 12000 routing platform. The MQC provides a common syntax in which a command results in a shared function or behavior. For example, the *bandwidth* command implements a minimum bandwidth guarantee. The Cisco 12000 Series makes the bandwidth reservation using MDRR the scheduling mechanism; the Cisco 7500 Series uses WFQ. The underlying algorithm complements the particular platform.

2.12.14 Congestion Avoidance/Management and Scheduling

The Service Provider Network Core, which consists of provider routers (as they are referred to on an MPLS network), is responsible for both avoiding and managing network congestion. Provider routers are also responsible for queuing and scheduling traffic as per the QoS policies, wherein traffic is queued as per the DiffServ markings.

2.13 Modular QoS CLI

As its name suggests, the *Modular QoS CLI* (MQC) is used to enable QoS functionality. The primary goal of the MQC is to provide a platform-independent interface for configuring QoS on Cisco platforms. To attain platform independence, the commands within the MQC define QoS functionality and behavior independent of the implementation or algorithm (that is, platform- or implementation-specific details are not exposed in the CLI). To this end, the MQC effectively defines a QoS behavioral model at an abstract level.

Examples of abstract behaviors configurable via the MQC include guaranteeing a minimum bandwidth allocation to a particular class of traffic, imposing a maximum transmission

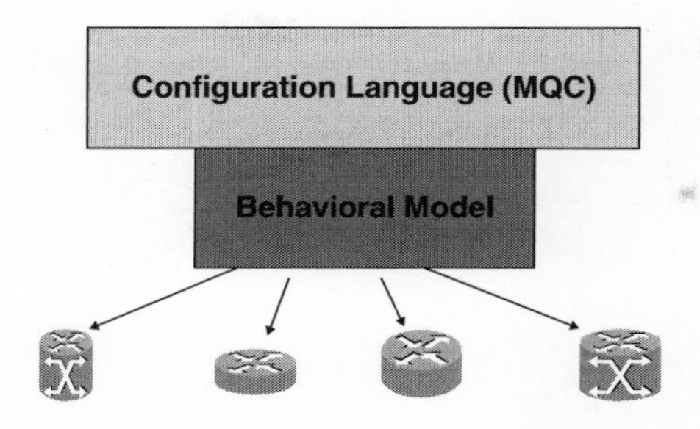

Figure 2.30: Abstraction of the QoS Model

rate on a class of traffic, and guaranteeing low latency to a class of traffic. Each of these examples illustrates a general behavior that is useful across platforms, and thus a common, consistent, and platform independent interface should be used to enable that behavior on all Cisco platforms. To further illustrate the importance of having a QoS CLI that is functional and behavioral rather than one that exposes platform- or implementation-specific details, consider the consequences of each platform having a different means to enable basic QoS functionality and each platform having unique internal system mechanics (such as switch fabrics), the resources of which must be managed directly (via platform-specific CLI) for the user to achieve basic QoS goals (for example, provide low latency for voice traffic). In such an environment, users must acquire knowledge and expertise of platform-specific architectural issues and essentially learn multiple ways to achieve what is really the same goal (that is, define QoS behavior on a given platform). Users should not be aware of platform-specific mechanisms or internal algorithms but instead should be able to specify abstract behaviors (for example, guarantee *X* mbps and low latency to class "foo" on interface *y*) that result in the automatic enabling of any and all appropriate platform mechanisms to achieve the stated behavioral goal. Different platforms can have different underlying mechanisms, but from the user's point of view, the requested behavior is the same. Therefore, hiding the underlying platform-specific details is of paramount importance. This greatly simplifies the user's task and thereby reduces operational costs and complexities for both enterprises and service providers. In summary, MQC provides a common and uniform CLI approach across Cisco platforms.

2.13.1 QoS Behavioral Model

This section defines the abstract Cisco QoS behavioral model that underlies the MQC (that is, the MQC is the configuration language for the abstract behavioral model). As discussed in the previous section, the motivation for defining a behavioral model and a configuration language for enabling that model are to ensure that any Cisco platform that implements QoS will do so in a way that will result in a behavior that is consistent with the behavior provided by other Cisco platforms. That is, all platforms should conform to the Cisco QoS behavioral model and present a common user interface (MQC), irrespective of the implementation details of the platforms. The relationship among MQC, the behavioral model, and Cisco platforms is illustrated in Figure 2.30.

The goals of the Cisco behavioral model are as follows:

- It should be intuitive and simple to understand.
- It should have a "you get what you dial approach"—that is, when a user specifies a certain behavior, this will be the resulting behavior, with no unexpected side effects.
- It should be flexible and should provide enough richness to accomplish a variety of tasks.

2.13.2 End-to-End QoS Operation

Typically, any SP IP/MPLS network is likely to have two types of encapsulation profiles:

- Traffic that is labeled: MPLS traffic
- Traffic that is unlabeled: plain IP traffic

2.14 Labeled Traffic

MPLS and MPLS VPN traffic can be categorized as *labeled traffic*. IP ToS, DSCP, or Layer 2 CoS values are used to classify traffic at the network edge. In the core, MPLS experimental bits are used as the classifier for mapping traffic into the various QoS classes. Figure 2.31 shows a general overview of how QoS would operate for labeled traffic between two CE devices in a SP IP/MPLS network and serves as a reference for understanding the functional flow of the various components that constitute the QoS framework for an IP NGN infrastructure.

A typical QoS operation in this category would be as follows:

- The provider edge (PE) receives IP traffic.
- The PE performs packet classification and applies the MPLS label and appropriate EXP bits pertaining to the service class for that destination.

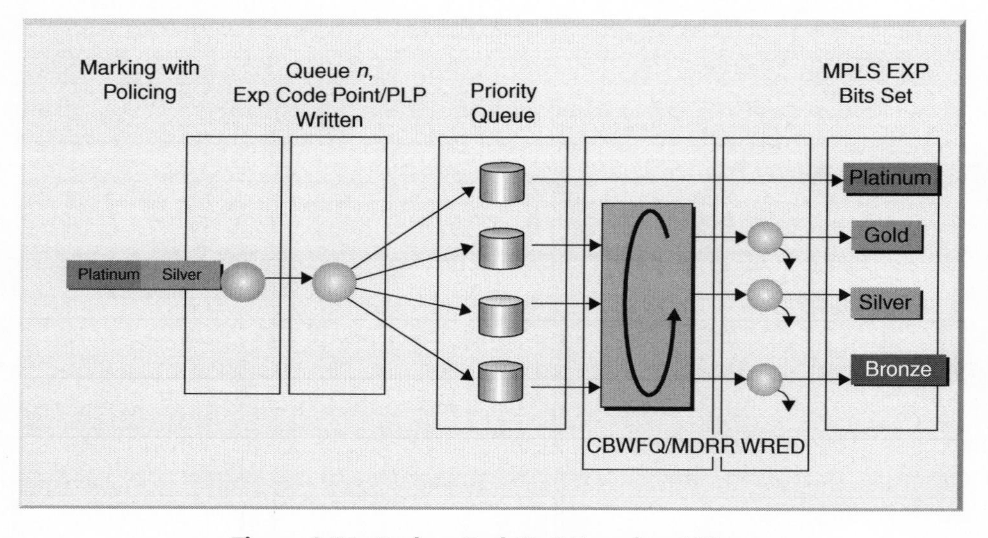

Figure 2.31: End-to-End QoS Functional Flow

- CBWFQ/WRED or MDRR is applied on the egress interface facing the network core.
- Depending on the platform type, egress queuing based on CBQFQ/MDRR is applied on all the provider router interfaces.
- WRED may be applied on the network core facing interfaces.
- The destination PE router forwards the IP packet based on the bottom label to its correct destination. Egress queuing from the PE router would be based on either the IP precedence or MPLS experimental bits, set at ingress to the MPLS network based on the DiffServ tunneling mode used. More on tunneling modes is provided later in this chapter.

2.15 Unlabeled Traffic

Traffic that has no MPLS Label association can be classified as *unlabeled* or *plain IP* traffic. The difference in treatment between labeled and unlabeled traffic is purely based on the remarking treatment at the network edge and queuing in the Network Core. In this case, appropriate IP precedence/DSCP bits are remarked/copied (from the customer IP precedence/DSCP values) at the edge, and queuing in the network core is based on the IP precedence/DSCP bits instead of the MPLS EXP code points, as in the case of the former.

2.16 Trust Boundaries

Although a CE device is traditionally owned and managed by the customer, an SP often provides managed CE service to a customer, where the CE is owned and managed by the service provider. The trust boundary for traditional unmanaged service delivery is at the PE–CE boundary, as shown in Figure 2.32, whereas in the case of managed service it lies behind the CE, between the CE and the rest of the enterprise network, as shown in Figure 2.33.

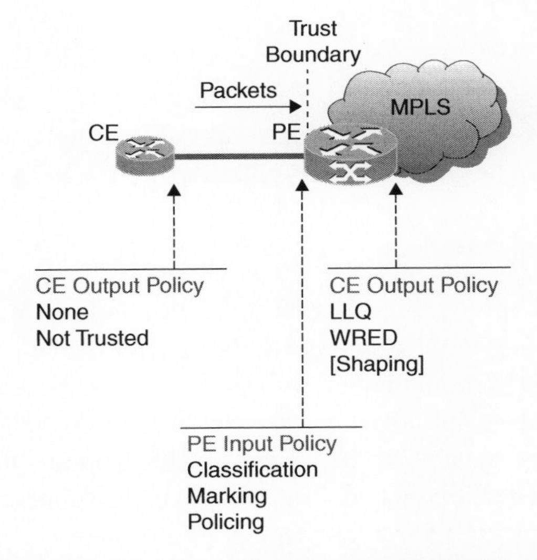

Figure 2.32: Trust Boundary for Unmanaged Services

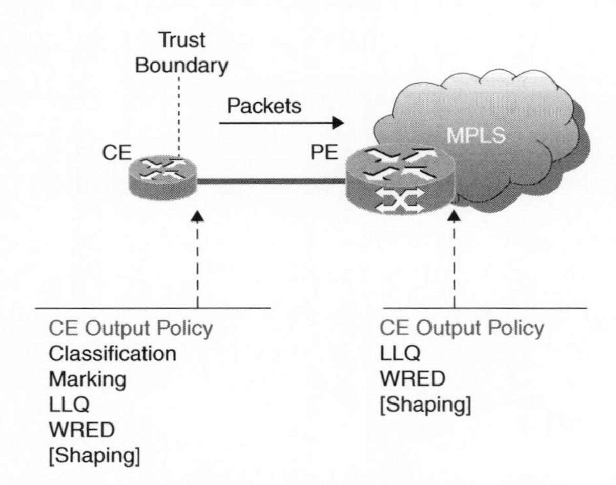

Figure 2.33: Trust Boundary for Managed Services

For unmanaged services, the SP maps enterprise traffic classes to aggregated SP traffic classes at the PE. Since traffic from multiple customers may be aggregated at a single PE, the PE needs to have separate configurations on a per-customer basis to implement such mappings and to enforce SLA. Naturally, the PE QoS configuration could be more complex in this case, depending on the extent of variations of individual customer QoS policies and SLAs. In a managed service, the SP owns and operates the CE (Figure 2.33) from a QoS prospective. One advantage of this is that it allows an SP to distribute the complexity of the enterprise-to-SP QoS policy mapping to the CE devices.

Since the SP owns the CE device, the enterprise-to-SP traffic class mapping as well as other SLA enforcements such as per-class policing can now be done in the CE itself, offloading the PE and thus simplifying the PE configuration.

2.17 QoS Transparency

Since enterprise traffic classification could be different from their SPs, enterprises would like to preserve the IP precedence or DSCP of their packets across the SP network. QoS transparency is a characteristic of an SP network to preserve the original IP precedence/DSCP across the network. This can be achieved in several ways by the SP, as Figure 2.34 summarizes.

2.18 DiffServ Tunnel Modes

DiffServ Tunneling Modes introduce a new PHB that allows differentiated QoS in an SP's MPLS network. The tunneling mode is defined at the edge of the network, normally in the PE label switch routers (LSRs), both ingress and egress. Consideration should be given on what occurs when the topmost label is removed from a packet due to penultimate-hop popping (PHP). It might be necessary to copy the MPLS EXP value from the top label that is being popped to the newly exposed label; this does not always apply to all scenarios, as illustrated in detail in the section "Explicit NULL Announcement by PE."

Service Type	IP Core	MPLS Core
Unmanaged	QoS Transparency is difficult to implement in the general case due to traffic aggregation of multiple enterprises, each with different QoS policies, on a single PE. Once the SP changes the IP precedence/DSCP at the ingress PE router, it is difficult to restore the original value at the egress PE. Possible for a traffic class if the SP can: 1. Classify traffic using ACLs based on criteria other than IP precedence/DSCP (e.g., protocol, port). This is often done with complex ACLs. 2. IP precedence/DSCP values are the same for a class between the SP and the enterprises (e.g., IP Precedence 5 for VoIP). **Note:** 1. NBAR classification, although popular in enterprise networks for its flexibility, is not usually recommended for a high-throughput PE due to its high CPU impact. 2. It is possible for an SP and an enterprise to agree that the enterprise marks its PE-bound traffic per SP policy and restore IP precedence/DSCP on traffic received from a PE according to an agreed scheme. This would preserve IP precedence/DSCP and, where possible, simplify PE configuration at the cost of CE config efforts. However, the increase in CE complexity might not be welcome by enterprises in all cases.	Since within the SP network an IP packet is encapsulated with MPLS label(s) that can carry the SP packet classification information in EXP bits, the original IP precedence/DSCP of a packet needn't be changed in the SP network. This makes it easier to implement QoS transparency in an MPLS network (compared to an IP Core.)
Managed	Since SP manages the CE, the QoS policy mapping is done at the CE itself, allowing the PE to be configured without knowledge of the per-customer traffic classification. Enterprise traffic classes are mapped to SP traffic classes at the CE in a mutually agreed way (SLA) by using ACLs or IP precedence/DSCP carried by the packets from the enrerprise. The IP precedence/DSCP is changed at the ingress CE to reflect SP traffic classification. The egress CE restores the original IP Precedence/DSCP using specific knowledge of IP precedence/DSCP mapping or via more involved ACLs.	The incoming enterprise IP packets are reclassified per SP policy at the CE per IP precedence/DSCP or via ACL. However, unlike the IP core case, the original IP precedence/DSCP is not changed to reflect the SP classification. Instead, the packet is marked by the EXP bits carried in the imposed MPLS label. in this case, packet reclassification is simplified by moving it out to the CE, and preserving original packet marking is simplified by using MPLS labels to carry classification information.

Figure 2.34: QoS Transparency Matrix

2.19 Business Objectives

The goal of CoS transparency is to allow an SP to offer differentiated services to its customers and still preserve customers' internal QoS policies. CoS transparency must be supported in a multiservice edge router to achieve its intended benefits.

2.20 The Tunnel Modes

There are different ways to deploy COS transparency in SP networks today. The most accepted way is through MPLS DiffServ tunnel modes. RFC-3270 describes three different modes: pipe mode, short-pipe mode, and uniform mode.

Pipe and *short-pipe modes* are typically used when a packet transits multiple DiffServ domains with different QoS policies. With pipe and short-pipe modes, an MPLS service provider can provide QoS treatment to packets without modifying the DiffServ information (coded in IP precedence/DSCP bits or MPLS EXP bits) on the received packet. These modes are two standard ways of providing end-to-end QoS transparency, also known as *CoS transparency*.

In *uniform mode*, a packet is assumed to transit a single DiffServ domain. As such, an MPLS service provider may modify the DiffServ information on the received packet to provide appropriate QoS treatment. When leaving the provider's MPLS network, the MPLS EXP bits get copied down to the IP precedence or DSCP field. Therefore a provider can, in effect, change the IP precedence of its customer's packet; thus this is not referred to as CoS transparency.

On Cisco routers, DiffServ modes are configured by applying the proper QoS policy on interfaces using MQC. All MPLS tunnel modes are defined by a specific PHB on all components of the network. In an MPLS network it makes sense to differentiate between the ingress PE behavior, the P behavior, and the egress PE behavior.

2.20.1 Explicit NULL Advertisement by PE

Let's take an example of an MPLS virtual private network (VPN) scenario in which the ingress PE imposes two labels on the incoming IP packet, the innermost label identifying the VPN, and the outermost label identifying the IGP label switched path in the core. In the short-pipe and pipe modes, the imposed labels are per the SP's QoS policy. The penultimate hop pops off one label before forwarding the packet with the remaining packet to the egress PE. The PE receives the packet and classifies it per service provider QoS policy using the single remaining label that still carries the EXP per service provider classification.

However, if the ingress PE imposes a single label on an incoming label (as can happen in some applications), the penultimate hop router pops off the label and forwards the IP packet without any label to the PE. In the absence of a label, the PE router has no knowledge of how the packet was classified by the service provider during transit (e.g., was it marked as out-of profile traffic?). The PE can only take decisions based on the IPP/DSCPs of the IP packet, which in reality identifies the packet classification per the enterprise's QoS policy. This might not always be desirable, in which case an option exists to let the PE advertise an explicit NULL to the penultimate-hop P (PHP) router via configuring the following command on its interface toward the P router:

```
mpls ldp explicit null
```

Because of explicit NULL advertisement, the PHP P router adds a label to the IP packet it sends to the PE router. Now the PE router can get the SP QoS classification information from the label. Note that this will also work in the MPLS VPN case; the PHP router imposes another label above the single one it sends to the PE router. So, instead of getting a packet with one label, the PE now gets it with two labels. Both labels can carry the SP classification information if set by the PHP router. The PE router uses this information and pops both labels.

This process can also be used in a managed CE setup, where the CE imposes an MPLS explicit NULL label on the packet being transmitted to the PE and marks the EXP bits per SP classification policy. Therefore, the PE router classifies the packet simply by using this label. Note that this is a Cisco-specific feature on the CE and PE. It is configured on the CE router via the same command:

```
mpls ip impose explicit null
```

on the egress interface toward the PE. This model is suitable when the SP provides a managed CE service to an enterprise. Please note that, though traffic from CE to PE carries the explicit NULL label, there is no label on the packets from the egress PE to CE. This is illustrated in Figure 2.35.

2.20.2 A Closer Look at Short-Pipe Mode

In short-pipe mode, the IP precedence values of the customer IP packet are copied to the MPLS EXP during imposition, or a policy could be configured for marking the SP EXP values. However, there is a slight difference on the egress PE router. Short-pipe mode will queue, based on the end customer's IP ToS values, on the egress interface of the PE router. Basically, the egress queuing is done based on the customer's QoS bits, not the SP's PHB layer.

2.20.3 Ingress PE Behavior

As stated, the SP's MPLS EXP bits might or might not be copied from the customer's IP ToS, DSCP, or MPLS EXP bits, because this is dependent on the platform and line card used. However, if this is not desired, prior to label imposition, the provider must configure a policer or MQC function on the ingress LSR to mark the packet. It is this new PHB that is marked

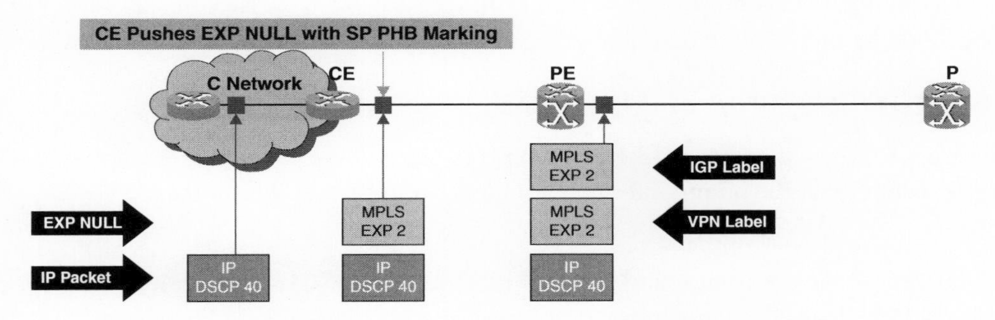

- The imposition of MPLS labels on the ingress PE is *the* default.
- The EXP of the received MPLS frame is copied in memory and later copied in the EXP field of *all* pushed labels. Treated as a default SWAP behavior.
- Could be useful for managed router service.

Figure 2.35: CE Imposed Explicit NULL

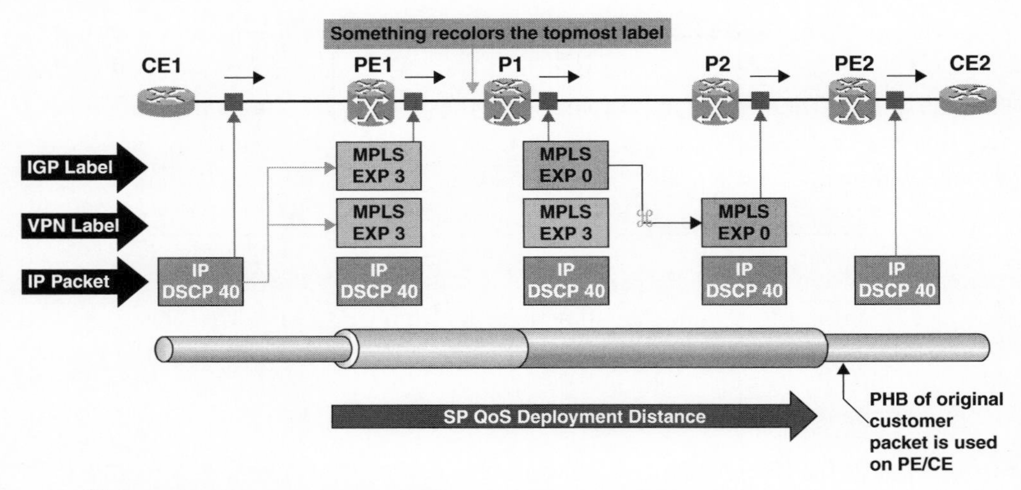

Figure 2.36: Short-Pipe Mode Architecture

only within the MPLS encapsulation for use in the MPLS network. The customer's IP/MPLS PHB marking will not be changed.

2.20.4 P Router Behavior

The MPLS EXP bits of individual MPLS packets might or might not be changed by P (core) routers using policers or MQC, because it is an optional task. For example, an ASBR router might need to change these bits because the ingress network might have different QoS policies. In short-pipe mode, this change must not be propagated to the customer PHB layer for those IP packets leaving the MPLS network. The SP PHB layer is used to classify the packet for discard and scheduling behavior at the output interface of each LSR.

2.20.5 Egress PE Behavior

On the egress PE the Customer PHB layer is used to classify the packet for discard and scheduling behavior at the output interface. Figure 2.36 illustrates the short-pipe mode behavior.

In this illustration, the CE router marks its traffic with an IP DSCP value of 40. At the SP edge, PE1 uses an MQC-based function to mark this traffic with an MPLS EXP value of 3. During imposition, the IGP and VPN labels are both marked with the same MPLS EXP values of 3. The provider router (Router P1 in this illustration) remarks all traffic with MPLS EXP 3 to a MPLS EXP value of 0. Note that this is not a mandatory step; it is used in Figure 2.36 to illustrate the impact of having multiple points of remarking in the overall network. Note that the EXP values in the VPN label and IP DSCP values in the IP header are untouched during the process of remarking the IGP label by the provider router. Finally, the egress PE router

Table 2.2: EXP Treatment in Short-Pipe Mode

	Push	Swap	Pop
ip2mpls	Copies the IP precedence into the EXP**	N/A	N/A
mpls2mpls	Copies the received EXP into the newly imposed EXP	Copies the received EXP into the newly imposed EXP	Copies the removed EXP into the newly revealed label
mpls2ip	N/A	N/A	Doesn't modify the DSCP; selects the PHB based on the DSCP

(PE2 in our illustration) uses the customer PHB layer for the appropriate classification and scheduling.

Table 2.2 illustrates the EXP treatment in short-pipe mode.

NOTE 2.3: Configuration Templates

This chapter provides the DiffServ tunneling mode configuration templates for IOS-based devices only. IOS-XR configuration templates for DiffServ tunneling modes are provided in Chapter 8, "Cisco IOS and IOS-XR Quality-of-Service Implementation for MPLS Layer 3 VPN Services."

2.20.6 Configuration Template

Short-pipe mode uses the customer IP precedence/DSCP values for queuing traffic toward the customer network (egress), since both the customer network (enterprise) and the SP network have their independent and distinct PHB layers. As a result, the PE routers do not need any additional configuration, apart from the configuration of queuing traffic toward the customer network, to achieve the short-pipe mode of operation.

The following configuration uses the following components to construct a DiffServ QoS deployment along with short-pipe mode of operation for CoS transparency:

- Class maps for classifying traffic and defining PHBs in the network core.
- Policy map (CORE-POLICY) for creating the various QoS classes and providing differential treatment in the network core. Three classes are defined, each with its own distinct characteristics. The policy map is applied in the direction facing the SP network core.
- Class maps for classifying customer IP precedence values to define PHBs toward the customer DiffServ domain.
- Policy map (SHORT-PIPE) that implements the short-pipe mode of operation by queuing traffic based on the customer IP precedence values and ensuring CoS transparency. The policy map is applied in the direction facing the CE device.

Short-Pipe Mode Configuration

```
!
class-map match-any Voice-Traffic
 description ### Matching Any ###
 match any
!
policy-map Voice-Traffic
 class Voice-Traffic
 set mpls experimental 5
!
class-map match-all Best-Effort
 match mpls experimental 0
!
class-map match-any Voice
 match mpls experimental 5
!
class-map match-any Video
 match mpls experimental 4
!
class-map match-any Voice-CE-Egress
 match ip precedence 5
!
class-map match-any Best-Effort-CE-Egress
 match ip precedence 0
!
class-map match-any Video-CE-Egress
 match ip precedence 4
!
policy-map CORE-POLICY
 class Voice
 priority
 police rate percent 30
 class Video
 bandwidth percent 50
 class Best-Effort
 bandwidth percent 20
!
policy-Map SHORT-PIPE
 Class Voice-CE-Egress
 Priority
 police rate percent 30
 Class Video-CE-Egress
 bandwidth percent 50
 Class Best-Effort-CE-Egress
 Bandwidth percent 20
!
```

```
Interface gi6/2
Description ### Network-Core-Interface ###
Service-policy output CORE-POLICY--- → Network CORE facing policy
!
Interface gi6/3
Description ### CE-Interface ###
Service-policy output SHORT-PIPE --→ Egress queuing to the customer!
!
End
```

2.20.7 A Closer Look at Pipe Mode

Pipe mode provides a distinct PHB through an MPLS SP network for use only within that network. Since each of the SP's customers can establish its own individual PHB layer marking scheme, the service provider's QoS is distinct from the PHB layer indicated in the SP's customer's IP or MPLS packets. The PHB marking of IP/MPLS packets entering an MPLS SP network might or might not be copied to the PHB marking of the MPLS packets. However, these are by definition different PHBs, and the SP changing the MPLS EXP bits will not affect the customer's IP precedence, DSCP, or MPLS EXP values.

2.20.8 Ingress PE Behavior

The ingress PE router behavior is similar to short-pipe mode, as stated earlier.

2.20.9 P Router Behavior

Once again, behavior on the provider routers is similar to short-pipe mode. The MPLS EXP bits of individual MPLS packets might or might not be changed by P (core) routers using policers or MQC, because it is an optional task.

2.20.10 Egress PE Behavior

On the egress PE the SP PHB layer is used to classify the packet for discard and scheduling behavior at the output interface. In fact, the customer PHB layer is ignored at this interface. Figure 2.37 illustrates the pipe mode behavior.

The only difference between short-pipe and pipe modes of operation is the PHB layer used for egress classification and appropriate scheduling. Pipe mode uses the SP PHB layer for this purpose. Based on the illustration in Figure 2.37, the egress PE router (PE2) uses MPLS EXP 0 as the classification criterion for the customer traffic instead of DSCP 40, which applies to the short-pipe mode of operation.

Table 2.3 illustrates the EXP treatment in pipe mode.

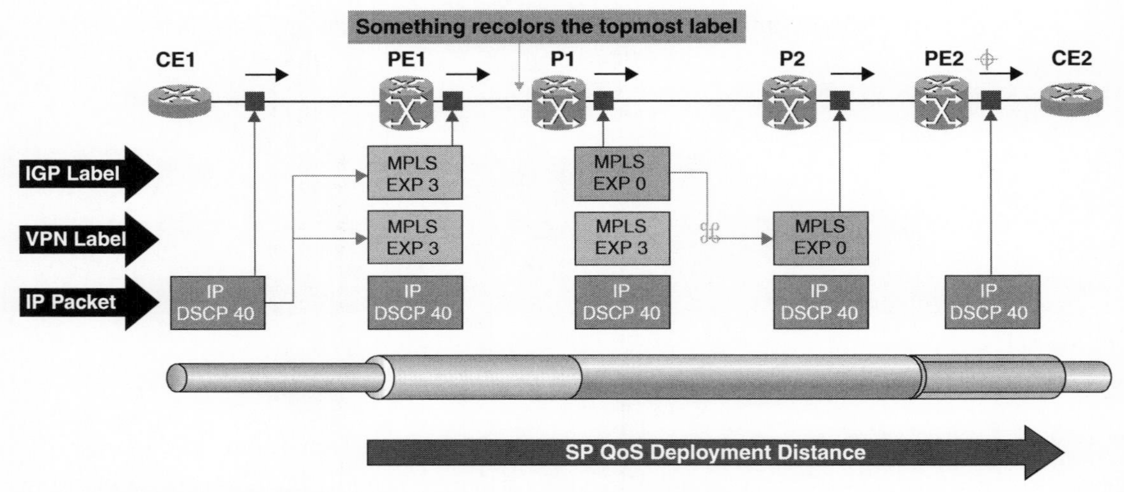

Figure 2.37: Pipe Mode Architecture

Table 2.3: EXP Treatment in Pipe Mode

	Push	Swap	Pop
ip2mpls	Copies the IP Precedence into the EXP**	N/A	N/A
mpls2mpls	Copies the received EXP into the newly imposed EXP	Copies the received EXP into the newly imposed EXP	Copies the removed EXP into the newly revealed label
mpls2ip	N/A	N/A	Doesn't modify DSCP; selects the PHB based on the EXP

2.20.11 Configuration Template

The following illustration provides the complete provider edge configuration required for deploying pipe mode:

- In this illustration, all the relevant EXP values are kept in a placeholder through the use of QoS groups prior to the MPLS disposition, that is, in the MPLS2IP path.
- A policy map called QoS group-in is attached to the network Core-facing interface on the egress PE router, which copies the appropriate EXP bits from each traffic class into individual placeholders.
- Finally, an egress policy map known as PIPE is attached to the CE-facing interface. This policy map makes reference to the EXP values copied to each of the placeholders and appropriately provides differentiated services. The illustration and configuration template achieves the characteristics needed for pipe mode behavior by using the SP PHB values for egress queuing into the end-customer DiffServ domain.

- A Core policy for defining the SP PHB layer has not been included for the sake of simplicity. The same policy map CORE-POLICY defined in the configuration provided for short-pipe mode can be used here as well.

Pipe Mode Configuration

```
!
class-map match-any Voice-Traffic
 description ### Matching Any ###
 match any
!
policy-map Voice-Traffic
 class Voice-Traffic
 set mpls experimental 5
!
class-map match-all Best-Effort
 match mpls experimental 0
!
class-map match-any Voice
 match mpls experimental 5
!
class-map match-any Video
 match mpls experimental 4
!
class-map match-any Voice-CE-Egress
 match qos-group 5
!
class-map match-any Best-Effort-CE-Egress
 match qos-group 0
!
class-map match-any Video-CE-Egress
 match qos-group 4
!
policy-map PIPE
 class Voice-CE-Egress --→ Refers to the Placeholder within the class-map!
 priority
 police rate percent 30
 class Video-CE-Egress
 bandwidth percent 50
 class Best-Effort-CE-Egress
 bandwidth percent 20
!
policy-Map qos-group-in --→ Place EXP values in Placeholders in MPLS2IP path!
 Class Voice
 set qos-group 5
 Class Video
 set qos-group 4
```

```
Class Best-Effort
set qos-group 0
!
Interface gi6/2
Description ### Network-Core-Interface ###
Service-policy input qos-group-in ---→ Copy EXP values into Placeholder
!
Interface gi6/3
Description ### CE-Interface ###
Service-policy input Voice-Traffic -→ Ingress Service Policy!
Service-policy output PIPE -→ Egress queuing to the customer!
!
end
```

2.20.12 A Closer Look at Uniform Mode

Uniform mode is identical to pipe and short-pipe mode on ingress PE and P routers. However, on the egress PE router, uniform mode will copy down the MPLS EXP bits from the label header to the customer's MPLS EXP bits or IP precedence field. Therefore, in this case an SP can alter the customer's packets, which is why it is usually only used with one DiffServ domain. In uniform mode, any changes made to the EXP value of the topmost label on a label stack are propagated both upward as new labels are added and downward as labels are removed.

2.20.13 Ingress PE Behavior

The ingress PE router behavior is similar to short-pipe and pipe modes of operation, as stated previously.

2.20.14 P Router Behavior

Once again, behavior on the provider routers is similar to short-pipe and pipe modes of operation. The MPLS EXP bits of individual MPLS packets might or might not be changed by P (core) routers using policers or MQC, because it is an optional task.

2.20.15 Egress PE Behavior

On the egress PE, the SP PHB layer is copied to the customer PHB layer. This means that the topmost MPLS EXP bits will be copied to the customer IP precedence/IP DSCP bits. Figure 2.38 illustrates the pipe mode behavior.

Based on Figure 2.38, we see that the SP PHB layer gets copied to the customer PHB layer. Therefore, MPLS EXP value 0 gets copied to the customer IP DSCP value, which now reflects the value of 0 instead of DSCP 40.

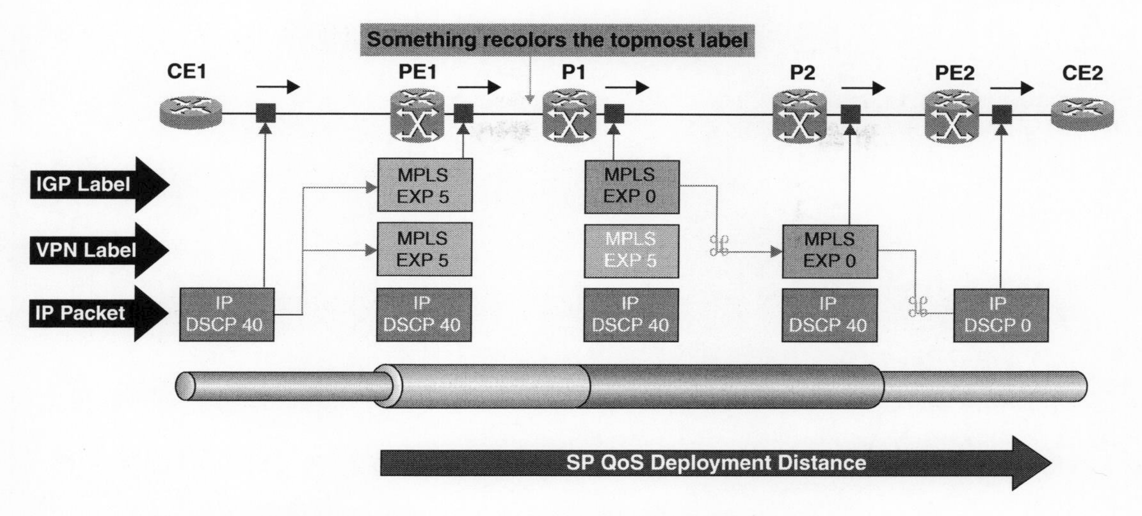

Figure 2.38: Uniform Mode Architecture

Table 2.4: EXP Treatment in Uniform Mode

	Push	Swap	Pop
ip2mpls	Copies the IP Precedence into the newly imposed label**	N/A	N/A
mpls2mpls	Copies the received EXP into the newly imposed EXP	Copies the received EXP into the newly imposed EXP	Copies the removed EXP into the newly revealed label
mpls2ip	N/A	N/A	Copies the removed EXP into DSCP

Table 2.4 illustrates the EXP treatment in uniform mode.

2.20.16 Configuration Template

Since uniform mode is only deployed within a single DiffServ domain, that is, when the SP and the end customer share the same QoS configurations, the customer PHB layer is a reflection of the SP QoS marking and policies. The configuration that follows illustrates that the PHB of the provider is copied to the customer PHB layer after MPLS disposition. As per the illustration, the network or provider edge marks incoming traffic with an MPLS EXP value of 4. On the egress PE router, QoS groups are used for copying the EXP values into the placeholder in the MPLS2IP path. This value is further copied to the end-customer IP precedence bits (an IP precedence value of 4 in this illustration). Finally, the egress queuing is based on the remarked IP precedence values.

Uniform Mode Operation

```
!
class-map match-any Data-Traffic
 description ### Matching Any ###
 match any
!
policy-map Data-Traffic-Marker
 class Data-Traffic
 set mpls experimental 4
!
class-map match-any Best-Effort
 match mpls experimental 0
!
class-map match-any Voice
 match mpls experimental 5
!
class-map match-any Data
 match mpls experimental 4
!
class-map match-any Voice-CE-Egress
 match qos-group 5
!
class-map match-any Best-Effort-CE-Egress
 match qos-group 0
!
class-map match-any Data-CE-Egress
 match qos-group 4
!
policy-map qos-group-in ------→ Placeholder QoS policy!
 class Voice
 set qos-group 5
 class Data
 set qos-group 4
 class Best-Effort
 set qos-group 0
!
policy-map UNIFORM ----→ Policy to overwrite Customer's IP TOS Values!
 class Voice-CE-Egress
 priority
 police rate percent 30
 set precedence 5
 class Data-CE-Egress
 bandwidth percent 50
 set precedence 4
 class Best-Effort-CE-Egress
 bandwidth percent 20
```

```
 set precedence 0
!
Interface gi6/2
 Description ### Core Interface ###
 Service-policy input qos-group-in
!
Interface gi6/3
 Description ### Core Interface ###
 Service-policy input Data-Traffic-Marker
 Service-policy output UNIFORM ---→ Egress queuing to the customer!
!
end
```

****NOTE 2.4: Copying of IP Precedence to EXP**

Not all platforms automatically copy the customer IP precedence bits to MPLS EXP during label imposition. The 7600 LAN cards are a classical example and an exception for this behavior. The behavior during imposition, in this case, largely depends on the defined "trust state." Trust states are detailed in the implementation chapters, later in this book.

2.20.17 A Word on Platform Support

It is important to determine the platform support prior to choosing the DiffServ tunneling mode for deployment. All devices in the network need to support the preferred tunnel mode or else the end result will not be as expected. This is especially important at the network edge, since it is this layer that influences the end result. For instance, the Cisco 7600 routing platform does not support the use of pipe mode; hence a network consisting of this platform would not be ideal for deploying pipe mode.

2.21 Summary

This chapter presented an overview of the DiffServ QoS framework, along with some of the most common tools and features offered by Cisco software used for deployment in IP/MPLS networks. It is worthy to note that QoS is not a panacea for an underprovisioned network, and hence proper capacity planning is the first step toward a successful QoS framework. An overutilized network with the best of QoS tools will fail to impress and result in unpredictable behavior and poor performance of end-user traffic. In other words, QoS in such a case will have little or no impact. The overall network design should keep in mind traffic patterns during normal operations as well as the impact in of a link failure.

Our next steps are to understand traffic characteristics and their needs. The QoS framework will need to employ the right set of tools for the right applications. For instance, voice traffic will need the services of the LLQ, whereas data traffic could be served by CBWFQ. A detailed brief on traffic types and their appropriate traffic-class mapping schemes is provided in Chapter 3, "Class-of-Service Requirements for Quad-Play Networks." In a nutshell, QoS design for an IP/MPLS network should be an evolving process that needs frequent reassessment as the network grows and newer applications are added. As a general rule, it is advisable to start as simply as possible, using only the tools that are deemed as necessary and mandatory. Cisco software provides a rich set of features and options, but not every tool needs to be deployed in the network on day one. An ideal approach is to deploy a set of tools that are needed and observe the behavior and trends that are set for a given period of time. It is of paramount importance that the behavior and trends be properly documented; this would greatly help us observe the delta of difference as and when newer features/changes to the QoS framework are made. QoS monitoring is covered in detail in Chapter 13, "Performance Monitoring and Measurement."

CHAPTER 3

Class-of-Service Requirements for Quad-Play Networks

3.1 Overview

The previous chapter focused on the building blocks for a QoS framework and the various tools available on Cisco software that are the enablers for building a DiffServ QoS model on IP next-generation networks. This chapter presents information on putting together the various building blocks to achieve a comprehensive framework to accommodate the requirements of the various applications within the Quad-Play suite, which includes voice, video, data, and mobility applications. This chapter starts by providing insight into possible options and methods for grouping enterprise applications into SP classes as per best practices and offers a deep dive into the requirements and appropriate recommendations for the most common traffic types.

3.2 Service-Level Agreements

Prior to stepping into the domain of classifying the requirements of application/traffic as well directing them into the appropriate QoS classes, it is imperative to understand the business driver for an efficient and effective QoS framework known as *service-level agreements* (SLAs). SLAs are essentially a business driver from an SP point of view and an agreement from a customer's standpoint. Before we get into discussing SLAs in more detail, let's look at some of the metrics that are the key to building them:

- *Loss.* A comparative measure of packets faithfully transmitted and received to the total number of packets that were transmitted. Loss is expressed as the percentage of packets dropped.
- *Delay.* The finite amount of time it takes a packet to reach the receiving endpoint after being transmitted from the sending endpoint. In the case of voice traffic, a useful measure is the "mouth to ear" delay—the time it takes for sound to leave a speaker's mouth and reach a listener's ear.
- *Delay variation (jitter).* The difference in the end-to-end delays between packets. For example, if one packet required 100 milliseconds (ms) to traverse the network from the source to the destination and the following packet required 125 ms to make the same trip, the delay variation would be calculated as 25 ms.

- *Throughput.* The available user bandwidth between an ingress point of presence (POP) and an egress POP (or between any two points of measurement).

An SLA is a contract between a service provider and a customer that specifies a required level of service and commits the service provider to it. An SLA typically contains a specified level of service, including availability (uptime or downtime), identification/classification of traffic into traffic classes, committed loss, latency, delay variation per traffic class, enforcement or penalty provisions for services not provided, and a specified level of customer support. In an effort to reduce complexity, a service provider typically provides its services with a small set of SLAs from which its customers can choose.

From a conceptual standpoint, a service provider could plan to offer several tiers of services with various levels of SLAs suitable for different types of applications run by its customers (e.g., best-effort service for nonmission-critical, nondelay-sensitive applications, intranet, and so on and a low-latency/high-priority service for VoIP traffic, to name a few). For example, an SP might opt to commit an SLA to limit VoIP traffic loss, latency, and jitter to 0%, 125 ms, and 30 ms, respectively, whereas the corresponding limits for low-latency data traffic (or another class) could be much higher. On the other hand, an SLA for best-effort traffic might be based on only availability and throughput.

In summary, SPs strive to provider tighter SLAs to distinguish themselves from the competition. SLA measurement and baselining can be achieved using some of the mechanisms presented here:

- Latency, loss, and jitter measurements can be carried out using Cisco's IP SLA or by available third-party measurement tools.
- Although service providers often measure round-trip delay (RTD), one-way delay needs to be measured as well, since services such as VoIP require one-way delay to be well within 150 ms.
- One-way delay measurement needs time synchronization between the measuring tools. Depending on the required accuracy, either NTP or GPS-based tools can be used for time synchronization.

When service providers commit to an SLA involving latency, jitter, and/or loss, they usually keep a margin of safety and design the network to meet tighter SLAs than what they commit to their customers. This is known as an *engineering SLA*. Such engineering SLAs are used for internal testing and certification purposes. Such a strict latency target might potentially be necessary in those cases where VoIP packets can be transmitted to another SP network (e.g., a transit provider's network) with higher latency. But SPs always design their networks to meet the stricter engineering SLA.

3.3 In-Contract Traffic

Traffic that adheres to the committed SLAs is considered to be *in-contract*. Typically this is related to the CIR that is agreed between the SP and the end customer. The default action for all traffic that falls within the contracted SLA is allowed to pass.

3.4 Out-of-Contract Traffic

Out-of-contract traffic refers to the traffic that exceeds the specified CIR. There are two possible options for handling such traffic. The first approach is to drop the excess traffic at the point at which the violation has been encountered. The second approach is to remark the excess traffic with a different code point (EXP/IP TOS/DSCP), which refers to a lower-priority queue. This way, an SP can allow the excess traffic to pass through but with a lower priority.

Figure 3.1 illustrates a snapshot of the treatment extended to traffic that classifies as in-contract and traffic that exceeds the CIR and is classified as out-of-contract.

3.5 DiffServ QoS and Traffic-Mapping Options

This section provides a reference on the possible combinations that SPs and even large enterprises use while deploying QoS frameworks for mapping customer traffic to CoS queues, with a goal of relating to many of the points discussed in earlier chapters.

SPs can't expect uniformity in traffic classification among their enterprise customers. Enterprises today use thousands of applications with varying delay, loss, and jitter requirements and place their traffic into a number of traffic classes. The number of classes can vary from a couple to six or seven (or more) from enterprise to enterprise. However, it should be noted that the number of classes in the SP core is much lower, and the provider edge typically consolidates the various enterprise traffic classes into the fewer provider classes. The applications an enterprise groups into a traffic class also vary depending on the relative importance of the applications to the enterprise's business objectives. Traditionally, an enterprise starts off with a few traffic classes and increases their number over a period of time

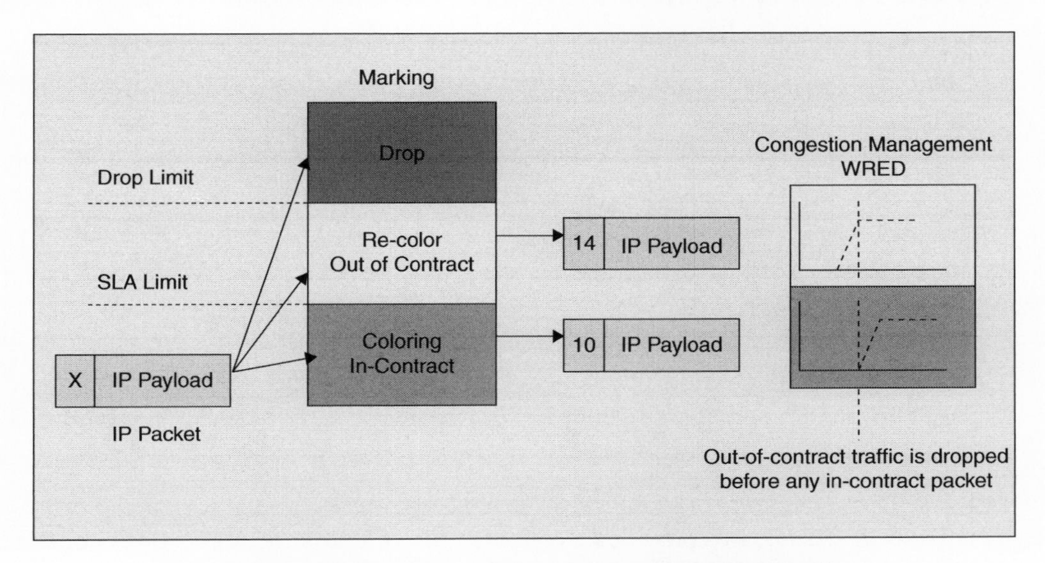

Figure 3.1: Treatment for In- and Out-of-Contract Traffic

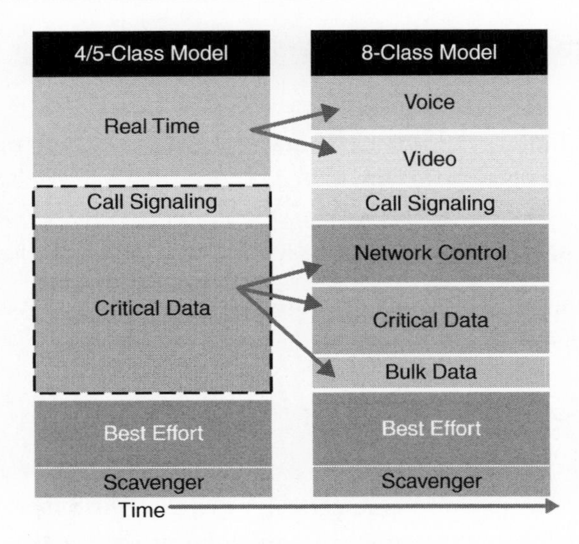

Figure 3.2: Possible Traffic-Class Evolution for an Enterprise

as their QoS requirements become more mature. For example, an enterprise can start with a four- or five-class model and migrate later to an eight-class model, as shown in Figure 3.2.

The kind of traffic carried in most of the classes is self-evident from the class names; a few might need clarification:

- In the leftmost column, the "critical data" traffic class includes traffic for applications that are really important to the business, e.g., SAP, financial applications, IP routing traffic, and network management. As the need to have more granular QoS grows, the critical class may be divided into multiple other classes as shown.
- In the next column, the critical data class includes applications for which response time is important, because in these applications users await response at computer terminals. Routing protocol traffic is classified and categorized in an independent class of its own known as *network control*, and less critical data are classified as *bulk data*. This indicates the level of granularity that gets evolved in the QoS model.
- Scavenger data class has significance today in the enterprise world only. It includes traffic from applications that the enterprise considers "less than best effort." Within the enterprise network this traffic class gets very little minimum bandwidth guarantee to reduce its traffic volume during periods of congestion. Internet download of music, for example, may be considered scavenger traffic by many enterprises. A service provider, however, doesn't distinguish between an enterprise's scavenger-class traffic and best-effort traffic.

3.6 Cisco QoS Baseline

Though the IETF RFC standards provided a consistent set of PHBs for applications marked to specific DSCP values, they never specified which application should be marked to which DiffServ code-point value. Much confusion and disagreements over matching applications

Application	L3 Classification		IETF
	PHB	DSCP	RFC
Routing	CS6	48	RFC 2474
Voice	EF	46	RFC 3246
Interactive Video	AF41	34	RFC 2597
Streaming Video	CS4	32	RFC 2474
Mission-Critical Data	AF31	26	RFC 2597
Call Signaling	CS3	24	RFC 2474
Transactional Data	AF21	18	RFC 2597
Network Management	CS2	16	RFC 2474
Bulk Data	AF11	10	RFC 2597
Best Effort	0	0	RFC 2474
Scavenger	CS1	8	RFC 2474

Figure 3.3: Cisco QoS Baseline

with standards-defined code points led Cisco in 2002 to put forward a standards-based marking recommendation in its strategic architectural QoS Baseline document. Eleven application classes that could exist within the enterprise were examined and extensively profiled, then matched to their optimal RFC-defined PHBs. The application-specific marking recommendations from Cisco's QoS Baseline are summarized in Figure 3.3.

The adoption of Cisco's QoS Baseline was a great step forward in QoS consistency, not only within Cisco, but also within the industry in general.

3.7 RFC-4594 Configuration Guidelines for DiffServ Classes

More than four years after Cisco put forward its QoS Baseline document, RFC-4594 was formally accepted as an informational RFC in August 2006. Before getting into the specifics of RFC-4594, it is important to comment on the difference between the IETF RFC categories of Informational and Standard. An *informational RFC* is an industry-recommended best practice; a *standard RFC* is an industry requirement for interoperability. Therefore RFC-4594 is a set of formal DiffServ QoS configuration best practices, not a requisite standard. RFC-4594 puts forward 12 application classes and matches these to RFC-defined PHBs. These application classes and recommended PHBs are summarized in Figure 3.4.

3.8 Cisco QoS Baseline vs. RFC-4594

It is fairly obvious that there are more than a few similarities between Cisco's QoS Baseline and RFC-4594, as there should be, since RFC-4594 is essentially an industry-accepted evolution of Cisco's QoS Baseline. However, there are some differences that merit attention. The first set of differences is minor, mainly involving nomenclature. Some of the application classes from the QoS Baseline have had their names changed in RFC-4594. These changes in nomenclature are summarized in Table 3.1.

Application	L3 Classification		IETF
	PHB	DSCP	RFC
Network Control	CS6	48	RFC 2474
VoIP Telephony	EF	46	RFC 3246
Call Signaling	CS5	40	RFC 2474
Multimedia Conferencing	AF41	34	RFC 2597
Real-time Interactive	CS4	32	RFC 2474
Multimedia Streaming	AF31	26	RFC 2597
Broadcast Video	CS3	24	RFC 2474
Low-Latency Data	AF21	18	RFC 2597
OAM	CS2	16	RFC 2474
High-Throughput Data	AF11	10	RFC 2597
Best Effort	DF	0	RFC 2474
Low-Priority Data	CS1	8	RFC 3662

Figure 3.4: RFC-4594 Marking Recommendations

Table 3.1: Nomenclature Changes, QoS Baseline to RFC-4594

Cisco QoS Baseline Class Names	RFC-4594 Class Names
Routing	Network Control
Voice	VoIP Telephony
Interactive Video	Multimedia Conferencing
Streaming Video	Multimedia Streaming
Transactional Data	Low-Latency Data
Network Management	Operations/Administration/Management
Bulk Data	High-Throughput Data
Scavenger	Low-Priority Data

The remaining changes are more significant. These include one application class deletion, two marking changes, and two new application class additions. Specifically:

- The QoS Baseline Locally Defined Mission-Critical Data class has been deleted from RFC-4594.
- The QoS Baseline marking recommendation of CS4 for Streaming Video has been changed in RFC-4594 to mark Multimedia Streaming to AF31.
- The QoS Baseline marking recommendation of CS3 for Call Signaling has been changed in RFC-4594 to mark Call Signaling to CS5.
- A new video class has been added to RFC-4594: Real-Time Interactive, which is to be marked CS4. This was done to differentiate between lower-grade desktop video telephony (referred to as Multimedia Conferencing) and higher-grade video

Application	L3 Classification		IETF
	PHB	DSCP	RFC
Network Control	CS6	48	RFC 2474
VoIP Telephony	EF	46	RFC 3246
Broadcast Video	CS5	40	RFC 2474
Multimedia Conferencing	AF41	34	RFC 2597
Real-Time Interactive	CS4	32	RFC 2474
Multimedia Streaming	AF31	26	RFC 2597
Call Signaling	CS3	24	RFC 2474
Low-Latency Data	AF21	18	RFC 2597
OAM	CS2	16	RFC 2474
High-Throughput Data	AF11	10	RFC 2597
Best Effort	DF	0	RFC 2474
Low-Priority Data	CS1	8	RFC 3662

Figure 3.5: Cisco Modified RFC-4594 Marking Values

applications such as TelePresence. Multimedia Conferencing uses the AF4 class and is subject to markdown policies; TelePresence uses the CS4 class and is not subject to markdown.

- A second new video class has been added to RFC-4594: Broadcast Video, which is to be marked CS3. This was done to differentiate between lower-grade desktop video streaming (referred to as Multimedia Streaming) and higher-grade Broadcast Video applications. Multimedia Streaming uses the AF3 class and is subject to markdown policies; Broadcast Video uses the CS3 class and is not subject to markdown.

The most significant of the differences between Cisco's QoS Baseline and RFC-4594 is the RFC-4594 recommendation to mark Call Signaling to CS5. Cisco has just completed a lengthy marking migration for Call Signaling from AF31 to CS3 (as per the original QoS Baseline of 2002), and as such, there are no plans to embark on another marking migration in the near future. It is important to remember that RFC-4594 is an informational RFC (i.e., an industry best practice) and not a standard. Therefore, lacking a compelling business case at the time of writing, Cisco plans to continue marking Call Signaling as CS3 until future business requirements arise that necessitate another marking migration. In summary, the Cisco modified version of RFC-4594 is very similar to RFC-4594, with the one exception of swapping Call Signaling marking and Broadcast Video. These marking values are summarized in Figure 3.5.

For the sake of simplicity, moving forward we follow the Cisco Modified RFC-4594 nomenclature as a reference for classifying traffic throughout this book.

3.9 Enterprise-to-Service-Provider Mapping Options

In reality, the number of classes in an SP network will be much less than the classes defined in both the Cisco QoS baseline and Cisco modified RFC-4594 models, which are ideally suited for enterprise deployment. An SP network ideally would host anywhere between three and seven aggregated classes, much less than the 11 to 12 classes described in the QoS Baseline and RFC-4594 models, respectively. Therefore consolidation of enterprise traffic classes to their SP counterparts is inevitable.

To help design SP traffic classes, this section describes examples of mapping 11 enterprise classes to three-, four-, or six-edge traffic classes of a service provider. The objective is to illustrate the fact that enterprises use many classes, typically aggregated into fewer classes at the SP edge. As mentioned earlier, SPs may choose different traffic classes and nomenclature to suit their business objectives and to accommodate their designs.

3.9.1 Three-Class Service Provider Model

In this model, the SP offers three classes of service: REALTIME (strict priority), CRITICAL-APPS (guaranteed minimum bandwidth), and BEST-EFFORT. Figure 3.6 illustrates this idea in more detail.

- The admission criterion for the REALTIME class is either DSCP EF or CS3.
- The admission criterion for CRITICAL-APPS is shown as DSCP CS6, AF41, AF21, or CS2.

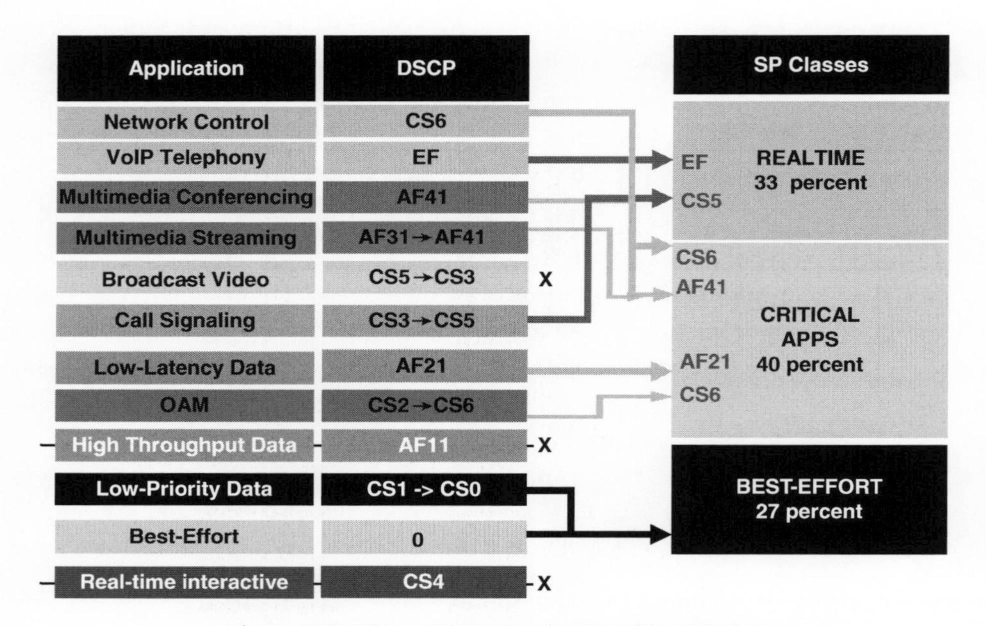

Figure 3.6: Three-Class Service Provider Model

- The other code points are remarked on the ingress PE to 0.
- In this model, there is no recommendation for protecting real-time interactive and broadcast video (because the CRITICAL-APPS queue hosts both low-latency data and multimedia video traffic that is less critical than both broadcast video and real-time interactive video; this queue will be subject to WRED, which is not suitable for delay and loss-sensitive video applications), nor is there a service provider class suitable for high-throughput data, which consists of large, nonbursty, TCP sessions that could drown out smaller data transactions.

The respective CE router configurations are given in Figures 3.7 and 3.8. The illustrations assume that the CE routers are managed by the SP; hence the appropriate markings are coordinated with the provider.

Figure 3.7 illustrates the various class maps required for traffic classification. The class maps refer to the various enterprise traffic classes and point to the respective DiffServ code points used by each class.

Figure 3.8 illustrates the respective policy-map configuration that remarks traffic in accordance with the SP ingress policy:

- The policy map CE-THREE-CLASS-SP-MODEL consists of all the enterprise traffic classes, with the exception of Realtime Interactive, Broadcast Video, and High Throughput Data classes, since there is no corresponding class on the SP network that can cater to the QoS requirements of the applications within these classes.

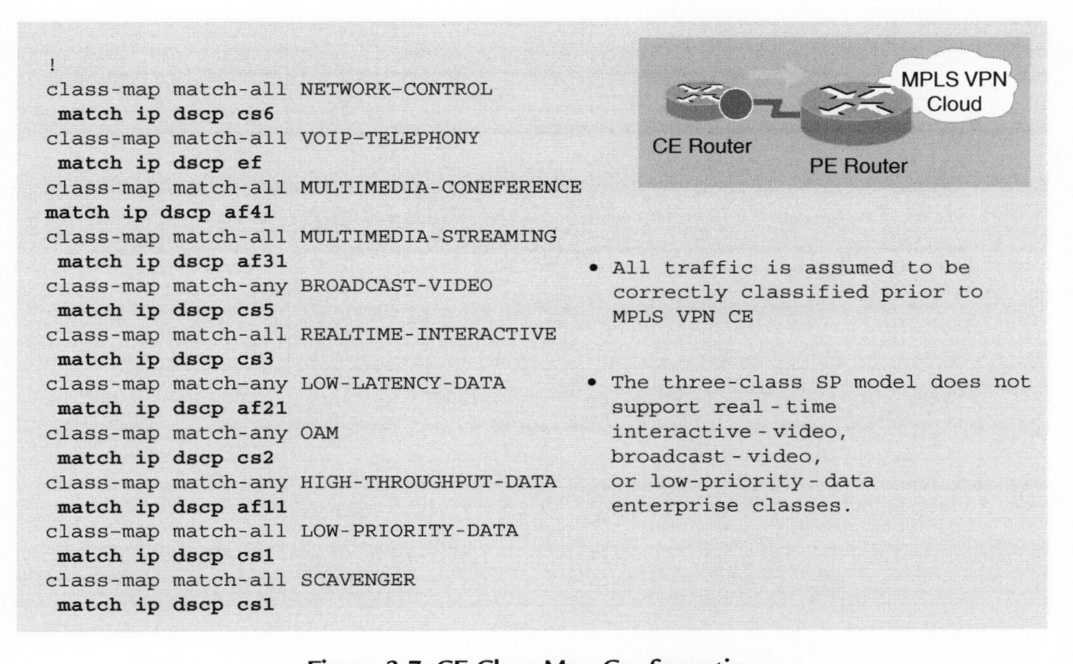

```
!
class-map match-all NETWORK-CONTROL
 match ip dscp cs6
class-map match-all VOIP-TELEPHONY
 match ip dscp ef
class-map match-all MULTIMEDIA-CONEFERENCE
match ip dscp af41
class-map match-all MULTIMEDIA-STREAMING
 match ip dscp af31
class-map match-any BROADCAST-VIDEO
 match ip dscp cs5
class-map match-all REALTIME-INTERACTIVE
 match ip dscp cs3
class-map match-any LOW-LATENCY-DATA
 match ip dscp af21
class-map match-any OAM
 match ip dscp cs2
class-map match-any HIGH-THROUGHPUT-DATA
 match ip dscp af11
class-map match-all LOW-PRIORITY-DATA
 match ip dscp cs1
class-map match-all SCAVENGER
 match ip dscp cs1
```


Figure 3.7: CE Class Map Configuration

```
policy-map CE-THREE-CLASS-SP-MODEL
 class NETWORK-CONTROL
  bandwidth percent 3
 class VoIP-TELEPHONY
  priority percent 15    ! Voice → SP-Realtime
 class MULTIMEDIA-CONFERENCE
  bandwith percent 15
 class CALL-SIGNALING
  priority percent 5     ! call-singaling gets LLQ for this(high—speed)scenario
 class MULTIMEDIA-STREAMING
  bandwidth percent 20   ! Multimedia-streaming is remarked + mapped to SP-Critical
  random-detect
  set ip dscp af41
  class LOW-LATENCY-DATA
  bandwidth precent 15
  random-detect
 class OAM
  bandwidth precent 2
 class LOW-PRIORITY-DATA
  bandwidth precent 1    ! Low Priority (choked at CE) will default to sp-Best effort
 class class-default
  bandwidth precent 24   ! Best Effort will default to SP-Best Effort class
  random-detect
!
```

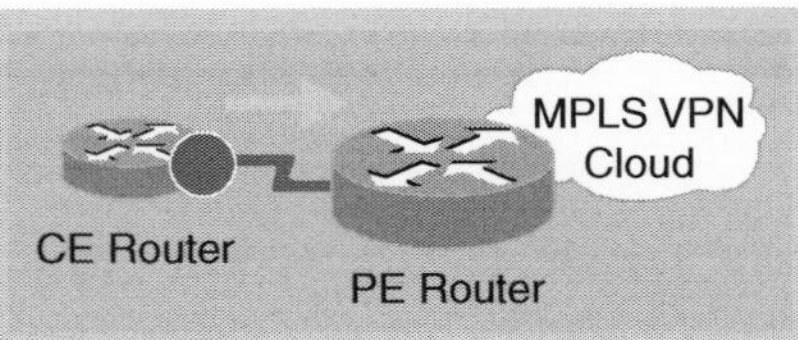

MPLS VPN Cloud
CE Router
PE Router

Figure 3.8: CE Policy Map Configuration

- In total there are nine classes, along with the class default. Looking back at Figure 3.4, Multimedia Streaming with a DSCP value of AF31 is remarked to DSCP AF41 to map to the SP CRITICAL APPS. This is reflected in the configuration template illustrated in Figure 3.8 using the `set ip dscp af41` command within the MULTIMEDIA-STREAMING class under the policy map.
- Classes VoIP-TELEPHONY and CALL-SIGNALING are assigned to the priority queue and have the highest preference within the scheduler.
- The LOW-PRIORITY-DATA class has minimal bandwidth guarantees and will be mapped to the BEST-EFFORT in the provider edge network.

Now that we've seen the CE configurations for creating the enterprise classes, this section helps us in mapping the "many" enterprise classes into fewer (three, as per our illustration in this section) SP classes.

Figure 3.9 illustrates the consolidation of enterprise classes into SP classes. The various enterprise classes with their respective DSCP values are consolidated in three classes at the SP edge. Policy map ENTERPRISE-SP-EDGE-MAP is used to mark the various traffic classes with corresponding MPLS experimental values. For instance, voice and Call Signaling traffic will be marked with an MPLS EXP value of 5; similarly, the other traffic classified under CRITICAL-APPS and BEST-EFFORT will be marked as per the SP's QoS policy.

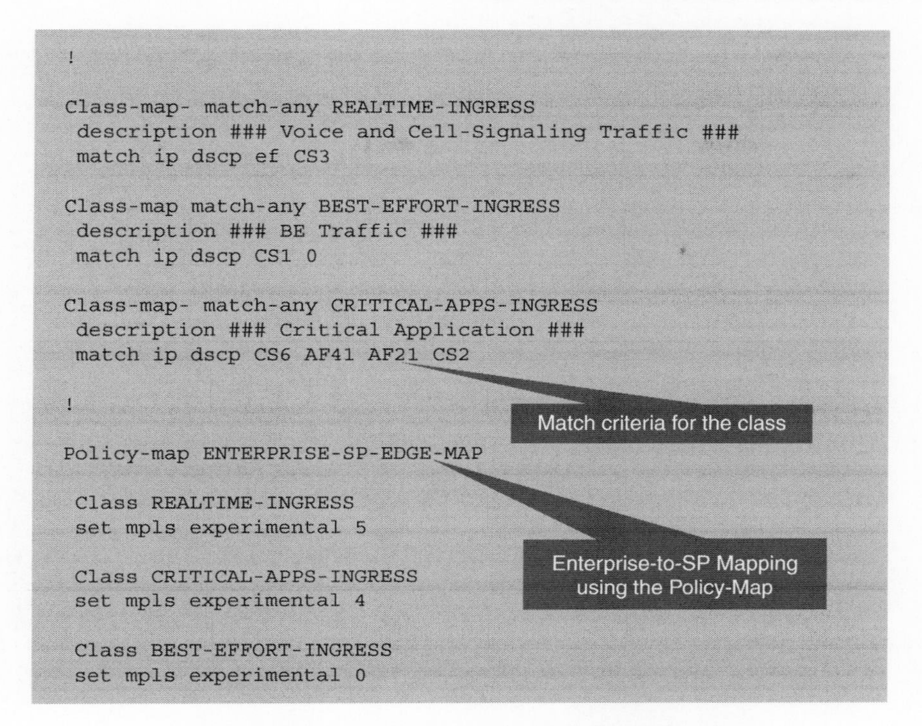

```
!

Class-map- match-any REALTIME-INGRESS
 description ### Voice and Cell-Signaling Traffic ###
 match ip dscp ef CS3

Class-map match-any BEST-EFFORT-INGRESS
 description ### BE Traffic ###
 match ip dscp CS1 0

Class-map- match-any CRITICAL-APPS-INGRESS
 description ### Critical Application ###
 match ip dscp CS6 AF41 AF21 CS2

!

Policy-map ENTERPRISE-SP-EDGE-MAP

 Class REALTIME-INGRESS
 set mpls experimental 5

 Class CRITICAL-APPS-INGRESS
 set mpls experimental 4

 Class BEST-EFFORT-INGRESS
 set mpls experimental 0
```


Figure 3.9: Enterprise-to-Service-Provider Mapping

3.9.2 Four-Class Service Provider Model

Building on the previous model, a fourth class known as VIDEO is added; it is used for carrying both broadcast video and real-time interactive video applications such as video-on-demand. The admission criterion for this new class can be DSCP CS4 or CS5. Figure 3.10 illustrates how this new class can be used for achieving a high-priority video service. There is no recommendation for high-throughput data.

The enterprise CS6 traffic is mapped to the CRITICAL-APPS class in the SP network. CS6 traffic requires adequate protection due to its critical nature, and providers typically need to ensure that this traffic does not get affected by WRED. This also applies to the discussion in the previous section, "Three-Class Service Provider Model."

3.9.3 Six-Class Service Provider Model

In this example, a fifth class, known as Bulk Data, can be used for low-priority data; a sixth class, Network Control, is added and again could be used for control and signaling traffic such as routing updates and so on. Figure 3.11 illustrates using these two new classes. The admission criterion for the Bulk Data is DSCP AF11, whereas the admission criterion for

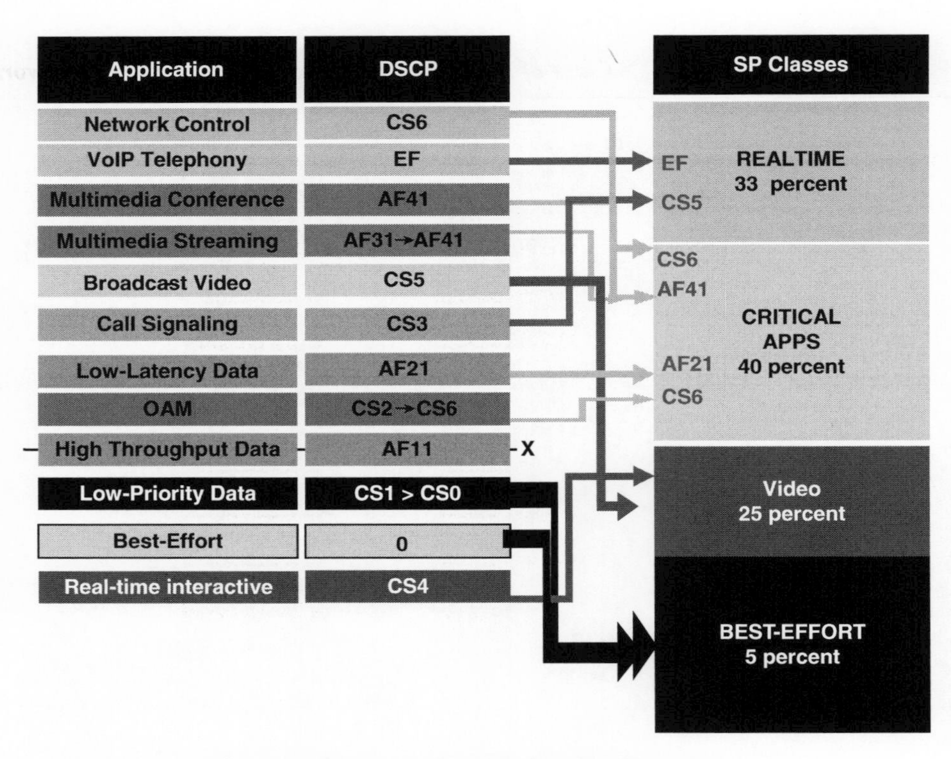

Figure 3.10: Four-Class Service Provider Model

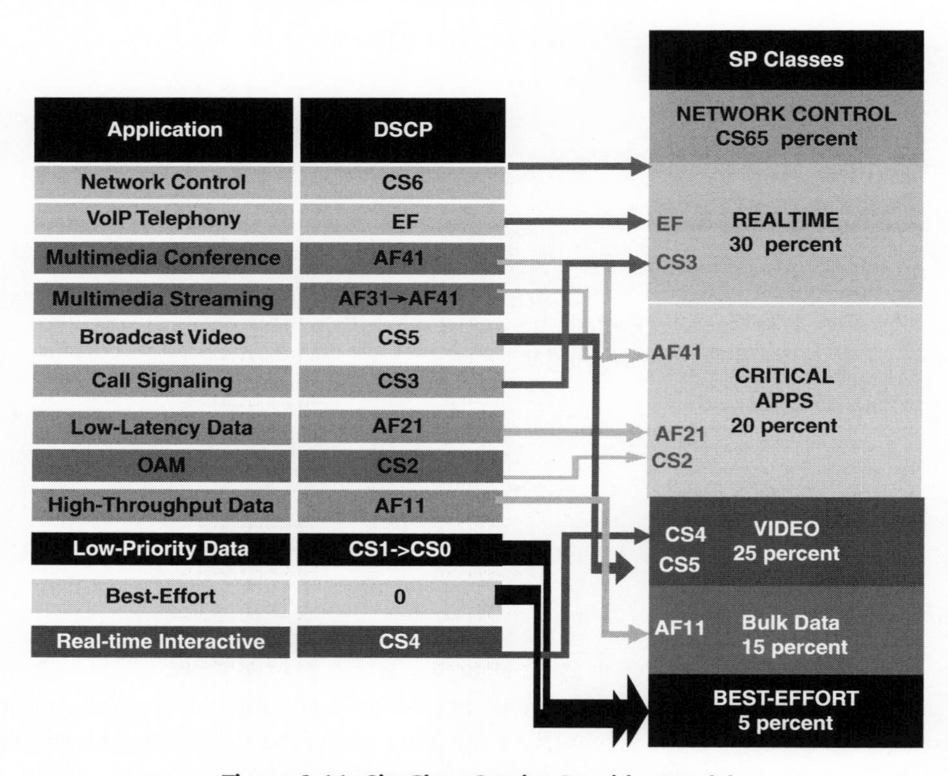

Figure 3.11: Six-Class Service Provider Model

Network Control is CS6. Figure 3.11 illustrates the use of the six-class model. A couple of points to be noted in this model are as follows:

- Service providers also need to ensure that the REALTIME class (low-latency/strict priority queue) is not oversubscribed due to the fact that the traffic from the enterprise network can flood this class. Ingress policing is used at the provider network to control incoming traffic and ensure that the REALTIME class does not exceed its configured bandwidth threshold. Once again, this applies to both the three-class and four-class SP models.

3.10 QoS Requirements and Design for Video Applications

The previous section provided recommendations on possible combinations for grouping many of today's commonly used enterprise applications/traffic classes into SP classes. This section focuses on some of the most common video applications and their inherent requirements from a QoS perspective. This section provides guidelines on classifying, queuing, and managing these sets of applications within the DiffServ QoS framework in an SP IP NGN infrastructure.

3.10.1 Real-Time Interactive Video: Cisco TelePresence

By definition, Cisco Telepresence classifies as a real-time interactive video application; hence we use Telepresence as an example providing insight into the QoS requirements of real-time interactive video applications. It is to be noted that the various details and algorithms provided in this section can be applied to other real-time interactive video applications as well.

Cisco TelePresence CTS-1000 and CTS-3000

Cisco TelePresence systems are currently available in one-screen (CTS-1000) and three-screen (CTS-3000) configurations. A CTS-3000 obviously has greater bandwidth requirements than a CTS-1000 but not necessarily by a full factor of three, as will be shown. Furthermore, the resolution of each CTS-1000 or CTS-3000 system can be set to 720 p or 1080 p (full HDTV). The resolution setting also significantly impacts the bandwidth requirements of the deployed TelePresence solution. Cisco TelePresence has even more levels of granularity in overall image quality within a given resolution setting because the motion-handling quality can also be selected. Therefore, TelePresence supports three levels of motion-handling quality within a given resolution—specifically, 720 p (Good), 720 p (Better), and 720 p (Best) as well as 1080 p (Good), 1080 p (Better), and 1080 p (Best). Each of these levels of resolution and motion-handling quality results in slightly different bandwidth requirements.

3.10.2 TelePresence Bandwidth Requirements

To keep the following sections and examples simple to understand, we'll break down only two cases for detailed analysis: 720 p (Good) and 1080 p (Best).

TelePresence CTS-1000

Let's break down the bandwidth requirements of the maximum bandwidth required by a CTS-1000 system running at 720p (Good) with an auxiliary video stream (for sharing Microsoft PowerPoint or other collateral via the data projector) and an auxiliary audio stream (for at least one additional person conferenced in by an audio-only bridge). The bandwidth requirements by component are:

- One primary video stream @ 1 Mbps: 1 Mbps
- One primary audio stream @ 64 Kbps: 64 Kbps
- One auxiliary video stream: 500 Kbps
- One auxiliary audio stream: 64 Kbps

Total audio and video bandwidth (not including burst and network overhead) is 1,628 Kbps (1.628 Mbps). The total bandwidth requirements without network overhead of such a scenario would be 1.628 Mbps. However, a 10 percent burst factor on the video channel, along with the IP/UDP/RTP overhead (which, combined, amounts to 40 bytes per packet) must also be taken into account and provisioned for, as must media-specific Layer 2 overhead. In general, video, unlike voice, does not have clean formulas for calculating network overhead because video packet sizes and rates vary proportionally to the degree of motion within the video image itself. From a network administrator's point of view, bandwidth is always provisioned at Layer 2, but with the variability in the packet sizes and the variety of Layer 2 media the packets may traverse from end to end and make it difficult to calculate the real bandwidth that should be provisioned at Layer 2. Cisco TelePresence video packets average 1100 bytes per packet. However, the conservative rule of thumb that has been thoroughly tested and widely deployed is to overprovision video bandwidth by 20 percent. This accommodates the 10 percent burst and the Layer 2/Layer 4 network overhead. With this 20 percent overprovisioning rule applied, the requisite bandwidth for a CTS-1000 running at 720p (Good) becomes 2 Mbps (rounded).

TelePresence CTS-3000

Now let's break down the maximum bandwidth required by a CTS-3000 system running at full 1080p (Best), with an auxiliary video stream and an auxiliary audio stream. The detailed bandwidth requirements are:

- Three primary video streams @ 4 Mbps each: 12,000 Kbps (12 Mbps)
- Three primary audio streams @ 64 Kbps each: 192 Kbps
- One auxiliary video stream: 500 Kbps
- One auxiliary audio stream: 64 Kbps

Total audio and video bandwidth (not including burst and network overhead) is 12,756 Kbps (12.756 Mbps). With the 20 percent overprovisioning rule applied, the requisite bandwidth for a CTS-3000 running at 1080p (Best) becomes 15 Mbps (rounded).

> **NOTE 3.1: TelePresence Bandwidth**
>
> Note that these bandwidth numbers represent the worst-case scenarios (i.e., peak bandwidth transmitted during periods of maximum motion within the encoded video). Normal use (i.e., average bandwidth), with users sitting and talking and gesturing naturally, typically generates only about 60–80 percent of these maximum bandwidth rates. This means that a CTS-3000 running at 1080 (Best) averages only 10–12 Mbps and a CTS-1000 running at 720 (Good) averages only 1.2–1.6 Mbps.

3.10.3 TelePresence Burst Requirements

Burst is defined as the amount of traffic (generally measured in bytes) transmitted per millisecond that exceeds the per-second average. For example, a CTS-3000 running at 1080 p (Best) at approximately 15 Mbps divides evenly into approximately 1966 bytes per millisecond (15 Mbps ÷ 1000 milliseconds). Cisco TelePresence operates at 30 frames per second. This means that a video frame is transmitted, every 33 ms; we refer to this as a *frame interval*. Each frame consists of several thousand bytes of video payload; therefore, each frame interval consists of several dozen packets, with an average packet size of 1100 bytes per packet. However, because video is variable in size (due to the variability of motion in the encoded video), the packets transmitted by the codec are not spaced evenly over each 33 ms frame interval but rather are transmitted in bursts measured in 1–2 ms intervals. Therefore, though the overall bandwidth (maximum) averages out to 15 Mbps over 1 second, when measured on a per-millisecond basis, the packet transmission rate is highly variable, and the number of bytes transmitted per millisecond for a 15 Mbps call bursts well above the 1966-byte average.

The following formula can be used to determine the recommended burst allowance:

$$B = R(T)$$

where R equals the maximum rate of Cisco TelePresence traffic traversing a given interface in bytes per second, T equals the time interval in milliseconds of the burst that must be sustained, and B equals the burst in bytes that must be sustained over T. To obtain R, simply take the maximum megabits per second (e.g., 15 Mbps) multiplied by 1024 to convert megabits per second to kilobits per second, multiplied again by 1024 to convert kilobits per second to bits per second, and then divided by 8 to convert bits per second to bytes per second. For example:

$$15\text{Mbps} * 1024 * 1024 \div 8 = 1{,}966{,}080 \text{ bytes/sec}$$

Take the result and use it as R in the burst formula. For T, test results have shown that a 200 ms burst time interval is adequate to accommodate Cisco TelePresence. This is denoted in decimal format in the formula, where 200 milliseconds = .2 seconds. Therefore the calculation is as follows:

$$B = 1{,}966{,}080 \text{ bytes/sec} * .2 \text{ seconds} = 393{,}216 \text{ bytes of burst}$$

3.10.4 TelePresence Latency, Jitter, and Loss Requirements

Cisco TelePresence has a network latency target of 150 ms; this target does not include codec processing time but purely network flight time. In some scenarios, however, this latency target might not always be possible to achieve due simply to the laws of physics and the geographical distances involved. Therefore, TelePresence codecs have been designed to sustain high levels of call quality, even up to 200 ms of latency.

Cisco TelePresence has a peak-to-peak jitter target of 10 ms. Jitter is defined as the variance in network latency. Thus if the average latency is 100 ms and packets are arriving between 95 ms and 105 ms, the peak-to-peak jitter is defined as 10 ms. Measurements within the Cisco TelePresence codecs use peak-to-peak jitter.

Cisco TelePresence is highly sensitive to packet loss and as such has an end-to-end packet loss target of 0.05 percent.

3.10.5 Classifying TelePresence

One of the first questions to be answered relating to TelePresence QoS design is: Should TelePresence be assigned to a dedicated class or should it be assigned to the same class as existing videoconferencing/video telephony (also known as multimedia conferencing, as per the Cisco modified RFC-4594 model)? The answer to this question directly relates to whether TelePresence has the same service-level requirements as these other two interactive video applications or whether it has unique service-level requirements. From the previously mentioned requirements it becomes apparent that TelePresence has unique (and higher/tighter) service-level requirements than do generic videoconferencing/video telephony applications; therefore, TelePresence requires a dedicated class along with a dedicated classification marking value.

Videoconferencing/video telephony applications have traditionally been marked to (RFC-2597) Assured Forwarding Class 4, which is the recommendation from both the Cisco QoS Baseline as well as the Cisco modified version of RFC-4594. However, the AF PHB includes policing (to conforming, exceeding, and violating traffic rates) as well as correspondingly increasing the drop preferences (to Drop Preference 1, 2, and 3, respectively), ultimately dropping traffic according to the drop preference markings. TelePresence traffic has a very low tolerance to drops (0.05 percent) and therefore would not be appropriately serviced by an AF PHB. Because of the low-latency and jitter service-level requirements of TelePresence, it might seem attractive to assign it an (RFC-3246) Expedite Forwarding (EF) PHB; after all, there is nothing in RFC-3246 that dictates that only VoIP can be assigned to this PHB. However, it is important to recognize that VoIP behaves considerably differently than video. VoIP has constant packet sizes and packet rates, whereas video packet sizes vary and video packet rates also vary in a random and bursty manner. Thus if both video and voice were assigned to the same marking value and class, (bursty) video could easily interfere with (well-behaved) voice. Therefore, for both operational and capacity-planning purposes, it is recommended not to mark both voice and video to EF. This recommendation is reflected in both the Cisco QoS Baseline as well as the Cisco modified RFC-4594 model.

What, then, should TelePresence be marked to? The best formal guidance is provided in the Cisco modified RFC-4594 model, where a distinction is made between a Multimedia Conferencing (i.e., generic Videoconferencing/Video Telephony) service class and a Real-Time Interactive service class. The Real-Time Interactive service class is intended for inelastic video flows, such as TelePresence. The recommended marking for this Real-Time Interactive service class, and thus the recommended marking for TelePresence, is Class Selector 4 (CS4).

3.10.6 Queuing Telepresence

The Cisco modified version of RFC-4594 specifies the minimum queuing requirement of the Real-Time Interactive service class to be a rate-based queue (i.e., a queue that has a guaranteed minimum bandwidth rate). However, the Cisco modified RFC-4594 makes an allowance that, though the PHB for Real-Time Interactive service class should be configured to provide high-bandwidth assurance, it may be configured as a second EF PHB that uses relaxed performance parameters, a rate scheduler, and a CS4 DSCP value. This means that, for example, TelePresence, which has been assigned to this Real-Time Interactive service class, can be queued with either a guaranteed rate nonpriority queue (such as a Cisco IOS CBWFQ) or a guaranteed-rate strict priority queue (such as a Cisco IOS LLQ) in cases where dual-priority queues are feasible. In either case, TelePresence is to be marked as CS4 (and not EF).Therefore, since the Cisco modified RFC-4594 model allows for the Real-Time Interactive service class to be given a second EF PHB and because of the low-latency, low-jitter, and low-loss requirements of TelePresence, it is recommended to place TelePresence in a strict-priority queue such as a Cisco IOS LLQ (on platforms that support the use of dual-priority queues) or a Cisco Catalyst hardware-priority queue whenever possible.

NOTE 3.2: TelePresence and the LLQ

It is recommended to place Telepresence within the LLQ only when the platform can support dual-priority queues.

However, an additional provisioning consideration must taken into account when provisioning TelePresence with a second EF PHB; this relates to the amount of bandwidth of a given link that should be assigned for strict-priority queuing. The well-established and widely deployed Cisco best-practice recommendation is to limit the amount of strict-priority queuing configured on an interface to no more than one third of the link's capacity. This has commonly been referred to as the *33 percent LLQ rule*. The rationale behind this rule is that if you assign too much traffic for strict-priority queuing, the overall effect is a dampening of QoS functionality for nonreal-time applications. Remember, the goal of convergence is to enable voice, video, and data to transparently coexist on a single network. When real-time applications such as voice and/or TelePresence dominate a link, data applications fluctuate significantly in their response times when TelePresence calls are present versus when they are absent, thus destroying the transparency of the converged network.

For example, consider a (45 Mbps) DS3 link configured to support two separate CTS-3000 calls, both configured to transmit at full 1080 p (Best) resolution. Each such call requires

15 Mbps of real-time traffic. Prior to TelePresence calls being placed, data applications have access to 100 percent of the bandwidth (to simplify the example, we are assuming there are no other real-time applications, such as VoIP, on this link). However, once these TelePresence calls are established, all data applications would suddenly be contending for less than 33 percent of the link. TCP windowing would take effect, and many data applications will hang, time out, or become stuck in an unresponsive state, which usually translates into users calling the IT help desk complaining about the network (which happens to be functioning properly, albeit in a poorly configured manner). To obviate such scenarios, extensive testing has found that a significant decrease in data application response times occurs when real-time traffic exceeds one third of link bandwidth capacity; therefore a general best-queuing practice is to limit the amount of strict-priority queuing to 33 percent of link bandwidth capacity.

On platforms that support only a single-priority queue/LLQ, Telepresence traffic can be placed on a dedicated CBWFQ queue, which has higher priority than multimedia conferencing and multimedia streaming traffic.

3.10.7 WRED and TelePresence

The use of WRED on the Real-Time Interactive class would have a serious impact on traffic. By virtue of being a congestion-avoidance mechanism, WRED starts dropping traffic ahead of the curve (i.e., before congestion actually happens). This could effectively mean that traffic well within the contractual boundary could actually be penalized. This also applies to other video classes such as Broadcast Video and Video on Demand.

Real-time interactive applications such as Telepresence, which have a stringent latency, loss, and jitter requirements, will be severely degraded in the event of random packet drops. Therefore it is strictly recommended that these classes not be configured for WRED. Instead, strict subscription policies need to be defined, wherein each of these classes is not oversubscribed and does not dominate the network bandwidth, starving other applications of access to the wire. In such cases, tail-drop will suit the bill.

3.10.8 Configurations and Recommendations

Figure 3.12 illustrates a configuration for the Real-Time Interactive Video class. In this illustration, the traffic is assigned to a strict-priority/LLQ, since the platform in this case supports dual-priority queues.

Table 3.2 illustrates the recommended characteristics for Real-Time Interactive Video traffic.

NOTE 3.3: Configurations

Detailed configurations and platform-specific details are provided in the implementation-specific chapters of this book.

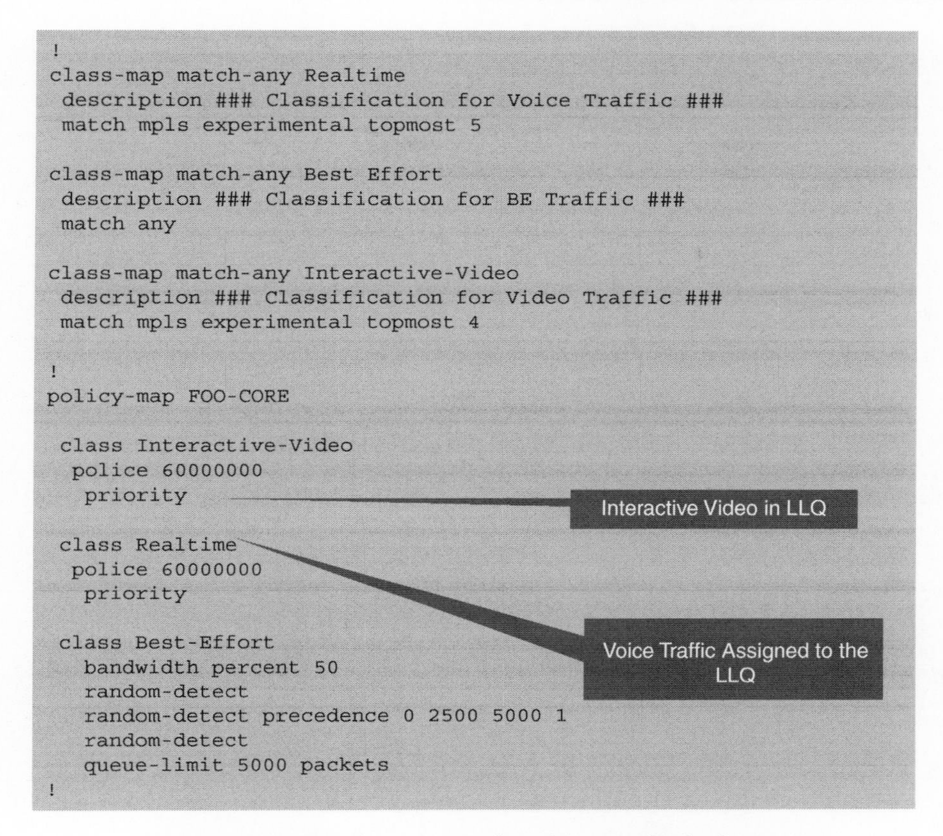

Figure 3.12: Real-Time Interactive Video Traffic in the LLQ

Table 3.2: Recommendations for Real-Time Interactive Video Traffic

PHB	Marking	WRED	Queue Limit	Queue	Bandwidth
Expedited Forwarding or Assured Forwarding PHB	CS4 in the Telepresence; CS4 may still be used for other applications as well	No; packet drop for this class is not desired	Large enough to accommodate maximum traffic bursts	LLQ in the case of platforms supporting dual-PQ or a dedicated nonpriority queue	In the case of LLQ, voice and video together should not exceed 33%; if used in a dedicated queue, adequate bandwidth with no "Oversubscription" should be allotted

In Figure 3.13, traffic within the Real-Time Interactive Video class is assigned to a nonstrict-priority queue with adequate guarantees. Here we see that the queue has adequate bandwidth guarantees and does not have any WRED (early packet drop), which can impact TelePresence or, for that matter, any interactive video application.

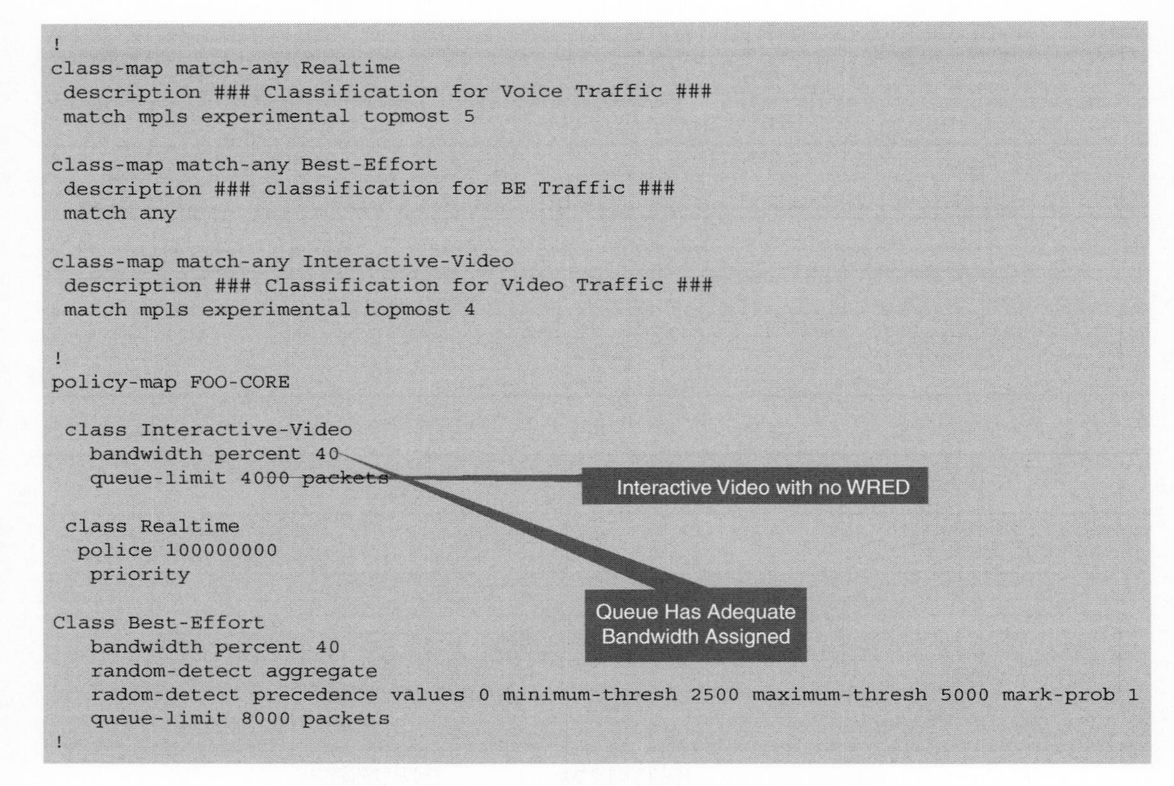

```
!
class-map match-any Realtime
 description ### Classification for Voice Traffic ###
 match mpls experimental topmost 5

class-map match-any Best-Effort
 description ### classification for BE Traffic ###
 match any

class-map match-any Interactive-Video
 description ### Classification for Video Traffic ###
 match mpls experimental topmost 4

!
policy-map FOO-CORE

 class Interactive-Video
   bandwidth percent 40
   queue-limit 4000 packets

 class Realtime
  police 100000000
   priority

Class Best-Effort
   bandwidth percent 40
   random-detect aggregate
   radom-detect precedence values 0 minimum-thresh 2500 maximum-thresh 5000 mark-prob 1
   queue-limit 8000 packets
!
```


Figure 3.13: Real-Time Interactive Video in Non-LLQ

3.11 Broadcast Video: Internet Protocol Television

The Broadcast Video service class is to be used for inelastic (instantaneous rate) traffic flows, which are intended for broadcast TV service and for transport of live video and audio events. By definition, Internet Protocol Television (IPTV) is categorized as a Broadcast Video application. IPTV delivers television programming to households via a broadband connection using Internet protocols. It requires a subscription and IPTV set-top box. IPTV is typically bundled with other services such as Video on Demand (VoD), Voice over IP (VoIP) or digital phone, and Web access, collectively referred to as *triple play*.

IPTV uses Internet protocols to provide two-way communication for interactive television. One application might be in game shows in which the studio audience is asked to participate by helping a contestant choose between answers. IPTV opens the door to real-time participation from people watching at home. Another application involves the ability to turn on multiple angles of a sporting event, such as a touchdown, and watch it from dual angles simultaneously using picture-in-picture viewing.

SPs typically offer multiple broadcast video channels for end users or subscribers connected to the network. In IPTV deployments, each broadcast video channel has a separate multicast group address. Users are provided access to the broadcast video channels in MPEG2/MPEG4 codec/s in SD/HD format, with each channel consuming bandwidth dependent on the type of codec or format.

IP Multicast technology is used to optimize the bandwidth requirements in the network. IP Multicast enables one-to-many communication in which multiple broadcast video clients (set-top boxes, or STBs) can receive the same stream from a video encoder/server. To receive a multicast stream, a client must have access to a multicast-enabled network. Hence the hardware and software in the network need to support the required features for transporting multicast packets.

3.11.1 IPTV Bandwidth Requirements

A standard-definition IP video stream that is carried as an MPEG4 SPTS stream uses about 2 to 2.75 Mbps of bandwidth. A high-definition IP video stream using the same type of compression and transport uses about 8 to 9 Mbps of bandwidth. These bandwidth requirements mean that the access infrastructure that is designed for real-time video transport must be capable of carrying significantly more bandwidth than what is needed for VoIP and Internet access services. For example, assuming that the access infrastructure is DSL based, the DSL line itself is typically constrained to carrying only one or two video streams simultaneously. The result is that video-over-DSL service offerings must limit the service to one or two simultaneous broadcast channels per household. Since broadcast video services use multicast, the amount of bandwidth required in the access and distribution networks scales with the number of channels offered. For example, a broadcast video service that uses MPEG4 compression and offers 100 channels of standard-definition content requires around 1 Gbps of capacity in the SP distribution network to handle worst-case usage patterns.

Multicast Admission Control mechanisms can also be used to limit or control bandwidth usage, as discussed in the following section.

IGMP Limit

SPs can enforce a maximum broadcast bandwidth limit by limiting the number of Internet Group Management Protocol (IGMP) joins on the ranges of multicast addresses associated with broadcast video to a configured maximum on the aggregation links that the router controls. The *ip igmp limit* command can be used to configure a limit on the number of IGMP states resulting from IGMP membership reports on a per-system or per-interface basis. It controls the maximum number of IGMP states allowed on a router or interface. Membership reports sent after the configured limits have been exceeded are not entered in the IGMP cache, and traffic for the excess membership reports is not forwarded.

Per-interface and per-system limits operate independently of each other and can enforce different configured limits. A membership state will be ignored if it exceeds either the per-interface limit or the global limit. If you do not configure the *except access-list* keyword and argument, all IGMP states resulting from IGMP are counted toward the configured cache limit on an interface. The *except access-list* keyword and argument exclude particular groups or channels from counting toward the IGMP cache limit. An IGMP membership report is counted against the per-interface limit if it is permitted by the extended access list specified by the *except access-list* keyword and argument. The command use is illustrated here.

IGMP Limits

```
!
ip igmp limit <number> [except access-list] (Enables per-system IGMP limit)
!
interface GigE x/y (Enables per-interface IGMP limit. DSLAM-facing intf)
 ip igmp limit <number> [except access-list]
!
```

3.11.2 IPTV Latency Jitter and Loss Requirements

To be considered optimal, IPTV (broadcast video) needs to achieve a latency of <150 ms one way. From a jitter standpoint, a value of <50 ms is required to provide consistent quality and a favorable user experience.

Coming to packet loss, the packet-loss ratio (PLR) should be well within the $<10^{-6}$ mark. To elaborate on this a little further, when broadcast and on-demand video (VoD, detailed in the next section) is carried over an IP network, there is an assumption that the video quality the subscriber experienced is comparable to that experienced by people watching MPEG4 video carried by cable and satellite networks today. To ensure that any degradation in video quality resulting from the IP transport network is negligible from a subscriber's point of view, most SPs allow only one visible degradation in video quality roughly every two hours. Though this allowance is similar to what is allowed for VoIP services, the resulting allowed packet-drop requirement for an IP transport network designed for video services is much more stringent. There are two reasons for this:

- Video is much more highly compressed, so losing a packet may result in the loss of more valuable encoded video information. If the network drops a single video packet, there is a visible degradation of video quality of anywhere from a single frame up to a loss of 1 second of video, depending on the kind of encoded information that is lost.
- The receiving decoders, such as the STBs, generally do not have loss-concealment algorithms, whereas VoIP phones and gateways typically support algorithms that conceal dropouts in the voice signal caused by lost packets. In the VoIP case, the network can drop a single voice packet without the listener perceiving any degradation in voice quality—unlike the case for video.

The DiffServ architecture needs to ensure that video flows meet the required 10^{-6} drop rate, even when links are congested. Packet drops due to bit errors on physical links must be addressed on a link-by-link basis. The link-layer technologies used in video networks employ cyclic redundancy check (CRC) algorithms to ensure that packets with errors are not delivered. This means that a single bit error in a video packet results in that packet being dropped when a CRC is performed. VoIP is typically carried in packets of approximately 1400 bytes. If bit errors are assumed to be distributed randomly, the resulting requirement for transport links is to ensure a bit-error rate (BER) less than 10^{-10}.

The BER on optical links can be engineered to 10^{-14} or less by ensuring a high signal-to-noise ratio (SNR) on those links. If optical connectivity is used in the access and distribution networks, degradation in video quality resulting from bit errors on these links should not be an issue. However, packet drops due to bit errors on links such as DSL can have a significant effect on video quality. The SNR on a DSL line varies as a result of many factors, including loop length, proximity to noise sources, and other factors. In addition, the SNR can vary over time because of factors such as corrosion at connection points, moisture, and so on. Consequently, it might be difficult to qualify a DSL line at the time of installation to ensure a BER of less than 10^{-10} over the life of the video service.

3.11.3 Classifying and Queuing Broadcast Video/IPTV

Broadcast video uses DSCP class selector CS3 as the classification criterion, as per the Cisco modified RFC-4594 model. However, due to the fact that Cisco marks Call Signaling traffic to CS3, the Cisco modified RFC-4594 model swaps Call Signaling with broadcast video, as mentioned in the earlier sections. Hence IPTV traffic is classified using CS5 instead of CS3.

Broadcast video needs to be assigned to a second EF queue (LLQ) on Cisco platforms that support dual-priority queues due to the strict latency, jitter, and packet-loss requirements. Alternately, on platforms that do not support dual-priority queues, broadcast video can be assigned to a dedicated class for video traffic. Some of the characteristics needed for this class are as follows:

- The Broadcast Video queue should never be oversubscribed. Oversubscription has the potential to drop traffic during congestion, which would have a negative impact on many channels of video traffic.
- Broadcast video traffic should not be combined with data traffic and hence needs a dedicated QoS queue. Other video applications such as Video on Demand (described in the next section) could optionally be combined with this traffic type.
- WRED should not be configured for broadcast video traffic.

3.11.4 Configurations and Recommendations

Figure 3.14 illustrates a configuration for the Broadcast Video class. In this illustration, the traffic is assigned to a strict priority/LLQ, since the platform in this case supports dual-priority queues.

Table 3.3 illustrates the recommended characteristics for broadcast video traffic.

In Figure 3.15, the traffic within the Broadcast Video class is assigned to a nonstrict-priority queue with adequate guarantees. Here we see that the queue has adequate bandwidth guarantees and does not have any WRED (early packet drop), which can impact IPTV and other types of broadcast video applications.

```
!
class-map match-any Realtime
 description ### Classification for Voice Traffic ###
 match mpls experimental topmost 5

class-map match-any Best-Effort
 description ### Classification for BE Traffic ###
 match any

class-map match-any Broadcast-Video
 description ### Classification for Video Traffic ###
 match mpls experimental topmost 4

!
policy-map FOO-CORE

 class Broadcast-Video
  police 60000000
   priority

 class Realtime
  police 60000000
   priority

 class Best-Effort
   bandwidth percent 50
   random-detect
   random-detect precedence 0 2500 5000 1
   queue-limit 5000 packets
!
```


Figure 3.14: Broadcast Video Traffic in LLQ

Table 3.3: Recommendations for Broadcast Video Traffic

PHB	Marking	WRED	Queue Limit	Queue	Bandwidth
Expedited Forwarding or Assured Forwarding PHB	CS5 as per the Cisco modified RFC-4594 model	No; packet drop for this class is not desired	Large enough to accommodate maximum traffic bursts	LLQ in the case of platforms supporting dual-PQ, or a dedicated nonpriority queue	In the case of LLQ, voice and video together should not exceed 33%; if used in a dedicated queue, adequate bandwidth with no "Oversubscription" should be allotted

NOTE 3.4: Broadcast and Real-Time Interactive Video

It is very common for SPs to combine both real-time interactive and broadcast video into a single VIDEO queue. In fact, this can be considered a recommended practice. Video on Demand, discussed in the following section, is also a potential candidate for this VIDEO queue, which helps in the consolidation of video applications with near to similar QoS requirements.

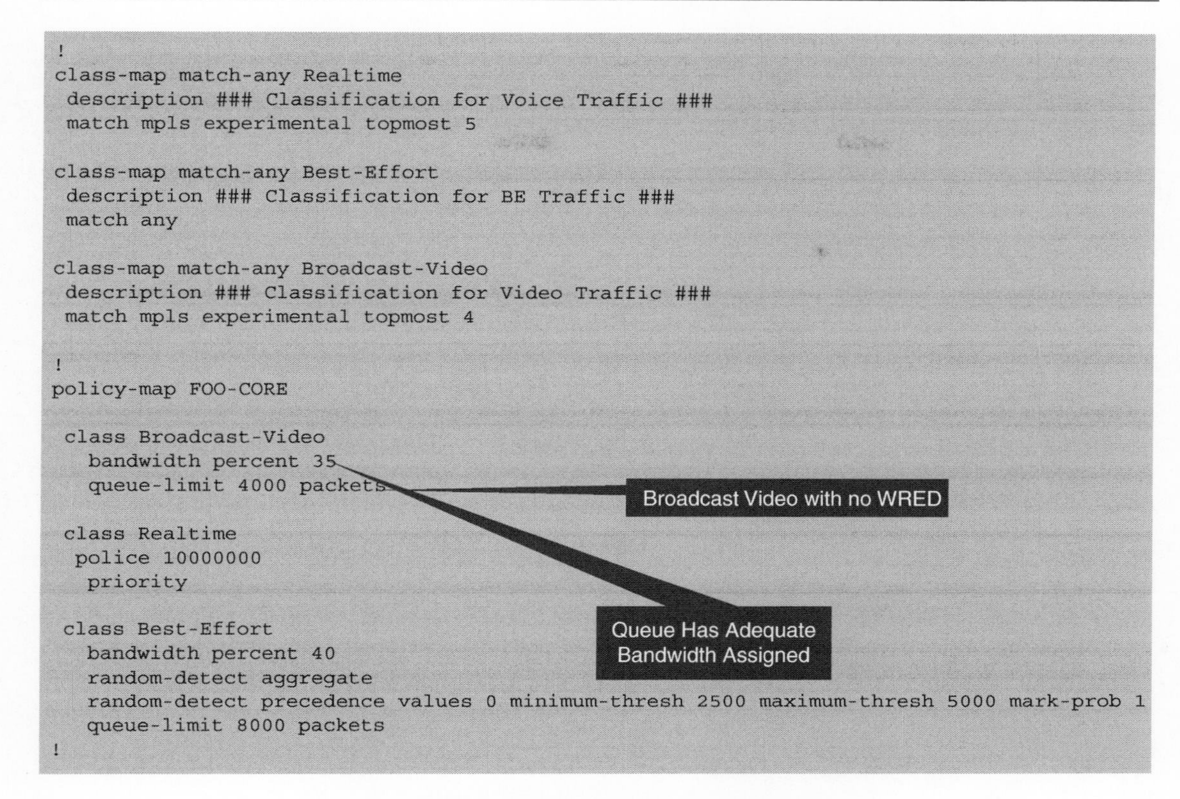

```
!
class-map match-any Realtime
 description ### Classification for Voice Traffic ###
 match mpls experimental topmost 5

class-map match-any Best-Effort
 description ### Classification for BE Traffic ###
 match any

class-map match-any Broadcast-Video
 description ### Classification for Video Traffic ###
 match mpls experimental topmost 4

!
policy-map FOO-CORE

 class Broadcast-Video
   bandwidth percent 35
   queue-limit 4000 packets

 class Realtime
  police 10000000
   priority

 class Best-Effort
   bandwidth percent 40
   random-detect aggregate
   random-detect precedence values 0 minimum-thresh 2500 maximum-thresh 5000 mark-prob 1
   queue-limit 8000 packets
!
```


Figure 3.15: Broadcast Video in Non-LLQ

3.12 Video on Demand

By definition, Video on Demand (VoD) refers to an SP hosting video titles in a centralized or distributed repository, which can be accessed on a demand basis at the subscriber's convenience. These VoD streams are encoded in MPEG4 SD format, consuming about 2.75 Mbps for each stream. Unicast technology is used to stream the video to end users; hence the bandwidth requirements can potentially be huge due to the streaming of a unique VoD stream for each subscriber. VoD services are offered by using an STB appliance in the subscriber home network and controlled by the SP using video middleware. The VoD server implements storage and real-time streaming functionality for on-demand services.

3.12.1 Video-on-Demand Bandwidth Requirements

On-demand services use unicast, so the amount of bandwidth required in the distribution network scales with the number of subscribers and peak on-demand utilization rates the network is designed to carry. For example, a distribution network that is designed to deliver MPEG4 compressed standard-definition content to 50,000 on-demand subscribers at a 10 percent peak take rate (5000 simultaneous users) requires about 13 Gbps of capacity.

3.12.2 Video-on-Demand Latency, Jitter, and Loss Requirements

VoD has similar latency, jitter, and loss requirements as broadcast video services. However, a little understanding of these two video applications (broadcast and VoD) is necessary. Broadcast video services are inherently real time. A subscriber who experiences an outage in the broadcast service cannot come back and continue watching at that point when the outage is over. Because of this and the higher usage rates associated with broadcast services, the availability associated with broadcast services must be very high. In contrast, the customer disruptions associated with an outage in VoD services are typically much less problematic. A subscriber who experiences an outage in a VoD service can come back at a later time and replay the content—either from the point of disruption or from the beginning. In addition, the peak usage rates associated with VoD are typically between 10 and 20 percent of the subscriber population.

Because of these factors, SPs have much higher link availability requirements for broadcast services than for on-demand services. Consequently, the differing availability requirements between the two services may result in differing transport requirements for each service. Therefore it is fair to state that VoD has higher-bandwidth and lower-availability requirements compared to broadcast video services, which have lower-bandwidth and higher-availability requirements.

The QoS architecture includes DiffServ marking for broadcast and on-demand services, allowing the network to drop VoD traffic preferentially over broadcast traffic in the event of a network outage.

NOTE 3.5: Drop Priority

To keep it simple, SPs typically offer QoS guarantees for VoD traffic in line with broadcast video; however, VoD traffic might have a higher drop priority compared to broadcast video applications.

3.12.3 Queuing Video-on-Demand Traffic

Typically VoD traffic can be combined with broadcast video and hosted on the same QoS queue. This means that both broadcast video and on-demand video obtain identical treatment from a QoS standpoint. Ideally this needs to be a decision based on the available classes in the SP network. For example, if the network has a five-class model, as illustrated in Figure 3.10, VoD and broadcast video may be placed in the same queue, as VoD will not be a fit in any of the data classes (due to factors such as early drop characteristics present in the data classes). On platforms that support dual-priority queues, VoD traffic may be also placed in the second EF class along with broadcast and real-time interactive video applications. However, this needs careful analysis, as the strict-priority queue should not become overloaded, which has a potential to starve other data classes. The 33 percent rule still applies, even if the LLQ hosts both voice and video traffic.

VoD Control Traffic

The middleware-STB/VoD control traffic needs to be considered as well. The recommendation here is to have the VoD control traffic placed in the queue that holds broadcast video traffic, due to its inherent critical nature.

3.12.4 Configurations and Recommendations

Figure 3.16 illustrates a configuration for VoD traffic. In this illustration, the traffic is assigned to a strict priority/LLQ along with broadcast video and real-time interactive video. The platform used in this case supports dual-priority queues.

Table 3.4 illustrates the recommended characteristics for VoD traffic.

Figure 3.17 illustrates a configuration for VoD traffic in a dedicated video queue (non-LLQ).

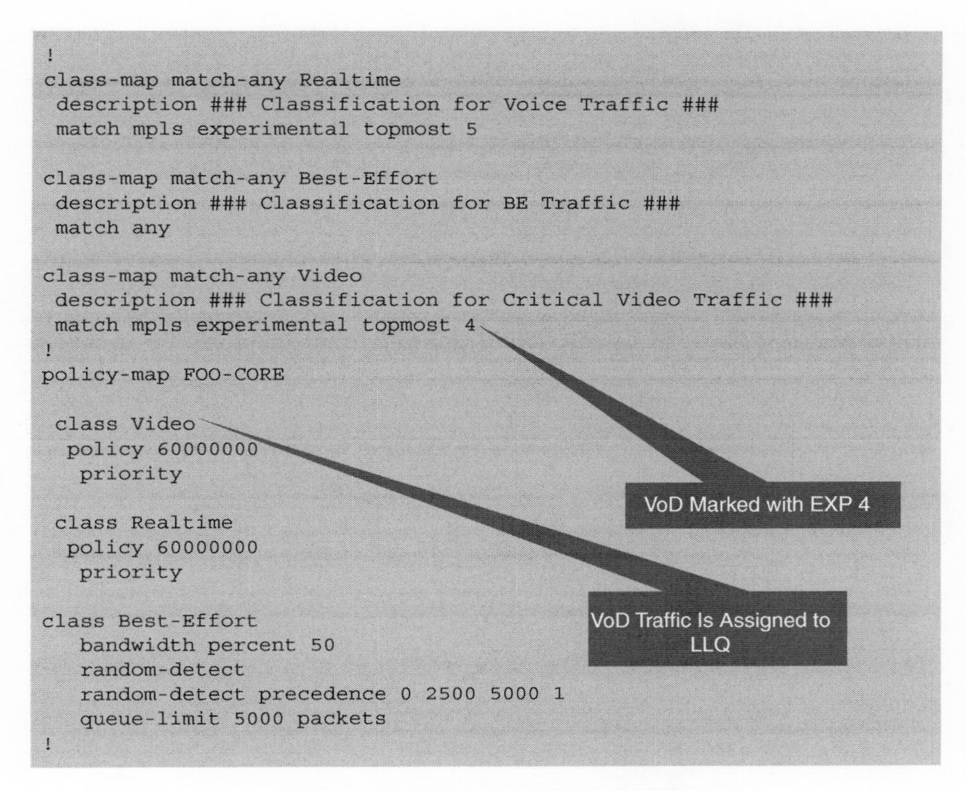

Figure 3.16: Video on Demand in LLQ

Table 3.4: Recommendations for Video-on-Demand Traffic

PHB	Marking	WRED	Queue Limit	Queue	Bandwidth
Expedited Forwarding or Assured Forwarding PHB	May be classified using CS5	No; packet drop for this class is not desired	Large enough to accommodate maximum traffic bursts	LLQ in the case of platforms supporting dual-PQ, or a dedicated nonpriority queue	In the case of LLQ, voice and video together should not exceed 33%; if used in a dedicated queue, adequate bandwidth with no "Oversubscription" should be allotted

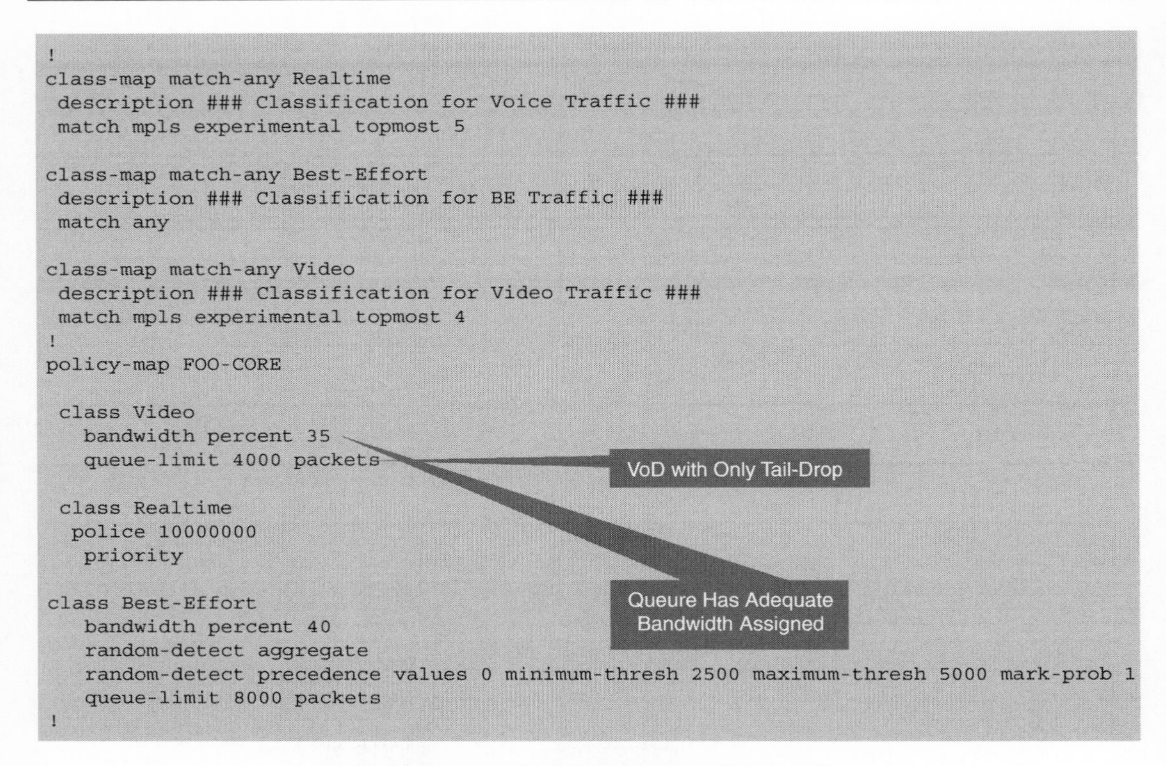

```
!
class-map match-any Realtime
 description ### Classification for Voice Traffic ###
 match mpls experimental topmost 5

class-map match-any Best-Effort
 description ### Classification for BE Traffic ###
 match any

class-map match-any Video
 description ### Classification for Video Traffic ###
 match mpls experimental topmost 4
!
policy-map FOO-CORE

 class Video
   bandwidth percent 35
   queue-limit 4000 packets

 class Realtime
  police 10000000
   priority

class Best-Effort
   bandwidth percent 40
   random-detect aggregate
   random-detect precedence values 0 minimum-thresh 2500 maximum-thresh 5000 mark-prob 1
   queue-limit 8000 packets
!
```


Figure 3.17: Video on Demand in Non-LLQ

3.13 Video Admission Control

Video Admission Control (VAC) is rapidly becoming an important new requirement for telecom equipment. It is most applicable to control dynamic admission of unicast VoD sessions, since VOD is a pay-per-use service and the most bandwidth-intensive (i.e., the most likely to cause resource contention when unchecked). Multicast VAC is being proposed for cases in which more broadcast channels are being offered than can be concurrently watched. Multicast VAC prevents bandwidth issues when changing channels—for example, when bringing up a new channel (one that has not been previously watched). This could potentially result in some of the least-watched channels being unavailable while ensuring that more popular channels are available, with the expected quality. The main goal of Multicast VAC is to conserve limited bandwidth that exists between aggregation routers and access layer devices such as DSLAMs/Layer 2 switches.

VAC is essentially a "safety valve" to ensure a flawless end-user experience for video streams by preventing additional streams from entering the network when remaining capacity is insufficient to support them (e.g., extreme VoD, concurrency peaks with a new movie release, or reduced capacity due to failures). Though VAC is a compromise between service quality and availability, the need to deny service requests due to insufficient network capacity should be an exception, not the rule. However, since the possibility of network congestion can never be ruled out, the implementation of an effective admission control strategy is an important issue involving network infrastructure, policy control systems, and video middleware. Denying too many requests should be a good indication that the capacity planning might have wrong assumptions on the concurrency take rates; thus more capacity would be needed.

The most common model for providing Video Call Admission Control (CAC) is described next.

On-Path CAC

On-path CAC (also known as *RSVP-based CAC*) is network aware and uses RSVP signaling to provide admission control decisions without using any external equipment for managing policy and bandwidth. Key features required to provide on-path CAC are support for RSVP over DiffServ on the network equipment, RSVP receiver proxy on the edge router, and RSVP integration on the VoD server. On-path CAC is highly accurate and provides 100 percent efficiency of bandwidth utilization.

3.14 RSVP-Based On-Path Admission Control

The RSVP VoD CAC solution relies on a very different QoS model, namely RSVP over DiffServ, whereby RSVP reservations are established over a DiffServ network. With RSVP over DiffServ, the router still maintains a soft-state reservation in the control plane but relies purely on regular DiffServ in the data path. As a result, an RSVP over DiffServ implementation would scale to tens of thousands of reservations per device because RSVP does not need to perform any policing or separate queuing for the admitted flows. All dataplane QoS is activated using the MQC. RSVP operates purely in the control plane and is solely responsible for admission control of flows over a configured bandwidth pool, which reflects the bandwidth allocated to the corresponding DiffServ queue.

The RSVP received proxy feature enables the edge access router (also known as the U-PE in a Metro Ethernet model; the U-PE connects to a PE device in the upstream direction) to respond to the RSVP messages and act as a proxy for the STB. It allows the RSVP signaling loop to be terminated by the PE-Aggregation router (instead of on the actual receiver, or STB, as per the regular RSVP end-to-end model). This enables the use of the RSVP VoD CAC in the access/aggregation network without any RSVP support of awareness on the access devices such as the DSLAM or STB.

The PE devices behave as regular RSVP nodes (that is, they forward RSVP messages after processing them), and the U-PE behaves as an RSVP receiver proxy (that is, it terminates the PATH messages toward the STB after processing them and generates an RSVP RESV message transmitted in the upstream direction).

In case of lack of sufficient bandwidth/resources, the intermediate routers send out an RSVP RESV error message to the receiver proxy interface. The receiver proxy immediately responds by sending an RSVP PATH Error message to the VoD server. This message contains the error code *Admission Control Failed*, analogous to a busy signal in the VoD service. The VoD server will respond by injecting an RSVP PATH Tear message to clean up the soft states and delete any reservations. Figure 3.18 illustrates the call flow for an unsuccessful admission control request.

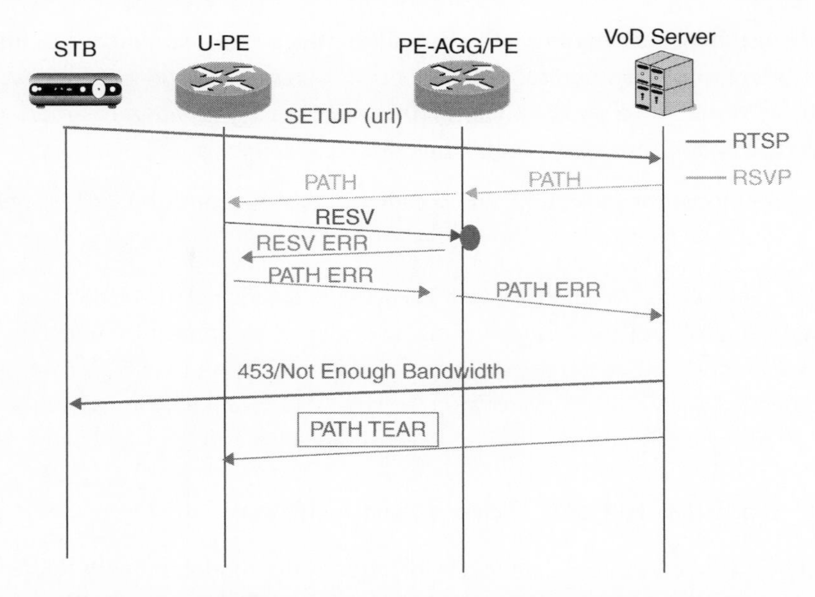

Figure 3.18: RSVP VoD CAC: Unsuccessful Admission Control

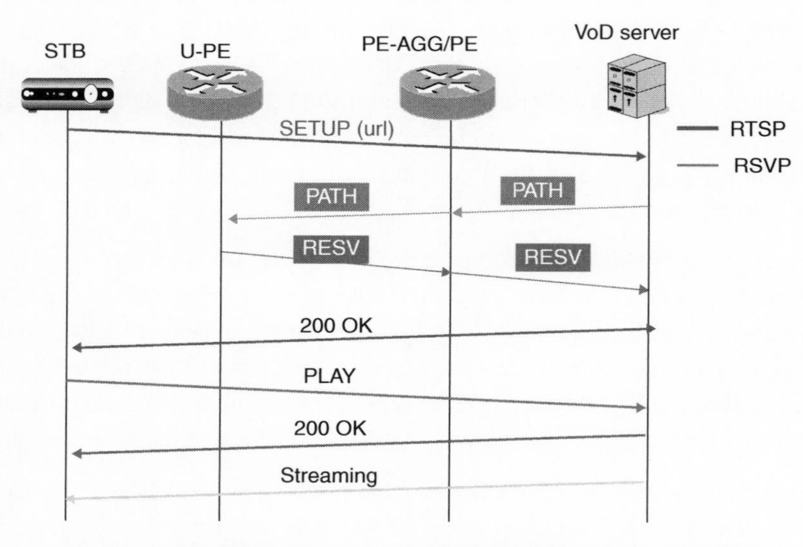

Figure 3.19: RSVP VoD CAC: Successful Admission Control

Figure 3.19 illustrates the call flow for a successful admission control request. The following steps are involved in the setup procedure:

1. The STB relays the customer request to the VoD server (at the application layer) for a new VoD session.
2. Before accepting the VoD session request at the application layer, the VoD Server requests the corresponding bandwidth reservation in the network by generating RSVP signaling (the RSVP Path message).

3. The U-PE router behaves as an RSVP receiver proxy so that it sinks the Path message and returns the corresponding RSVP reservation request (RESV) message. The U-PE may also consult a policy server that can provide a policy-based admission control decision for that reservation.
4. The RSVP RESV travels back toward the video server and is processed at every hop that performs bandwidth-based admission control. If the admission control decision is successful at every hop, the video server will receive the RESV message confirming the reservation.
5. The VoD server can then confirm, at the application level, that the new VoD session is accepted and can then start unicasting the corresponding media stream toward the end user.

3.15 Multimedia Conferencing and Streaming: Video Streaming and Telephony

Multimedia conferencing service class is best suited for applications that require very low delay and have the ability to change encoding rate (rate adaptive), such as H.323/V2 and later videoconferencing service. Multimedia Streaming service class is best suited for variable-rate elastic streaming media applications in which a human is waiting for output and whereby the application has the capability to react to packet loss by reducing its transmission rate, such as streaming video and audio and Webcasting. These applications can operate from the end-customer's network or could even be offered by an SP.

The Multimedia Conferencing service class is for videoconferencing solutions that have the ability to reduce their transmission rate on detection of congestion. These flows can therefore be classified as rate adaptive. Since currently two types of videoconferencing equipment are used in IP networks (ones that generate inelastic, or instantaneous rate, traffic and ones that generate rate-adaptive traffic), two service classes are needed. The Real-Time Interactive service class (which we discussed in the previous section) is used for equipment that generates inelastic video flows; the Multimedia Conferencing service class is for equipment that generates rate-adaptive video flows.

The Multimedia Streaming service class is to be used for elastic multimedia traffic flows. This multimedia content is typically stored before being transmitted. It is also buffered at the receiving end before being played out. The buffering is sufficiently large to accommodate any variation in transmission rate that is encountered in the network. Multimedia entertainment over IP delivery services that are being developed can generate both elastic and inelastic traffic flows; therefore, two service classes are defined to address this space, respectively: Multimedia Streaming and Broadcast Video (which was discussed in the previous section).

3.15.1 Latency, Jitter, and Loss Requirements

Multimedia conferencing and streaming applications do not have stringent requirements, as do broadcast video, real-time video, and video-on-demand. Latency for this category to be considered optimal is around 400 ms; jitter and packet loss constitute around 50 ms and 1 percent, respectively.

3.15.2 Classifying and Queuing Multimedia Conferencing and Streaming Video

Multimedia conferencing and multimedia streaming are classified using AF41 and AF31, respectively, as per the Cisco modified RFC-4594 model. Since both these categories belong to the Assured Forwarding class, each of these applications can be placed into one of the classes that belong to the AF category, which could ideally be the CRITICAL-APPS class, as illustrated in Figure 3.10. Also note that both these application types can be subject to markdown policies (for out-of-contract traffic).

There are no special guidelines on the drop probability of multimedia conferencing and streaming traffic, but since both these traffic classes are mapped to the AF41 and AF31 categories, respectively, the fundamental requirement is to have a "Low" drop probability. SPs may typically offer an EIR for these two traffic types, and the excess traffic can be marked down. This excess (out-of-contract) traffic does not ideally carry the same SLA guarantees as offered to the in-contract traffic and might be subject to a more aggressive drop probability.

Since both the traffic types are "rate adaptive" in nature and capable of adjusting the transmission rates based on network congestion, both these traffic classes can be configured for WRED.

3.15.3 Configurations and Recommendations

Figure 3.20 illustrates that multimedia conferencing and streaming are placed in the CRITICAL-APPS queue. This queue may host data applications in addition to the two video traffic types. Two different drop profiles have been configured, one for in-contract (EXP3) and one for out-of-contract (EXP2) traffic, wherein the former has a low drop profile and the latter has a more aggressive drop rate, as expected. The configuration also illustrates the use of a dedicated video queue for broadcast video, interactive video, and VoD traffic.

Table 3.5 illustrates the recommended characteristics for multimedia conferencing and streaming traffic.

3.16 QoS Requirements and Design for Voice Over IP

In an IP network, delay budgeting typically starts with the Real-Time class (the most delay-sensitive traffic class that carries voice traffic), with the expectation that if latency requirements can be satisfied for this class, latency for other classes will be easier to deal with.

NOTE 3.6: Definition of the Real-Time Class

The term *Real-Time class* denotes the LLQ that carries VoIP traffic. This term will be used interchangeably with the term LLQ for the rest of this book.

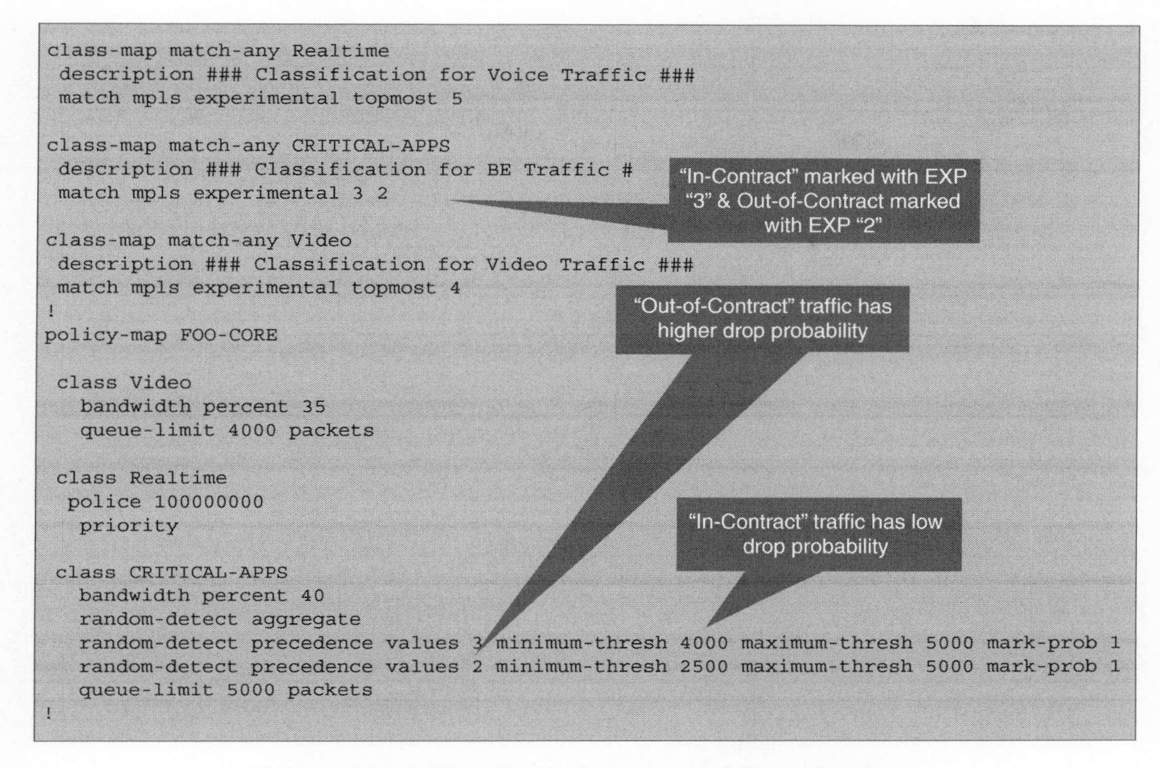

```
class-map match-any Realtime
 description ### Classification for Voice Traffic ###
 match mpls experimental topmost 5

class-map match-any CRITICAL-APPS
 description ### Classification for BE Traffic #
 match mpls experimental 3 2

class-map match-any Video
 description ### Classification for Video Traffic ###
 match mpls experimental topmost 4
!
policy-map FOO-CORE

 class Video
  bandwidth percent 35
  queue-limit 4000 packets

 class Realtime
  police 100000000
  priority

 class CRITICAL-APPS
  bandwidth percent 40
  random-detect aggregate
  random-detect precedence values 3 minimum-thresh 4000 maximum-thresh 5000 mark-prob 1
  random-detect precedence values 2 minimum-thresh 2500 maximum-thresh 5000 mark-prob 1
  queue-limit 5000 packets
!
```


Figure 3.20: Multimedia Conferencing and Streaming Class

Table 3.5: Recommendations for Multimedia Conferencing and Streaming Traffic

PHB	Marking	WRED	Queue Limit	Queue	Bandwidth
Assured Forwarding PHB	AF41 for Multimedia Conferencing and AF31 for Multimedia Streaming	Low drop profile for in-contract traffic; "medium drop rate for out-of-contract" traffic	Large enough to accommodate maximum traffic bursts	Could be placed in a CRITICAL-APPS queue along with critical data applications	Adequate bandwidth to handle out-of-contract traffic

3.16.1 SLA Requirements for Voice Over IP

VoIP traffic has very strict SLA requirements, including strict latency, loss, and jitter limits. G.114 recommends a mouth-to-ear latency not exceeding 150 ms for toll-quality voice service. A higher latency may be acceptable in some situations (transcontinental calls or calls through satellites), albeit with perceived loss of voice quality. The contribution of the network components/destination devices to the end-to-end delay for voice is described here, with samples to help you more clearly understand the role of the network:

- *Codec delay.* Fixed delay due to encoding the packet by the codec (varies per codec type and packetization interval). We use 35 ms in examples of this section.

- *Ingress and egress access network delay.* This is the variable delay in the ingress access network due to propagation, switching, queuing, and serialization of packets. Slower-speed access links could make the serialization delay to be the major part of the access network delay for voice traffic.
- *Core delay.* This is the variable delay in the core network due to propagation, switching, queuing, and serialization of packets. Depending on the span of the network, propagation delay could form the major part of a core network delay.
- *Jitter buffer delay.* A jitter buffer can exist in the VoIP phone (or soft phone) or in the voice gateway inside the access network to remove jitter from incoming VoIP packets by buffering them in a queue and dequeuing them at the VoIP stream rate. Jitter buffer size can be fixed or can change per traffic pattern (adaptive). A jitter buffer's maximum possible size (configurable) would determine the maximum buffering delay that it could introduce.

3.16.2 Example of Delay and Jitter Allocation for Voice Traffic

In the following example, we have assumed an engineering mouth-to-ear VoIP latency target of 125 ms. Note that this value is for illustrative purposes only.

As shown in Figure 3.21, the delay budget for the backbone and each access network is 5 ms and 15 ms, respectively. Codec delay is assumed to be 35 ms. Assuming there are 10 hops in the backbone, each backbone router gets a delay budget of 5 ms / 10 = 500 micro secs in this example. However, a service provider might consider higher or lower values based on specific backbone span in terms of distance and hops and the routers used.

The maximum jitter buffer size that can be supported in this example is 125 − 35 − 15 − 35 − 15 = 25 ms. Note that the jitter buffer might exist in the voice gateway or in the phones themselves. Adaptive jitter buffers will automatically adjust their size in response to measured changes in jitter values; however, to limit the end-to-end jitter, a max jitter buffer size needs to

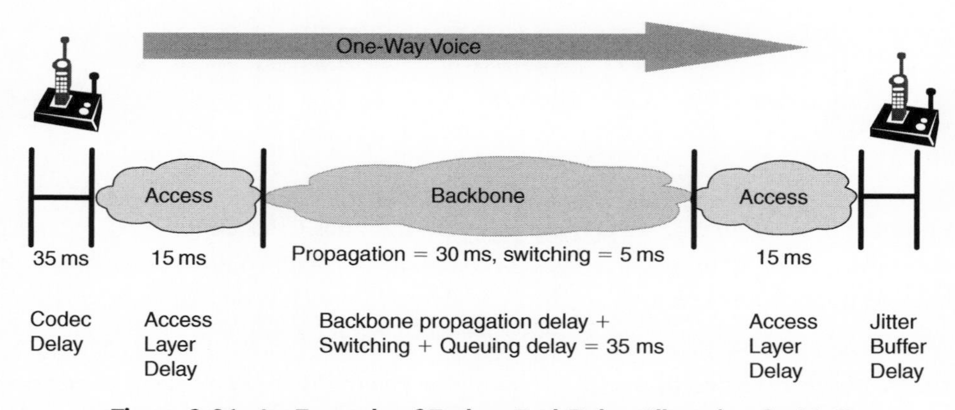

Figure 3.21: An Example of End-to-End Delay Allocation for VoIP

be set (25 ms, as per the delay budget allocation of this example; other delay budget allocations and codec types can have different values as appropriate).

Some enterprises use 30 ms maximum end-to-end jitter as a rule of thumb and might have that value as a requirement. However, note that max end-to-end jitter need not be 30 ms always and can vary to some extent in specific networks. Therefore the target maximum core and access network jitter can be lower or higher than 30 ms as long as the end-to-end delay + end-to-end maximum jitter is within the latency goal for VoIP, and the jitter buffer can accommodate the maximum jitter.

It is to be noted that, jitter being variations in delay, jitter across a single router can never exceed the difference between the max and the min latency across the same router. For example, if the max latency of a core router is <500 ms, it implies that the jitter across that router will be less than (probably much less than) 500 ms. Similarly, as in Figure 3.14, the jitter introduced by the access network (ingress or egress) can't exceed 15 ms (this is well within our budget of the jitter buffer in the example).

Budgeting jitter accurately is rather difficult due to its dependency on traffic mix and traffic burstiness, link utilization, and the nonadditive property of jitter (i.e., jitter across a network path is not the sum of jitters across consecutive parts of the path). However, the fact that maximum jitter in any router (or network) for a flow can't exceed the maximum latency for the flow in the same router (network) can be utilized to find an upper bound for jitter, once the max latency limit is estimated or budgeted. So, one possible way to engineer jitter is to design a network so that the max latency is less than or equal to the required max jitter limit. If that is feasible, no separate jitter budgeting is necessary.

NOTE 3.7: Jitter

Jitter is not additive; that is, if two routers connected to each other generate a jitter of X and Y ms, respectively, then their combined jitter is typically going to be less than X + Y, probably closer to max (X, Y). Therefore, dividing the core jitter budget by the number of hops to arrive at the per-router jitter budget, though not accurate, results in a much tighter per-hop jitter budget allocation, with the expectation that if the network can meet such a tight jitter budget, in real life the jitter would be much more likely to stay within the budgeted value.

3.16.3 Packet Loss for VoIP Traffic

Voice traffic ideally needs to have zero packet loss. Current Packet Loss Concealment (PLC) technology in DSPs can conceal the effect of a single packet loss but not for more than one consecutive lost packet. SPs typically target 0 percent drop for VoIP traffic.

3.16.4 Classifying and Queuing VoIP

The Cisco modified RFC-4594 assigns VoIP to the Expedited Forwarding (EF) class. Hence VoIP traffic is always assigned to the LLQ, also known as the Real-Time class, to adhere to the strict latency, packet loss, and jitter requirements. By virtue of being the LLQ, voice traffic is not subject to any early drop characteristics (WRED) and buffering, since traffic in the LLQ is emptied immediately and before other CBWFQ classes.

Controlling Latency in the LLQ

As mentioned earlier, VoIP needs to have a maximum one-way delay of no more than 150 ms to be considered optimal and effective for a conversation to take place. Since the LLQ receives strict priority, the only delays for the Real-Time class are the serialization and propagation delays (if any) in the network. Therefore network designers need to take into account these delays while designing an SLA for VoIP traffic. On platforms that process QoS in hardware (ASICs), the traffic in the LLQ is subject to a per-hop delay only in units of microseconds rather than milliseconds, which would ideally guarantee the latency requirements of VoIP traffic. However, this largely depends on the platform, line cards used, network links, and their respective utilization. SPs engineering the network core need to be aware of the various components in the entire path, from the VoIP source to destination and the delays that get accumulated in the process, prior to designing an SLA for the Real-Time class.

Minimizing Jitter in the LLQ

A dejitter buffer can be set up on the receiving end to collect and feed packets to the application layer with consistent interpacket gaps. This requires further buffering and can increase delay. As mentioned earlier in this chapter, Cisco IP telephones consist of in-built jitter buffers that can compensate for some amount of jitter. Finally, LLQ reorders packets on each link to make sure that jitter-sensitive flows (VoIP) are transmitted first and no sensitive flows are buffered, minimizing delay variation (jitter).

Packet Loss in the LLQ

Packet drop is a function based on class subscription rates and available link buffer space. A packet will only be dropped in the network where a link has been oversubscribed and runs out of buffer space. For some classes it is more important for traffic to be dropped than for it to be delayed. This would be the case for applications such as voice or video. A late packet will be discarded by the application and hence should have been discarded by the network to save network resources such as bandwidth and buffer space. Other classes are more reliant on delivery and less on delay. Applications such as Web browsing and database replication are examples.

For delay-sensitive traffic, low buffer thresholds limit the amount of variable delay induced by the network in times of congestion. For delivery of sensitive traffic, high buffer thresholds increase the chance of delivery. In short, QoS is only one of the aspects in a larger framework that addresses packet loss, since loss of traffic is directly proportional to network uptime and the amount of resiliency built into the network such as device and link protection schemes at various layers. Table 3.6 presents a matrix on network uptime and associated values for your reference.

From a QoS perspective, the LLQ will ensure that there are no packet drops, since the LLQ is not subject to WRED or excessive buffering. However, VoIP traffic needs to conform to the reserved bandwidth, since any excess or violation to the prescribed bandwidth would result

Table 3.6: Service Uptime/Downtime

Tier	Service Uptime	Service Downtime/Year
1	99.999%	5.2 minutes
2	99.9%	525 minutes, or 8 hours 42 minutes
3	99%	5256 minutes, or 87 hours 36 minutes

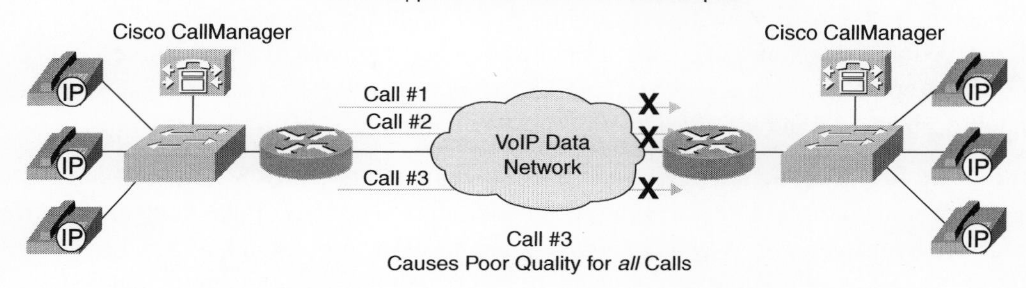

Figure 3.22: Call Admission Control

in the packet drops. However, this only applies from a QoS perspective; other factors such as network resiliency, high availability at the various layers in the network, and fast network convergence contribute to the overall end result.

3.16.5 Connection Admission Control for VoIP

By definition, network bandwidth is finite, and points of congestion do occur. All traffic types do encounter congestion at some given point of time. If packets cannot be dropped to resolve congestion, packet flows that cause congestion should not be allowed onto the network. This makes the case for the deployment of CAC tools; these are, in essence, the congestion avoidance mechanism for real-time applications. After it is admitted, a real-time flow such as voice must be carried; if there are insufficient bandwidth resources to carry the flow within the delay and loss bounds of the application, the flow must be rejected or redirected before it is admitted to the network.

Another way to look at CAC is that most of the QoS tools discussed in this book so far strive to protect voice traffic from other traffic types. CAC protects voice traffic from voice traffic itself. For example, if there is sufficient bandwidth provisioned through the LLQ to carry only two calls across a link, admitting a third call will cause packet drops and will impair the voice quality of all three calls in progress. Such scenarios necessitate the use of CAC to ensure that no more voice calls are admitted into the network beyond that allowed by the QoS engineering of the nodes.

CAC systems allow VoIP systems to make an informed decision before admitting a new call based on the condition of the network. If the call is not admitted, the call can be given the reorder (or overflow) tone, or a recorded announcement can inform the caller that the network is too busy to complete the call attempt.

3.16.6 RSVP CAC for Voice Over IP

The VoIP CAC using the RSVP feature, Cisco IOS Release 12.1(5)T, synchronizes RSVP signaling with H.323 Version 2 signaling to ensure that the bandwidth reservation is established in both directions before a call moves to the alerting phase (ringing). This ensures that the called party's phone rings only after the resources for the call have been reserved. Using RSVP-based admission control, VoIP applications can reserve network bandwidth and react appropriately if bandwidth reservation fails.

Synchronized RSVP is attempted for an IP call when the requested QoS for the associated dial peer is set to controlled load or guaranteed delay, as long as RSVP has been enabled for the interface by using the *ip rsvp bandwidth* command. If the requested QoS level is set to the default of best effort or if RSVP is not enabled, bandwidth reservation is not attempted.

If RSVP reservation is attempted but fails, the accepted QoS for the dial peer determines the outcome of the call. When the acceptable QoS is configured for best effort, the call setup proceeds but without any bandwidth reservation in place. When the acceptable QoS on either gateway is configured for other than best effort and the RSVP reservation fails, the call is released.

Figure 3.23 summarizes the results of nine call setup scenarios using fast connect based on the QoS levels configured in the VoIP dial peers at the originating and terminating gateways. Figure 3.16 does not include cases in which the requested QoS is best effort and the acceptable QoS is other than best effort because those configurations are considered invalid. The following convention is used in the Requested QoS and Acceptable QoS columns to indicate the configuration for the scenario:

- CL: Controlled Load
- GD: Guaranteed Delay
- BE: Best Effort

3.17 Summary of Requirements for Voice and Video Classes

This section summarizes the requirements for the various video classes and is illustrated in Table 3.7.

3.18 QoS Requirements and Design for Data Applications

Looking back at the Cisco modified RFC-4594 model, data applications can be traditionally classified as low latency, high throughput, or low priority. Each of these categories indicates

Call Scenario	Originating Gateway		Terminating Gateway		
	Requested QoS	Acceptable QoS	Requested QoS	Acceptable QoS	Results
1	Controlled-load or guaranteed-delay	Controlled-load or guaranteed-delay	Controlled-load or guaranteed-delay	Controlled-load or guaranteed-delay	Call proceeds only if both RSVP reservations succeed.
2	Controlled-load or guaranteed-delay	Controlled-load or guaranteed-delay	Controlled-load or guaranteed-delay	Best-effort	Call proceeds only if both RSVP reservations succeed.
3	Controlled-load or guaranteed-delay	Controlled-load or guaranteed-delay	Best-effort	Best-effort	Call is released.
4	Controlled-load or guaranteed-delay	Best-effort	Controlled-load or guaranteed-delay	Controlled-load or guaranteed-delay	Call proceeds only if both RSVP reservations succeed.
5	Controlled-load or guaranteed-delay	Best-effort	Controlled-load or guaranteed-delay	Best-effort	Call proceeds regardless of RSVP results. If RSVP reservation fails, call receives best-effort service.
6	Controlled-load or guaranteed-delay	Best-effort	Best-effort	Best-effort	Call proceeds with best-effort service.
7	Best-effort	Best-effort	Controlled-load or guaranteed-delay	Controlled-load or guaranteed-delay	Call is released.
8	Best-effort	Best-effort	Controlled-load or guaranteed-delay	Best-effort	Call proceeds with best-effort service.
9	Best-effort	Best-effort	Best-effort	Best-effort	Call proceeds with best-effort service.

Figure 3.23: Call Results Based on Configured QoS Levels

Table 3.7: Voice and Video Service Requirements

Traffic Class	Delay	Jitter	Bandwidth	Packet Loss
Voice	150 ms one way	<=30 ms	<=33% of the link bandwidth, since voice is always assigned to the LLQ	Nil
Interactive Video (TelePresence)	150 ms (can accept delays up to 200 ms)	<=10 ms	2 Mbps for CTS-1000 and 15 Mbps for CTS-3000	0.05%
Broadcast Video (IPTV)	150 ms	<=50 ms	<2.75 Mbps for standard definition stream and <9 Mbps for high-definition stream	$<10^{-6}$
Video on Demand (Unicast Based)	150 ms	<=50 ms	<2.75 Mbps for standard definition stream and <9 Mbps for high-definition stream	$<10^{-6}$
Multimedia Conferencing and Streaming (PC-based Conferencing)	>400 ms	<=50 ms	<=460 Kbps per video call	1%

the characteristics of applications that may classify as candidates. For instance, Oracle database updates, e-commerce transactions, and terminal connections are both interactive in nature and highly critical to an enterprise and can be classified as applications that need guaranteed delivery and low latency. File transfers, database queries, and corporate intranet applications, on the other hand, need guaranteed delivery but are not very sensitive to latency. These applications classify as being high throughput in nature. Low-priority applications could include Internet access and Web surfing, which is categorized as expecting best-effort service.

Typically an SP has two or three classes for catering to data traffic. Based on Figure 3.10, each of these classes offers a unique set of services. However, the key aspect to be noted is the fact that data applications traditionally do not require any jitter guarantees; neither are they tied to a strict latency norm. Guaranteed bandwidth and delivery are the most common and accepted characteristics for data applications. Hence data applications are always grouped into the AF PHB. Service providers can differentiate between low-latency data and high-throughput data classes by assigning different weights for each CBWFQ queue that services these data applications. For instance, low-latency data might be assigned a higher weight (in essence, more bandwidth) compared to the high-throughput class, which might have a relatively lesser assigned weight. This will result in the system spending more cycles for the low-latency data class.

Another differentiating factor is the use of WRED for congestion avoidance.

3.18.1 WRED and Data Traffic Classes

WRED plays a major role in altering the bandwidth and is essentially offered throughout to a given class. Depending on the priority of a data class, drop profiles (WRED) can be configured as being either aggressive or moderate. For example, low-latency data can inherit a less aggressive drop profile compared to high-throughput data, which might be subject to a relatively more aggressive drop rate. Finally, each class could have a moderate to high buffering scheme, which is also an option for providing differentiated services between data classes. All this put together would result in each class inheriting different bandwidth, throughput, and latency guarantees.

As an example, let's look at some sample SLAs in the three data classes, as illustrated in Figure 3.10:

- Low-latency data have a requirement for a delay of no more than 200 ms in the SP core.
- High-throughput data need a delay threshold of 250 ms in the SP core.
- Best effort has no guarantees, as its name suggests.

To achieve these requirements, an SP has to baseline the bandwidth allotted for each class, because a highly oversubscribed class will result in unpredictable results and violate all service-level guarantees. So, the first step is to plan on the bandwidth allotments for each class. The next step is to define the drop profiles and subsequently the buffer size per class. For example, let's assume that the network diameter in the SP core has four hops (provider edge to provider edge). To achieve the latency of 200 ms for low-latency data, the delay at each hop in the network needs to be well within 50 ms; this includes serialization, propagation, and delays introduced by virtue of buffering traffic. As per this example, it is worth noting that the maximum WRED values and queue limit definition need to be well within 50 ms of threshold to have traffic that exceeding this value has to be dropped rather than delayed further.

The same principles apply for the high-throughput data, with the exception that per-hop latencies in this case could be around 60 ms because the end-to-end latency requirements are 250 ms, as per the example.

3.18.2 Best-Effort Traffic

This class usually has no latency, jitter, or loss commitments and includes all traffic that is not included in the other edge classes. Some characteristics of this class are given here:

- *Marking.* Traffic of this class is typically marked with DSCP 0 and EXP 0 in the MPLS core.
- *Link bandwidth allocation for Best-Effort class.* Service providers may provision different fractions of link bandwidth to this class, based on their business requirements. Note that this class can potentially carry traffic from thousands of applications from a large enterprise; hence assigning too little bandwidth to this class can lead to end-user dissatisfaction. In case of a five-class implementation, an SP may provision a fixed minimum bandwidth for best-effort class. A value of 20–30% is usual in multiservice environment, although it can be lower or higher depending on the SP's provided services.
- *PHB.* This traffic class is assigned the class default and receives best-effort treatment.
- *WRED.* WRED is configured for this class to avoid TCP synchronization. WRED can also be used to drop certain types of best-effort traffic prior to other types of best-effort traffic.

3.18.3 Class for Routing and Management Traffic

An SP may define additional traffic classes at the edge, such as Routing class and/or Management class, to further control the minimum bandwidth for these types of traffic.

3.18.4 Network Control Class

Bandwidth allocation is the type of routing packets, packet sizes, the routing burst to be supported, and the planned convergence time for the burst would determine the bandwidth allocated to the Routing class. A starting value for the bandwidth can be calculated based on the following formula (its accuracy will depend on the accuracy of the routing burst and convergence durations).

NOTE 3.8: Bandwidth Calculation

Bandwidth in Kbps for Network Control class = (Routing packets in a burst * Packet size in Kbits) / (Desired routing convergence time in secs)

Table 3.8 illustrates the recommended characteristics for network control traffic.

3.19 QoS Treatment of Locally Sourced Traffic

Locally sourced traffic identifies the traffic that is originated from the local router and does not refer to traffic that is being forwarded. Cisco IOS and IOS-XR software treats routing and several other types of control plane traffic in a special way to ensure that they are not dropped (or are dropped last) during congestion. Interior Gateway Protocol (IGP) traffic, such as Routing Information Protocol (RIP) and Enhanced Interior Gateway Routing Protocol (EIGRP), typically don't require explicit traffic provisioning, as they benefit from Cisco's internal mechanism (PAK_PRIORITY) of flagging a packet as important so that it can override the packet-drop algorithms of WRED. However, for OSPF Protocol, only the hellos are marked with the PAK_PRIORITY, whereas the other OSPF traffic gets marked with IP DSCP 48/IP Precedence 6, and BGP traffic (while also marked IPP6/CS6) does not get marked PAK_PRIORITY; hence they may need to be explicitly protected to maintain peering sessions. If a service provider has a separate class for routing, this traffic can be protected. A detailed discussion on this topic follows:

- *How locally sourced traffic is marked.* The marking of locally sourced traffic may be used for local classification, but is also important where the traffic is destined for nondirectly connected neighbors and hence will transit intermediary routers en route to the destination, e.g., iBGP and SNMP. In the latter case, if the traffic has been correctly marked at the source, the DSCP/IP Precedence field is used for classification at the intermediary routers and the design goal is achieved by allocating this traffic to a class (and hence a queue), which has been provisioned to receive good service with low loss. It is therefore not recommended to allocate this traffic to the Best-Effort class.
- *How locally sourced traffic is classified and queued.* Assuming that the locally sourced traffic has been correctly marked, consideration then needs to be given to how this traffic is queued locally.

The following sections describe these considerations in more detail.

Table 3.8: Recommendations for Network Control Class

PHB	Marking	WRED	Queue Limit	Bandwidth
Assured Forwarding PHB	DSCP48, IP Precedence 6, and MPLS EXP 6; Cisco IOS and XR software generates OSPF, BGP, and RIP Version 2 with this marking	No; packet drop for this class is not desired	Large enough to accommodate maximum traffic bursts	Typically around 3–5% of the link bandwidth

3.19.1 Marking of Locally Sourced Traffic

Figure 3.24 shows the default IOS behavior with respect to the marking of locally sourced traffic for some of the most common control/routing/management traffic.

If local traffic marking is required outside the IOS default scheme shown, an outbound service policy can be used on some platforms to set the DSCP/prec of locally generated traffic, as shown in Figure 3.25. An ACL is used to identify the traffic, and the policy map POLICY is configured to mark the DSCP values as per the requirement.

Application	Default DSCP / Precedence Marking	Notes
APS control packets	DSCP 48 / PRECEDENCE 6	
BGP	DSCP 48 / PRECEDENCE 6	
LDP	DSCP 48 / PRECEDENCE 6	
OSPF	DSCP 48 / PRECEDENCE 6	
RADIUS	DSCP 0 / PRECEDENCE 0	
RIP	DSCP 48 / PRECEDENCE 6	
SNMP	DSCP 0 / PRECEDENCE 0	Configurable via SNMP-server ip [dscplprec] from 12.0(26)S

Figure 3.24: Marking of Locally Sourced Traffic

```
access-list 103 permit ip host <loopback_addr> <mgt_prefix> <mgt_mask>
!
class-map MGT
  match access-group 103
!
policy-map POLICY
  ...
  class MGT
   Bandwidth 8
   queue-limit 40
   set ip dscp 32
  ...
!
interface <int>
  service-policy output POLICY
```

Figure 3.25: Using an Outbound Service Policy

3.19.2 Queuing Treatment of Locally Sourced Traffic

To ensure that locally sourced traffic receives good service with low loss, SPs typically dedicate a class for this purpose. This class needs to have minimal bandwidth assurances, as illustrated in Table 3.8.

3.20 Management Class

SNMP, Syslog, NTP, NFS, Telnet, TFTP, and other traffic used for managing the network can also be assigned a separate traffic class such as the Network Control class. Assigning a separate class to management traffic may help a service provider get Telnet access to a heavily congested router. Some of the characteristics are:

- Bandwidth allocation per expected traffic load
- WRED is not typical in this class, since most traffic is SNMP, which is UDP based

3.21 Summary

This chapter focused on providing guidelines on mapping enterprise applications to SP classes of service using two reference models in the Cisco QoS Baseline and the Cisco modified RFC-4594 framework. Various application types, along with their respective QoS requirements, that provide a quality of experience to the end user have also been elaborated. These guidelines are crucial in ensuring a favorable experience to end subscribers.

As mentioned earlier, both Cisco modified RFC-4594 and Cisco QoS Baseline are intended only to assist in developing a framework for deployment and are not "must adhere to" recommendations. Both the QoS Baseline and Cisco modified RFC-4594 recommend markings as well as what applications should be grouped together. It is important to understand that there are multiple approaches to deploying QoS. One option is not more correct than the other. The option that best adheres to the overall QoS strategy and allows you to meet your goals/SLAs will dictate what solution is chosen. In some cases, it could be a combination of the two. The key is to ensure that the PHB is consistent for traffic classes because applications are serviced from end to end within the network, based on the requirements from the network. However, despite the subtle differences between the two recommendations, the approaches are very similar in nature.

However, the bottom line is that SPs and enterprise customers can still choose to differ on both the traffic-to-class mapping as well as the acceptable metrics for the various applications that are deployed. Metrics and SLAs for measuring performance can vary on a case-by-case basis, and the choice lies in what suits a given environment.

CHAPTER 4

Carrier CE Services in Cisco IP NGN Networks

4.1 Overview

This chapter delves a little deeper into the discussion of both managed and unmanaged CE services that a carrier might provide. In Chapter 3, we discussed possible combinations of mapping enterprise classes into the SP classes and the relative impact on each approach. Here we build on these discussions with more details on the configurations and, more important, present some very common carrier product offerings from a QoS standpoint. Having seen requirements in the previous chapters and moving toward QoS implementation and case studies in the chapters ahead, this chapter provides some real-life examples of how carriers build and offer SLA metrics for managed services (services wherein the customer premises equipment, or CPE, is provided and managed by the carrier).

4.2 Customer Requirements

Spending most of our time in discussion from a carrier viewpoint, let's look at a bit of background on the adoption of IP by enterprises and the importance of their communication needs.

An enterprise's decision to move to IP delivers the most value when a substantial ratio of its applications and facilities has been migrated to the converged network. Encouragingly, a global survey of 395 senior executives conducted by the Economist Intelligence Unit for a leading carrier shows that the pace of migration has become inexorable: By mid-2007, about 50 percent of firms globally—and two-thirds of U.S. firms—had shifted their voice and data applications over to IP. By mid-2008 this figure had risen to an average of 72 percent of firms, based on the survey results. Among the various approaches to IP migration, the "big bang," or enterprisewide, implementation is most popular among firms worldwide, although in the United States.

A phased, department-by-department strategy is much more likely. Fewer than one in five firms uses small-scale trials, though this can be a highly effective way to iron out difficulties in advance and avoid disrupting business. Surveyed executives view disruption to day-to-day business as the principal risk involved with migration of applications to IP. Migration prepares the way for the integration of applications. Research shows that most companies today have

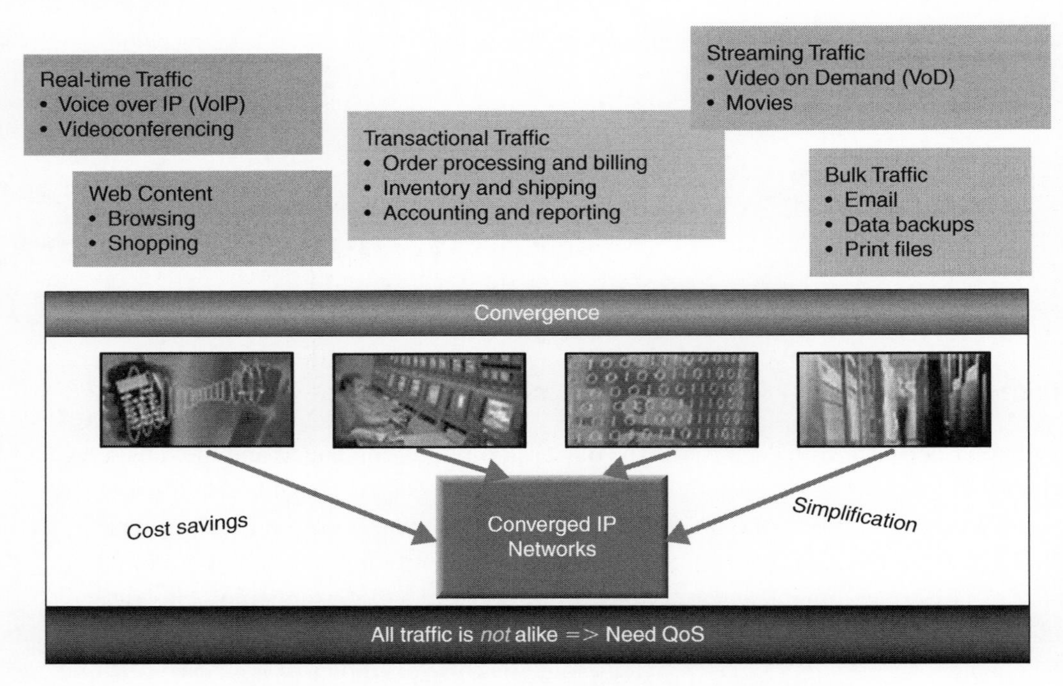

Figure 4.1: IP Convergence for Enterprise Networks

a strategy in place to integrate applications on IP and that the market for integration software is burgeoning. Companies are generally adopting "Web services" to provide a standardized way to carry out the difficult task of integration.

Looking a little deeper to understand how a converged IP network delivers the benefits we've discussed, we find that the single large advantage lies in enabling any mix of applications to coexist and be optimally delivered via DiffServ QoS on this converged infrastructure. Figure 4.1 provides a snapshot of this aspect.

4.3 Challenges Faced by Customers

Having discussed the trend in enterprise adoption of IP, we look at some underlying challenges and some guidelines for enterprises to this effect. This discussion applies to enterprise customers of a carrier who subscribe to both IP VPN services (in effect, managed services) as well as pure Layer 2 circuits (such as MPLS Layer 2 VPN services, for instance), where management of the enterprise perimeter is done by the end customer. The reason we discuss this topic here is to ensure that SPs understand these nuances and are sensitive to these needs while designing and deploying QoS for customers at the network edge.

Of all the issues faced by enterprises in managing their networks and traffic, capacity planning is one of the most important. Until recently more art than science, network capacity planning is all about balancing the need to meet user performance expectations against the realities of capital budgeting. WAN bandwidth is expensive, and many enterprises attempt to control costs by acquiring the minimum bandwidth necessary to handle traffic on a circuit. Unfortunately, this strategy can lead to congestion and degraded application performance.

A WAN circuit running at 80 percent capacity is too full. Even a circuit that averages 65 percent of capacity may well peak at 95 percent capacity for several periods during a day, reducing user productivity and negatively affecting business activities. Many enterprises rely on SNMP to monitor overall WAN bandwidth utilization. Measuring overall traffic, however, does little to characterize network traffic, which is essential to deciding if additional capacity is warranted. Without knowing what types of traffic are using the network, it is impossible to know whether QoS parameters for applications such as voice and video within the enterprise support these target levels. Complicating the challenges of traffic characterization is the reality that many new applications use a range of dynamic ports. These dynamic ports may also be used by several applications within the enterprise.

In general, many IT staffs of large enterprises believe that networks built with high-capacity switching/routing gear and high-speed links would never need QoS management. They believe that the more bandwidth that is available, the less QoS is needed. All networks have congestion points where packets can be dropped—WAN links where a larger trunk funnels data into a smaller one or a location where several trunks funnel data into fewer outputs. Applying QoS at the enterprise-to-carrier border does not create additional bandwidth. Rather, it helps smooth the peaks and valleys of network circuit utilization. In these cases, QoS provides more consistent network performance from the point of view of end users. Deploying QoS uniformly across the network protects important real-time voice and video applications guaranteeing bandwidth and/or low latency from occasional traffic spikes than can affect performance.

Due to this measure of protection, QoS settings must be deployed on all networking devices, such as all switches and routers. Later in this chapter we take a look at some configurations as well. Another aspect that is worth a mention is that though most capacity planning occurs at the circuit level, it is also desirable where possible to plan within individual classes of service. It is possible to oversubscribe one or more classes of service without reaching utilization levels that would affect a circuit's overall performance. It is increasingly important to do this planning while using MPLS Layer 3 VPN services. Carriers, in addition to charging for a circuit, also charge for these classes of service. Managing the bandwidth levels of these individual classes of service ensures proper application performance without overspending for a particular class of service. This activity generally needs proper coordination between the enterprise and the SP.

4.4 Managed and Unmanaged CE Services

Customers have the option of choosing between managed or unmanaged services when they subscribe to a carrier offering for connectivity. The option chosen is largely based on the end customer requirements and may also be a policy decision. Before we look at some important aspects influencing this decision, let's have a closer look at both these service types.

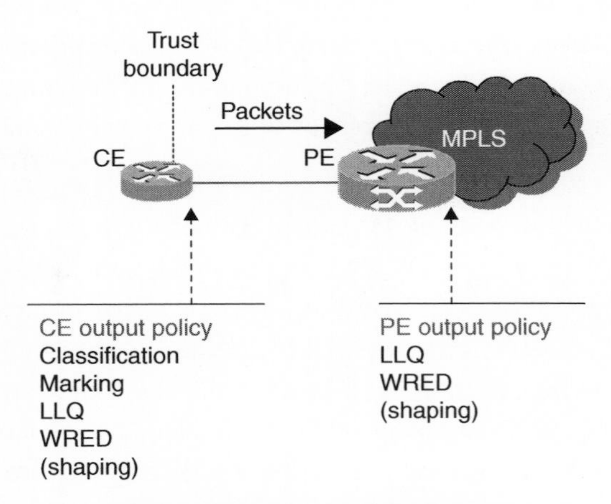

Figure 4.2: Managed CE Setup

4.4.1 Managed CE Services

The primary difference between managed CE and unmanaged CE services is that the CE device is provided, configured, and managed by the carrier in the case of the former. To recap, let's look at this in a little more detail. In Figure 4.2, we notice that the trust boundary is extended to the perimeter of the customer network. In other words, the provider domain is extended to the CE device. By definition, "trust" indicates that the job of classification and marking is no more a function of the PE (only in regard to a given PE-CE connection) and has been entrusted to the CE device. Managed CE services offer better coordination in QoS policies between the customer and carrier. "Better coordination" indicates that the customer and carrier can effectively coordinate the QoS policies in regard to the enterprise traffic to carrier QoS class mapping and results in distribution of key functions such as marking and classification, as mentioned previously.

A typical scenario occurs when the CE device can be used for remarking customer traffic to facilitate enterprise traffic to carrier QoS classes. This becomes very handy, since the number of QoS classes within the enterprise network is typically large compared to the carrier classes, which are fewer. Having the CE router remark traffic to suit the carrier QoS classes results in offloading much of the load from the PE devices in the carrier network. Let's look at an example as illustrated in Figure 4.3.

In the illustration, we notice that the enterprise edge (the CE router) has 11 classes, compared to three classes of service within the carrier network. Each class at the enterprise is mapped to a corresponding carrier class. Also we notice that the Multimedia Streaming and Broadcast Video classes are remarked at the CE (at the enterprise class level) to a corresponding carrier class, since their original marking values of CS5 and AF31 do not map to any of the classes in the carrier network. This helps in offloading the marking function from the PE layer, providing an opportunity to distribute functions.

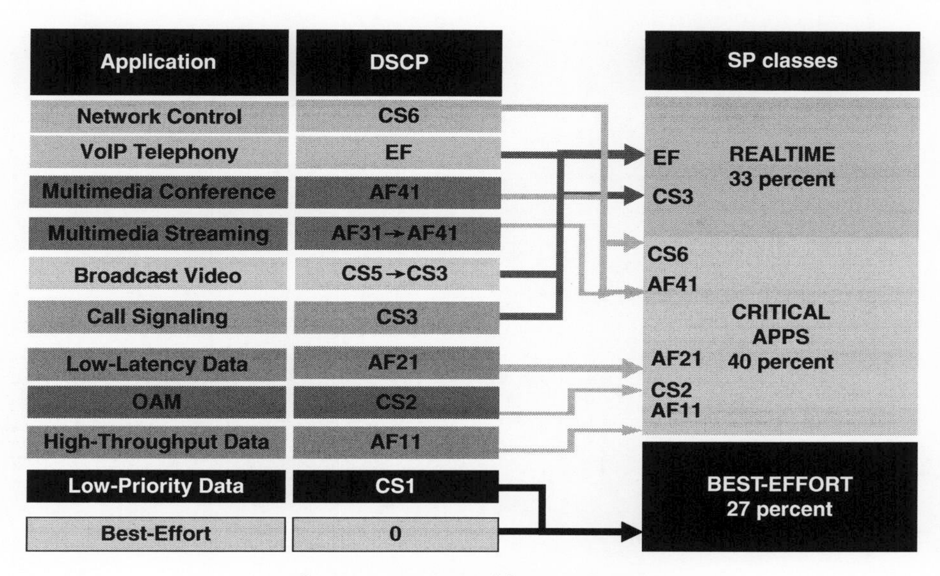

Figure 4.3: Remarking at the CE

Let's look at the device configuration for the CE router for a managed CE scenario, as illustrated in Figure 4.2. In the configlet we notice that the CE device classifies traffic based on the marked IP precedence (we use IP precedence in this example to provide variety) and appropriately schedules traffic on the CE-PE link. The CE device is not configured for any marking and instead relies on other devices in the network (such as the IP phones and Ethernet switches) to mark appropriate traffic. However, the CE router uses functions such as WRED and LLQ for managing congestion and scheduling traffic on the CE-to-PE link. Detailed illustrations and examples, along with explanations of device configurations for the various QoS functions based on various hardware platforms and line-card combinations, are provided in the implementation chapters, starting with Chapter 8.

CE Router Configuration

```
!
!
class-map match-any Control
 match ip precedence 6 7
class-map match-all Realtime
 match ip precedence 5
class-map match-any Video
 match ip precedence 4
class-map match-any Premium
 match ip precedence 2
class-map match-all BestEffort
 match ip precedence 0
```

```
!
policy-map router-ce-Edge_Egress
 class Control
 Bandwidth percent 2
 class Realtime
 Priority percent 25
 class Video
 bandwidth percent 40
 class Premium
 Bandwidth percent 28
 random-detect
 random-detect exponential-weighting-constant 13
 random-detect precedence 1 35ms 40ms 1
 random-detect precedence 2 40ms 45ms 1
 queue-limit 45ms
 class BestEffort
 bandwidth percent 4
 random-detect
 random-detect exponential-weighting-constant 13
 random-detect precedence 0 30ms 100ms 1
 queue-limit 100ms
!
interface GigabitEthernetx/x
 service-policy output router-ce-Edge_Egress
!
End
```

Let's look at the device configuration for the CE device for a managed CE scenario using a switch instead of a router, as illustrated in Figure 4.4.

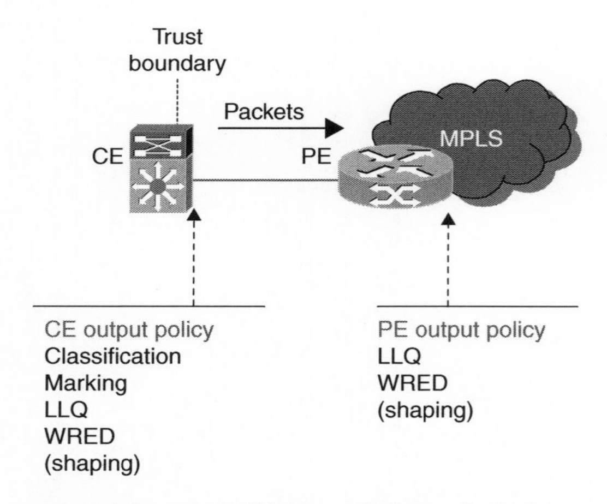

Figure 4.4: Managed CE Setup Using a Switch as a CE

In the configuration that follows, we notice that the CE has two policy maps configured under the ingress and egress interfaces. The ingress policy map named *switch-ce-Edge_Ingress* is used to police incoming traffic based on a configured CIR and to remark traffic. Out-of-contract traffic is also remarked to a lesser precedence value, to indicate a lower priority. The egress policy map named *switch-ce-Edge_Egress* is used for scheduling traffic on the CE-PE link. This is used to ensure protection for the various traffic types on the upstream interface, toward the carrier network.

CE Switch Configuration

```
!
!
class-map match-any Control
 match cos 6 7
class-map match-all Realtime
 match cos 5
class-map match-any Video
 match cos 4
class-map match-any Premium
 match cos 1 2
class-map match-all BestEffort
 match cos 0
!
policy-map switch-ce-Edge_Ingress
 class Control
 police cir <rate>
 conform-action set-qos-transmit 6
 exceed-action drop
 class Realtime
 police cir <rate>
 conform-action set-qos-transmit 5
 exceed-action drop
 class Video
 Police cir <rate>
 conform-action set-qos-transmit 4
 exceed-action drop
 class Premium
 police cir <rate>
 conform-action set-qos-transmit 2
 exceed-action set-qos-transmit 1
 violate-action drop
 class BestEffort
 police cir <rate>
 conform-action set-qos-transmit 0
 exceed-action drop
!
```

```
policy-map switch-ce-Edge_Egress
 class Control
 bandwidth <rate>
 class Realtime
 priority
 police cir <rate>
 conform-action transmit
 exceed-action drop
 class Video
 bandwidth <rate>
 class Premium
 bandwidth <rate>
 class BestEffort
 bandwidth <rate>
!
interface FastEthernetx/x
 service-policy input switch-ce-Edge_Ingress
!
interface FastEthernetx/y
 service-policy output switch-ce-Edge_Egress
 End
```

Finally we look at the PE device configuration. Here we notice that traffic policers are enforced at the network edge. This step may be redundant in the case of managed CE deployments, since the policing function can be shifted to the CE device. However, there might be cases wherein the carrier expects a more granular traffic rate in terms of burst rate and so on, which can only be deployed at the PE router, since the CE scheduler configuration might not always support this configuration for all classes. It is worth noting that only the LLQ may have a policer configured in terms of burst rate and so on, whereas other traffic classes might simply consist of a *bandwidth* command.

PE Router Configuration

```
!
!
class-map match-any Control
 match ip precedence 6 7
class-map match-all Realtime
 match ip precedence 5
class-map match-any Video
 match ip precedence 4
class-map match-any Premium
 match ip precedence 2
class-map match-all BestEffort
 match ip precedence 0
!
```

```
policy-map PE-CE-Edge_Ingress
 class Control
 police cir <rate> conform-action set-mpls-exp-topmost-transmit 6 exceed-
action drop
 class Realtime
 police cir <rate> conform-action set-mpls-exp-topmost-transmit 5 exceed-
action drop
 class Video
 police cir <rate> conform-action set-mpls-exp-topmost-transmit 4 exceed-
action drop
 class Premium
 police cir <rate> conform-action set-mpls-exp-topmost-transmit 2 exceed-
action drop
 class BestEffort
 police cir <rate> conform-action set-mpls-exp-topmost-transmit 0 exceed-
action drop
!
policy-map SP-CORE-POLICY
 class Control
 Bandwidth percent 2
 class Realtime
 Priority percent 25
 class Video
 bandwidth percent 40
 class Premium
 Bandwidth percent 28
 random-detect
 random-detect exponential-weighting-constant 13
 random-detect precedence 1 35ms 40ms 1
 random-detect precedence 2 40ms 45ms 1
 queue-limit 45ms
 class BestEffort
 bandwidth percent 4
 random-detect
 random-detect exponential-weighting-constant 13
 random-detect precedence 0 30ms 100ms 1
 queue-limit 100ms
!
interface GigabitEthernetx/x
 Description ### Link to CE device ###
 service-policy output PE-CE-Edge_Ingress
!
interface GigabitEthernetx/y
 Description ### Link to Carrier Network Core ###
 service-policy output SP-CORE-POLICY
!
End
```

NOTE 4.1: Edge Layer

In both these examples, we can notice that the CE and PE classes are identical, wherein there is an easy one-one mapping. This might or might not be the case in most enterprise deployments, since the number of classes in the enterprise network may be more in number due to the large number of applications. However, this is more related to the mapping, and examples in this regard are provided in Chapter 2. What we notice in these examples is the consistency in both the mapping and QoS configurations, which is important. Often the CE router will also need to remark traffic to conform to the QoS policy in the carrier network, as illustrated in Figure 4.3.

4.4.2 Unmanaged CE Services

Unmanaged CE services merely indicate that the CE device is not owned by the carrier; therefore the carrier boundary ends at the PE layer. The CE device is part of the customer network in all aspects, and from a QoS configuration point as well. In this case, the carrier extends no "trust" CE. Therefore the functions of classification and marking are performed at the PE device. The CE device can perform its own set of QoS functions, such as scheduling and congestion avoidance; this is completely independent of the carrier's QoS structure. An illustration of unmanaged CE services is provided in Figure 4.5.

4.5 Guidelines for Carriers Deploying Managed CE Services

Often SPs might need to act as trusted advisors to end customers in helping them make the right choices in regard to many aspects of their networks, such as capacity planning and network engineering, in addition to enabling a QoS framework in the network. This can largely depend on the level of managed services being offered by the carrier. Some services

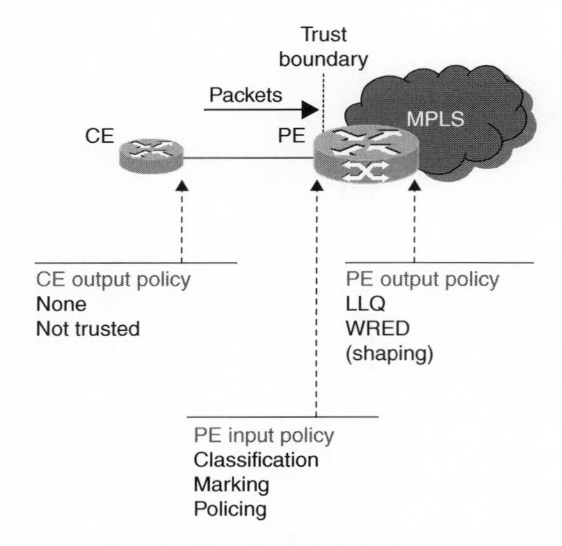

Figure 4.5: Unmanaged CE Setup

might simply involve providing a managed CE service that can involve provisioning the last-mile circuit and configuring QoS at the network edge, in line with the enterprise classes and relative mapping to the carrier classes, whereas other services can involve the carrier getting involved with the complete network engineering/design in the enterprise network. Whatever the level of involvement, the following facts help both the enterprise and the carrier with some guidelines on overcoming the most common challenges in regard to enterprise networks and their requirements.

The most important exercise lies in ensuring proper categorization of network traffic. Generally speaking, enterprises can begin by categorizing network traffic into three types, as follows.

4.5.1 Legitimate Business-Related Traffic

Enterprises build their networks to accommodate legitimate business-related traffic. If a link is at capacity and all traffic is legitimate, a network/link upgrade might be necessary. A factor influencing this decision is that some legitimate traffic, backups, file transfers, or VoD replication can be scheduled outside peak utilization hours. The ability to make scheduling changes can often postpone the need for an upgrade. "When we first implemented a new application to back user PC hard drives across the network, we seriously underestimated the impact it would have on the WAN—especially smaller branch WAN links," said an IT manager of a large enterprise. "While backups were done incrementally, the initial backup was always large—and when we first deployed the application, they were all initial backups. After looking at the performance problems and realizing they were created by a legitimate application that would eventually stop needing so much bandwidth, we decided to avoid WAN upgrades. Instead we asked the application developers to schedule all initial backups after hours. When they did so, the problem was solved."

4.5.2 Inappropriate Traffic

Traffic in the inappropriate category can include everything from recreational Internet downloads to viruses, worms, or distributed denial-of-service (DDoS) attacks. In general it has been observed that it's not important to eliminate recreational traffic entirely until it begins to significantly affect bandwidth availability and compete with the top 10 applications.

4.5.3 Bulk Traffic

Harder to describe than inappropriate or legitimate traffic, bulk traffic can result from how and where business-related applications are used. Backups or database synchronizations performed at inappropriate times or even over inappropriate segments of the network are obvious offenders. Traffic consuming significant bandwidth during peak hours that can be safely moved or rescheduled can be called bulk traffic. Many times categorizing such traffic as Scavenger class will automatically throttle such traffic during peak utilization and allow it to flow through during availability of resources is an effective way of handling such traffic.

4.5.4 Consistent QoS Policy

Once traffic has been categorized, the next important step is to deploy a consistent QoS policy/configuration in the network. It is important that all devices are configured for QoS and essentially are aware of the QoS policy enforced in the enterprise network. For instance, marking of traffic may be a function implemented in all the wiring closet switching equipment to which the end user's device is physically connected. In many cases, the end-user equipment such as a Cisco IP phone might have the ability to mark traffic with a predefined QoS code point. However, the important fact is that the entry points for traffic should be responsible for categorizing traffic. This scheme should be extended to the entire network and should be reflected in the edge device (CE) that connects to the carrier network. Normally, the link would be relatively smaller compared to the links within the enterprise LAN or compared to the scale within the carrier core infrastructure. Therefore it is at this point that a lot of care needs to be provided in terms of a robust QoS policy to achieve needed service levels. Features such as LLQ and WRED need to be configured not just within the carrier network; they are of paramount importance at the network edge, too. Most of the recommendations made in the previous chapters in regard to applications and their inherent needs from a QoS standpoint within a carrier core network also apply to the network edge. So, consistent deployment and protection for critical applications by virtue of QoS configurations at the network edge result in achieving tighter SLAs.

4.6 Sample Carrier Service Offerings

Here we look at some sample SLAs that carriers offer to managed CE customers. The offerings illustrated here apply to managed CE customers, since they are all applicable end to end, that is, from CE to CE. End-to-end SLAs can be offered only if the CE and the last mile are managed by the carrier. These metrics may be unique to a given carrier, but what is important for an enterprise is to choose the product and service offering (from a QoS standpoint) that suits the applications and traffic types. In the previous sections, we discussed in detail the requirements for each traffic type (such as voice, various types of video, and data applications). Most of the guidelines apply to both carriers and enterprises and hence may be used as a ready reference. Having said that, certain applications within the enterprise could have some special requirements, so choosing the appropriate service becomes imperative.

4.6.1 Sample Offering 1

In this section we look at a sample QoS offering from a carrier who offers Internet and VPN services. This carrier offers xDSL-based access services and has a portfolio of QoS offerings consisting of three classes. The Platinum class caters to voice and video traffic, and the carrier classifies this traffic to adhere to strict service-level guarantees, achieving the same by ensuring that this class is not oversubscribed, hence the description of 1:1.

The Gold class caters to mission-critical applications; therefore it is safe to state that this class is predominantly a data-only class. Voice and video in this context refer to PC-based videoconferencing applications that have some amount of voice and video content and are considered less critical than VoIP and video applications such as TelePresence. This class is oversubscribed to an extent of 5:1, since data traffic is expected to have periodic bursts, which could, in effect, mean that bandwidth is not completely utilized during long periods of time. The ratio of oversubscription, however, is a call; the carrier needs to keep an accounting of the number of subscribers, application types, SLAs, and so on.

The Bronze class is the best-effort equivalent, catering to noncritical applications. This class is supposed to have a high oversubscription ratio compared to the Gold class. Figure 4.6 provides a synopsis of the service offerings.

Looking at the service offering in Figure 4.6, we see that some of the key metrics missing in the illustration are metrics such as delay, jitter, and, of course, packet loss. It is extremely essential for an enterprise to have this information prior to choosing the appropriate class. Similarly, an enterprise's requirements in terms of SLAs will not always fit into the carrier's categorization of applications to respective classes. For instance, an enterprise can require that its corporate email traffic/groupware applications require a higher priority than traditional best-effort treatment. Now when we compare this requirement with the grouping as shown in Figure 4.1, there is a direct mismatch. In this case, the carrier would need flexibility in accommodating traffic into various classes based on customer requirements rather than having a rigid policy of categorization. That said, certain classes in the carrier network would not be open to all traffic types. Examples are the class that hosts voice traffic (also known as the LLQ); the exclusive Video class (if any) may not host traffic other than video.

4.6.2 Sample Offering 2

In this example, we look at another carrier that has a more detailed representation of the QoS framework being offered to customers. Even though the metrics apply to both managed

Class of Service	IP Precedence	Typical Use
Platinum	5	Multimedia applications such as voice and video only. Expected performance is equivalent to a 1:1 DSL service.
Gold	3	Mission-critical data applications such as voice, video, SAP, Citrix, etc. Expected performance is equivalent to a 5:1 DSL service.
Bronze	1	Best-effort data applications such as Internet, email, and FTP. Expected performance is equivalent to a standard 20:1 DSL service.

Figure 4.6: Synopsis of the QoS Classes

and unmanaged subscribers, the details on the last-mile circuit apply to only the managed subscribers, since this portion of the network is under the carrier's administrative boundary. In this example, as illustrated in Figure 4.7, there are four classes of service: Real-Time, Multimedia, Business, and Best-Effort. Looking at what each class stands for:

- The Real-Time class hosts all VoIP traffic.
- The Multimedia class hosts only video traffic.
- The Business class hosts all mission-critical data traffic.
- The Best-Effort class hosts other generic applications that are not critical in nature.

The carrier in this case has provided a chart on expected metrics with regard to various interface types. The first column, Link Speed, indicates the various link types, starting from E1 circuits, T3 links, STM-1, and Gigabit Ethernet links. Figures 4.6 and 4.7 provide two charts with the expected metrics for both the access circuits between the CE and PE devices as well as metrics within the carrier core network. This is to help in clearly identifying parameters such as delay in both the edge and core network infrastructures. Moreover, link types are illustrated in the "access network" portion of the illustration in Figure 4.6 to clearly highlight variations in the metrics based on the access circuit type. This information is masked in Figure 4.7 because the links used are irrelevant from a customer standpoint; the metrics that can be achieved are all that matters.

Let's take a closer look at the illustration in Figure 4.6. Taking the case of E1 links, the carrier has indicated a "serialization delay" of 6 ms for this link type. Serialization delays are an indication of low-speed circuits, and in this case it might be possible that the carrier is offering subrate access or fractional E1 circuits (in the scale of nx64 kbps) to end subscribers.

The Packet Size column indicates that these metrics apply to all traffic with packet sizes up to 1500 bytes. This is merely an indication that all traffic types fit into the scheme of this calculation by the carrier.

Minimum WRED and maximum WRED thresholds indicate the amount of time that traffic belonging to a given class can be subject to the early drop characteristics configured at each hop. Furthermore, they are an indication of the maximum amount of time that traffic will be allowed to spend at a given hop before being permanently discarded. Once again, each class has a policy configuration based on its priority—the higher the priority, the less aggressive the WRED profile. Looking at the Real-Time class, we notice a value of 4 ms in the Engineered Max Delay column. A clever reader may ask: How does WRED apply to the Real-Time class that hosts voice traffic? This is just an indication of the maximum time needed for this class of traffic to make it across a single hop. Comparing this with the other classes in the Engineered Max Delay column, we notice that the Real-Time class is engineered to have only a maximum

Link speed	Class of service	Packet size (bytes)	Serialization delay (msec)	Engineered min delay (wred min threshold)	Engineered max delay (wred max threshold)	Max per hop delay	PLR
E1	Cos-1 (realtime)	1500	6 msec	n/a	4 msec	10 msec	0%
E1	Cos-2 (multimedia)	1500	6 msec	50 msec*	50 msec*	56 msec	0%
E1	Cos-2 (out-of-contract)	1500	6 msec	40 msec	50 msec	56 msec	n/a
E1	Cos-3 (business)	1500	6 msec	35 msec	75 msec	81 msec	<0.5%
E1	Cos-3 (out-of-contract)	1500	6 msec	30 msec	75 msec	81 msec	n/a
E1	Cos-4 (best-effort)	1500	6 msec	25 msec	100 msec	106 msec	n/a
T3	Cos-1 (realtime)	1500	n/a	n/a	2 msec	2 msec	0%
T3	Cos-2 (multimedia)	1500	n/a	50 msec*	50 msec*	50 msec	0%
T3	Cos-2 (out-of-contract)	1500	n/a	40 msec	50 msec	50 msec	n/a
T3	Cos-3 (business)	1500	n/a	35 msec	75 msec	75 msec	<0.5%
T3	Cos-3 (out-of-contract)	1500	n/a	30 msec	75 msec	75 msec	n/a
T3	Cos-4 (best-effort)	1500	n/a	25 msec	100 msec	100 msec	n/a
STM-1	Cos-1 (realtime)	1500	n/a	n/a	1 msec	1 msec	0%
STM-1	Cos-2 (multimedia)	1500	n/a	50 msec*	50 msec*	50 msec	0%
STM-1	Cos-2 (out-of-contract)	1500	n/a	40 msec	50 msec	50 msec	n/a
STM-1	Cos-3 (business)	1500	n/a	35 msec	75 msec	75 msec	<0.5%
STM-1	Cos-3 (out-of-contract)	1500	n/a	30 msec	75 msec	75 msec	n/a
STM-1	Cos-4 (best-effort)	1500	n/a	25 msec	100 msec	100 msec	n/a
GigE	Cos-1 (realtime)	1500	n/a	n/a	0.5 msec	0.5 msec	0%
GigE	Cos-2 (multimedia)	1500	n/a	50 msec*	50 msec*	50 msec	0%
GigE	Cos-2 (out-of-contract)	1500	n/a	40 msec	50 msec	50 msec	n/a
GigE	Cos-3 (business)	1500	n/a	35 msec	75 msec	75 msec	<0.5%
GigE	Cos-3 (out-of-contract)	1500	n/a	30 msec	75 msec	75 msec	n/a
GigE	Cos-4 (best-effort)	1500	n/a	25 msec	100 msec	100 msec	n/a

Figure 4.7: Metrics for Access Network

delay of 4 ms, whereas other classes are subject to higher delays. For instance, the Multimedia class is engineered to have 50 ms, Business to have 75 ms, Best-Effort 100 ms, and so on.

Moving to the next column, Max Per-Hop Delay is an indication of the maximum per-hop delay that can be expected per class. This accounts for all delays—in our case, serialization and forwarding delays.

***NOTE 4.2: Edge Layer**

The Multimedia class has no early drop characteristics—an indication that this class will host video traffic that is sensitive to packet loss.

Figure 4.8 provides the SLA metrics for the core network— "end to end" across the carrier core. Therefore an end customer will need to add up these values along with associated metrics for the access network; we have discussed this in Figure 4.6. One point to note: Here we notice that out-of-contract traffic does not have any associated packet-loss commitments. This is due

Class of service	End-to-end delay	End-end jitter	PLR
Cos-1 (Real-Time)	4 msec	2 ms	0%
Cos-2 (Multimedia)	200 msec	n/a	0%
Cos-2 (Out-of-Contract)	200 msec	n/a	n/a
Cos-3 (Business)	300 msec	n/a	<0.5%
Cos-3 (Out-of-Contract)	300 msec	n/a	n/a
Cos-4 (Best-Effort)	400 msec	n/a	n/a

Figure 4.8: Metrics for the Carrier Core

to the fact that out-of-contract traffic is excess traffic for a given class and is subject to a more aggressive drop rate. Similarly, only the Real-Time class has commitments for jitter.

4.7 Summary

In this chapter, we discussed the details of managed and unmanaged CE deployments and looked at some of the important differences between the two. We also discussed the advantage that a managed CE deployment offers in distributing key functions between the PE and CE layers, to offload tasks from the PE layer. We also took a look at sample carrier offerings for managed CE customers from a QoS standpoint and discussed some important points to be considered for establishing a well-coordinated QoS policy. These sample offerings and metrics are provided with the intention of helping the reader understand QoS models from a carrier's perspective before we move into the implementation chapters that follow.

CHAPTER 5

Quality of Service for IP Mobile Networks

5.1 Overview

This chapter explores the quality-of-service (QoS) framework required for mobile networks over an NGN infrastructure.

There is no question that the advent of mobile broadband speeds and native IP communications for voice and data, courtesy of third-generation (3G) technology, are some of the important drivers for the NGN story among providers. Developments in WiMAX, often referred to as *fourth generation*, or 4G, are further fuelling the converged NGN vision.

In this chapter we explore an introduction to mobile network evolution, with emphasis on 3G standards and transport options through the various releases. More recent work in the area of legacy radio access network transport to the cell sites is also discussed. Finally, a framework for QoS is developed for 2.5G GSM, 3G Release 99, Release 4, and Release 5. For specific CLI commands, refer to the MPLS VPN and Multicast QoS chapters.

5.2 The First-Generation Mobile Network

The concept of cellular handheld devices was conceived by Bell Labs in the late 1950s. The framework was based on optimizing the use of frequency bands into geographic regions referred to as *cells*—hence the term *cellular network*.

As shown in Figure 5.1, Bell Labs groups frequency bands into clusters of seven cells, allowing reuse of frequencies while ensuring enough separation to avoid overlap between base stations.

The late 1970s and early 1980s saw the first real mobile network implementations across the United States and Japan (using Advanced Mobile Phone Service, or AMPS), northern Europe (using Nordic Mobile Telephony, or NMT), and the United Kingdom (using Total Access Communication System, or TACS).

5.3 The Second-Generation Mobile Network

As technology improved and customer expectations grew, the functionality and services on the mobile network infrastructure evolved. The second-generation networks delivered superior, more efficient voice as well as basic data capabilities from 2.5G onward.

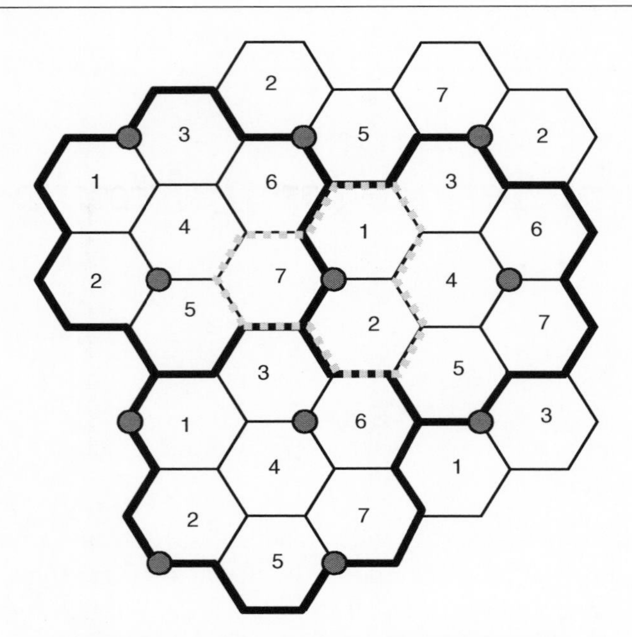

Figure 5.1: Cellular Network Frequency Reuse

The second generation of mobile networks is digital transmission based. Although there were many standards in the 2G space, of most interest was the emergence of the two most prolific technologies in the mobile space today:

- Code Division Multiple Access (CDMA)-based IS-95
- Time Division Multiple Access-based Global System for Mobile Communications (GSM)

Given that GSM is by far the most dominant technology in the mobile space, currently considered to carry up to 90 percent of mobile traffic today, this chapter explores the GSM network evolution toward 3G and transport over an IP/MPLS infrastructure.

The initial 2G networks for GSM were voice only with no data services. Digital transmission techniques led to superior voice quality, improved spectrum efficiency, and reliability over analog first-generation networks, driving mobile providers to upgrade infrastructure to the second generation.

The reference model for GSM 2G is shown in Figure 5.2.

The user equipment (UE) is used by the subscriber to access services. The UE connects to the nearest base transmission station (BTS) over an air interface. The BTS connects to a base station controller (BSC) through a TDM network via point-to-point transport such as E1/T1 or microwave via SONET/SDH rings. The BTS and BSC combined are often referred to as the *base station subsystem* (BSS).

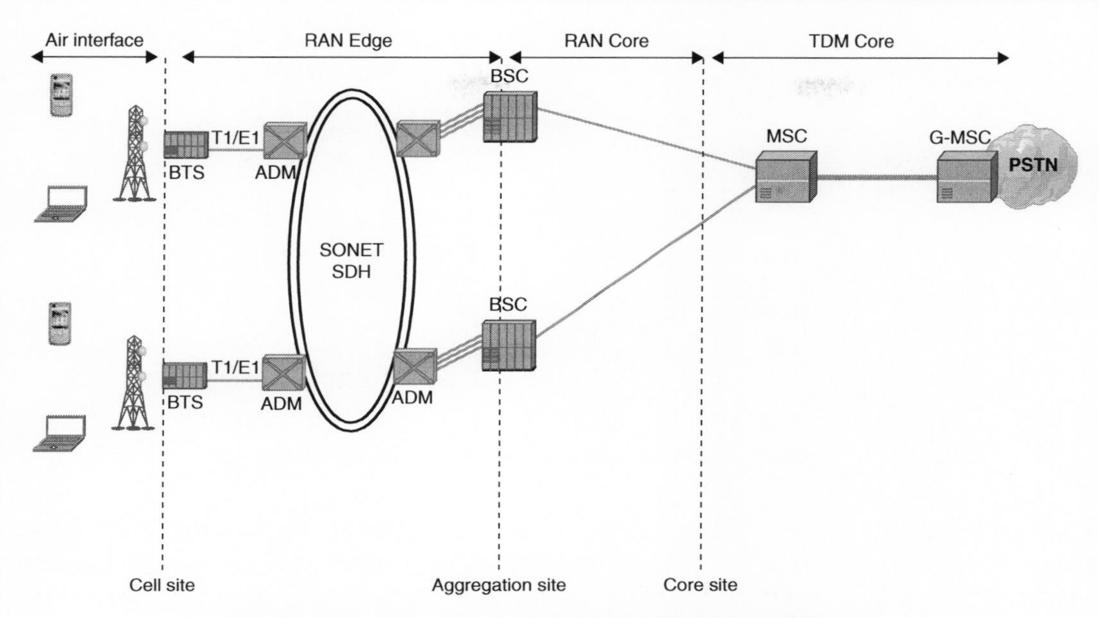

Figure 5.2: Second-Generation GSM Reference Architecture

The BSCs are aggregated at the mobile switching center (MSC), once again over TDM infrastructure. The MSC is the node that resides between the access network, including the radio access network (RAN) core, RAN edge and air interface, and other networks such as partner mobile vendors and the PSTN. Among other duties, the MSC is responsible for keeping track of where users are located at any given point in time and for setting up and tearing down calls to and from mobile terminals. Mobile telephone calls originating in or destined for the PSTN traverse a purpose-built device called the *gateway MSC* (G-MSC).

In terms of traffic flow in the 2G network, Figure 5.3 shows the call signaling and voice flow as well as an overview of the responsibilities of major components in the call path.

Voice traffic enters the mobile network at the BTS in the RAN edge, then flows through to a designated regional BSC on a circuit-switched 64 Kbps channel within the bundled E1/T1 transmission link. The voice traffic then moves through the BSC to an MSC, which will route the call to other users in the mobile network or via the gateway MSC (G-MSC) to the PSTN or other mobile vendors, as required. All voice calls and signaling are circuit switched over a TDM-based T1/E1 or microwave infrastructure, typically supported by an underlying SONET/ SDH layer in the RAN edge, RAN core, and network core, where the G-MSC is required. Refer to later sections in this chapter for protocol stacks through the network.

5.4 The 2.5G Mobile Network

The requirement for data services emerged rapidly as handsets and users became more sophisticated, particularly given the competing standard CDMA, which had data capabilities

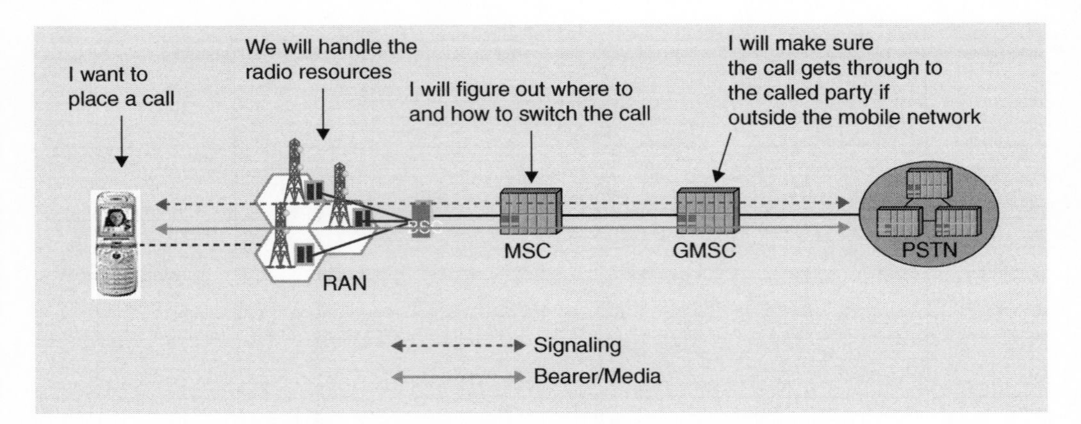

Figure 5.3: 2G Mobile Network Voice Traffic Flow

from the outset of deployment. The additional of General Packet Radio Service (GPRS) gave the data service capabilities required, albeit at relatively slow data rates and typically through cumbersome gateways. This step in GSM evolution was referred to as *enhanced GSM* or 2.5G, with a data transfer capability of up to 115 Kbps. Enhanced GSM was deployed from the mid-1990s and represents the most widely deployed GSM standard today.

2.5G was a step between 2G and 3G mobile technologies, enabling data without any true multimedia capabilities. The GPRS concept was developed by the ITU and would ultimately be continued through the 3GPP standards, as discussed in detail in this chapter. The 2.5G term actually describes 2G systems that have implemented a packet-switched domain for data in addition to the circuit-switched domain for voice; however, it should be noted that 2.5G is a marketing term rather than an officially defined standard.

A commonly implemented architecture for 2.5G is shown in Figure 5.4.

The introduction of the Serving GPRS Support Node (SGSN) and the Gateway GPRS Support Node (GGSN) connected to the BSC via Frame Relay enabled the data packet capabilities in the GSM network through the addition of a packet-switched (PS) domain.

A Serving GPRS Support Node is responsible for the delivery of data packets to and from mobile devices. The SGSN is generally specific to a geographical region. The SGSN is responsible for packet routing, mobility management, logical link management, authentication, and charging functions. The SGSN includes a location register for connected users that stores information such as current cell, current visitor location register (VLR), and user profiles.

A Gateway GPRS Support Node is a gateway between a wireless data network user and other data networks such as the Internet or private networks. The GGSN is the data anchor point enabling the mobility of the user terminal in GPRS networks. The GGSN is effectively the GPRS equivalent of a home agent in mobile IP. It maintains routing necessary to tunnel the Protocol Data Units (PDUs) to the SGSN that service a particular mobile subscriber (MS).

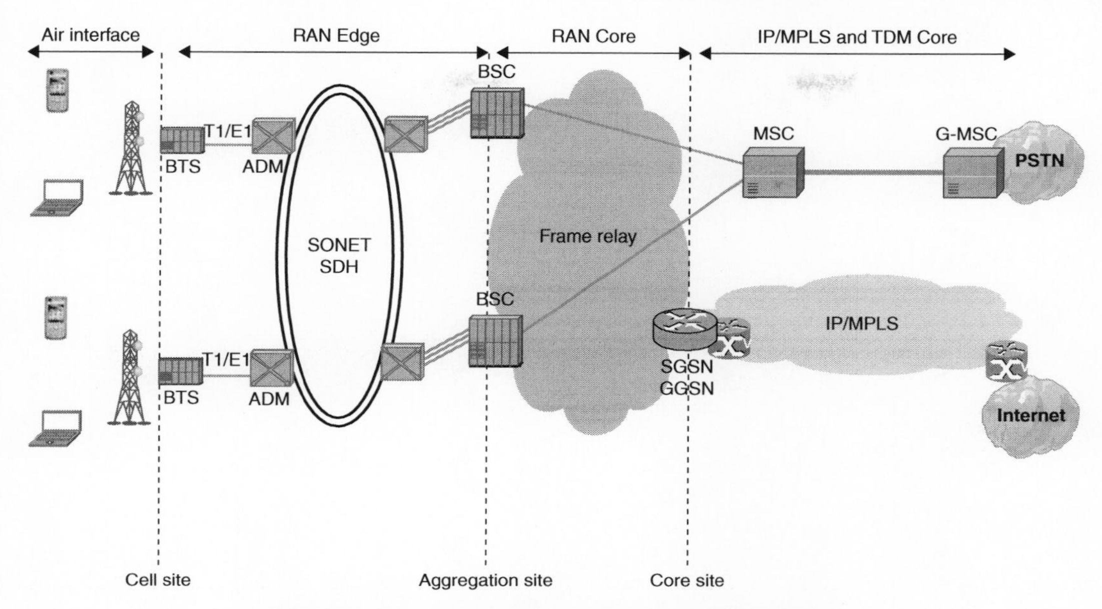

Figure 5.4: 2.5G Mobile Architecture with GPRS

Other functions include subscriber screening, IP pool management, address mapping, QoS, and Packet Data Protocol (PDP) context enforcement.

The air interface standards did not change to the UE with the introduction of GPRS; instead, slices of spectrum could be allocated to data traffic as well as voice.

5.5 The Third-Generation Mobile Vision

The standards for a third-generation network are governed by the ITU. The ITU umbrella name for 3G standards is IMT-2000, which stands for International Mobile Telecommunications 2000. In Europe IMT-2000 is typically referred to as Universal Mobile Telephone Service (UMTS).

Wideband CDMA is the standard for Universal Mobile Telephone Service. UMTS is the committed standard for Europe and the likely migration path for other GSM operators globally. UMTS leverages GSM's dominant position as the preferred mobile standard by building on the 2.5G standard architecture for the access aggregation and core, however it requires substantial new spectrum and significant investment at the base station level as the radio standards are CDMA based.

There are two specific groups aligned with the dominant mobile technologies of GSM and CMDA. The 3rd Generation Partnership Project (3GPP) is focused on GSM and UMTS evolution. The 3rd Generation Partnership Project Two (3GPP2) is a separate organization focused on the evolution of CMDA toward the 3G vision. The goal of an ultimate merger

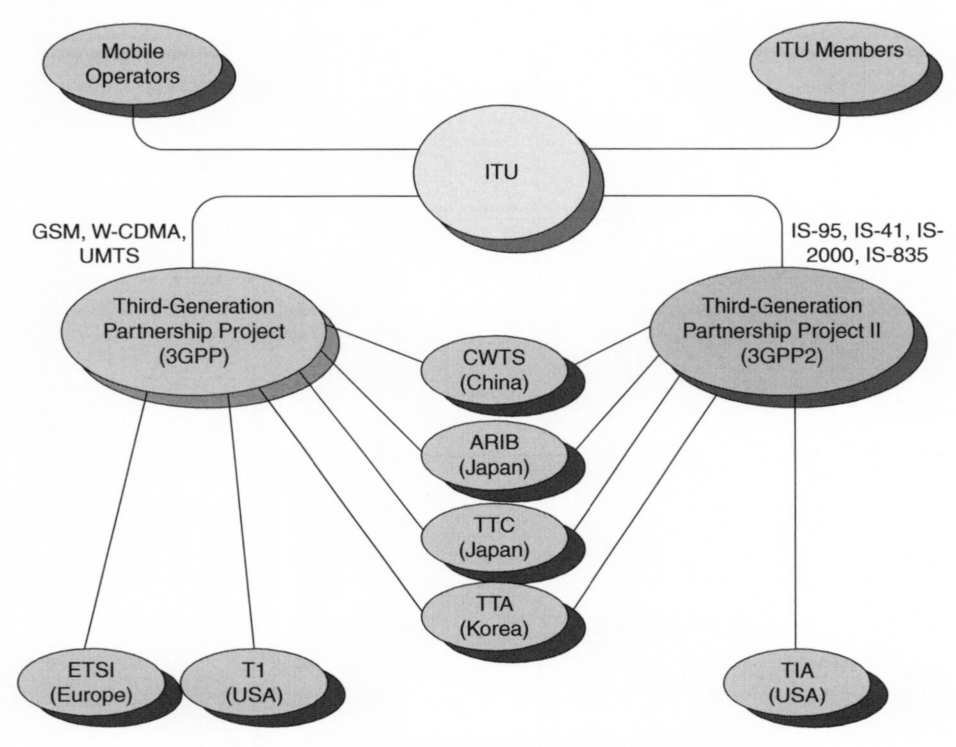

Figure 5.5: 3G Mobile Standards Organizations

(3GPP + 3GPP2) remains a priority and talking point in the ITU, although an exact framework has not been formalized.

National and regional standards bodies across the globe such as ARIB, TIA, TTA, TTC, CWTS, T1, and ETSI are collaborating with ITU in the 3G Partnership Projects, as shown in Figure 5.5.

Note that although there are groups aligned with GSM and CDMA, with GSM the dominant technology, the accepted 3G radio standards (CDMA2000, W-CDMA, and TD-SCDMA) are all CDMA based. As such the migration of GSM to W-CDMA requires extensive forklift upgrades at the radio access layer, as mentioned previously, whereas CDMA to CMDA2000 can be achieved with additions to the existing infrastructure.

The IMT-2000 framework envisages coverage provided by a combination of cell sizes ranging from "in-building" pico/femto cells to global cells provided by satellite, giving service to the more remote regions of the world.

According to the ITU, "The IMT-2000 third-generation mobile standard enables mobile users to harness the full power of the Internet through efficient high-speed radio transmission, optimized for multimedia communications."

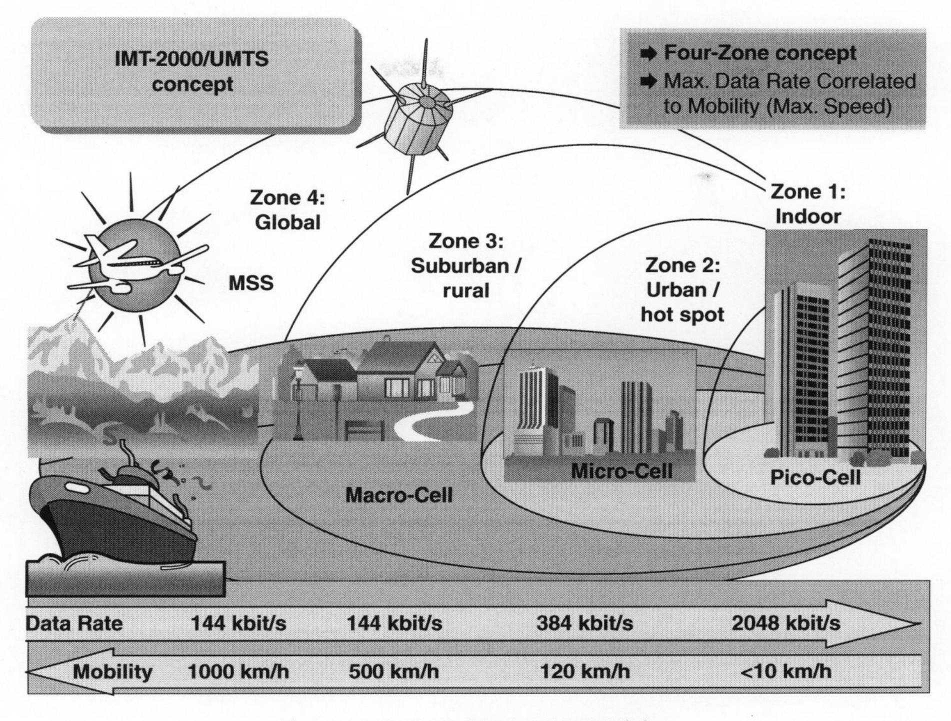

Figure 5.6: IMT-2000 UMTS Vision

The overall IMT-2000 vision is shown in Figure 5.6.

Some stated goal for the third-generation network are as follows:

- Universal global roaming
- Genuine multimedia support for voice, data, and video
- Increased data rates up to broadband speeds: 384 Kbps while moving, 2 Mbps when stationary at specific locations
- Increased capacity over the same frequency spectrum, so more spectrally efficient
- A native IP architecture

5.6 The Evolution Toward 3G

As shown in Figure 5.7, the path toward the third-generation network vision is complex and must take into account the dominant mobile technologies, GSM and CDMA, as well as a variety of less popular standards deployed in various regions around the globe. The evolutionary steps within the dominant technologies, 2.5G and 2.75G (commonly referred as Enhanced Data Rates for GSM Evolution, or EDGE), add further challenge to the convergence toward a 3G standard.

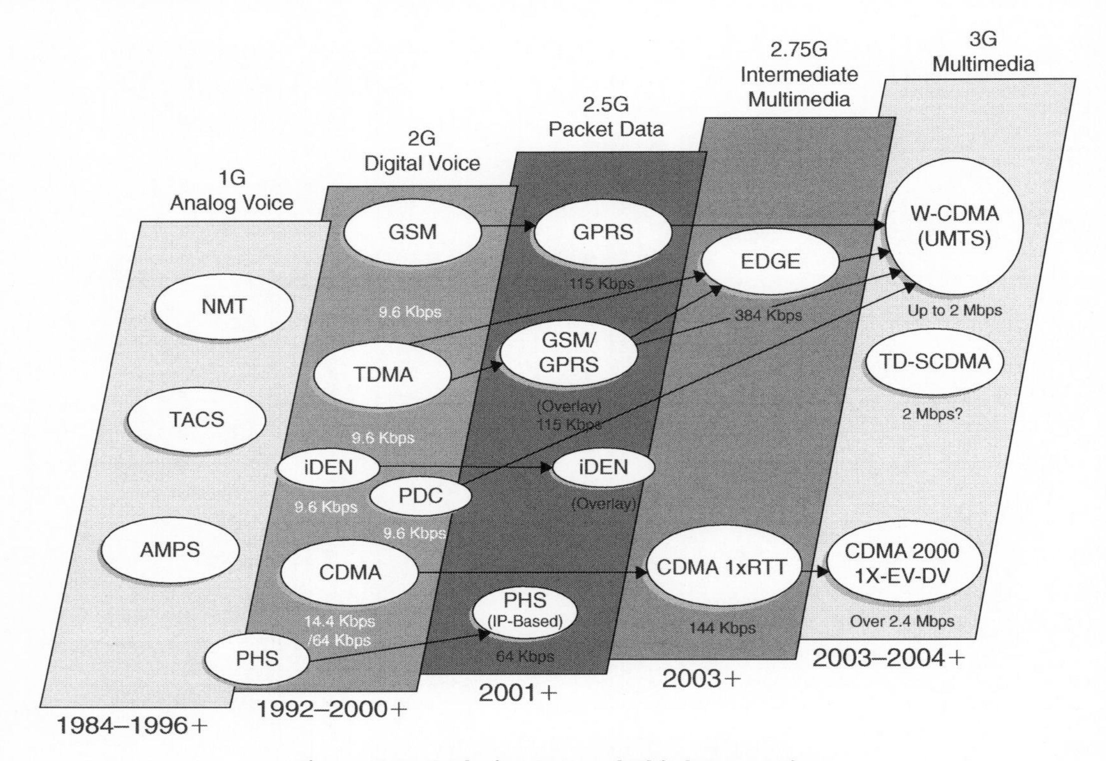

Figure 5.7: Evolution Toward Third Generation

5.7 Third-Generation Evolution for GSM

The 3G Partnership Project (3GPP) has defined specific releases for GSM within the third-generation framework. The intention is to define a smooth migration path from GSM to UMTS (W-CDMA) with allowances for 2G infrastructure and handsets to remain active, given global providers' investment in this technology.

The GSM release high-level road map is defined here:

- *3GPP Release 99.* Adds 3G radio devices, voice services, emergency call capability, short-message service, and Internet access.
- *3GPP Release 4.* Adds soft switch/voice gateways, optimization of the UMTS Terrestrial Radio Access Network (UTRAN), removal of legacy MSC, QoS, and preparation for all IP packet core.
- *3GPP Release 5.* All IP Multimedia Services (IMS) with SIP and QoS, all IP UTRAN, open systems architecture, and high-speed downlink packet access phase 1.
- *3GPP Release 6.* All-IP network, HSDPA phase 2.

The following section gives a complete description of the terminology used for the 3G network. Briefly, UTRAN refers to Node B base stations and radio network controllers, which make up the UMTS radio access network. UTRAN allows connectivity between the UE and the core network carrying voice and data traffic. Within UTRAN, the RNC and its corresponding Node Bs are called the *radio network subsystem* (RNS). There can be more than one RNS present in a UTRAN.

Another common term in the radio access layer is the GSM EDGE Radio Access Network (GERAN). GERAN is a key part of GSM and of combined UMTS/GSM networks existing during the evolution from GSM to 3G. GERAN is the radio part of GSM/EDGE, together with the circuit-switched network that joins the base stations and the base station controllers. A mobile phone operator's network can be comprised of one or more GERANs, together with UTRANs in the case of a UMTS/GSM hybrid network.

The IP Multimedia Subsystem (IMS) is an architectural framework for delivering IP multimedia to mobile users. The IMS concept is defined by the 3rd Generation Partnership Project (3GPP) as part of the vision for evolving mobile networks beyond GSM. The original specification (3GPP R5) represented an approach to delivering Internet services over GPRS.

The 3G standards rely on two important technologies in the evolution of the radio network from narrowband data services to true broadband capabilities. High Speed Data Packet Access (HSDPA) and CDMA 1x Evolution-Data Optimized (EV-DO) are the standards that will achieve this transformation.

HSDPA is a critical feature of R5/6 in the 3G standards. There are three phases increasing in speed and ability to support real-time applications, all relying on IP as the converged transport. The first phase, specified in 3GPP Release 5, will see the introduction of several new basic functions with the objective of achieving a peak data rate of 10.8 Mbit/s. The second phase, specified in 3GPP Release 6, will introduce antenna array processing technologies to optimize the air interfaces and enhance the potential peak data rate to around 30 Mbit/s. The third phase is intended to encompass additional access technologies beyond radio-based mobile.

The advent of "all IP" from Release 5 onward refers to handsets and user equipment that rely on IP for data and voice applications. 3GPP has positioned IP as the converged network layer that will ultimately meet the IMT2000 vision across all access technologies. Using IP for data and voice will allow consistent service delivery across any device type and any transport media. Note that the original standards for IMS were IPV6 based only; however, industry pressure forced the ITU to allow IPV4 and/or IPV6 in the IMS standards. This issue is discussed in a later section.

5.8 Converged NGN Infrastructure for Mobile Transport

As discussed in Chapter 1, network operators are consolidating disparate networks to reduce their capital expenses (CapEx) and operating expenses (OpEx). Mobile networks evolving toward 3G standards are perfect candidates for this convergence. The drive toward a consolidated IP/MPLS NGN framework is changing mobile operators' approach to the 3G evolution road map, including R99 onward and the RAN.

The 3G technology standards implementation is by far the easiest part of the evolution story. The challenge facing operators is to support the evolving standards in a cost-effective manner. The transport network infrastructure from the edge cellular base station through the aggregation network is the greatest expense facing operators when considering upgrades to support 3G. Current backhaul networks for 2G were designed using narrowband, point-to-point TDM technologies such as leased lines or microwave.

Upgrading the existing TDM-based backhaul infrastructure to support capacity demanded by 3G with multimedia capabilities is prohibitively expensive. Hence operators must find alternative approaches. Operators are seeking to take advantage of cost-effective IP transport prior to the full IP Release 5 implementation. Furthermore, operators recognize that their networks will spend a large amount of time on the transition to the final goal; hence converging the transport first will extend their investment return in radio equipment.

Operators have taken steps to introduce the GPRS network for data handling; now they are deploying packet-based technology in the voice core, such as soft switches and media gateway nodes as defined in 3GPP standards. Clearly the path to optimizing CapEx and OpEx for these operators is to extend the IP packetization into the backhaul network. As discussed in Chapter 1, this goal is driven by the NGN vision of convergence across all packet-based services onto a single IP/MPLS infrastructure.

The 3G standards intend to ultimately achieve the goal of IP packetization from the handset through the RAN to the core, as previously discussed, starting with ATM-defined interfaces in R99, as discussed in the following sections. Clearly, the optimum path lies in an IP interface at the base station to realize an IP Radio Access Network (IPRAN), which is a goal of the 3GPP standards. One possible interim solution while evolving toward 3G IMS is the Mobile Transport over Pseudowire (MTOP), discussed later in this chapter. The overall position of IP in the mobile operator network is defined in the following section.

The Cisco IP Next-Generation Network (IP NGN) architecture for mobile operators is a road map to realize the vision of next-generation mobile services—the delivery of data, voice, and video anywhere and anytime across virtually any access or core transport technology. The Cisco IP NGN provides mobile operators a migration path to an IP foundation prior to the implementation of the all-IP 3G IMS vision starting in Release 5. This IP foundation can reduce OpEx and allow operators, and indeed handset owners, additional time to depreciate their investment in technology implementing 3G Release 4 or earlier.

The NGN framework also allows interoperability with various radio access technologies and vendors. This is possible with convergence at application, service control, and network layers, as shown in Figure 5.8.

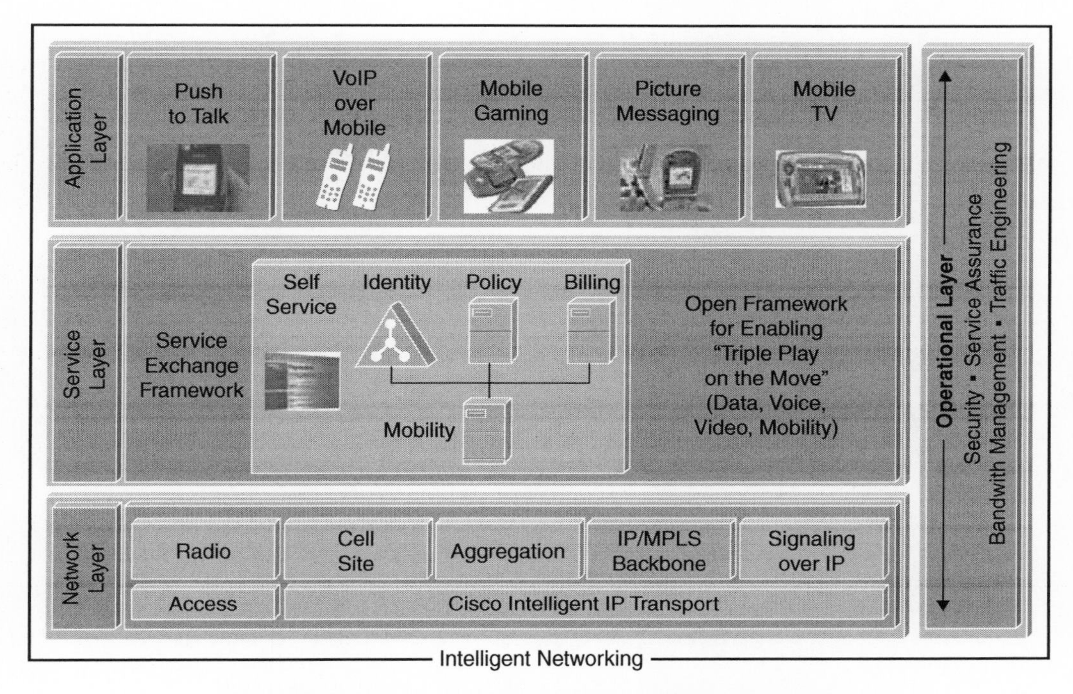

Figure 5.8: Cisco NGN Vision for Mobile Operators

Mobile operators need an application layer that interfaces with the customer device—a network layer that creates and delivers the services and a service layer enabling the delivery, operations, features, and billing of the services portfolio across all access types. The service layer is known as the Cisco Service Exchange Framework (SEF). Refer to Chapter 1 for a full description of the NGN framework.

5.9 Third-Generation Release 99 Overview

In the introduction of 3G specifications for GSM, ATM has figured prominently, starting from the Release 99 specifications. ATM was the obvious choice, given the relatively high speed and class-of-service capabilities at the time of drafting the standards in the 1990s.

The introduction of ATM into mobile standards was intended to be a solution for integrated voice, data, and video for speed and differentiation of service types. However, scalability and management of ATM transport quickly became concerns under increasing expected IP data traffic loads on mobile networks. As identified in Chapter 1, QoS capabilities in native IP environments across faster, cheaper Layer 2 technologies such as Ethernet were also maturing, putting further pressure on the ATM approach for mobile networks. Although ATM represented a cost-effective solution compared to upgrading existing 2G point-to-point, E1/T1 TDM links, it cannot compete with a converged IP infrastructure over more cost-effective media running the providers' full services suite, which is the goal of NGN. Had the standards

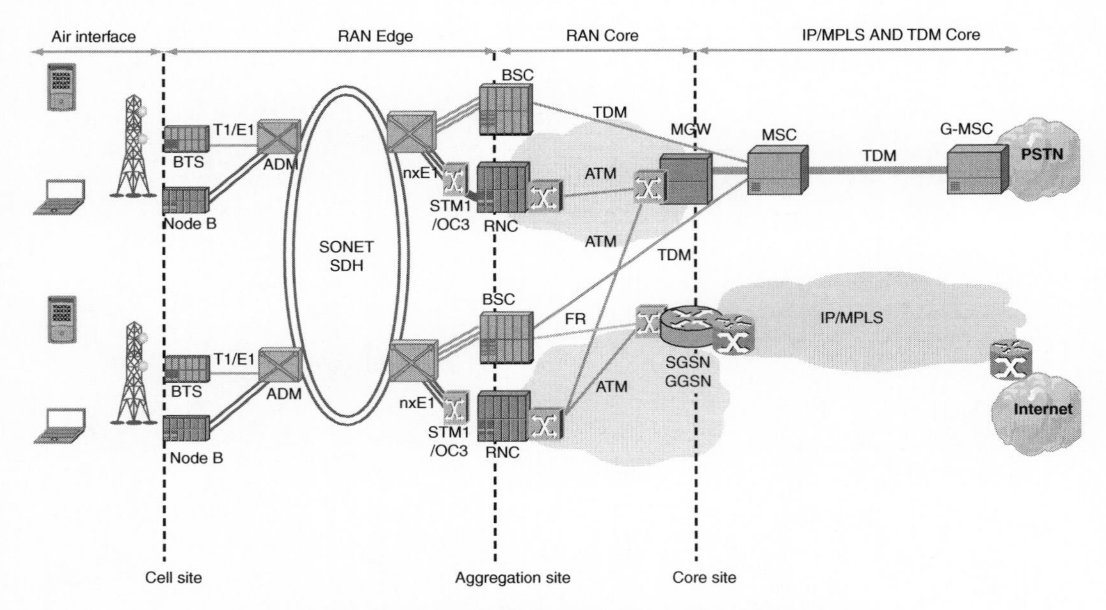

Figure 5.9: Mobile 3G R99 Transport Architecture

been drafted some five years later, the adoption of IP as a converged network layer would have been very likely; in fact, the standards for Release 4 onward clearly defined a road map toward this concept.

The reference architecture for 3G Release 99 is shown in Figure 5.9.

The Release 99 specifications started the path toward multimedia and broadband data speeds to the end user through the introduction of new equipment and an ATM-based RAN. The RAN must still support the 2.5G architecture with voice over TDM and data over Frame Relay to the SGSN, as shown in the diagram. 3G Release 99 voice is carried over ATM as far as the media gateway in this release, then offloaded to the MSC over TDM to minimize network changes in this step.

ATM extends from the 3G Node-B through the 3G Radio Network Controller (RNC) to the media gateway (MGW) for voice and the SGSN for data. The RNC is effectively a 3G version of the 2G BSC, responsible for routing calls and regulating bandwidth. The MGW is introduced to voice-over-ATM-to-TDM conversion and signaling for the first step of the 3G evolution. The MGW takes on a greater role in subsequent releases, including retiring the 2G MSC.

Figure 5.10 shows the interfaces within the 3G Release 99 specified RAN. 2G interfaces are also shown for reference.

As mentioned previously, the new interfaces for the 3G Release 99 RAN are ATM based. The data capabilities of GPRS through the SGSN are still used by Release 99; hence an additional ATM interface in the SGSN router is required from the BSC or, alternatively, a dedicated

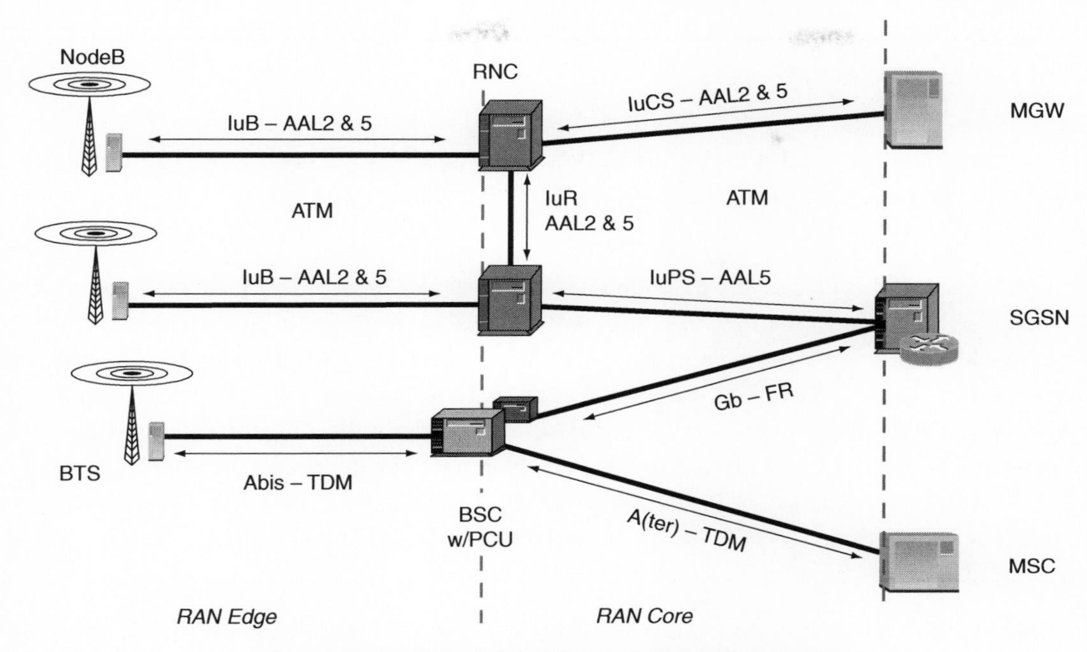

Figure 5.10: 2G and 3G Release 99 Interface Types

3G SGSN/GGSN pair can be implemented, which tended to be the most common approach by providers adopting Release 99 standards.

The intention of the Release 99 specifications is to position the mobile network for the subsequent Release 4, and beyond, evolution. Careful consideration is given to maintaining the providers' investment in the 2G infrastructure when the 3G standards and releases were conceived.

5.10 Third-Generation Release 99 Convergence Over IP/MPLS

The intention of introducing the ATM interfaces in the 3G standards was to allow providers to leverage more cost-effective ATM backhaul rather than expanding existing costly and inefficient TDM-based E1/T1 transport. In fact, the majority of mobile providers already had expansive ATM networks for enterprise customers and backhaul of broadband Internet traffic using ADSL. Contributors drafting the 3G standards saw this ATM network as the obvious evolutionary step for faster data rates and more efficient bandwidth usage for voice and signaling as discussed in the previous section.

Ultimately, as discussed in Chapter 1, with the drive toward a consolidated IP/MPLS infrastructure, converging voice and data over a single packet-switched IP/MPLS network as early as possible is the preferred option for providers. This requires multiple Gigabit speeds, enhanced availability in the IP infrastructure, and QoS to match ATM to ensure that strict requirements are met for mobile network traffic, including multimedia, voice, and signaling.

Leveraging IP/MPLS for transport of the ATM links would achieve this goal with the necessary requirements across transport and QoS.

A network with 2G and 3G R99, with IP/MPLS extending to the RAN core network for the 3G services, including voice and data, is as shown in Figure 5.11. This is the logical first step toward network consolidation of the RAN and packet-switched data networks for the mobile provider.

The IP/MPLS cloud is effectively extended to include the RAN core ATM interfaces north from the 3G RNC toward the network core. Any Transport over MPLS (AToM), specifically ATM over MPLS, is used to transport the cells with the required QoS over the IP infrastructure. Interfaces transported over AToM are IuCS for voice, IuPS for data, and IuR, which carries both voice and data; these interfaces are clearly defined later in this chapter. The existing 2G TDM infrastructure is not carried by the IP/MPLS network at this stage in the evolution; however, Mobile Transport over Pseudowire (MToP) can be used as discussed later in this chapter. The 2.5G Frame Relay interface between the BSC and SGSN will also be transported over IP/MPLS at this stage in the convergence if required.

The goal of converging to an NGN infrastructure is to carry all traffic over IP/MPLS in a single network infrastructure. This would ultimately include the RAN access layer from the BTS or Node B toward the provider core network. True convergence would see all aspects of the mobile network infrastructure using IP/MPLS as the transport technology. The introduction of ATM-based 3G into the existing 2G network builds a complex stack of protocols, including SONET/SDH, ATM, Frame Relay, and IP.

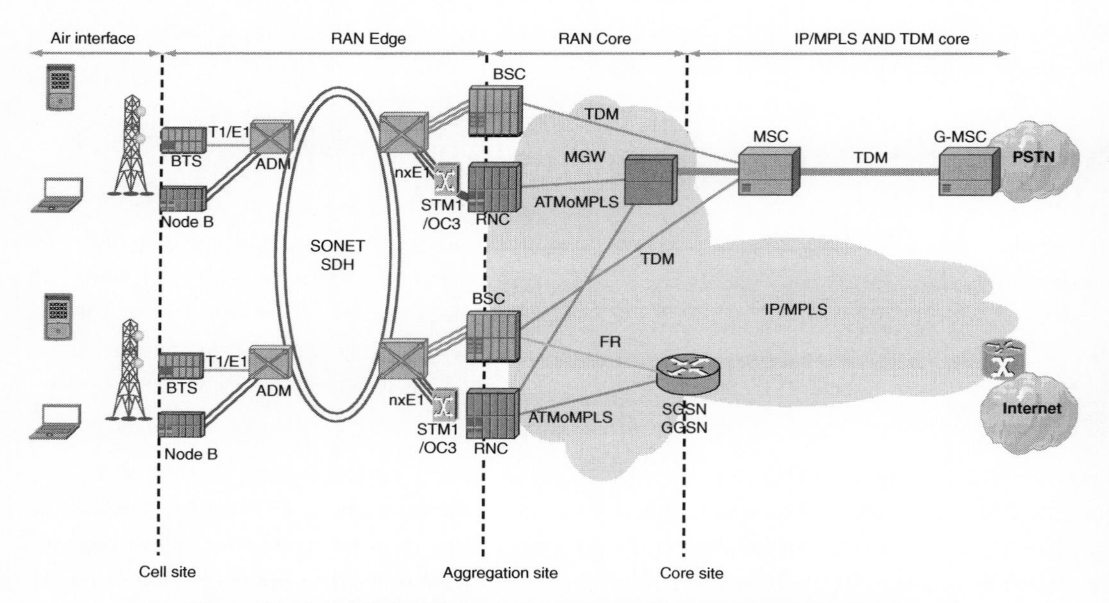

Figure 5.11: Mobile 3G R99 Transport with IP/MPLS RAN Core

Figure 5.12 depicts the network with 2G/3G in the existing protocol stack evolving into the converged NGN vision.

As shown in the diagram, the IP/MPLS network can run over DWDM or directly over fiber. Given IP/MPLS as the converged communications layer, any physical infrastructure can potentially be used for transport, including Ethernet, PoS, ADSL, cable, or metro-Ethernet, assuming that the necessary traffic requirements for delay, jitter, and packet loss can be implemented adequately.

5.11 Third-Generation Release 4 Overview

The 3GPP Release 4 (R4) framework introduces two new key architectural changes: the split architecture and removal of the MSC.

From a mobile voice-switching point of view, the split framework, commonly referred to as the *bearer-independent circuit-switched* architecture, means that the centralized TDM mobile switching center (MSC) responsible for signaling and voice switching in 2G are now being decommissioned, with the functions decoupled and separated into two new devices: the existing MGW from the Release 99 deployment and a new MSC Server installed as part of Release 4. Similarly, the gateway MSC (GMSC) is split into a GMSC server coupled with one or more CS-MGW devices. The GMSC handles the mobility and call control duties and the CS-MGW manages the bearer plane.

An overview of the evolution to split architecture is shown in Figure 5.13.

With this split architecture, the voice services are no longer handled by the MSC and GMSC. Interest in this split architecture for voice is based on the desire of mobile operators to retire their traditional TDM-based MSCs. In some cases, the circuit-switched infrastructure is approaching end of life and often entails very high OpEx. Few mobile operators want to invest further in what is seen as the legacy circuit-switched technology, which is difficult to scale

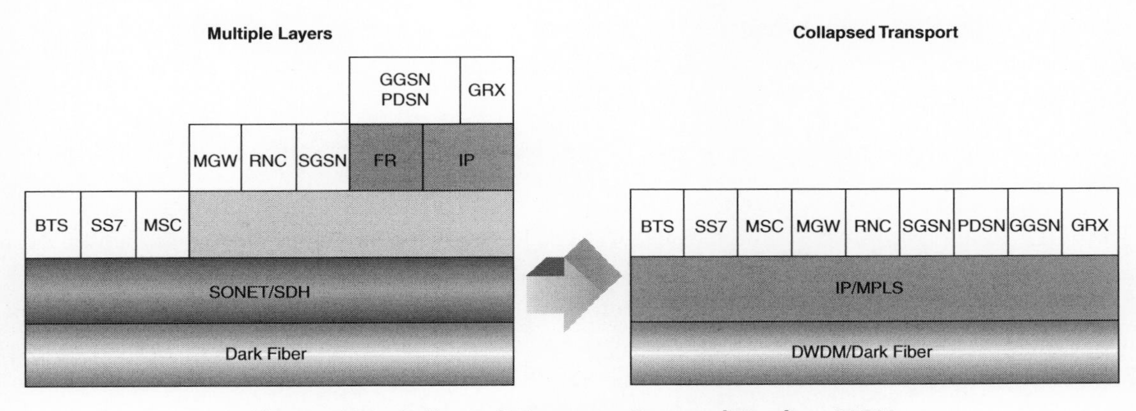

Figure 5.12: Collapsed Transport Protocol Stack to NGN

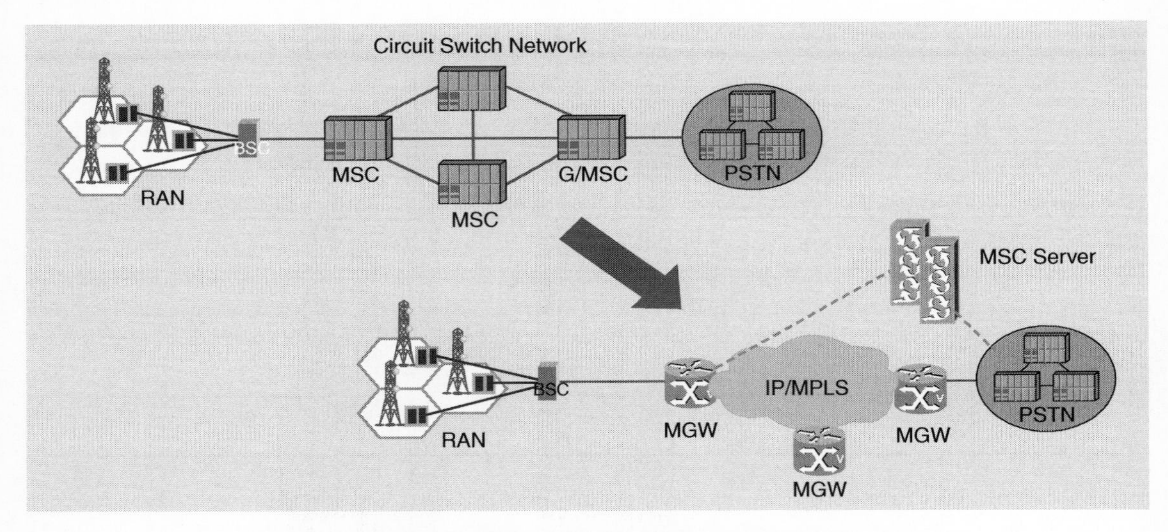

Figure 5.13: 3G Release 4 Split Architecture Overview

to the demands of 3G services. VoIP is also considered much less expensive when mobile operators use a converged IP/MPLS network instead of traditional transport over T1/E1 lines. Introduction of VoIP in the core at this stage positioned the network for IP voice to the handset as part of IMS in Release 5.

The MSC server and MGW combined basically perform the same functions as the legacy MSC. The separation of these functions allows greater scalability, support of legacy 2G services, introduction of VoIP, support of new 3G services, and a graceful evolution toward the ultimate 3G vision with multimedia over IP transport.

Note that the R4 evolution to a split architecture does not entail changes to the radio access network from the Release 99 phase. This ensures minimum changes to the mobile network in the 3G R4 evolution step. The CS-MGW (CS for *circuit-switched* domain) provides the physical interfacing between the radio access network and the core network for voice and related signaling. It is also responsible for processing, and converting if required, bearer traffic that in some cases traverses different networks running different technologies (ATM for 3G and TDM for 2G).

Figure 5.14 shows the resulting separation of the signaling and voice traffic in the 3G R4 split architecture framework.

The 3GPP Release 4 framework defines the ATM as the transport of circuit-switch domain traffic same as the Release 99 specifications. This essentially means that according to the standards, both signaling and bearer traffic going between MSC servers, GMSC servers, and CS-MGW nodes must be transported using ATM. The signaling traffic leverages SCTP transport and the bearer is transported using AAL2/ATM. Some radio vendors preferred to move to IP-based protocol stacks from the Release 5 standards rather than stay with Release 99 and 4 ATM options.

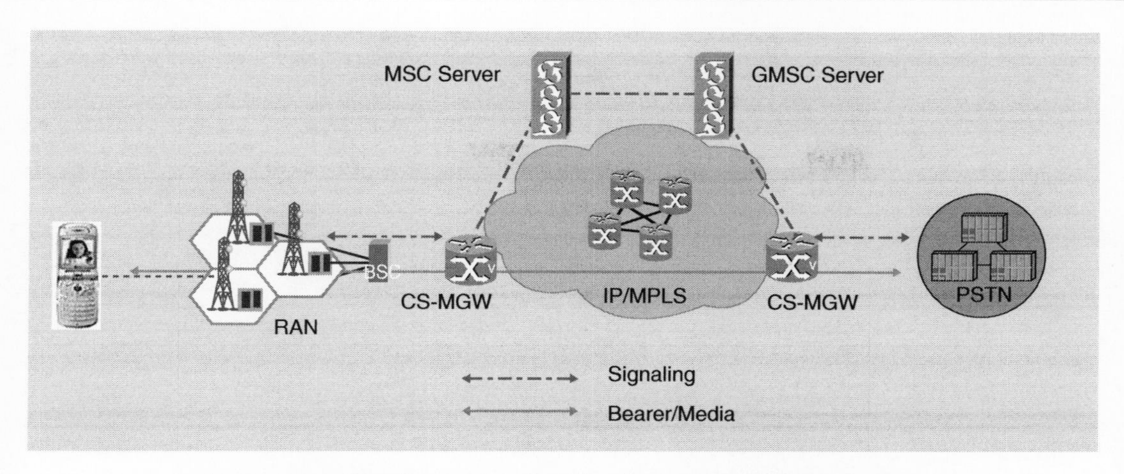

Figure 5.14: Signaling and Voice Flow in 3G R4 Split Architecture

5.12 Third-Generation Release 4 Convergence Over IP/MPLS

The 3G Release 4 standard introduces the concept of a split architecture, as previously discussed. For 3G voice traffic, the connection between the MGWs has a control plane and a user plane. The control plane is IP-based Signaling System 7 (SS7), as defined by SIGTRAN, enabled through the MSC server. The user plane must handle TDM for 2G and ATM or IP for 3G R4.

SIGTRAN is the Internet Engineering Task Force (IETF) working group responsible for producing protocol specifications that provide reliable datagram service and user layer adaptations for SS7 and Integrated Services Digital Network (ISDN) communications protocols. SIGTRAN is an extension of the SS7 protocol supporting the same application and call management standards as SS7 using an IP transport called Stream Control Transmission Protocol (SCTP). In the mobile network, SCTP is used to carry PSTN signaling over IP.

The real savings and simplicity for the mobile operators come courtesy of the MGWs transforming 3G and 2G voice services into VoIP across the IP/MPLS RAN core, therefore removing the legacy 2G MSC and inefficient TDM transport. The interconnects for the user plane and the control plane for all voice services, 2G and 3G, beyond the MGW are based on IP technology from Release 4 onward. Some operators are even deploying the Release 4 split architecture for 2G-only network solutions to retire the existing TDM infrastructure in the core and make use of converged IP-based interconnects.

For the ATM RAN, 3G ATM voice traffic can be carried over IP/MPLS in the RAN core using Cisco Any Transport over MPLS (AToM) technologies exactly as per the Release 99 approach previously discussed. For providers who have taken the R99 step (many did not, choosing instead to move directly to R5, as previously mentioned), transporting the mobile traffic over an IP/MPLS core using AToM in the R4 step required no additional effort. Note that from 3G

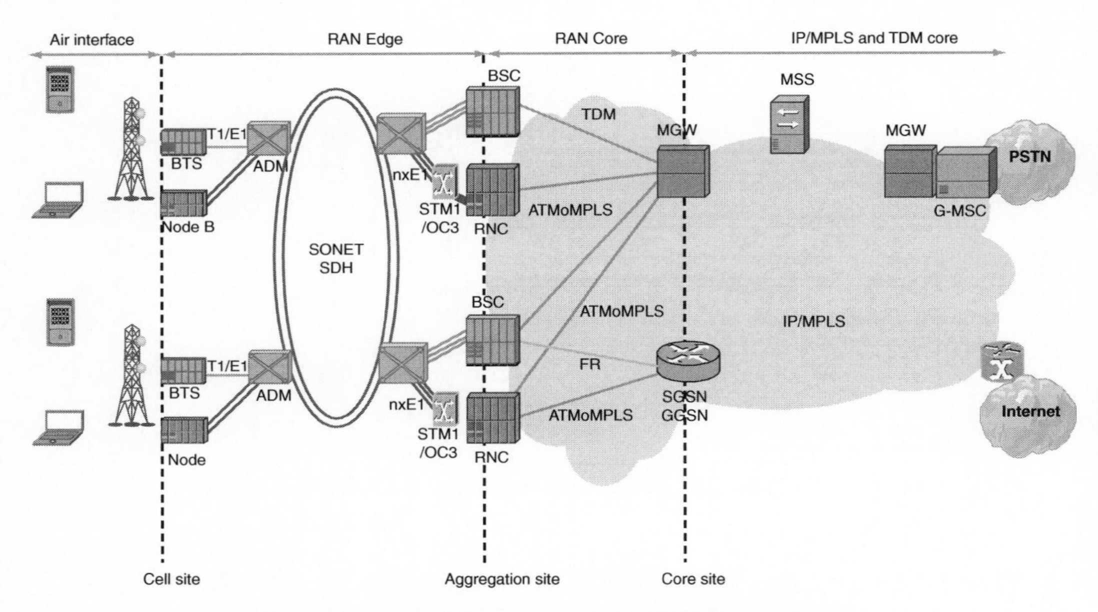

Figure 5.15: Mobile 3G R4 with IP/MPLS Transport

R99, GTP tunnels for data are terminated to the RNC, which actually means that the interface for packet-switched data (Iu-ps) is IP transported over ATM from the RNC.

Figure 5.15 shows the connectivity and transport in the 3G Release 4 standards mobile network. Note the absence of the legacy MSC device. The MSS is the MSC Server as previously defined.

Once again, note that the Frame Relay connection between the 2G BSC and the SGSN can converge over the IP/MPLS core if the providers choose this option.

Figure 5.16 shows the interface type in the 3G R4 network with the 2G coexistence.

As shown, the legacy BSC now connects to the MGW with the retirement of the MSC. The interface remains TDM based, since upgrading the BSC to packet based is not seen as cost effective by providers.

5.13 Third-Generation Release 5/6 Overview

Releases 5 and 6 were defined with the concept of the IP Multimedia Subsystem (IMS). The IP Multimedia Subsystem is an architectural framework for delivering multimedia to mobile users, including voice, data, and video over IP. The original specifications were drafted by the wireless standards body 3rd Generation Partnership Project (3GPP) as part of the vision for evolving mobile networks beyond 2.5G.

In the standards original form, known as 3G R5, IMS represented an approach to delivering multimedia services over GPRS. Later standards by 3GPP, 3GPP2, and TISPAN expanded

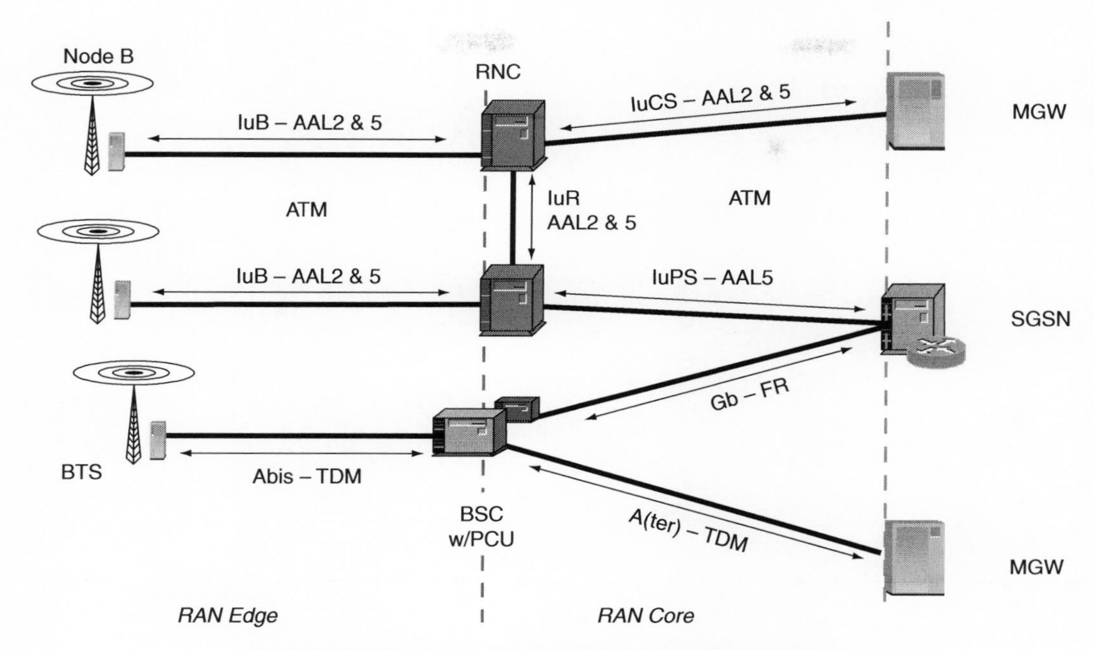

Figure 5.16: 2G and 3G Release 4 Interface Types

to networks other than GPRS, such as Wireless LAN, CDMA2000, and fixed line, which leveraged the move to IP and SIP protocols.

With the move to IMS based on IP, the 3GPP opted for the IETF Session Initiation Protocol (SIP). The IMS standard is not intended to define applications but instead addresses the access of multimedia and voice applications across wireless and wireline terminals, with a view to fixed mobile convergence (FMC). As with the Cisco NGN vision, this is achieved using a horizontal control layer between the access network and the service layer to allow any media.

The uptake of IMS has thus far been slow in the mobile operator community. Handsets are being developed utilizing SIP; however, the current 3G handsets not yet enabled with SIP already include Internet capabilities around messaging and multimedia that meet consumer demands. Ultimately the consumer will not be aware of whether the voice call is IP based or not; the introduction of native IP is of benefit to the mobile provider.

A disruptive new standard such as WiMAX, requiring development of a new handset anyway, could drive the 3G IMS vision with handset and radio vendors.

The reference architecture for the 3G IMS includes R5 and R6, as shown in Figure 5.17.

The evolution from Release 5 onward saw introduction of additional functionality and media types. Of more interest in this chapter is the RAN convergence toward IP for the mobile network RAN.

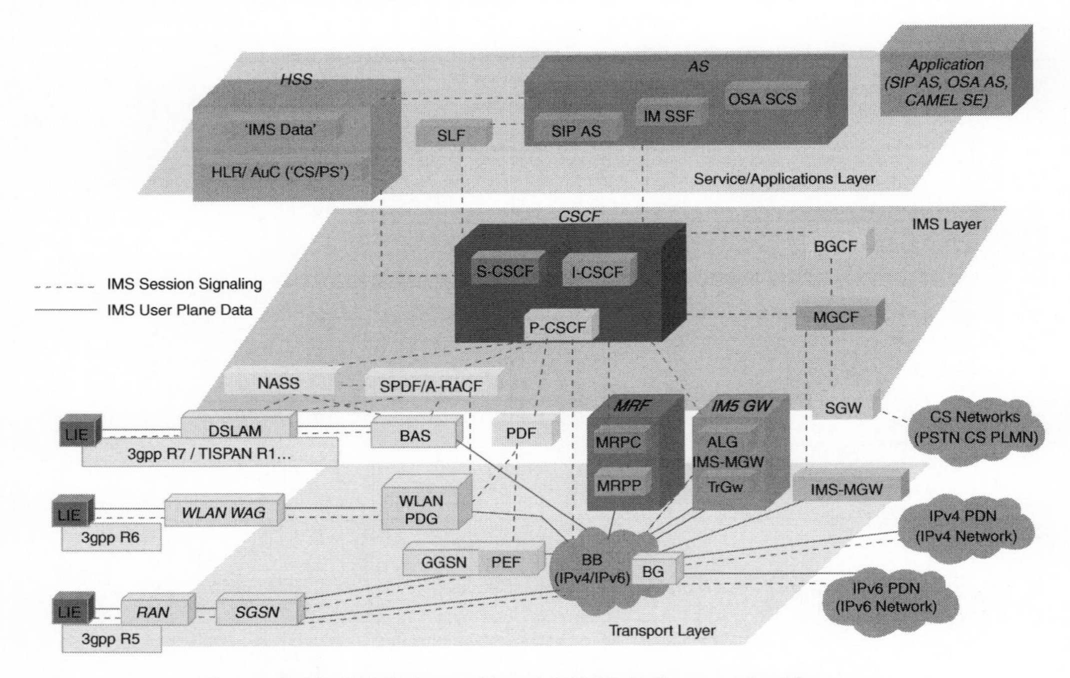

Figure 5.17: 3G Release 5 and 6 IMS Reference Architecture

The UTRAN specifications up to Release 4 define ATM as the transport method in the RAN access. Within 3GPP Release 5, the radio access transport can be IP or ATM. Release 5 specifications allow IP from Node B, which enables any data link layer in the RAN access, including ATM if preferred. Note that ATM is still an option in the standards if desired by the provider.

The interface definitions and options for Release 5 in the RAN access and core are shown in Figure 5.18.

5.14 Third-Generation Release 5/6 Convergence Over IP/MPLS

Increased use of IP/MPLS to RAN access with 3G Release 5 and beyond will simplify and accelerate the introduction of VoIP over the converged IP network end to end, which is one of the stated goals of IMS. As shown in Figure 5.19, eventually IP/MPLS will become the transport technology in the RAN access and core infrastructure. With an IP/MPLS-based RAN and core, mobile operators will be able to reap cost savings, simplify network operations, and accelerate time to market for new services.

Figure 5.19 shows a converged network for the 3G Release 5 and onward infrastructure. Note that the 2G will remain TDM based through the RAN, leaving MToP as the only option for converging this network over IP/MPLS.

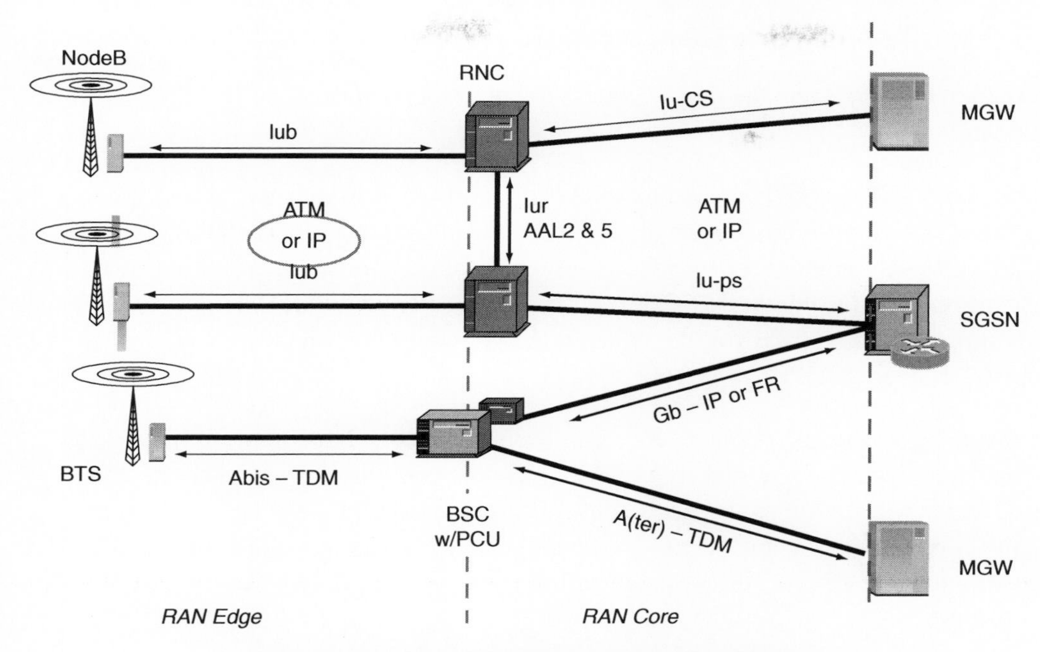

Figure 5.18: 2G and 3G Release 5 Interface Types

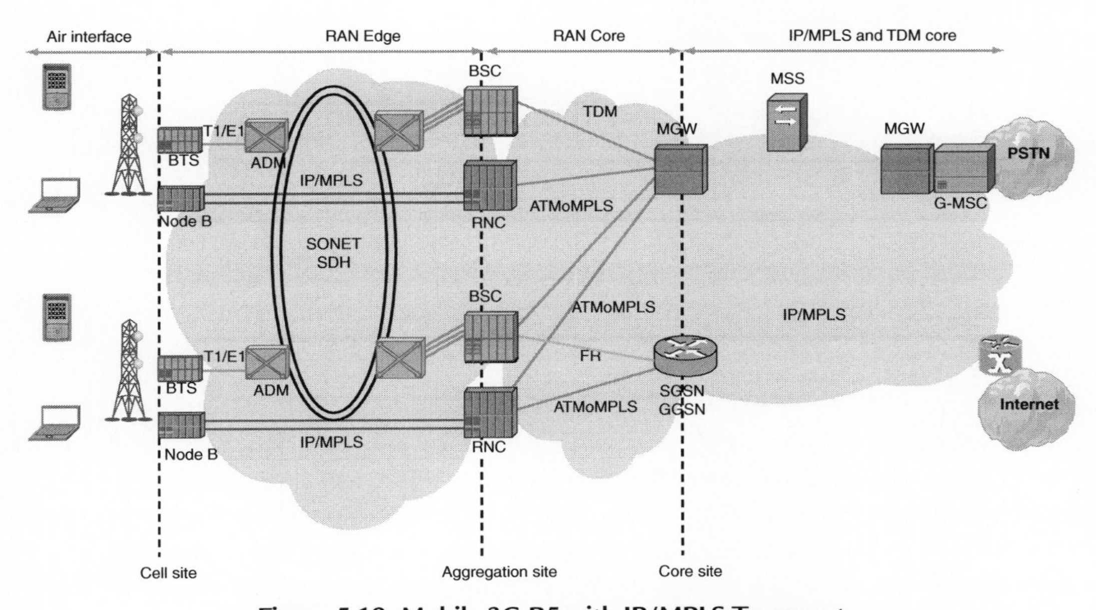

Figure 5.19: Mobile 3G R5 with IP/MPLS Transport

The introduction of the packet-based B-Node capabilities makes extending the IP/MPLS cloud to the edge a relatively simple technical task. Any technology at the access layer can be used, assuming that the strict SLAs as defined by 3GPP can be met. Some common access technologies considered by mobile providers so far include metro-Ethernet.

5.15 Mobile Network RAN Access

This section briefly covers the mobile access transport options using an IP/MPLS infrastructure.

The 3G goal of IP convergence in the mobile core network drove providers and vendors to consider extension of this vision beyond the RNC into the access. With the advent of standards allowing higher data speeds to user equipment, more and more of the costly E1 access transmission would be utilized by IP-based data applications. Providers saw the value in transporting the access layer for 3G, which is ATM over E1/T1, and legacy 2G, which is TDM using E1/T1, over IP/MPLS.

To achieve the access layer convergence goal, vendors realized that new interface cards and standards would be required. Networking vendors and providers alike could safely assume that aging equipment in the 2G network, such as the BTS and BSC, would not be natively upgraded to allow packet-based connectivity. As such, equipment capable of interfacing to the BTS and BSC and converting from cells to packets was the fastest path to convergence.

The technology for transport at the RAN layer is Mobile Transport over Pseudowire (MToP). MToP relies on Circuit Emulation over Packet (CEoP) standards to convert TDM or ATM traffic into packets, as the name suggests. These packets are sent across an IP network in MPLS pseudowires to the selected destination. It's important to note that this technology is designed to transport both TDM for 2G and ATM for 3G to optimize the benefits to the provider. MToP gives significant benefits in terms of availability in the access layer as well, allowing rerouting of pseudowires in the event of layer device failure in the IP network.

The existing RAN structure for a 2G and 3G infrastructure is as shown in Figure 5.20.

As previously discussed, the backhaul for the legacy BTS for 2G is TDM using E1/T1 transport. The TDM links are terminated at the BSC, which connects through to the core using TDM over SDH.

The new-generation Node Bs for 3G rely on ATM encapsulation, still over E1/T1 transmission. For the 3G transmission, ATM switches were required to terminate and aggregate the connection to the RNC. Likewise, ATM was used from the RNC to the core mobile network over the SDH transmission. Remember that the 3GPP evolution sought to reduce new infrastructure investment as much as possible; hence the SDH transmission into the MGW in the core network remained.

Figure 5.21 shows the extension of MPLS to the network edge. The Node-B sites can be connected at strategically located aggregation sites to optimize the backhaul without placing IP transport equipment at every base station site.

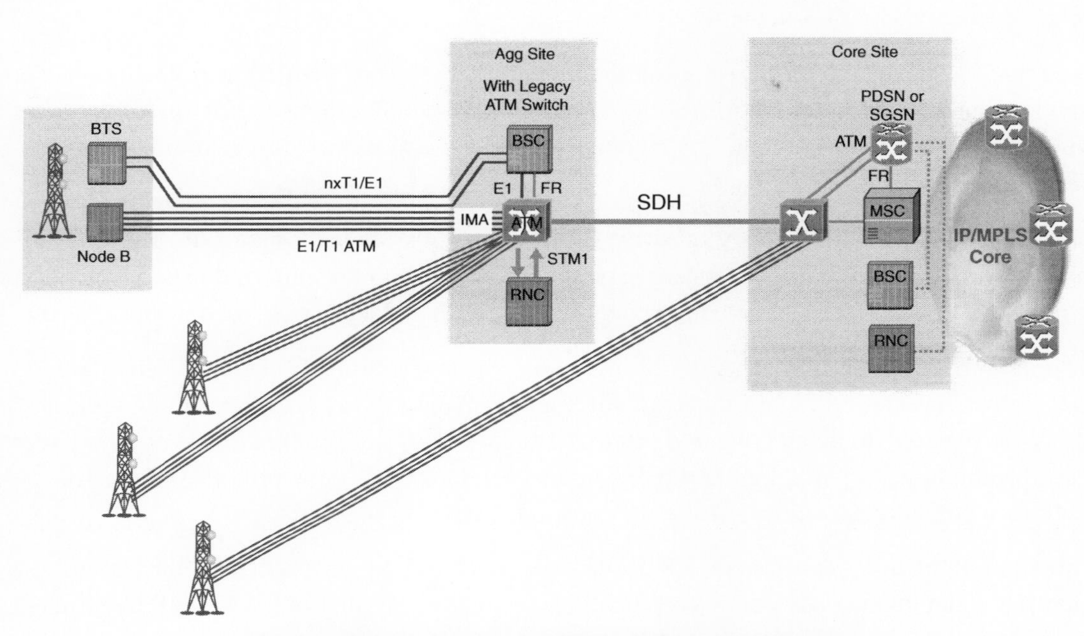

Figure 5.20: 2G and 3G R99 RAN and Core Transport

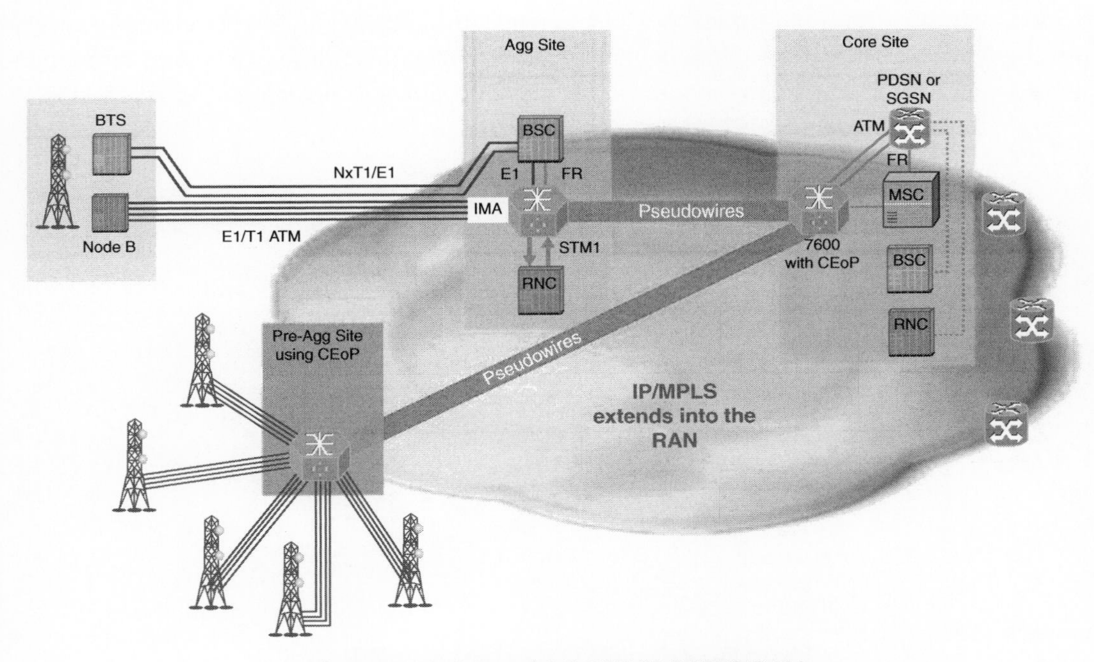

Figure 5.21: 2G and 3G R99 IP/MPLS RAN

Multiple Node Bs are transporting over traditional E1/T1 TDM links to the pre-aggregation site that connects to the MPLS network.

Given that the capability for transporting the mobile access over IP/MPLS was now in place, providers realized the potential for further savings. The QoS requirements for voice, signaling, and data were vastly different, giving an opportunity to use more cost-effective transport options for the less important traffic.

Voice and signaling traffic is very sensitive to any packet loss, delay, or jitter. If received traffic strays outside the strict parameters user experience can be severely impacted. Effectively all the traffic in these categories can be considered as requiring highest possible forwarding priority.

The data traffic, however, is generally of much lower priority. Some of the traffic could be video, which has similar requirements to voice and signaling; however, the vast majority of data is not sensitive to delay, loss, and jitter parameters. As such, sending this traffic over more cost-effective transport could greatly reduce transmission costs for the provider while still meeting customer expectations. This data transport model is shown in Figure 5.22.

Vendors implementing the B Node and RNC have standard PVC mappings for the signaling, voice, and data, making separation technically possible by mapping to the VC/VP identifiers. The ATM-interfacing device simply needs to route a given VC/VP over the alternative transport paths based on vendors' mapping standards.

The data path can utilize standard broadband access types, such as metro-Ethernet or xDSL, to provide a cost-effective, high-capacity channel for the less sensitive traffic traversing the access layer. If video is a data service implemented by the provider, this traffic can be sent through the data path with higher priority to other traffic. If the data path does not support the necessary

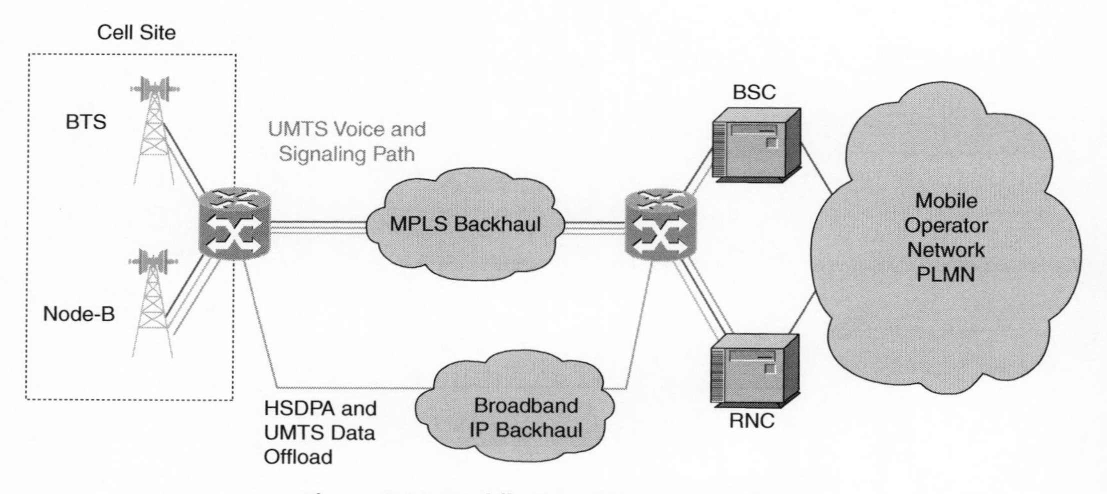

Figure 5.22: Mobile Data Transport Offload

QoS for the video traffic, the provider can choose to forward the video over the voice and signaling path to ensure that QoS parameters are met.

5.16 IPv6 in 3G Networks

The 3G working groups are encouraging the adoption of Internet Protocol Version 6 (IPv6) within the mobile community. Given the IP capabilities to the handset envisaged by IMS, the number of IP-addressable devices could potentially explode as 3G gains momentum beyond Release 4.

Support for IPv6 in IP backbones, and eventually the RAN, is a clear direction stated in 3GPP specifications. An MPLS-enabled IP network provides a simple path for support of IPv4, IPv6, and ATM protocols that will all be required as mobile operators evolve their infrastructures from the initial Release 99 step. The IPv6 provider edge (6PE) router approach is a straightforward method of integrating IPv6 into an IP/MPLS infrastructure.

Compelling reasons for IPv6 include the expansion of the address space required to enable the growth of mobile multimedia applications. IPv6 has been proposed as a primary technology enabler for wide-scale adoption of IMS. Even with commercial deployment of IMS as per the standards being slowed, the drivers for IPv6 remain.

One strategy for SPs is to insert IPv6 support only at the edge of their current IP networks, where feasible, to minimize changes to the core of the network. It is likely that IPv6 traffic will grow slowly, which is one reason that the previous 3GPP mandate of IMS as exclusively using IPv6 is no longer the case. MPLS 6PE is the simplest solution for mobile network operators requiring IPv6 support.

The 6PE approach allows existing IP/MPLS networks to carry the IPv6 packets using MPLS labels; hence only the PE device needs to support the IPv6 protocol and addressing. As shown in Figure 5.23, the core transport remains IPv4 with MPLS labeling while the 6PE at the edge of the network labels the traffic.

5.17 3GPP Specifications for IPv6

The wireless mobile market is only one of the factors for IPv6 adoption. In many regions, including Asia/Pacific, there is currently a lack of IPv4 address space, which will only increase in the future. Growing Internet adoption in emerging countries such as China and India and the adoption of new Internet-connected appliances are fueling the IPv6 drive.

According to the 3GPP IMS standards, IPv6 can be used in any area where IPv4 is currently the protocol of choice. As shown in Figure 5.24, IPv6 can be adopted at the data-bearer level for user applications and the transport-bearer level for user data transport.

At the user layer, IPv6 may be used for GPRS data for some or all applications. Clearly, to support IPv6 at the user layer, all network elements, including mobile station, SGSN

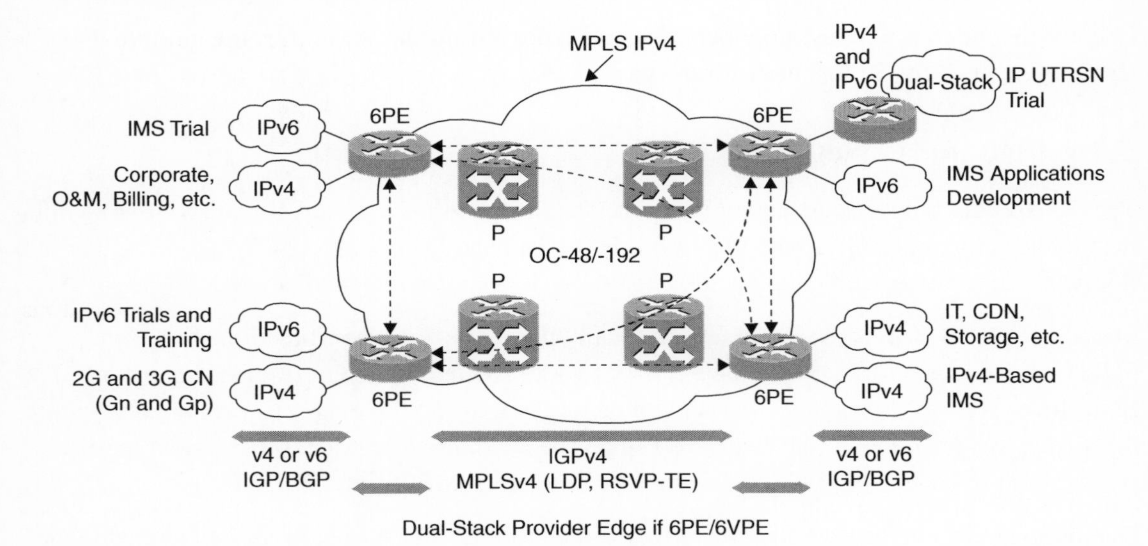

Figure 5.23: IPv6 Transport in an MPLS Network

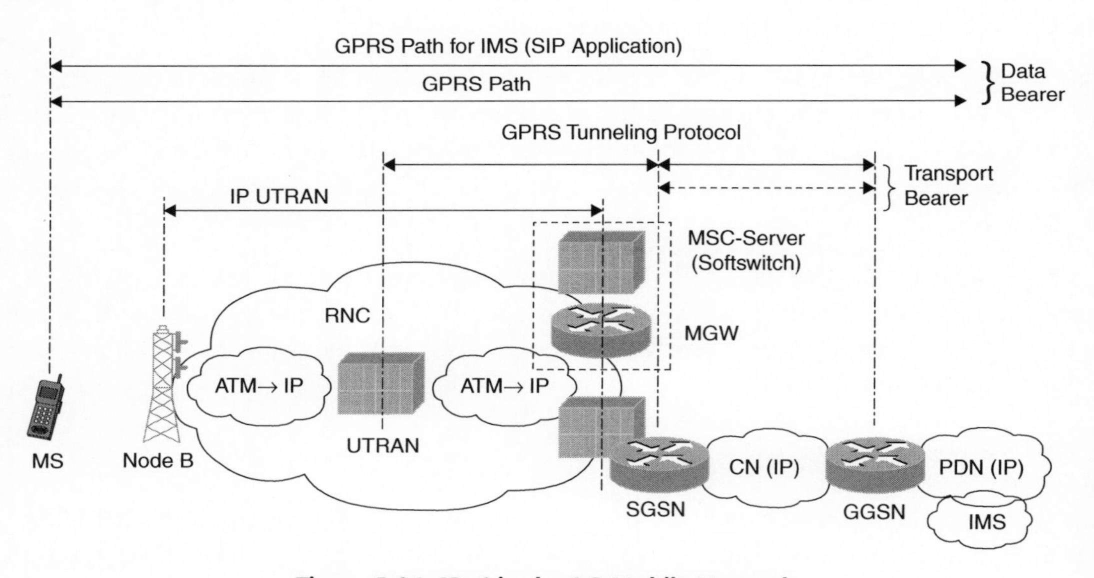

Figure 5.24: IPv6 in the 3G Mobile Network

recognizing the IP address field for charging purposes, GGSN, address provisioning, and name services such as Domain Name System (DNS) must support IPv6. As of today, the main focus area is in the delivery of commercial IPv6 services at the two endpoints: the user equipment and applications. Internetworking beyond the mobile provider network will also be a prerequisite for applications if services are to span outside the local provider domain or if complex gateways are to be avoided.

The concept of IMS was not an application but rather a framework to offer Session Initiation Protocol (SIP)-based applications on a GPRS bearer. This capability is based on three primary technologies:

- SIP as the control plane for the establishment of IMS sessions
- IPv6 as the transport
- Authentication, authorization, and accounting (AAA) and billing

Examples of IMS-based applications include Push-to-Talk over cellular or rich voice applications based on VoIP. New messaging capabilities far beyond current handset functionality are also examples of an SIP implementation. Other aspects of IMS are QoS enforcement at Layer 2 (radio bearer) and Layer 3 (IP), authentication and security, and charging and support of multiple types of devices.

Mobile operators quickly realized the advantages of developing new applications using SIP; however, they remained concerned about the IMS mandate for IPv6. Clearly, despite its limited scalability in the future, IPv4 was widely deployed from 2.5G onward and technically could be used within the initial 3GPP IMS model for SIP deployments. In response to mobile operator and radio vendor pressure, 3GPP modified the exclusive statement of IPv6 to allow IPv4. The 3GPP TS23.221 specification states: "3GPP specifications design the IM CN subsystem elements and interfaces to exclusively support IPv6. However, early IMS implementations and deployments may use IPv4." This statement reinforced the discussions and the work on SIP, IPv6, and IPv4 and IPv6 internetworking.

Currently, most IP traffic from the mobile station is IPv4 with the exception of some experimental work by selected vendors. Adoption of IPv6 will probably take a few more years because of multiple factors, including availability of IPv6 mass-market handsets, applications for IMS based on an SIP framework supported by both 3GPP and IETF, and the IMS and GPRS support-node infrastructure.

Ultimately, in the context of QoS, the specifications for IPv6 and IPv4 will be identical in an MPLS-labeled network. Refer to later sections in this chapter for details on the QoS framework in 3G networks.

5.18 Overview of QoS and the 3GPP Standards

There are many documents arising from the 3GPP working groups regarding the issue of Quality of Service (QoS). The foundation standard is QoS Concept and Architecture (3GPP TS 23.107), which defines the overall framework for QoS within the 3G mobile network. This document is discussed in the following section.

5.19 QoS Concept and Architecture (3GPP TS 23.107)

This document gives an overview of the QoS framework to be adopted in the 3G network infrastructure. The definitions are across all traffic types in the UMTS, including voice, signaling, and data. The parameters for QoS are given in specific terms, albeit not commonly understood ATM or IP network terms; hence a mapping is required.

General requirements for QoS are identified as follows:

- QoS attributes (or mapping of them) should not be restricted to one or few external QoS control mechanisms, but the QoS concept should be capable of providing different levels of QoS by using UMTS-specific control mechanisms (not related to QoS mechanisms in the external networks).
- All attributes must have unambiguous meaning.
- QoS mechanisms have to allow efficient use of radio capacity.
- Allow independent evolution of core and access networks.
- Allow evolution of UMTS network (i.e., eliminate or minimize the impact of evolution of transport technologies in the wireline world).
- All attribute combinations must have unambiguous meaning.

In terms of general high-level technical requirements for the UMTS, QoS will be defined with a set of generic attributes. The attributes should meet the following criteria:

- UMTS QoS control mechanisms shall provide QoS attribute control on a peer-to-peer basis between UE and 3G gateway node.
- The UMTS QoS mechanisms shall provide a mapping between application requirements and UMTS services.
- The UMTS QoS control mechanisms shall be able to efficiently interwork with current QoS schemes. Further, the QoS concept should be capable of providing different levels of QoS by using UMTS-specific control mechanisms (not related to QoS mechanisms in the external networks).
- A session-based approach needs to be adopted for all packet mode communication within the 3G serving node with which the UMTS QoS approach shall be intimately linked; essential features include multiple QoS streams per address.
- The UMTS shall provide a finite set of QoS definitions.
- The overhead and additional complexity caused by the QoS scheme, as well as the amount of state information transmitted and stored in the network, should be kept reasonably low.
- QoS shall support efficient resource utilization.
- The QoS attributes are needed to support asymmetric bearers.

- Applications (or special software in the UE or 3G gateway node) should be able to indicate QoS values for their data transmissions.
- QoS behavior should be dynamic, that is, it will be possible to modify QoS attributes during an active session.
- The number of attributes should be kept reasonably low (increasing the number of attributes increases system complexity).
- User QoS requirements shall be satisfied by the system, including when a change of SGSN within the core network occurs.

As can be seen, these attributes are high level at best, with generic statements giving no indication of methods or measurable criteria.

The network architecture presented is end to end, from terminal equipment (TE) to the remote TE for all services. The reference mode defined in the standard is shown in Figure 5.25.

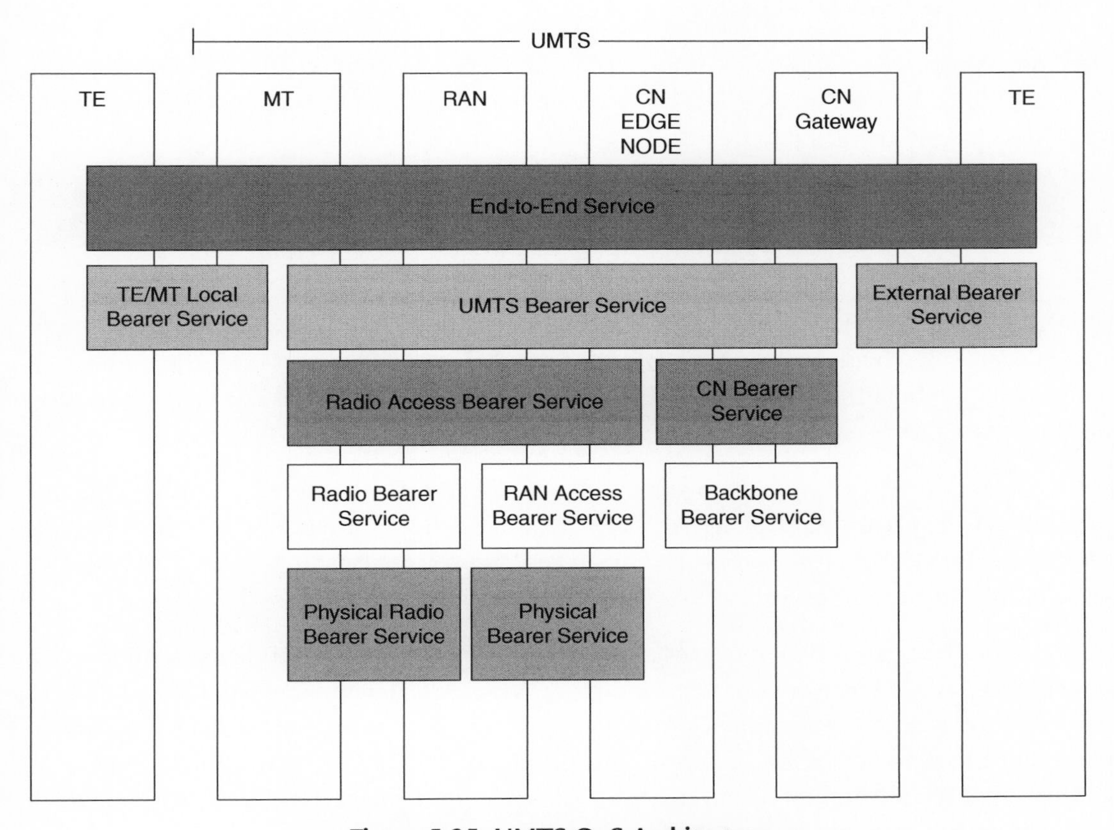

Figure 5.25: UMTS QoS Architecture

Traffic flowing from TE to TE traverses different bearer services of the network. By 3GPP definition, a TE is connected to the UMTS network through a Mobile Termination (MT) device. The End-to-End Service on the application level uses the bearer services of the underlying network.

The End-to-End-Service used by the TE will traverse a TE/MT Local Bearer Service, a UMTS Bearer Service, and an External Bearer Service as shown in the figure. The TE/MT Local Bearer Service is actually outside the 3G network and is not discussed further in the standards. An example is an Ethernet or USB connection to some sort of mobile network modem or even a communications card in a computer PC Card slot.

The UMTS Bearer Service is within the boundaries of the operator; it is this bearer service that provides the QoS for traffic. By definition, as shown in the figure, the UMTS Bearer Service consists of two parts: the Radio Access Bearer Service and the Core Network Bearer Service.

The Radio Access Bearer Service provides secure transport of signaling and user data between the MT and CN Edge Node, with QoS enforced to meet the negotiated UMTS Bearer Service or with the default QoS for signaling.

The Core Network Bearer Service of the UMTS core network connects the UMTS CN Edge Node with the CN Gateway that interfaces to external networks. Once again, this layer must honor the QoS as contracted to the UMTS bearer service. The UMTS packet core network must support different backbone bearer services for variety of QoS parameters.

The Radio Access Bearer Service is further broken down into a Radio Bearer Service and an RAN Access Bearer Service, as shown in the figure.

The Radio Bearer Service includes all the aspects of the radio interface transport. This bearer service is provided by the UTRAN FDD/TDD or the GERAN. QoS at this level requires honoring requirements per user subflow, equating to an application the TE is using, typically belonging to a flow.

The RAN Access Bearer Service, together with the Physical Bearer Service, provides the transport between RAN and CN. RAN Access Bearer Services for packet traffic shall provide different bearer services for a variety of QoS. The RAN Access Bearer Service is provided by the Iu or the Gb Bearer Service.

The Core Network Bearer Service uses a generic Backbone Network Service according to the standard. The Backbone Network Service provides transport functionality, and although it must fulfill the QoS requirements of the Core Network Bearer Service, no further details are given in the standard as to how this will happen. According to 3GPP 23.107, "Backbone Network Service is not specific to UMTS but may reuse an existing standard," further reinforcing the fact that QoS enforcement is up to the mobile network operator.

5.20 3G Traffic Classes

One challenge facing the drafters of the 3G standards was enforcement of the QoS over the air interface. Any complexity in the standards would lead to problems in application to the air interface, hence potentially jeopardizing the end-to-end QoS goal. As such the standards were kept as simple as possible to ensure seamless QoS from user to user.

The 3rd Generation Partnership Program (3GPP) has four classes of QoS:

- Conversational
- Streaming
- Interactive
- Background

Figure 5.26 shows the class definitions, characteristics of each class, and an example of the traffic types that can be expected in each class.

The most notable difference between these QoS classes is the delay parameter. The Conversational class is intended for traffic which is extremely delay sensitive. The Background class is the most delay-insensitive traffic class.

Conversational and Streaming classes are intended to be used for real-time traffic. Once again, the difference between these classes is delay sensitivity. Conversational real-time services, such as video telephony, are highly delay sensitive and should be classified as Conversational.

Interactive and Background classes are intended for traditional Internet applications such as Internet, email, Telnet, and FTP. The Interactive class is used by interactive applications

	Conversational class	Streaming class	Interactive class	Background class
Characteristics	Preserve time relation (variation) between information entities of the stream Conversational pattern (very low delay and jitter)	Preserve time relation (variation) between information entities of the stream Delay and jitter requirements not as stringent as conversational	Request response pattern Retransmission of payload content in route	Destination is not expecting the data within a stringent time Retransmission of payload content in route may occur
Example of Application	Voice over IP	Streaming video	Web browsing	Email download

Figure 5.26: 3G Traffic Class Definitions

such as interactive email or interactive Web browsing. The Background class is intended for background traffic, such as download of emails or files. As would be expected, traffic in the Interactive class has higher priority over Background class traffic, so background applications use transmission resources only when the other traffic classes are not using them.

5.21 Bearer Service Attributes

Bearer service attributes describe the services the network provides to the end user. A set of QoS attributes are used to specify a given service. At bearer service establishment for a user application, QoS profiles mapping to the application needs must be classified and subsequently enforced.

These attributes are as follows:

- Traffic class
- Maximum bit rate
- Guaranteed bit rate
- Delivery order
- Maximum service data unit (SDU) size
- SDU format information
- SDU error ratio
- Residual bit error ratio
- Delivery of erroneous SDUs
- Transfer delay
- Traffic-handling priority (THP)
- Allocation and retention priority
- Source statistics descriptor
- Signaling indication

Details of these attributes are not given here; however, the specifications give an exhaustive view of recommendations for each attribute to each service class at each layer of the reference model.

5.22 Mobile Network Protocol Stacks

To understand the QoS requirements in a mobile network, it is important to understand the traffic and protocols in detail that must be transported across the network infrastructure.

The General Protocol Model is described in standard 3G TS 25.401. The UTRAN interface consists of a set of horizontal and vertical layers, as shown in Figure 5.27. The UTRAN requirements are addressed in the horizontal radio network layer across various types of control and user planes.

Control planes are used to control a link or a connection, as the name suggests. User planes are used to transparently transmit user data from the higher-layer applications.

Five major protocol blocks are shown in the figure as follows:

- Signaling bearers are used to transmit higher layers' signaling and control information.
- Data bearers are the frame protocols used to transport user data streams generated from higher-layer applications.
- Application protocols refer to UMTS—specific signaling and control within UTRAN rather than user applications. An example is establishing bearers in the radio network layer.
- Data streams contain the user data that are transparently transmitted between the network elements. User data comprised the subscriber's personal data and mobility management information that are exchanged between the peer entities MGW/MSC and UE.
- Access Link Control Application Part (ALCAP) protocol layers are provided in the Transport Network Control Plane (TN–CP). ALCAP manages the radio network layer's demands to set up, maintain, and release data bearers. The primary objective of introducing the TN–CP was to totally separate the selection of the data bearer

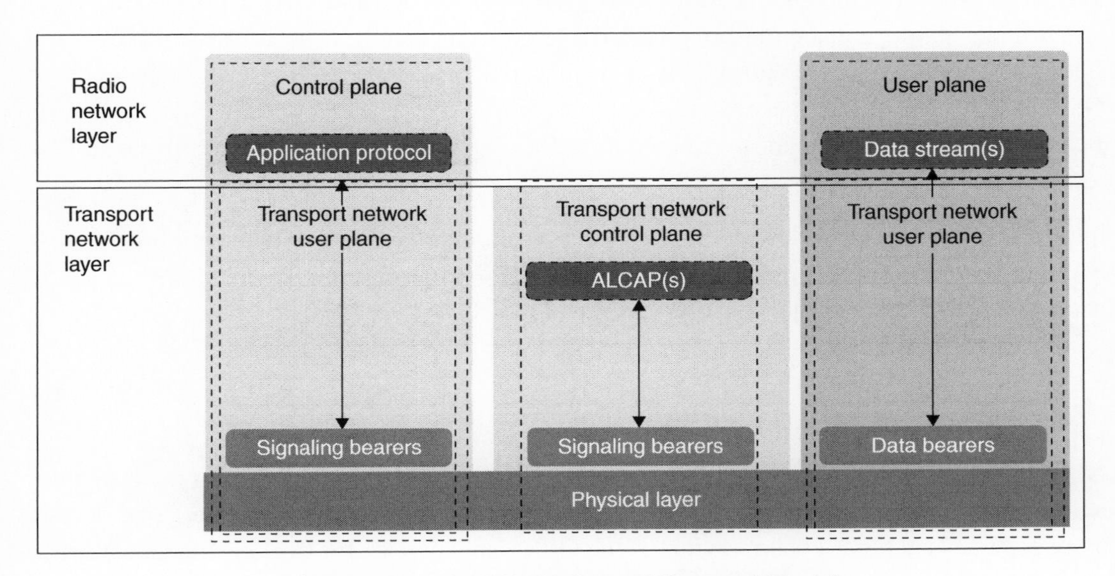

Figure 5.27: 3G UTRAN General Protocol Model

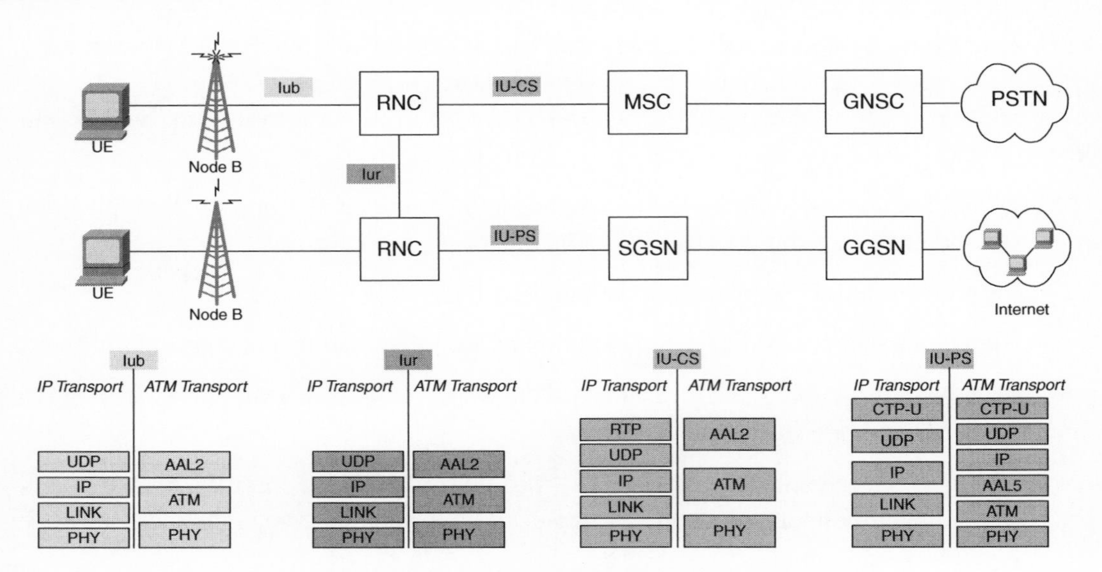

Figure 5.28: 3G Interface Protocol Stacks

technology from the control plane where the UTRAN–specific application protocols are located. The TN–CP is present in the Iu–CS, Iur, and Iub interfaces.

As discussed in previous sections, in 3GPP R99 ATM is the dominant transport technology from Node B through the CN. With Release 5, both ATM and IP are equally valid transport technologies, with IP as the converged network layer.

For 3G Release 99 and 4, transport is either AAl2 or AAL5. AAL2 offers synchronous mode, connection-oriented connections with VBR (e.g., voice traffic). AAL5 offers asynchronous mode, connection-oriented VBR (e.g., packet data). Currently, within the UTRAN, AAL5 carries all control data, as well as user data, over the Iu-PS interface to the SGSN. AAL2 carries user voice data in the circuit-switched domain over Iu-CS. However, since 3GPP Release 5, IP is the converged transport for all data, including control and Iu-PS user data.

Figure 5.28 shows an overview of the protocol stacks in the UMTS network with both ATM and IP options at the relevant network interface reference points. A detailed view of the protocol stacks transported for both GSM and 3G per release is given in the rest of this section.

5.23 Packet-Switched Domain Network Protocol Stacks

The GPRS subnetwork is responsible for user application data transport. As per the previous sections, there must be connectivity for 2.5G and 3G services in the mobile operator's network. Figure 5.29 gives a high-level overview of the GPRS subnetwork for the GSM legacy users and the 3G UMTS RAN.

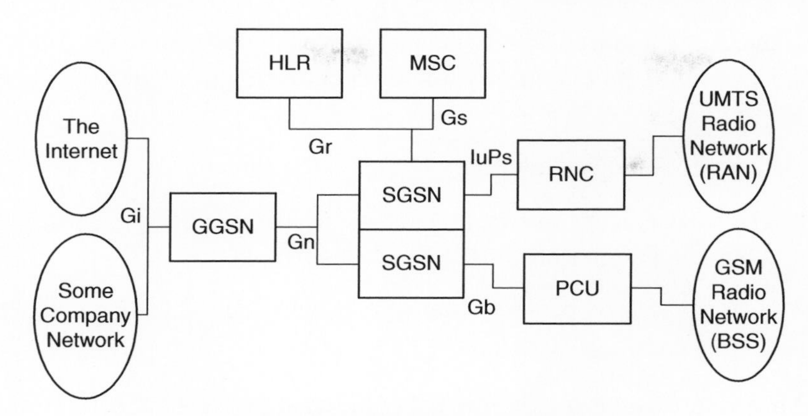

Figure 5.29: GPRS Core Network

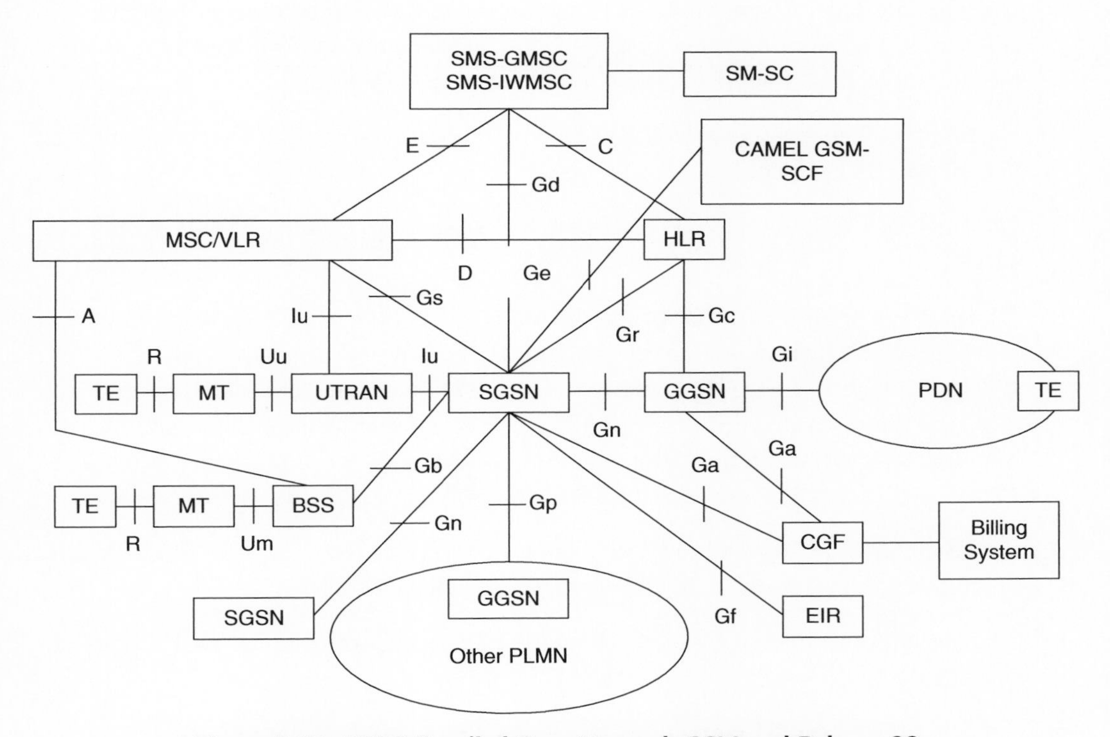

Figure 5.30: GPRS Detailed Core Network GSM and Release 99

Figure 5.30 presents a detailed diagram of the converged GSM 2.5G and 3G GPRS subnetwork as per the specification 3GPP TS123060. Note that the reference interfaces in the data path do not change through to Release 5; only the underlying transport protocol changes from ATM to IP.

There are many interfaces required within the data packet-switched domain. These interfaces span the UTRAN and GSM BSS connectivity; however, the majority are after the SGSN, which is the same for either 2.5G or 3G.

Here is a complete list of reference interfaces in the GPRS network:

- *Gb.* Interface between the base station subsystem and the SGSN. The transmission protocol could be Frame Relay or IP.
- *Gn.* IP-based interface between SGSN and other SGSNs and (internal) GGSNs. DNS also shares this interface. Uses the GTP Protocol.
- *Gp.* IP-based interface between internal SGSN and external GGSNs. Between the SGSN and the external GGSN is the border gateway (which is essentially a firewall). Also uses the GTP Protocol.
- *Ga.* The interface servers the CDRs (accounting records) which are written in the GSN and sent to the charging gateway (CG). This interface uses a GTP-based Protocol, with modifications that supports CDRs (Called GTP′ or GTP prime).
- *Gr.* Interface between the SGSN and the HLR. Messages going through this interface use the MAP3 Protocol.
- *Gd.* Interface between the SGSN and the SMS Gateway. Can use MAP1, MAP2, or MAP3.
- *Gs.* Interface between the SGSN and the MSC (VLR). Uses the BSSAP+ Protocol. This interface allows paging and station availability when it performs data transfer. When the station is attached to the GPRS network, the SGSN keeps track of which routing area (RA) the station is attached to. An RA is a part of a larger location area (LA). When a station is paged, this information is used to conserve network resources. When the station performs a PDP context, the SGSN has the exact BTS the station is using.
- *Gi.* The interface between the GGSN and a Public Data Network (PDN), either directly to the Internet or through a WAP gateway. Uses the IP protocol.
- *Ge.* The interface between the SGSN and the Service Control Point (SCP). Uses the CAP Protocol.
- *Gx.* The online policy interface between the GGSN and the Charging Rules Function (CRF). It is used for provisioning service data flow-based charging rules. Uses the Diameter Protocol.
- *Gy.* The online charging interface between the GGSN and the Online Charging System (OCS). Uses the Diameter Protocol (DCCA application).
- *Gz.* The offline (CDR-based) charging interface between the GSN and the CG. Uses GTP′.

- *Gmb.* The interface between the GGSN and the Broadcast Multicast Service Center (BM-SC), used for controlling MBMS bearers.

Not all of these interfaces are of interest in the context of QoS within the mobile provider's infrastructure. The following section identifies the interfaces in the GPRS subnetwork that require QoS enforcement.

5.24 GSM 2.5G GPRS Protocol Stacks

Figure 5.31 shows the protocol stack for the 2.5G GPRS traffic flow from the end-user terminal to the GGSN gateway. The first diagram shows the user plane; the second shows the control plane.

Note that the network service interface for Gb between the BSC in the BSS and the SGSN is generally Frame Relay.

Figure 5.32 shows the protocol stack for the control plane. Note that the protocol stack for the control plane is identical to the user plane up to the SGSN.

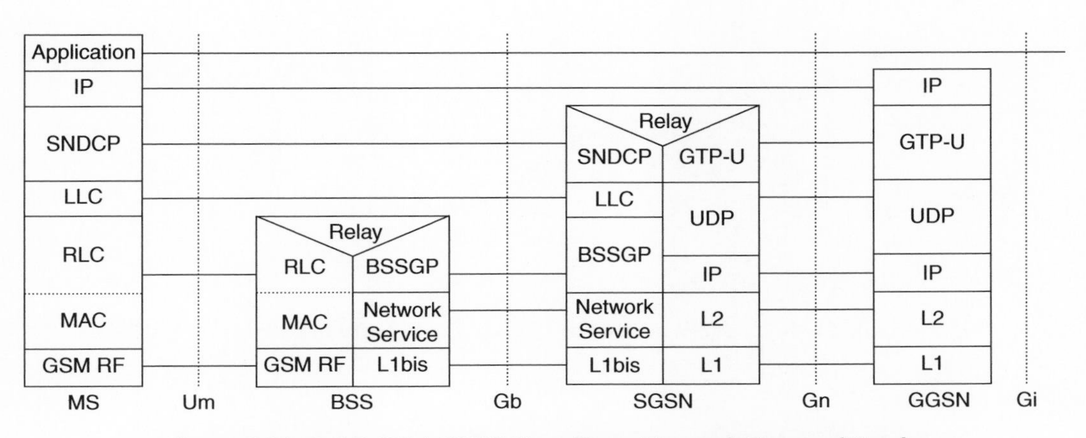

Figure 5.31: 2.5G GSM GPRS User Plane Network Protocol Stacks

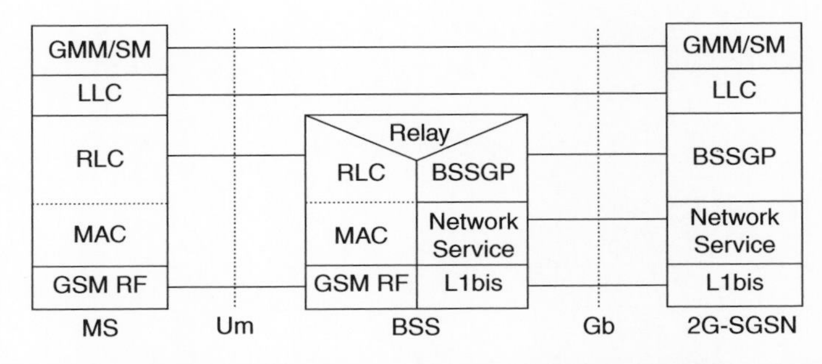

Figure 5.32: 2.5G GSM GPRS Control Plane Network Protocol Stacks

Once again, as for the data bearer plane, the network service for the Gn connection typically uses Frame Relay.

Note that the control plane data only as far as the SGSN in the figure. Control and signaling for connections are handled exclusively by the SGSN device. The GGSN accepts tunneled data and forwards as requested by the SGSN. This is the case for all the 3G releases, as shown in the subsequent control protocol stack figures.

5.25 3G Release 99 and Release 4 GPRS Protocol Stacks

The 3G Release 99 and Release 4 protocol stacks for GPRS are identical. Both these releases rely on ATM for transport, as shown in Figures 5.33 and 5.34 for the user and control planes.

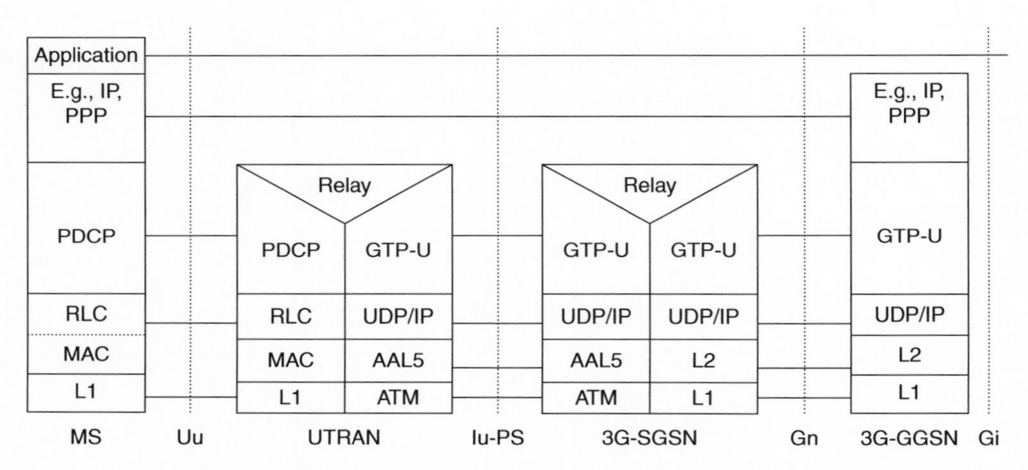

Figure 5.33: 3G Release 99 and 4 GPRS User Plane Network Protocol Stacks

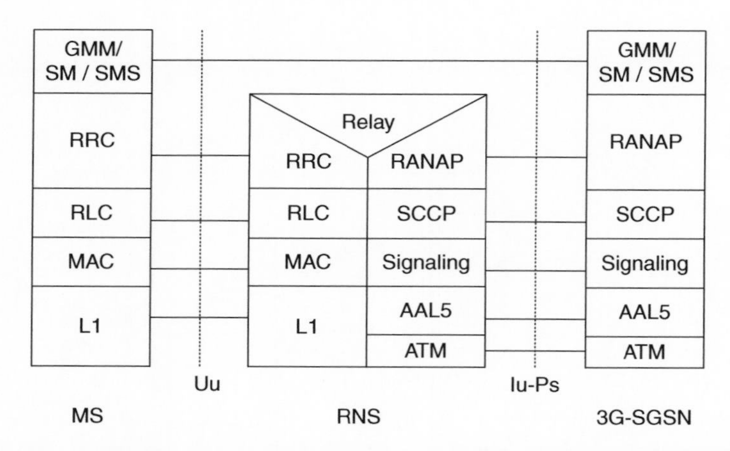

Figure 5.34: 3G Release 99 and 4 GPRS Control Plane Network Protocol Stacks

The connection from the UTRAN RNC through to the SGSN for both user and control data utilizes the AAL5 adaption layer for both the control and user planes. Also worthy of note is the extension of the GPRS Tunneling Protocol (GTP-U) through to the RNC. In the GSM network the GTP protocol is exclusively between the SGSN and the GGSN.

5.26 3G Release 5 GPRS Protocol Stacks

Release 5 introduces IP as an option in the transport from the RNC, as previously discussed in this chapter. Although IP becomes the converged network layer, providers with ATM investment may still use this technology as the Layer 2 network if desired.

The protocol stack for 3G Release 5 GPRS in the user and control planes is shown in Figure 5.35.

With IP as the converged Layer 3 from the UTRAN RNC through to the GGSN, any Layer 1 and 2 transport technology can be used. This is an important step on the path to IP-enabled multimedia applications. Once again, note that throughout the evolution of 3G releases, the SGSN to GGSN Gn interface remains unchanged.

In practice, many mobile providers have opted to implement dedicated 3G SGSN/GGSN pairs in parallel with the existing GSM pairs. Additionally, many providers preferred to move to the Release 5 standards (see Figure 5.36) directly rather than implementing the release 99 and 4 specifications using ATM.

As shown in the Iu-PS figures, the protocol stack on the interface supports Radio Access Network Application Part (RANAP) in the control plane. RANAP is the Radio Network Layer signaling protocol for the Iu interface, including Iu-PS and Iu-CS. It manages the signaling and

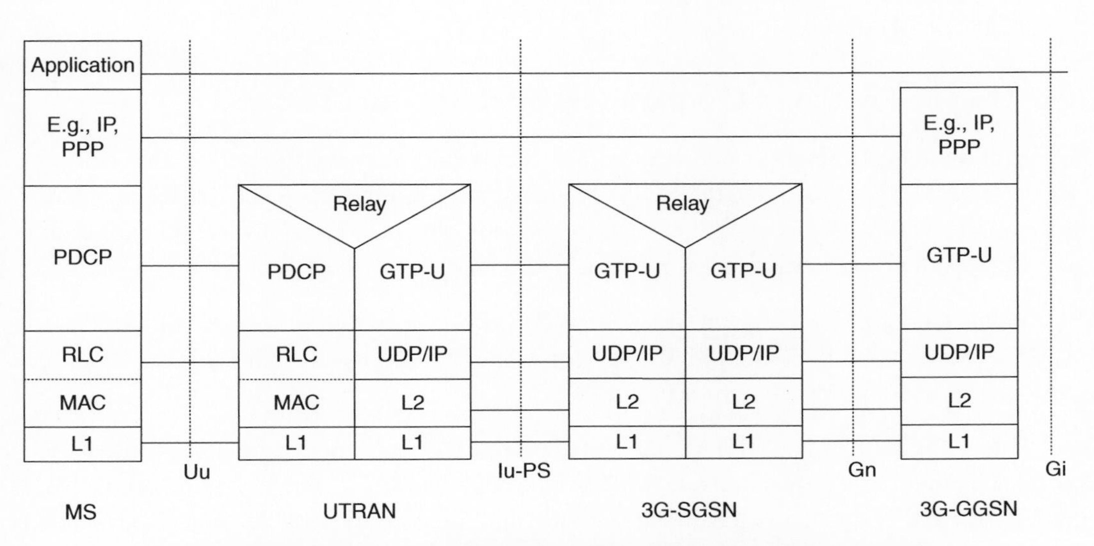

Figure 5.35: 3G Release 5 GPRS User Plane Network Protocol Stacks

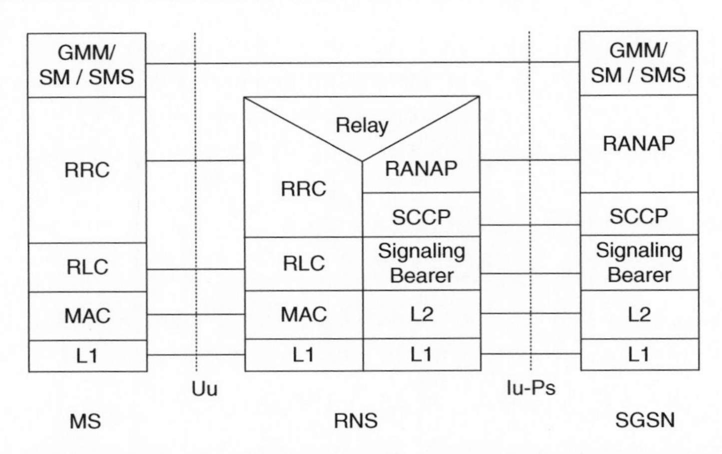

Figure 5.36: 3G Release 5 GPRS Control Plane Network Protocol Stacks

GTP connections between RNC and 3G-SGSN. It also manages signaling and circuit-switched connections between RNC and 3G MGW on the Iu interface.

RANAP also provides a signaling channel to transparently pass messages between UE and the core network. HSS RANAP protocol implementation provides elementary procedures for accomplishing radio access bearer management, serving RNS relocation, transport of NAS information between UE and CN, paging UE, and release of Iu resources.

RANAP gives three types of services:

- General control services
- Notification services
- Dedicated control services

5.27 Circuit-Switched Domain Network Protocol Stacks

The circuit-switched domain contains protocols specifically for voice signaling and transport. In the Release 99 specifications, the MGW is placed between the RNC and the legacy MSC connected via TDM. As discussed in previous sections, this is to allow a graceful evolution to bearer independent infrastructure from Release 4 onward.

With the introduction of Release 4, the MSC and GMSC are retired in favor of the MGW plus MSC server and GMSC server. The reference model used by the 3GPP for the Release 4 circuit-switched domain is shown in Figure 5.37.

According to the standards: "The Mc reference point in the present document considers the aspects of the interface between the G-MSC server and the MGW. The H.248 protocol [5] together with 3GPP specific extensions/packages shall be used over the Mc interface. The Network-Network based call control is used over the Nc interface. Any suitable call control

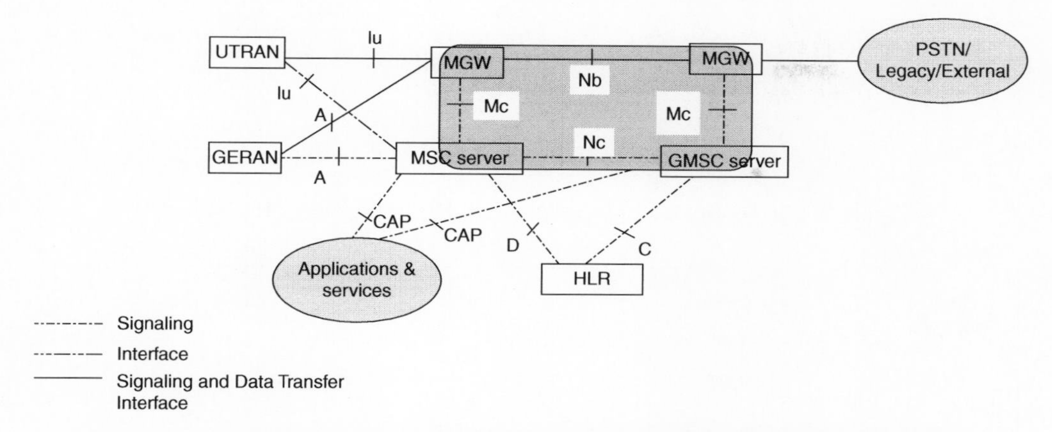

Figure 5.37: 3G Bearer Independent Circuit-Switched Domain Core Network

AAL-2 SAR SSCS (I.366.1)
AAL2 (I.363.2)
ATM

Figure 5.38: 3G Bearer Independent CS Nb Interface User Plane

AAL2 Connection Signaling (Q.2630.2)
AAL2 Signaling Transport Converter for MTP3b (Q.2150.1)
MTP3b
SSCF-NNI
SSCOP
AAL5
ATM

Figure 5.39: 3G Bearer Independent CS Nb Interface User Control

protocol may be used over the Nc interface (e.g., BICC). The bearer control signaling and transport are carried over the Nb interface."

The Nb interface user plane protocol stack can be ATM or IP based. Figures 5.38 and 5.39 show the ATM options for the user plane and the control plane.

The IP option for the Nb interface for the control and user plane is as shown in Figure 5.40.

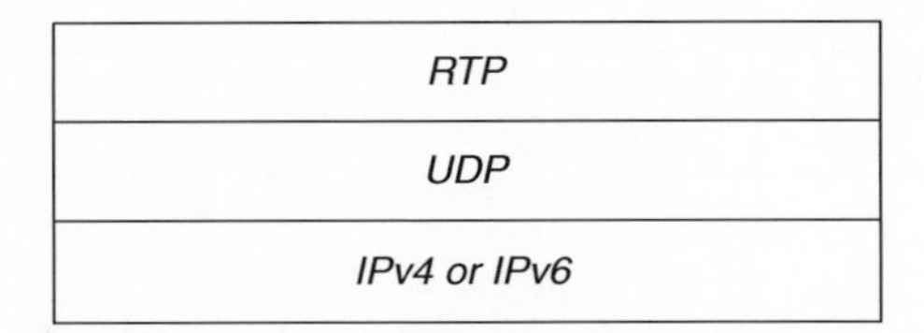

Figure 5.40: 3G Bearer Independent CS Nb IP Interface User Plane

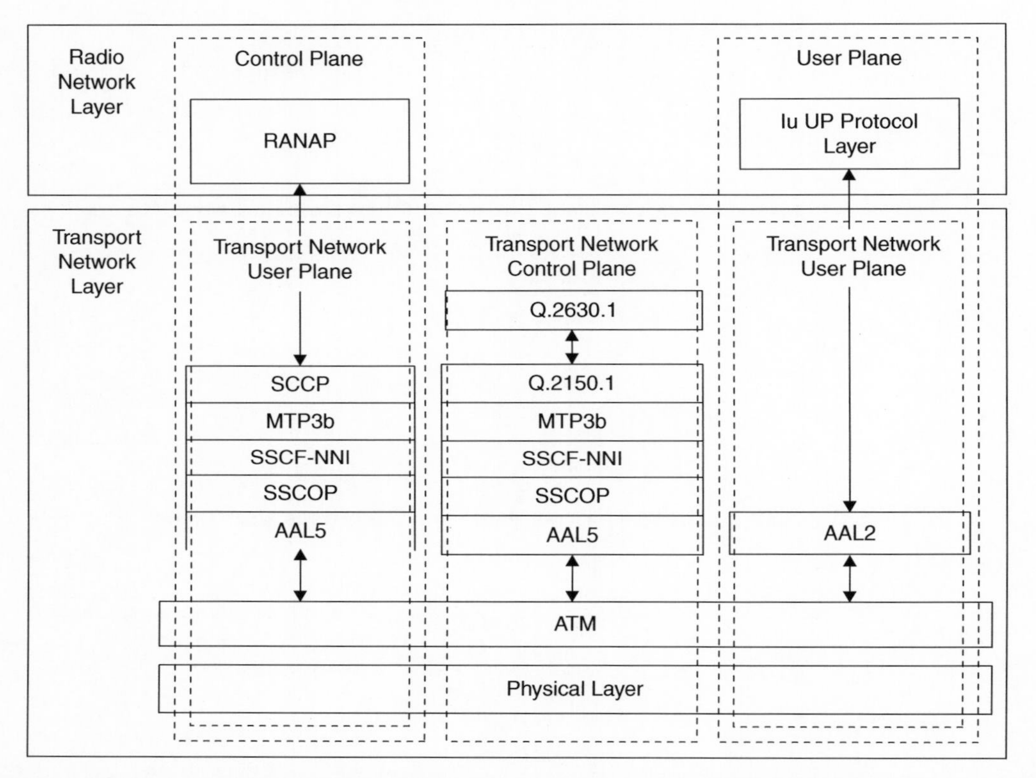

Figure 5.41: 3G Release 99 and 4 Circuit-Switched Domain Control Plane Network Protocol Stacks

Note that IPv4 or IPv6 are valid options for the transport. Also note that Layer 1 and 2 protocols are not shown since IP is the converged Layer 3, making the choice of transport at lower layers irrelevant. In the case of the control path, the upper-layer protocol will be RCTP; otherwise the protocol stack is identical to the user plane.

For the remainder of this chapter, IP is assumed as the chosen transport option for the Nb, Nc, and Mc interfaces.

5.27.1 Iu Interface in the Circuit-Switched Domain

The Iu interface toward the circuit-switched domain is Iu-CS. This interface is between the 3G RNC and the MGW. This interface services the voice traffic and signaling to and from the core

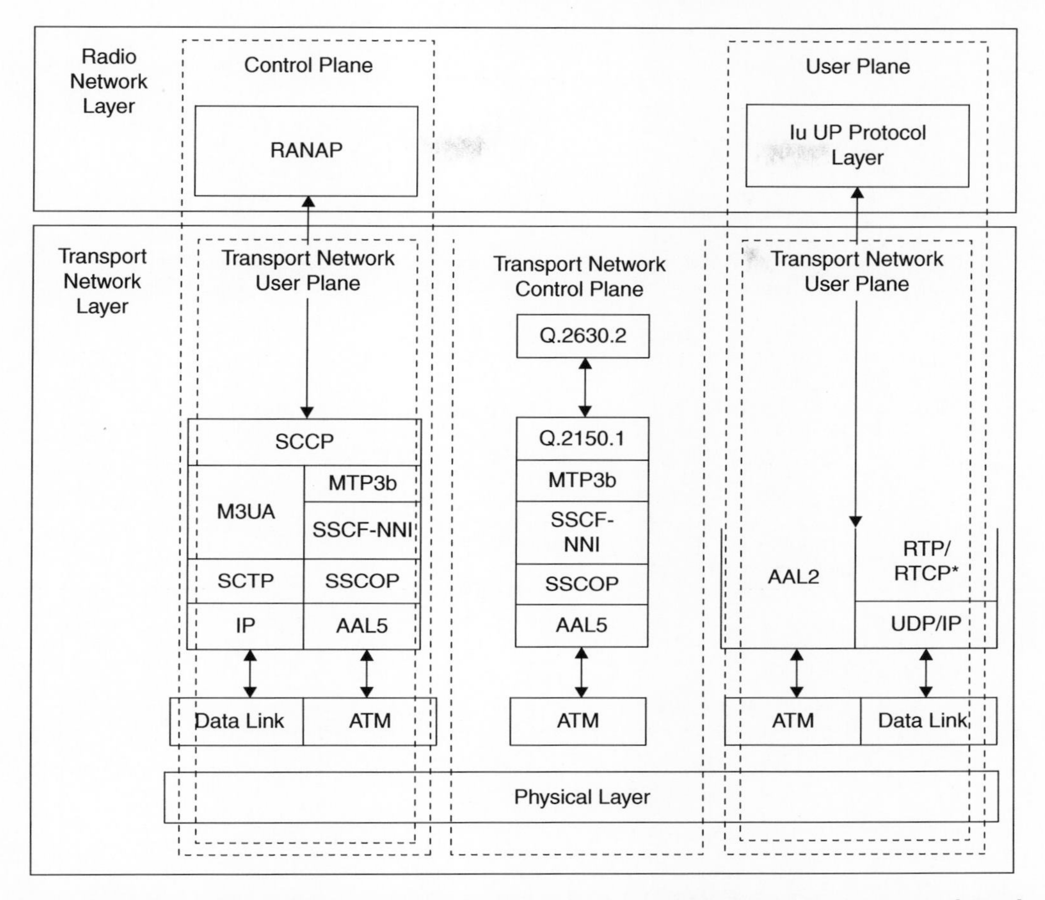

Figure 5.42: 3G Release 5 Circuit-Switched Domain Control Plane Network Protocol Stacks

network. In the Release 99 specification, the interface from the RNC into the MGW is ATM, which the MGW then converts to TDM for connection to the legacy MSC. In Release 4, VoIP is introduced and the MSC retired; however, the Iu-CS interface remains ATM and unchanged from Release 99.

Figure 5.41 shows a detailed breakdown of the Iu-CS protocol stack for the control and user planes in the Release 99 and Release 4 specifications.

Note that in the user plane for the circuit-switched domain traffic the transport is ATM AAL2. The control and network planes rely on AAL5.

As was the case with the Iu-CS protocol stack, from Release 5 the option exists for IP transport on the Iu-CS interface for both the control and user plane. Figure 5.42 shows the Iu-CS protocol stack for Release 5 onward.

Note that both ATM and IP are valid transport options in Release 5 to support legacy equipment from Releases 99 and 4.

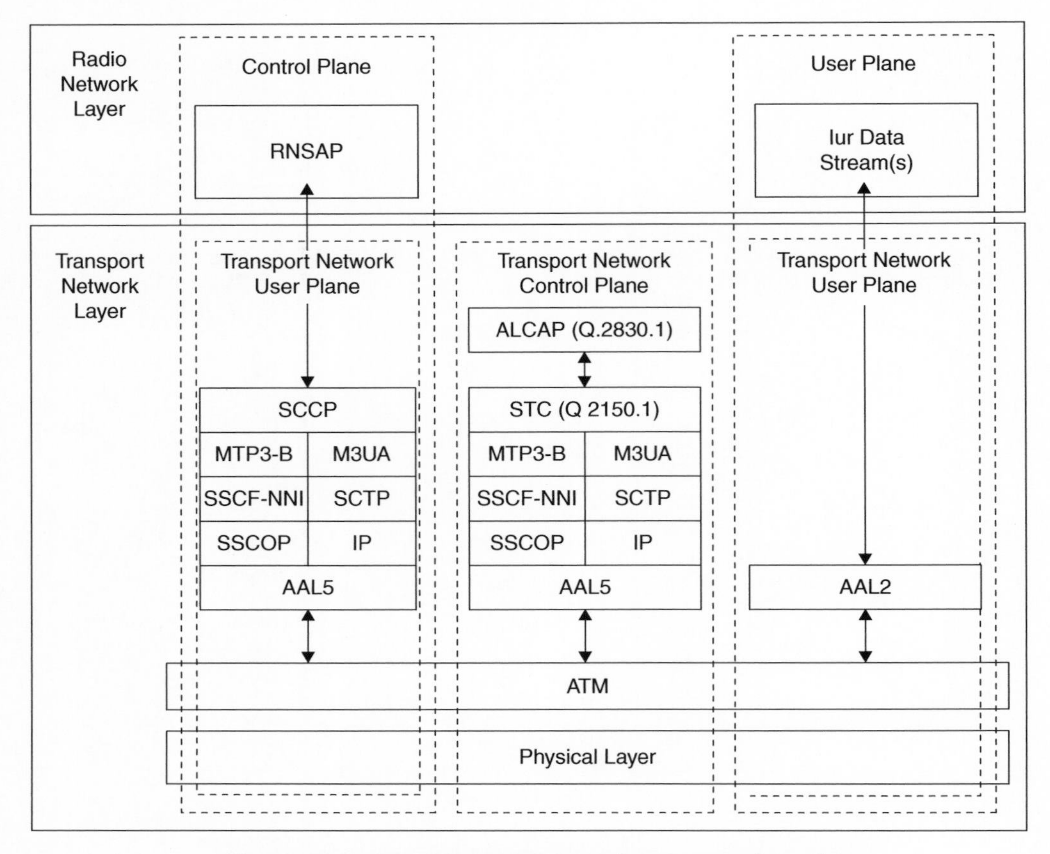

Figure 5.43: 3G UTRAN IuR Interface Protocol Stack

The IuR interface connects the 3G RNC's together for both control and user plane. The protocol stack for IuR is shown in Figure 5.43.

The control plane relies on AAL5 whereas the user plane relies on AAL2. This is the same as the Iu-CS interface.

5.28 Mobile Network Transport Framework

This section covers the transport of mobile traffic through the provider network. Layer 3 VPN-based transport is the preferred option for mobile traffic. The recommended structure for VPNs is outlined. The QoS framework and requirements for the mobile network supporting legacy 2G data and 3G Release 99 through Release 5 connectivity are defined in Figure 5.44. As previously mentioned, for specific details of the QoS configurations, refer to the later MPLS VPN and multicast QoS chapters.

Note that in the Release 99 specification, the legacy MSC remains; however, since it is TDM connected, no reference will be made to the MSC in the QoS framework. Also note that the

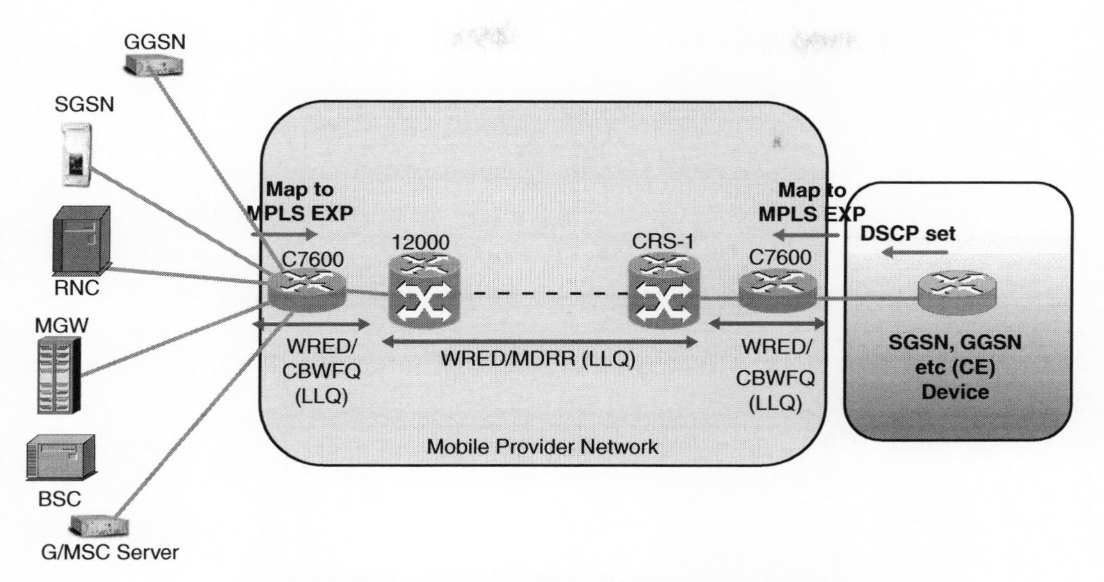

Figure 5.44: Mobile Provider Device Connectivity

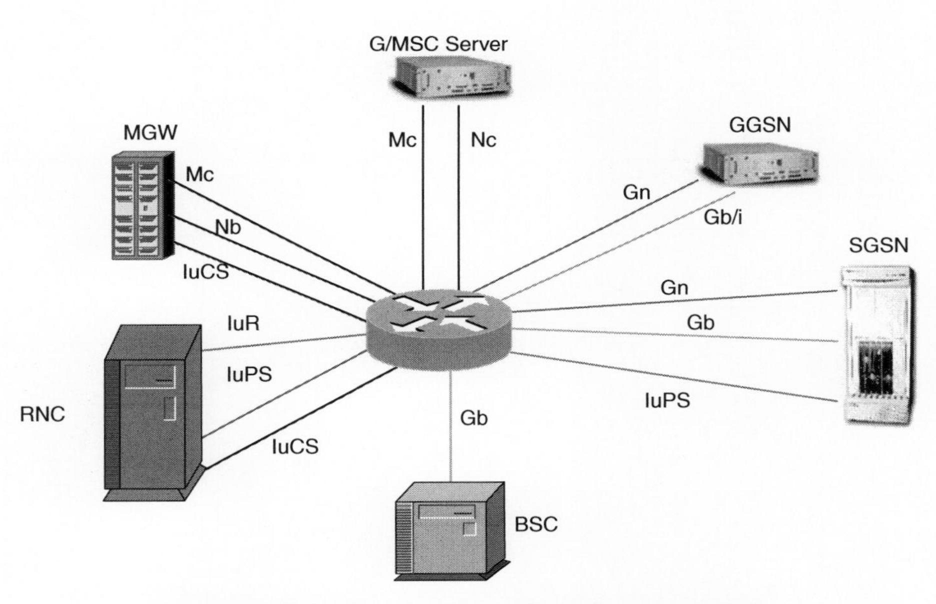

Figure 5.45: Mobile Provider POP Device Connectivity

MSC server and GMSC servers are shown in the diagram with reference to Release 4 and beyond. These devices are not included in the Release 99 specifications.

Figure 5.45 gives a more detailed view of the connections from each of the devices to the edge PE router.

Table 5.1: Mobile Network Interfaces for 2.5G, 3G Release 99, 4, and 5

Mobile Generation	Interface Name	Interface Type
2.5G GSM	Um	Air/radio
	Abis	TDM
	A	TDM
	Gb	Frame Relay
	Gn	IP
	Gi	IP
3G Release 99	Uu	Air/radio
	Iub	ATM AAL2/5 E1
	A	TDM
	IuCS	ATM AAL2/5
	IuPS	ATM AAL5
	IuR	ATM AAL2/5
	Gn	IP
	Gi	IP
3G Release 4	Uu	Air/radio
	Iub	ATM AAL2/5 E1
	A	TDM
	IuCS	ATM AAL2/5
	IuPS	ATM AAL5
	IuR	ATM AAL2/5
	Gn	IP
	Gi	IP
	Nb	IP
	Nc	IP
	Mc	IP
3G R5	Uu	Air/radio
	Iub	ATM AAL2/5 E1
	A	TDM
	IuCS	IP
	IuPS	IP
	IuR	ATM AAL2/5
	Gb	Frame Relay or IP
	Gn	IP
	Gi	IP
	Nb	IP
	Nc	IP
	Mc	IP

The interface names and associated types are shown in Table 5.1. Building on the previous sections, the mobile network infrastructure must support the following interfaces within a mobile network on the evolutionary path to 3G. Entries for 2.5G, 3G Release 99, 4, and 5 are shown.

MPLS Layer 2 VPN for ATM traffic and Layer 3 VPN for all IP traffic are accepted as leading practice for transporting mobile traffic through the provider network.

5.29 Quality-of-Service Framework

As discussed in Chapter 3, this book prefers to use the Cisco modified informational RFC-4594 recommendations as the baseline for classification. The classification guidelines used for this book are shown again in Figure 5.46 for reference.

Vendors of the mobile network equipment must classify the traffic prior to transport across the core network. Particularly for the data transport, this is the only option available within the network, since there is no scalable way for the edge PE to implement a classification policy. When the data context is initiated, the mobile equipment will mark the traffic with the appropriate DiffServ fields.

Figure 5.47 shows a mapping of DSCP bits to the four data classes as defined by 3GPP. This gives a reference for the typical QoS model that may be used by a mobile equipment vendor in the GGSN and SGSN.

According to the GSMA PRD IR.34 recommendations, six classes of service are strictly required; however, the interactive class contains three subclasses that can be aggregated into

Application	L3 Classification		IETF
	PHB	DSCP	RFC
Network Control	CS6	48	RFC 2474
VoIP Telephony	EF	46	RFC 3246
Broadcast Video	CS5	40	RFC 2474
Multimedia Conferencing	AF41	34	RFC 2597
Real-Time Interactive	CS4	32	RFC 2474
Multimedia Streaming	AF31	26	RFC 2597
Call Signaling	CS3	24	RFC 2474
Low-Latency Data	AF21	18	RFC 2597
OAM	CS2	16	RFC 2474
High-Throughput Data	AF11	10	RFC 2597
Best Effort	DF	0	RFC 2474
Low-Priority Data	CS1	8	RFC 3662

Figure 5.46: Cisco-Modified RFC4594 Marking Values

3GPP QoS Information		DiffServ PHB	DSCP	QoS Requirement on GRX				Service Example
Traffic Class	THP			Max Delay	Max Jitter	Packet Loss	SDU Error Ratio	
Conversational	N/A	EF	101110	20 ms	5 ms	0.5%	10^{-6}	VoIP, Video Conferencing
Streaming	N/A	$AF4_1$	100010	40 ms	5 ms	0.5%	10^{-6}	Audio/video Streaming
Interactive	1	$AF3_1$	011010	250 ms	N/A	0.1%	10^{-8}	Transactional Services
	2	$AF2_1$	010010	300 ms	N/A	0.1%	10^{-8}	Web Browsing
	3	$AF1_1$	001010	350 ms	N/A	0.1%	10^{-8}	Telnet
Background	N/A	BE	000000	400 ms	N/A	0.1%	10^{-8}	E-mail Download

Figure 5.47: QoS Mapping for 3G Data from GSMA PRD IR.34

a single class if required by the provider. Hence, the minimum requirement is for four classes to carry the 3GPP data classes. Remember that ultimately the provider may have a converged network carrying many services including mobile traffic, and hence the QoS framework must be in the context of the network as a whole.

5.30 QoS Traffic Management for Mobile

With the classification established for the traffic, important aspects of the traffic management must now be agreed:

- Mapping of data DiffServ classes to MPLS EXP bits for enforcement through the provider network
- Clearly defining the treatment for out-of-contract traffic in each class
- Clearly understanding the requirement for WRED to further optimize traffic patterns

Traffic levels that are beyond what has been agreed to are referred to as *out-of-contract* traffic and should be defined for each class to make sure that all traffic uses the same out-of-contract behavior in that class. If the traffic in one class exceeds what the GPRS/UMTS operator has allocated in the CoS traffic contract, various options can be performed.

5.30.1 Conversational Class

The Conversational traffic class will be marked as DiffServ Expedited Forwarding. To preserve the low-latency queuing behavior, the out-of-contract Conversational class is defined to be dropped. To accommodate the burst nature of conversational traffic, metering with token bucket algorithms can be used to determine whether traffic is out of contract.

The proposed marking is as follows:

- EF in-contract conversational traffic class
- Out-of-contract conversational traffic is dropped

The Expedited Forwarding behavior aggregate uses LLQ, as described in Chapter 2. Strict-priority queuing allows delay-sensitive data such as voice to be sent in preference to other queued traffic, effectively giving delay-sensitive data preferential treatment. This can lead to a situation where the LLQ traffic can starve other queues of bandwidth potential impacting other services. Typically the LLQ is limited to a maximum of 30 percent of the total link capacity for this reason. Configuration of traffic management will include a bandwidth argument that gives *maximum* bandwidth for this behavior aggregate. If congestion occurs, when the allocated bandwidth for the strict-priority queue is exceeded, policing is used to drop packets.

Given that the traffic in the conversational class is UDP based and there is a hard out-of-contract policy enforced, WRED is not used.

5.30.2 Streaming Class

As recommended by GSM Association PRD IR.34, streaming traffic class is marked as Assured Forwarding (AF4x). Video traffic, because of its usually limited burst behavior and large packet size, is typically more complex to manage than voice.

As with conversational traffic, in the event of traffic in this class exceeding the allocated bandwidth, packets will be dropped rather than remarked.

- AF41 in-contract streaming class is passed
- Out-of-contract streaming traffic class is dropped

Given that the majority of traffic in the streaming class is UDP based and there is a hard out-of-contract policy enforced, WRED is not used.

5.30.3 Interactive Class

Interactive traffic classes use the remaining Assured Forwarding classifications. According to GSM Association PRD IR.34, the difference among AF3x, AF2x, and AF1x traffic classes is the priority of the queuing behavior and the maximum buffer size, which is defined to accommodate the high delay possibilities for the lower-priority traffic.

- AFx1 in-contract interactive traffic class
- AFx2 exceeded-contract interactive traffic class
- AFx3 violated-contract interactive traffic class

The provider may choose to map each of these Interactive subclasses into a single class within the IP/MPLS core or they may keep them separate. Both these options are explored in the following sections.

Interactive traffic class will mainly contain TCP traffic. TCP congestion-avoidance techniques can therefore be used. WRED is recommended to manage traffic in this class.

5.30.4 Background Class

The Background class is recommended to be marked as best effort by the standards document by GSM. Given that the traffic in this class has traversed the radio interface in the case of ingress traffic from the UE, marking this class as best effort has caused the use of valuable resources to possibly see the data dropped. The provider may choose to give the Background class priority through the network beyond best effort if they determine other network traffic is of lower priority.

5.30.5 Alternative QoS Models

There are many alternative models for the QoS framework. Figure 5.48 gives an example five-class QoS model.

Note that the interactive classes are all configured as a single IP precedence and MPLS EXP class for management in the provider network. This gives fewer classes to manage in the network, making issues such as capacity planning less complex for the network operator. The disadvantage is that the delay differences between the Interactive classes are combined, giving a single profile for transactional services and general Web browsing.

A more granular QoS class approach also gives the provider greater visibility into the network bandwidth usage. This enables more effective understanding of the traffic profiles and hence more accurate capacity planning.

3GPP Class	DiffServ	DSCP	IP Prec	MPLS Exp
Routing/Signaling	AF	48	6	6
Conversational	EF	40	5	5
Streaming	AF	32	4	4
Interactive Gold	AF	24	2	2
Interactive Silver	AF	16	2	2
Interactive Bronze	AF	8	2	2
Background	BE	0	0	0

Figure 5.48: Mobile Network Five-Class QoS Model

Ultimately the parameters for the Interactive classes are identical except for delay parameters, leading many providers to the five-class model.

Where the provider prefers a more granular model, the Interactive class can be split into separate classes as shown in Figure 5.49.

As mentioned before, the chosen scheme will depend on:

- The implementation of classes from the vendor equipment such as the GGSN and RNC
- The QoS framework adopted by the provider in the context of all services carried through the network

Given the recommendations in GSMA PRD IR.34, the seven-class scheme supporting the 3GPP QoS framework is preferred where possible. As noted, many providers consider the five-class model adequate, given the close alignment of requirements in the three Interactive category subclasses.

The QoS scheme extends beyond the 3GPP QoS framework for the provider. The network must also support traffic for the Iu interface types being transported. The QoS framework for all traffic in the provider network for 3G Release 99 through Release 5/6 is discussed in the following sections.

5.31 Quality-of-Service Mapping for 2.5G and 3G Release 99

The interface mappings shown in Figure 5.50 and Table 5.2 give an example of ways in which a provider may map the IP precedence and MPLS EXP bits at the edge of the network for the 2.5G and 3G Release 99 mobile standards.

Note that the 2.5G and 3G GGSN may be the same device; however, as discussed previously, separating these devices is common practice with providers implementing the 3G road map.

3GPP Class	DiffServ	DSCP	IP Prec	MPLS Exp
Routing/Signaling	AF	48	6	6
Conversational	EF	40	5	5
Streaming	AF	32	4	4
Interactive Gold	AF	24	3	3
Interactive Silver	AF	16	2	2
Interactive Bronze	AF	8	1	1
Background	BE	0	0	0

Figure 5.49: Mobile Network Seven-Class QoS Model

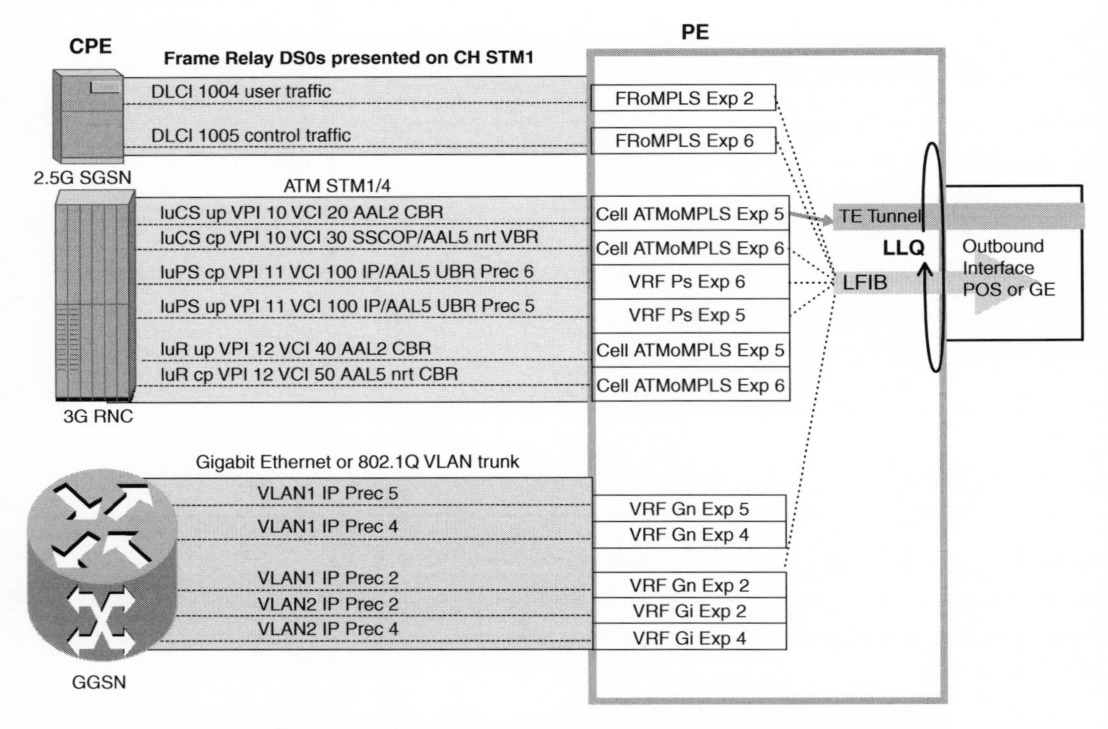

Figure 5.50: Mobile Network Edge QoS Mapping for 3G Release 99

Table 5.2: QoS Mapping for 2.5G and 3G Release 99

Release	Interface Name	Interface Type	QoS Requirement	IP Prec/MPLS EXP
2.5G GSM	Um	Air/radio	N/A	
	Abis	TDM	N/A	
	A	TDM	N/A	
	Gb	Frame Relay	User traffic Control traffic	2 6
	Gn	IP	User traffic	2
	Gi	IP	User traffic	2
3G Release 99	Uu	Air/radio	N/A	
	Iub	ATM AAL2/5 E1	MTOP N/A	
	A	TDM	N/A	
	IuCS	ATM AAL5 ATM AAL2	Control plane User plane	6 5
	IuPS	ATM AAL5	Control plane User plane	6 5
	IuR	ATM AAL5 ATM AAL2	Control plane User plane	6 5

Continued

Table 5.2 **Continued**

Release	Interface Name	Interface Type	QoS Requirement	IP Prec/MPLS EXP
	Gn	IP	Conversational	5
			Streaming	4
			Interactive 1	3
			Interactive 2	2
			Interactive 3	1
			Background	0
	Gi	IP	Conversational	5
			Streaming	4
			Interactive 1	3
			Interactive 2	2
			Interactive 3	1
			Background	0

The Gb interface between the SGSN and the BSC is represented on the SGSN only in the diagram for simplicity. Likewise, the Gn interface between the SGSN and the GGSN is shown on the GGSN only. The MGW is not shown as the Iu-CS interface is represented on the RNC device and the interface from the MGW to the MSC is TDM; hence QoS is not required.

The Gn and Gi VRF show multiple VLANs and IP precedence or DSCP settings. This is vendor dependent and has been shown as an example. Likewise, the mapping for VPI and VCI from the RNC, and the Frame Relay DCLI's from the 2.5 GGSN is to illustrate the QoS principle only.

Note that the seven-class model from the previous section is used for the QoS mapping.

5.32 Quality-of-Service Mapping for 3G Release 4

The interface mappings in Figure 5.51 and Table 5.3 give an example of ways in which a provider may map the IP precedence and MPLS EXP bits at the edge of the network for the 3G Release 4 mobile standards.

The RNC, GGSN, and SGSN interfaces are identical to those in the previous section. The MGW requires ATM and Ethernet interface types for the Release 4 specifications. The Nc interface between the MGW and the MSC server is shown on the MSC server only.

5.33 Quality-of-Service Mapping for 3G Release 5

The interface mappings in Figure 5.52 and Table 5.4 give an example of ways in which a provider may map the IP precedence and MPLS EXP bits at the edge of the network for the 3G Release 5 mobile standards.

The GGSN, SGSN, and MSC server interfaces are identical to those in the previous sections. The 3G RNC Iu-PS and Iu-CS interfaces are IP based over Ethernet interfaces. The IuR interface is shown as IP; however, it may be ATM or IP according to the standards.

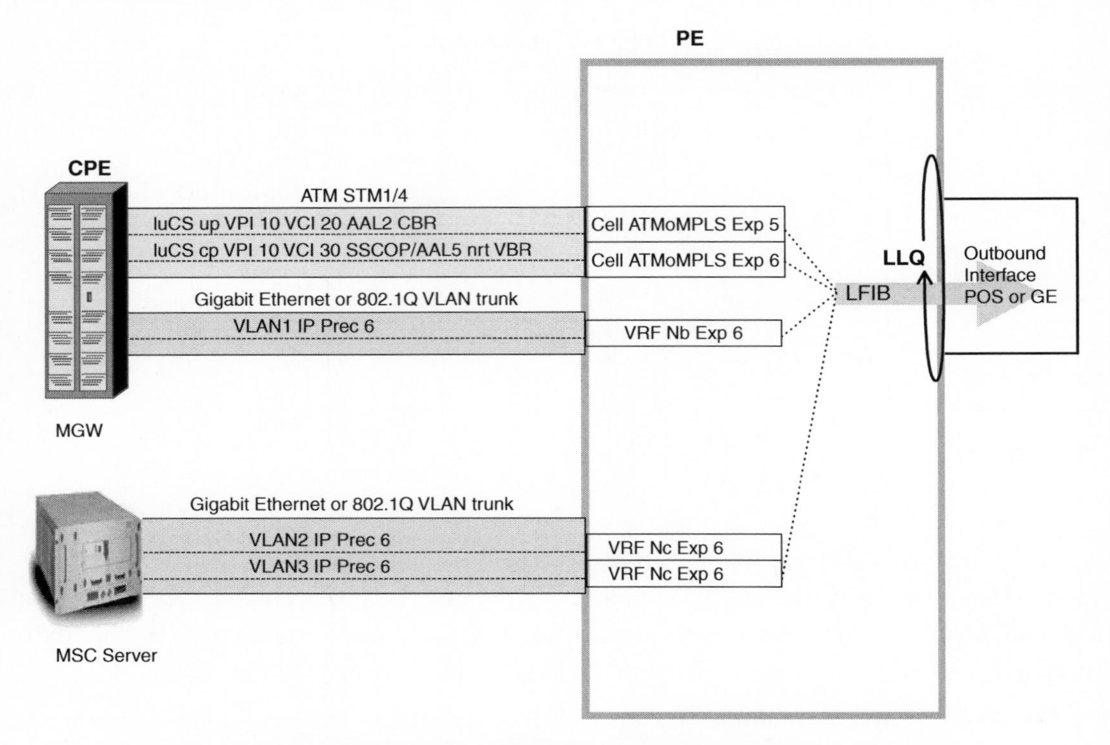

Figure 5.51: Mobile Network Edge QoS Mapping for 3G Release 4

Table 5.3: QoS Mapping for 2.5G and 3G Release 4

Release	Interface Name	Interface Type	QoS Requirement	IP Prec/MPLS EXP
3G Release 4	Uu	Air/radio	N/A	
	Iub	ATM AAL2/5 E1	MTOP N/A	
	A	TDM	N/A	
	IuCS	ATM AAL5 ATM AAL2	Control plane User plane	6 5
	IuPS	ATM AAL5	Control plane User plane	6 5
	IuR	ATM AAL5 ATM AAL2	Control plane User plane	6 5
	Gn	IP	Conversational Streaming Interactive 1 Interactive 2 Interactive 3 Background	5 4 3 2 1 0

Continued

Table 5.3 *Continued*

Release	Interface Name	Interface Type	QoS Requirement	IP Prec/MPLS EXP
	Gi	IP	Conversational Streaming Interactive 1 Interactive 2 Interactive 3 Background	5 4 3 2 1 0
	Nb	IP	Signaling	6
	Nc	IP	Signaling	6
	Mc	IP	Signaling	6

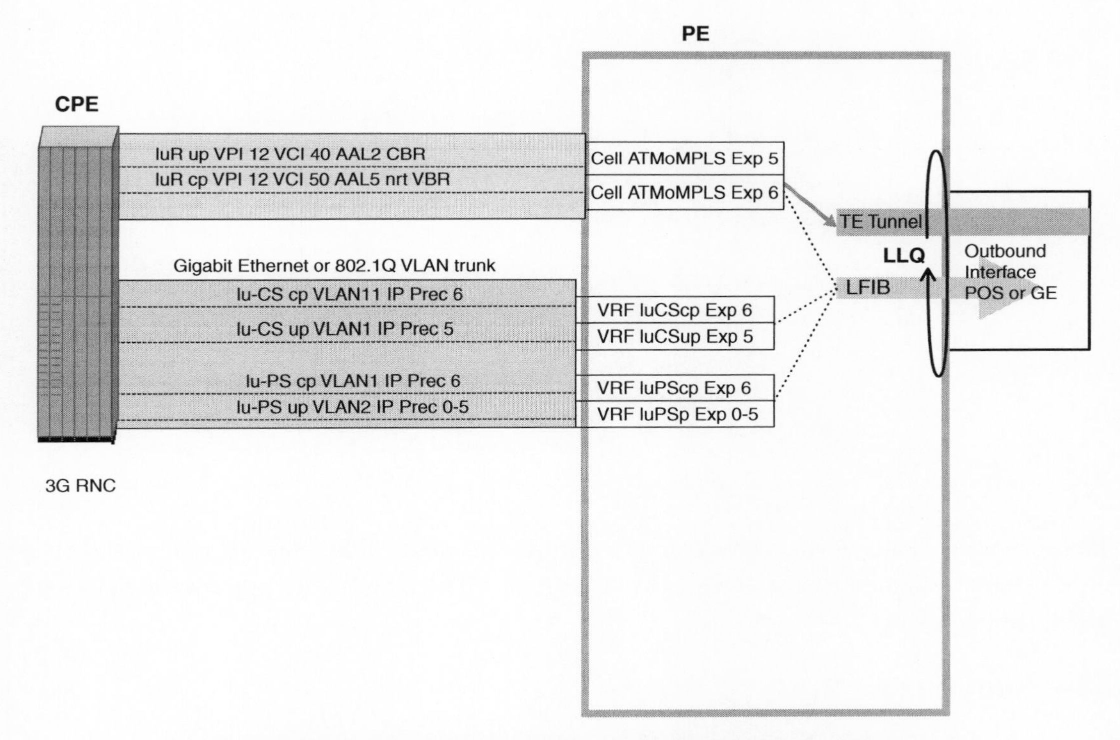

Figure 5.52: Mobile Network Edge QoS Mapping for 3G Release 5

Table 5.4: QoS Mapping for 3G Release 5

Release	Interface Name	Interface Type	QoS Requirement	IP Prec/MPLS EXP
3G Release 5	Uu	Air/Radio	N/A	
	Iub	ATM AAL2/5 E1	MTOP N/A	
	A	TDM	N/A	
	IuCS	IP	Control plane	6

Continued

Table 5.4 Continued

Release	Interface Name	Interface Type	QoS Requirement	IP Prec/MPLS EXP
		IP	User plane	5
	IuPS	IP	Control plane Conversational Streaming Interactive 1 Interactive 2 Interactive 3 Background	6 5 4 3 2 1 0
	IuR	ATM AAL5 ATM AAL2	Control plane User plane	6 5
	Gn	IP	Conversational Streaming Interactive 1 Interactive 2 Interactive 3 Background	5 4 3 2 1 0
	Gi	IP	Conversational Streaming Interactive 1 Interactive 2 Interactive 3 Background	5 4 3 2 1 0
	Nb	IP	Signaling	6
	Nc	IP	Signaling	6
	Mc	IP	Signaling	6

The Iu-PS user plane interface now carries the traffic based on 3GPP classification based on conversational, streaming, interactive, and background. The DSCP or IP precedence markings will be applied by the RNC.

5.34 Summary

The mobile provider network is rapidly evolving toward an end-to-end IP infrastructure. The mobile network is an important aspect of the NGN vision driving toward a single converged infrastructure.

This chapter identified the key architectural standards in the 3G evolution, from 2.5G networks through the full IP as defined in 3G Release 5 onward. The expansion of IP/MPLS into the mobile space has been explored, together with the appropriate QoS framework for ensuring successful mobile network execution throughout the 3G evolution road map.

Subsequent chapters in this book give details of recommended configurations required to implement the QoS framework as defined.

CHAPTER 6

QoS Service Assurance

6.1 Overview

This section focuses on creating an understanding of a critical topic known as *service assurance*. The importance of analyzing key metrics and creating a baseline for measuring QoS and application performance is the objective of this chapter. This chapter does not focus on specific tools and software for achieving the same; those are addressed in Chapter 13, "Performance Monitoring and Measurement." Furthermore, this chapter will help you identify some of the key requirements to look for in a tool or software that is to be used for service assurance.

6.2 Revisiting Service-Level Agreements

Providers are under increasing pressure to offer SLAs to their customers (enterprises) and to verify and measure outsourced SLAs. SPs have an incentive to offer SLAs, improve customer satisfaction, and guarantee their customers certain service levels. Management requires contractual assurance that the network will meet business objectives; end users want some assurance that their critical network applications and services will be available as needed. A service-level verification is often required before a company will deploy a new technology, business critical applications, or IP service such as voice over IP (VoIP). It can be difficult to determine exactly what to monitor, how to take measurements, and how frequently to collect data. With the proliferation of heterogeneous and multiservice networks, it is also difficult to monitor the service from end to end. The challenge is compounded by the need to demarcate the timing of problems and to provide customers with reports at the appropriate level of granularity.

Figure 6.1 illustrates a sample framework used by SPs to build end-customer SLAs.

In developing SLAs, it is critical that SPs focus on translating business objectives to SLAs so that tangible service metrics are measured, reported, and validated. Long, complex, and unrealistic agreements are often to blame when SPs fail to manage by service level. They also have a tendency to fail to monitor the negotiated SLAs parameters. A clear understanding of the objective and proper validation of key aspects (some of them given here) is critical prior to building SLAs. For example:

- Verify that the SLA accurately measures delay in both the SP access and core network. This calculation should include all delays in the network, which include serialization, propagation, and switching delays.

Typical Customer Site SLA

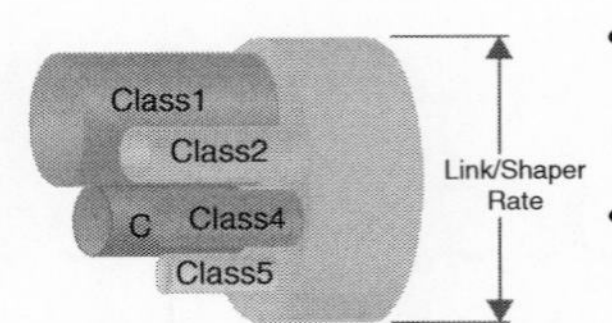

Class	Committed Bandwidth	Delay	Jitter	Loss
Real-time	X	Low	Low	Low
Interactive	Y	Low	*NA*	Low
Business	Z	*NA*	*NA*	Low
Best-Effort	*NA*	*NA*	*NA*	*NA*

- Typically from three to five classes (Real-Time, Video, Interactive, Business, Best-Effort)
- Delay, jitter, and loss guarantees for conforming real-time traffic
- Combination of delay and loss guarantees for data traffic
- Sum of committed bandwidth (per-class CIR) not to exceed link/shaper rate
- Additional classes not visible to customer may exist (e.g., management, control traffic)

Figure 6.1: Sample SLA Framework

- Understand the minimum required delay, packet-loss ratios, and jitter values for the various application types. Also an understanding of the acceptable performance values (which might be an increase by a delta), which help in having a leeway and some amount of margin to operate while building end-customer SLAs.
- Derive an engineering SLA (also called an *internal SP SLA*), which typically consists of more aggressive threshold values. The network should adhere to this SLA under all conditions. However, the engineering SLA should not be marketed to the end customer. For instance, if a given service demands 200 ms of delay, the internal SLA should be designed to probably achieve 175 ms, thus providing a buffer of 25 ms that could come in handy due to unforeseen outages or failures in the SP network.
- Develop a service SLA, which is offered to the end customer. There should not be any violations to this SLA, since this would ideally be a contractual agreement between the SP and the customer.
- Appropriate performance management and baselining tools for developing and managing SLAs need to be deployed.
- Web-based tools that can generate performance reports for the various metrics, which can be viewed on a periodic basis, need to be deployed. The tools are used to facilitate end customers in verifying the SP's SLA adherence and are considered critical.

6.3 Calculating Delay

Having discussed the need to estimate metrics that influence SLAs, this section provides information on understanding delay calculations. We take an example of real-time traffic (voice and video) and assess the impact of the various elements that influence delay for this class.

This is a manual method of achieving a reasonably close figure on delays in an SP network, and there are automated tools that help in the calculation of various SLA metrics. However, the objective of this section is to provide an insight into this process.

Examining this further: In IP backbone terms, network one-way delay characterizes the time difference between the reception of an IP packet at an ingress point of presence (POP) and its transmission at an egress POP. Network and service one-way delays are made up of the following components:

- *Propagation delay.* Propagation delay is constrained by the speed of light in a medium and for optical fiber is around 5 ms per 1000 km. Propagation delay can vary as network topology changes—when a link fails, for example, or when an underlying network (e.g., SDH/SONET) reroutes its circuit paths.
- *Switching delay.* Switching or processing delay is the time difference between receiving a packet on an incoming router interface and the enqueuing of the packet in the scheduler of its outbound interface. Switching delays on today's high-performance routers are negligible, typically on the order of 10–20 μs per packet.
- *Scheduling delay.* Scheduling (or queuing) delay is defined as the time difference between the enqueuing of a packet on the outbound interface scheduler and the start of clocking the packet onto the outbound link. This is a function of the scheduling algorithm used and of the scheduler queue utilization, which is in turn a function of the queue capacity and the offered traffic load and profile. This effect is analyzed in more detail later in this chapter.
- *Serialization delay.* Serialization delay is the time taken to clock a packet onto a link and is dependent on the link speed and the packet size. Serialization delay is considered negligible at link speeds above STM-1/OC3.
- *Service delays.* These delays are caused by end-user equipment.

The goal commonly used in designing networks to support real-time applications is a delay budget of 150 ms. A design should apportion this budget to the various components of network delay (propagation delay through the backbone, scheduling delay due to congestion, and the access link serialization delay) and service delays. Propagation delay is often budgeted for using the widest diameter in the network, which, for example, in a national network in the United States would give a worst case (coast-to-coast) of 6000 km or 30 ms of one-way propagation delay.

Figure 6.2 illustrates the various types of delay introduced in each point of an SP NGN infrastructure, starting from the CPE (a.k.a. customer edge routers) to the label edge routers (LERs, a.k.a. PE routers) and label switch routers (LSRs, a.k.a. provider routers).

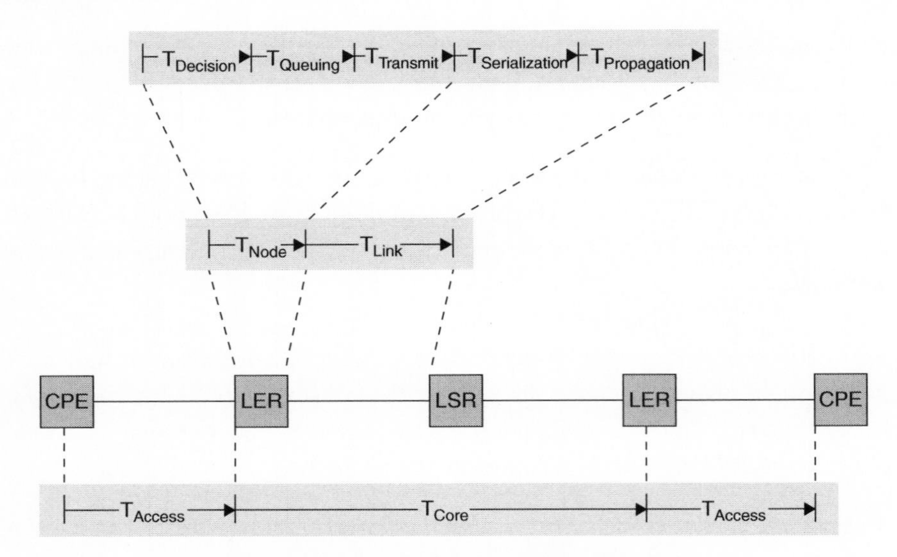

Figure 6.2: End-to-End Delay Segments

6.3.1 Uncongested Delay on Backbone Routers: Dealing with the Laws of Physics

As we discuss the design of backbone routers, we first ask the question, "What is acceptable delay for an uncongested router to add to a packet?" Essentially we are looking at how much time the router must spend processing the packet: optical to electrical conversions, packet header parsing, performing the packet lookup, internal queuing, any backplane or switch fabric transmissions, and ultimately, a conversion back from electrical to optical and the transmission onto the destination interface. We measure this independently from any actual queuing behavior: At this point we're simply interested in how fast the router can move a packet from one side of the box to the other. From testing, we know that the worst-case uncongested delay of the Cisco 12000 and 7600 series routers is on the order of 20–200 microseconds (a microsecond is a millionth of a second, or one thousandth of a millisecond). On the CRS-1 routers, the uncongested delay is higher, measuring between 50–500 microseconds. Why such a difference? In essence, we're looking at a function of the device complexity and the laws of physics; the CRS-1 is significantly more complex from a hardware standpoint than the Cisco 12000 and 7600 series. However, this does not include propagation delays, as the platform does not play a role in altering this delay.

The larger number of ASICs that provide more complex features and the highly scalable switch fabric also mean the packet has more "steps" in the forwarding chain. This accounts for the difference that we see in the two devices. That being said, it's important to look at this added delay in relationship to the overall delay budget of the network. If we look at the worst-case scenarios, as illustrated in Figure 6.3, that is, by looking at the Cisco CRS-1 or Cisco 12000/7600 routers and assume that we have 20 of these routers in the network path, we're looking at uncongested delay addition of no more than 1000 microseconds

propagation delay added by 1000km of optical fiber	500ms
propagation delay added by 100km of optical fiber	50ms
propagation delay added by 10km of optical fiber	5ms
typical uncongested delay of the c12000 system	4ms
worst-case uncongested delay of the c12000 system	20ms
typical uncongested delay of the CRS-1 system	30ms
worst-case uncongested delay of the CRS-1 system	50ms
1 MTU (1500B) queueing latency @ GigabitEthernet (1000Mbps)	1.2ms
1 MTU (1500B) queueing latency @ OC3/STM1 (155Mbps)	7.7ms
1 MTU (1500B) queueing latency @ DS3 (45Mbps)	26.6ms
1 MTU (1500B) queueing latency @ T1 (1.544Mbps)	777.2ms
1 MTU (1500B) queueing latency @ 256kbps (fractional T1)	4689ms
1 MTU (1500B) queueing latency @ 64kbps (1xDS0)	18750ms

Figure 6.3: Various Components of Delay

(50 microseconds × 20 routers); this substitutes to only a very small amount of the entire delay budget of real-time traffic (which requires 150 ms). Let's put this in perspective: Light propagates through optical fiber at about 200 km each millisecond, meaning that a 1000 km fiber run adds as much delay to the system as *10* routers in the worst case. Our point is fairly simple: The addition of even a couple hundred microseconds by a router has virtually zero impact on the real-world quality of the network. If this is the case, the router is typically never the bottleneck in terms of achieving latencies as per SLAs. The two important factors to look out for in this case are propagation delays and delays introduced by transport equipment such as the optical ADM switches.

6.3.2 Congested Delay on Backbone Routers: Dealing with the Laws of Physics

As we look at router designs, a far more important measure of service impact is the way that the device deals with a congested environment—one in which the router is forced to not only do the basic packet-forwarding functions but also to smartly manage multiple queues with packets from various classes of service. It is in this environment where the design and implementation of router QoS becomes critically important. Backbone routers platforms such as the Cisco 12000 and the CRS-1 systems utilized a fully hardware-based queuing system that provides a strict-priority scheme for high-value traffic. The hardware in both devices is capable of making packet-scheduling decisions at wire rate on a packet-by-packet basis; this allows the system to ensure that traffic in the low-latency/high-priority queue is always serviced immediately. If we have this type of queuing system, the worst-case scenario becomes one in which a low-latency/high-priority packet arrives immediately after we begin transmitting a low-priority packet. In less ideal queuing schemes, the system may be unable to immediately schedule the LLQ/priority packet, resulting in more than one low-priority packet getting "in the way" of the important traffic. The strict-priority scheduler of the Cisco 12000 and the CRS-1 guarantees that only one packet-time (i.e., 1 MTU) of delay is introduced for priority/LLQ traffic. Again, for the purposes of comparison, Figure 6.3 shows some components of delay (all measured in microseconds for consistency).

Looking at these numbers, we can see that the uncongested delay of any modern hardware-based routing system is orders of magnitude lower than the end-to-end delay budget. However, looking at the serialization delay on a very slow link, it becomes clear that optimizing the behavior of the queuing system under congested situations is actually far more important. Rather than being concerned with a few hundred microseconds, SPs need to be careful that on low-speed links the queuing system introduces as little delay as possible and that an improperly configured or designed system is not introducing tens of milliseconds into the system.

6.4 Calculating Jitter

It is well known that to contain jitter, real-time traffic should not exceed a certain percentage of the line bandwidth. This percentage varies in different studies, from as low as about 15 percent to as high as nearly 70 percent, and a consistent recommendation is difficult to obtain. However, many service providers try not to allocate more than 33 percent of the link bandwidth for real-time traffic.

Network congestion is another important factor that has a bearing on jitter and needs to be kept under control. As a general practice, SPs need to look at bandwidth upgrades when the link utilization exceeds around 70 percent. Several tools can also be used to proactively run probes in a live network (in a nondestructive manner) to determine the jitter in both SP access and core networks. The maximum jitter can never exceed the maximum delay in the network; it can also be used as a simple mechanism to create a jitter budget.

6.5 Calculating Packet Loss

Packet loss can be caused by a number of factors, including signal degradation over the network medium, oversaturated network links, corrupted packets rejected in transit, faulty networking hardware, or maligned system drivers or network applications, or it can even be caused by normal routing routines. When caused by network problems, lost or dropped packets can result in highly noticeable performance issues or jitter with streaming technologies, VoIP, online gaming, and other video applications and will affect all other network applications to a degree.

Some network transport protocols such as TCP provide for reliable delivery of packets. In the event of packet loss, the receiver asks for retransmission or the sender automatically resends any segments that have not been acknowledged. Although TCP can recover from packet loss, retransmitting missing packets causes the throughput of the connection to decrease. This drop in throughput is due to the sliding window protocols used for acknowledgment of received packets. In certain variants of TCP, if a transmitted packet is lost, it will be resent along with every packet that had been sent after it. This retransmission causes the overall throughput of the connection to drop. It is worthy to note that too many retransmissions can increase both delay and jitter for real-time applications. Protocols such as UDP provide no recovery for lost packets. Applications that use UDP are typically designed to handle this type of packet loss. However, it might differ based on the application and it could vary on a case-by-case basis.

From a QoS perspective, typically packet loss is controlled by assigning traffic to high-priority queues such as the strict-priority/LLQ, which ensures that such traffic is forwarded ahead of others in the event of network congestion. That said, this does not justify the existence of network congestion over long periods, because congestion can alter the behavior of every traffic class and have its own side effects. Furthermore, traffic that is very sensitive to packet loss, such as voice and video, is never configured in QoS classes that permit early packet discard techniques such as WRED.

Link failures in the network are another important factor that causes packet loss. The time to converge after a failure can determine the amount of packet loss in the network. Voice traffic, for instance, typically requires a "zero" percent packet loss, and if the network suffers an outage for a long period, it can have a severe bearing on overall performance. SPs typically deploy fast convergence features such as MPLS Traffic Engineering and IGP Fast Convergence to achieve subsecond convergence in the network. When deployed, these features are known to react to a failure within 50–100 ms and help in reducing packet loss to a very negligible level or even to none, depending on the network configuration.

Therefore the key to building a successful SLA is to have a periodic and comprehensive assessment of the network infrastructure based on the three key metrics of delay, jitter, and packet loss, prior to building end-customer SLAs.

6.6 The Need for Performance Management

Many SPs suffer poor credibility with customers because the business value of the IT investment on services or outsourcing is not rewarding. Proper processes and procedures are needed to improve operational efficiency and restore credibility. Efficiency can be achieved via proven processes as well as attention to technologies that automate execution of these processes.

Performance management is the process of converting raw IP traffic measurements into meaningful performance measures. It can be divided into real-time (or near-real-time/short-term) and long-term management. Real-time performance management typically includes snapshots of the behavior of bottleneck network elements (e.g., backbone link elements that affect the operation of the entire network) as well as mission-critical applications. It is intended for SPs to make certain that network capacity is used efficiently by the mission-critical applications most important to the business (e.g., the most profitable services).

The real-time performance management process is a mechanism of constant monitoring of high-priority customer services (e.g., voice and video) as well as customers who have been complaining about the performance of their services.

Long-term performance management, on the other hand, supports studies that monitor the ability of the existing IP networks to meet service objectives. The purpose of this type of study is to identify situations in which corrective planning is necessary. This is needed when objectives are not being satisfied and, where possible, to provide early warning of potential service degradation so that a corrective plan can be formulated before service is affected.

Typically, raw traffic measurements are collected, validated by data collection systems (or element management systems), and then stored in batch mode in a database. One of the most critical steps in developing comprehensive management methods is to define the required traffic measurements that are the basis for performance, fault, and service-level agreements (SLAs). Examples of IP performance raw traffic measurements include:

- Number of packets received per interface
- Number of packets transmitted per interface
- Number of packets dropped due to mild congestion per interface
- Number of packets dropped due to severe congestion per interface
- Number of packets dropped due to protocol errors
- Amount of time a network element is in a mild congestion state
- Amount of time a network element is in a severe congestion state
- Number of times a network element enters a mild congestion state
- Number of times a network element enters a severe congestion state

6.7 Performance Management Tools and Software

End-to-end performance monitoring can be extremely useful as a proactive method for both rapid troubleshooting and performance management of SP networks. It has been successfully implemented to quickly identify and resolve the myriad performance issues associated with networks, servers, and applications.

The use of end-to-end performance-monitoring tools can uncover serious inefficiencies with poorly designed applications and badly designed networks. They can provide the "big-picture" view of networks and applications, answering questions that are critical for the end-user (enterprise) perspective and experience: "What impact will outsourcing my hosted applications have on my users?" "Which will work better on my network, thick or thin clients?" "Is the SP delivering the SLA as promised?" and "Which web pages are the slowest to download?" This method offers drill-down troubleshooting capabilities to reveal metrics that can save you weeks or months of time in identifying and resolving issues.

Analyses that previously required weeks to complete with packet-sniffing tools can be accomplished in minutes when end-to-end performance-monitoring appliances are properly configured. Because they continuously monitor applications, such tools notice and report even difficult intermittent issues that cannot readily be reproduced. If a problem occurred at 3:00 a.m. the previous day, their stored reports can be used for a post-mortem analysis. There is no need to wait for a recurrence to capture the behavior, as legacy troubleshooting tools require. End-to-end performance-monitoring appliances with intelligent thresholds can alert the various SP operations teams to a developing problem before end customers are severely impacted.

In essence, proactive management allows you to discover new ways to optimize the network—they can "find new money" at a time when you need it most. Not all end-to-end performance-monitoring offerings are created equal. Some are focused on a specific task or application that limits their broader value. Others focus on providing a comprehensive portfolio of elements that can monitor various applications, give metrics for SLA adherence, provide intelligent thresholds and performance maps, and finally, act as a proactive agent in helping the SP make an informed decision on capacity planning.

The following discussion presents some of the key offerings of performance management systems.

6.8 Network Investigations

6.8.1 Measuring Delay

Performance management tools bring in the ability to create delay and loss maps of the network. Typically, performance management systems have the ability to set incident-based thresholds to detect degradation of performance within networks due to retransmissions. Some of the reasons for retransmissions could be congestion on the network, physical errors, and overloaded devices. An SP may use this information prior to offering SLAs across a given path in the network or indeed look at this information as a baseline for future capacity planning.

6.8.2 Measuring Packet Loss

Performance management also includes the ability to determine packet-loss percentage across the various paths in the network. Figure 6.4 shows a sample output revealing the top 25 customer regions (sites connected across the SP network) with the worst loss. Packet-loss percentage is defined as the percentage of data lost on the monitored network and the loss rate in packets/second. Loss is perceived when seeing either the same sequence number twice or seeing a gap in the sequence numbers. High loss rates may be caused by errors or congestion;

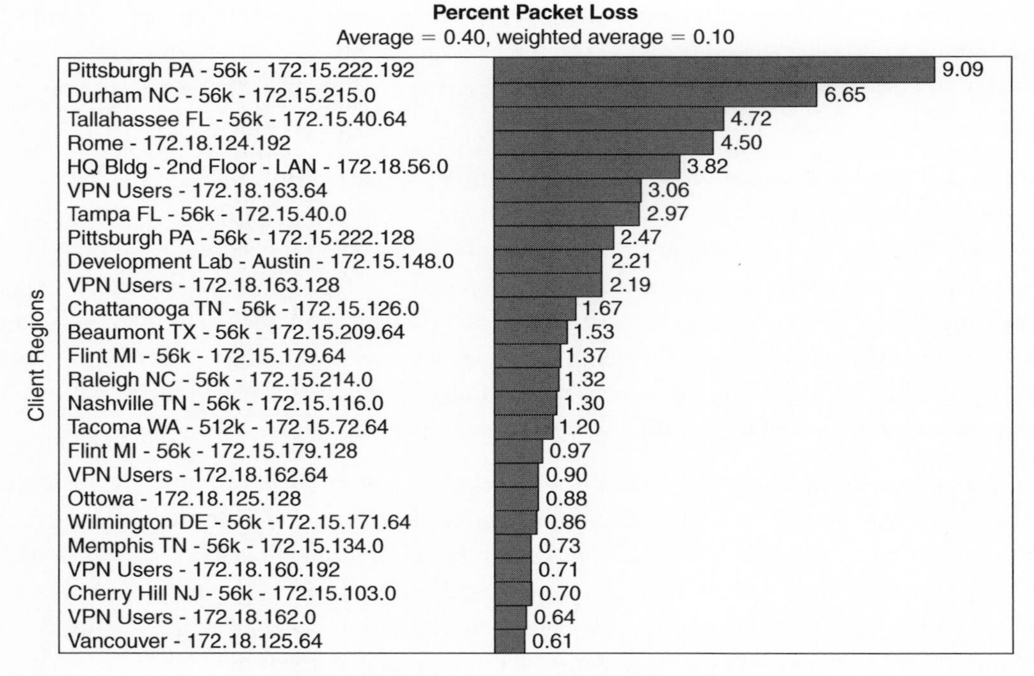

Figure 6.4: Baselining Network Packet Loss

in either case they represent significant inefficiencies and opportunities for improvement. Packet loss not only causes the data to be retransmitted, it causes TCP to reduce the window size, which slows the transfer time for future packets. Retransmitted packets increase the load on the network. In the example, the productivity of users in Pittsburgh, PA, 172.15.222.192 in Figure 6.4, is severely limited because of the network conditions.

6.8.3 Measuring Application Responses

Another common practice is to baseline network services such as VoIP and video. Apart from delay and packet loss, described earlier in this chapter, it is important to measure the amount of jitter for such traffic types. Performance management tools typically have the ability to measure the variance in interpacket delay in both directions (source to destination and destination to source). The probes used by such tools ideally send out a series of packets at a specified interval. The timestamps and sequence numbers of those packets and the responses to those packets are collected and used to calculate the variance in the packet delay. This measurement is useful in verifying solid VoIP and video-based services and the packet loss. Figure 6.5 illustrates a sample report created for measuring jitter for voice and video applications.

6.9 Summary

This chapter provided an overview of the need for a holistic approach toward managing SLAs and creating baseline information for trend analysis. Performance management is

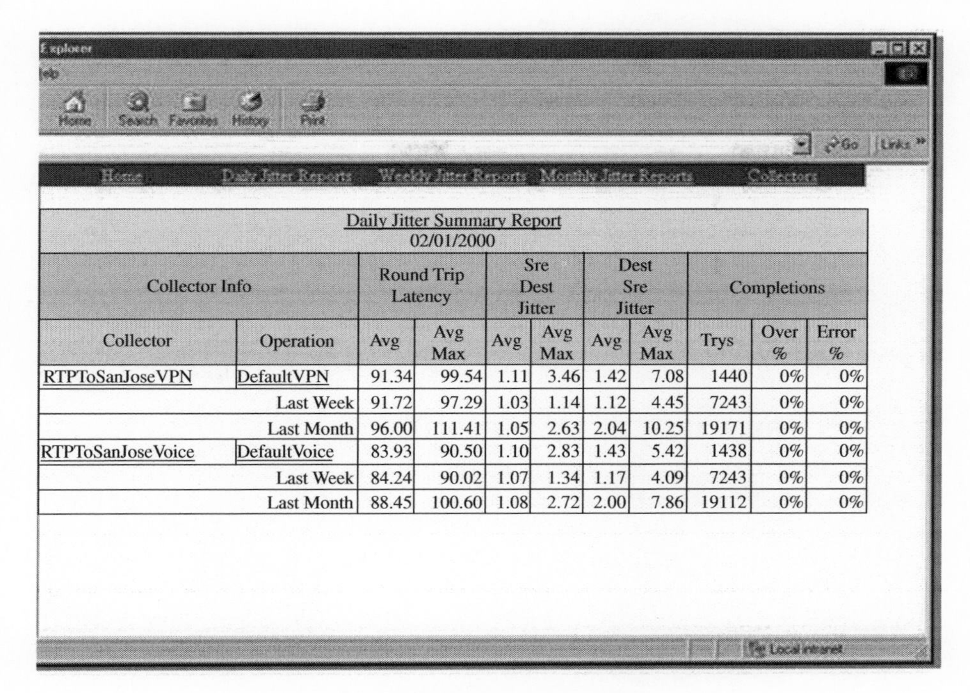

Daily Jitter Summary Report
02/01/2000

Collector Info		Round Trip Latency		Sre Dest Jitter		Dest Sre Jitter		Completions		
Collector	Operation	Avg	Avg Max	Avg	Avg Max	Avg	Avg Max	Trys	Over %	Error %
RTPToSanJoseVPN	DefaultVPN	91.34	99.54	1.11	3.46	1.42	7.08	1440	0%	0%
	Last Week	91.72	97.29	1.03	1.14	1.12	4.45	7243	0%	0%
	Last Month	96.00	111.41	1.05	2.63	2.04	10.25	19171	0%	0%
RTPToSanJoseVoice	DefaultVoice	83.93	90.50	1.10	2.83	1.43	5.42	1438	0%	0%
	Last Week	84.24	90.02	1.07	1.34	1.17	4.09	7243	0%	0%
	Last Month	88.45	100.60	1.08	2.72	2.00	7.86	19112	0%	0%

Figure 6.5: Baselining Jitter

an integral part of validating a QoS framework and plays a pivotal role in helping an organization periodically reassess its QoS needs. For instance, trend analysis aids a service provider that intends to deploy a new application or service, because available baseline information serves as a quick reference in making a decision as to whether the available resources or QoS deployment would serve the purpose. In effect, this aspect of performance management complements the process of capacity planning. More on the available tools and configurations on this topic are covered in Chapter 13, "Performance Monitoring and Measurement."

CHAPTER 7

Cisco CRS-1, 12000, 7600, and ASR1000 Router Architecture

7.1 Overview

This chapter focuses on the architecture of the Carrier Routing System (CRS), 12000, 7600, and Aggregation Services Router ASR1000 series router platforms. These platforms represent the best of core, Ethernet, and edge routers available to service providers building a high-performance, highly available network infrastructure.

The chapter presents an overview of the chassis, line card options, architecture, switch fabric, and QoS implementation.

7.2 Cisco Carrier Routing System Series Routers

The Carrier Routing System (CRS) is Cisco's next-generation core router family. The CRS platform is a carrier-grade, fully distributed, modular architecture that can be a standalone router, starting with 640 gigabits for second (Gbps) capacity through to a multishelf system, interconnecting through a central switch fabric shelf, providing capacity up to 92 terabits per second (Tbps).

There are three basic chassis options available in the CRS series: the CRS-4/S, CRS-8/S, and CRS-16/S. There is also a multichassis option available, enabled by a dedicated switch fabric shelf called the CRS-Multi-Chassis (MC), to extend the total throughput capacity to 92 Tbps.

Figure 7.1 shows the three basic chassis and the multichassis.

The chassis and high-level specifications are as follows:

- CRS-16/S: 1.2 Tbit/s, 16-slot 40 G/slot line-card chassis
- CRS-8/S: 640 Gbit/s, eight-slot 40 G/slot line-card chassis
- CRS-4/S: 320 Gbit/s, four-slot 40 G/slot line-card chassis
- CRS-MC: Switch fabric capable of scaling to 72 line-card chassis and eight-switch fabric chassis

The major components of the CRS platform are the Route Processor (RP), the optional Distributed Route Processor (DRP), the Modular Services Card, the Physical Line Interface Module or Shared Port Adaptor (SPA) Interface Processor (SIP), the chassis midplane and the three-stage switch fabric. Note that the SIP is also referred to as a Flexible MSC.

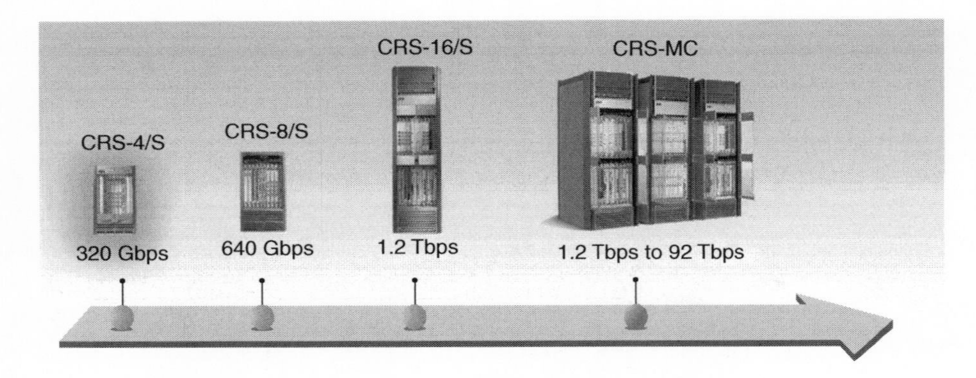

Figure 7.1: Cisco Carrier Routing System Series Routers

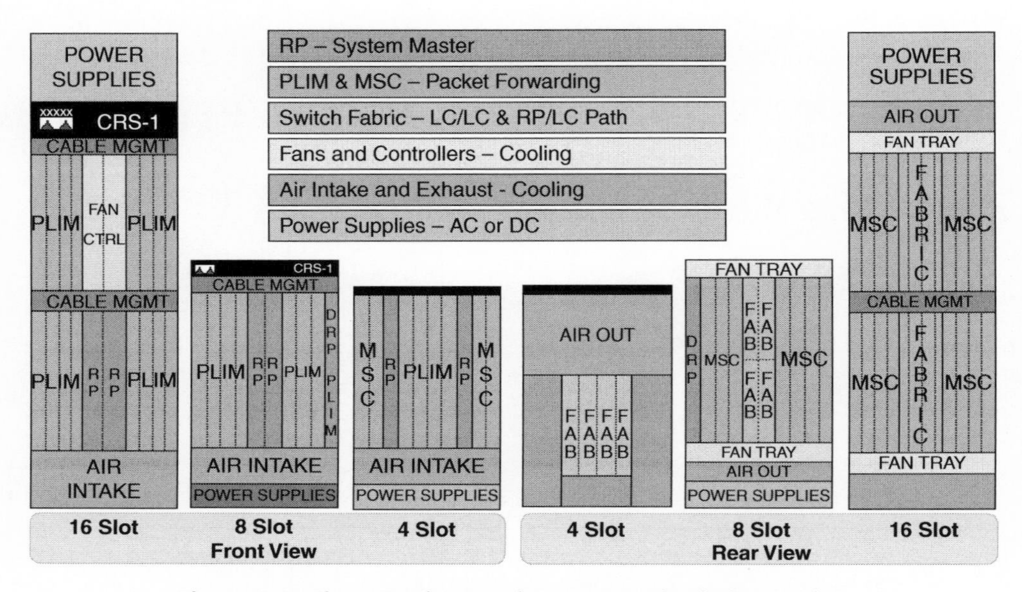

Figure 7.2: Cisco Carrier Routing System Physical Overview

Figure 7.2 shows each of the chassis options with physical configuration details.

The CRS 16-slot line-card chassis has the following specifications:

- Up to 16 line cards (modular services cards) that are inserted into the rear
- Up to 16 physical layer interface modules (PLIM or SIP) that are inserted into the front
- Two route processors (RPs) inserted into the front
- Two shelf controllers (SCs) inserted into the front
- Eight switch fabric cards inserted into the rear

The CRS eight-slot line-card chassis has the following specifications:

- Up to eight line cards (modular services cards) that are inserted into the rear
- Up to eight physical layer interface modules (PLIM or SIP) that are inserted into the front
- Two route processors (RPs) inserted into the front (note that when ordering the CRS 8 slot, you have to specify the redundant processor)
- Four switch fabric cards inserted into the rear; each fabric card comprises two switch fabric planes

The CRS four-slot line-card chassis has the following specifications:

- Up to four line cards (modular services cards) that are inserted into the front
- Up to four physical layer interface modules (PLIMs) that are inserted into the front
- Two route processors (RPs) inserted into the front
- Four switch fabric cards inserted into the rear; each fabric card comprises one switch fabric plane

7.2.1 CRS Series Routers Architecture

The CRS router is based on contemporary best practices for high-end router design. The CRS architecture is based on three key components: the Interconnect mechanism, the forwarding plane, and the control plane.

Figure 7.3 gives an overview of the CRS architecture.

Route processors are connected to the MSC via a switch fabric based on a three-stage Benes topology. This switch fabric design allows a modular approach to the switching fabric stages, allowing the CRS to scale from one line-card chassis to 72 line-card chassis. The CRS Multi Chassis can act as an external Stage 2 (S2) switching fabric, enabling scaling beyond a single line-card platform.

The following sections give an overview of the CRS components.

7.2.2 CRS Route Processor and Distributed Route Processor

The CRS Route Processor (RP) is responsible for the system initialization and operation, including coordination of the fabric, MSC, and PLIM boot processes. On booting, the RPs will negotiate to determine the primary controller.

The RP provides physical console access, management Ethernet, and boot media. There is an onboard disk for logging. The RP executes protocols, including BGP, OSPF, ISIS, EIGRP, RIP, LDP, and MPLS-TE. The RP uses these protocols to build forwarding tables that are downloaded to the MSC. Each RP includes two gigabit Ethernet ports specifically for multichassis control.

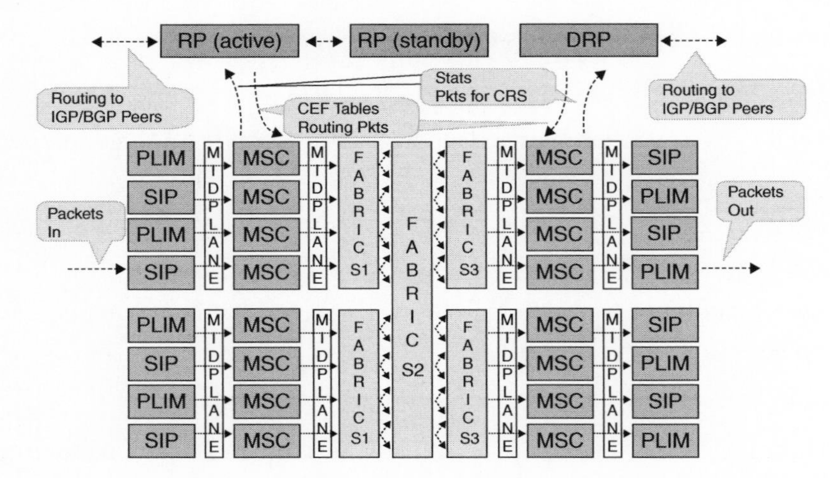

Figure 7.3: Cisco Carrier Routing System Architecture Overview

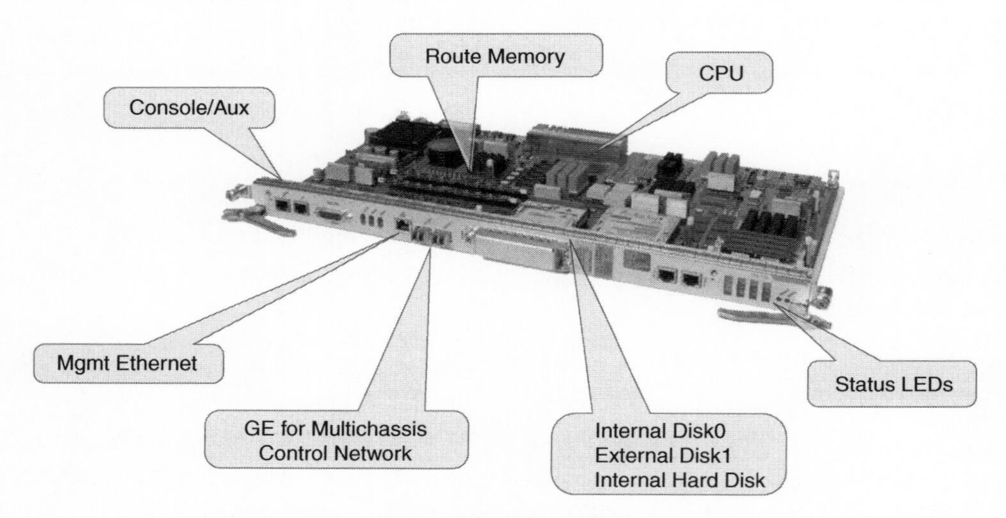

Figure 7.4: Cisco Carrier Routing System Route Processor

Figure 7.4 shows the CRS route processor hardware.

The RP is available in two models: the RP-8 and RP-16. Specifications for the RP options are given at the end of this section.

The CRS also supports a distributed route processor, which is used for process offload from the RP or to provide secure domain router (SDR) functionality. The SDR functionality effectively provides two additional routers on a single CRS chassis. The DRP is comprised of two cards, a DRP PLIM and DRP CPU, which can be inserted into any PLIM and MSC slot pair. The DRP has independent route memory, Flash, disk and dual CPUs.

Figure 7.5 shows the PLIM and CPU cards used as a single DRP.

Table 7.1 gives high-level specifications for the RP-8, RP-16, and DRP.

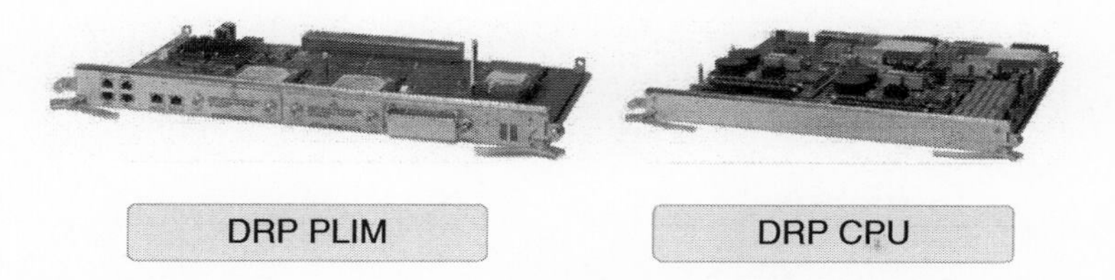

Figure 7.5: Cisco Carrier Routing System Distributed Route Processor

Table 7.1: CRS-1 RP and DRP Hardware Overview

	RP-8	RP-16	DRP
CPU	1 × 1.2 GHz PPC	2 × 800 MHz PPC (2 × 1.2 GHz in rev B)	2 × (2 × 1.2 GHz) PPC
Chassis support	CRS-1/8 CRS-1/4	CRS-1/16	All
Memory options	2–4 GB	2–4 GB	2 × 4 GB
Management Ethernet	1 × 10/100/1000	1 × 10/100/1000	2 × 10/100/1000
Flash PCMCIA	1 GB internal 1 GB external	1 GB internal 1 GB external	2 × 1 GB internal 2 × 1 GB external
Hard disk	40 GB	40 GB	2 × 40 GB

7.2.3 CRS Modular Services Card, Physical Line Interface Module, and SPA Interface Processor

Line cards are a combination of a Modular Services Card (MSC) and either a Physical Layer Interface Module (PLIM) or a Shared Port Adaptor (SPA) Interface Processor (SIP), connected via a midplane.

The MSC receives a routing forwarding table from active RP/DRP to enable ingress and egress packet forwarding for IPv4/v6 and MPLS. The MSC also performs packet forwarding, buffering, and features such as ACL, WRED, policing, MDRR, and other per-packet features. The MSC is responsible for sending and receiving packets on the switch fabric.

The PLIM or SIP, paired with MSC, implements OSI L1/L2 protocol requirements (see Figure 7.6).

The SIP module gives flexibility and investment protection to the network operator by allowing the use of Shared Port Adapter (SPA) modules for physical interfaces. The SPAs are a portfolio of interfaces interchangeable between a range of Cisco platforms, including the 7300, 10000, and XR12000 series routers. Based on a single architecture, SPAs offer the latest Layer 1 and Layer 2 technology across a broad array of transport types, including Ethernet (FE and GE), SONET (OC3-OC192), ATM, and channelized and copper interfaces.

The MSC effectively provides the processing power for the MSC/PLIM or SIP line-card pair. Figure 7.7 highlights the architecture of the MSC in the context of the CRS platform.

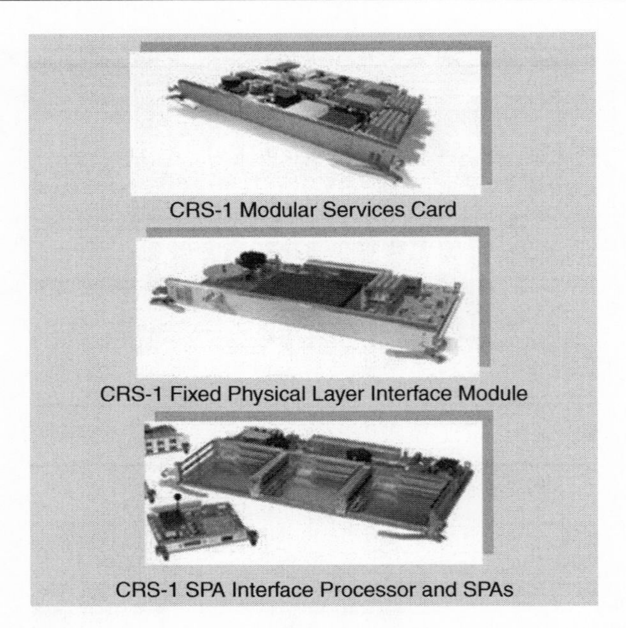

Figure 7.6: Cisco Carrier Routing System MSC, PLIM, and SIP Hardware

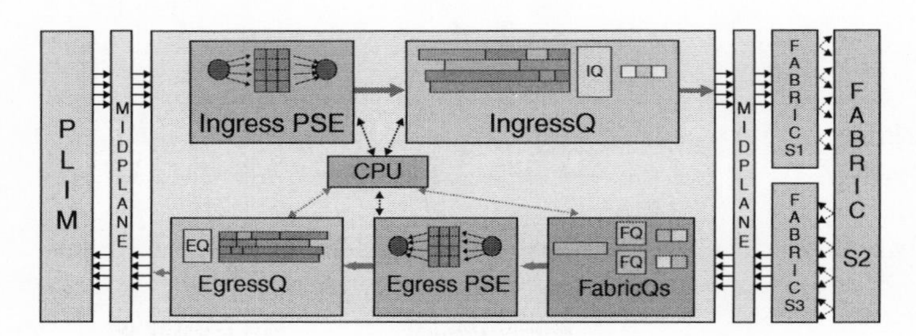

Figure 7.7: CRS Line-Card Architecture Overview

The function of the various components is as follows:

- *Ingress Packet Switching Engine (PSE).* Also referred to as Silicon Packet Processor (SPP). Packet receive forwarding and feature enforcement.
- *IngressQ.* Queuing and shaping for fabric cell segmentation.
- *FabricQs.* Fabric cell reassembly.
- *Egress Packet Switching Engine (PSE).* Packet transmit forwarding and feature enforcement.
- *EgressQ.* Queuing and shaping for transmitted packets.

As previously noted, the PLIM can be a fixed configuration in which the ports are not able to be changed, or it can be a flexible PLIM, also referred to as a SIP, where various interface types can be installed in the carrier card.

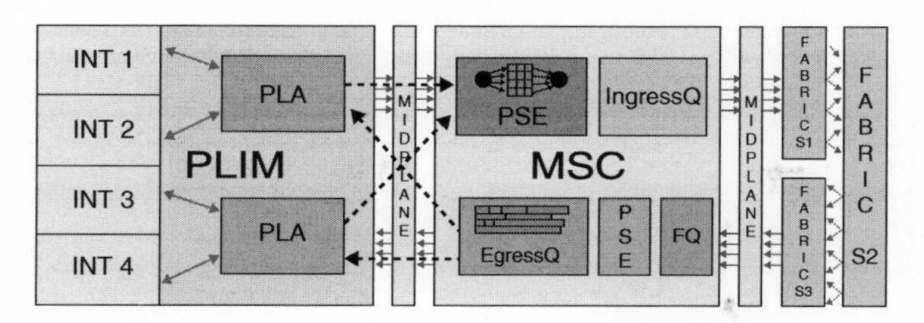

Figure 7.8: CRS Line Card with PLIM Architecture Overview

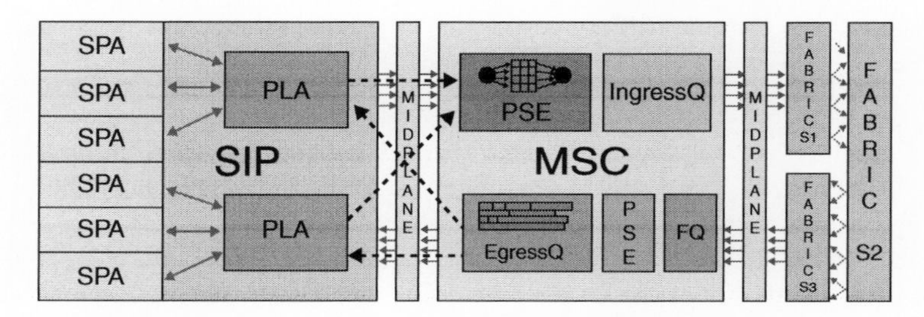

Figure 7.9: CRS Line Card with SIP Architecture Overview

Figure 7.8 shows the line-card architecture with the fixed PLIM.

Figure 7.9 shows the line-card architecture with the flexible SIP.

The PLIM ASIC (PLA) supports basic functionality including packet statistics, combining and separating packets to and from the MSC, and managing interface oversubscription.

7.2.4 CRS Switch Fabric

As previously described, the switch fabric in the CRS router is based on a three-stage switch architecture. The resilient and redundant, 1296 × 1296 buffered, nonblocking fabric uses a three-stage Benes topology with eight logical planes of fabric elements that enables the system to scale to full capacity.

Figure 7.10 gives an overview of the CRS architecture, including the switch fabric stages.

The interconnect mechanism is a multistage switch fabric giving an internal, high-speed, nonblocking data path connecting ingress and egress interfaces within the router. The forwarding plane consists of interface modules and packet-forwarding components for applying features without degrading performance. The control plane processes all network-level control functions in a timely and reliable manner.

The interconnect mechanism, or switch fabric, must fulfill requirements as follows:

- *Nonblocking.* The switch fabric must be a point of congestion in the router architecture. However, the switch fabric must be capable of dealing with congestion elsewhere in the router—for example, many ingress interfaces routing to a single egress interface.

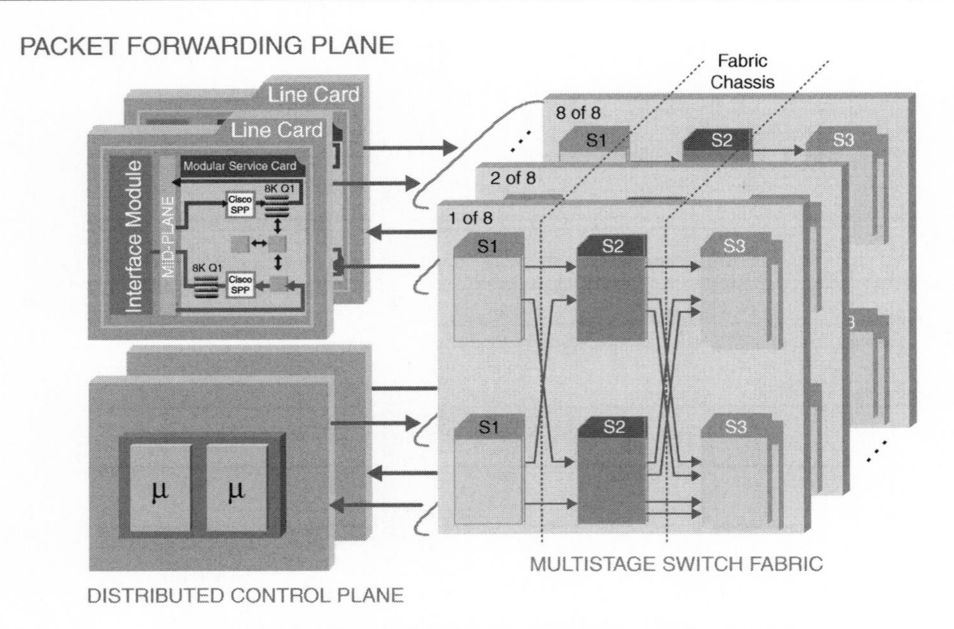

Figure 7.10: CRS Switch Fabric Architecture Overview

- *Service-aware.* The switch fabric must be capable of differentiating service types identified by QoS classification. The CRS switch fabric has buffering mechanisms and queues designated for both unicast and multicast traffic in different priorities.
- *Availability.* Failure of an individual component must not fail the entire system. With a fabric speedup and 1:*N* redundancy, the fabric can support a full traffic load in the event of any single fabric component failing.
- Scalability. The three-stage fabric design allows CRS-1 to physically scale from 1.2 to 92 Tbps of capacity without service disruption with the addition of an external fabric chassis shelf.

The three stages have specific functions in the forwarding of a packet through the CRS platform. Refer to the Quality of Service section on page 209 for details.

The eight-slot chassis has eight fabric planes split across four fabric boards to give the three-stage fabric. Each line card in the chassis connects to all eight planes, with a total raw throughput of 80 Gbps allowing a full-duplex 40 Gbps interface in each line card.

The four-slot chassis has four fabric planes split across four fabric boards—that is, one fabric plane per board. To maintain the 80 Gbps bandwidth into and out of the fabric, the number of links from the MSC into the fabric has doubled in density.

The Stage 2 fabric can be cards within the CRS router chassis or an external fabric shelf allowing scalability to 92 Tbps. Figure 7.11 shows where the fabric chassis may be used in the three-stage fabric path.

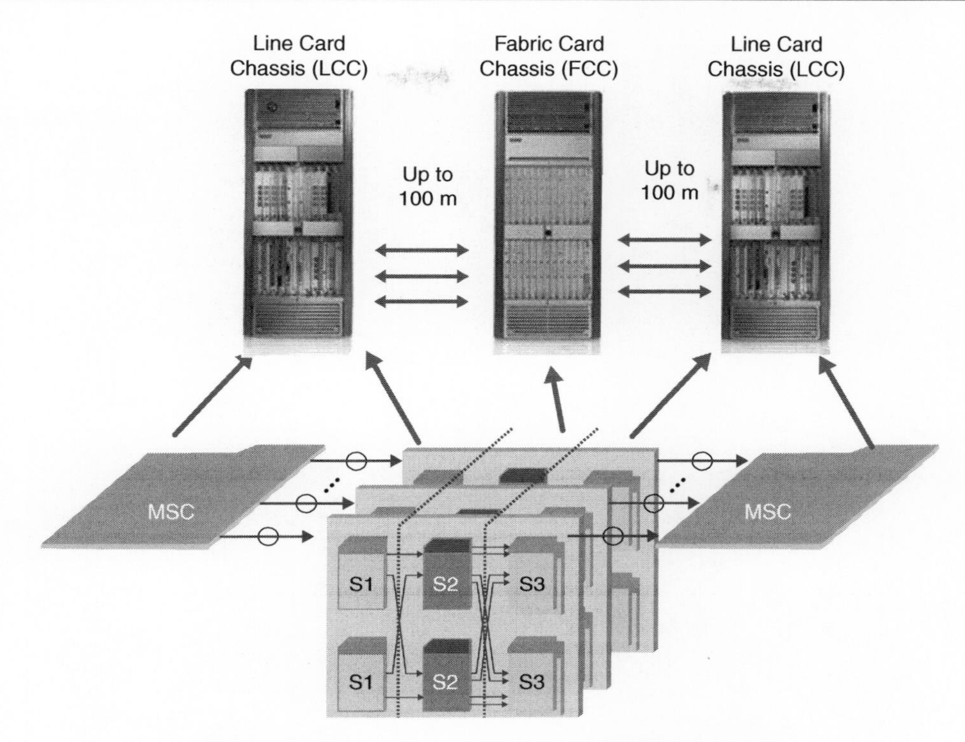

Figure 7.11: CRS Fabric Chassis Architecture Overview

The CRS Multi Chassis system supports the placement of all the optical interface modules and fabric cards in a single chassis or across multiple chassis. The CRS Multi Chassis system supports configurations with one, two, or four Fabric Chassis. An additional chassis can be used to add fabric redundancy in a 1:1 fashion. Note that this is only for redundancy, not additional capacity.

Figure 7.12 shows an example of a single-fabric chassis and dual-fabric chassis in redundant mode as they would be used to connect two CRS-16 line-card chassis.

As shown in the figure, the convention for system configuration is $N + M$, where N is the number of line-card chassis and M is the number of fabric chassis.

The Multi Chassis system requires connection of a control network, referred to as the *shelf controller*, to allow management of fabric chassis components. The shelf controller manages processes such as boot and initialization of the SFCs, the optical interface module LED (OIM-LED) card, alarms, power supplies, and fans.

The fabric chassis includes an integrated GE Ethernet Switch Interface, which provides out-of-band interchassis control network. An external Cat6500 chassis may also be used for the management network. Full mesh connectivity is required to enable communication from the line-card chassis RP to the fabric chassis.

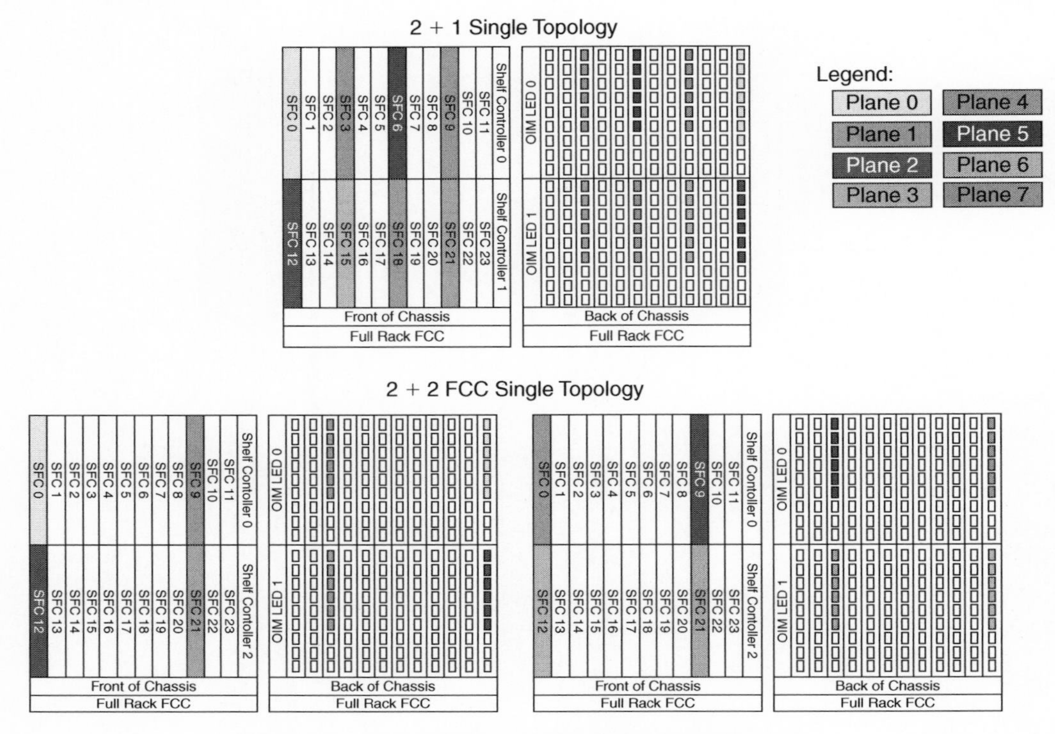

Figure 7.12: CRS Fabric Chassis Redundancy

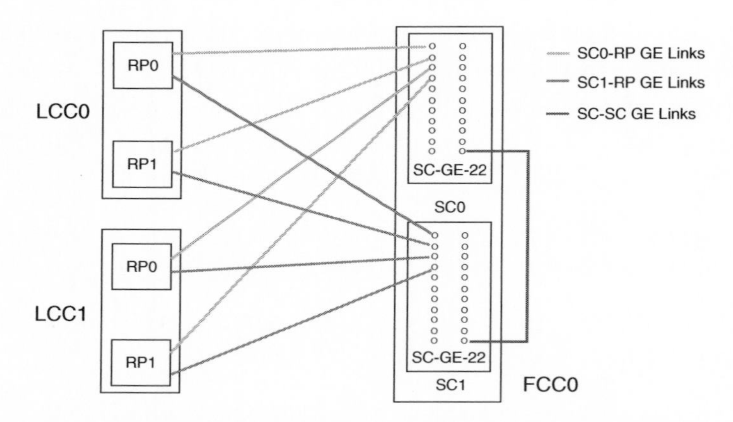

Figure 7.13: CRS Switch Fabric Control Network Connectivity

Figure 7.13 gives an example of connectivity of the control management network in a 2 + 1 system.

Note that the integrated switch is not connected to the fabric. The control Ethernet network is used for system boot, node availability (heartbeat) checks, and all communication from the LCC to the FCC. As shown in the figure, the control network is redundant and must

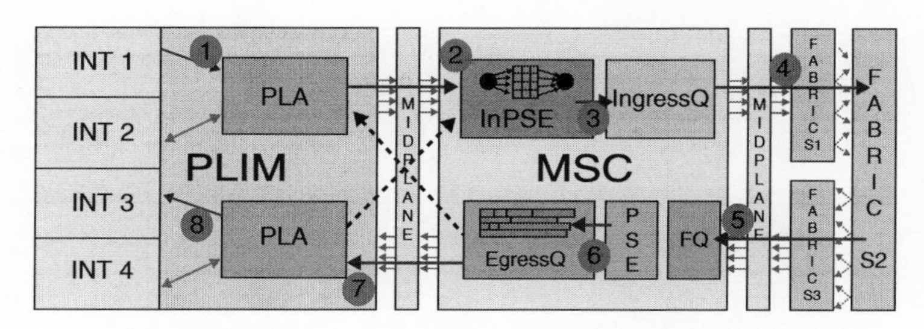

Figure 7.14: CRS Quality-of-Service Reference Architecture

be connected in a fully meshed configuration to all active and standby RPs and SCs. The control network uses Spanning Tree Protocol (STP) to determine which paths to use for communication.

7.2.5 CRS Quality of Service

For quality of service to be effective, the entire path through the CRS, including the ingress line card, switch fabric, and egress line card, must ensure that classified traffic is treated with the required priority.

Figure 7.14 shows the path of a packet through the CRS platform.

A packet that is forwarded by the Cisco CRS-1 takes the following path through the system:

1. The framer on the PLIM receives a frame carrying the IP packet. The framer removes the Layer 1 encapsulation as well as the CRC. The remaining Layer 2 and Layer 3 frames are sent to the RX PSE.
2. The RX PSE performs the destination lookup and ingress feature processing, including access lists, QoS classification, policing, WRED, and policy routing. The result of the destination lookup includes the destination line card, which fabric path will be taken.
3. The packet is passed to the ingress-queuing ASIC, which performs shaping and P2MDRR on the packet as well as the segmentation of the packet for transmission across the switch fabric. The ingress-queuing ASIC has shape queues and fabric queues for precise control over packets transiting the fabric.
4. Cells are sent into the fabric. The cells arrive at the stage 1 (S1) of the switch fabric. The S1 simply distributes the incoming cells across the available S2. Note that S2 may be an external fabric chassis.
5. The S2 stage performs a lookup on the cell header to determine to which S3 ASIC within the switch fabric the cell is to be sent. The S2 fabric supports different priority queues for both unicast and multicast traffic.
6. The packet is passed to the TX PSE, which performs full Layer 3 processing, including route lookup, access-list processing, QoS classification, and WRED. The appropriate

Layer 2 encapsulation is also applied before the TX PSe hands the updated packet the egress-queuing ASIC.

7. The egress-queuing ASIC supports thousands of shape queues, which are user configurable. These queues are mapped into groups or subinterfaces and in turn mapped into physical ports.

8. When the packet has been queued and shaped, it is then passed to the interface module ASIC on the PLIM. Finally, the packet is sent through the egress port and onto the physical link.

7.3 Cisco 12000 Series Router

The Cisco 12000 product line was released in 1997 as a high-end IP router platform specifically for the service provider market. The 12000 Series has since been expanded into a variety of chassis and interface options, including edge functions, with the introduction of the CRS as Cisco's premier core router. The first 12000 router supported OC3/STM-1 and OC12/STM-4 speeds, later supporting OC48/STM-16 interfaces. Later chassis and fabric upgrades gave 10 Gbps and subsequently 40 Gbps per slot, allowing greater density and higher-speed interfaces.

Figures 7.15 and 7.16 show the entire 12000 Series router family.

The basic chassis options are the 12404, the 12 × 06, the 12 × 10, and the 12 × 16, where the last two numbers identify the number of slots in the chassis. The third number identifies the

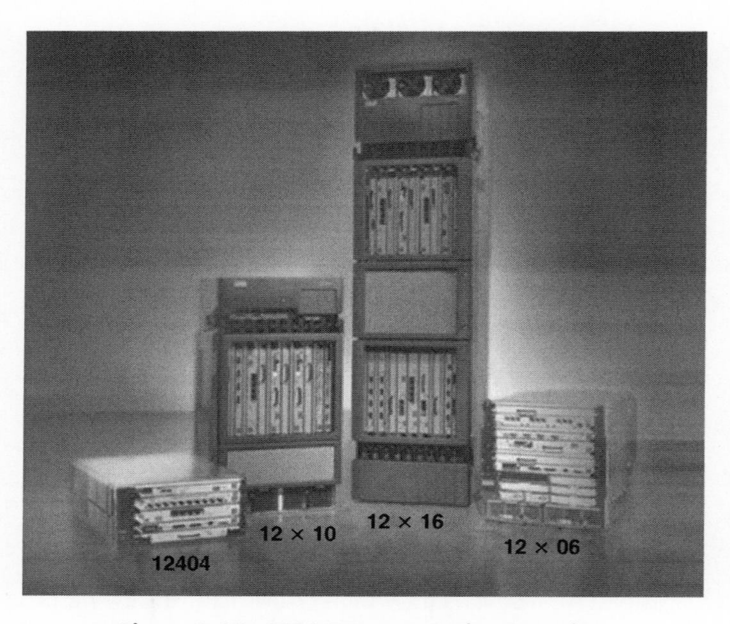

Figure 7.15: 12000 Router Series Overview

fabric generation, with 0 referring to 2.5 Gbps full duplex per slot, 4 referring to 10 Gbps full duplex per slot, and 8 referring to 40 Gbps full duplex per slot.

Figure 7.17 shows the 12000 platform range with switching capacity and associated packet-processing performance.

As shown in the figure, the 12816 router has a 40 Gbps slot capacity giving a total of 1.28 Tbps throughput with 750 million packets-per-second performance.

7.3.1 12000 Series Routers Architecture

The basic components of the Cisco 12000 product line are the chassis, passive backplane, power supply, route processor, switch fabric, and interface-line cards.

Figure 7.18 gives an overview of the 12000 router architecture.

	4 slots 6 RU 120/208 VAC		Cisco 12404 80 Gbps	
	6 slots 10 RU 120/208 VAC or 48 DC	Cisco 12006 30 Gbps Upgradeable to 120 Gbps	Cisco 12406 120 Gbps	
	10 slots 20 RU 208 VAC or 48 DC	Cisco 12010 50 Gbps Upgradeable to 200 or 800 Gbps	Cisco 12410 200 Gbps Upgradeable to 800 Gbps	Cisco 12810 200 Gbps
	16 slots 20 RU 208 VAC or 48 DC	Cisco 12016 80 Gbps Upgradeable to 320 Gbps or 1.28 Tbps	Cisco 12416 320 Gbps Upgradeable to 1.28 Tbps	Cisco 12816 1.28 Tbps

Figure 7.16: 12000 Router Series Platform Overview

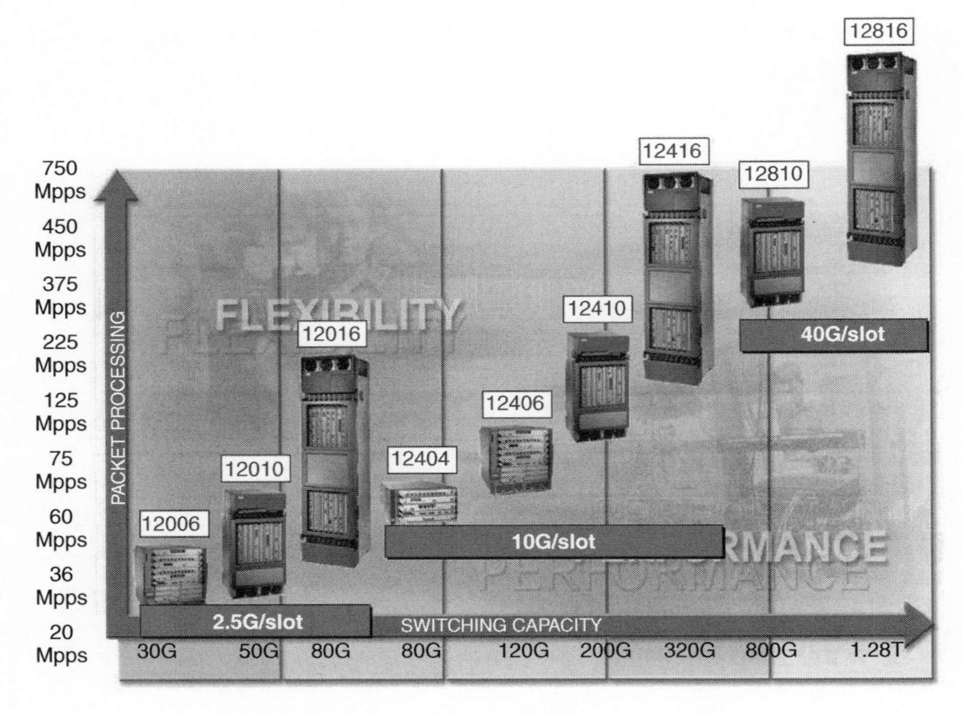

Figure 7.17: 12000 Router Series Platform Performance

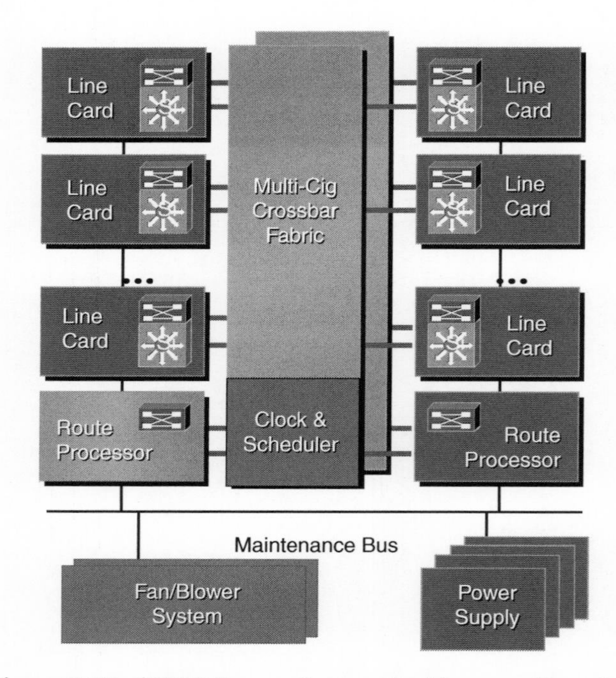

Figure 7.18: 12000 Router System Architecture Overview

The power supply and switch fabric cards are specific to the chassis type, whereas route processors and line cards may be shared between the various systems. High-capacity line cards must be matched to chassis with higher fabric capacity. The 12000 router system architecture is a distributed system with no active bus or backbone. The route processor runs the routing protocols and builds the forwarding tables, which are downloaded to the individual line cards in the chassis. The line cards then use the forwarding tables to forward packets—egress through the interfaces and ingress across the chassis switch fabric.

The switch fabric is a crossbar design, chosen for its scalability and performance beyond shared memory and bus-based router architectures. The switch fabric is discussed in more detail in a later section.

The Cisco 12000 Series routers utilize a sophisticated Maintenance Bus (MBUS) system. The MBUS is a resilient 1 Mbps serial bus known as a Controller Area Networks (CAN) bus. All active components in the chassis are connected to the MBUS with a purpose-built controller. Active components include router processors, line cards, switch fabric cards, power supplies, and fan assemblies.

At system startup, the route processor uses the MBUS to discover the active components installed in the router. The MBUS is used to gather environmental information such as temperatures, voltages, and fan speeds from the relevant active components.

7.3.2 12000 Series Route Processor

The 12000 Series router processor (RP) acts as the centralized processing card for the entire chassis, effectively acting as the control plane for the distributed architecture. The RP stores and runs the IOS or IOS XR software image.

Figure 7.19 shows an example of the RP used for the 12000 Series routers.

The RP executes all IP and MPLS routing protocols used to build forwarding tables, which are subsequently downloaded to line cards. General router utilities, such as CDP and NTP, are run on the RP.

Figure 7.19: 12000 Series Route Processor

Table 7.2: 12000 Series GRP and PRP Hardware Overview

	GRP	PRP-1	PRP-2	PRP-3
CPU	R5000 200 MHz	PPC 667 MHz	PPC 1.3 GHz	DCP 1.33 GHz
Memory	64–512 MB	512 MB–2 GB	1–4 GB	4–16 GB
NVRAM	512 KB	2 MB	2 MB	4 MB
Ethernet	1 × 10	2 × 10/100	2 × 10/100/1000	2 × 10/100/1000
IOS XR	Unsupported	Supported	Recommended	Required

The RP includes Ethernet ports providing access to the device for management tasks such as loading images and core dumps.

Various RPs are available for the 12000 Series routers, depending on the memory, processing power, and software required to run. Table 7.2 gives an overview of the Gigabit Route Processor, Performance Route Processor 1 and 2, and the latest-generation PRP-3.

The PRP-3 is a significant step in performance for tasks such as route convergence, access list compilation, and router bootup. The PRP-3 includes flexible storage options with a PCMCIA Flash (1 GB default, 512 MB option), a 1 GB internal Compact Flash (optional FRU), and an 80 GB hard drive (optional FRU).

7.3.3 12000 Series Line Cards

In a fully distributed architecture, as employed by the 12000 Series routers, the line cards are autonomous components in the router. The 12000 Series router relies on as much processing as possible being done on the ingress-side line card.

The basic building blocks of a line card are the fabric interface, the forwarding engine, and the physical layer interface, as shown in Figure 7.20.

The physical layer interface module provides the connectors, framing, and support circuitry for the physical type of interface of the line card. The physical layer tests the integrity of the link layer frame, decapsulates the data, and hands the packet to the forwarding engine. In the opposite direction, it takes the IP packet from the forwarding engine, encapsulates the packet in the appropriate frame, calculates necessary checksums, and sends the frame onto the link.

The forwarding engine is the processing power on the line card. It consists of several custom ASICs, packet buffers, a CPU, and memory. The CPU runs a subset of the software on the route processor and has full control over all components on the line card. The line card receives the forwarding table information from the route processor and programs the forwarding ASICs. Class-of-service settings are enforced at the line-card CPU.

The memory buffers are used to store packets. The transmit- and receive-side buffers are separate on the line card. The buffer size is matched to the aggregate speed of the line card and is managed by dedicated buffer management ASICs (BMAs). The BMAs assist the lookup

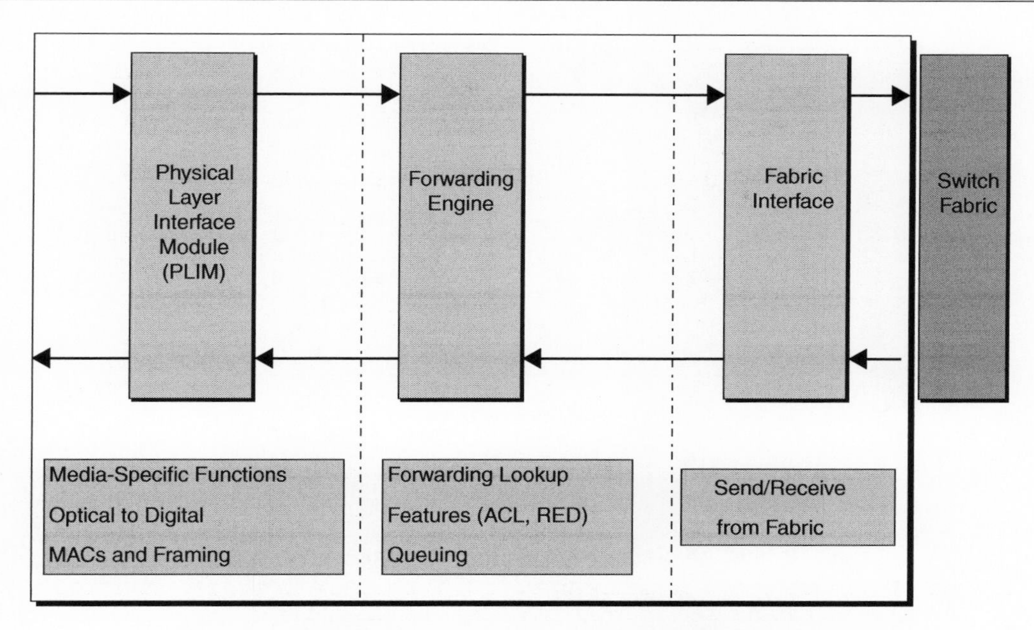

Figure 7.20: 12000 Router Line-Card Architecture Overview

engines and enforce class-of-service (CoS) queuing and Weighted Random Early Detection (WRED).

The fabric interface, connecting to the switch fabric, segments and reassembles data to and from the fabric and interfaces the request/grant protocol to the scheduler. The fabric interface also generates and verifies checksums for the CiscoCells transiting the fabric.

Through the evolution of the 12000 Series platform, there have been various generations of line cards. Figure 7.21 shows the various generations of line cards, referred to as *engines*, available for the 12000 Series router.

As shown in the figure, the horizontal axis shows the throughput performance of the line card, the vertical axis shows the features supported with edge-focused IP Services Engine (ISE) cards providing the most feature-rich options.

Engines 0, 1, 2, and 4 line cards are now end of life and end of sale and have been replaced by engines 3, 5, and 6 (see Table 7.3).

The edge engine 3 and 5 line cards are often referred to as the IP Services Engine (ISE). The ISE is available for all chassis options in a modular SPA Interface Processor (SIP) architecture, allowing various physical interface types to be installed in a carrier module.

Figure 7.22 shows the SIP and SPA options for the 12000 Series routers.

Table 7.4 summarizes the SPA Interface Processors available for the 12000 Series router.

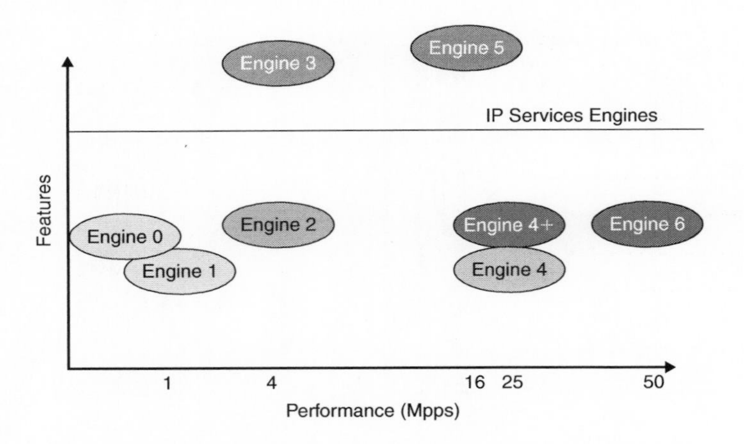

Figure 7.21: 12000 Router Line-Card Engine Overview

Table 7.3: 12000 Series Router Line Card Engine Specification

	Edge/Backbone	Packets per Second	Chassis
Engine 3	Edge	4 Mpps	2.5 G/10 G/40 G chassis
Engine 4+	Backbone	25 Mpps	10 G/40 G chassis
Engine 5	Edge	16 Mpps	10 G/40 G chassis
Engine 6	Backbone	50 Mpps	40 G chassis

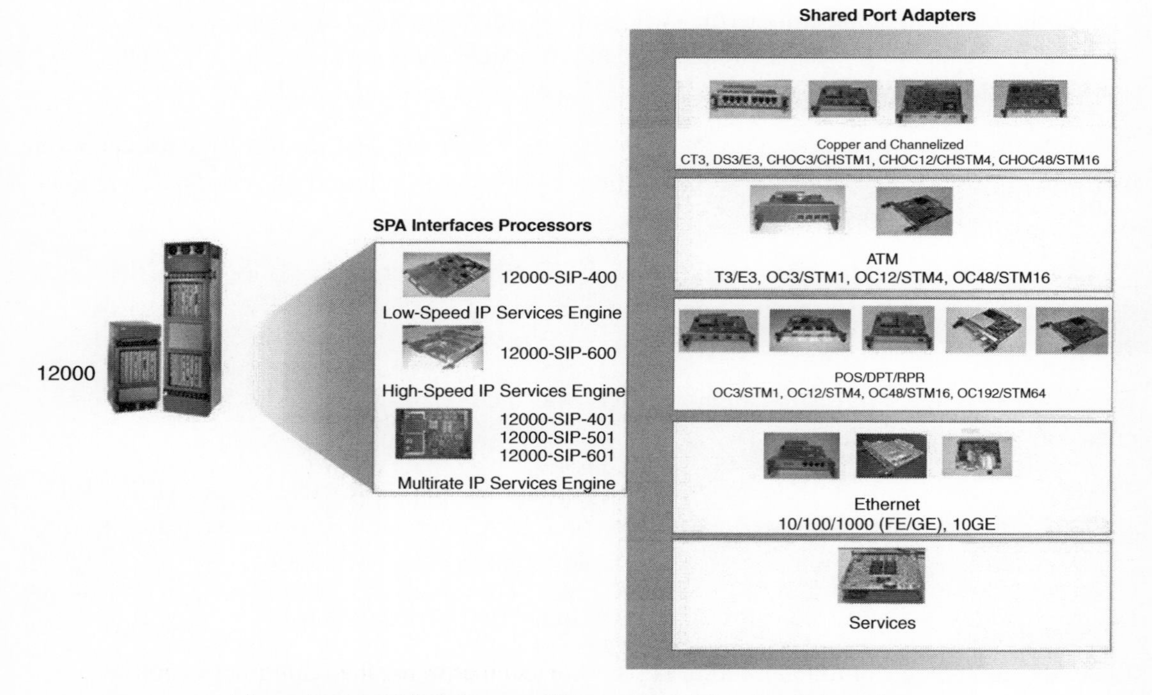

Figure 7.22: 12000 Router SIP and SPA Line-Card Overview

Table 7.4: SPA Interface Processor Specifications

SPA Interface Processor Module	Description	Forwarding Engine
12000-SIP-601	Multirate 10 G IP Services Engine (Modular)	5
12000-SIP-501	Multirate 5 G IP Services Engine (Modular)	5
12000-SIP-401	Multirate 2.5 G IP Services Engine (Modular)	5
12000-SIP-600	10 Gbps IP Services Engine (modular)	5
12000-SIP-400	2.5 Gbps IP Services Engine (modular)	3

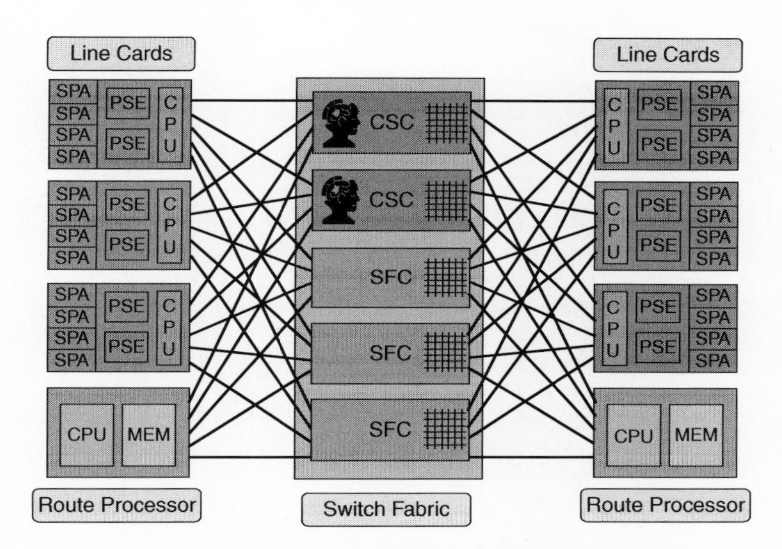

Figure 7.23: 12000 Series Router Switch Fabric Overview

Note that the engine 3 line cards are also available in fixed interface configuration as well as the flexible SIP-400.

7.3.4 12000 Series Switch Fabric

The 12000 series routers use a state-of-the-art gigabit switching fabric designed for high-performance, nonblocking and high-availability packet forwards between line cards.

Figure 7.23 gives an overview of the 1200 architecture with emphasis on the switch fabric components.

As shown in the figure, the Cisco 12000 Series switch fabric comprises two card modules: the Switch Fabric Card (SFC) and the Clock and Scheduler Card (CSC).

The SFC comprises the crossbar switching fabric and transceivers. The switch fabric is a mesh of connections implemented in an ASIC. The transceivers provide a standard physical interface between the line cards and the crossbar switch fabric.

The CSC is a superset of the SFC. It comprises the same crossbar switching fabric and transceivers as the SFC. The CSC also contains the scheduler and system timing ASIC for handling requests from the line cards to access the crossbar switching fabric. The CSC also provides a reference clock to all cards in the system, which synchronizes data transfer across the crossbar switch fabric. A second CSC provides clock, scheduler, and switch fabric redundancy.

Each slot in the 12000 Series router has multiple point-to-point serial lines to each SFC and CSC. The number of lines determines the bandwidth to and from each line card specifically to ensure that bandwidth for the card is matched or exceeded.

The 12000 router switch fabric design includes innovative technologies to provide a highly efficient, scalable system, including:

- Multiple fabric queues per line card to allow mapping to each possible egress line card, therefore eliminating head-of-line blocking (HoLB) effects
- An intelligent, efficient scheduling algorithm to improve fabric efficiency
- Hardware-based replication for multicast traffic and support of partial fulfillment to provide a highly efficient platform for multicast traffic
- Use of pipelining to improve switch fabric performance

Packets are forwarded across the switch fabric using cells, as shown in Figure 7.24.

Data packets are chopped into CiscoCells by the line cards before being sent across the switching fabric. A CiscoCell is 64 bytes of data consisting of 8 bytes of header, 48 bytes of payload, and 8 bytes of CRC.

7.3.5 12000 Quality of Service

QoS implementation on the 12000 Series router is based on either the IP precedence bits located in the ToS field or the MPLS EXP bits in the MPLS label. This section gives an

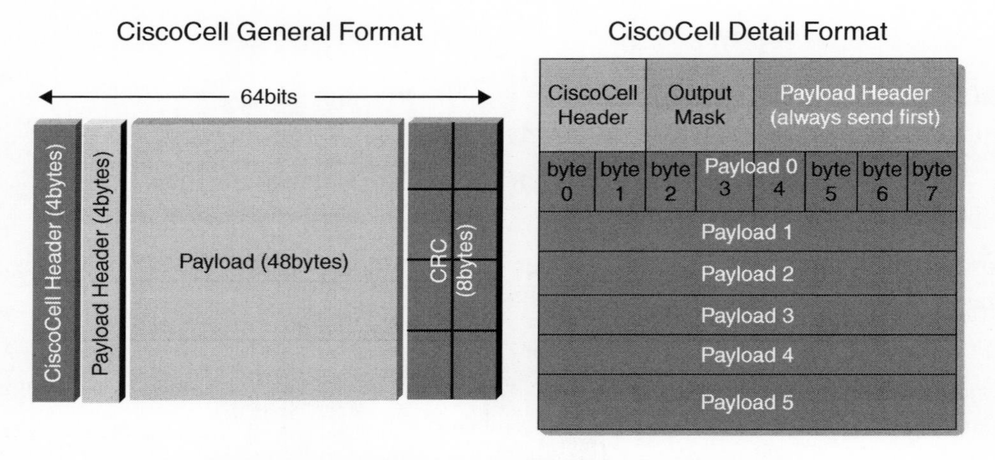

Figure 7.24: 12000 Series Router Switch Fabric Cells

overview of QoS on the 12000 Series routers. For exhaustive descriptions of mechanisms such as MDRR, WRED, and policing, refer to Chapter 2.

Figure 7.25 shows the enforcement of QoS through the 12000 Series router.

Considering the receive-side processing, the first step is a lookup of the destination. This lookup determines the egress-line card using the forwarding table downloaded from the 12000 RP.

The next step is policing and marking of traffic. Policing involves the rate limiting of traffic with packets that exceeds a max rate being dropped. Marking of packets is used to set IP, MPLS, or DSCP precedence.

The third step involves traffic shaping. As described in previous chapters, rate limiting allows buffering of traffic to manage transmission rates in accordance with configurations.

Weighted Random Early Detection (WRED) allows congestion control by dropping traffic in a controlled manner.

Packets are then queued to the fabric and passed through Modified Deficit Round Robin (MDRR) before being forwarded across the fabric.

7.4 Cisco 7600 Series Router

The Cisco 7600 Series Internet Routers are distributed routing and switching systems that provide 10/100 Ethernet, 10/100/1000 Ethernet, Gigabit Ethernet, 10 Gigabit Ethernet,

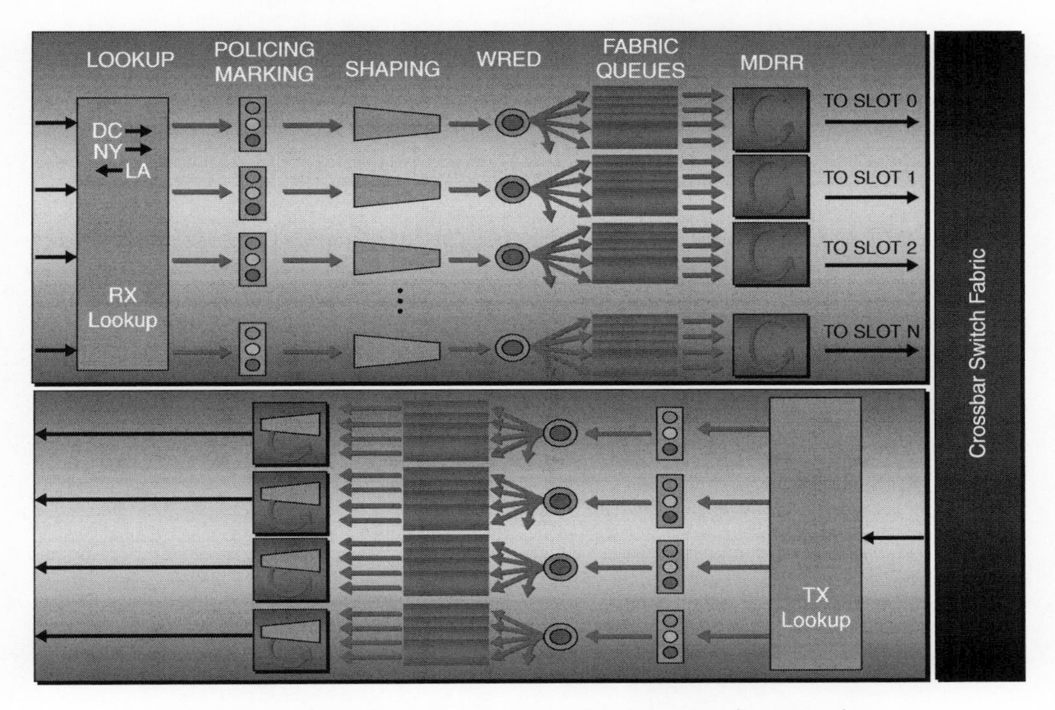

Figure 7.25: 12000 Series Router Quality-of-Service Overview

SONET/SDH, and other high-speed interfaces for a variety of networks and network applications.

The 7600 also supports an integrated services architecture allowing feature-specific modules such as firewalls, VPNs, intrusion detection, Secure Socket Layer encryption, network analysis, and content switching, to be inserted in the chassis.

The 7600 architecture separates packet forwarding from the system control operations. Performance scalability is assured through the extensive use of application-specific integrated circuits (ASICs) dedicated to selected features and functions within the 7600 system.

The 7600 router series range is shown in Figure 7.26.

As shown, there are five chassis options providing form factor and slot density appropriate for edge-through-to-core-layer applications. The chassis scales from three to 13 slots with performance as shown in Figure 7.27.

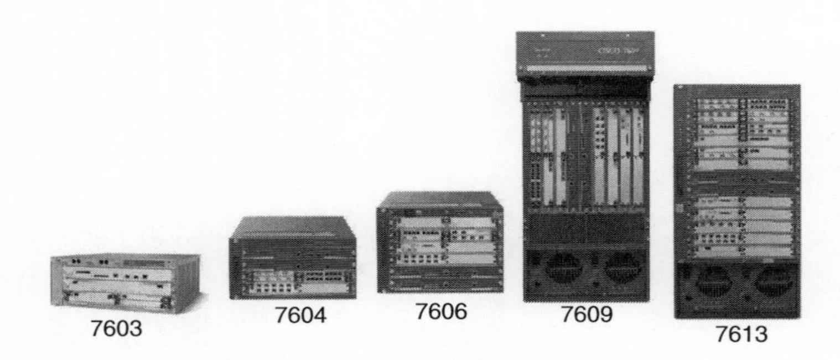

Figure 7.26: 7600 Router Series Overview

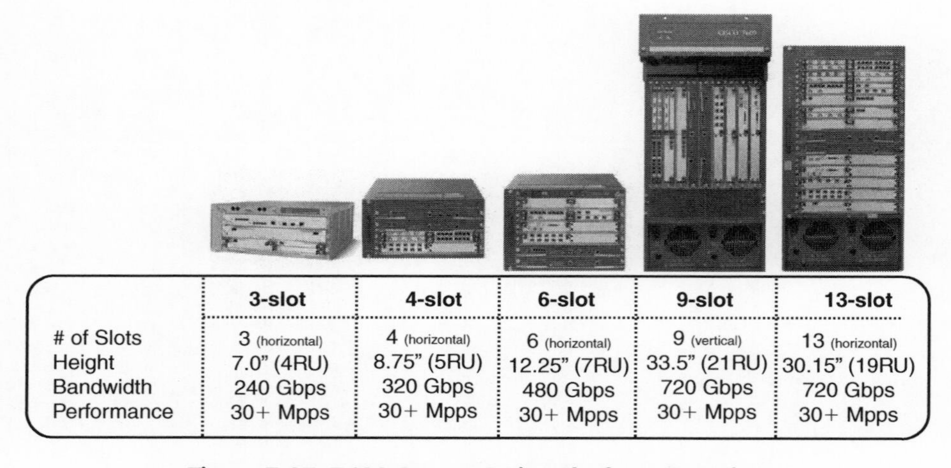

	3-slot	4-slot	6-slot	9-slot	13-slot
# of Slots	3 (horizontal)	4 (horizontal)	6 (horizontal)	9 (vertical)	13 (horizontal)
Height	7.0" (4RU)	8.75" (5RU)	12.25" (7RU)	33.5" (21RU)	30.15" (19RU)
Bandwidth	240 Gbps	320 Gbps	480 Gbps	720 Gbps	720 Gbps
Performance	30+ Mpps	30+ Mpps	30+ Mpps	30+ Mpps	30+ Mpps

Figure 7.27: 7600 Router Series Platform Overview

7.4.1 7600 Series Routers Architecture

The 7600 supports centralized or distributed performance, allowing scalability for edge, aggregation, and core applications in an SP network. Packet forwarding on the 7600 takes place in ASICs on the Policy Feature Card (PFC) or the Distributed Forwarding Card (DFC), depending on the line card and route processor versions in the chassis. Packet-forwarding features include layer bridging, routing, QoS marking and policing, ACLs, and NetFlow statistics collection.

All control and management operations for the system are performed on the route processor engine by a group of purpose-built processors. This processor architecture uses dual CPUs to ensure scalable control plane performance.

As shown in the previous section, the platform is a chassis-based system available in 3, 4, 6, 9, or 13 slot varieties and can be configured with a range of network media types scaling to over 1000 10/100 ports, 600 10/100/1000 Ethernet ports, 400 Gigabit Ethernet ports, or 30 10 Gigabit Ethernet ports for the 7613 chassis option.

The 7600 allows scalable performance with bandwidth capacity from 32 Gbps to 720 Gbps and with full redundancy for supervisor, switch fabric, and power supply.

Figure 7.28 gives an overview of the 7600 architecture.

As shown in the figure, the 7600 has both a shared bus and a switch fabric option for connectivity of line cards. The supervisor provides route calculation and centralized packet forwarding for line cards not equipped with distributed forwarding capabilities.

Refer to the "7600 Series Shared Bus and Switch Fabric" section for details of the shared bus, switch fabric, and line-card types: Classic, Fabric Enabled and Fabric Only.

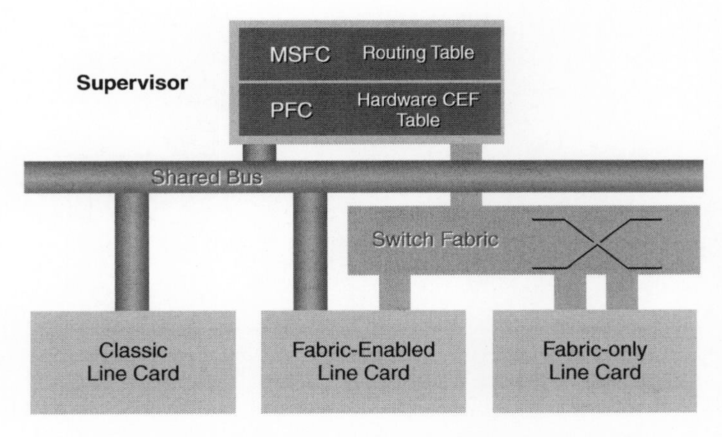

Figure 7.28: 7600 Router System Architecture Overview

Each of the chassis options provides preferred slots for Supervisor Engines and line cards as shown in Figure 7.29.

The chassis has slots that are specifically enabled for insertion of the Supervisor Engine, as shown, but note that these slots may also be used for line cards if required. The 7600 may be installed with dual Supervisor Engines for redundancy if additional availability in the network is a requirement.

7.4.2 7600 Series Route Processor

The Supervisor Engine provides the processing power for the Cisco 7600 router. The 7600 allows scalable performance with route processor options as follows:

- Supervisor Engine 1a
- Supervisor Engine 2
- Supervisor Engine 32
- Supervisor Engine 2 + Switch Fabric Module
- Supervisor Engine 720 variants

This section focuses on the Supervisor Engine 720 variants, which are default on the 7600 Series routers used for SP networks.

	7603-S	7604	7606-S	7609-S	7613	
Slot 1	Sup or LC	Sup or LC	LC Only	LC Only	LC Only	Slot 1
Slot 2	Sup or LC	Sup or LC	LC Only	LC Only	LC Only	Slot 2
Slot 3	LC Only	LC Only	LC Only	LC Only	LC Only	Slot 3
Slot 4		LC Only	LC Only	LC Only	LC Only	Slot 4
Slot 5			Sup or LC	Sup or LC	LC Only	Slot 5
Slot 6			Sup or LC	Sup or LC	LC Only	Slot 6
Slot 7			LC Only	LC Only	Sup or LC	Slot 7
Slot 8			LC Only	LC Only	Sup or LC	Slot 8
Slot 9			LC Only	LC Only	LC Only	Slot 9
Slot 10					LC Only	Slot 10
Slot 11					LC Only	Slot 11
Slot 12					LC Only	Slot 12
Slot 13					LC Only	Slot 13

Figure 7.29: 7600 Router Series Slot Allocations

The Supervisor 720 family represents the third generation of Supervisor Engines released by Cisco. The Supervisor 720 Engine options include the following:

- Supervisor 720 (WS-SUP720), referred to as the Supervisor 720-3 A. This is the first-generation Supervisor 720.
- Supervisor 720-3B (WS-SUP720-3B), an update of the original Supervisor 720-3 A, adding support for a number of new hardware-based features including MPLS.
- Supervisor 720-3BXL (WS-SUP720-3BXL), based on the Supervisor 720-3B, has increased performance and memory for storing up to 1 million IPv4 routes.
- Supervisor 720-3C-10GE and Supervisor 720-3CXL-10GE, which adds 2 × 10GE uplink ports on the supervisor card and hardware acceleration for features.

Figure 7.30 shows the 7600 Supervisor 720 module with critical hardware components highlighted.

All Supervisor 720 models have an integrated high-capacity crossbar switching fabric, a Policy Feature Card (PFC) hardware forwarding engine, and a Multi-layer Switch Feature Card (MSFC). As shown in the figure, the PFC3 and MSFC are daughter cards, with the switching fabric component consolidated onto the Supervisor baseboard. A Supervisor Engine 720 requires a PFC3 and an MSFC3 for operation; both are standard additions to the baseboard.

The Supervisor Engine 720 and its switch fabric provide a 1:1 redundancy capability, with one active and one backup Supervisor. The active Supervisor Engine will also act as the active switch fabric, MSFC, and PFC. The Supervisor Engine 720, including the switch fabric, PFC, and MSFC, operate as a single entity; hence all components must be operational for the supervisor to be operational. A supervisor failover automatically causes a fabric, PFC, and MSFC failover on the 7600 router.

Figure 7.30: 7600 Router Series Supervisor Hardware

7.4.3 7600 Series Line Cards

The 7600 has a variety of interface module types depending on the connectivity and performance requirements. The module type options are as follows:

- Ethernet Services Modules (ES-20)
- SPA Interface Processors (SIPs)
- FlexWAN Module
- Optical Service Modules (OSMs)
- High-density Ethernet Connectivity Modules

Figure 7.31 shows the module types.

The Ethernet Services Module (ES-20) is designed for Carrier Ethernet, IP/MPLS PE Edge, in midsize and smaller service provider and enterprise WAN applications. The ES20 supports 20 Gbps of bandwidth with 20 ports of Gigabit Ethernet or two ports of 10 G Ethernet interface models. The card features hierarchical QoS and up to 32 K VLAN IDs per line card. The ES20 provides both Layer 2 and Layer 3 services on the same line card, allowing Layer 2 switching, bridging, VPLS, Ethernet over MPLS (EoMPLS), and Layer 3 IP/MPLS routing.

The SPA Interface Processor (SIP) is based on the Cisco I-Flex design, combining shared port adapters (SPAs) and SPA interface processors (SIPs). This architecture gives improved slot efficiency, allowing a granular interface mix on a single line card. The SIP is also optimized for edge performance, allowing full-feature configuration without impacting throughput.

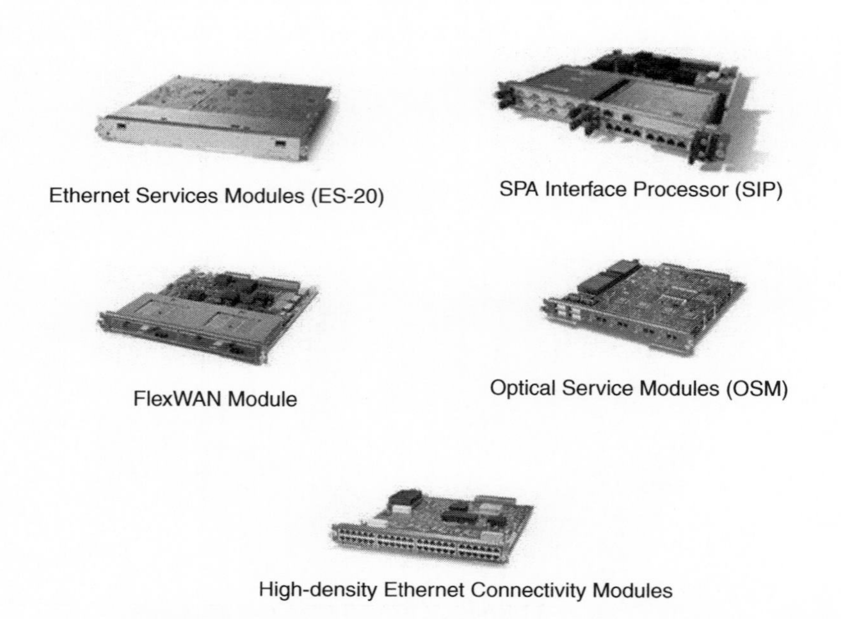

Figure 7.31: 7600 Router Series Interface Modules Overview

The SIP is available in three versions, as shown in Figure 7.32.

The figure shows the performance and features on the SIP interface modules available on the 7600. The SIP-600 is the premier line card; it offers 10 Gbps performance with all features enabled.

The Enhanced FlexWAN module provides aggregate throughput of over 600 kpps per module, more than double the throughput of its predecessor, and it is switch fabric enabled, enabling high-performance, intelligent MAN and WAN services. It supports Cisco 7000 Series Port Adapters, allowing customers to reduce OpEx and provide investment protection to customers migrating from the Cisco 7500 Series.

The Optical Service Modules (OSMs) provide optical WAN interfaces, PXF IP Services Processors for high-speed IP service application, and large packet buffers appropriate for high-speed WAN applications. Each OSM line card provides an additional four ports of GBIC-based switched Gigabit Ethernet in addition to the high-speed WAN interfaces. The OSM provides an 8 Gbps full-duplex connection to the switch fabric (with dual connectivity to redundant crossbar fabrics).

The high-density Ethernet Connectivity Modules provide a set of fixed configuration Ethernet modules. These modules provide a high port count of FE, GE, or 10GE in either copper or optical interface implementations with fixed, GBIC, or SFP interface options.

7.4.4 7600 Series Shared Bus and Switch Fabric

The switch fabric is a crossbar architecture integrated into the Supervisor Engine 720. The crossbar functions as a switch, providing dedicated bandwidth to modules in each slot.

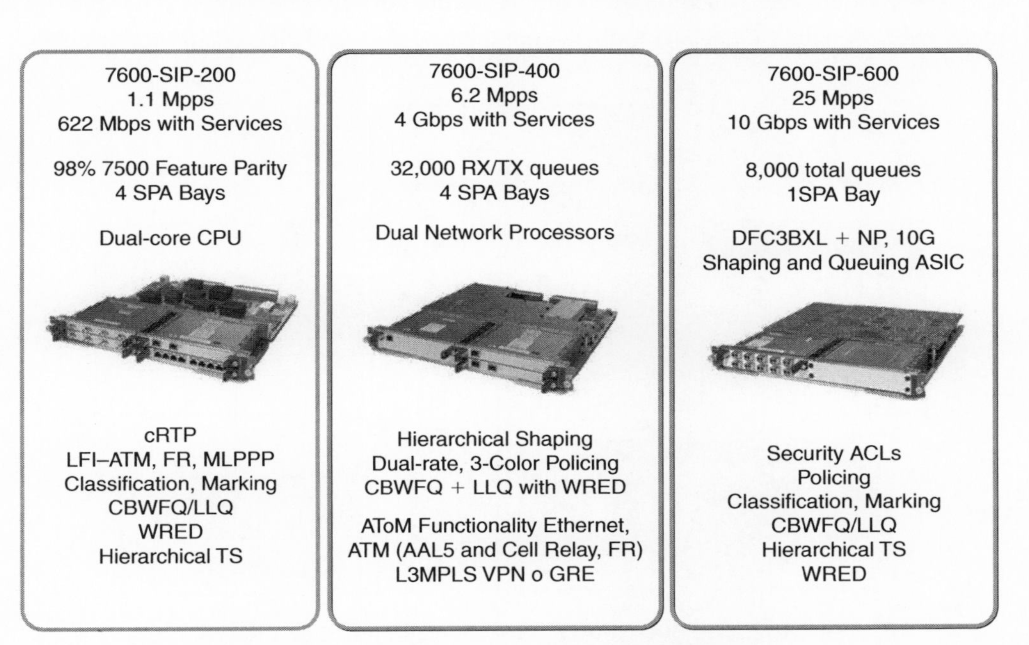

Figure 7.32: 7600 Router Series SIP Performance

The fabric comprises purpose-built ASICs, which make up the crossbar switching complex connecting to line-card modules via serial channel connections.

Figure 7.33 gives an overview of the switch fabric and the connected line cards.

As shown, the speed of the fabric channel can be at either 8 Gbps or 20 Gbps, depending on the module type. The CEF256 and dCEF256 Series modules connect to the switch fabric at 8 Gbps per channel, and the CEF720 Series modules connect to the switch fabric at 20 Gbps per channel.

The Supervisor Engine 720 switch fabric is capable of connecting at 20 Gbps per slot if required. The Supervisor 720-10GE actually provides 20 fabric channels, with the two additional fabric channels used to connect to the two 10GE ports on the Supervisor module.

Within the interface card types available on the 7600 platform, the connection architecture to the bus or switch fabric defines the performance potential of the line card. The card types, as shown in the figure, are as follows:

- Classic modules
- CEF256 modules
- DCEF256
- CEF720
- DCEF720

Classic Series modules are based on the original architecture of the Catalyst 6500 bus introduced in 1999. Classic Series modules connect to the shared 32 Gbps Switching bus.

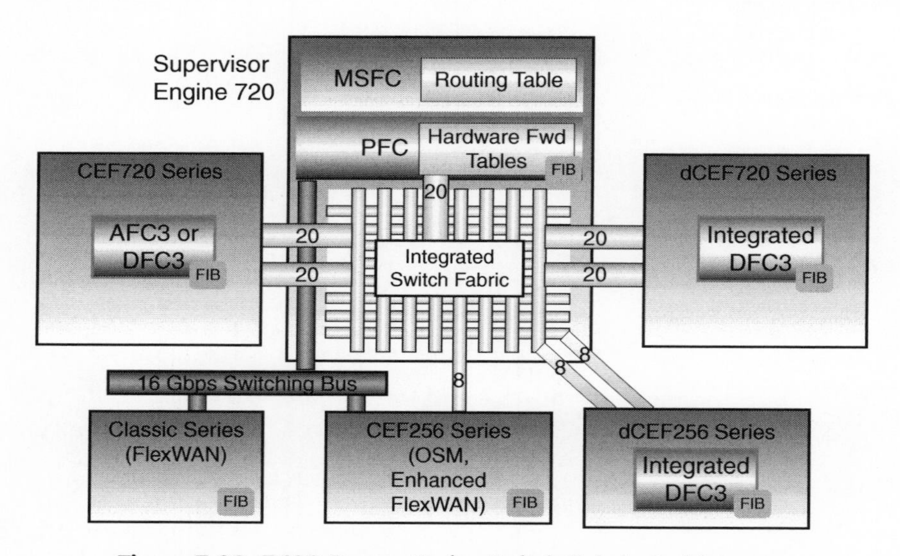

Figure 7.33: 7600 Router Series Switch Fabric Architecture

They rely on the route processor PFC forwarding engine for all packet-forwarding decisions. The maximum forwarding rate for these modules is 15 Mpps per system. Examples of Classic Series line cards include the original FlexWAN and original LAN modules.

CEF256 Series modules have connectivity to both the shared 32 Gbps Bus and a 256 Gbps switch fabric. CEF256 Series modules utilize the central PFC for all forwarding decisions in the same way as the Classic Series modules. The maximum centralized forwarding rate of these modules is 30 Mpps per system with the Sup720, which requires all modules in the system to be CEF256 Series or higher. The switch fabric connection is via a single 8 Gbps fabric channel. CEF256 Series modules can be upgraded to use a distributed forwarding architecture with the addition of the DFC daughterboard, which allows 15 Mpps distributed performance. Examples include the Enhance FlexWAN and OSM line cards.

The dCEF256 Series module has a dual 8 Gbps fabric channel to a 256 Gbps switch fabric, with no connection to the shared 32 Gbps bus. The dCEF256 module has an integrated DFC for distributed forwarding decisions by default. This module type supports a forwarding rate for this module is up to 24 Mpps per slot.

CEF720 Series Modules provide the highest port density available on the platform, requiring a Supervisor Engine 720 route processor to operate. They have either single or dual 20 Gbps fabric interfaces to the switch fabric on the Supervisor Engine 720. CEF720 modules use the centralized PFC on the route processor for all forwarding decisions by default; however, another distributed forwarding card may be added for additional performance.

DCEF720 Series modules use an integrated Centralized Forwarding Card daughter card to provide accelerated connectivity to the switching bus. This CFC does not provide any forwarding intelligence; the Distributed Forwarding Card is available as an option to provide high-performing distributed CEF forwarding (dCEF).

7.4.5 7600 Quality of Service

The path of the packet through the 7600, and hence the implementation of QoS, depends on whether the line requires centralized forwarding at the Supervisor Engine or has distributed forwarding capabilities.

Figure 7.34 shows the packet path through the 7600 with centralized forwarding.

CEF256-type line cards are used in this example. The classic line cards have the same forwarding path with the exception that forwarding is across the 32 Gbps shared bus rather than the switch fabric.

The packet forwarding from source to destination is as follows:

1. The packet is received on the line card port ASIC, where the framing is stripped. The packet is then forwarded to the fabric buffer memory.

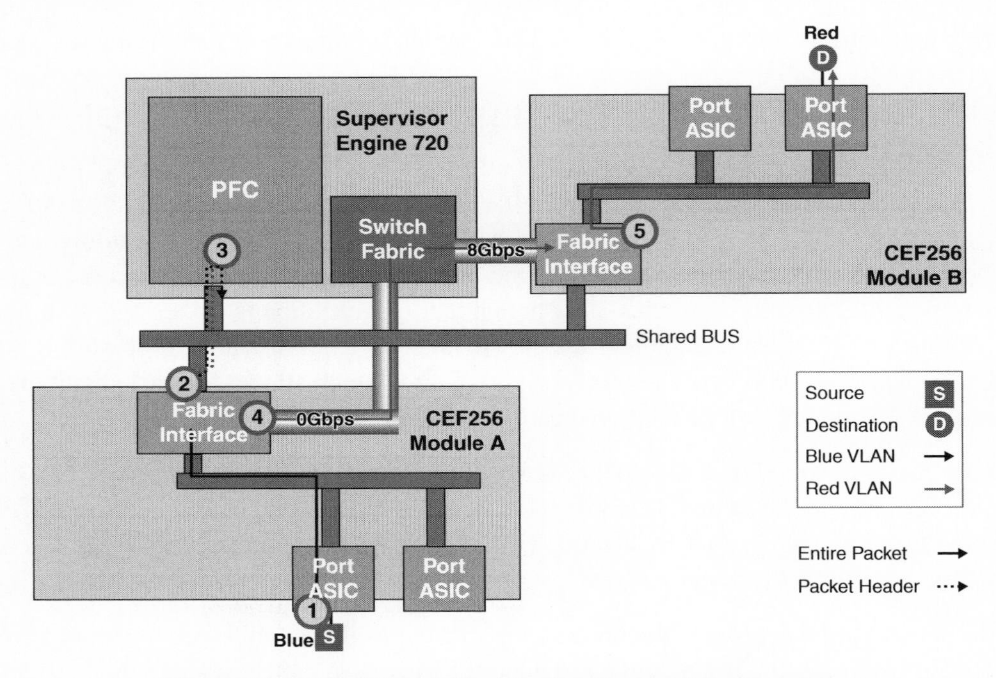

Figure 7.34: 7600 Centralized Packet Forwarding Overview

2. The packet is stored in buffer memory with the header copied and forwarded to the Supervisor Engine PFC for processing.
3. The header information, including source, destination, port, and ToS/DiffServ, is processed by the PFC to determine destination. It is at this point that QoS features, including policing, WRED, and queuing, are implemented. The PFC determines the egress line card for the packet, which is signaled to the ingress line card and switch fabric.
4. Header changes are applied to the packet in ingress line card memory, if required. The packet is then forwarded across the switch fabric (or shared bus for classic line cards) to the egress line card.
5. The packet is forwarded to the appropriate egress port ASIC where the layer 1/2 framing is applied and sent on the physical transmission media.

Figure 7.35 shows the packet path through the 7600 with distributed forwarding.

CEF720-type line cards with the DFC option are used in this example.

The packet forwarding from source to destination is as follows:

1. The packet is received on the line-card port ASIC where the framing is stripped. The packet is then forwarded to the fabric buffer memory.

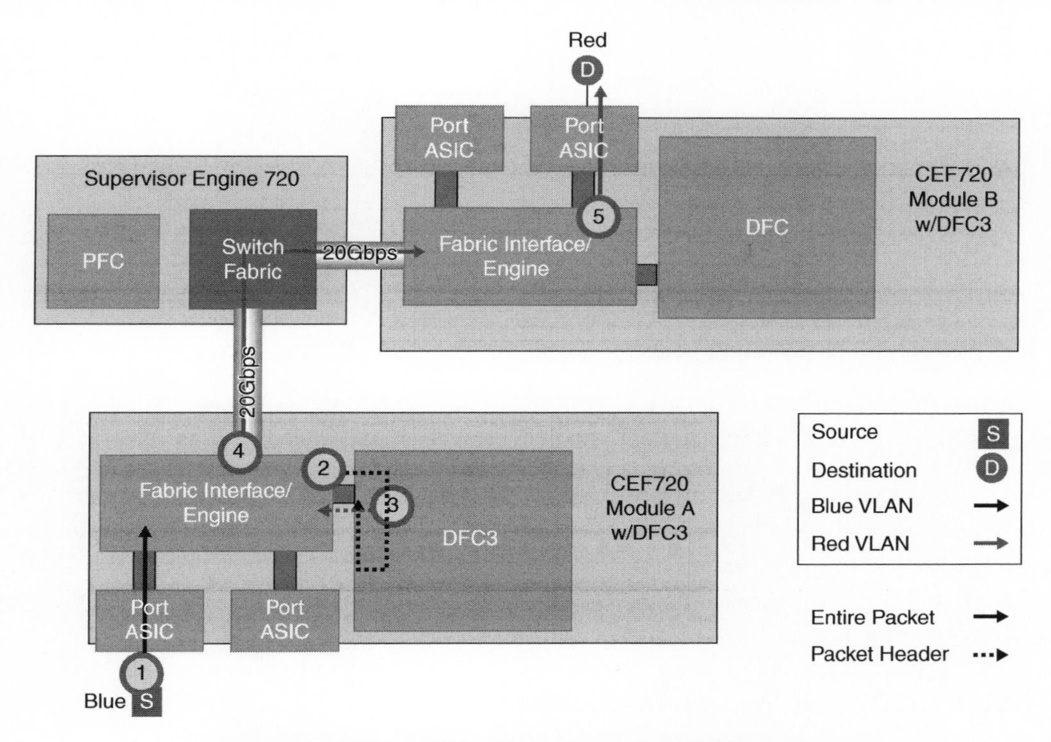

Figure 7.35: 7600 Distributed Packet Forwarding Overview

2. The packet is stored in buffer memory, with the header copied and forwarded to the line card DFC for processing.
3. The header information, including source, destination, port, and ToS/DiffServ, is processed by the ingress line-card DFC to determine destination. It is at this point that QoS features, including policing, WRED, and queuing, are implemented. The DFC determines the egress line card for the packet, which is signaled to the ingress line-card and switch fabric.
4. Header changes are applied to the packet in ingress line-card memory, if required. The packet is then forwarded across the switch fabric to the egress line card.
5. The packet is forwarded to the appropriate egress port ASIC, where the layer 1/2 framing is applied and sent on the physical transmission media.

7.5 Cisco ASR1000 Series Router

The Cisco ASR 1000 Series Aggregation Services Router is a next-generation, modular, highly scalable midrange routing platform designed to support up to 8 Mpps packet forwarding and 10 Gbps system bandwidth, regardless of features enabled. The ASR is designed as an edge aggregation device with features and performance required for modern SP applications.

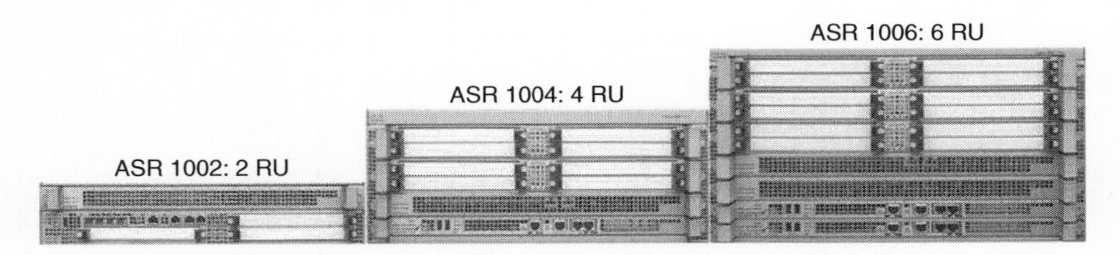

Figure 7.36: ASR1000 Router Series Overview

The platform has three form factors as shown in Figure 7.36.

As shown, three chassis options provide form factors to meet edge requirements from small to large aggregation POPs. Specific details of each chassis are as shown in Figure 7.37.

The ASR1000 relies on a Route Processor and Embedded Services Processor for packet forwarding, as described in the following section. All interfaces are connected via Shared Port Adapters (SPAs) attached to fixed slots or SPA Interface Processors (SIPs). As previously mentioned, the SPA hardware can be used across a variety of router platforms to ensure a cost-effective network solution.

7.5.1 ASR1000 Series Routers Architecture

The architecture on the Cisco ASR 1000 Series Router has taken lessons learned from high-end routers to develop a high-performance and scalable midrange router. Traditionally, low- to midrange devices collapse the forwarding plane and control plane into a single CPU to ensure a cost-effective solution. This limits the platform's ability to scale and adapt, particularly with ever-increasing throughput and feature requirements from SP networks.

The ASR 1000 Series Routers rely on hardware separation of control and forwarding functions into dedicated processors as follows:

- The Route Processor (RP) handles control-plane traffic, that is, executes IP routing protocols and manages the system.
- The Embedded Services Processor (ESP) handles forwarding-plane traffic that is, performs packet-processing functions such as firewall inspection, ACLs, encryption, and QoS.
- The Services Port Adapter Interface Processor (SPA SIP) houses the SPAs, which provide interface (I/O) connectivity.

Figure 7.38 shows the architecture for the Cisco ASR 1000 router, specifically the ASR1006.

The ASR1006 features redundant RPs and ESPs in an active/standby mode, as shown in the figure. The line cards are connected via a passive midplane design specifically architected to

	Cisco ASR 1002	Cisco ASR 1004	Cisco ASR 1006
Chassis	Size: 2 rack units (2RU) DC power (maximum): 590W AC power (maximum): 560W Scalable to 10 Gbps Software failover	Size: 4RU DC power (maximum): 1020W AC power (maximum): 960W Scalable to 40 Gbps Software failover	Size: 6RU DC power (maximum): 1700W AC power (maximum): 1600W Scalable to 40 Gbps Hardware failover
Forwarding cards	One 5-Gbps Cisco ASR 1000 Series ESP (ESP5) (part number ASR1000-ESP5) or one 10-Gbps Cisco ASR 1000 Series ESP (ESP10) (part number ASR1000-ESP10) 4–8 millions of packets per second (Mpps) 5-Gbps forwarding	One Cisco ASR 1000 Series ESP10 (ASR1000-ESP10) 8 Mpps 10-Gbps forwarding	One or two Cisco ASR 1000 Series ESP10s (ASR1000-ESP10) 1 + 1 redundancy 8Mpps 10-Gbps forwarding
Route processor	Integrated 4-GB memory	One Cisco ASR 1000 Series Route Processor 1 (RP1) (ASR1000-RP1) 2-or 4-GB memory Optional 40-GB hard disk drive	One or two Cisco ASR 1000 Series RP1s (ASR1000-RP1) 1 + 1 redundancy 2- or 4-GB memory Optional 40-GB hard disk drive
Carrier card	Integrated: 3 SPA slots	Up to two Cisco ASR 1000 Series SPA Interface Processors (SIPs) (ASR1000-SIP10) 8 SPA slots	Up to three Cisco ASR 1000 Series SIPs (ASR1000-SIP10) 12 SPA slots

Figure 7.37: ASR1000 Router Series Platform Overview

provide meshed connections between the RPs and ESPs and between the interface processors and ESPs. The Cisco ASR 1004 and 1002 routers each have a single RP and ESP.

One innovative feature on the ASR1000 router is that the Cisco IOS Software supports dual software packages in a single RP for software redundancy on the Cisco ASR 1002 and the Cisco ASR 1004 chassis. This allows redundancy in software for the lower-end ASR1000 chassis without the expense of the additional hardware in the ASR1006 chassis.

The ASR 1000 Series Routers have a distributed control plane in which each of the RP, ESP, and SIP line cards has its own dedicated CPU to run the various control tasks and perform any required housekeeping.

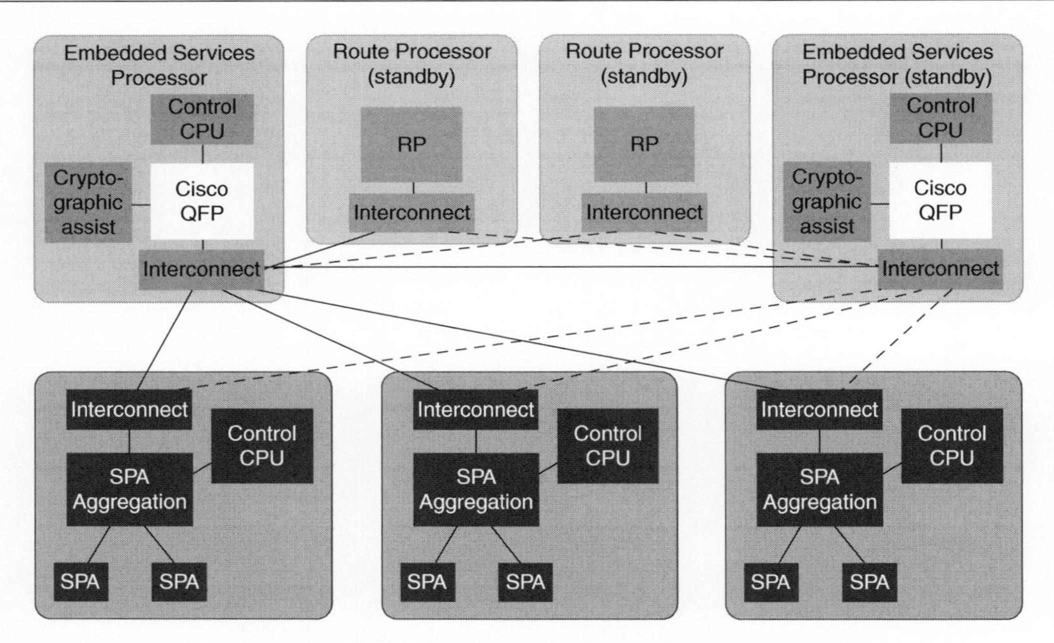

Figure 7.38: ASR1000 Router System Architecture Overview

Cisco ASR 1000 Series Routers is a centralized forwarding architecture. All traffic flows go through the centralized ESP where packet processing (firewall, ACLs, encryption, QoS, and so on) is executed. The SIP line cards are responsible for framing and forwarding packets. The ESP relies on multiple functions to be executed in parallel to ensure that the platform can achieve the required scale and performance.

7.5.2 ASR1000 Series Route Processor and Embedded Service Processor

The ASR 1000 Series Route Processor 1 (RP1) is responsible for building the route and forwarding tables for IP and Multi Protocol Label Switching (MPLS) packets. These tables are subsequently downloaded to the Embedded Services Processor (ESP), discussed later in this section. The RP1 also monitors and manages the other components in the router chassis, such as the ESP and SIP.

Figure 7.39 shows the ASR1000 RP line card.

The first-generation Route Processor offers the following additional embedded features:

- Runs the modular Cisco IOS XE Software, which is a new-generation, modular code base, evolved from the IOS code
- Provides optional redundant-processor support for the ASR1006 chassis
- Provides dual Cisco IOS Software support for the single route processor ASR1002 and ASR1004

Figure 7.39: ASR1000 Router Series Route Processor

- Provides 40 GB hard disk drive (HDD) for code storage, boot, configuration, logs, and the like
- Provides USB port for 1 GB Compact Flash memory support
- Provides built-in eUSB memory support: 1 GB on ASR1000-RP1; 8 GB on the built-in RP1 on the Cisco ASR 1002 Router (partitioned: 1 GB for bootflash; 7 GB for mass storage)
- Provides Stratum-3 clock circuitry and input ports
- Provides memory scalability up to 4 GB DRAM

The RP1 is responsible for the following processes in the ASP1000 router:

- Building and distributing forwarding information to the Embedded Services Processor (ESP)
- Implementing session border controller (SBC) setup and teardown
- Offering a portal for stateful firewall policy configuration and distribution to the ESP forwarding engine
- Negotiating and maintaining IP Security (IPsec1) authentication, encryption methods, and encryption keys (Internet Key Exchange [IKE])
- Loads the operating system software system images to all installed line cards at powering up
- Synchronizes the dynamic state conditions for the redundant operating system, the route processor, and embedded services processor components
- Performs failover for redundant components
- Provides out-of-band system console and auxiliary ports, a USB, and an Ethernet port for router configuration and maintenance

- Allows direct system access through the operating system kernel if catastrophic Cisco IOS Software failure occurs
- Monitors and manages the power and temperature of system components such as line cards, power supplies, and fans

The ASR 1000 Series Embedded Service Processors (ESPs) are based on a technology known as the QuantumFlow Processor for packet forwarding and queuing in hardware. The ESP is available in two models with 5 and 10 Gbps performance, respectively.

Figure 7.40 shows the Embedded Services Processor (ESP) hardware.

The ESP is responsible for the data-plane processing tasks and all associated traffic flows through the ASR1000 routing platform. This includes all baseline packet-routing operations such as MAC classification, Layer 2 and Layer 3 forwarding, QoS classification, policing and shaping, security ACLs, VPNs, load balancing, and NetFlow. The ESP is also responsible for advanced features such as firewalls, intrusion prevention, Network-Based Application Recognition (NBAR), Network Address Translation (NAT), and flexible pattern matching.

The 5 Gbps ESP supports 5 Gbps bandwidth and is supported exclusively on the Cisco ASR1002 Router chassis option. The 10 Gbps ESP supports 10 Gbps bandwidth and is

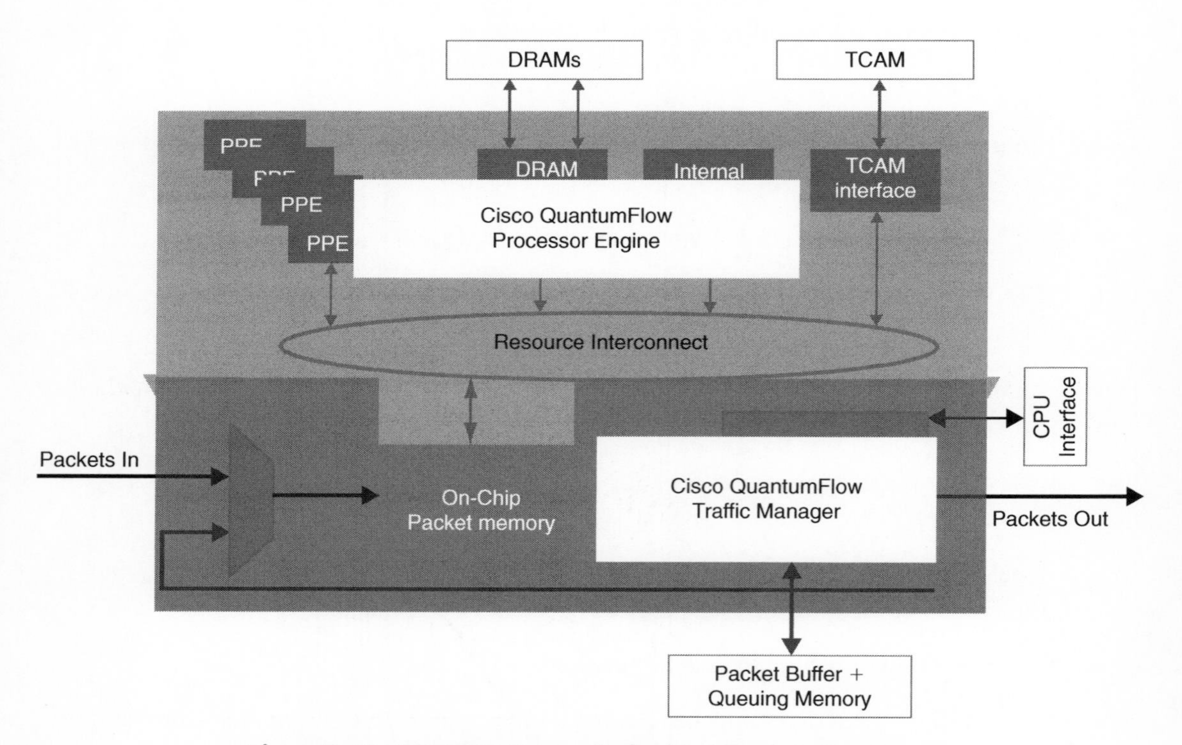

Figure 7.40: ASR1000 Router Embedded Services Processor

supported on all Cisco ASR 1000 Series chassis options. The ESP can optionally be deployed in a 1:1 redundant configuration.

7.5.3 Embedded Services Processor QuantumFlow Processor

As mentioned, the ESP uses a QuantumFlow Processor (QFP) complex for scalable and high-performance implementation of features. This processor complex uses both purpose-built ASICs and general-purpose network processors to provide hardware-accelerated packet forwarding while maintaining feature enhancement flexibility in the future.

Figure 7.41 shows an overview of the QuantumFlow Processor complex.

As shown in the figure, the QFP consists of two main components:

- *Cisco QuantumFlow Process Engine.* A set of powerful packet-processing engines (cores) running at 900 MHz to 1.2 GHz. This parallel-processing complex allows the entire payload and headers of frames to be processed simultaneously. Essentially this chip is dedicated to accelerating features such as firewall, NBAR, and NetFlow and reduces the need for external service blades inside the router.
- *Cisco QuantumFlow Traffic Manager.* A hardware-queuing engine with hundreds of customized network processor resources, each capable of flexible flow processing for

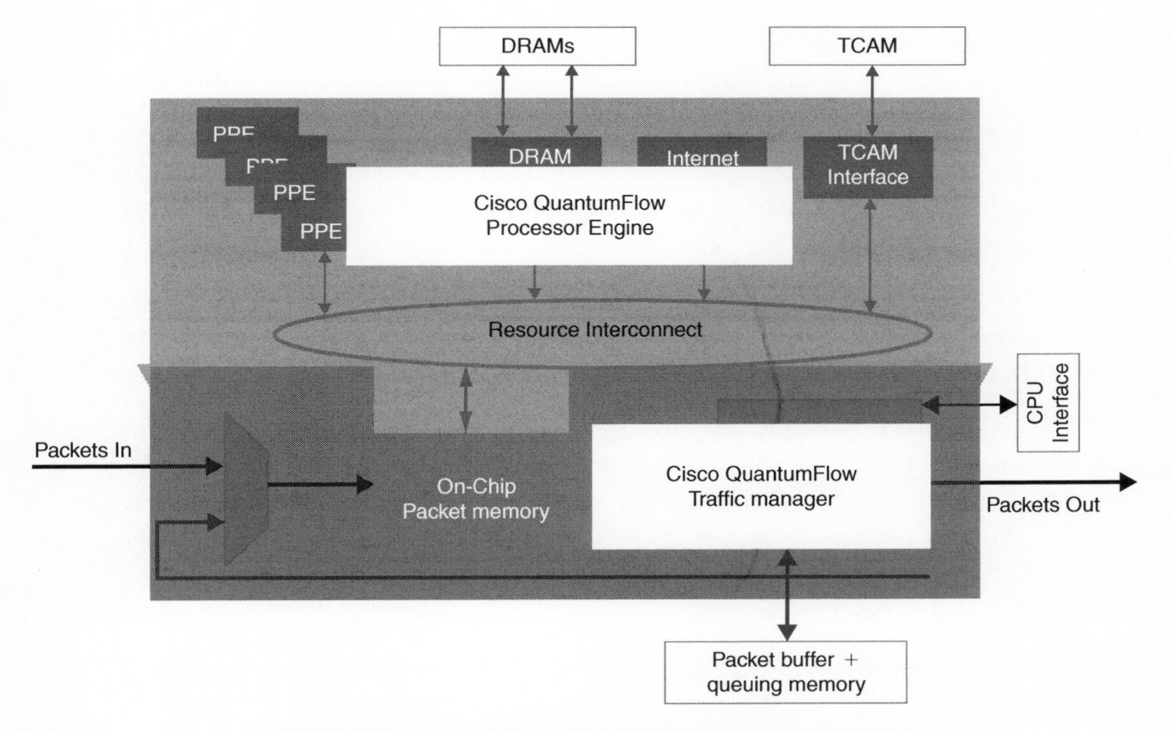

Figure 7.41: ASR1000 Router QuantumFlow Processor

many applications into more than 100,000 queues. This chip enables accelerated and highly scalable QoS with minimum penalty for highly intensive tasks such as shaping, policing, and WRED.

In addition, on- and off-chip resources on the ESP assist QFP in accelerating specific features:

- The cryptographic engine (CE) features multiple packet-processing cores to accelerate cryptographic functions, delivering up to 2.5 Gbps IPsec throughput with IMIX traffic. The cryptographic engine is accessed from the PPE via the traffic manager, where it is buffered, queued, and scheduled to the cryptographic engine. When the cryptographic operation is completed, the packet returns to a PPE for additional packet processing.
- In regard to scalable IP multicast encryption, three mechanisms, namely the multiple cores in the CE, full-circle back pressure mechanisms between the CE and QFP, and a large CE buffer, are all designed to enable highly scalable IP multicast encryption, avoiding packet drops in situations in which bursts of replicated packets are directed at the cryptographic engine.
- Other resources assist the QFP in hardware feature acceleration of network address and prefix lookups, hash lookups, WRED, traffic policers, range lookups, and TCAM for advanced classification and ACL acceleration as it processes packets.

The Cisco QuantumFlow Processor is built around 40 custom Cisco QuantumFlow Processor Packet Processing Engines (PPEs), each of which supports individual threads of program execution. This allows hundreds of independent processor threads running in parallel.

This hardware architecture allows the Cisco QuantumFlow Processor to provide concurrent deployment of multiple features and services such as firewalling, intrusion detection, Network Address Translation (NAT), and deep packet inspection, without risk of CPU overload or excessive processing delays.

The Cisco QuantumFlow Processor includes a sophisticated memory management architecture with high-speed, multilevel instruction caches to allow immediate access to the necessary code to apply multiple services to any packet.

The PPEs on the Cisco QuantumFlow Processor have access to the entire packet, not just packet headers, as is the case in other architectures. This enables complex operations requiring deep packet inspection to be immediately executed, therefore dramatically reducing overall processing time.

7.5.4 ASR1000 Series Line Cards

The Cisco I-Flex design combines SPAs and SIPs. This allows portability of interface hardware across multiple platforms in the Cisco range of routers and switches.

As previously described, the SIP is built into the ASR1002 chassis and supported as a modular component on the Cisco ASR1004 and Cisco ASR1006 chassis options. The first-generation SIP, both fixed and modular, supports up to 10 Gbps throughout.

Figure 7.42 shows the modular SIP used in the ASR1004 and ASR1006.

The Cisco ASR 1000 Series SIP provides the physical termination for selected SPAs, accepting up to four half-height or two full-height SPAs supporting Ethernet, ATM, Packet over SONET/SDH (PoS), and serial interfaces.

The ASR 1000 platform is built on a centralized forwarding architecture; hence the SIP does not participate in forwarding decisions. The SIP provides ingress classification and buffering capabilities before passing traffic to the Embedded Services Processor (ESP) for packet processing.

The SIP has built-in network clock circuitry to receive and distribute clocking information between the Route Process (RP) and the SPAs. The software architecture of the ASR1000 router allows SPAs installed on the SIP to be hot-swapped individually, without impact to the remaining SPAs installed in the same SIP or the same chassis.

7.5.5 ASR1000 Quality of Service

A midrange router positioned at the edge of an SP network requires high-speed, advanced QoS mechanisms as a prerequisite. QoS processing on the ASR1000 router is executed on the SIP line card and the centralized ESP line card. The Cisco QuantumFlow Processor on the ESP utilizes more than 100,000 hardware queues allocated in an arbitrary hierarchy, allowing a flexible, sophisticated, tiered traffic management system.

Figure 7.43 shows the QoS capabilities on the SPA Interface Processor line card.

Figure 7.42: ASR1000 Router Series SPA Interface Processor

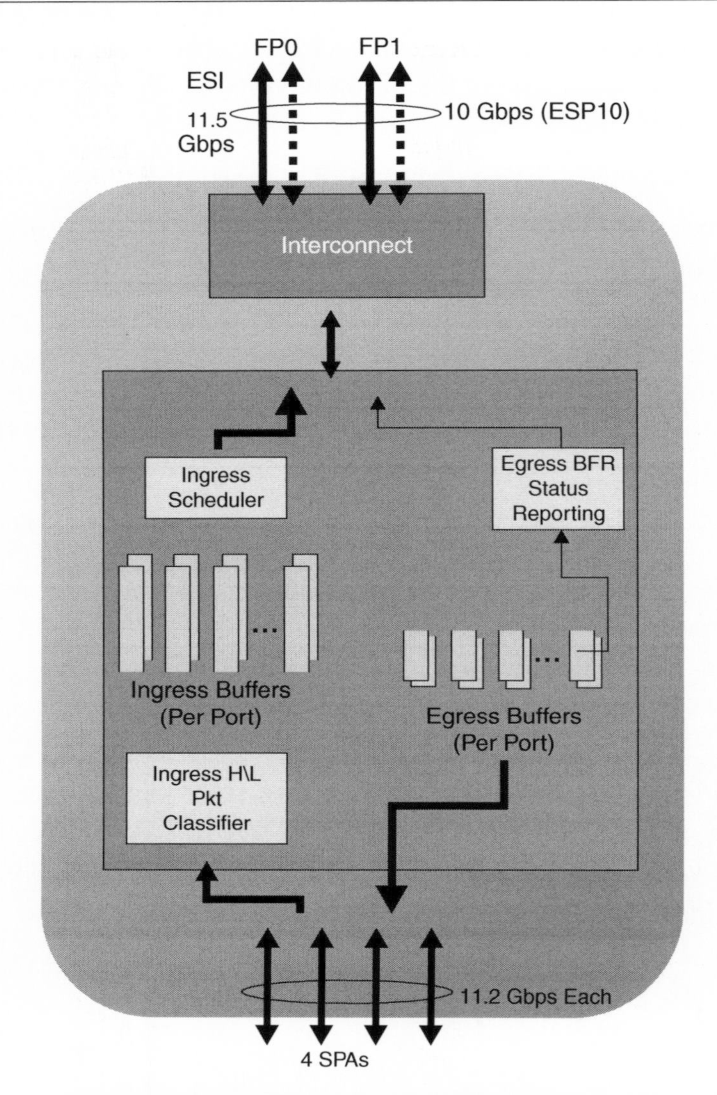

Figure 7.43: ASR1000 Router SIP Quality of Service

The SIP line card has the following QoS features for ingress traffic:

Ingress packet priority classification:

- Identifies ingress packets as low- or high-priority traffic to match scheduling to ESP
- Classifies based on 802.1P, IPv4 TOS, IPv6 TC, MPLS EXP

Ingress scheduler for packets to ESP:

- Queues packet to ESP across high-speed interconnect links
- Weighted fair scheduling is default but can be configured

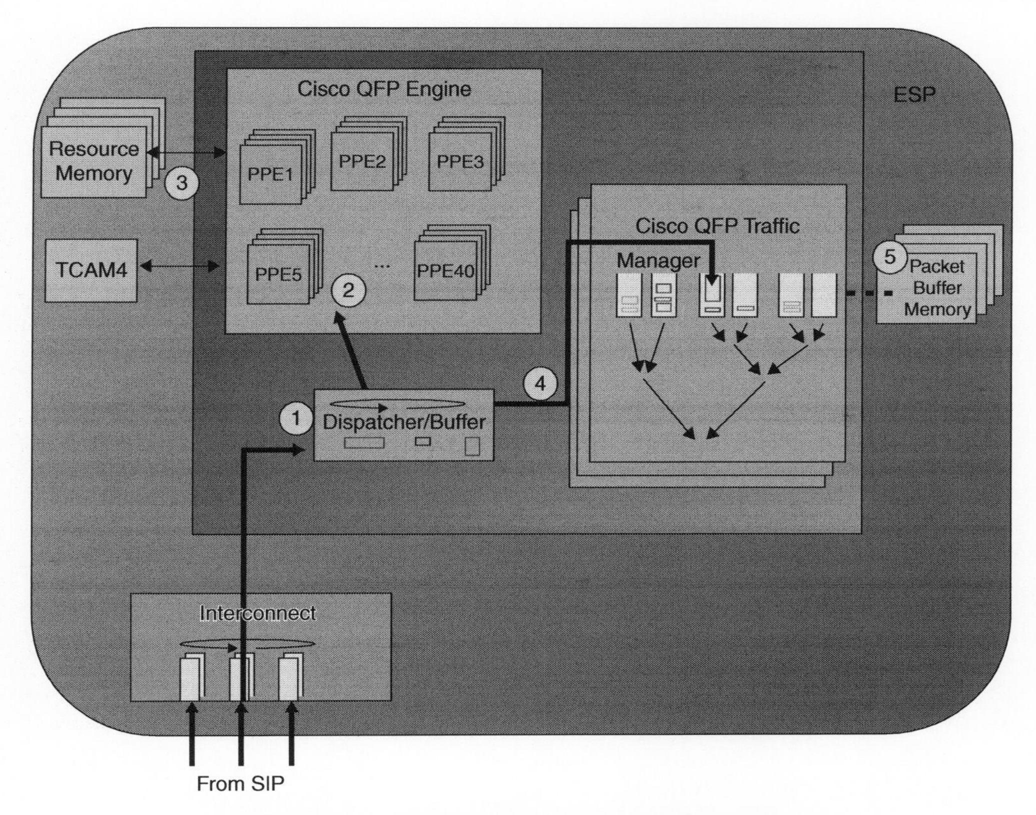

Figure 7.44: ASR1000 Router ESP Quality of Service

Ingress buffering when ESP oversubscribed:

- Line card accepts packets at line rate
- Buffers packets based on high- and low-priority queues per port
- Total ingress buffer pool is 128 MB per SIP

The SIP line card has the following QoS features for egress traffic:

Egress buffering from ESP:

- Shallow buffers per port for accepting packets from the ESP

Egress scheduler for packets to interface:

- Queues packet to interface
- Weighted fair scheduling is default but can be configured using MQC

The majority of QoS functions in the ASR1000 router are executed on the Embedded Services Processor as previously noted. Figure 7.44 can be used as a reference for describing the packet path through the ESP.

The packet path steps are as follows:

1. Ingress packets are temporarily stored in the internal dispatcher packet buffer until processed.
2. The first free QFP Engine is allocated for this packet and begins processing packets (MAC classification, QoS classification, ACLs, forwarding lookup, policing, WRED, etc.), including modifying packet contents as required (e.g., DSCP/ToS rewrite).
3. The QFP Engine accesses tables in resource DRAM and TCAM to perform lookups for features required for this packet, update statistics, and update states for stateful features.
4. Once packet processing is complete and the packet has been modified, if required, the software issues a request to enqueue the packet to an output queue for transmission to the appropriate SIP.
5. The packet is copied from the internal packet buffer to the deep output packet buffer, where it awaits scheduling for output.

The Cisco QFP Traffic Manager monitors millions of events per second across multiple channels, allowing very accurate scheduling, which is essential for effective QoS enforcement. Other hardware resources in the packet path, such as the encryption engine, SPAs, and the route processor, rely on sophisticated traffic management capabilities to ensure that oversubscription within the router platform is avoided while maintaining appropriate priority from the input to the output interface.

7.6 Summary

This chapter gave a high-level overview of the most popular Cisco routers used in service provider networks today. The CRS is the premier core routing platform capable of scaling from 640 Gbps to 92 Tbps with a distributed, multishelf architecture. The 12000 Series routers are appropriate for core, aggregation, or edge applications scaling from 30 Gbps to 1.28 Tbps, with wire rate edge feature line-card options available. The 7600 Series routers are designed for high-density, high-speed Ethernet applications at the edge and aggregation layers in an SP network. The 7600 supports various chassis and performance options scaling from 240 Gbps to 720 Gbps. The ASR1000 is a highly scalable, feature-rich edge router scaling to 10 Gbps and 8 million packets per second throughput with all features enabled.

CHAPTER 8

Cisco IOS and IOS-XR Quality-of-Service Implementation for MPLS Layer 3 VPN Services

8.1 Overview

The previous section focused on highlighting the architectural nuances of the QoS implementation on Cisco hardware that is widely used in service provider (SP) deployments. This section intends to take the lessons forward and help in translating them into building QoS classes for MPLS Layer 3 VPN services. This chapter and subsequent chapters focus on QoS implementation for the most common network services in a given IP/MPLS network rather than focusing on individual applications, since traffic in an SP network is grouped within network services. Applications within these services are typically classified and eventually grouped into traffic classes to provide unique separation from a QoS standpoint and, in effect, to provide differential treatment within the same network. For instance, an MPLS Layer 3 VPN used by Customer FOO may carry voice, video, and data applications, each subscribed to a different QoS class in the SP network.

In effect, SPs deploy QoS for their various network services to achieve the following:

- Provides the SP with an opportunity to deploy a consistent service (in effect, product) definition for the current generation or new services that are being planned. Deployment of QoS ensures predictable network behavior and service performance, even during times of congestion that are short term in nature.
- Comply with service-level agreements (SLAs) offered to end customers/subscribers. This becomes increasingly important for services such as voice- and video-based applications that have strict service-level requirements.
- Provides the SP with an opportunity to price and position products based on the Class-of-Service (CoS) category. Even though network resources may be in abundance/excess, it becomes increasingly important for an SP to offer services based on the type of subscription a customer may opt for, thus providing flexibility for the end customer in choosing a service type.

8.2 QoS Implementation for MPLS Layer 3 VPN Services

This section provides the various edge and core MQC configuration templates for the Cisco CRS-1-, Cisco 12000-, Cisco 7600-, and Cisco 7200-based platforms. Looking back at Chapter 2, "Introduction to Cisco's Quality-of-Service Architecture for IP Networks," the network edge is responsible for classification and marking and in essence creates a platform for per-hop behaviors for each traffic class, whereas the network core introduces queuing based on behavior aggregates. To elaborate further, Figure 8.1 provides an illustration of the IP NGN infrastructure owned by an SP named *FOO*. This network is used as a reference for building the configuration templates for this chapter and serves as a case study for developing an SP NGN framework and its subsequent implementation.

In Figure 8.1, the IP NGN core consists of Cisco CRS-1 and Cisco 12000 routers, and the edge layer consists of 7600 and 7200 routers dedicated as provider edge (PE) devices. The PE-AGG devices are 7600 routers, and UPE devices are Cisco Catalyst Ethernet switches.

NOTE 8.1: Edge Layer

In addition to Cisco 7600 and 7200 devices, edge configuration and implementation templates for the Cisco 12000 and CRS-1 platforms are included for the sake of completeness.

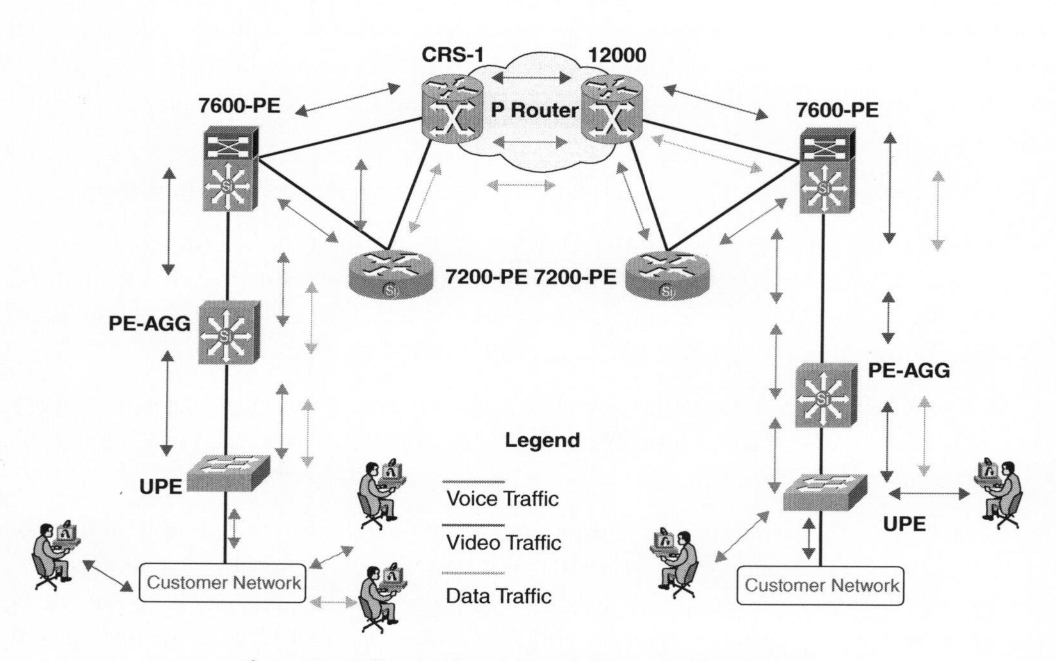

Figure 8.1: Illustration of an IP NGN Infrastructure

An Ethernet access layer is shown to indicate a Carrier Ethernet (also known as *Metro Ethernet*) access, which essentially serves as an extension to the SP network. The Carrier Ethernet access layer increases the scope and reach of the SP (FOO, in this case study), enabling more extensive coverage in reaching end customers and offering a broader range of quad-play services. In our case study, Figure 8.2 illustrates that the IP NGN of Service Provider FOO is a converged network that hosts voice, video, mobility, and data traffic. Therefore the QoS framework needs to address these needs in great detail.

By definition, the User PE (UPE) layer provides the user-to-network interconnect (UNI) and directly interfaces with the end customer or subscriber of the SP. The PE Aggregation (PE-AGG) layer acts as an aggregator for multiple UPE devices in a given region or area. For instance, an SP point of presence (POP) in New York can have one or more PE-AGG devices per suburb, which would consolidate the traffic from all the UPE devices. The PE-AGG layer converges at the PE layer. One of the primary differences between the Ethernet access layer in the path up to the PE layer and the SP PE and provider (core layers) lies in the marking of traffic and the appropriate classifiers used for queuing. By virtue of being a Layer 2 domain, the Ethernet access layer uses 802.1P bits for marking and queuing. On the contrary, the network core uses MPLS EXP or IP DSCP values based on the network/service type.

It is assumed that SP FOO needs to support a wide range of traffic types within its network. The various traffic types that will be transported over this network are as follows:

- Voice over IP
- Broadcast video (IPTV is used here)

		SLA Characteristics						
Service Class	Application	Loss	Delay	Jitter	BW	EXP	Markdown	Oversub
Control	Routing and Control	☑	☑	-	~2%	6,7	No	No
Real-time	Voice	☑	☑	☑	~25%	5	No	No
Video	IPTV and Telepresence	☑	☑	-	~40%	4	No	No
Premium	Streaming video, intranet, OAM, and premium data applications	☑	-	-	~28%	2	1	Low
Best-Effort	Broadband users and low-priority data	—	—	—	~5%	0	No	Med./High

Figure 8.2: Five-Class Model as Reference

- Streaming video (3G applications)
- TelePresence (which is used by the SP's end customers)
- Intranet applications and financial transactions
- Internet and broadband services

Based on the various traffic types, a five-class QoS framework has been used for SP FOO, as illustrated in Figure 8.2. In our example, VoIP traffic has been allocated a dedicated class and queue structure and is by choice the candidate for the LLQ. A dedicated class known as Video will host broadcast video and TelePresence applications. Premium data applications and other video services such as "streaming video and 3G-based mobile video applications" are grouped together in a separate class referred to as the Premium category. A dedicated class, referred to as Control, is reserved for control and signaling traffic. Finally, a Best-Effort class will serve the remaining applications that do not categorize in either of the previously mentioned.

NOTE 8.2: Queue Characteristics

Each queue will be configured as per the recommendations made in Chapter 3, "Class-of-Service Requirements for Quad-Play Networks." The same principle applies to all the implementation-specific chapters.

Going forward, all the chapters focusing on the implementation of QoS will use this five-class model (as illustrated in Figure 8.2) for illustrating the configuration templates, to maintain consistency across the various chapters. This class model was deemed broadly suitable for the demonstration network but does not necessarily address the requirements of all service providers. Therefore, in real-time deployments, you might choose to opt for a different QoS model based on both the business and technical requirements. Therefore all configurations will reflect the characteristics of the classes, as illustrated in Figure 8.2.

NOTE 8.3: The Reference Five-Class Model

Markdown indicates that the class supports forwarding of out-of-contract traffic with a lesser service guarantee. The Premium class in Figure 8.2 remarks out-of-contract traffic.

In Figure 8.3, we discuss the various SLAs offered by SP FOO for each class in the NGN core. The SLAs offered are categorized into delay, jitter, and packet loss. These metrics are in line with the recommendations provided in Chapter 3, "Class-of-Service Requirements for Quad-Play Networks." In fact, some of the SLAs used by SP FOO are more aggressive than the standard recommendations provider in Chapter 3. Therefore all the configuration templates will be tuned to this effect. We take a look at these values in Figure 8.3.

		SLA Characteristics						
Service Class	Application	Loss	Delay	Jitter	BW	EXP	Markdown	Oversub
Control	Routing and Control	0%	<250 ms	N/A	~2%	6,7	No	No
Real-time	Voice	0%	100 ms	20 ms	~25%	5	No	No
Video	IPTV and Telepresence	0%	<150 ms	<50 ms	~40%	4	No	No
Premium	Streaming video, intranet, OAM, and premium data applications	N/A	<175 ms	N/A	~28%	2	1	Low
Best-Effort	Broadband users and low-priority data	N/A	N/A	N/A	~5%	0	No	Med./High

Figure 8.3: Per-Class SLA Offerings by Service Provider FOO

It is worth noting that these SLAs and associated metrics are offered on a per-class basis and globally apply to all users or end customers subscribed to a given class. In the DiffServ QoS model, there are no per-customer SLAs in the network core.

8.3 Edge QoS Configurations

This section illustrates QoS configuration templates for MPLS Layer 3 VPN services. The core and edge configurations for the various engine and line-card types are provided separately for the sake of uniqueness. It is assumed that SP FOO uses various line cards and engine types in its IP NGN infrastructure.

There are multiple methods of classifying traffic, and the various examples are not repeated here on a per-line-card basis. Instead the various methods are distributed in their illustrations, wherein each line-card configuration chooses a given scheme. It is to be noted that the edge QoS configurations in the Cisco MQC are almost identical on IOS-based platforms, with the exception of a few keywords that change on certain platforms. These differences are highlighted in this chapter. Similarly, there are minor differences between IOS and IOS-XR-based platforms, and they follow in subsequent sections.

Various examples on classification and marking using a given hardware and line-card type are provided in this chapter. However, not all classes are chosen for illustration under a given hardware/line-card type. Various scenarios are chosen throughout this chapter and, based on a given scenario, one class of traffic is chosen for the illustration.

NOTE 8.4: QoS Configuration Templates

The configurations provided in this chapter are intended to illustrate the various options available for configuring both edge and core QoS. These parameters will need to be tuned as per the exact requirements in a given SP network. The configuration templates in this chapter use various values for configuring the various parameters (such as WRED) to help the reader understand that various combinations can be used.

8.3.1 Cisco 12000 Series Routers

This section focuses on providing the configuration templates for building the needed QoS framework at the edge layer. Various line-card combinations on the Cisco 12000 are used to illustrate this idea. Subtle variations in the configurations across the line cards are highlighted wherever appropriate.

NOTE 8.5: Reference

From this section onward, we refer to the term *customer* to identify the end customers of SP FOO.

Engine 3 Line Cards

Regarding customer requirements: The customer HAY-BANK has subscribed to a Layer 3 VPN service to interconnect his various offices via the Service Provider core, for building an inter-office VoIP infrastructure. All traffic originating from the customer in this scenario is VoIP. Service Provider FOO manages the Customer Edge (CE) device for this customer; hence all VoIP traffic is marked with the DSCP value of Expedited Forwarding (EF) prior to entering the provider edge network. The customer has procured a connection worth 10 Mbps; hence SP FOO also needs to control all inbound traffic to be within the contractual rate.

The following illustration highlights the configuration required for classifying VoIP traffic and appropriately marking the MPLS Experimental bits. Class-map VoIP is used to match all traffic marked with a DSCP value set to EF, which is normally assigned to voice traffic. Typically Cisco VoIP phones mark all voice traffic with a DSCP value equal to EF. The policy map Real-time is used to mark all the EF traffic with an MPLS Experimental value of 5. The value of 5 will typically correspond to the LLQ in the network core. (QoS configuration templates for the core are described in subsequent sections.) Finally, the policy map is attached to the CE-facing interface at the Provider Edge layer.

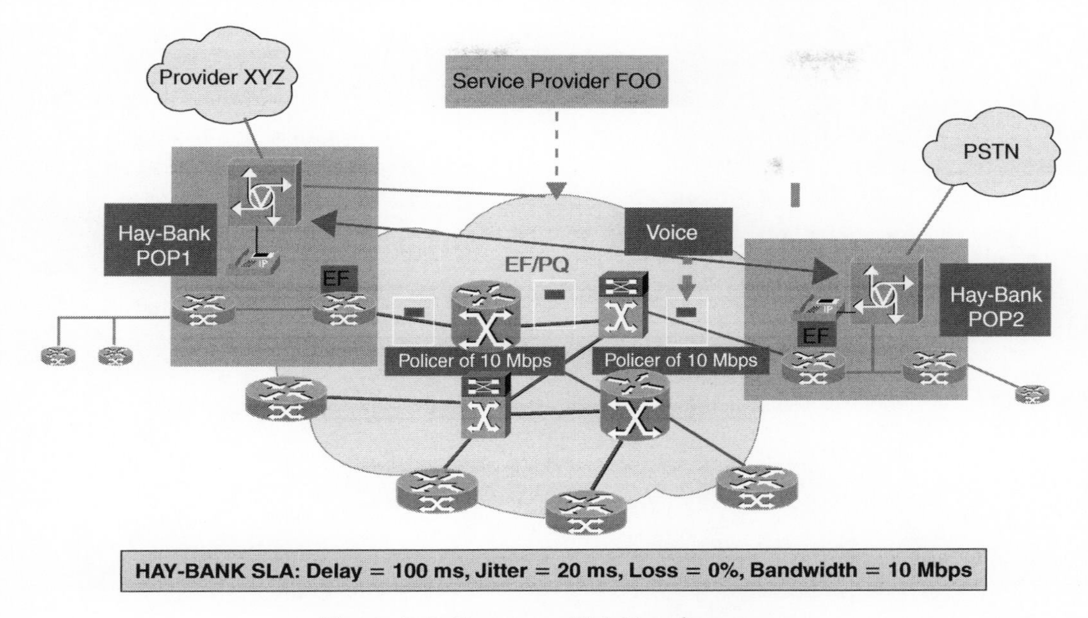

Figure 8.4: Customer SLA Requirements

Figure 8.4 illustrates the customer requirements as well as the overall flow in more detail.

Configuration

```
!
class-map match-any VoIP
 description ### Matching VoIP traffic marked with DSCP Class - EF ###
 match ip dscp EF
!
policy-map Realtime
 class VoIP
police cir 10240000 bc 128000 be 128000 conform-action set-mpls-exp-
topmost-transmit 5 exceed-action drop --------→ Set MPLS EXP 5!
!
interface GigabitEthernet6/3.1000 -------→ PE-CE interface!
 description ### User to Network Interface for Customer-HAY-BANK ###
 encapsulation dot1Q 1000
 ip vrf forwarding HAYBANK-L3VPN
 ip address 8.8.8.1 255.255.255.252
 no ip directed-broadcast
 service-policy input Realtime --→ Ingress Service Policy applied!
!
End
```

NOTE 8.6: Match Criteria

Care needs to be taken prior to the decision to use the appropriate match criteria. The preceding illustration matches all traffic based on a particular DSCP value. Essentially, an SP may match on IP DSCP, precedence, or 802.1P bits if the CE device is managed and maintained by the provider; otherwise, there is always a potential risk involved due to misconfigurations at the SP's end-customer network. For instance, a misconfiguration in the marking policies in the CE device can cause "nonvoice" traffic to also be marked with a DSCP value of EF. This will result in the actual voice traffic being starved of network resources because the SP edge will drop all traffic that exceeds or violates the SLA and, since more than voice may have EF values, assuming there is a misconfiguration, the chances are high that traffic will exceed the committed rate earlier.

Verification

```
!
12416#show policy-map interface gigabitEthernet 6/3.1000
 GigabitEthernet6/3.1000
  Service-policy input: RealTime (432)
   Class-map: Realtime (match-any) (13255777/1)
     11105 packets, 1110500 bytes -----------------> Hits from the edge!
     5 minute offered rate 12000 bps, drop rate 0 bps
     Match: ip dscp EF (15304930)
     Set Policy:
       set mpls experimental imposition 5
```

The output shown here verifies the classification and marking process at the network edge. In our illustration, traffic with DSCP values set to EF is marked with an MPLS EXP value of 5. An account of the number of packets matching this criterion is visible in the output of the *show policy-map interface* command.

Engine 4 and 4+ Line Cards

In terms of customer requirements, the customer ABC-CORP has subscribed to a Layer 3 VPN service to interconnect various offices via the SP core. The customer has both data and video traffic within the enterprise, but it only subscribes to the Premium class. This is a typical example of customers having a mix of traffic but still subscribing to only a single class in the provider network. In this example, customer ABC-CORP considers the SLAs in the Premium class adequate for both data and video applications. In our illustration, the customer has subscribed to a 10 Mbps interconnect; hence all incoming traffic will be policed to this limit.

The same configuration used on the Engine 3 line cards can also be applied to the Engine 4 series as well. An identical configuration used in the illustration for Engine 3-based interfaces is used on an Engine 4 interface as follows, and the same result can be expected. However, there are certain match criterions that are not supported on the Engine 4 line cards. For instance, a match using access groups *match access-group* and match criteria using the *any* keyword (match *any*) cannot be used here.

Once again SP FOO provides a managed CE service for the customer; hence all traffic is marked with DSCP AF41 prior to entering the SP edge. The classified traffic is marked with EXP 2, which corresponds to the Premium class.

Figure 8.5 illustrates the customer requirements as well as the overall flow in more detail.

Engine 5 Line Cards

In terms of customer requirements, the customer XYZ-CORP has subscribed to a Layer 3 VPN service to interconnect various offices via the SP core. The customer uses the VPN only for interoffice email and file-sharing purposes. Hence the customer has opted for only a Best-Effort service. Similarly the subscription is for 1 Mbps.

The same configuration used on the Engine 3 and Engine 4 line cards can also be applied to the Engine 5 series. The illustration for Engine 5 cards follows on page 250.

The classified traffic is marked with EXP 0, which corresponds to the Best-Effort class. Figure 8.6 illustrates the customer requirements as well as the overall flow in more detail.

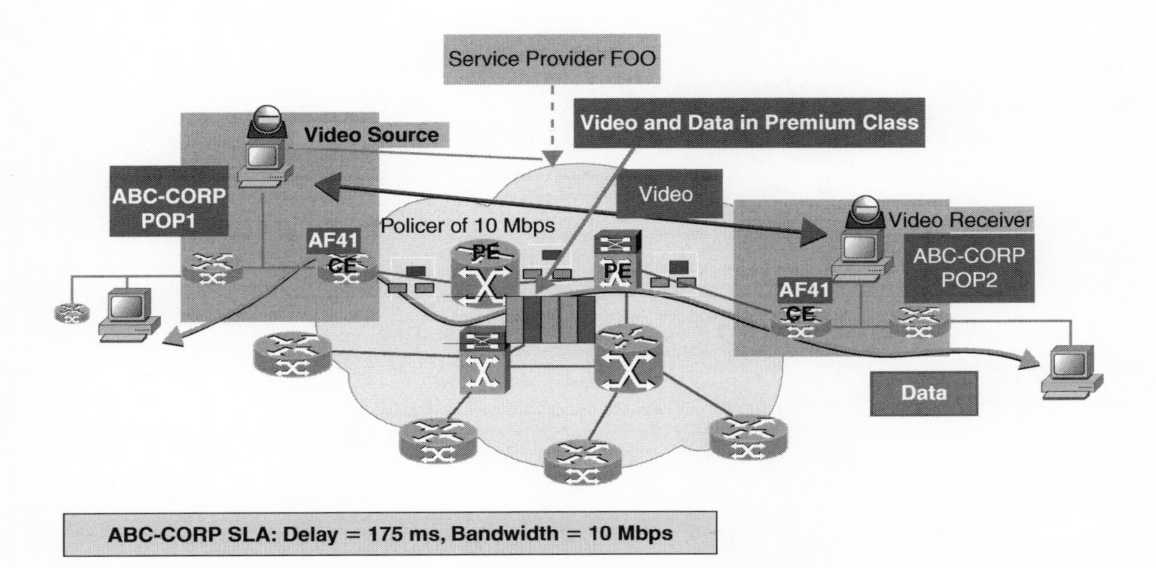

Figure 8.5: Customer SLA Requirements

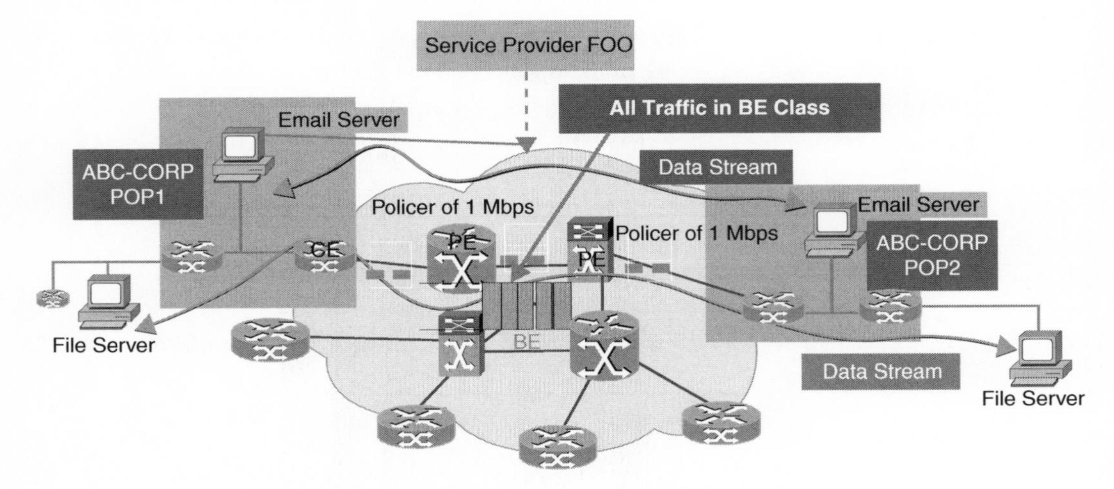

Figure 8.6: Customer SLA Requirements

Configuration

```
!
class-map match-any BE
  description ### Matching all incoming traffic ###
  match any
!
policy-map BE
  class BE
police cir 1024000 bc 128000 be 128000 conform-action set-mpls-exp-topmost-
transmit 0 exceed-action drop --------→ Set MPLS EXP 0!
!
interface GigabitEthernet6/2.1000 ------→ PE-CE interface!
  description ### User to Network Interface for XYZ-CORP ###
  encapsulation dot1Q 1000
  ip vrf forwarding XYZCORP-L3VPN
  ip address 8.8.8.9 255.255.255.252
  no ip directed-broadcast
  service-policy input BE → Ingress Service Policy applied!
!
End
```

TIP 8.1: Use of Policers

It is a recommended practice for SPs to use policers at the network ingress to both enforce SLAs and mark the appropriate QoS values. This is an effective tool in the process of network capacity planning and helps in keeping a tab on the oversubscription of customer traffic that is considered acceptable.

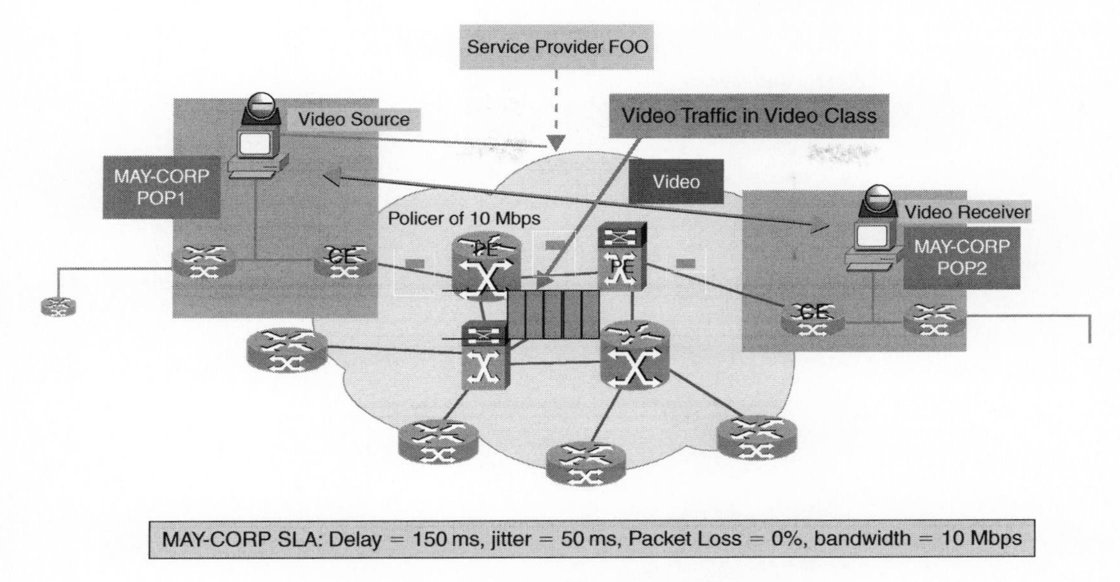

Figure 8.7: Customer SLA Requirements

8.3.2 Edge Configurations for the Cisco 7200 Series Routers

In this section, the edge configurations for the 7200 series of routers are illustrated.

In terms of customer requirements, the customer MAY-CORP has subscribed to a Layer 3 VPN service to establish a corporate videoconferencing network via the SP core. The customer has subscribed to the Video class in the FOO network for a 10 Mbps interconnect. Since all incoming traffic is videoconferencing based, the *match any* keyword is used in the following configuration.

Figure 8.7 illustrates the customer requirements as well as the overall flow in more detail.

Configuration

```
!
class-map match-any Video
 description ### Matching all traffic ###
 match any
!
policy-map Video
 class Video
police cir 10240000 bc 128000 be 128000 conform-action set-mpls-exp-
topmost-transmit 4 exceed-action drop --------→ Set MPLS EXP 4!
!
interface GigabitEthernet0/1 -------→ PE-CE interface!
```

```
 description ### User to Network Interface for MAY-CORP ###
 ip vrf forwarding MAYCORP-L3VPN
 ip address 8.8.8.13 255.255.255.252
 no ip directed-broadcast
 duplex auto
 speed auto
 media-type gbic
 negotiation auto
 service-policy input Video → Ingress Service Policy applied!
!
End
```

Verification

```
7206B#show policy-map interface gigabitEthernet 0/1
 GigabitEthernet0/1
  Service-policy input: Video (16)
    Class-map: Video (match-any) (2909697/10)
      105641 packets, 159639474 bytes --------> Hits on the ingress
interface!
      5 minute offered rate 2923000 bps, drop rate 0 bps
      Match: any (8846562)
        105641 packets, 159639474 bytes
        5 minute rate 2923000 bps
      QoS Set
        mpls experimental imposition 4
          Packets marked 105641 ---→ Indicates the number of packets marked!
```

The output shown here verifies the classification and marking process at the network edge. In our illustration, all traffic entering the network ingress from the customer is marked with an MPLS EXP value of 4. An account of the number of packets matching this criterion and having its QoS values set is visible in the output of the *show policy-map interface* command.

NOTE 8.7: QoS on the 7200

The Edge QoS configuration provided can be applied to any of the supported interfaces on the 7200. This includes interfaces on the Network Processing Engine (NPE) as well as the port adapters.

8.3.3 Edge Configurations for the Cisco 7600 Series Routers

In this section, the edge configurations for the 7600 series of routers are illustrated. Configuration templates for various interfaces such as the Enhanced FlexWan and LAN (WS-67xx-based interface modules) interfaces are provided in the following sections.

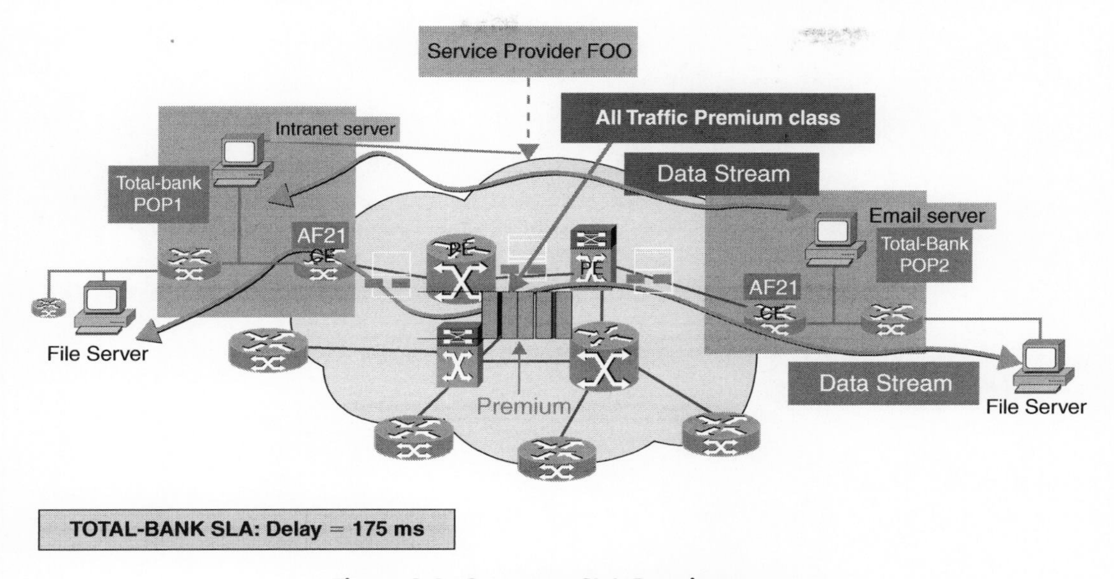

Figure 8.8: Customer SLA Requirements

WS-67xx Line Cards

In terms of customer requirements, the customer TOTAL-BANK has subscribed to a Layer 3 VPN service to interconnect his various offices via the SP core. The customer traffic is a combination of Intranet applications, email, and other traditional data applications. The customer has purchased the Premium service for all his traffic and has a subscription rate of full GE port. The customer has coordinated the marking scheme for all its traffic, and the agreement is that all traffic will be marked with a DSCP value of 18 (Assured Forwarding–AF21) prior to entering the SP edge layer.

The following illustration matches traffic with DSCP value of 18 (Assured Forwarding–AF21) and sets the MPLS EXP bits to a value of 2. EXP value of 2 corresponds to the Premium class in the SP FOO network core. The command *mls qos vlan-based* is required to enable SVI- or VLAN-based QoS on the Cisco 7600 router. Finally, the policy map is applied to the ingress interface for the required processing.

Figure 8.8 illustrates the customer requirements as well as the overall flow in more detail.

Configuration

```
!
class-map match-any data
description ### Matching all traffic marked with DSCP 18 ###
match ip dscp 18
!
policy-map Premium
```

```
class data
 set mpls experimental imposition 2 --------→ Set MPLS EXP 2!
!
interface GigabitEthernet1/1
 description ### User to Network Interface for Customer-XYZ ###
 switchport
 switchport trunk encapsulation dot1q
 switchport mode trunk
 mls qos vlan-based -------→ Required to enable SVI based QoS!
!
interface Vlan1000
 description ### L3VPN Interface XYZ-L3VPN###
 ip vrf forwarding XYZ-L3VPN
 ip address 2.2.2.1 255.255.255.252
 no snmp trap link-status
 service-policy input Premium--→ Ingress Service-Policy!
!
End
```

Trust IP Precedence on WS-67xx Line Cards

The use of Trust states introduces a scalable method of distributing QoS functions in an NGN infrastructure. It largely helps in automating the QoS classification and marking functionalities at the edge of the network, wherein the SP edge layer can merely rely on the QoS marking enforced by the access layer. This access layer can be the CE device (in the case of a Managed CE scenario) or even UPE or PE-Aggregation devices (in the case of a Carrier Ethernet-based access environment). Based on the type of trust established, the SP edge may automatically copy these QoS values into the MPLS Experimental bits for further processing in the network core. This section details the possible Trust states that are configurable on the 7600 LAN (WS67xx) interface modules.

In terms of customer requirements, customer ROYAL-BANK has subscribed to a Layer 3 VPN services and has indicated his preference of subscribing to the Premium class. SP FOO offers a Managed CE service to this customer; hence the CE router is configured to mark all traffic destined for the SP core with IP precedence 2. By virtue of using a Trust Precedence state, we may instruct the PE layer to instruct the router to copy this value to the outgoing MPLS EXP bits. The end result would have an IP precedence value of 2 being copied to an MPLS EXP value of 2.

The following illustration uses Trust IP precedence, which indicates that the incoming IP precedence value set on the IP packet gets copied to the outbound MPLS Experimental and CoS bits. From an MPLS SP infrastructure standpoint, the MPLS EXP bits being rewritten as per the IP precedence values are of specific interest because queuing and scheduling in the network core is essentially based on these values (see Figure 8.9).

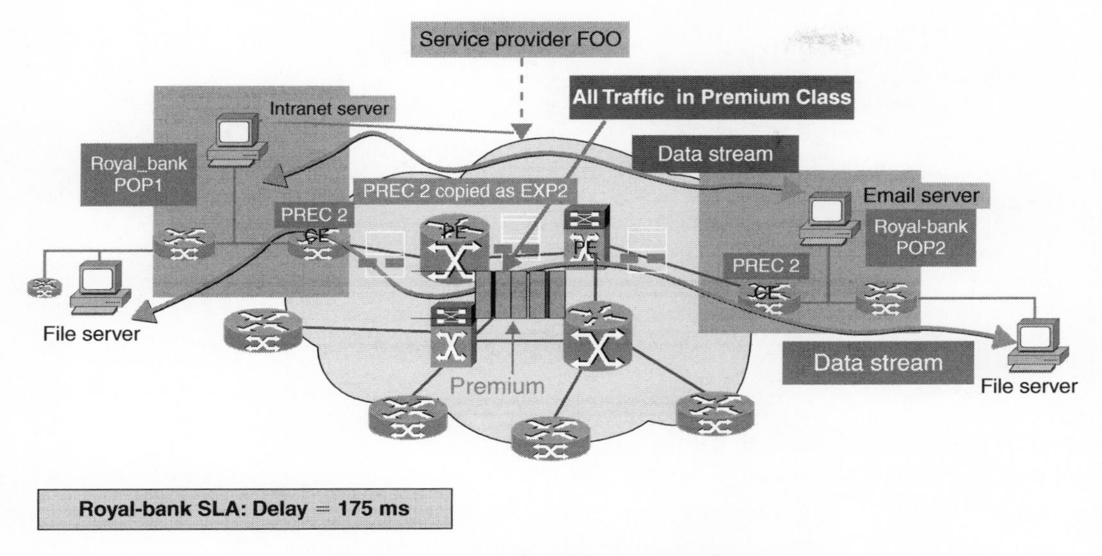

Figure 8.9: Result of Trust Precedence

Configuration

```
!
interface GigabitEthernet1/1
 switchport
 switchport trunk encapsulation dot1q
 switchport mode trunk
 mls qos vlan-based
 mls qos trust ip-precedence ----------> Trust state defined!
end
!
interface Vlan1000 -------> No Service Policy or ingress marking defined!
 description ### L3VPN Interface to Customer ROYAL-BANK ###
 ip vrf forwarding ROYALBANK-L3VPN
 ip address 2.2.2.1 255.255.255.252
 no snmp trap link-status
!
End
```

This can be verified in the output given as follows. The egress policy map indicates that the Premium class corresponds to MPLS EXP values 2 and indicates packet matches that indeed verify the behavior.

Verification

```
7609#show policy-map interface ge-WAN 3/1 output class Premium
 GE-WAN3/1
  Service-policy output: FOO-CORE
```

```
  Class-map: Premium (match-any)
   164 packets, 20008 bytes -------------→ Indicates Egress hits!
   5 minute offered rate 0 bps, drop rate 0 bps
   Match: mpls experimental topmost 2 1 -→ EXP Values 2 is matched
   Queueing
   queue limit 5000 packets
   (queue depth/total drops/no-buffer drops) 0/0/0
   (pkts output/bytes output) 164/20008
  bandwidth 28% (280000 kbps)
   (bandwidth parameter is rounded to 278431 kbps due to granularity)
[Output is Truncated]
```

Trust IP DSCP on WS-67xx Line Cards

Similar to precedence, Trust DSCP can be used at the network ingress (edge). This feature can be used if an SP intends to automatically map certain DSCP values into CoS/EXP values. By default the 7600 will only use the first 3 bits for transferring the value to the outbound CoS/EXP code points, since both these values consist of only 3 bits. This might not be desirable at all points, since copying only 3 bits can result in a behavior that is not expected. The 7600 uses an internal DSCP-CoS map table to decide on the appropriate mappings, as illustrated in Figure 8.10.

If the default behavior is undesirable, the maps can be altered and are user configurable using the command *mls qos map dscp-cos,* wherein up to eight DSCP values can be mapped to single CoS value. Multiple statements can be issued to further modify this on a per-CoS value basis. The following illustration provides a closer view of this topic.

Configuration

```
!
mls qos map dscp-cos 18 26 to 4 ------→ DSCP to CoS Map!
!
interface GigabitEthernet1/1
 description ### Physical interface ###
 switchport
 switchport trunk encapsulation dot1q
 switchport mode trunk
 mls qos vlan-based
 mls qos trust dscp ---------> Trust state defined!
end
!
interface Vlan1000 -------> No Service Policy or ingress marking defined!
 description ### L3VPN Interface to Customer-ABC ###
 ip vrf forwarding ABC-L3VPN
 ip address 2.2.2.1 255.255.255.252
 no snmp trap link-status
!
end
```

DSCP-to-CoS Mapping Table

DSCP Value	0–7	8–15	16–23	24–31	32–39	40–47	48–55	56–63
CoS Value	0	1	2	3	4	5	6	7

Figure 8.10: Default DSCP-to-CoS Map Table

To help understand this configuration template, consider that the PE router is configured for a DSCP-to-CoS map that maps DSCP values 26, 18 to CoS/EXP value 4 (which is the Video queue). Assuming that a CE router is used to send traffic with a DSCP value of 18, the corresponding output queue should be the Video queue. Let's verify the output of this illustration as shown here to confirm the operation.

Verification

```
7609#show policy-map interface ge-WAN 3/1 output
 GE-WAN3/1
  Service-policy output: FOO-CORE
   Class-map: Video (match-any)
    72 packets, 8784 bytes -----------------------> Indicates hits!
    5 minute offered rate 0 bps, drop rate 0 bps
    Match: mpls experimental topmost 4
    Queueing
    queue limit 4167 packets
[Output is Truncated]
```

NOTE 8.8: Default Behavior on Cisco Platforms

By default, Cisco platforms such as the CRS-1, 12000, and 7200 trust DSCP on an incoming interface. Cisco 7600 LAN interfaces need an explicit Trust state to influence a particular behavior.

Trust States and Explicit Policies on WS-67xx Line Cards

It is important to understand the behavior of using a given Trust state on an interface along with an explicit policy map. An interface (physical) cannot have both a policy map and a Trust state configured. Typically either one of the two is supposed to be used. If the user configures both, the Trust state takes precedence. The following illustrates the behavior.

Configuration

```
!
class-map match-any data
  description ### Matching all traffic on a given interface ###
  match any
```

```
!
policy-map Premium
   class data
    set mpls experimental imposition 3 --------→ Set MPLS EXP 3!
!
interface GigabitEthernet1/1
description ### Physical Interface ###
 switchport
 switchport trunk encapsulation dot1q
 switchport mode trunk
 mls qos vlan-based
 mls qos trust dscp ----------> Trust state defined!
end
!
interface Vlan1000
 description ### User to Network Interface to Customer-ABC ###
 ip vrf forwarding ABC-L3VPN
 ip address 2.2.2.1 255.255.255.252
 no snmp trap link-status
service-policy input Premium -----> Service policy marking all traffic to EXP 3!
!
End
```

The preceding illustration shows that an explicit policy, used along with Trust DSCP configured on the Physical interface, does not take effect. As per our illustration, we check the behavior by instructing the CE device to send traffic with DSCP18, and when this is converted to EXP (taking the first 3 bits), it becomes 4, which is mapped into the Video queue as per the QoS framework recommended for SP FOO. A detailed illustration is shown in Figure 8.11, and the output follows.

Verification

```
7609#show policy-map interface ge-WAN 3/1 output class Video
GE-WAN3/1
Service-policy output: FOO-CORE
Class-map: Video (match-any)
72 packets, 8784 bytes ----------> Traffic still gets into this queue!
     5 minute offered rate 0 bps, drop rate 0 bps
     Match: mpls experimental topmost 4
     Queueing
     queue limit 4167 packets
     (queue depth/total drops/no-buffer drops) 0/0/0
     (pkts output/bytes output) 72/8784
[Output is Truncated]
```

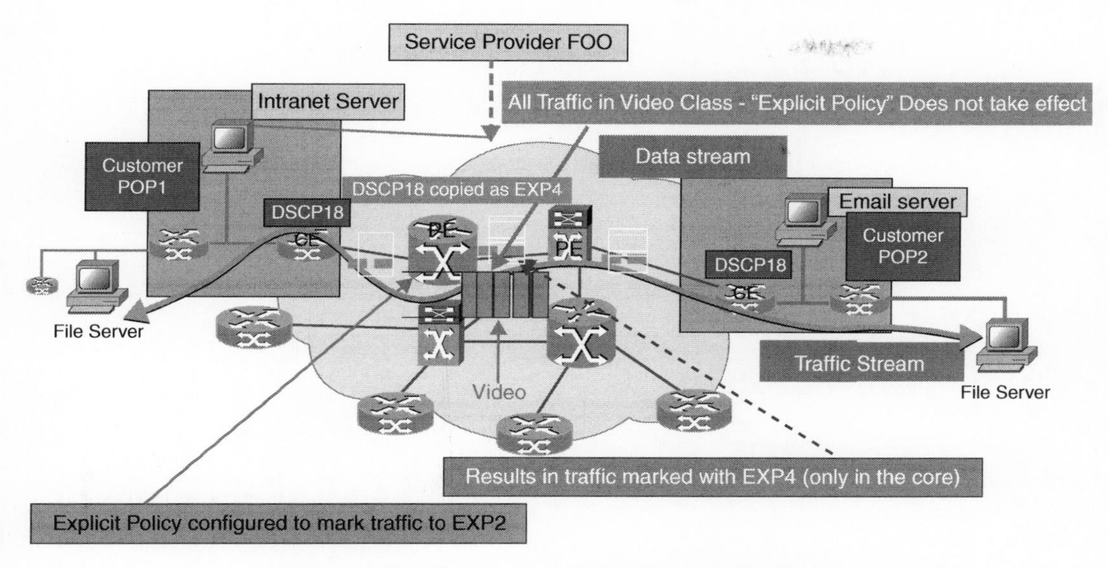

Figure 8.11: Trust State vs. Explicit Service Policies

Ignoring Trust States on WS-67xx Line Cards

Port trust can be ignored by using the command *mls qos marking ignore port-trust*. This command enables you to use a Trust state on the ingress interface and still use remarking at the ingress (on any of the subinterfaces that belong to the physical interface). This way, traffic that matches the ingress policy will be remarked. The illustrations that follow verify this behavior, wherein all the ingress traffic from the CE device gets remarked as per the ingress service policy (Policy-Map Voice) that is attached instead of the Trust state Trust DSCP, defined on the parent interface. The CE device is instructed to generate ICMP traffic with a DSCP value of 18, which corresponds to an MPLS Experimental value of 4. However, the policy map takes precedence in this scenario, and all traffic is remarked to EXP 5 based on the policy-map association. The configuration and relevant output for verifying this are provided here.

Configuration

```
!
mls qos marking ignore port-trust ----→ Ignores configured Trust States!
!
class-map match-any VoIP
  description ### Matching all traffic on a given interface ###
  match any
!
policy-map Voice
  class VoIP
   set mpls experimental imposition 5 --------→ Set MPLS EXP 5!
!
```

```
interface GigabitEthernet1/2
 description ### Physical Interface ###
 switchport
 switchport trunk encapsulation dot1q
 switchport mode trunk
 mls qos vlan-based
 mls qos trust dscp ----------> Trust state defined!
end
!
interface Vlan1001
  description ### User to Network Interface to Customer-ABC ###
  ip vrf forwarding ABC-L3VPN
  ip address 2.2.2.5 255.255.255.252
  no snmp trap link-status
service-policy input Voice -----> Service policy marking all traffic to EXP 5!
!
End
```

Verification

```
7613#show policy-map interface ge-WAN 3/1 output
 GE-WAN3/1
  Service-policy output: FOO-CORE
   Class-map: RealTime-Core (match-any) -→ Matches on MPLS EXP 5!
     712 packets,28784 bytes ---> Hits indicating matches on EXP 5!
     5 minute offered rate 0 bps, drop rate 0 bps
       Match: mpls experimental topmost 5
     police:
        cir 25 %
        cir 250000000 bps, bc 7812500 bytes
       (Police cir is rounded to 250019840 bps due to granularity)
     Priority: 0% (0 kbps), b/w exceed drops: 0
[Output is Truncated]
```

NOTE 8.9: Ignore Port-Trust

The *mls qos marking ignore port-trust* command does two things. First, it instructs the router to ignore any configured port-trust states. Second, it resets the port-trust state to Trust DSCP. Therefore, if no policy maps are attached to an interface, the incoming DSCP values are copied to the frame's outgoing EXP values.

Multiple Trust States on WS-67xx Line Cards

Multiple UNI service types per interface are a common requirement in a Carrier Ethernet access network. Let's look at the following customer requirement.

In terms of customer requirement, customer CLAY-BANK uses a single physical interface to connect to SP FOO. Within this interface, the customer has subscribed to more than one service type (MPLS Layer 2 VPN and MPLS Layer 3 VPN) using multiple VLANs. The customer also requires various QoS settings per service type. This would mean that an individual service type can require a particular Trust state. In this scenario, the L3 VPN needs to Trust DSCP and the Layer 2 VPN service on the same physical interface needs to Trust CoS. Let's look at an illustration for the same.

Configuration

```
!
class-map premium-dscp
match ip dscp AF41
!
class-map business-dscp
match ip dscp AF31
!
  <one for every class>
  !
policy-map set-ingress-trust
  class premium-dscp
   trust dscp
  class business-dscp
   trust dscp
!
!
interface GigabitEthernet1/2
 description ### Physical Interface ###
 switchport
 switchport trunk encapsulation dot1q
 switchport mode trunk
 mls qos vlan-based
 mls qos trust cos ----------> Trust state defined!
!
interface Vlan2000
 description ### MPLS L2VPN User to Network Interface to CLAY-BANK ###
 no ip address
 no snmp trap link-status
 xconnect 10.159.253.1 9000 encapsulation mpls
!
interface Vlan1001
 description ### MPLS L3VPN User to Network Interface to CLAY-BANK ###
 ip vrf forwarding CLAYBANK-L3VPN
 ip address 2.2.2.5 255.255.255.252
 no snmp trap link-status
 service-policy input set-ingress-trust → policy for Trusting DSCP!
!
End
```

Enhanced Flex-WAN Line Cards

In terms of customer requirements, customer ABC-ENTERPRISE has subscribed to a Layer 3 VPN service, and the requirement is to provide a Premium service for certain types of traffic. Essentially, the traffic destined for certain subnets is to be provided a Premium service, whereas the remaining traffic may be offered Best-Effort treatment. The customer has subscribed to a full port, and hence no ingress policers are required at the PE layer.

The following illustration provides the edge configuration for Enhanced Flex-WAN modules on the Cisco 7600. In this example, ACLs are used to classify traffic. ACL 188 is used to classify the group of source and destination subnets to mark the required EXP bits.

Configuration

```
!
access-list 188 remark ##############################
access-list 188 remark Tier-1 Sites
access-list 188 permit ip any 150.163.0.0 0.0.255.255
access-list 188 remark ##############################
access-list 188 remark Tier-2 Sites
access-list 188 permit ip any 150.135.0.0 0.0.255.255
access-list 188 permit ip any 172.22.106.0 0.0.0.255
access-list 188 permit ip any 172.22.102.0 0.0.0.255
access-list 188 permit ip any 172.22.103.0 0.0.0.255
access-list 188 permit ip any 172.22.100.0 0.0.0.255
access-list 188 permit ip any 172.22.101.0 0.0.0.255
access-list 188 permit ip any 10.252.100.0 0.0.0.255
access-list 188 permit ip any 10.250.0.0 0.0.255.255
access-list 188 permit ip any 150.114.0.0 0.0.255.255
access-list 188 permit ip any 150.64.1.0 0.0.0.255
access-list 188 permit ip any 150.153.0.0 0.0.255.255
access-list 188 permit ip any 150.164.0.0 0.0.255.255
access-list 188 permit ip any 150.142.0.0 0.0.255.255
access-list 188 permit ip any 150.149.0.0 0.0.255.255
access-list 188 permit ip any 150.166.0.0 0.0.255.255
!
class-map match-all critical-data
 match access-group 188 -------------→ Match criteria based on ACL 188
!
policy-map Premium
  class critical-data
  set mpls experimental imposition 2
!
interface Serial5/1/0
 ip vrf forwarding ABC-ENTERPRISE-L3VPN
 ip address 1.1.1.1 255.255.255.252
```

```
framing g751
dsu bandwidth 34010
service-policy input Premium
!
End
```

Enhanced Flex-WAN Line Cards Using NBAR

In terms of customer requirements, customer ABC-BANKING-CORP has subscribed to a Layer 3 VPN service, and the requirement is to provide a Real-time service for VoIP traffic. The customer has subscribed to a full port; hence no ingress policers are required at the PE layer.

In this case, NBAR is used to classify VoIP traffic; hence the keyword *rtp* is used. NBAR is an effective tool that aids in classifying applications using a keyword that otherwise might need ACLs for the same purpose. However, it is to be noted that NBAR with a Supervisor 720 on the 7600 is only supported on FlexWAN, Enhanced FlexWAN, and the 7600-SIP-200 modules. It is also worthy to note that NBAR is run on the processors in the case of these modules.

Configuration

```
!
class-map match-all Voice
 match protocol rtp audio -------→ Match using Protocol (RTP)
!
policy-map Voice
 class Voice
  set mpls experimental imposition 5
!
interface Serial5/1/0
 ip vrf forwarding ABC-L3VPN
 ip address 1.1.1.1 255.255.255.252
 framing g751
 dsu bandwidth <bandwidth>
 service-policy input Voice
!
end
```

8.3.4 Edge Configurations for the Cisco CRS-1 Series Routers

In this section, the edge configurations for the CRS-1 series of routers are illustrated. The configuration variants illustrated in the previous sections are not repeated, since the Cisco CRS-1 and IOS-XR supports the Cisco MQC framework, and certainly some of the previously illustrated configurations can be reused in IOS-XR. As mentioned before, the CRS-1 routers are not used as PE devices in the Service Provider FOO network, but the configurations are provided to ensure completeness in the chapter.

IOS XR Configuration

The following illustration uses a class-map named VoIP to classify all traffic the customer edge marked with a DSCP value pertaining to Expedited Forwarding, which has the corresponding MPLS EXP bits set to 5 during the MPLS label imposition.

Configuration

```
!
class-map match-any VoIP
match dscp ef
!
policy-map Voice
  class VoIP
    set mpls experimental imposition 5
!
interface TenGigE0/0/0/0
 description ### MPLS Layer 3 VPN UNI to Customer ABC ###
 cdp
 service-policy input Voice
 ipv4 address 10.10.3.2 255.255.255.0
!
end
```

IOS XR Configuration Using Access Lists

In this example, we look at the use of a combination of ACLs and DSCP values used together to classify traffic at the network ingress using IOS-XR software. ACL VoIP prefixes are used to classify a group of prefixes or voice subnets that need to be categorized for queuing within the Real-time class or LLQ within the SP FOO network core.

Configuration

```
!
class-map match-any VoIP
 match dscp ef
 match access-group ipv4 VoIP-Prefixes
!
ipv4 access-list VoIP-Prefixes
 10 permit ipv4 10.0.0.0 0.255.255.255 any
 20 deny ipv4 any any
!
```

```
policy-map Voice
 class VoIP
  set mpls experimental imposition 5
!
interface TenGigE0/0/0/0
  description ### MPLS Layer 3 VPN UNI to Customer ABC ###
  cdp
  service-policy input Voice
  ipv4 address 10.10.3.2 255.255.255.0
!
end
```

8.3.5 Core Configurations for the Cisco 12000 Series Routers Using IOS

Having seen the various options used for classifying and marking of traffic at the network edge, this section lays emphasis on the required configurations for queuing and scheduling traffic in the network core. In this section, we look at the various engine types on the Cisco 12000 router and examine the options available for building the QoS framework in the core for SP FOO based on the five-class model.

Engine 3 Line Cards

The Engine 3 line card supports only four egress queues by default. Since we need five queues in total for SP FOO, including the Best-Effort queue, the following command is needed on the Cisco 12000: *hw-module slot <number> qos interface queues 8*. A micro reload on the given line card is needed for this command to take effect. The policy map FOO-CORE is a construct of the core-facing policy and consists of the various parameters that define the scheduler behavior. The class Real-time is nominated as the LLQ or strict-priority queue by virtue of using the Priority keyword under this class. A hard policer is used under this class to enable strict policing of voice traffic and prevent nondeterministic behavior. In our illustration, the policer is configured as follows: *police cir percent 25 bc 20 ms be 20 ms*. This indicates that the committed and excess burst sizes can scale a maximum of 20 ms, which is derived as follows: We compute 20 ms of the link speed and use that number. So 20 ms of a GE link would be (1,000,000,000 bits * 0.20 sec = 20 Mbits of burst), which we then convert to 2.5 Mbytes, and is considered an optimal value for making a start with the LLQ configuration.

Classes other than the strict-priority queue have bandwidth allotments configured through the *bandwidth percent* command. This specifies the bandwidth allocation as a percentage of the underlying link rate. The bandwidth command can be entered in different variations, as given in Figure 8.12.

Command syntax	Description
Bandwidth {kbps}	Specifies bandwidth allocation as a bit rate.
Bandwidth percent {value}	Specifies bandwidth allocation as a percentage of the underlying link rate.
Bandwidth remaining percent {value}	Specifies bandwidth allocation as a percentage of the bandwidth that has not been allocated to other classes.

Figure 8.12: Use of the Bandwidth Command

Configuration

```
!
hw-module slot 6 qos interface queues 8 ---→ Enables 8 egress queues!
!
class-map match-any Control
  description ### Classification for Control Traffic ###
  match mpls experimental 6 7
class-map match-any Realtime
  description ### Classification for Voice Traffic ###
  match mpls experimental 5
class-map match-any Premium
  description ### Classification for Premium Applications ###
  match mpls experimental 2 1
class-map match-any Video
  description ### Classification for Video Traffic ###
  match mpls experimental 4
class-map match-any Best-Effort
  description ### Classification for BE Traffic ###
  match any
!
policy-map FOO-CORE
  class Control
   bandwidth percent 2
  class Video ---→ The Video queue does not use WRED!
   bandwidth percent 40
   queue-limit 35 ms
  class Premium
   bandwidth percent 28
   random-detect
   random-detect precedence 1 35 ms 40 ms
   random-detect precedence 2 40 ms 45 ms ---→ Max hold-time is 45ms!
   queue-limit 45 ms
  class Realtime
   priority
  police cir percent 25 bc 20 ms be 20 ms
```

```
  class Best-Effort
   bandwidth percent 5
   random-detect
   random-detect precedence 0 30 ms 100 ms
   queue-limit 100 ms ---→ High Hold-Time since BE is not delay sensitive!
!
interface GigabitEthernet6/2
 description ### Link to the Network Core ###
 ip address 10.159.255.5 255.255.255.252
 no ip directed-broadcast
 ip ospf network point-to-point
 negotiation auto
 mpls label protocol ldp
 mpls ip
 service-policy output FOO-CORE -----→ Egress Policy applied!
!
end
```

TIP 8.2: Queue Limit and WRED

The queue limit and WRED thresholds define the maximum time that a packet can spend in the system buffer.

The command *show policy-map interface <interface-name> output class <class-name>* can be used to verify the traffic entering a given class in the egress direction. Various counters are provided that include traffic matches and drops. The following illustration verifies this behavior.

Verification

```
!
12416#show policy-map interface gigabitEthernet 6/2 output class Realtime
 GigabitEthernet6/2
  Service-policy output: FOO-CORE (242)
   Class-map: Realtime (match-any) (8414465/6)
    1115 packets, 115960 bytes ------------------> Hits towards the Core
    5 minute offered rate 0 bps, drop rate 0 bps
    Match: mpls experimental 5 (12943090)
    Class of service queue: 23
    Queue-limit: 65536 packets (default)
    Current queue-depth: 0 packets, Maximum queue-depth: 0 packets
    Average queue-depth: 0.000 packets
    Priority
    police:
     cir 25%, burst 250 ms, extended burst 250 ms
```

```
      250000000 bps, 7812500 limit, 7812500 extended limit
      conformed 1115 packets, 115960 bytes; actions:
        transmit
      exceeded 0 packets, 0 bytes; actions: drop
      conformed 0 bps, exceed 0 bps
```

Engine 3 Line Cards Using GE Subinterfaces

A very common configuration is the use Gigabit Ethernet subinterfaces or dot1q interfaces for connectivity to the network core. As Ethernet has increasingly found favor in the access layer, so has it found increased usage in the core layer as well. A classical example is the use of Ethernet-over-SDH transport as the mode of connectivity in the network core. SPs use multiple subinterfaces on a given physical interface to build multiple Ethernet Virtual Circuits across an Ethernet-over-SDH infrastructure; hence QoS policies will need to be applied over each individual interface in this case.

NOTE 8.10: Ethernet Virtual Circuits

The Ethernet Virtual Circuits referred to in this section are different from the Martini MPLS Layer 2 Pseudo Wires (Layer 2 VPNs), and is a term used in the Ethernet over SDH (EoSDH) deployments.

The following illustration focuses on the configurations for deploying QoS on Gigabit Ethernet subinterfaces on Engine 3 line cards.

Configuration

```
!
hw-module slot 6 qos interface queues 8 ---→ Enables 8 egress queues!
!
class-map match-any Control
  description ### Classification for Control Traffic ###
  match mpls experimental 6 7
class-map match-any Realtime
  description ### Classification for Voice Traffic ###
  match mpls experimental 5
class-map match-any Premium
  description ### Classification for Premium Applications ###
  match mpls experimental 2 1
class-map match-any Video
  description ### Classification for Video Traffic ###
  match mpls experimental 4
class-map match-any Best-Effort
  description ### Classification for BE Traffic ###
```

```
 match any
!
policy-map FOO-CORE
 class Control
   bandwidth percent 2
 class Video ---→ The Video queue does not use WRED!
   bandwidth percent 40
   queue-limit 35 ms
 class Premium
   bandwidth percent 28
   random-detect
   random-detect precedence 1 35 ms 40 ms
   random-detect precedence 2 40 ms 45 ms ---→ Max hold-time is 45ms!
   queue-limit 45 ms
 class Realtime
   priority
  police cir percent 25 bc 20 ms be 20 ms
 class Best-Effort
   bandwidth percent 5
   random-detect
   random-detect precedence 0 30 ms 100 ms
   queue-limit 100 ms ---→ High Hold-Time since BE is not delay sensitive!
!
!
policy-map FOO-CORE-PARENT -----→ Parent Hierarchical Policy!
 class class-default
  shape average percent 100
 service-policy FOO-CORE -------→ Refers the actual service policy!
!
interface GigabitEthernet6/2
 description ### Main Interface ###
 no ip address
 no ip directed-broadcast
 negotiation auto
!
interface GigabitEthernet6/3.1000
 description ### Link to the Network Core ###
 encapsulation dot1Q 1000
 ip address 10.159.255.5 255.255.255.252
 no ip directed-broadcast
 ip ospf network point-to-point
 mpls label protocol ldp
 mpls ip
 service-policy output FOO-CORE-PARENT ----→ Egress Hierarchical Policy!
!
End
```

The Engine 3 line card requires a Hierarchical service policy while applying egress QoS service policies on subinterfaces. This means that the FOO-Core service policy, which consists of the various CoS-specific attributes, will need to be referenced via a Parent policy that has only a Class-Default reference. The Class-Default queue will need to be shaped to 100 percent of the actual bandwidth, which is the aggregate, and each individual queue under the FOO-Core policy map will have its respective share of bandwidth.

Engine 3 Line Cards Using L3/nC/mD Model

Extending this idea a bit further, another common scenario is based on a model known as the L3/nC/mD. This model allows support for multiple customers, where each customer has multiple VLANs. A parent-shaping policy is applied across a group of VLANs, and a child (queuing) policy is applied to the parent-shaping policy. In this model, there are m VLANs configured under a single physical interface, and these are distributed among n customers, hence $n < m$. The customer-specific MQC configuration is also attached to the physical interface, and match {vlan} type semantics are required to distinguish the traffic of each customer.

In the following example, we define two "blocks" of VLANs, the first containing VLANs 101–105 and the second containing VLANs 106–110. Each of these blocks is assigned to a separate class in the parent policy. This is the only model in which you configure something other than class default in the parent policy. Within the two blocks of VLANs we define four queues each. Notice that the two child policy maps are not required to use the same set of MQC parameters. In this specific example, all traffic destined for VLANs 101–105 will be shaped in aggregate to 100 Mb and within that 100 Mb will be treated as defined in the policy map child-101–105. All traffic destined for VLANs 106–110 will be shaped in aggregate to 200 Mb, and within that 200 Mb will be treated as defined in the policy map child-106–110. The full configuration illustration is given in Figure 8.13.

Engine 4 and 4+ Line Cards

Now we move on to the section on Engine 4 and Engine 4+ line cards. These series of line cards differ slightly from a configuration perspective compared to their other counterparts, such as the Engine 3 and Engine 5 (which we discuss a little later in this chapter). The difference is that the Engine 4 and 4+ line cards do not accept the use of strict-priority queuing, with the *bandwidth/bandwidth percent* commands to be used on the non-LLQ classes. Instead, the other classes need to have the *bandwidth remaining percent* command used. The Engine 4 line cards do not accept the use of a strict policer within the LLQ; hence it is mandatory to use ingress policing to restrict the bandwidth usage of traffic within this class. The Engine 4+ line cards do accept the usage of a strict policer; hence the use of the *bandwidth remaining percent* command within non-LLQ classes is considered merely a method of implementation within the IOS code since the LLQ can be hard-policed.

Ethernet interface L3/nC/mD configuration:	L3/nC/mD policy-map & class-map configuration:

interface GigabitEthernet 6/0
 no ip address
 service-policy output parent
!
interface GigabitEthernet6/0.101
 encapsulation dot1q 101
 ip address 20.101.1.1 255.255.255.252
!
interface GigabitEthernet6/0.102
 encapsulation dot1q 102
 ip address 20.102.1.1 255.255.255.252
!
interface GigabitEthernet6/0.103
 encapsulation dot1q 103
 ip address 20.103.1.1 255.255.255.252
!
interface GigabitEthernet6/0.104
 encapsulation dot1q 104
 ip address 20.104.1.1 255.255.255.252
!
interface GigabitEthernet6/0.105
 encapsulation dot1q 105
 ip address 20.105.1.1 255.255.255.252
!
interface GigabitEthernet6/0.106
 encapsulation dot1q 106
 ip address 20.106.1.1 255.255.255.252
!
interface GigabitEthernet6/0.107
 encapsulation dot1q 107
 ip address 20.107.1.1 255.255.255.252
!
interface GigabitEthernet6/0.108
 encapsulation dot1q 108
 ip address 20.108.1.1 255.255.255.252
!
interface GigabitEthernet6/0.109
 encapsulation dot1q 109
 ip address 20.109.1.1 255.255.255.252
!
interface GigabitEthernet6/0.110
 encapsulation dot1q 110
 ip address 20.110.1.1 255.255.255.252
	class-map match-any voice
	 match ip precedence 5
	class-map match-any gold
	 match ip precedence 3
	class-map match-any silver
	 match ip precedence 1
	!
	class-map VLAN101-105
	 match vlan 101 102 103 104 105
	!
	class-map VLAN106-110
	 match vlan 106 107 108 109 110
	!
	policy-map parent
	 class VLAN101-105
	shape average 100000000
	service-policy child-101-105
	 class VLAN106-110
	shape average 200000000
	service-policy child-106-110
	!
	policy-map child-101-105
	 class voice
	  priority
	  police cir percent 10
	 class gold
	  bandwidth percent 50
	 class silver
	  bandwidth percent 30
	 class class-default
	  bandwidth percent 10
	!
	policy-map child-106-110
	 class voice
	  priority
	  police cir percent 30
	 class gold
	  bandwidth remaining percent 20
	 class silver
	  bandwidth remaining percent 30
	 class class-default
	  bandwidth remaining percent 10

Figure 8.13: Hierarchical QoS on E3 Line Cards

Configuration

```
!
class-map match-any Control
  description ### Classification for Control Traffic ###
  match mpls experimental 6 7
class-map match-any Realtime
  description ### Classification for Voice Traffic ###
  match mpls experimental 5
class-map match-any Best-Effort
  description ### Classification for BE Traffic ###
  match mpls experimental 0
```

```
class-map match-any Premium
  description ### Classification for Premium Applications ###
  match mpls experimental 2 1
class-map match-any Video
  description ### Classification for Video Traffic ###
  match mpls experimental 4
!
policy-map FOO-CORE
  class Control
    bandwidth remaining percent 2
  class Video
    bandwidth remaining percent 40
    queue-limit 35 ms
  class Premium
    bandwidth remaining percent 28
    random-detect
    random-detect precedence 1 35 ms 40 ms
    random-detect precedence 2 40 ms 45 ms ---→ Max hold-time is 45ms!
    queue-limit 45 ms
  class Realtime
    priority
  class Best-Effort
    bandwidth remaining percent 5
    random-detect
    random-detect precedence 0 30 ms 100 ms
    queue-limit 100 ms ---→ High Hold-Time since BE is not delay sensitive!
!
interface GigabitEthernet6/4
  description ### Link to the Network Core ###
  ip address 10.159.255.5 255.255.255.252
  no ip directed-broadcast
  ip ospf network point-to-point
  negotiation auto
  mpls label protocol ldp
  mpls ip
  service-policy output FOO-CORE -----→ Egress Policy applied!
!
end
```

Engine 4+ Line Cards Using "Always-on Policer"

The following illustration indicates the configuration of an Engine 4+ line card and the support for an "Always-on Policer" within the LLQ.

Configuration

```
!
class-map match-any Control
```

```
 description ### Classification for Control Traffic ###
 match mpls experimental 6 7
class-map match-any Realtime
 description ### Classification for Voice Traffic ###
 match mpls experimental 5
class-map match-any Best-Effort
 description ### Classification for BE Traffic ###
 match mpls experimental 0
class-map match-any Premium
 description ### Classification for Premium Applications ###
 match mpls experimental 2 1
class-map match-any Video
 description ### Classification for Video Traffic ###
 match mpls experimental 4
!
policy-map FOO-CORE
 class Control
  bandwidth remaining percent 2
 class Video
  bandwidth remaining percent 40
  queue-limit 35 ms
 class Premium
  bandwidth remaining percent 28
  random-detect
  random-detect precedence 1 35 ms 40 ms
  random-detect precedence 2 40 ms 45 ms ---→ Max hold-time is 45ms!
  queue-limit 45 ms
 class Realtime
  Priority
  police cir percent 25 bc 20 ms be 20 ms ---→ Always on Policer!
class Best-Effort
  bandwidth remaining percent 5
  random-detect
  random-detect precedence 0 30 ms 100 ms
  queue-limit 100 ms ---→ High Hold-Time since BE is not delay sensitive!
!
interface POS 2/0
 description ### Link to the Network Core ###
 ip address 10.159.255.9 255.255.255.252
 no ip directed-broadcast
 ip ospf network point-to-point
 negotiation auto
 mpls label protocol ldp
 mpls ip
 service-policy output FOO-CORE -----→ Egress Policy applied!
!
End
```

Engine 5 Line Cards

The following illustration provides the QoS configuration for the Engine 5 line cards. The QoS configurations for the Engine 5 line cards are similar to their Engine 3 counterparts. The only exception or difference between the Engine 3 and Engine 5 cards is that egress QoS policies on the Engine 5 subinterfaces do not require a hierarchical policy map. The policy map FOO can be applied directly at the subinterface level.

Configuration

```
!
class-map match-any Control
  description ### Classification for Control Traffic ###
  match mpls experimental 6 7
class-map match-any Realtime
  description ### Classification for Voice Traffic ###
  match mpls experimental 5
class-map match-any Premium
  description ### Classification for Premium Applications ###
  match mpls experimental 2 1
class-map match-any Video
  description ### Classification for Video Traffic ###
  match mpls experimental 4
class-map match-any Best-Effort
  description ### Classification for BE Traffic ###
  match any
!
policy-map FOO-CORE
  class Control
    bandwidth percent 2
 class Video ---→ The Video queue does not use WRED!
    bandwidth percent 40
    queue-limit 35 ms
    class Premium
    bandwidth percent 28
    random-detect
    random-detect precedence 1 35 ms 40 ms
    random-detect precedence 2 40 ms 45 ms ---→ Max hold-time is 45ms!
    queue-limit 45 ms
class Realtime
    priority
  police cir percent 25 bc 20 ms be 20 ms
class Best-Effort
    bandwidth percent 5
    random-detect
    random-detect precedence 0 30 ms 100 ms
    queue-limit 100 ms ---→ High Hold-Time since BE is not delay sensitive!
```

```
!
interface GigabitEthernet6/7
   description ### Link to the Network Core ###
   ip address 10.159.255.13 255.255.255.252
   no ip directed-broadcast
   ip ospf network point-to-point
   negotiation auto
   mpls label protocol ldp
   mpls ip
   service-policy output FOO-CORE -----→ Egress Policy applied!
!
end
```

Configuration Using Subinterfaces

```
!
class-map match-any Control
  description ### Classification for Control Traffic ###
  match mpls experimental 6 7
class-map match-any Realtime
  description ### Classification for Voice Traffic ###
  match mpls experimental 5
class-map match-any Premium
  description ### Classification for Premium Applications ###
  match mpls experimental 2 1
class-map match-any Video
  description ### Classification for Video Traffic ###
  match mpls experimental 4
class-map match-any Best-Effort
  description ### Classification for BE Traffic ###
  match any
!
policy-map FOO-CORE
  class Control
   bandwidth percent 2
  class Video ---→ The Video queue does not use WRED!
   bandwidth percent 40
   queue-limit 35 ms
  class Premium
   bandwidth percent 28
   random-detect
   random-detect precedence 1 35 ms 40 ms
   random-detect precedence 2 40 ms 45 ms ---→ Max hold-time is 45ms!
   queue-limit 45 ms
  class Realtime
   priority
```

```
    police cir percent 25 bc 20 ms be 20 ms
  class Best-Effort
    bandwidth percent 5
    random-detect
    random-detect precedence 0 30 ms 100 ms
    queue-limit 100 ms ---→ High Hold-Time since BE is not delay sensitive!
!
interface GigabitEthernet6/7
  description ### Link to the Network Core ###
  ip address 10.159.255.13 255.255.255.252
  no ip directed-broadcast
  ip ospf network point-to-point
  negotiation auto
  mpls label protocol ldp
  mpls ip
  service-policy output FOO-CORE -----→ Egress Policy applied!
!
end
```

NOTE 8.11: Egress QoS Policies

The default values for the Exponential Weighting Constant and Max Probability Denominator on the Cisco 12000 Series platform are considered optimal and do not need any further adjustments.

Egress Queuing on Engine 5 Line Cards

Finally, let's look at the policy map association for egress interfaces (customer edge facing).

Irrespective of the DiffServ Tunneling mode chosen, egress policies are always based on IP ToS values. The following illustration provides a configuration template for this purpose.

Configuration

```
!
class-map match-any Control-Egress
  description ### Classification for Control Traffic ###
  match ip precedence 6 7
class-map match-any Realtime-Egress
  description ### Classification for Voice Traffic ###
  match ip precedence 5
class-map match-any Premium-Egress
  description ### Classification for Premium Applications ###
  match ip precedence 2 1
class-map match-any Video
  description ### Classification for Video Traffic ###
```

```
  match ip precedence 4
class-map match-any Best-Effort-Egress
  description ### Classification for BE Traffic ###
  match any
!
policy-map FOO-EGRESS
 class Control-Egress
   bandwidth percent 2
 class Video-Egress ---→ The Video queue does not use WRED!
   bandwidth percent 40
   queue-limit 35 ms
 class Premium-Egress
   bandwidth percent 28
   random-detect
   random-detect precedence 1 35 ms 40 ms
   random-detect precedence 2 40 ms 45 ms ---→ Max hold-time is 45ms!
   queue-limit 45 ms
 class Realtime-Egress
   priority
  police cir percent 25 bc 20 ms be 20 ms
 class Best-Effort-Egress
   bandwidth percent 5
   random-detect
   random-detect precedence 0 30 ms 100 ms
   queue-limit 100 ms ---→ High Hold-Time since BE is not delay sensitive!
!
interface GigabitEthernet1/7
   description ### Link to the Customer ABC ###
   ip vrf forwarding ABC-L3VPN
   ip address 172.10.200.13 255.255.255.252
   no ip directed-broadcast
   negotiation auto
   service-policy output FOO-EGRESS -----→ Egress Policy applied!
!
end
```

8.3.6 Core Configurations for the Cisco 12000 Series Routers Using XR

In this section we look at the QoS configuration on the Cisco 12000 routers using IOS-XR. The configurations on the core-facing interfaces are identical to the CRS-1 platforms. The following illustration provides insight into this setup.

Configuration

```
!
class-map match-any Control
 match mpls experimental topmost 6 7
```

```
!
class-map match-any Video
 match mpls experimental topmost 4
!
class-map match-any Premium
 match mpls experimental topmost 2 1
!
class-map match-any Voice
 match mpls experimental topmost 5
!
class-map match-any Best-Effort
 match mpls experimental topmost 0
!
! ======================================
!
policy-map FOO-CORE
 class Voice
  police rate percent 25
   conform-action transmit
   exceed-action drop
  priority
!
class Control
  bandwidth percent 2
!
class Premium
 random-detect exp 2 40 ms 45 ms
 random-detect exp 1 35 ms 40 ms
 bandwidth percent 28
 queue-limit 45 ms
!
class Video
 bandwidth percent 40
 queue-limit 35 ms
!
class Best-Effort
 random-detect exp 0 30 ms 100 ms
 bandwidth percent 5
 queue-limit 100 ms
! ======================================
!
interface GE 0/0/1/0
description <Core facing interface>
service-policy output FOO-CORE
!
end
```

The *show qos interface <interface> output* command has a few variants when used on the 12000 platform, compared to the CRS-1. The command output is shown next.

Verification

```
RP/0/6/CPU0:NGN-P5#show qos interface gigabitEthernet 0/0/1/0 output
Interface GigabitEthernet0_0_1_0 -- output policy
Total number of classes: 6
---------------------------------------------------
LEVEL1 class: classid       =    0x1
class name                  =    Voice
queue ID (Priority)         =    17
Queue Limit                 =    16384 packets (16384 pkts)
Policer average             =    25 % (249984 kbps)
Policer conform action      =    Just TX
Policer exceed action       =    DROP PKT
LEVEL1 class: classid       =    0x2
class name                  =    Control
queue ID                    =    12
Queue Min. BW.              =    2 % (20000 kbps) --→ bandwidth percent
reserved!
Weight                      =    1
Queue Limit                 =    2048 packets (2048 pkts)
LEVEL1 class: classid       =    0x3
class name                  =    Premium
queue ID                    =    13
Queue Min. BW.              =    28 % (280000 kbps)
Weight                      =    1
Queue Limit                 =    45 ms (21973 pkts) --→ queue-limit
EXP        Label        Min. Threshold            Max. Threshold
1          1            35 ms (17483 pkts)        40 ms (19531 pkts)
EXP        Label        Min. Threshold            Max. Threshold
2          2            40 ms (19925 pkts         45 ms (21973 pkts)
LEVEL1 class: classid       =    0x4
class name                  =    Video
queue ID                    =    14
Queue Min. BW.              =    40 % (400000 kbps)
Weight                      =    1
Queue Limit                 =    35 ms (17090 pkts)
LEVEL1 class: classid       =    0x5
class name                  =    Best-Effort
queue ID                    =    15
Queue Min. BW.              =    5 % (50000 kbps)
Weight                      =    1
Queue Limit                 =    100 ms (48828 pkts)
EXP    Label    Min. Threshold        Max. Threshold
0      1        30 ms (16060 pkts)    100 ms (48828 pkts)
LEVEL1 class: classid       =    0x0
```

```
class name          =        class-default
queue ID            =        16
Weight              =        1
Queue Limit         =        16384 packets (16384 pkts)
```

Fabric QoS

A constant burst of traffic for extended periods of time results in exhaustion of all the I/O memory. In such a situation, prior to this feature, the 12000 router drops high-priority traffic (such as voice) as well as low-priority traffic. Fabric QoS provides the facility of configuring MQC policies on the switch fabric queues; in effect this feature protects high-priority traffic against drops under these circumstances. The configurations are shown next.

The Configuration illustration provides maximum protection to voice traffic by virtue of configuring the LLQ without any policer. This is indicative of the fact that voice traffic may have an absolute protection in the line of the fabric. Two other classes, Video and Critical Data, are defined with the *bandwidth remaining percent* command, which indicates that they may receive fabric space/bandwidth in the event of voice traffic not using any bandwidth.

Configuration

```
!
!
class-map match-any Video
  match mpls experimental topmost 1
  end-class-map
!
class-map match-any Voice
  match mpls experimental topmost 5
  end-class-map
!
class-map match-any Critical-data
  match mpls experimental topmost 4 3
  end-class-map
!
policy-map tofabqos
 class Voice
  priority
!
class Video
  bandwidth remaining percent 30
!
class Critical-data
  bandwidth remaining percent 10
!
 class class-default
```

```
 !
 end-policy-map
!
switch-fabric
 service-policy tofabqos
!
end
```

8.3.7 Core Configurations for the Cisco 7200 series routers

This section illustrates the configurations on the 7200 platform; the following illustration provides insight into the details. By default only 75 percent of interface bandwidth is available for CBWFQ use, which means that the sum of bandwidth allotments for the various classes within a policy map needs to be within this limit. This default behavior can be modified using the interface command *max-reserved-bandwidth*, as shown here.

Maximum Reserved Bandwidth

```
!
! interface GigabitEthernet0/2
   ip address 192.168.1.13 255.255.255.252
   max-reserved-bandwidth 98    ←Changed to 100% of bandwidth
!
end
```

It is important to note that the sum of total bandwidth allocation on the 7200 cannot exceed 99 percent. Hence the bandwidth allocation for the Best-Effort queue within the network core of SP FOO has been reduced from 5 percent to 4 percent. This only applies to the 7200 platform. The exponential weighting constant can be adjusted as per the link speeds on the 7200 and is considered a good practice. Figure 2.17 in Chapter 2 provides a list of recommended values for this purpose.

Configuration

```
!
class-map match-any Control
 description ### Classification for Control Traffic ###
 match mpls experimental 6 7
class-map match-any Realtime
 description ### Classification for Voice Traffic ###
 match mpls experimental 5
class-map match-any Premium
 description ### Classification for Premium Applications ###
 match mpls experimental 2 1
class-map match-any Video
```

```
 description ### Classification for Video Traffic ###
 match mpls experimental 4
class-map match-any Best-Effort
 description ### Classification for BE Traffic ###
 match any
!
policy-map FOO-CORE
 class Control
  bandwidth percent 2
 class Video ---→ The Video queue does not use WRED!
  bandwidth percent 40
  queue-limit 35 ms
 class Premium
  bandwidth percent 28
  random-detect
  random-detect exponential-weighting-constant 13 -→ Value for GE Link!
  random-detect precedence 1 35 ms 40 ms 1
  random-detect precedence 2 40 ms 45 ms 1 ---→ Max hold-time is 45ms!
  queue-limit 45 ms
 class Realtime
  priority percent 25
 class Best-Effort
  bandwidth percent 4 ---------→ Reduced from 5% to 4%!
  random-detect
  random-detect exponential-weighting-constant 13
  random-detect precedence 0 30 ms 100 ms 1
  queue-limit 100 ms ---→ High Hold-Time since BE is not delay sensitive!
!
interface GigabitEthernet0/3
  description ### Link to Network Core ###
  ip address 10.159.255.6 255.255.255.252
  no ip directed-broadcast
  ip ospf network point-to-point
  duplex auto
  speed auto
  media-type gbic
  negotiation auto
  mpls label protocol ldp
  mpls ip
  service-policy output FOO-CORE ----→ Egress Policy!
!
End
```

Egress Queuing on 7200

The following illustration for creating an egress policy map for queuing on the CE-facing direction follows. Once again, the classification criterion for this policy needs to be based on IP ToS.

Configuration

```
!
class-map match-any Control-Egress
 description ### Classification for Control Traffic ###
 match ip precedence 6 7
class-map match-any Realtime-Egress
 description ### Classification for Voice Traffic ###
 match ip precedence 5
class-map match-any Premium-Egress
 description ### Classification for Premium Applications ###
 match ip precedence 2 1
class-map match-any Video
 description ### Classification for Video Traffic ###
 match ip precedence 4
class-map match-any Best-Effort-Egress
 description ### Classification for BE Traffic ###
 match any
!
policy-map FOO-EGRESS
 class Control
  bandwidth percent 2
 class Video ---→ The Video queue does not use WRED!
  bandwidth percent 40
  queue-limit 35 ms
 class Premium
  bandwidth percent 28
  random-detect
  random-detect exponential-weighting-constant 13 -→ Value for GE Link!
  random-detect precedence 1 35 ms 40 ms 1
  random-detect precedence 2 40 ms 45 ms 1---→ Max hold-time is 45ms!
  queue-limit 45 ms
 class Realtime
  priority percent 25
 class Best-Effort
  bandwidth percent 4 ---------→ Reduced from 5% to 4%!
  random-detect
  random-detect exponential-weighting-constant 13
  random-detect precedence 0 30 ms 100 ms 1
  queue-limit 100 ms ---→ High Hold-Time since BE is not delay sensitive!
!
interface GigabitEthernet0/1
  description ### Link to the Customer ABC ###
  ip vrf forwarding XYZ-L3VPN
  ip address 172.12.200.13 255.255.255.252
  no ip directed-broadcast
```

```
  negotiation auto
  service-policy output FOO-EGRESS -----→ Egress Policy applied!
!
end
```

8.3.8 Core Configurations for the Cisco 7600 Series Routers

This section illustrates the configurations for the various line cards on the 7600 platform. Illustrations for both Layer 3 line cards that support the MQC framework and LAN cards that support only PFC QoS are covered here.

Enhanced OSM Line Cards

The Enhanced OSM modules require WRED and queue-limit thresholds to be entered in the units of packets and not time, as illustrated in the following configuration.

Configuration

```
!
class-map match-any Control
 description ### Classification for Control Traffic ###
 match mpls experimental topmost 6 7
class-map match-any Realtime
 description ### Classification for Voice Traffic ###
 match mpls experimental topmost 5
class-map match-any Premium
 description ### Classification for Premium Applications ###
 match mpls experimental topmost 2 1
class-map match-any Video
 description ### Classification for Video Traffic ###
 match mpls experimental topmost 4
class-map match-any Best-Effort
 description ### Classification for BE Traffic ###
 match any
!
!
policy-map FOO-CORE
 class Control
  bandwidth percent 2
 class Video
  bandwidth percent 40
  queue-limit 4167 packets
 class Premium
  bandwidth percent 28
  random-detect
  random-detect precedence 1 2916 4167
  random-detect precedence 2 4167 5000
```

```
   queue-limit 5000 packets
  class Best-Effort
   bandwidth percent 5
   random-detect
   random-detect precedence 0 3333 8333
   queue-limit 8333 packets
  class Realtime
   police cir percent 25
   priority
!
 interface GE-WAN3/1
  description ### Link to Network Core ###
  ip address 10.159.240.6 255.255.255.252
  no ip directed-broadcast
  ip ospf network point-to-point
  duplex auto
  speed auto
  media-type gbic
  negotiation auto
  mpls label protocol ldp
  mpls ip
  service-policy output FOO-CORE -----→ Egress Policy!
!
end
```

Enhanced Flex-WAN Line Cards

Next we examine the core configuration templates for Enhanced Flex-WAN (E-Flex-WAN) modules, given in the following illustration. The Enhanced Flex-WAN modules indeed support the use of the Exponential Weighting constant in the configurations, and it is a good practice to enter the values as per the recommendations in Chapter 2. Similarly, the use of the max probability denominator is mandatory, and setting this to a value of 1 is considered optimal.

Configuration

```
!
class-map match-any Control
 description ### Classification for Control Traffic ###
 match mpls experimental topmost 6 7
class-map match-any Realtime
 description ### Classification for Voice Traffic ###
 match mpls experimental topmost 5
class-map match-any Premium
 description ### Classification for Premium Applications ###
 match mpls experimental topmost 2 1
class-map match-any Video
```

```
  description ### Classification for Video Traffic ###
  match mpls experimental topmost 4
class-map match-any Best-Effort
  description ### Classification for BE Traffic ###
  match any
!
policy-map FOO-CORE
  class Control
   bandwidth percent 2
  class Video
   bandwidth percent 40
   queue-limit 2920
  class Premium
   bandwidth percent 28
   random-detect
   random-detect exponential-weighting-constant 13
   random-detect precedence 1 3000 3200 1
   random-detect precedence 2 3200 3700 1
   queue-limit 3700
  class Realtime
   priority
   POLICE CIR PERCENT 25
  class Best-Effort
   bandwidth percent 5
   random-detect
   random-detect exponential-weighting-constant 13
   random-detect precedence 0 2500 8333 1
!
!
interface Hssi5/0/1
  ip address 2.1.1.1 255.255.255.252
  service-policy output FOO-CORE
!
end
```

SIP-600 Line Cards

The following is an illustration for the QoS configuration on the SIP-600 modules. Similar to the other line cards on the 7600, WRED and queue-limit thresholds need to be entered in units of packets and not time. It is recommended that the queue limits be manually configured within the class, even when using WRED. It is a good practice to always manually configure the queue limits to match the maximum threshold of WRED. The following illustration adheres to this practice.

The SIP-600 reserves 1 percent of the link bandwidth for routing protocols and other purposes. Hence only 99 percent of the link bandwidth should be reserved for CBWFQ. In this illustration, we configure the LLQ to be policed at 240 Mbps to follow this rule. The *random-detect* commands are replaced with *aggregate random-detect* statements on the SIP-600. The aggregate is supported on platforms that are restrictive in the number of WRED colors that can be supported. The SIP-600 supports four colors (unique minimum and maximum thresholds) per queue and hence uses aggregates for this purpose, since they provide a way to limit the number of colors per queue. This is an internal mechanism of functionality, and from a functionality standpoint, both *aggregate random-detect* and *normal random-detect* provide exactly the same functionality.

Configuration

```
!
class-map match-any Control
 description ### Classification for Control Traffic ###
 match mpls experimental topmost 6 7
class-map match-any Realtime
 description ### Classification for Voice Traffic ###
 match mpls experimental topmost 5
class-map match-any Premium
 description ### Classification for Premium Applications ###
 match mpls experimental topmost 2 1
class-map match-any Video
 description ### Classification for Video Traffic ###
 match mpls experimental topmost 4
class-map match-any Best-Effort
 description ### Classification for BE Traffic ###
 match any
!
policy-map FOO-CORE
 class Control
  bandwidth percent 2
 class Video
  bandwidth percent 40
  queue-limit 4000 packets
 class Premium
  bandwidth percent 28
  random-detect aggregate
  random-detect precedence values 2 minimum-thresh 3500 maximum-thresh 4000
mark-prob 1
  random-detect precedence values 1 minimum-thresh 3000 maximum-thresh 3500
mark-prob 1
queue-limit 4000 packets -----→ Queue-limits equal to WRED Max-Threshold!
 class Realtime
  police 1000000000
   priority
 class Best-Effort
  bandwidth percent 5
```

```
  random-detect aggregate
  random-detect precedence values 0 minimum-thresh 2500 maximum-thresh 5000
mark-prob 1
  queue-limit 5000 packets
!
interface TenGigabitEthernet4/0/0
 ip address 2.2.1.1 255.255.255.252
 service-policy output FOO-CORE
!
end
```

NOTE 8.12: Bandwidth for the Real-Time Class

A different bandwidth allocation has been used for the Real-time class for some of the line cards on the 7600 platform, just to illustrate that various combinations can be used for configuring the "Always-on Policer" within the low-latency (Real-time) queue.

SIP-600 Line Cards Using Subinterfaces

Here we examine the QoS configuration on subinterfaces for the SIP-600 line cards. The SIP-600 requires a hierarchical QoS policy to be applied to subinterfaces. The parent policy merely needs a shaper and would also need to reference a child policy (which is a construct of all the classes and bandwidth statements). The 1 percent reservation by the SIP-600 needs to be considered while configuring the parent shaper. The following configuration illustrates that the shaper is configured for 9900 Mbps instead of 10 Gbps prior to attaching the policy to the TenGigabitEthernet interface. If the same policy is to be applied to multiple subinterfaces on a single physical interface, the shaper needs to reflect this by having the bandwidth shared across the various interfaces. For instance, if the policy is applied on two subinterfaces, the shaper bandwidth will need to be shared across both the interfaces as follows: (9900 Mb/2 = 4950 Mb). Therefore the parent policy will shape bandwidth to the amount of 4950 Mbps and not 9900 Mbps, as illustrated in the following configuration. Care should also be taken to ensure that the policer in the LLQ is well within the shaper value given under the parent policy. If the objective is to restrict voice traffic to 25 percent of the link rate, the policer should be configured to restrict traffic to 25 percent of the configured shaper (4950 Mb in the case of our illustration and not 10 G, which is the actual interface rate).

Configuration

```
!
class-map match-any Control
 description ### Classification for Control Traffic ###
 match mpls experimental topmost 6 7
class-map match-any Realtime
 description ### Classification for Voice Traffic ###
 match mpls experimental topmost 5
```

```
class-map match-any Premium
 description ### Classification for Premium Applications ###
 match mpls experimental topmost 2 1
class-map match-any Video
 description ### Classification for Video Traffic ###
 match mpls experimental topmost 4
class-map match-any Best-Effort
 description ### Classification for BE Traffic ###
 match any
!
policy-map FOO-CORE
 class Control
  bandwidth percent 2
 class Video
  bandwidth percent 40
  queue-limit 40000 packets
 class Premium
  bandwidth percent 28
  random-detect aggregate
  random-detect precedence values 2 minimum-thresh 35000 maximum-thresh
40000 mark-prob 1
  random-detect precedence values 1 minimum-thresh 30000 maximum-thresh
35000 mark-prob 1
queue-limit 40000 packets
 class Realtime
  police 1000000000
  priority
 class Best-Effort
  bandwidth percent 5
  random-detect aggregate
  random-detect precedence values 0 minimum-thresh 25000 maximum-thresh
 50000 mark-prob 1
  queue-limit 50000 packets
!
policy-map FOO-PARENT ----→ Hierarchical Policy!
 class class-default
  shape average 4950000000 ----→ Shaper for class-default traffic!
  Service-policy FOO-CORE
!
interface TenGigabitEthernet4/0/0
 no ip address
!
interface TenGigabitEthernet4/0/0.1000
 ip address 1.1.1.1 255.255.255.252
 service-policy output FOO-PARENT ----→ Hierarchical Policy applied!
!
interface TenGigabitEthernet4/0/0.2000
```

```
 ip address 1.1.1.5 255.255.255.252
 service-policy output FOO-PARENT
!
end
```

SIP-400 Line Cards with "Priority Levels"

Next we examine the QoS configuration on subinterfaces for the SIP-400 line cards. The SIP-400 line cards support the use of dual priority queues. In the following illustration, we demonstrate the use of the two priority queues for both voice and video. The Real-time class is configured for Priority Level 1, which indicates it has higher preference than the Video class, which is configured for Priority Level 2. Whenever traffic enters the Real-time class it is immediately serviced before any other queues, and the Video class is immediately serviced ahead of the other queues except the Real-time class, which—as a result of being the Priority Level 1 queue—has the highest preference. The output is verified using the *show policy-map interface* command.

Configuration

```
!
class-map match-any Control
 description ### Classification for Control Traffic ###
 match mpls experimental topmost 6 7
class-map match-any Realtime
 description ### Classification for Voice Traffic ###
 match mpls experimental topmost 5
class-map match-any Premium
 description ### Classification for Premium Applications ###
 match mpls experimental topmost 2 1
class-map match-any Video
 description ### Classification for Video Traffic ###
 match mpls experimental topmost 4
class-map match-any Best-Effort
 description ### Classification for BE Traffic ###
 match any
!
policy-map FOO-CORE
 class Control
  bandwidth percent 2
 class Video
  police 60000000
  priority level 2 ----→ Priority Level 2 for Video traffic!
 class Premium
  bandwidth percent 28
  random-detect
  random-detect precedence 1 3000 3500
  random-detect precedence 2 3500 4000
```

```
   queue-limit 40000 packets
  class Realtime
   police 60000000
   priority level 1 ----→ Priority Level 1 for Voice traffic!
  class Best-Effort
   bandwidth percent 5
   random-detect
   random-detect precedence 0 2500 5000
   queue-limit 5000 packets
!
interface POS2/0/0
  ip address 10.255.248.6 255.255.255.252
  crc 32
  clock source external
  service-policy output FOO-CORE
!
end
```

Verification

```
7600-CE#show policy-map interface POS2/0/0
 POS2/0/0
  Service-policy output: FOO-CORE
  Counters last updated 00:00:00 ago
   queue stats for all priority classes:
     Queueing
     priority level 2
     queue limit 15000 packets
     (queue depth/total drops/no-buffer drops) 0/0/0
     (pkts output/bytes output) 0/0

   queue stats for all priority classes:
     Queueing
     priority level 1
     queue limit 15000 packets
     (queue depth/total drops/no-buffer drops) 0/0/0
     (pkts output/bytes output) 0/0
 Class-map: Video (match-any)
   0 packets, 0 bytes
   5 minute offered rate 0 bps, drop rate 0 bps
   Match: mpls experimental topmost 4
   police:
      cir 60000000 bps, bc 1875000 bytes
     conformed 0 packets, 0 bytes; actions:
      transmit
     exceeded 0 packets, 0 bytes; actions:
```

```
      drop
     conformed 0 bps, exceed 0 bps
    Priority: Strict, burst bytes 1500000
    Priority Level: 2 ----→ Video is assigned Priority Level 2!
   Class-map: Realtime (match-any)
    0 packets, 0 bytes
    5 minute offered rate 0 bps, drop rate 0 bps
   Match: mpls experimental topmost 5
   police:
      cir 60000000 bps, bc 1875000 bytes
    conformed 0 packets, 0 bytes; actions:
      transmit
    exceeded 0 packets, 0 bytes; actions:
      drop
    conformed 0 bps, exceed 0 bps
   Priority: Strict, burst bytes 1500000
   Priority Level: 1 ----→ Voice is assigned Priority Level 1!
[Output is Truncated]
```

SIP-400 Line Cards Without "Priority Levels"

In the following illustration, we configure the dual priority queues without the *Priority level* keywords. This allocates equal preference to both the Video and Real-time classes. Therefore, the two classes are serviced with equal preference and traffic is emptied in a round-robin fashion. The output of the policy map illustrated here provides details on the dual priority queues.

Configuration

```
!
class-map match-any Control
 description ### Classification for Control Traffic ###
 match mpls experimental topmost 6 7
class-map match-any Realtime
 description ### Classification for Voice Traffic ###
 match mpls experimental topmost 5
class-map match-any Premium
 description ### Classification for Premium Applications ###
 match mpls experimental topmost 2 1
class-map match-any Video
 description ### Classification for Video Traffic ###
 match mpls experimental topmost 4
class-map match-any Best-Effort
 description ### Classification for BE Traffic ###
 match any
!
policy-map FOO-CORE
```

```
  class Control
   bandwidth percent 2
  class Video
   police 60000000
   priority ----→ Priority without the level keyword!
  class Premium
   bandwidth percent 28
   random-detect
   random-detect precedence 1 3000 3500 1
   random-detect precedence 2 3500 4000 1
   queue-limit 40000 packets
  class Realtime
   police 60000000
   priority ----→ Priority without the level keyword!
  class Best-Effort
   bandwidth percent 5
   random-detect
   random-detect precedence 0 2500 5000 1
   queue-limit 5000 packets
!
interface POS3/0/0
 ip address 10.252.248.6 255.255.255.252
 crc 32
 clock source external
 service-policy output FOO-CORE
!
end
```

Verification

```
!
7613#show policy-map interface pos3/0/0
 POS3/0/0
  Service-policy output: FOO-CORE
  Counters last updated 00:00:00 ago
   queue stats for all priority classes:
   queue limit 311000 packets
    (queue depth/total drops/no-buffer drops) 0/0/0
    (pkts output/bytes output) 0/0
   Class-map: Video (match-any)
    0 packets, 0 bytes
    5 minute offered rate 0 bps, drop rate 0 bps
    Match: mpls experimental topmost 4
    police:
     cir 60000000 bps, bc 1875000 bytes
     conformed 0 packets, 0 bytes; actions:
```

```
      transmit
    exceeded 0 packets, 0 bytes; actions:
      drop
    conformed 0 bps, exceed 0 bps
   Priority: Strict, burst bytes 1500000 ----→ Priority Class!
  Class-map: Realtime (match-any)
    0 packets, 0 bytes
    5 minute offered rate 0 bps, drop rate 0 bps
    Match: mpls experimental topmost 5
    police:
       cir 60000000 bps, bc 1875000 bytes
     conformed 0 packets, 0 bytes; actions:
       transmit
     exceeded 0 packets, 0 bytes; actions:
       drop
     conformed 0 bps, exceed 0 bps
    Priority: Strict, burst bytes 1500000 ----→ Priority Class!
[Output is Truncated]
```

ES20 Line Cards

In the following illustration, we configure the egress QoS policy on an ES-20 Ten Gigabit Ethernet module. The configurations on the SIP-600 and ES-20 modules are very similar in nature, and it is worth noting that both these line cards use a similar buffering algorithm.

Configuration

```
!
class-map match-any Control
  description ### Classification for Control Traffic ###
  match mpls experimental topmost 6 7
class-map match-any Realtime
  description ### Classification for Voice Traffic ###
  match mpls experimental topmost 5
class-map match-any Premium
  description ### Classification for Premium Applications ###
  match mpls experimental topmost 2 1
class-map match-any Video
  description ### Classification for Video Traffic ###
  match mpls experimental topmost 4
class-map match-any Best-Effort
  description ### Classification for BE Traffic ###
  match any
!
policy-map FOO-CORE
  class Control
   bandwidth percent 2
```

```
 class Video
  bandwidth percent 40
  queue-limit 40000 packets
 class Premium
  bandwidth percent 28
  random-detect aggregate
  random-detect precedence values 2 minimum-thresh 35000 maximum-thresh
40000 mark-prob 1
  random-detect precedence values 1 minimum-thresh 30000 maximum-thresh
35000 mark-prob 1
  queue-limit 40000 packets
 class Realtime
  police 1000000000
  priority
  class Best-Effort
  bandwidth percent 5
  random-detect aggregate
  random-detect precedence values 0 minimum-thresh 25000 maximum-thresh
50000 mark-prob 1
  queue-limit 50000 packets
!
interface TenGigabitEthernet1/0/1
 ip address 172.16.2.1 255.255.255.252
 service-policy output FOO-CORE
!
end
```

ES20 Line Cards Using Subinterfaces

In the following illustration, we look at the QoS configuration on ES-20 subinterfaces. The same rules of the SIP-600 configurations apply to the ES-20 subinterface-based QoS policies.

Configuration

```
!
class-map match-any Control
 description ### Classification for Control Traffic ###
 match mpls experimental topmost 6 7
class-map match-any Realtime
 description ### Classification for Voice Traffic ###
 match mpls experimental topmost 5
class-map match-any Premium
 description ### Classification for Premium Applications ###
 match mpls experimental topmost 2 1
class-map match-any Video
 description ### Classification for Video Traffic ###
 match mpls experimental topmost 4
```

```
class-map match-any Best-Effort
 description ### Classification for BE Traffic ###
 match any
!
policy-map FOO-CORE
 class Control
  bandwidth percent 2
 class Video
  bandwidth percent 40
  queue-limit 40000 packets
 class Premium
  bandwidth percent 28
  random-detect aggregate
  random-detect precedence values 2 minimum-thresh 35000 maximum-thresh
40000 mark-prob 1
  random-detect precedence values 1 minimum-thresh 30000 maximum-thresh
35000 mark-prob 1
  queue-limit 40000 packets
 class Realtime
  police 1000000000
  priority
 class Best-Effort
  bandwidth percent 5
  random-detect aggregate
  random-detect precedence values 0 minimum-thresh 25000 maximum-thresh
50000 mark-prob 1
  queue-limit 50000 packets
!
policy-map FOO-PARENT
 class class-default
   shape average 4950000000
  service-policy FOO-CORE
!
interface TenGigabitEthernet1/0/2
 no ip address
!
interface TenGigabitEthernet1/0/2.666
 encapsulation dot1Q 1500
 ip address 172.16.1.9 255.255.255.252
 service-policy output FOO-PARENT
!
interface TenGigabitEthernet1/0/2.667
 encapsulation dot1Q 1501
 ip address 172.16.1.5 255.255.255.252
 service-policy output FOO-PARENT
!
end
```

PFC QoS on LAN Interfaces

In the following illustration, we look at the core configuration on a Layer 2 interface (also known as a LAN interface) using PFC-based QoS. We use a WS-X6748-GE-TX card for this illustration. Configuration commands across LAN interfaces are almost similar in nature, with the exception of the number of queues and thresholds supported, which is largely dependent on the transmit queue structure. For instance, this interface supports a transmit structure of 1P3Q8T (which stands for 1 Priority Queue, 3 Standard Queues, each capable of hosting 8 thresholds).

The priority queue is defined by means of the command *priority-queue cos-map <queue-id> <cos-value>*. The command *wrr-queue random-detect* defines the minimum and maximum thresholds for each threshold within a given queue. Queues 2 and 3 host video and control traffic, respectively. Hence no WRED thresholds have been defined, and instead tail-drop for these classes has been configured. This mirrors the configuration used in MQC for the various interfaces. The command *no wrr-queue random-detect <queueid>* disables WRED for a given queue.

NOTE 8.13: WRR CoS Values

The values entered against individual queues represent Layer 2 CoS values, since LAN cards are Layer 2 based. However, when we use a given CoS value in the match criteria, it also implies that MPLS Experimental values would be matched. No explicit command is needed to enable support for labeled packets.

Configuration

```
!
interface gigabitethernet 3/3
  wrr-queue cos-map 1 1 2 -----→ CoS 2 mapped to threshold 1 of queue 1
  wrr-queue cos-map 1 2 1 -----→ CoS 1 mapped to threshold 2 of queue 1
  wrr-queue cos-map 1 3 0 -----→ CoS 0 mapped to threshold 3 of queue 1
  wrr-queue cos-map 2 1 4 -----→ CoS 4 mapped to threshold 1 of queue 2
  wrr-queue cos-map 3 1 6 7 -----→ CoS 6 & 7 mapped to threshold 1 of queue 3
  priority-queue cos-map 1 5 -----→ CoS 5 mapped to Priority queue
  wrr-queue queue-limit 40 50 10
  wrr-queue bandwidth 40 50 10
  no wrr-queue random-detect 2 -----→ Disables WRED for queue 2
  no wrr-queue random-detect 3 -----→ Disables WRED for queue 3
  wrr-queue random-detect min-threshold 1 40 35 30 100 100 100 100 100
  wrr-queue random-detect max-threshold 1 45 45 100 100 100 100 100 100
  wrr-queue random-detect min-threshold 2 100 100 100 100 100 100 100 100
  wrr-queue random-detect max-threshold 2 100 100 100 100 100 100 100 100
  wrr-queue random-detect min-threshold 3 100 100 100 100 100 100 100 100
  wrr-queue random-detect max-threshold 3 100 100 100 100 100 100 100 100
```

The following illustration verifies the queuing configuration on a given interface. Class-to-queue mapping can be verified using this command. Also visible are the WRED thresholds for each queue, bandwidth ratios, and the tail-drop profiles for each threshold within a given class. Transmit and Receive queue structures are clearly illustrated along with "packet drops" per queue. This command is important in the operation and management of PFC-based QoS.

Verification

```
7600-2#show queuing interface gigabitEthernet 3/3
Interface GigabitEthernet3/3 queuing strategy: Weighted Round-Robin
  Port QoS is enabled ----→ Indicates Port is configured for QoS
  Port is untrusted
  Extend trust state: not trusted [COS = 0]
  Default COS is 0
  Queuing Mode In Tx direction: mode-cos
  Transmit queues [type = 1p3q8t]: ----→ Transmit queue structure
  Queue Id     Scheduling     Num of thresholds
  -----------------------------------------------
   01             WRR              08
   02             WRR              08
   03             WRR              08
   04             Priority         01 ----→ Priority queue mapping
 WRR bandwidth ratios:     40[queue 1]   50[queue 2]   10[queue 3]
 queue-limit ratios:       40[queue 1]   50[queue 2]   10[queue 3]
 queue tail-drop-thresholds
 ---------------------------
 1    70[1]   100[2]  100[3]   100[4]   100[5]   100[6]   100[7]   100[8]
 2    70[1]   100[2]  100[3]   100[4]   100[5]   100[6]   100[7]   100[8]
 3    100[1]  100[2]  100[3]   100[4]   100[5]   100[6]   100[7]   100[8]
 queue random-detect-min-thresholds ----→ WRED Min-thresholds
 ----------------------------------
 1    40[1]    35[2]    30[3]    100[4]   100[5]   100[6]   100[7]   100[8]
 2    100[1]   100[2]   100[3]   100[4]   100[5]   100[6]   100[7]   100[8]
 3    100[1]   100[2]   100[3]   100[4]   100[5]   100[6]   100[7]   100[8]
 queue random-detect-max-thresholds ----→ WRED Max-thresholds
 ----------------------------------
 1    45[1]   45[2]   100[3]   100[4]  100[5]   100[6]  100[7]   100[8]
 2    100[1]  100[2]  100[3]   100[4]  100[5]   100[6]  100[7]  100[8]
 3    100[1]  100[2]  100[3]   100[4]  100[5]   100[6]  100[7]   100[8]
 WRED disabled queues:2 3 ----→ WRED is disabled for queue 2 & 3
 queue thresh cos-map ----→ CoS to Queue map as per the configuration
 ---------------------------------------------
 1    1    2
 1    2    1
 1    3    0
 1    4
```

```
1      5
1      6
1      7
1      8
2      1      4
2      2      3
2      3
2      4
2      5
2      6
2      7
2      8
3      1      6     7
3      2
3      3
3      4
3      5
3      6
3      7
3      8
4      1      5
Queuing Mode In Rx direction: mode-cos
Receive queues [type = 2q8t]:
Queue Id    Scheduling        Num of thresholds
-------------------------------------------------
 01          WRR                      08
 02          WRR                      08
WRR bandwidth ratios:    100[queue 1]     0[queue 2]
queue-limit ratios:      100[queue 1]     0[queue 2]
queue tail-drop-thresholds
--------------------------
1    100[1]   100[2]   100[3]   100[4]  100[5]   100[6]  100[7]   100[8]
2     100[1]   100[2]   100[3]   100[4]  100[5]   100[6]  100[7]   100[8]
queue thresh cos-map ----→ No Rx QoS enabled
----------------------------------------
1     1      0 1 2 3 4 5 6 7
1     2
1     3
1     4
1     5
1     6
1     7
1     8
2     1
2     2
2     3
```

```
2       4
2       5
2       6
2       7
2       8
Packets dropped on Transmit: ----→ Packet drop statistics on transmit side
 queue       dropped     [cos-map]
---------------------------------------------
1                  0     [2 1 0 ]
2                  0     [4 3 ]
3                  0     [6 7 ]
4                  0     [5 ]
Packets dropped on Receive:
 queue       dropped     [cos-map]
---------------------------------------------
1                  0     [0 1 2 3 4 5 6 7 ]
2                  0     []
```

The *show interface <interface-name> capabilities* command can be used to determine the QoS capabilities of the port in addition to providing generic information that could be useful for the operator. In this illustration, we use this command to determine the queuing structure in both directions (Tx and Rx).

Verifying Port Capabilities

```
7600-2#show interfaces gigabitEthernet 3/3 capabilities
GigabitEthernet3/3
  Dot1x:                      yes
  Model:                      WS-X6748-GE-TX
  Type:                       10/100/1000BaseT
  Speed:                      10,100,1000,auto
  Duplex:                     half,full
  Trunk encap. type:          802.1Q,ISL
  Trunk mode:                 on,off,desirable,nonegotiate
  Channel:                    yes
  Broadcast suppression:      percentage(0-100)
  Flowcontrol:                rx-(off,on,desired),tx-(off,on,desired)
  Membership:                 static
  Fast Start:                 yes
  QOS scheduling:             rx-(2q8t), tx-(1p3q8t) ----→ Queue structure
  CoS rewrite:                yes
  ToS rewrite:                yes
  Inline power:               no
  SPAN:                       source/destination
  UDLD                        yes
```

```
Link Debounce:               yes
Link Debounce Time:          no
Ports on ASIC:               1-12
Port-Security:               yes
```

8.3.9 Core Configurations for the Cisco CRS-1 Series Routers

QoS in the CRS-1 is distributed in many locations and is performed end to end. This means that QoS is present not only in the line card but also in the fabric. This section provides a very brief overview of QoS on the CRS-1 platform as well as necessary configuration templates for the following:

- Fabric QoS (to-fabric and from-fabric)
- Core-facing interface QoS

Fabric QoS

Fabric QoS affects the following QoS components in CRS-1:

IngressQ ASIC:

- Classification into HP/LP To-Fabric queues to achieve strict-priority scheduling of real-time traffic across the switch fabric.

NOTE 8.14: Fabric QoS

From the switch-fabric perspective it would be sufficient and simpler to classify the HP/LP traffic using the ingress interface service policy. However, the FabricQ QoS provides more flexibility for handling the traffic at egress of switch fabric, that is, the possibility of AF queues in addition to HP/LP.

FabricQ ASIC:

- Classification (on FabricQ ASIC) into HP, AF, and BE From-Fabric queues.
- MDRR control when dequeuing the From-fabric queues, that is, just before the packet is handed over to TX-PSE in EgressQ ASIC. The main objective of three-class MDRR at this level is to distinguish AF class (mission-critical and multimedia traffic) from BE data in case of oversubscribed TX-PSE. The TX-PSE can get oversubscribed in terms of pps when several ingress MSCs send to the same egress MSC. The oversubscription of each separate egress interface is handled by EgressQ ASIC.
- The Backpressure mechanism involves broadcasting a "discard" message to all IngressQs when a particular From-Fabric queue becomes congested (that is, has exceeded the tail-drop threshold).

NOTE 8.15: Fabric QoS and Bandwidth

Bandwidth Remaining Percent values for FabricQ queues must be configured in multiples of 5.

Configuration

```
!
class-map match-any FABRIC_AF_VIDEO_PREMIUM
 match mpls experimental topmost 2 4
 match precedence ipv4 2 4
!
! VIDEO and PREMIUM applications travel in AF queue
!
class-map match-any FABRIC_PQ_VOICE_CONTROL
 match mpls experimental topmost 5 6 7
 match precedence ipv4 5 6 7
!
! VOICE and CONTROL applications travel in HP queue
!
policy-map FABRIC_QOS
 class FABRIC_PQ_VOICE_CONTROL
  priority
!
! Video and Premium services scheduled in AF queue (protected from
! best-effort)
!
class FABRIC_AF_VIDEO_PREMIUM
 bandwidth remaining percent 45
!
! BE and OUT-OF-CONTRACT PREMIUM DATA scheduled in class-default
!
class class-default
 bandwidth remaining percent 55
!
!
switch-fabric
 service-policy FABRIC_QOS -------→ Policy applied to the Switch Fabric!
!
end
```

Core-Facing Interface QoS

In this section, we take a look at the QoS configurations for the core-facing interfaces (egress QoS) on the CRS-1 platforms. Two interface types are chosen for the illustration: (1) 10GE SPA and (2) POS OC192-SPA.

The CRS-1 platform supports the keyword *EXP* while configuring WRED-based profiles. This support is not available on IOS software. However, the use of the keyword *PRECEDENCE* on IOS-based platforms will also match MPLS Experimental values; hence there are no differences from a functional standpoint.

The *show qos interface <interface> output* command provides a comprehensive output on the functionality of the policy map applied to the egress interface. It can be viewed as a command that enables the operator to verify and validate the QoS configurations for a given interface. Policer configuration for the LLQ, maximum and minimum available bandwidth for a given queue, WRED profiles, and queue-limit/tail-drop values are provided. An operator typically uses this command to verify the applied policy and its parameters immediately after attaching a policy map to an interface.

Configuration

```
!
class-map match-any Control
 match mpls experimental topmost 6 7
!
class-map match-any Video
 match mpls experimental topmost 4
!
class-map match-any Premium
 match mpls experimental topmost 2 1
!
class-map match-any Voice
 match mpls experimental topmost 5
!
class-map match-any Best-Effort
 match mpls experimental topmost 0
!
! ====================================
!
policy-map FOO-CORE
 class Voice
  police rate percent 25
   conform-action transmit
   exceed-action drop
  priority
 !
 class Control
  bandwidth percent 2
 !
 class Premium
  random-detect exp 2 40 ms 45 ms
  random-detect exp 1 35 ms 40 ms
  bandwidth percent 28
  queue-limit 45 ms
```

```
  !
  class Video
   bandwidth percent 40
   queue-limit 35 ms
  !
  class Best-Effort
   random-detect exp 0 30 ms 100 ms
   bandwidth percent 5
   queue-limit 100 ms
! ====================================
!
interface TenGigE 0/0/0/3
 description <Core facing interface>
 service-policy output FOO-CORE
!
end
```

Verification

```
RP/0/RP0/CPU0:CRS-E#show qos interface tenGigE 0/0/0/3 output
Fri Apr 25 09:42:10.081 GMT EDT
Interface TenGigE0_0_0_3 -- output policy
Total number of classes: 6
-------------------------------------------------------
LEVEL1 class: classid                    =       0×1
class name                               =       Voice
No explicit weight assigned for this class
Sharq Queue ID                           =       16
This Q belongs to Group                  =       12
Queue Max. BW.                           =       10000128 kbps --→ Max
bandwidth available!
TailDrop Threshold(bytes)                =       12500160
WRED not configured for this class
Policer slot #                           =       225
Policer avg. kbps                        =       2500000 kbps
Policer peak kbps                        =       0 kbps
Policer conform burst configured         =       0 Kbits
Policer conform burst programmed         =       2097120 bytes
Policer conform action                   =       Just TX
Policer conform action value             =       0
Policer exceed action                    =       DROP PKT
Policer exceed action value              =       0
LEVEL1 class: classid                    =       0×2
class name                               =       Premium
No explicit weight assigned for this class
Sharq Queue ID                           =       32
```

```
This Q belongs to Group              =     12
Queue Max. BW.                       =     10000128 kbps --→ Max bandwidth
                                           available!
Queue Min. BW.                       =     2800128 kbps --→ Min assured
                                           bandwidth!
TailDrop Threshold(bytes)            =     56250000
WRED profile for EXP 1
WRED Min. Threshold                  =     43962880 bytes
WRED Max. Threshold                  =     49999872 bytes
WRED First Segment                   =     189
WRED Segment Size                    =     9
WRED profile for EXP 2
WRED Min. Threshold                  =     50212864 bytes
WRED Max. Threshold                  =     56249856 bytes
WRED First Segment                   =     189
WRED Segment Size                    =     9
Policer not configured for this class
LEVEL1 class: classid                =     0x3
class name                           =     Control
No explicit weight assigned for this class
Sharq Queue ID                       =     33
This Q belongs to Group              =     12
Queue Max. BW.                       =     10000128 kbps
Queue Min. BW.                       =     199936 kbps
TailDrop Threshold(bytes)            =     250003200
WRED not configured for this class
Policer not configured for this class
LEVEL1 class: classid                =     0x4
class name                           =     Video
No explicit weight assigned for this class
Sharq Queue ID                       =     34
This Q belongs to Group              =     12
Queue Max. BW.                       =     10000128 kbps
Queue Min. BW.                       =     4000000 kbps
TailDrop Threshold(bytes)            =     43750000
WRED not configured for this class
Policer not configured for this class
LEVEL1 class: classid                =     0x5
class name                           =     Best-Effort
No explicit weight assigned for this class
Sharq Queue ID                       =     35
This Q belongs to Group              =     12
Queue Max. BW.                       =     10000128 kbps
Queue Min. BW.                       =     499968 kbps --→ 5% of 10Gbps
TailDrop Threshold(bytes)            =     125000000
WRED profile for EXP 0
WRED Min. Threshold                  =     41038848 bytes
```

```
WRED Max. Threshold                    =          124999680 bytes
WRED First Segment                     =          169
WRED Segment Size                      =          13
Policer not configured for this class
LEVEL1 class: classid                  =          0x0
class name                             =          class-default
No explicit weight assigned for this class
Sharq Queue ID                         =          15
This Q belongs to Group                =          12
Queue Max. BW.                         =          10000128 kbps
TailDrop Threshold(bytes)              =          250003200
WRED not configured for this class
Policer not configured for this class
!
end
```

NOTE 8.16: Bandwidth Allocations

Looking at the preceding output, we see that the maximum bandwidth allocations for all queues are similar and indicate 10000128 Kbps, which is 10 Gbps. It means that each queue can scale up to 10 Gbps of bandwidth while other queues are idle and not using the link bandwidth.

The *show policy-map interface* command can be still used for verifying traffic counters and the respective traffic to queue mappings. The following illustration provides insight into the command usage.

Verification

```
RP/0/RP0/CPU0:CRS-E#show policy-map interface TenGigE 0/0/0/3
Fri Apr 25 10:23:48.473 GMT EDT
TenGigE0/0/0/3 output: FOO-CORE
Class Voice
 Classification statistics               (packets/bytes)     (rate-kbps)
  Matched              :                       3/450                0
  Transmitted          :                       3/450                0
  Total Dropped        :                       0/0                  0
 Policing statistics                     (packets/bytes)     (rate-kbps)
  Policed(conform)     :                       3/450                0
  Policed(exceed)      :                       0/0                  0
  Policed(violate)     :                       0/0                  0
  Policed and dropped  :                       0/0
  Queuing statistics
  Vital (packets)      :                       0
  Queue ID             :                       16
```

```
  High watermark (bytes)                  :0
  Inst-queue-len (bytes)                  :0
  Avg-queue-len (bytes)                   :0
  Taildropped(packets/bytes)              :0/0
Class Premium
  Classification statistics                 (packets/bytes)     (rate-kbps)
   Matched             :                          10/2000              0
   Transmitted         :                          10/2000              0
   Total Dropped       :                           0/0                 0
  Queuing statistics
   Vital (packets)                          :0
   Queue ID                                 :32
   High watermark (bytes)                   :0
   Inst-queue-len (bytes)                   :0
   Avg-queue-len (bytes)                    :0
   Taildropped(packets/bytes)               :0/0
   RED random drops(packets/bytes)          :0/0
   RED maxthreshold drops(packets/bytes)    :0/0
   WRED profile for EXP 1
   RED Transmitted (packets/bytes)          :0/0
   RED random drops(packets/bytes)          :0/0
   RED maxthreshold drops(packets/bytes)    :0/0
   WRED profile for EXP 2
   RED Transmitted (packets/bytes)          :10/2000
   RED random drops(packets/bytes)          :0/0
   RED maxthreshold drops(packets/bytes)    :0/0
   [Output is Truncated]
```

Core QoS Using OC-192 POS Interface Modules

Let's examine a QoS configuration on the OC-192 POS interface. The configurations on the PoS and 10 GE interfaces are identical and have no differences. It is worth noting that the QoS configurations on the CRS-1 platform are not line-card specific.

Configuration

```
!
class-map match-any Control
 match mpls experimental topmost 6 7
!
class-map match-any Video
 match mpls experimental topmost 4
!
class-map match-any Premium
 match mpls experimental topmost 2 1
!
```

```
class-map match-any Voice
 match mpls experimental topmost 5
!
class-map match-any Best-Effort
 match mpls experimental topmost 0
!
! ========================================
!
policy-map FOO-CORE
 class Voice
  police rate percent 25
   conform-action transmit
   exceed-action drop
  priority
 !
 class Control
  bandwidth percent 2
 !
 class Premium
  random-detect exp 2 40 ms 45 ms
  random-detect exp 1 35 ms 40 ms
  bandwidth percent 28
  queue-limit 45 ms
 !
 class Video
  bandwidth percent 40
  queue-limit 35 ms
 !
 class Best-Effort
  random-detect exp 0 30 ms 100 ms
  bandwidth percent 5
  queue-limit 100 ms
! ========================================
!
interface POS 0/3/0/1
 description <Core facing interface>
 service-policy output FOO-CORE
!
end
```

8.4 DiffServ Tunneling Modes on IOS-XR

In Chapter 2 we discussed the implementation of DiffServ Tunneling modes on IOS-based platforms. In this section we discuss the implementation specific details on XR-based platforms.

8.4.1 Configuration Example of Short-Pipe Mode

The following is a definition of class maps used for classifying traffic at the ingress PE router of an MPLS network. Since this is the first entry point in the MPLS network, this PE will receive an IP packet, and an ingress line card will do an imposition of MPLS labels. By default the MPLS EXP will copy the precedence values in the IP header; therefore it is not necessary to specify the matching of DSCP default AF11 and AF21 as a match criteria as per the following class map. However, in this example the SP wants to use the same class map at all ingress and egress PEs and specifies a generic set of match criteria that can be used at both the ingress and the egress PE. Matching on DSCP at ingress might seem redundant, but it can provide an advantage in terms of standardizing and minimizing the number of class maps used throughout the SP's network.

Defining Class Maps for Short Pipe

```
# Defining classification for Normal Price Traffic
class-map match-any BE
 match mpls experimental topmost 0
 match dscp default
!
#Defining classification for Priority-Price
class-map match-any PP
 match mpls experimental topmost 1
 match dscp af11
!
#Defining classification for Business traffic
class-map match-any BUS
 match mpls experimental topmost 2
 match dscp af21
!
#Defining classification for Interactive Traffic
class-map match-any INT
 match mpls experimental topmost 3
 match dscp af31
!
#Defining classification for Real Time traffic
class-map match-any RT
 match mpls experimental topmost 5
 match dscp ef
!
#Defining classification for Real Time and INT traffic for Internal qos policy
class-map match-any RT_INT
 match mpls experimental topmost 3 5
!
```

Now let's examine the egress policy, which is illustrated next. Note that the customer's PHB markings are not remarked by the SP. Though the class map defines EXP and DSCP as match criteria, the actual match is only done on the IP packet's DSCP value, since the MPLS label attributes are not extended to the egress line card.

Egress Policy for Short Pipe

```
policy-map edge_egress
  class RT
   police rate percent 20
   !
queue-limit 1000 packets
priority
  !
  !
  class INT
  queue-limit 1000 packets
   bandwidth percent 20
  !
  class BUS
   bandwidth percent 20
   bandwidth remaining percent 20
  !
  class PP
   bandwidth percent 15
   bandwidth remaining percent 10
  !
  class BE
   bandwidth percent 10
   bandwidth remaining percent 10
 !
end
```

8.4.2 Configuration Example of Pipe Mode

In this section we look at the required configurations for the pipe mode of operation. The following illustration provides insight into the required configurations on the ingress interface (core facing) on the egress PE router. As mentioned in Chapter 2, all other configurations are similar to the short-pipe mode of operation. The egress PE router uses two mechanisms, *qos-group* and *discard-class*, to deploy this mode of operation. However, the use of *discard-class* is optional here.

Qos-group is an internal marking on the packet header buffer. This value is used for classification within the local router and does not have significance beyond the local router. On Cisco IOS XR software, it is currently possible to set *qos-group* values from 0–31. Alternatively, an option is available for specifying another internal marking, called *discard-class,* in the range from 0 to 7. The *discard-class* setting is useful in the match criteria for egress as well as for performing WRED directly on *discard-class* labels.

Pipe Mode Configuration

```
class-map match-any exp0
 match mpls experimental topmost 0
!
class-map match-any exp1
 match mpls experimental topmost 1
!
class-map match-any exp2
 match mpls experimental topmost 2
!
class-map match-any exp3
 match mpls experimental topmost 3
!
class-map match-any exp4
 match mpls experimental topmost 4
!
class-map match-any exp5
 match mpls experimental topmost 5
!
Class qos-group0
 Match qos-group 0
!
Class qos-group1
 Match qos-group 1
!
Class qos-group2
 Match qos-group 2
!
Class qos-group3
 Match qos-group 3
!
Class qos-group4
 Match qos-group 4
!
Class qos-group5
 Match qos-group 5
!
policy-map ingress_PE ------→ attached to the core facing interface!
 class exp0
  set qos-group 0
 !
 class exp1
  set qos-group 1
 !
 class exp2
  set qos-group 2
 !
```

```
  class exp3
   set qos-group 3
  !
  class exp4
   set qos-group 4
  !
  class exp5
   set qos-group 5
  !
!
policy-map edge_egress_4 ----→ attached to the egress interface!
  class qos-group5
   police rate 30 mbps
   !
   queue-limit 50 ms
   priority
  !
  class qos-group4
   queue-limit 100 ms
   bandwidth remaining percent 40
   !
  class qos-group3
   bandwidth remaining percent 30
   !
  class qos-group2
   bandwidth remaining percent 5
   !
  class qos-group1
   bandwidth remaining percent 5
   !
  class qos-group0
   bandwidth remaining percent 3
   !
!
policy-map edge_egress_PIPE
  class class-default
   shape average 450 mbps
   service-policy edge_egress_4
  !
!
End
```

8.4.3 Configuration Example of Uniform Mode

In this section we look at the required configurations for the uniform mode of operation. Once again, as mentioned in Chapter 2, all configurations are similar to the short-pipe and pipe modes of operation with the exception of the egress PE. At the egress PE, the configuration is similar to the pipe mode model. The only exception is that the SP PHB is copied to the customer PHB. In the following illustration, we only examine this bit.

Uniform Mode Configuration

```
policy-map edge_egress_4
 class qos-group5
 police rate 30 mbps
 !
 queue-limit 50 ms
 priority
 !
 class qos-group4
 set precedence flash
 queue-limit 100 ms
 bandwidth remaining percent 40
 !
 class qos-group3
 set precedence immediate
 bandwidth remaining percent 30
 !
 class qos-group2
 set precedence priority
 bandwidth remaining percent 5
 !
 class qos-group1
 set precedence routine
 bandwidth remaining percent 5
 !
 class qos-group0
 set precedence routine
 bandwidth remaining percent 3
 !
 !
end
```

8.5 Summary

This chapter provided guidelines and implementation specific details on configuring QoS for MPLS Layer 3 VPN services. A case study was also chosen to illustrate these details using guidelines provided in the previous chapters. It is recommended that this information be used to create a broad framework in an SP network, but the finer details will always need optimization based on a wide variety of requirements, and there cannot be any hard and fast rules for deployment.

CHAPTER 9

Cisco IOS and IOS-XR Quality-of-Service Implementation for Carrier Ethernet and Virtual Leased-Line Services

9.1 Overview

Carrier Ethernet and virtual leased-line (VLL) services refer to a group of technologies that allow the carriage of ISO Layer 2 protocols on a Layer 3 IP/MPLS network. These services are enabled by the encapsulation of Layer 2 frames in a standards-based manner: RFC-4619 for Frame Relay, RFC-4448 for Ethernet IEEE 802.3, and RFC-4717 for Asynchronous Transfer Mode, to name a few. Apart from Ethernet, each of these services provides point-to-point service only, encapsulating frames between two logical interfaces. Carrier Ethernet, on the other hand, provides either a point-to-point or a point-to-multipoint service.

Tables 9.1 and 9.2 provide illustrations of some Carrier Ethernet and VLL service types. In Table 9.1 we notice that a Carrier Ethernet offering may consist of both point-to-point and multipoint services. Multipoint services are also known as *virtual private LAN service* (VPLS).

As mentioned, VLL services are only point-to-point in nature and are considered alternatives to traditional leased-line circuits. VLL-based services are encapsulation specific and can be transparently hosted on an IP/MPLS infrastructure.

This chapter focuses on the aspects needed for building a Carrier Ethernet and VLL infrastructure and places more emphasis on the aspects that are relevant at the network edge, since this is the only difference between these services and MPLS L3VPN and other service types. Hence, to avoid repetition, core configurations that are the nerve center for building and controlling SLAs are not discussed, since they were addressed in the previous chapter.

NOTE 9.1: Carrier Ethernet and Virtual Leased Line

Throughout this chapter, all Ethernet-based services are referred to as Carrier Ethernet services; this includes both point-to-point and multipoint services. Non-Ethernet-based services are referred to as virtual leased-line, or VLL, services.

Table 9.1: Carrier Ethernet Service Types

Carrier Ethernet	Service Type
Ethernet Relay Service	Point-to-point VLAN-based service
Ethernet Wire Service	Point-to-point port-based service
Ethernet Relay Multipoint Service	Multipoint VLAN-based service
Ethernet Wire Multipoint Service	Multipoint port-based service

Table 9.2: Virtual Leased-Line Service Types

Virtual Leased Line	Service Type
ATM over MPLS	Point-to-point-based service
PPP over MPLS	Point-to-point-based service
HDLC over MPLS	Point-to-point-based service
Frame Relay over MPLS	Point-to-point-based service

Table 9.3: Possible Service Examples

Service Delineator	Example Value	User
ToS	1	Customer A
	2–4	Customer B
802.1Q VLAN Tags	100	Customer D
	200–300	Customer E
802.1Q in 802.1Q VLAN Tags	S = 100, C = 100	Customer F
	S = 101, C = 200–250	Customer G

9.2 Carrier Ethernet Service

Carrier Ethernet is a combination of point-to-point and multipoint services for the carriage of Ethernet frames across an MPLS network. In the case of multipoint-based services, forwarding is based on Mac learning and loop prevention is based on split horizon. Service delineation in Carrier Ethernet can be classified by any part of the Ethernet header, such as the VLAN ID or Type of Service (IEEE 802.1p) field in the IEEE 802.1q header. However, services are commonly delineated by a customer's vlan (C-VLAN), a service provider's VLAN (S-VLAN), a combination of both, or a combination of service provider VLAN and ranges of customer VLANs. For example, in a simple scenario, each VLAN on an IEEE802.1q-enabled port could be considered a discrete service. Table 9.3 shows a set of possible service examples.

9.3 An Introduction to Ethernet Virtual Circuits

Ethernet has gone far beyond its traditional calling of LAN connectivity; it is now ubiquitous, being present in the LAN, MAN, and WAN and going far beyond the original plans for

Ethernet. As Ethernet technology has evolved, so have the requirements for Ethernet services, new platforms, and enhancements to existing platforms (such as the Cisco 7600) are becoming more Ethernet services aware. This means that these platforms are required to handle a wide breadth of services on a single port, with the ability to flexibly map Ethernet frames into varying services, independently of the actual service, whether locally switched, P2P, and P2MP. There is also an increasing demand to scale the number of Ethernet-supported services through many techniques, including QinQ, Mac-in-Mac, and VLAN local significance.

To be aligned with this flexibility, 7600 supports a new infrastructure for Ethernet provisioning, called the Ethernet Virtual Circuit Infrastructure (EVC).[1] The goal of the EVC infrastructure is to extend the functionality of the Ethernet from both a control and a forwarding plane perspective. It is designed to empower Ethernet technology into the service provider arena. In short, EVC is the new-generation infrastructure providing Ethernet-based point-to-point and multipoint services.

NOTE 9.2: Supported Platforms

At present, EVC infrastructures and deployment are supported on the 7600 platform only. The most common line card used for building EVCs is the ES-20; hence we focus all our discussions in the chapter around this line card.

9.3.1 EVC CLI

The general goal for the new EVC CLI is to provide a flexible and uniform approach to provisioning Ethernet services for both routing and switching platforms. The EVC CLI accommodates the following requirements:

- Low-touch provisioning: CLI should be simple and kept to a minimum.
- Uniform touch and feel for all Ethernet L2 services, and for L3 services.
- Consistent across platforms.
- Extensible, for future additions and enhancements.
- Flexible, to accommodate various service offerings.
- Supports coexistence of L2 and L3 features on the same physical port.
- Scalable, in terms of service instance count and configuration file size.

The new EVC CLI has a hierarchical structure. Figure 9.1 shows the high-level structure of EVC CLI.

[1] The Metro Ethernet Forum (MEF) defines an Ethernet Virtual Connection, or EVC, as an association between two or more UNIs that identifies a point-to-point, multipoint-to-multipoint, or point-to-multipoint path within a service provider's network.

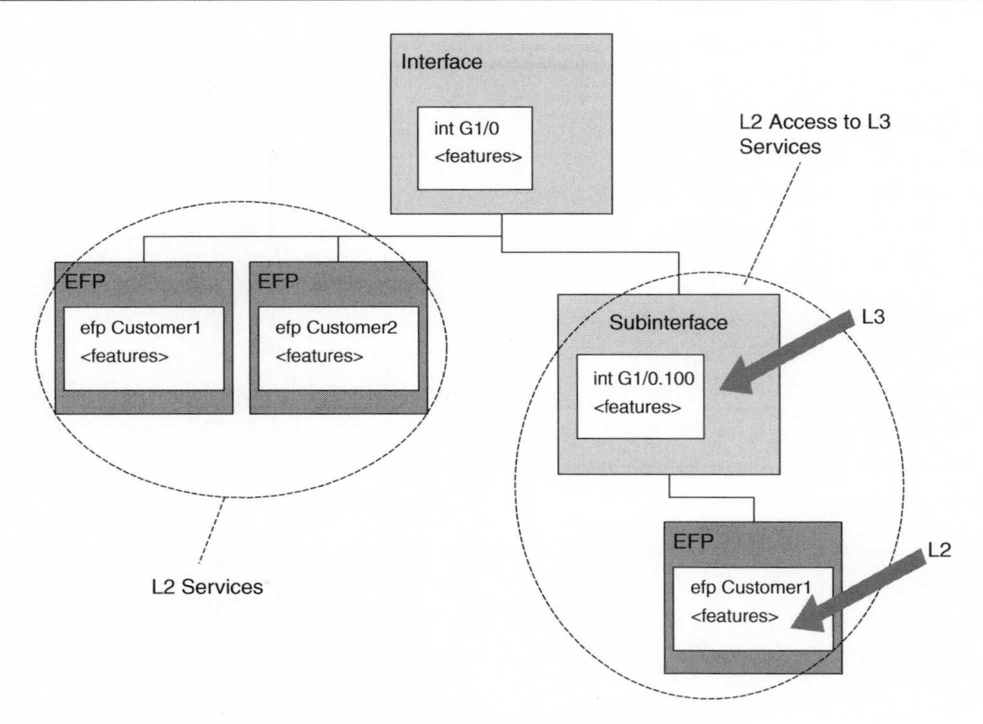

Figure 9.1: EVC Hierarchical CLI Structure

The software and hardware implementation of EVC CLI decouples the forwarding from the control plane, effectively eliminating scalability limitations in terms of number of VLANs and interfaces. When the EVC infrastructure is involved, a new command-line interface (CLI) is implemented to create Ethernet virtual circuits using the *service instance* command. The syntax and the options for the *service instance* command is given next. This CLI enables far more flexibility than previous interface-based commands. More details on the EVC architecture are discussed in the following sections.

Service Instance CLI

```
interface <type><slot/port>
 service instance <id> ethernet   !(ID unique/int, evc-name
   <evc-name>                        unique/network)
  <match criteria commands>       !(VLAN tags, MAC, CoS, Ether type)
  <rewrite commands>              !(VLAN tags pop/push/translation)
  <forwarding commands>           !(L2 P2P or Multipoint Bridging)
  <feature commands>              !(QoS, ACL, etc)
```

The EVC infrastructure offers increased flexibility, which includes the following Flexible Edge-related features:

- *Independent Ethernet encapsulation.* This allows the EVC infrastructure to operate independent of the Ethernet encapsulation (Ethernet, 802.1Q, QinQ, 802.1ah etc.).

- *Flexible frame matching.* Flexible frame matching allows for a wide range of flexible-matching techniques to be able to map Ethernet frames into services. Flexible QinQ options such as matching a single or range of 802.1Q tags or even flexibly matching on a range of inner and outer tags within a QinQ environment make this flexibility an extremely powerful feature.
- *Flexible VLAN manipulation.* This feature allows the SP some flexibility with the incoming tagged frames, options such as mapping frames on a 1:1, 1:2, or 2:1 basis provide the SP with some flexibility as the frames come into the network. In addition to these mappings, inner or outer tags can be pushed, popped, or rewritten (as described previously) in varying combinations to provide flexibility.
- *Flexible services mapping.* Flexible service mapping enables multiple Ethernet services to be configured on a single port. Sample services include EoMPLS, locally L2 connected services, VPLS, L3 VPN, and Ethernet MultiPoint Bridging (E-MPB). Additionally, Ethernet frames can be flexibly mapped into a single service—for example, a range of VLANs, or a specific combination of a single outer tag with varying inner tags can be mapped to a single Ethernet service. This offers the ability to reduce the number of required services while providing great flexibility for the service provider.
- *Ethernet scaling.* As mentioned earlier, with Ethernet extending its reaches beyond the traditional campus/LAN environment, Ethernet scale becomes a challenge. The EVC infrastructure allows for local VLAN significance on a per-port basis, which means that each port can host 4000 VLANs that are (for certain service types) independent of the same VLAN numbers configured on other ports throughout the same node. Additionally, with the flexible services offerings available with the EVC infrastructure, we can map these locally significant VLANs from various ports into a single common service, should this be desired.
- *OAM protocols.* The EVC infrastructure today supports varying OAM protocols, including CFM and LDP, and E-LMI interworking. However, in the future this will be expanded to support additional protocols such as 802.3AH and so on.

9.3.2 EVC Architecture

The Ethernet Virtual Circuit Architecture illustrated in Figure 9.2 is made up of several components:

- On the very top is a Control Point, which basically provides cross-platform command line and gives a structured command line to the configuration.
- On the service Abstraction Layer, we define the Ethernet Flow Point (EFP) on the Ethernet interface to represent an Ethernet flow. The Ethernet flow point is independent of the Ethernet encapsulation.

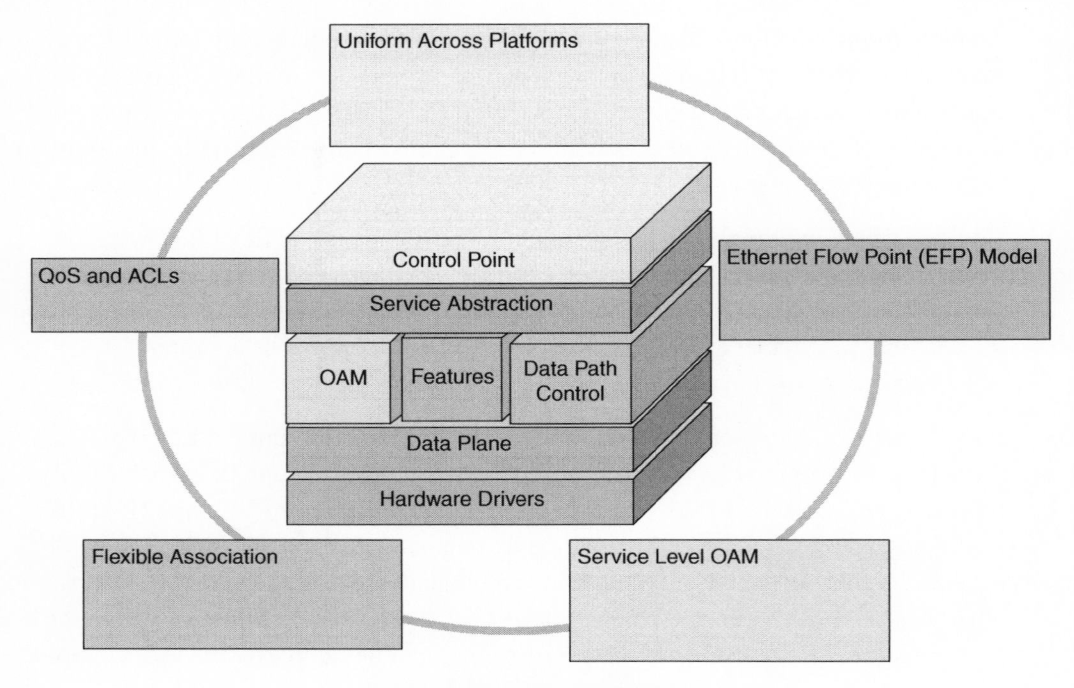

Figure 9.2: EVC Architecture

- Operations and Maintenance features for Ethernet.
- For features, we can basically have QoS and ACL features. These features can directly apply to the EFP.
- Data Path Control.

9.3.3 EVC/EFP Forwarding Model

Figure 9.3 illustrates the forwarding model in great detail. From the following illustration, it can be seen that the large pipe on the left side is an Ethernet interface and that the small pipes are Ethernet flow points.

Some of the highlights of EVC and EFP are as follows:

- *Ethernet Flow Points (EFPs)* are very similar to Layer 3 subinterfaces, but the difference is that Ethernet flow points are for Layer 2 services, and subinterfaces are for Layer 3 services. Another difference is that for subinterfaces where the *encapsulation vlan* command is used, this can only match a unique VLAN ID, whereas for Ethernet flow points these can match multiple VLAN IDs or a range of the VLAN IDs at a time. The Ethernet flow point could represent greater than 4000 VLANs of configuration thus making it scale far more efficiently. The EFP can map to different

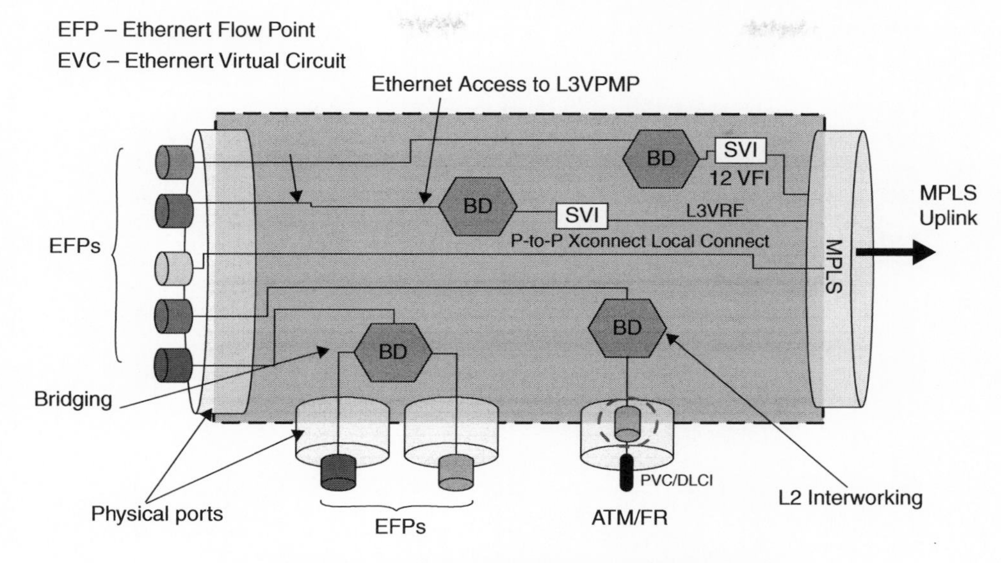

Figure 9.3: EVC/EFP Forwarding Model

services, and from Figure 9.2 it can be seen that a single service can be mapped to a point-to-point cross-connect and the local connect, which also applies to a multipoint service.

- *Bridge domain (BD)* equates to a global VLAN on a 7600 and allows mapping Ethernet flow points to a bridge domain. The bridge domain, since it is equal to the global VLAN, can have an SVI interface. Under the SVI interface it is possible to configure VPLS, EoMPLS, or Layer 3 termination. Multiple Ethernet flow points can be mapped to the same bridge domain and, as shown in Figure 9.2, the flow points can cross different physical interfaces to the same bridge domain.

9.3.4 EVC Packet Flow

The following section gives an understanding of the EVC packet flow and an explanation of the various blocks that make up the end-to-end flow. A graphic showing this model appears in Figure 9.4.

Matching Features

On ingress the packet at Tier 1 (the input feature), the match actually takes place. On each Ethernet flow point it is possible to match on the following criteria:

- Unique VLAN tag
- Multiple or a range of VLAN tags

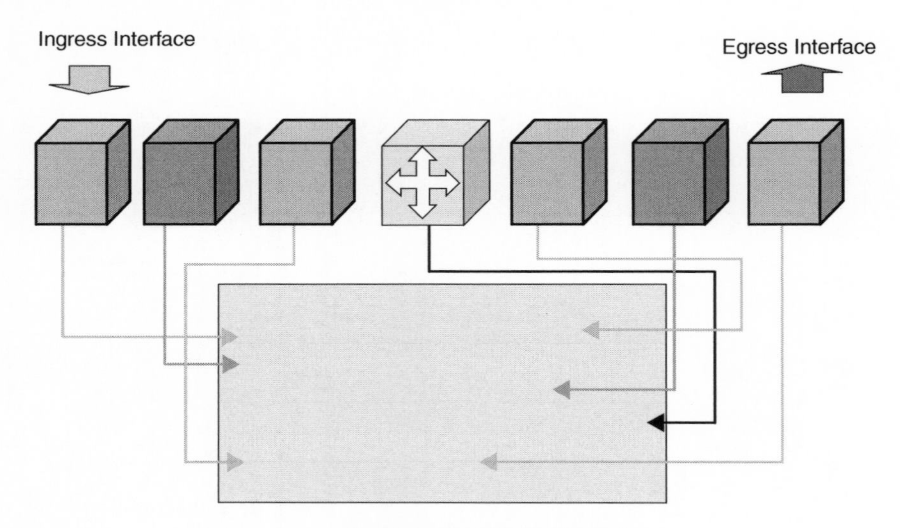

Figure 9.4: EVC Packet Flow

- Any combination of up to two VLAN tags
- There can only be a single "match untag," which is used to match the untagged frame

For example, Layer 2 control protocols usually go as untagged, so you need to define the Ethernet flow point for those protocols that have untagged frames. There is also the match default, whereby if there is no match for any specific Ethernet flow point, it just all falls into the class default. The command-line interface (CLI) for flexible frame matching is shown in the following configuration example. The CLI with explanations is provided in the configuration template.

CLI for Match Criteria

```
interface <type><slot/port>
 service instance <ID> ethernet
!
! Single tagged frame
! Vlan tag can be single, multiple or range or any (1-4096).
encapsulation dot1q {any | "<vlan-id>[, <vlan-id>[-<vlain-id>]]"}
!
! Double tagged frame
! First vlan tag must be unique, second vlan tag can be any, unique, range or
multiple
! Only look up to 2 tags if receive more than 2 tagged frames
```

```
   encapsulation dot1q <vlan-id> second-dot1q {any | "<vlan-id>[,<vlan-id>[-
<vlain-id>]]"}
!
! Default tag
! Match all frames tagged or untagged that are not matched by other more
specific service
! instances
   encapsulation default
!
! Untagged
! Match no tagged frames, for example native vlan
   encapsulation un tagged
```

Matching Types

The EVC infrastructure only supports nonexact matching; this means that a configuration can match many different combinations. For instance, the command *Encapsulation dot1q 10* will match any packets with the outer (also known as the Service Provider) tag set to 10 by default. As shown in Figure 9.5, both of these frames will be matched by the configuration *encapsulation dot1q 10*.

Similarly, a configuration with the command *encapsulation dot1q 10 second-dot1q 200* will match any frames with the mentioned inner and outer tags. This being said, the EVC model supports longest-tag matching, first matching the longest matching tag identifier and then matching the shorter tag and so on. As shown in Figure 9.6, we can have truly flexible QinQ mappings, and the longest or more specific match is chosen out of all the available options. The ordering for encapsulation matching is as follows:

- Longest match
- No exact match using outer tag
- Untagged encapsulation matches untagged packets
- Default encapsulation catches all remaining traffic that doesn't have a more specific match as previously described; this will also catch untagged packets, should there be no service instance configured with Encapsulation untagged

The flexible VLAN tag-matching facility is performed on the GE ASIC. On the ES20 there are two of these ASICS: the first covers ports 0–9 and the second covers ports 10–19 on the GE version of the ES20. On the 10 GE version, each ASIC covers a single 10 GE port. Each of the GE ASICS can handle 8 K entries. Unique (single- or double-tag encapsulations), untagged encapsulations and the default encapsulation consume a single entry out of these 8000 entries.

For a range of matching entries (i.e., dot1q 100–300) the number of entries borrows a concept from IP routing summarization whereby each entry can cover a number (in base 2) of entries.

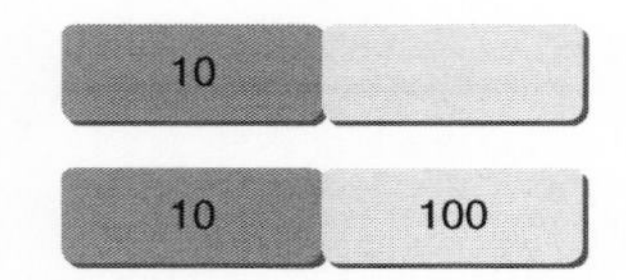

Figure 9.5: Single-Match Clause

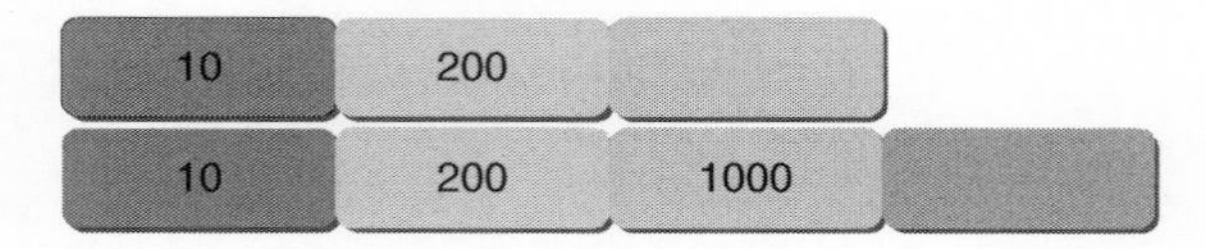

Figure 9.6: Double-Match Clause

For example, for the range 128–133 we need to use two entries (128–131 and 132–133); a range of 1–133 requires three entries (1–128, 128–131, and 132–133).

Encapsulation Adjustment

The ingress encapsulation adjustment is where any manipulation of VLAN tags takes place:

- Option 1: Translate VLAN tag (one to one/two to one/one to two/two to two).
- Option 2: Add VLAN tag (add one new tag/add two new tags).
- Option 3: Remove VLAN tag (remove one/remove two).

The encapsulation rewrite is always symmetrical, meaning that whatever is rewritten in the ingress direction should have the reverse rewrite on the egress direction for the same interface and same EFP. For example, if the outer VLAN tag on ingress is removed, the original VLAN tag needs to be added back on the egress direction. For the configuration, this would have resulted in always requiring two lines of rewrite configuration: one for rewrite ingress, the other for rewrite egress. To make configuration simple and avoid misconfiguration, the mandatory keyword *symmetric* is used, and the *rewrite egress* CLI is blocked for this purpose.

NOTE 9.3: Rewrite

The *symmetric* command will be accepted only when a single VLAN is configured in encapsulation. If a list of VLANs or a range of VLANs is configured in encapsulation, the symmetric will be accepted only for push rewrite operations; all other rewrite operations *will be rejected!*

The encapsulation rewrite CLI is outlined in the following configuration template. The commands have explanations above them within the configuration template.

Encapsulation Rewrite CLI

```
interface <type><slot/port>
 service instance <id> ethernet
   encapsulation dot1q <match criteria>
!
! Option 1 Translate Vlan Tag(s)
! e.g. translation of ingress Vlan tag (match criteria) to specified vlan-ID
   rewrite ingress tag translate 1-to-1 dot1q <vlan-ID> symmetric
!
! other options:
   rewrite ingress tag translate 2-to-1 dot1q <vlan-ID> symmetric
   rewrite ingress tag translate 1-to-2 dot1q <vlan-ID> symmetric second-dot1q
<vlan-ID>
   rewrite ingress tag translate 2-to-2 dot1q <vlan-ID> symmetric second-dot1q
<vlan-ID>
!
! Option 2 Add Vlan Tag(s)
! e.g. add single Vlan tag
   rewrite ingress tag push dot1q <vlan-ID>
!
! other options:
   rewrite ingress tag push dot1q <vlan-ID> second-dot1q <vlan-ID> ---→ Add
two tags
!
! Option 3 Remove Vlan Tag(s)
! e.g. remove single Vlan tag
   rewrite ingress tag pop 1 ---→ Remove the outermost tag
!
! other options:
   rewrite ingress tag pop 2 ---→ Remove the two outermost tags
```

Egress Tag Filtering

Two-stage filtering is implemented for EVC-based E-MPB[2] (discussed in the next section) configurations to prevent leaking broadcast/multicast bridge domain traffic packets from one EFP to another. Egress tag filtering is based on the encapsulation and rewrite configuration and is performed before and after egress tag rewrite (called the Encapsulation tag filter and the Rewrite tag filter):

- *Rewrite tag filter.* Performed *before* the tag rewrite operation. For flooded packets, all EFPs belonging to the same bridge domain will receive the copy. Before the egress

[2] Ethernet Multipoint Bridging allows us to group dot1q tagged VLAN(s) on different EFPs under the same bridge domain. Traffic from EFPs in the same bridge domain can be directed through whatever L2 interface is configured to access the bridge domain, including legacy LAN cards and L2 Gigabit Ethernet ports.

rewrite operation, the filter will check the VLAN tag from the source EFP against the tag applied through the ingress *rewrite* command on the destination EFPs. The packet is filtered if it doesn't match.

- *Encapsulation tag filter*. Performed *after* the tag rewrite operation. For flooded packets, all EFPs belonging to the same bridge domain will receive the copy. After the egress rewrite operation, the filter will check the VLAN tag from the source EFP against the encapsulation tag applied through the ingress encapsulation *match* command on the destination EFPs. The packet is filtered if it doesn't match.

9.3.5 Mandatory Rewrite Options and E-MPB

An important Layer 2 service that can be offered on 7600 routers as part of an EVC is support for Ethernet bridging (E-MPB) among physical and virtual interfaces that are heterogeneous in nature (EFPs, VFIs, and the like).

The frame encapsulations for all interface types are essentially Ethernet. It is therefore a useful abstraction to consider all members of a bridge domain as Ethernet pseudoports.

It is important to understand the requirements in terms of VLAN tag rewrite when heterogeneous Ethernet pseudoports are bridged into the same bridge domain. The aim of the bridge domain is the flexibility to map it to various services, including L3, P2P and P2MP EoMPLS, and so on. This also requires certain attention regarding VLAN tag rewrite on EFPs, described in greater detail in the next section.

As far as the basic Ethernet bridging functionality is concerned, all members of the bridge domain are Ethernet ports. All the usual bridging operations (MAC address learning, forwarding, flooding) occur among the pseudoports. The broadcast domain is identified by a number, namely the VLAN ID, that equals the global VLAN on the 7600. Every ingress frame is associated with a VLAN ID and thereby the broadcast domain it needs to be seen on.

The following sections describe the E-MPB packet flow for various module combinations and service mappings.

EFP-to-EFP (E-MPB)

For EFP-based configuration, the *bridge-domain <vlan-ID>* defines the broadcast domain on which frames from this EFP must be available. This command alone will *not* add or modify any VLAN header in the packet because this operation, if desired, is solely performed by the *rewrite ingress* command. Internally the bridge domain VLAN is updated in the 7600 DBUS header VLAN field and the frame is left intact on ingress if no rewrite action is configured.

As shown in Figure 9.7, the resulting frame on the wire totally depends on the rewrite configuration. LAN tag rewrite is *not* mandatory for bridging between EFPs, since the original VLAN ID is preserved through the internal switching process.

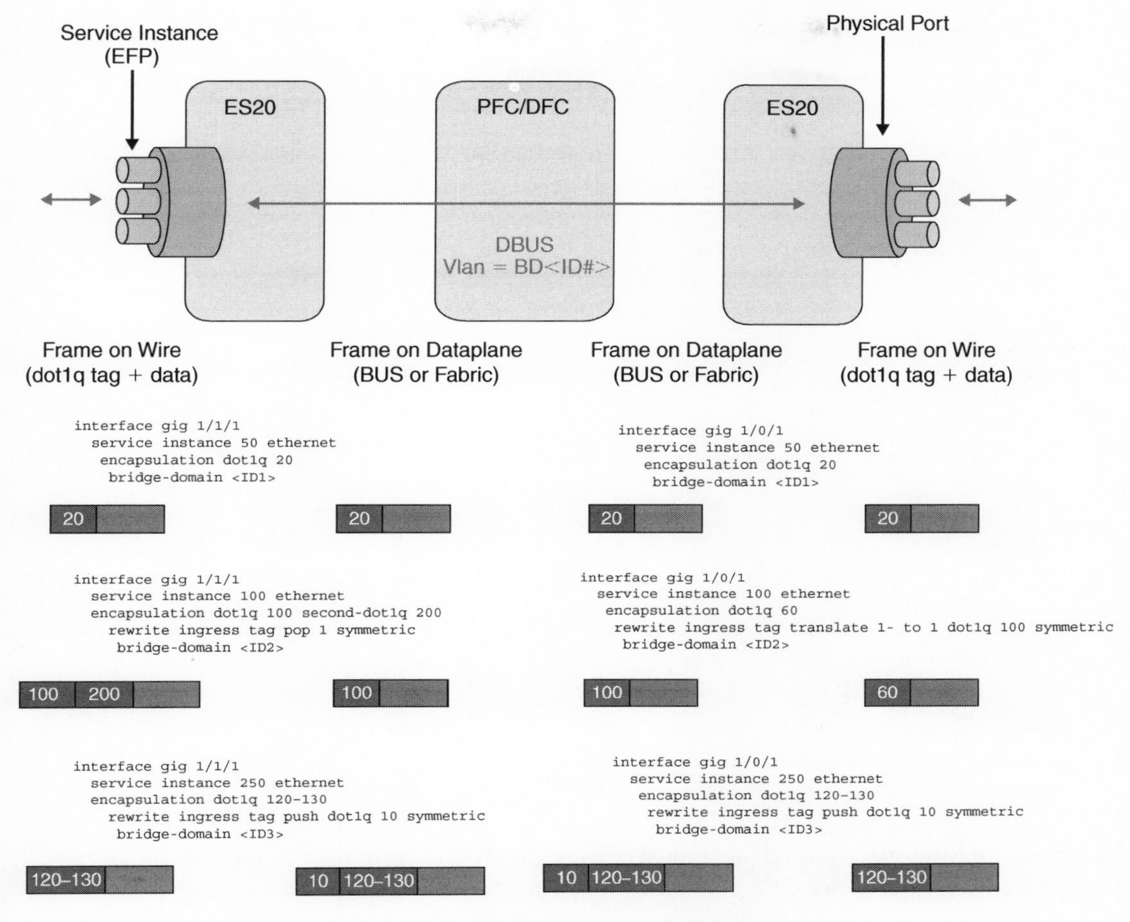

Figure 9.7: EFP-to-EFP (E-MPB)

EFP-to-L3 (E-MPB)

VLAN tags must be removed from data plane frames if L3 service termination is required—that is, *rewrite ingress pop 1* (single tagged frames) or *rewrite ingress pop 2* (double tagged frames) is *mandatory* in this case. Figure 9.8 illustrates this behavior.

EFP-to-EFP (EoMPLS)

For EoMPLS or VPLS there are different VC types: VC Type 5, used for the Port mode, and VC Type 4, used for VLAN mode. The difference between these is that for the VC Type 5 service, the delimiter VLAN tag will be removed and will not be transmitted across MPLS, whereas for the VC Type 4 service, the delimiter VLAN will be added and rewritten by the peer PE. This is not something that needs to be configured since it is automatically negotiated between 7600 peers.

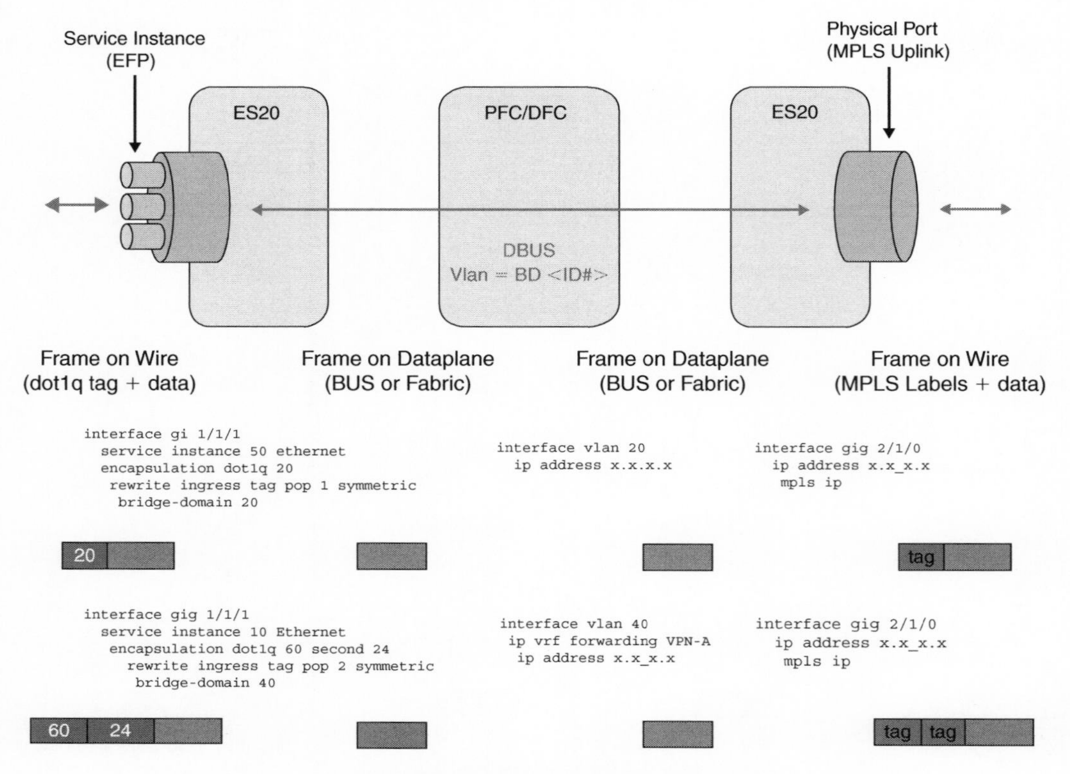

Figure 9.8: EFP-to-L3 (E-MPB)

An important thing needs to be taken into consideration if an xconnect is applied under EFP. Since the EFP has its own rewrite configuration, all the decisions on whether to keep or remove the VLAN tags are based on the rewrite configuration and *not* on the negotiation result. The VLAN tag that remains after the rewrite operation is treated as payload for EoMPLS and will be tunnelled regardless of VC type. Therefore, for this reason, if VC Type 5 is used, it is *recommended* to manually configure the removal of delimiter VLAN to avoid waste of bandwidth when transmitting the frame through the core.

Both peers must be 7600 routers because this is currently the only platform supporting EFP. If both peers are 7600 routers, the VC Type 5 will be used for all types of EoMPLS configurations by default.[3] It can autonegotiate to different VC types if the peer device does not support VC Type 5. Figure 9.9 illustrates this discussion graphically.

EFP-to-Non-EFP (EoMPLS)

Removal of the service delimiter VLAN is *mandatory* if the peer PE is not using an EFP-based configuration. If the service delimiter VLAN tag is not removed, it can cause duplicated VLAN tags to be sent out by the peer PE using a non-EFP-based configuration (e.g., SVI-based

[3] VC type can be autonegotiated to a different VC type if the peer device does not support VC Type 5.

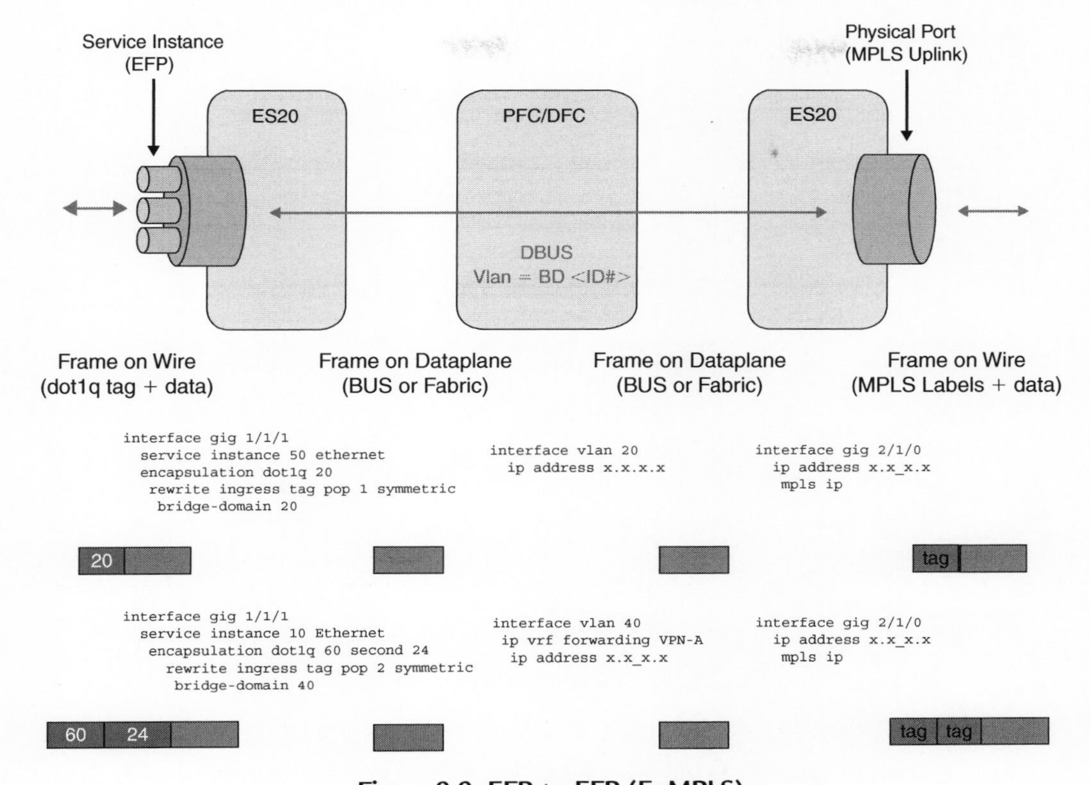

Figure 9.9: EFP-to-EFP (EoMPLS)

EoMPLS), as shown in Figure 9.10. On the EFP site, received frames are sent out untagged because the rewrite configuration is missing.

9.3.6 Flexible Service Mapping

The EFP can be used to designate how frames belonging to a particular Ethernet flow are mapped to a particular service. The following services are available in the EVC model:

Layer 2 Switched Services (bridging):

- The service instance is mapped to a bridge domain, where frames are switched based on their destination MAC address. This includes multipoint scenarios:
- Ethernet-to-Ethernet Bridging
- VPLS

Layer 2 Stitched Services (connect):

- This covers point-to-point Layer 2 associations that are statically established and do not require a MAC address lookup and thus no MAC address learning.

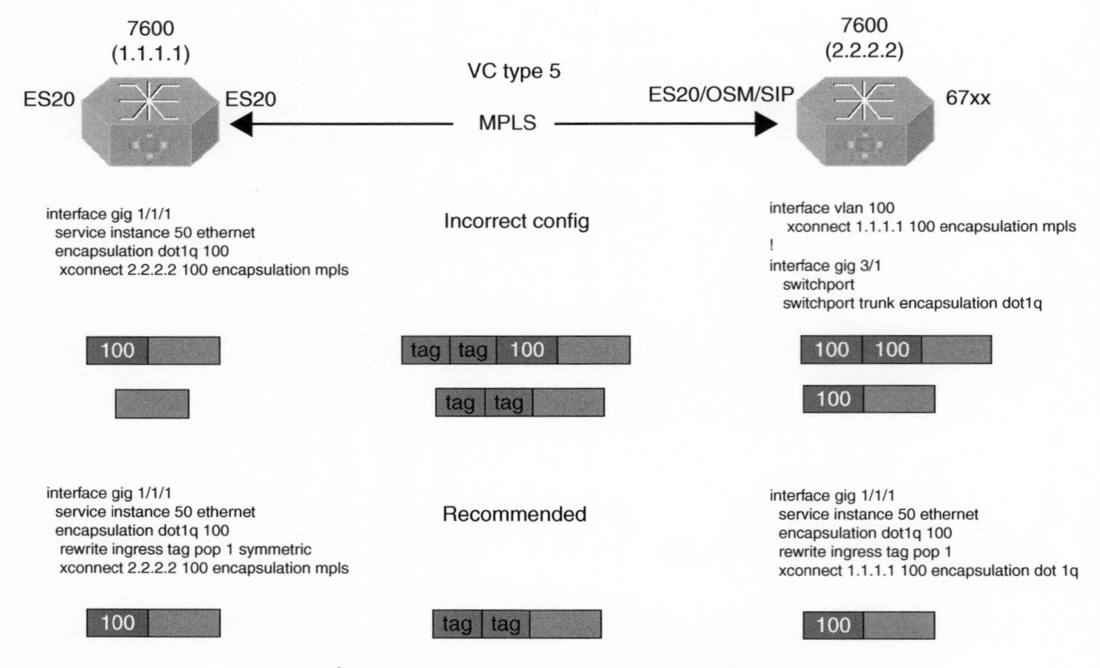

Figure 9.10: EFP-to-Non-EFP (EoMPLS)

- Ethernet-to-Ethernet Local Switching. The service instance is mapped to an S-VLAN on either the same port or another port. The S-VLANs may be identical or different.

Tunneled Services (xconnect):

- The service instance is mapped to a Layer 3 tunnel. This covers point-to-point scenarios only.
- EoMPLS
- L2TPv3
- GRE

Layer 3 Terminated Services (Ethernet access to Layer 3 service):

- The service instance is mapped to an IP interface that has a global address or belongs to a VRF (includes both IP and MPLS L3 VPNs).

Figure 9.11 illustrates the capabilities of flexible service mapping. The two physical interfaces are defined with multiple Ethernet flow points. A local connect could be defined between two Ethernet Flow Points (L2 Stitched Service).

There is the ability to have EoMPLS cross-connects directly from the Ethernet flow points, and multiple Ethernet flow points can be put into the bridge domain and have a split horizon option

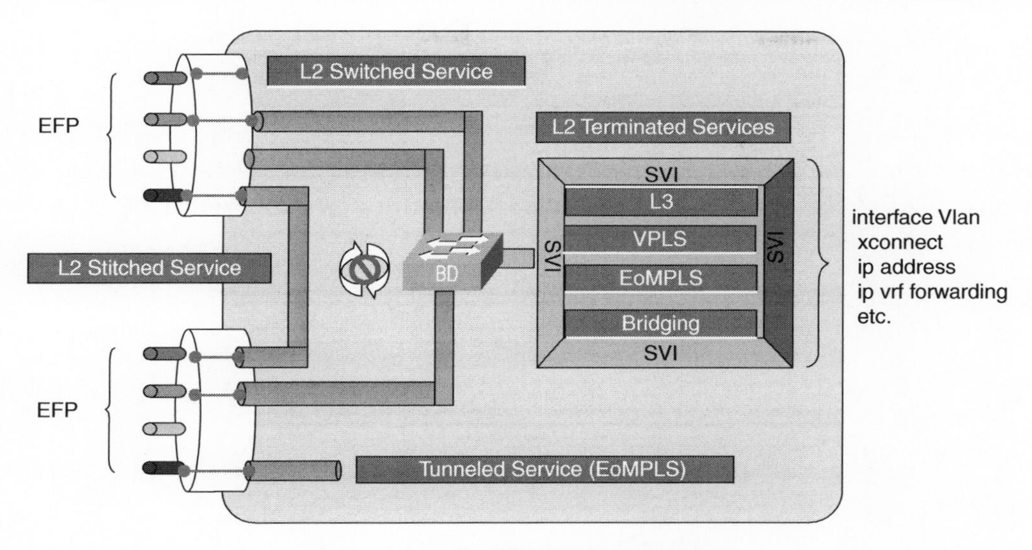

Figure 9.11: Flexible Service Mapping

that will either enable or disable Layer 2 communication between the two Ethernet flow points. The bridge domain equates to the global VLAN, which is effectively the SVI. Under the SVI the configuration is applied for Layer 3, VPLS, EoMPLS, or just for Layer 2 bridging.

9.4 EVC Configuration

The following sections bring the EVC services in context with the specific configuration that is required to implement them.

9.4.1 L2 Switched Services

Ethernet Multipoint Bridging (E-MPB)

The idea of E-MPB is to tie multiple EFPs matching different 802.1q VLANs into the same L2 bridging domain (BD) and at the same time keep the dot1q VLANs locally significant. This concept differs from what IEEE 802.1q or IEEE 802.1ad defines. These protocols establish a one-to-one mapping between a BD and a VLAN and assume that the VLAN has global significance per device. BD extends this concept by decoupling the notion of VLAN as an encapsulation from VLAN as a broadcast domain. Thus the VLAN gains local significance per port, and VLAN tags can be reused for separate service instances and separate broadcast domains on different ports.

The flexibility of E-MPB allows connecting EFPs configured on one ES20 port to other L2 ports or features by utilizing a single broadcast domain. The broadcast domain equals the number of VLANs that are globally unique on a given chassis (i.e., per 7600 chassis). In essence, E-MPB provides L2 switchport-like features without the full implementation of a "real" switchport. In addition, L2 and L3 services such as L2 VPN, L3 VPN, and L2 bridging can be simultaneously configured on the same physical port.

For E-MPB Service, the packet is forwarded based on a MAC address table, that is, frames are switched within a BD based on their destination MAC address. Multicast and unknown destination unicast frames are flooded within the confines of a BD, and source MAC address learning is performed transparently.

To set up E-MPB we need to configure the bridge domain and assign a unique *bridge ID*, which equals a global VLAN ID. This is shown in the following configuration template.

E-MPB

```
interface GigabitEthernet4/1/0
 service instance 101 ethernet
  encapsulation dot1q 101-1000
  bridge-domain 100
interface GigabitEthernet4/1/1
 service instance 101 ethernet
  encapsulation dot1q 101-1000
  bridge-domain 100
interface GigabitEthernet3/1
  switchport access vlan 100
  switchport mode dot1q-tunnel
```

The *split-horizon* command can be used to disable L2 communication between two EFPs belonging to the same BD. With the following configuration, L2 communication is allowed only between EFPs and the switchport, *not* between EFPs.

E-MPB Split Horizon

```
interface GigabitEthernet4/1/0
 service instance 30 ethernet
  encapsulation dot1q 10
  bridge-domain 400 split-horizon
interface GigabitEthernet4/1/1
 service instance 30 ethernet
  encapsulation dot1q 10
  bridge-domain 400 split-horizon
interface GigabitEthernet3/1
  switchport
  switchport trunk encapsulation dot1q
```

E-MPB for VPLS

E-MPB is used to combine VPLS with EVC-based attachment circuits (ACs). VPLS builds a single bridge domain across a packet-switched network, such as MPLS. L2 frames from

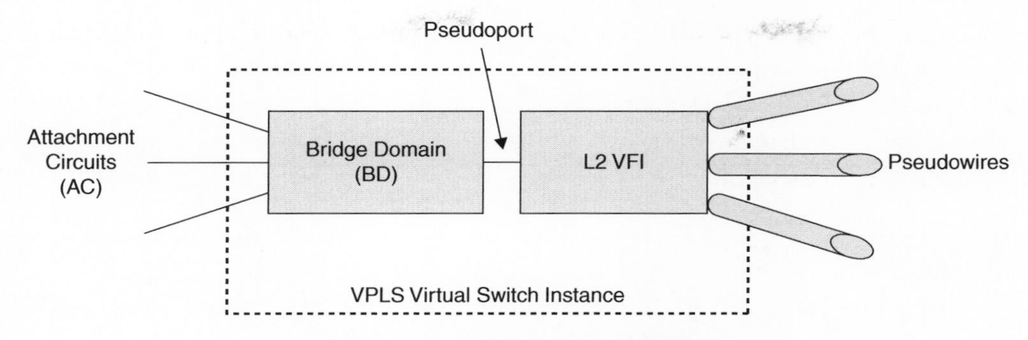

Figure 9.12: E-MPB and VPLS VFI

various EFPs are bridged into a virtual forwarding instance (VFI) that is used for the multipoint EoMPLS cross-connect. The VFI is tied to an SVI and appears as an emulated LAN interface (pseudoport) to the bridge domain. Hence the individual pseudowires that interconnect the VPLS forwarders are opaque to the bridge domain and appear as though they were a single interface. Figure 9.12 depicts this model.

Frames are forwarded into the BD based on MAC address, that is, MAC learning, forwarding, aging, and so on are involved. The VPLS and E-MPB configuration is described here.

E-MPB for VPLS

```
vfi vpls-120
 vpn id 120
 neighbor x.x.x.x encapsulation mpls
 neighbor x.x.x.x encapsulation mpls
!
interface GigabitEthernet4/1/0
 service instance 30 ethernet
  encapsulation dot1q 120
  rewrite ingress tag pop 1 symmetric
  bridge-domain 120 split-horizon
interface GigabitEthernet4/1/1
 service instance 30 ethernet
  encapsulation dot1q 120
  rewrite ingress tag pop 1 symmetric
  bridge-domain 120 split-horizon
interface Vlan 120
 xconnect vfi vpls-120
```

9.4.2 L2 Stitched Services

A *point-to-point stitched service* is defined as a service in which frame forwarding is done based on a statically stitched relationship between the ingress and egress ports (ports in this context may be physical or virtual) and no bridging function is performed (no MAC learning or lookup). One of the commonly used services is EFP-to-EFP Local Switching, which is applicable for Ethernet Access Domain (intra-EAD) point-to-point communication between two EFPs. These EFPs may be on the same interface or distinct interfaces. Frames ingress on one EFP are switched to the other, and vice versa, without performing MAC address learning.

NOTE 9.4: Local Connect

In the current IOS release local connect is *not* supported if the two EFPs come from the same physical interface (hairpin connection). This will be supported in a future release.

In the following configuration example, a service instance is defined that equates to the Ethernet flow point. To perform a local connection, we need to define two service instances. The global *connect* command is used to connect the two service instances.

Point-to-Point Local Switching

```
interface GigabitEthernet4/1/0
 service instance 3 ethernet
  encapsulation dot1q 51
  rewrite ingress tag translate 1-to-2 dot1q 52 second-dot1q 52 symmetric
interface GigabitEthernet4/1/1
 service instance 3 ethernet
  encapsulation dot1q 52 second-dot1q 52
connect eline-3 GigabitEthernet4/1/0 3 GigabitEthernet4/1/1 3
```

9.4.3 Tunneled Services

Tunneled service is similar to L2 stitched service with the difference that it is used for inter-EAD communication. In this scenario, exactly one EFP and one Pseudowire are statically stitched together. Frames ingress on the EFP are forwarded on the Pseudowire, and vice versa. No MAC address learning is performed. The Pseudowire may be EoMPLS, L2TPv3, or any other tunnelling technology.

To cross-connect the EFP and Pseudowire requires us to apply the EoMPLS configuration (xconnect) under the service instance, as given in the following configuration sample.

Point-to-Point Xconnect

```
interface GigabitEthernet4/1/1
  service instance 11 ethernet
  encapsulation dot1q 101 second-dot1q 60-70
  rewrite ingress tag pop 1 symmetric
  xconnect 10.0.0.3 101 encapsulation mpls
```

9.4.4 L3 Terminated Services

For terminating Layer 3 services and at the same time utilizing the common EVC-based configuration, it is important that IP routed frames received on EFPs are bridged to a particular SVI, depending on their destination MAC address. The service instance is configured on a trunk port (UNI or L2 NNI) facing a customer. It is assumed in this case that the service instance on this port uniquely identifies the customer or service by matching the dot1q encapsulation tag (EFP match). The IP termination typically results in all the traffic coming in on an EFP being sent to the internet, a voice gateway, or to a particular L3VPN, for example.

Three configuration options are available for terminating Layer 3 services:

- Option 1: L2 Switchport-based termination in combination with L3 SVI-based termination
- Option 2: L2 EVC-based termination in combination with L3 SVI-based termination
- Option 3: Direct L3 termination on subinterface

> **NOTE 9.5: Termination of Layer 3 Services**
>
> Option 1 is *not* discussed further in this chapter, since it does not allow double-tag termination, as Options 2 and 3 do.

The main difference between Options 2 and 3 is the way single- or double-tag termination provides port-local or global VLAN significance. For Option 2, the service instance does not consume any internal VLAN resources on 7600. In fact, 16K service instances are supported on an ES20 line card, compared to 4 K L3 subinterfaces. For Option 2 it is the bridge domain that consumes a global VLAN resource (4 K total), but it supports local significance of the encapsulation VLAN *even* for single tag termination.

For Option 3, a hidden/internal 7600 VLAN is used for every subinterface, which limits the total number of interfaces to 4 K. Local VLAN significance could only be achieved for double-tag termination; see the configuration templates that follow.

> **NOTE 9.6: MAC Learning**
>
> Turning off MAC address learning is optional and can be used if BD has only one EFP (point-to-point CE-PE link).

L3 Single-Tag Termination

```
Option (2)
interface GigabitEthernet4/1/1
```

```
 service instance 100 ethernet
  encapsulation dot1q 100     <--- VLAN ID port local significant
  rewrite ingress tag pop 1 symmetric
  bridge-domain 100           <--- VLAN ID globaly significant (Bridge
domain)
no mac address-table learning vlan 100    <--- optional
interface Vlan100
 ip address 100.1.100.1 255.255.255.0
Option (3)
interface GigabitEthernet4/1/1.100
encapsulation dot1q 100              <--- VLAN ID globaly significant
(internal VLAN)
 ip address 100.1.100.1 255.255.255.0
```

L3 Double-Tag Termination

```
Option (2)
interface GigabitEthernet4/1/1
 service instance 100 ethernet
  encapsulation dot1q 100 second 200    <--- VLAN IDs port local significant
  rewrite ingress tag pop 2 symmetric
  bridge-domain 100                 <--- VLAN ID globaly significant (BC
domain)
no mac address-table learning vlan 100  <--- optional
interface Vlan100
 ip address 100.1.100.1 255.255.255.0
Option (3)
interface GigabitEthernet4/1/1.100
encapsulation dot1q 100 second 200   <---- VLAN ID 100 globaly significant ;
VLAN ID
 address 100.1.100.1 255.255.255.0         200 port local significant
```

EVC Local VLAN Significance

In the context of EVCs, a VLAN no longer has global scope within the switch. For example, Ports P1, P2, and P3 could belong to VLAN 10 and be mapped using the EVC infrastructure to bridge domain 100. At the same time, ports P4, P5, and P6 could carry VLAN 10 and be mapped using the EVC infrastructure to bridge domain 200.

This implies that there is one VLAN 10 used by ports P1, P2, and P3 and another VLAN 10 used by ports P4, P5, and P6. Here the VLAN is port-local and is important primarily to identify EFPs and to serve as encapsulations on the wire. The VLAN thus loses its "broadcast domain" semantics. Local VLAN significance is especially useful in the Carrier Ethernet space, where the same VLAN needs to be used by different customers. One can then create small islands of customer-local VLANs without any change in VLAN IDs or VLAN translation requirements for customers.

In terms of VLAN scalability on a 7600 platform equipped with Ethernet Service line cards (ES20), it is important to differentiate between the following categories of VLANs:

- *Classical VLANs* used for L2 IEEE bridging or E-MPB (a.k.a. bridge domain). The maximum number of this type of VLANs for the whole 7600 system is 4 K, whether ES20 is used or not. A configuration sample follows.

Classical VLAN

```
!
interface gig 1/1/1
  switchport
  switchport access vlan 10    <-- VLAN 10 equals a Layer 2 broadcast domain

interface gig 1/1/2
 service instance 1 ethernet
  encapsulation dot1q 100
  rewrite ingress tag pop 1 symmetric
  bridge-domain 200           <-- VLAN 200 equals a Layer 2 broadcast domain
!
```

- *Local VLAN* is locally significant per port and the service provided for this VLAN is point-to-point (EoMPLS xconnect or local connect). In this case the ES20 can support 16 K point-to-point "xconnect" or 8 k "local connect" services per line card/chassis. A sample configuration illustrating the same is as follows.

Local VLAN

```
!
interface gig 1/1/2
 service instance 2 ethernet
  encapsulation dot1q 102
  rewrite ingress tag pop 1 symmetric
  xconnect 1.1.1.1 100 encap mpls     <-- No system VLAN (16K Pseudowires
per ES20)
!
```

- *Encapsulation VLAN* is the VLAN ID that can be configured per port or per module (EFP match). With ES20, each port can have single tag and/or double tag configured. For single-tag configuration, each port can have all 4 K local VLANs with EVC EFPs, meaning 4 K × 20 (ES20-GE3) VLANs configured per module. For double-tag configuration, since each outer tag VLAN can have 4 K inner VLANs, it can support 4 K × 4 K VLAN tag combinations per port.

Encapsulation VLAN

```
!
interface gig 1/1/2
 service instance 102 ethernet
  encapsulation dot1q 2-4000    <-- encap VLAN (4K per port)
  rewrite ingress tag pop 1 symmetric
  xconnect 1.1.1.1 100 encap mpls
!
 service instance 103 ethernet
  encapsulation dot1q 100 second 1-4096    <-- 4K inner tag per outer tag
(4k×4k = 16M)
  rewrite ingress tag pop 1 symmetric
  xconnect 1.1.1.1 100 encap mpls
```

9.5 EVC QoS Overview

EVC QoS uses the IOS MQC-based CLI. An MQC policy map is applied to a service instance. Under the same physical port it can have both service instance and subinterface configured. On ES20 line cards, both service instance and subinterface can have a QoS policy map applied, as shown in the following example. The following illustration shows the acceptable configurations for both service instance and subinterface with double tags.

Supported Configuration Sample

```
!
interface GigabitEthernet1/0/1
 service instance 1 ethernet
  encapsulation dot1q 20
  bridge-domain 20
  service-policy input in-policy1 --→ QoS policy applied at service instance level
  service-policy output out-policy1
Interface GigabitREthernet1/0/1.1
  encapsulation dot1q 30 second 40
  ip address 1.1.1.1 255.255.255.0
  service-policy input in-policy2 → QoS policy applied at subinterface level
  service-policy output out-policy2
!
End
```

Note that for ES-20 line cards, as soon as a service instance or subinterface with double-tag encapsulation is configured, port-level QoS policy is *not* supported. The following configuration template illustrates this idea.

Unsupported Example (ES20 Only)

```
!
interface GigabitEthernet1/0/1
service-policy input in-policy1  ← QoS policy can't be applied at port level if service instance is configured
  service instance 1 ethernet
    encapsulation dot1q 20
    bridge-domain 20
!
end
router(config-if)#service-policy out out-policy1
Service-policy cannot be applied to main interface when service instances are configured.
```

An EVC service instance is double-tag aware by design. It has flexibility to classify frames based on both inner and outer CoS or VLAN ID or a combination of CoS and VLAN ID. Also, since EVC is double-tag aware, it also has the flexibility to mark both inner and outer CoS. It can mark MPLS EXP for VPLS and EoMPLS encapsulation. Similarly, for the queuing/shaping, ES-20 line cards support hierarchical shaping/queuing, LLQ/CBWFQ, and WRED.

Figures 9.13 and 9.14 provide a summary of the EVC QoS classification and marking capabilities.

Classification Criteria	ES-20
Outer and/or inner CoS	•Yes
Outer and/or inner VLAN ID	•Yes
Combination of CoS and VLAN ID	•Yes
IPP/DSCP/EXP[1]	•Future

Figure 9.13: EVC Classification

Feature	ES-20
Outer and/or inner CoS	•Yes
IPP/DSCP	•Future
EXP	•Yes

Figure 9.14: EVC Marking

9.5.1 EVC Classification and Marking

EVC service instances could have various service-mapping configurations such as local connect, xconnect under service instance (also known as Scalable EoMPLS), and bridge domain-based configurations. In essence, it includes two types of services: point-to-point and multipoint Layer 2 service. Each of the service types has been discussed in the "Flexible Service Mapping" section earlier in this chapter. The internal packet flow is quite different for these two types of services; thus the QoS marking is different as well. Now let's discuss the behavior for both point-to-point and multipoint configurations.

Point-to-Point Layer 2 Service (Local Connect and Scalable EoMPLS)

For scalable EoMPLS, the ingress line card does all the VLAN tag rewrite and EoMPLS encapsulation. The 7600 Enhanced Address Resolution Logic (EARL) is doing only the MPLS label switching. EARL is not involved in QoS. The original DSCP is not touched, regardless of whether it is a tagged or untagged frame. The Port Trust configuration options (discussed in Chapter 8) do not apply. Finally, the DBUS CoS is always copied from outer CoS.

For local connect, the ingress and egress line card does the VLAN tag rewrite, including CoS marking. The original DSCP is not touched, whether it is a tagged or untagged frame. EARL is not involved in QoS. Port Trust configuration options do not apply. DBUS CoS is always copied from outer CoS.

Multipoint Layer 2 Service (Layer 2 Bridging, VPLS and SVI-Based EoMPLS)

A global VLAN resource for the multipoint bridging is always required. A service instance is treated as a pseudo-port and coexists with switchport in the bridge domain. A frame is forwarded based on MAC address by EARL. After packet rewrite by the ingress line card and EARL, it is forwarded to the egress line card for packet encapsulation. In the case of Layer 2 bridging, the egress line card does dot1q encapsulation. In the case of VPLS and SVI-based

EoMPLS, the egress line card does the EoMPLS packet encapsulation. DBUS CoS is used to set outer CoS or MPLS EXP bits.

QoS marking policy map could be applied to SVI, but it is not recommended to configure marking to both service instance and SVI. This chapter focuses on the marking under service instance.

The following highlights the classification and marking support under SVI for the sake of reference.

Marking Under SVI

- For untagged packet, it is possible to mark DSCP/IPP.
- It is possible to mark MPLS EXP bits.
- It is not possible to mark CoS.

Classification Under SVI

- For untagged packet, it is possible to classify based on DSCP/IPP and ACL.
- Can't classify based on CoS.

9.5.2 EVC QoS Marking Packet Flow Overview

This section describes the internal EVC QoS marking packet flow. Be aware that this is only from the logical point of view. It is meant to help explain the various components of EVC QoS marking.

Let's look at the various steps involved and the behavior of QoS marking for EVC-based point-to-point and multipoint services in Figure 9.15.

EVC QoS Marking Packet Flow: Ingress

0. Frame received on the ingress port. QoS classification is based on the CoS and VLAN of the frame received on the wire.
1. Ingress VLAN tag rewrite (see Figure 9.16). It includes POP, push, and xlate configuration. This could cause three different results:
   - Same number of tags (1-to-1, 2-to-2 xlate); it keeps the original CoS.
   - Tag(s) removed (pop, 2-to-1 xlate); it keeps the original CoS.
   - New tag added (push, 1-to-2 xlate); CoS of new tag is copied from the original outer CoS.

   Note that if the frame is an untagged frame, the outer CoS is always zero.

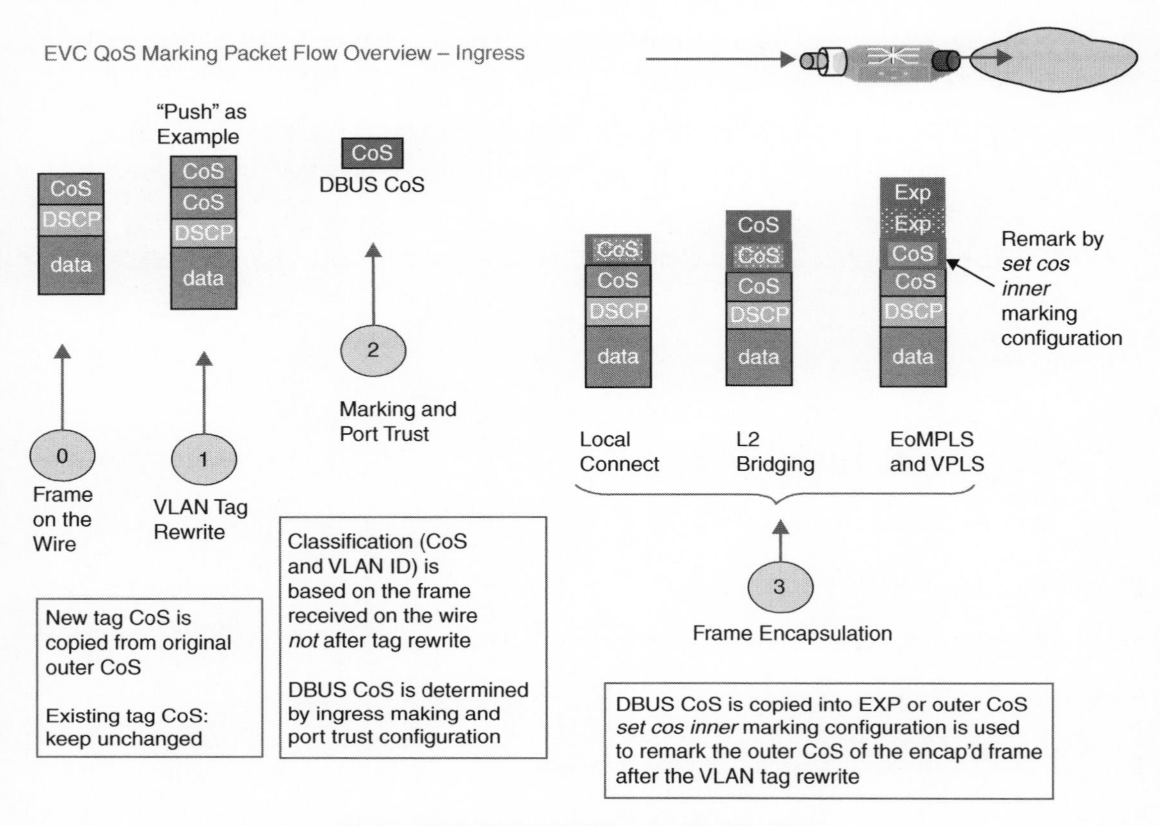

Figure 9.15: EVC QoS Ingress Packet Flow

NOTE 9.7: Inner and Outer CoS

The inner CoS is the value set on the top, and the outer CoS is set at the bottom of the frame.

2. Ingress marking and port trust configuration. Here DBUS CoS is determined by ingress marking and/or port trust configuration. The behavior is different for point-to-point and multipoint service types and hence depends on whether it is a point-to-point or multipoint deployment.

In the case of point-to-point service, "port trust" does not apply. The DBUS CoS is copied from the outer tag CoS. If the frame is untagged, DBUS CoS is set to zero. However, DBUS CoS can be changed by ingress marking configuration. The command *set cos* sets the DBUS CoS in case of a local connect. For scalable EoMPLS the command *set mpls exp imp* is used to set the DBUS CoS (although *set cos* has the same result as *set mpls exp imp* in this case, so it is not a recommended configuration). The DBUS CoS value is copied to both tunnel

Rewrite	Outer CoS	Inner CoS
POP 1	NA	NA
POP 2	NA	NA
PUSH 1	Outer CoS	NA
PUSH 2	Outer CoS	Outer CoS
1-1 TRANSLATE	Original Outer CoS	NA
1-2 TRANSLATE	Outer CoS	Original Outer CoS
2-1 TRANSLATE	Original Outer CoS	NA
2-2 TRANSLATE	Original Outer CoS	Original Inner CoS

Figure 9.16: VLAN Tag Rewrite Configuration Results

and VC label EXP. The command *set cos inner* configuration is used to remark the outer CoS of the original frame after tag rewrite. The original inner CoS or DSCP can't be changed.

> **NOTE 9.8: Point-to-Point Service**
>
> A VLAN-based QoS policy does not apply to a point-to-point service. More details on this topic can be found at www.cisco.com/en/US/docs/routers/7600/ios/12.2SR/configuration/guide/qos.html.

In essence, the case of multipoint service has a two-stage marking configuration. On the port and service instance policy level, port trust and marking configuration determine the DBUS CoS sent to EARL. Then EARL can also have VLAN-based policy marking as well. DBUS CoS is copied from the original outer CoS. This can be changed by service instance ingress marking configuration using the commands *set cos* or *set mpls exp imp*. Then DBUS CoS and port trust information is sent to EARL. From here EARL can apply the policy and perform the packet rewrite as follows:

Without VLAN based QoS policy (configured under an SVI interface) configuration:

- If the port is untrusted, DBUS CoS is ignored. Internal DSCP is set to zero.
- If the port has a *trust cos* configuration, DBUS CoS is honored. Internal DSCP is copied from the DBUS CoS.
- If the port is trust DSCP, but the frame is tagged, DBUS CoS is honored. Internal DSCP is copied from DBUS CoS.
- If the port has a trust DSCP configuration and the frame is untagged, internal DSCP is copied from original packet DSCP.

With VLAN-based QoS policy (configured under an SVI interface) configuration—for example, marking DSCP/EXP:

- If the port is untrusted, VLAN marking set the internal DSCP based on the marking configuration.
- If the port is trusted, VLAN marking is ignored. It follows the preceding situation. To make VLAN marking works, it require *mls qos marking ignore port-trust* global configuration. Then internal DSCP is set by the VLAN marking.

The internal DSCP is mapped to DBUS CoS on egress, which is used for the packet encapsulation in the next step (Step 3).

The outer tag of the original frame after tag rewrite could be changed using the command *set cos inner*, which is same as the point-to-point service.

3. Ingress packet encapsulation. Depending on the service, the packet encapsulation is done in different places and hardware components:

   - For local connect, after the VLAN tag rewrite, there is no additional packet rewrite. The packet is forwarded to the egress service instance. The egress port does the egress VLAN tag rewrite.
   - For scalable EoMPLS, after VLAN tag rewrite, the ingress line card also does the EoMPLS encapsulation. Both tunnel and VC label EXP are copied from DBUS CoS.
   - For Layer 2 local bridging, after ingress VLAN tag rewrite and service instance marking, the packet is sent to EARL. As mentioned in Step 2, at this stage the EARL is involved in QoS marking and rewrite. DBUS CoS is mapped from the internal DSCP, which is determined by port trust, service instance marking, and VLAN marking configuration. DSCP could be rewritten as well if it is an untagged frame. Egress port does the 802.1q encapsulation, and the new CoS is copied from DBUS CoS.
   - VPLS and SVI-based EoMPLS follow the same behavior as Layer 2 local bridging. The only difference is egress packet encapsulation. It is EoMPLS instead of 802.1q. By default, both tunnel and VC label EXP are copied from DBUS CoS. However, with the command *platform vfi dot1q-transparency* configuration, VC label EXP is copied from the original outer CoS instead of DBUS CoS. This is used for end-to-end dot.1p transparency. Refer to Example TBD for details.

Figure 9.15 illustrates an example of "pushing" one tag. Figure 9.16 describes the behavior with various VLAN tag rewrite configurations.

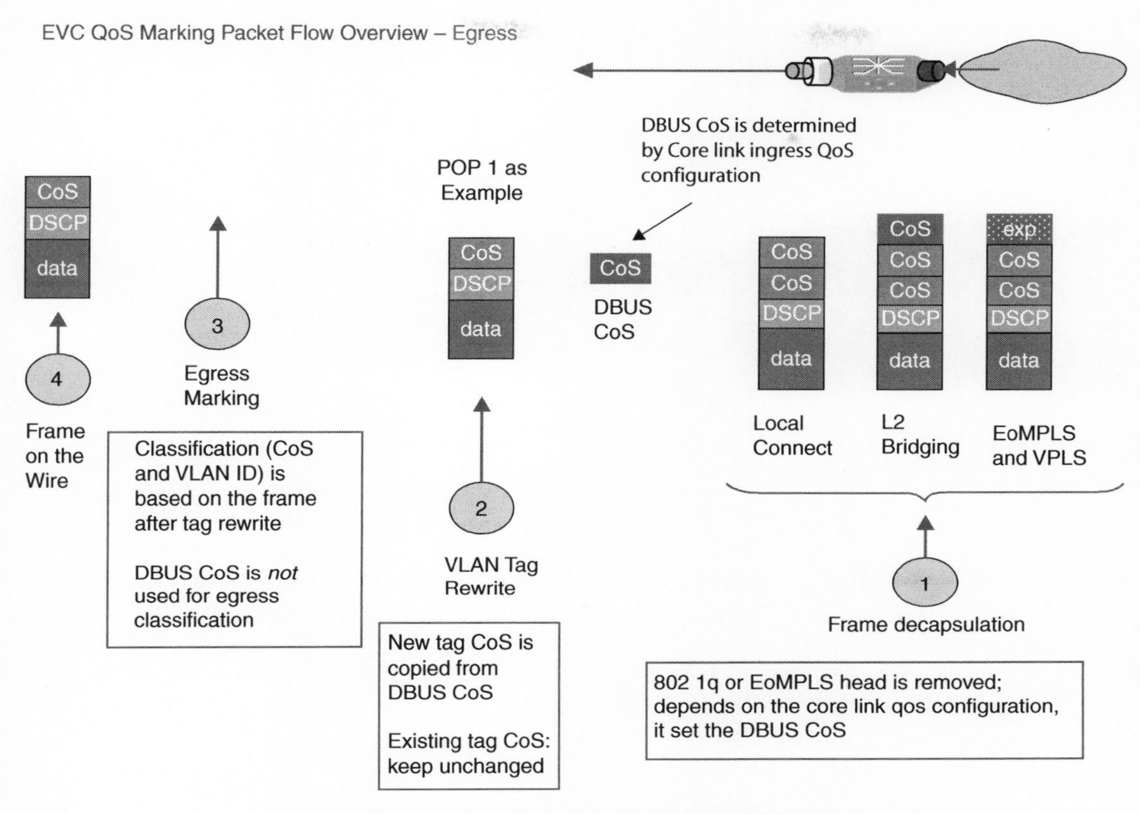

Figure 9.17: EVC QoS Egress Packet Flow

EVC QoS Marking Packet Flow: Egress

In Figure 9.17, we look at this discussion on egress packet flows in more detail.

1. Packet decapsulation on egress:

   - For local connect, the ingress and egress PE are the same box. In this case, DBUS CoS is kept for egress packet rewrite as well.
   - For scalable EoMPLS, the DBUS CoS is copied from MPLS EXP. The egress line card (which has a service instance xconnect configuration) does the EoMPLS packet decapsulation.
   - For VPLS and SVI-based EoMPLS, the DBUS CoS is copied from MPLS EXP. Ingress line card (the MPLS core) does the EoMPLS packet decapsulation. After that, the packet is forwarded to EARL for MAC-based Layer 2 forwarding. At this stage, DSCP could be rewritten if it is an untagged frame.
   - For Layer 2 local bridging, the DBUS CoS is determined by the ingress Layer 2 port trust and marking configuration. The ingress line card does the 802.1q packet

Rewrite	Outer CoS	Inner CoS
POP 1	NA	NA
POP 2	NA	NA
PUSH 1	DBUS CoS	NA
PUSH 2	DBUS CoS	DBUS CoS
1-1 TRANSLATE	Original Outer CoS	NA
1-2 TRANSLATE	DBUS CoS	Original Outer CoS
2-1 TRANSLATE	Original Outer CoS	NA
2-2 TRANSLATE	Original Outer CoS	Original Inner CoS

Figure 9.18: VLAN Tag Rewrite Configuration Results

decapsulation. After that, packet is forwarded to EARL for the Layer 2 switching. In this stage, DSCP could be rewritten if it is an untagged frame.

2. Egress VLAN tag rewrite. This happens on the egress service instance. VLAN tag rewrite includes POP, push, and xlate configuration. This could cause three different results, as follows:

   - Same number of tags (1-to-1, 2-to-2 xlate); it keeps the original CoS.
   - Tag(s) removed (pop, 2-to-1 xlate); it keeps the original CoS.
   - New tag added (push, 1-to-2 xlate); CoS of new tag is copied from DBUS CoS.

   The key here is that DBUS CoS is used to set CoS on any new added tag. Otherwise, the original CoS is kept unchanged. Figure 9.18 describes the behavior with different VLAN tag rewrite configurations.

3. Egress marking. Both inner and outer CoS can be remarked before they are transmitted to the wire. The command *set cos* will remark the outer CoS and the command *set cos inner* can be used to remark the inner CoS of the frame sent to the wire. Be aware that the classification on the egress is based on frame CoS after egress VLAN tag rewrite (Step 2). It is not based on DBUS CoS.

4. Frame is sent out of the egress port.

9.5.3 EVC Marking for Point-to-Point Layer 2 Services

Having seen an overview in the previous sections, let's delve deeper in this section. Figure 9.19 illustrates two typical scalable EoMPLS configurations. Two examples are used here: Example 9.1

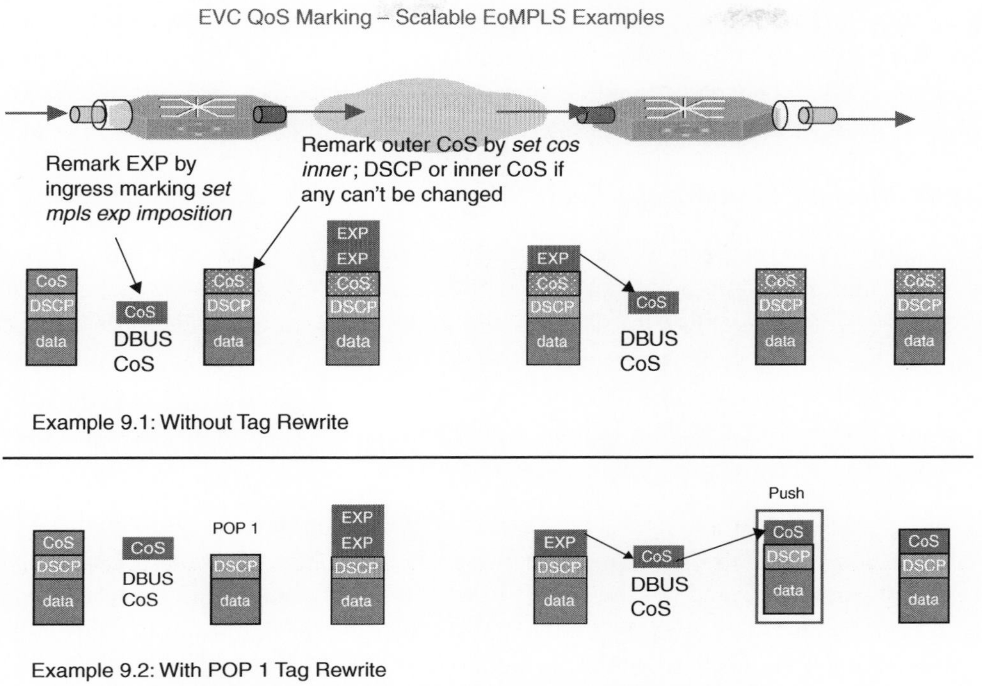

EVC QoS Marking – Scalable EoMPLS Examples

Remark EXP by ingress marking *set mpls exp imposition*

Remark outer CoS by *set cos inner*; DSCP or inner CoS if any can't be changed

Example 9.1: Without Tag Rewrite

Example 9.2: With POP 1 Tag Rewrite

Figure 9.19: Typical Scalable EoMPLS Configurations

illustrates the process of EVC QoS marking without a VLAN tag rewrite; Example 9.2 illustrates the process with a POP 1 VLAN tag rewrite.

> **NOTE 9.9: Tag**
>
> The reference to the word *tag* in this section and subsequent sections refers to the VLAN tag.

Example 9.1: Marking for Scalable EoMPLS, No VLAN Tag Rewrite

This is the easiest configuration option. With default configuration, end-to-end DSCP and CoS transparency can be achieved. Typically this configuration applies if both PE routers (ingress and egress) use EVC configuration. One of the drawbacks is the link efficiency, since the VLAN tag is not needed across the network. If the service provider wants to remark the EXP, explicit marking at the network edge may be used. With explicit marking, the original CoS is still kept intact on the egress.

Example 9.2: Marking for Scalable EoMPLS, POP 1 VLAN Tag Rewrite

This is a typical configuration, especially if the remote PE does not use EVC configuration. By default, on ingress PE, the DBUS CoS is copied from the outer CoS, which is used to set EXP. On egress PE, EXP is used to set DBUS CoS, which is used to set CoS of the new added tag. So the original CoS is not changed with default configuration. However, if the SP wants to remark the EXP to be different than the ingress CoS, the CoS may change on the egress PE. To remark the EXP and get end-to-end CoS transparency, one of the options is described as Example 9.1. Another option is explicit marking on the egress PE to restore the original CoS.

9.5.4 EVC Marking to Multipoint Layer 2 Services

An EVC multipoint Layer 2 service includes Layer 2 local bridging and VPLS/SVI-based EoMPLS. For multipoint Layer 2 services, one bridge domain consumes one global VLAN. Frames are forwarded based on MAC address within the bridge domain. EARL is involved for the Layer 2 forwarding and packet rewrite. Here port trust applies. However, different line cards have different behavior for the port trust feature. The ES20 supports port trust configuration, and trust DSCP is the default if not configured. However, the SIP-400 and ES+ do not have port trust configuration and always trust DSCP.

Since EARL is involved for the packet rewrite, VLAN policy marking is supported. DSCP could be rewritten by DBUS CoS. The key point is whether EARL is aware of Layer 3 DSCP to make use of trust DSCP and rewrite DSCP. Frames must be untagged in the bridge domain to make EARL aware of Layer 3 DSCP. Here are some examples that result in a tagged frame in the bridge domain. In this case, EARL is not aware of DSCP.

For EVC port:

- Receive single tag without “pop 1” configuration
- Receive double tag without “pop 2” configuration
- Receive untagged frame but with “push” configuration

For switchport:

- Dot1q trunk but receive double-tagged frame
- Dot1q tunnel, receive single- or double-tagged frame

Here are some examples that result in an untagged frame in the bridge domain. In this case, EARL is aware of DSCP.

For EVC port:

- Receive single tag with “pop 1” configuration
- Receive double tag with “pop 2” configuration
- Receive untagged frame

For switchport:

- Dot1q trunk, receive single-tagged frame

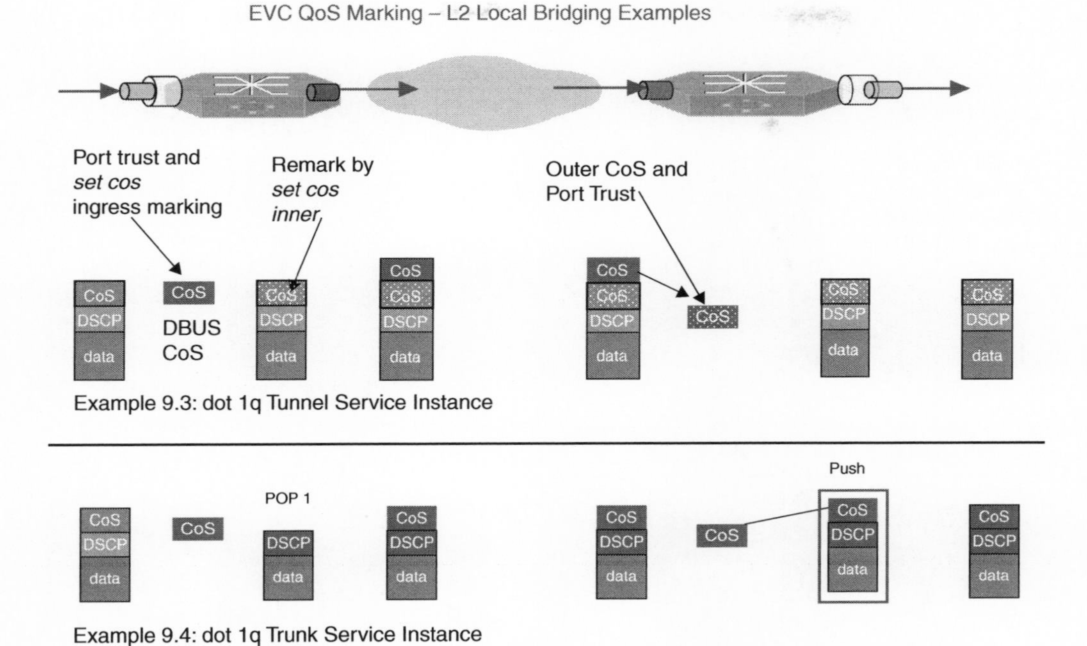

Figure 9.20: Marking for Multipoint Local Bridging Service

The following section gives a series of typical configuration examples to describe the EVC marking for a multipoint Layer 2 local bridging service, illustrated in Figure 9.20. Typically the service instance has two configuration options for Layer 2 bridging. One is the 802.1q trunk function; the other is the 802.1q tunnel function.

Example 9.3: Marking for Layer 2 Bridging: Service Instance Function as Switchport dot1q Tunnel

Here there is no VLAN tag rewrite and the original customer tag is kept unchanged end to end. Since it is a tagged frame, DSCP cannot be changed or trusted. DBUS CoS is determined by port trust and ingress marking configuration. By default, it is *trust DSCP*. Since it is a tagged frame, the actual result is *trust CoS*. So the DBUS CoS is copied from the outer CoS. This can be changed by explicit marking configuration command *set cos*. The DBUS CoS is used for the egress Layer 2 802.1q CoS rewrite. The original outer CoS can be remarked by the *set cos inner* marking configuration, although it is not commonly used.

On the egress PE, 802.1q decapsulation is performed by the system on the incoming Layer 2 trunk port and the outer tag is removed. Depending on the port trust and marking configuration, the DBUS CoS is either copied from outer CoS (port trust configuration) or reset to zero (port untrusted) or explicitly remarked (marking configuration). Since there is no VLAN tag rewrite, the original CoS remains unchanged. In short, for this example, with or without explicit marking, the end-to-end DSCP and CoS are not changed.

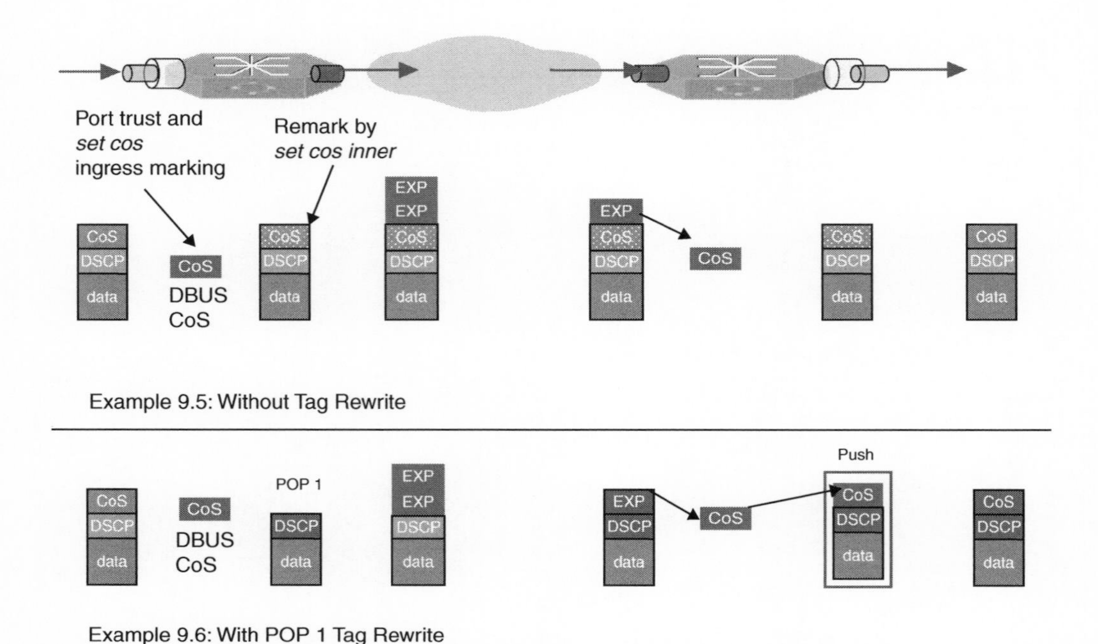

Figure 9.21: EVC Marking for VPLS and SVI-Based EoMPLS, Example 9.4

Example 9.4: Marking for Layer 2 Bridging: Service Instance Function as Switchport dot1q Trunk

If there is a single tagged frame after POP 1, it becomes an untagged frame (as described in Figure 9.21). EARL is aware of the DSCP and as a result the DSCP is rewritten as well. If *trust cos* is used on the ingress port, DSCP is mapped from the original outer CoS. If *trust DSCP* is used, DBUS CoS is mapped from the original DSCP. On the egress PE, the original CoS is not restored, since the CoS of the pushed VLAN tag is copied from the DBUS CoS.

To get both DSCP and CoS transparency, it is required to configure the *no mls qos ip dscp rewrite* and the *trust cos* configurations.

Now let's move to discussion of VPLS and SVI-based EoMPLS. The following illustrations show the EVC marking configuration for the typical scenarios of the VPLS and SVI-based EoMPLS deployments. SVI-based EoMPLS and VPLS have the same EVC QoS behavior and packet flow, and therefore only VPLS is discussed here, for the sake of simplicity.

Example 9.5: Marking for VPLS Without Tag Rewrite Configuration

In this example there is no VLAN tag rewrite. The original customer tag is kept unchanged end to end. Since there is a tagged frame, DSCP can't be changed or trusted. The DBUS CoS is determined by port trust and ingress marking configuration. By default, it is *trust dscp*. Since it

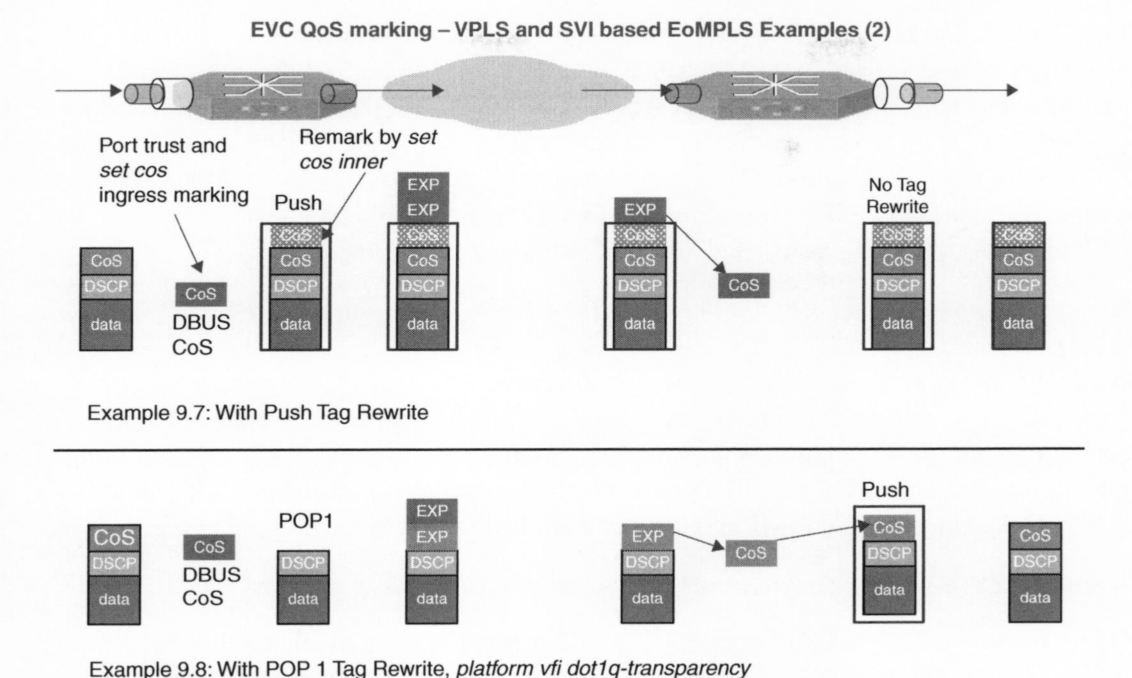

Figure 9.22: EVC Marking for VPLS and SVI-Based EoMPLS, Example 9.6

is a tagged frame, it is an implicit *trust cos*. Therefore the DBUS CoS is copied from the outer CoS. This can be changed by explicit marking configuration using the command *set mpls exp imp*. DBUS CoS is used for the egress EoMPLS encapsulation, and both the tunnel and VC label EXP are copied from DBUS COS by default.

The original outer CoS can be remarked by the *set cos inner* marking configuration, although it is not commonly used. On the egress PE, the VC label EXP is copied to DBUS CoS. Since there is no VLAN tag rewrite, the original CoS is not changed. Note that with or without explicit marking, the DSCP and CoS values are not changed.

Example 9.6: Marking for VPLS with POP 1 Tag Rewrite Configuration

If there is a single tagged frame after POP 1, it becomes an untagged frame. EARL is aware of the DSCP. As a result, DSCP is rewritten as well. If *trust cos* is set on the ingress port, DSCP is mapped from the original outer CoS, and DSCP is changed. If *trust DSCP* is used, DBUS CoS is mapped from original DSCP, which is used to set both tunnel and VC label EXP. On the egress PE, the VC label EXP is used to set DBUS CoS, which is used to set the CoS of the pushed tag. Therefore CoS is changed. To get both DSCP and CoS transparency requires the *no mls qos ip dscp rewrite* and *platform vfi dot1q transparency* configurations (see Figure 9.22).

Example 9.7: Marking for VPLS with PUSH Tag Rewrite Configuration
This configuration is used in the Cisco Tahoma solution for DSLAM data services and EoMPLS backhaul. The pushed tag is used to identify the DSLAM since the subscribers use the same VLAN range on the different DSLAM. The BRAS side terminates a double-tagged frame. With this configuration, DSCP can't be changed since it is a tagged frame. CoS is not changed with the default *port trust* configuration. However, if SP FOO intends to remark the EXP explicitly, the new pushed tag CoS is different from the original CoS.

Example 9.8: Marking for VPLS with POP 1 Tag Rewrite Configuration with DSCP/CoS Transparency
Basically, this example provides the solution to achieve DSCP and CoS transparency for Example 9.6. The command *no mls qos ip dscp rewrite* will keep DSCP unchanged. With the command *platform vfi dot1q transparency* configuration, the VC label EXP is copied from the original CoS instead of the DBUS CoS. On the egress PE, the VC label EXP is used to set DBUS CoS, which is used to set the CoS of the pushed tag. Thus the original CoS is restored.

9.5.5 DSCP and CoS Transparency: A Deeper Dive

While keeping DSCP and CoS unchanged, an SP might also need to remark the MPLS EXP on the ingress PE device. Therefore, the EXP value could be different from the customer CoS or DSCP values. Figure 9.23 summarizes the DSCP/CoS transparency for an EVC Layer 2 VPN service.

NOTE 9.10: Core Policies

Core policies are highlighted in detail in Chapter 8.

9.5.6 ES-20 EVC Queuing and Scalability

The ES-20 does not support the commands "bandwidth remaining ratio", and "shaper rate oversubscription" in the present IOS release, but will be supported in future releases. ES-20 does not support ingress shaping, and there is no plan to support it in the future.

ES-20 has two ASICs that provide the queuing functionality. For parent queues (referred to as *sublinks*) there is 1 K and for child queues there are 8 K for each instance of the ASIC. The area of most concern is the number of sublinks. To maximize the number of sublinks, it was proposed to allow flat policies to be applied to subinterfaces or service instances that would eliminate having to configure sublinks. All classes in the flat policy would need to be configured with the *shape ave* command to limit the customer bandwidth.

The configuration model is to apply flat policy maps to residential Carrier Ethernet customers, including a priority class for voice and other data classes. Due to the static nature of video traffic, the residents' video class will be separated in a different VLAN. Due to the diverse traffic in the business customer, a hierarchical policy map will be used.

•DSCP/CoS Transparency for EVC Layer 2VPN Service

Service	DSCP Transparency	CoS Transparency	Configuration Option
Local Connect	• Yes	• Yes	• Default Configuration
Scalable EoMPLS	• Yes	• Yes	• No VLAN tag rewrite • Example 9.1
	• Yes	• Yes with *trust cos* (by default); SP can't remark the EXP	• POP 1 • Example 9.2
Layer 2 Bridging – dot1q Tunnel	• Yes	•Yes	• NO VLAN tag rewrite • Example 9.3
Layer 2 Bridging – dot1q Trunk	• *no mls qos rewrite ip dscp* for single tagged frame received on ingress	• Yes with *trust cos* configuration; SP can't remark the CoS	• POP 1 • Example 9.4
VPLS- and SVI-Based EoMPLS	• Yes	• Yes	• NO VLAN tag rewrite • Example 9.5
	• *no mls qos rewrite ip dscp* for single tagged frame received on ingress	• Yes with *platform vfi dot1q-transparency* configuration	• POP 1 • Example 9.8
	• Yes	• Yes	• Push • Example 9.7

Figure 9.23: Transparency Matrix

The following policy map gives one example of configuring egress queuing for a DSLAM aggregation port on the aggregation PE box. Since ES-20 supports dual priority queues, video (IPTV/VOD) can be put into one of the high-priority queues. But it can also be put into the regular queue with shape and bandwidth, with no excess bandwidth. The following example explains the ES-20 EVC queuing scalability.

Configuration

```
!
policy-map video
  class class-default
    police ...
    priority
policy-map residential
  class voice
    police ...
    priority
```

```
   class class-default
      bandwidth ...
      shape ave ...
policy-map business-child
   class priority
      police ...
      priority
   class class2
      bandwidth ...
   class class3
      bandwidth ...
   class class-default
      shape ave ...
policy-map business-parent
   class class-default
      shape ave ...
      service-policy business-child
interface GigabitEthernet1/0/1
  service instance 1 ethernet → Video
   encapsulation dot1q 10
   rewrite ingress tag pop 1 symmetric
   bridge-domain 101
   service-policy output video
service instance 2 ethernet → data and VoIP
   encapsulation dot1q 11-1011
   rewrite ingress tag push dot1q 101 symmetric
   bridge-domain 100 split-horizon
   service-policy output residential
service instance 3 ethernet → business customer 1
   encapsulation dot1q 20 second any
   xconnect ...
   service-policy output business-parent
interface vlan 101
   ip address 10.1.101.1 255.255.255.0
   ip pim sparse-mode
interface vlan 100
   xconnect ...
!
End
```

Up to 2 K business customers with four queues are supported per ES-20 (uses 2 K sublinks and 8 K physical queues). In addition, it can also support around 8 K residential customers. Each residential customer needs one queue for the default class. For VoIP priority queues, all the residential priority queues will be configured to a single HW queue per port. The same applies for the video priority queue.

9.6 Virtual Leased-Line Service

VLL services are point-to-point services for the carriage of common Layer 2 protocols such as Ethernet, Frame Relay, Asynchronous Transfer Mode (ATM), Point to Point Protocol (PPP), and High Level Data Link Control (HDLC). Each of these link layer protocols are in ubiquitous use in global data and voice communication systems. In an attempt to provide a common transport for these protocols, a series of IETF RFCs was developed to encapsulate them in MPLS Label packets. This encapsulation is commonly referred to as the Martini Encapsulation, after Luca Martini, the original author.

From a QoS perspective, each of these protocols requires a particular service level. For example, ATM can be deployed in one of five modes: Constant Bit Rate (CBR), Real-time Variable Bit Rate (RT-VBR), Non-Real-time Variable Bit Rate (NRT-VBR), Available Bit Rate (ABR), and Unspecified Bit Rate (UBR). Each of these modes requires a different treatment, both at the edge and on the core of an MPLS network.

In general, these link layer protocols have the QoS attribute tolerances shown in Table 9.4.

Note that Table 9.4 is not taking into account the type of information being carried in each of the link layer protocols and assumes that the correct service type is used in the right context and can only be used as a general guide.

Service delineation on HDLC/PPP links is per physical link; Ethernet, Frame Relay, and ATM, however, have the ability to multiplex multiple services on a single physical interface. Cisco IOS provides a command-line interface to support multiple subinterfaces on a single physical interface. A typical example of marking QoS at the edge is shown next. In the illustration, we notice that policy maps are attached to individual subinterfaces for various encapsulation types. In our illustration, we look at Ethernet, ATM, and Frame Relay encapsulation types, and each of them represent a Layer 2 point-to-point VPN.

Table 9.4: Virtual Leased-Line Protocol QoS Attributes

Link Layer Protocol	Delay	Jitter	Loss
HDLC/PPP	Low	Low	Low
Frame Relay	Medium	Medium	Medium
ATM CBR	Low	Low	Low
ATM RT-VBR	Medium	Low	Low
ATM NRT-VBR	Medium	Medium	Medium
ATM ABR	Medium	High	High
ATM UBR	High	High	High
Ethernet	Low	Medium	Medium

Virtual Leased-Line Configuration

```
!
interface GigabitEthernet11/4
!
interface GigabitEthernet11/4.100
 encapsulation dot1Q 150
 xconnect 1.1.1.1 100 encapsulation mpls
 service-policy input <policy-map)
!
!
interface Serial0
 encapsulation frame-relay
!
interface Serial0.1 point-to-point
 ip address 3.1.3.1 255.255.255.0
 frame-relay interface-dlci 140
 service-policy input <policy-map)
!
interface ATM2/0
!
interface ATM2/0.1 point-to-point
ip address 1.1.0.13 255.255.255.0
 no ip directed-broadcast
 pvc 0/100
 service-policy input <policy-map)
!
End
```

More sample configurations follow to help the reader understand this concept in more detail. In our "ATM-over-MPLS Configuration" illustration, we create a policy map named ATMoMPLS with a policer to enforce a CIR and appropriately mark traffic with an MPLS Experimental value of 5. This policy map is further attached to an ATM interface, which hosts an ATM-over-MPLS Layer 2 VPN.

ATM-over-MPLS Configuration

```
!
!
 class-map match-any ATMoMPLS
  match input-interface ATM6/0 ← All traffic on Main interface/Subinterface
is matched
!
policy-map ATMoMPLS
 class ATMoMPLS ← Common policy for all traffic on interface/sub interfaces
```

```
   police cir 128000 bc 16000 be 16000
    conform-action set-mpls-exp-transmit 5
    exceed-action drop
!
interface ATM6/0
 service-policy input ATMoMPLS
 xconnect 192.168.2.1 20000 encapsulation mpls
!
End
```

In our “EoMPLS Port-Based Configuration” illustration, a policy map named REALTIME-Ingress is created to mark all traffic with an MPLS Experimental value of 5. This policy map is further attached to an Ethernet interface, which hosts an Ethernet-over-MPLS Layer 2 VPN.

EoMPLS Port-Based Configuration

```
!
!
!
Mls qos
!
mls qos marking ignore port-trust
!
class-map match-any REALTIME-Ingress
  description ### Matching Any ###
  match any
!
policy-map REALTIME-Ingress
  class REALTIME-Ingress
   set mpls experimental imposition 5 -------- Set MPLS EXP 5!
!
!
interface GigabitEthernet1/3
 description ### Link to CE - EWS Layer2 VPN Customer ###
 no ip address
 xconnect 3.3.3.3 1001 encapsulation mpls
 service-policy input voice-customer
!
End
```

9.7 Summary

In this chapter, we discussed in detail the Cisco EVC architecture and associated services that are made possible using this infrastructure. EVC-styled configurations, along with the

ES-20 line cards, provide a powerful tool for deploying scalable and flexible Carrier Ethernet services. Therefore it is becoming the de facto standard for deploying Layer 2-based services. We examined the nuances and associated aspects that need to be understood for deploying QoS at the edge for each of these service types. Many possibilities bring in more challenges, since it is common to deploy every feature that is available. Therefore, a common word of caution is to be careful in choosing the number of features required for deployment by always staying in line with requirements. Therefore, even if the possibilities are large, only the required level of functionality should be deployed.

We also discussed virtual leased-line services and took a look at some of the configurations required for deploying QoS at the carrier edge, since QoS policies in the core are not impacted by the services deployed at the network edge. Detailed core configurations were provided in Chapter 8.

CHAPTER 10

Cisco IOS and IOS-XR Quality-of-Service Implementation for IP Internet Services

10.1 Overview

Now that we've discussed the implementation of QoS for MPLS VPN service that is categorized as labeled traffic, this section takes a look at the various IOS and IOS-XR configuration templates for unlabeled traffic. By definition, unlabeled traffic does not consist of an MPLS header, and hence the QoS policies will need to use an alternate scheme of marking and classifying within the SP network core, instead of MPLS Experimental bits. Hence IP traffic that is unlabeled can use IP precedence or IP DSCP bits for this purpose. Using IP DSCP bits for QoS marking and classification provides more flexibility for reasons mentioned in Chapter 2, "Introduction to Cisco's Quality-of-Service Architecture for IP Networks." IP precedence may also be used if the existing deployment uses this scheme. Most SPs use a combination of the two to support both schemes.

Many ISPs built their IP infrastructures before MPLS evolved as an alternative to traditional IP forwarding/routing. Therefore, Internet services in these networks operated as native/pure IP traffic wherein each device in the network has a role in the forwarding decision. Routing tables are built and maintained in each device, including both the edge and core devices. QoS classification and scheduling in these environments are based on IP precedence and IP DSCP (essentially IP ToS-based) values. In this section, we look at implementing QoS for native IP traffic, with the assumption that Internet services fall into this category.

NOTE 10.1: Internet Traffic

Note that Internet traffic may also be deployed within an SP core to be label switched, which means that Internet traffic can utilize one or two labels, depending on the type of deployment within a given network. In such cases, MPLS EXP bits may be used for classification and queuing. In such environments, the implementation details provided in Chapter 8, "Cisco IOS and IOS XR Quality-of-Service Implementation for MPLS Layer 3 VPN Services," can be used.

Once again, we use the same IP NGN infrastructure as mentioned in the various implementation chapters, starting with Chapter 8, to illustrate the QoS configuration templates. Figure 10.1 recaptures the IP NGN topology for the sake of refreshing our memory.

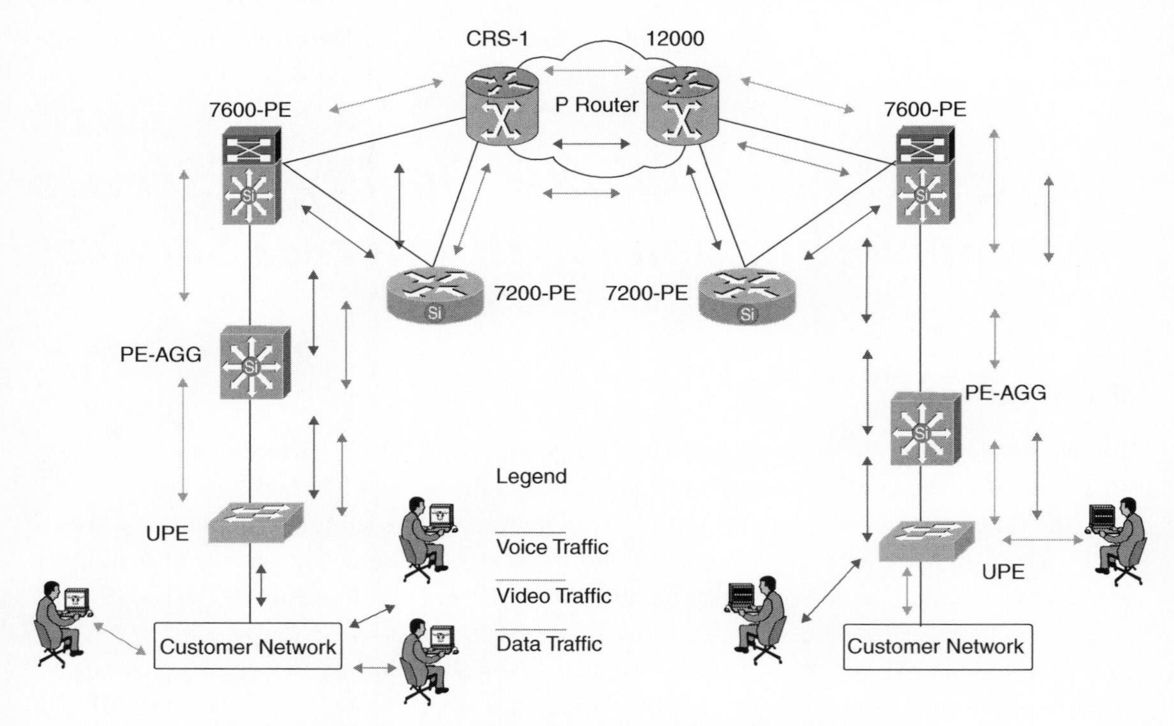

Figure 10.1: Illustration of an IP NGN Infrastructure

10.2 QoS Implementation for IP Internet Services

This section provides some sample edge and core MQC configuration templates for the Cisco CRS-1, Cisco 12000, Cisco 7600, and Cisco 7200-based platforms. Once again, all the configuration templates will follow the QoS framework, as proposed in the implementation chapters starting with Chapter 8. The QoS framework is once again illustrated in Figure 10.2, which provides the modified framework for IP Internet services.

10.3 QoS Configurations

This section illustrates QoS configuration templates for IP Internet services. The Core and Edge configurations for the various engine and line card types are provided separately for the sake of uniqueness.

> **NOTE 10.2: Edge Layer**
>
> In addition to Cisco 7600 and 7200 devices, edge configuration and implementation templates for the Cisco 12000 and CRS-1 platforms are also included for the sake of completeness. This is to aid in the overall understanding of QoS on these platforms.

		SLA Characteristics							
Service Class	Application	Loss	Delay	Jitter	BW	IP Prec	DSCP	Mark down	Oversub
Control	Routing and Control	☑	☑	-	~2%	6,7	48,56	No	No
Real-time	Voice	☑	☑	☑	~25%	5	46	No	No
Video	IPTV and TelePresence	☑	☑	-	~40%	4	32	No	No
Premium	Streaming video, intranet, OAM, and Premium data applications	☑	-	-	~28%	2	16	IPP->1 DSCP->8	Low
Best-Effort	Broadband users and low-priority data	-	-	-	~5%	0	0	No	Med./ High

Figure 10.2: The Six-Class Model

There are multiple methods of classifying traffic, and the various examples are not repeated here on a per-line-card basis. The various approaches were illustrated in Chapter 8. From a QoS standpoint, "unlabeled" IP Internet services differ only in the marking of traffic at the network edge and classification and queuing in the network core. Classification criteria at the edge remain the same and similar to MPLS VPN services. Therefore this chapter focuses only on the aspects that are unique to this category of traffic and does not provide illustrations that overlap with the previous sections.

10.3.1 Edge Configurations for the Cisco 12000 Series Routers

This section focuses on providing the configuration templates for building the needed QoS framework at the edge layer and the appropriate marking scheme required for building a QoS infrastructure using the Cisco 12000 Series routers.

In terms of customer requirements, the customer CORP-CONSULTING has subscribed to an Internet service. The customer intends to use the Internet infrastructure for two purposes: (1) to access the Internet and (2) to connect the voice infrastructure of the various offices via the public IP Internet. The customer has two requirements in this regard:

- Voice traffic between the various sites essentially forms a closed user group (CUG), which means that all sites of the customer are connected only via Service Provider FOO. This traffic needs to have a subscription to the Real-time class.
- Traffic destined for the Internet may have only a Best-Effort privilege.

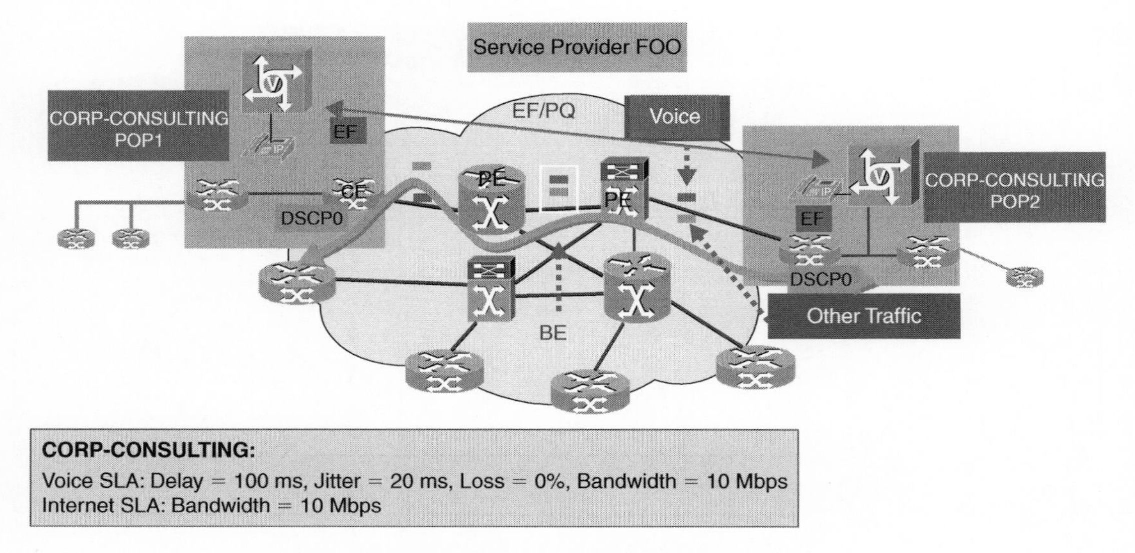

Figure 10.3: Customer SLA Requirements

The customer has procured a connection worth 20 Mbps wherein voice traffic has a contractual rate of 10 Mbps and Internet access has a contract worth 10 Mbps as well. Service Provider FOO has coordinated with the customer that all voice traffic will have a DSCP value of EF, which corresponds to the LLQ, and the remaining traffic that is to be categorized in the Best-Effort class will be left to defaults. In effect, Service Provider FOO does not remark any of the traffic at the network ingress. Policers are used in the ingress to ensure that there are no contractual violations for either of the traffic types.

QoS configuration templates for the core are described in subsequent sections. Finally, the policy map is attached to the CE-facing interface at the PE layer. Figure 10.3 illustrates this concept in more detail.

Configuration

```
!
class-map match-any VoIP
  description ### Matching all EF traffic ###
  match ip dscp EF
!
class-map match-any Internet
  description ### Matching all other traffic ###
  match any
!
policy-map CORP-CONSULTING
  class VoIP
```

```
   police cir 10240000 bc 128000 be 128000 conform-action transmit exceed-
   action drop
!
class Internet
   police cir 10240000 bc 128000 be 128000 conform-action set-dscp-transmit
   0 exceed-action drop
!
interface GigabitEthernet6/4.2000 ------→ PE-CE interface!
   description ### User to Network Interface for CORP-CONSULTING ###
   encapsulation dot1Q 2000
   ip address 8.8.8.1 255.255.255.252
   no ip directed-broadcast
   service-policy input CORP-CONSULTING -→ Ingress Service Policy applied!
!
End
```

10.3.2 Edge Configurations for the Cisco 7200 Series Routers

In this section, the edge configurations for the 7200 series of routers are illustrated.

In terms of customer requirements, the customer TOTAL-BANK has subscribed to an Internet service. The customer has purchased the Premium service for Internet traffic and has a subscription rate of full GE PORT. The customer edge layer is not configured for any marking of the IP Internet traffic; hence the Provider Edge devices will remark all incoming traffic to DSCP 16, which corresponds to the Premium class.

Figure 10.4 illustrates the customer requirements as well as the overall flow in more detail.

In the following illustration, it is assumed that all traffic entering the SP network ingress from a given customer is subscribed to the Premium class. Hence the keyword *match any* is used here. The policy map Premium is used to mark all incoming traffic to DSCP 16. Below the configuration template, the illustration verifying the marking at the network edge is provided. In the illustration, we can see that all incoming traffic is marked as DSCP 16 by means of the input service policy (policy map).

Configuration

```
!
class-map match-any Premium-traffic
   description ### Matching all traffic ###
   match any
!
```

```
policy-map Premium
   class Premium-traffic
    set ip dscp 16 --------→
!
interface GigabitEthernet0/2 ------→ PE-CE interface!
   description ### User to Network Interface for Customer-XYZ ###
   ip address 8.8.8.5 255.255.255.252
   no ip directed-broadcast
   duplex auto
   speed auto
   media-type gbic
   negotiation auto
   service-policy input Premium -→ Ingress Service Policy applied!
!
End
```

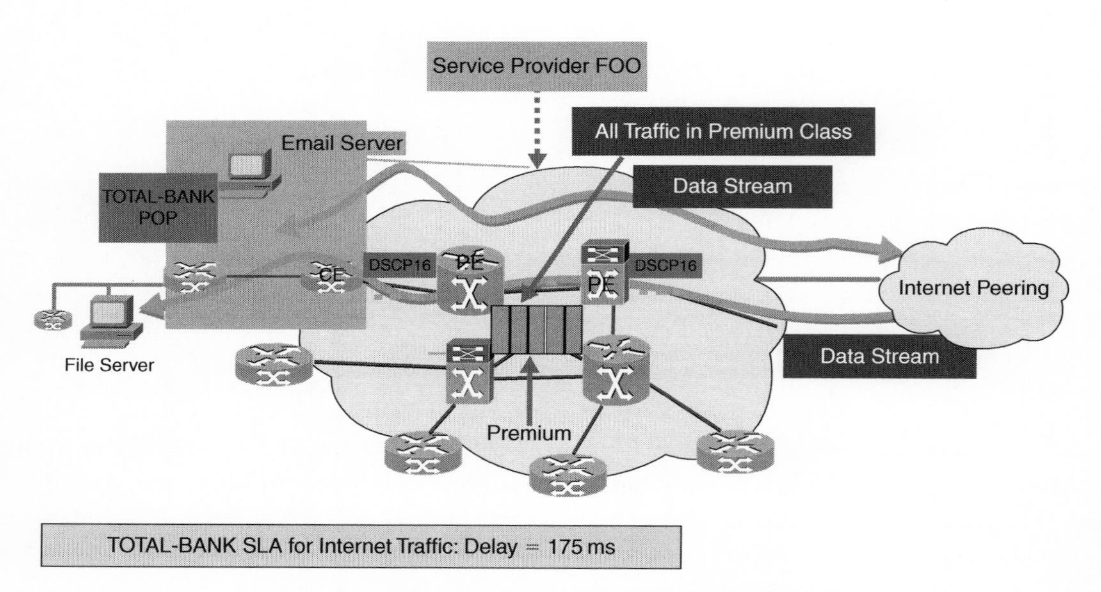

Figure 10.4: Customer SLA Requirements

Verification

```
7206B#show policy-map interface gigabitEthernet 0/2
 GigabitEthernet0/2
   Service-policy input: Premium (16)
     Class-map: Premium-traffic (match-any) (2909697/10)
```

```
  105641 packets, 159639474 bytes --------> Hits on the ingress
interface!
  5 minute offered rate 2923000bps, drop rate 0bps
  Match: ip dscp 46 (13558290)
   0 packets, 0 bytes
   5 minute rate 0 bps
  Match: any (8846562)
   105641 packets, 159639474 bytes
   5 minute rate 2923000 bps
  QoS Set
   Dscp 16
    Packets marked 105641 ---→ Indicates the number of packets marked!
```

10.3.3 Edge Configurations for the Cisco 7600 Series Routers

This section illustrates the edge configurations for the 7600 Series of routers. Configuration templates are provided. The following illustration matches all traffic on VLAN 1000 and appropriately marks the IP DSCP values to DSCP 16.

Configuration

```
!
class-map match-any Premium
  description ### Matching all traffic ###
  match any
!
policy-map Premium
  class data
  set ip dscp 16 ---------→ Set IP DSCP 16!
!
interface GigabitEthernet1/1
  description ### User to Network Interface for Customer-XYZ ###
  switchport
  switchport trunk encapsulation dot1q
  switchport mode trunk
  mls qos vlan-based -------→ Required to enable SVI based QoS!
!
interface Vlan1000
  description ### Internet Access Service###
  ip address 2.2.2.1 255.255.255.252
  no snmp trap link-status
  service-policy input Premium--→ Ingress Service-Policy!
!
End
```

10.3.4 Edge Configurations for the Cisco CRS-1 Series Routers

In this section, the edge configurations for the CRS-1 series of routers are illustrated. The following illustration uses a class map named VoIP to classify all traffic flowing via a given interface and marks the DSCP values to reflect the need for Expedited Forwarding (EF). IOS-XR does not support the use of the keyword *match-any* under a class map; hence an access list *acl 104* is used to match all traffic entering a given interface. Once classified, this traffic is marked with DSCP EF for mapping it into the LLQ.

Match Criteria Using IP DSCP

```
!
ipv4 access-list 104
  10 permit ipv4 any any
!
class-map match-any Voice
  match access-group ipv4 104
  end-class-map
!
policy-map Voice
  class Voice
   set dscp ef
!
interface TenGigE0/0/0/0
  description ### Internet Access UNI to Customer ABC ###
  cdp
  service-policy input Voice
  ipv4 address 10.10.3.2 255.255.255.0
!
End
```

Verifying the Output

```
RP/0/RP1/CPU0:CRS-E#show policy-map interface tenGigE 0/0/0/0
Mon Mar 24 07:18:17.669 EST EDT
TenGigE0/0/0/0 input: Voice
Class Voice
  Classification statistics          (packets/bytes)         (rate-kbps)
    Matched            :                    5/750                  0
    Transmitted        :                    5/750                  0
    Total Dropped      :                    0/0                    0
  Marking statistics (S/W only)      (packets/bytes)
    Marked             :                    5/750
```

```
   Queuing statistics
   Vital              (packets)                  : 0
   Queue ID                                      : 32
   High watermark     (bytes)                    : 0
   Inst-queue-len     (bytes)                    : 0
   Avg-queue-len      (bytes)                    : 0
   Taildropped(packets/bytes)                    : 0/0
Class class-default
   Classification statistics          (packets/bytes)           (rate-kbps)
   Matched            :                    0/0                        0
   Transmitted        :                    0/0                        0
   Total Dropped      :                    0/0                        0
[Output is Truncated]
```

10.3.5 Core Configurations for the Cisco 12000 Series Using IOS

Now that we've seen the various options used for classifying and marking traffic at the network edge, this section puts emphasis on the required configurations for queuing and scheduling traffic in the network core. In this section we look at the configurations in the network core for supporting "unlabeled" Internet traffic. Configurations in the SP network core need to reflect the values that have been used for marking traffic in the network edge.

Engine 3 and 5 Line Cards

The following configuration includes IP precedence and IP DSCP values within the various class maps in addition to MPLS Experimental bits. This is required for classifying and appropriately queuing and scheduling traffic in the network core. As mentioned earlier in this section, IP traffic will not have any label associations and hence will be routed in the network core rather than being label switched (which is the case for MPLS VPNs), so the IP DSCP/IP precedence values will be used for QoS functionality.

Configuration

```
!
class-map match-any Control
   description ### Classification for Control Traffic ###
   match mpls experimental 6 7
   Match ip dscp 48 56
   Match ip precedence 6 7
class-map match-any Realtime
   description ### Classification for Voice Traffic ###
   match mpls experimental 5
   Match ip dscp 46
```

```
   Match ip precedence 5
class-map match-any Premium
   description ### Classification for Premium Applications ###
   match mpls experimental 2 1
   Match ip dscp 16 8
   Match ip precedence 2 1
class-map match-any Video
   description ### Classification for Video Traffic ###
   match mpls experimental 4
   Match ip dscp 32
   Match ip precedence 4
class-map match-any Best-Effort
   description ### Classification for BE Traffic ###
   match any
!
policy-map FOO-CORE
   class Control
      bandwidth percent 2
   class Video ---→ The Video queue does not use WRED!
      bandwidth percent 40
      queue-limit 35ms
   class Premium
      bandwidth percent 28
      random-detect
      random-detect precedence 1 35  ms 40  ms
      random-detect precedence 2 40  ms 45  ms ---→ Max hold-time is 45ms!
      queue-limit 45  ms
   class Realtime
      priority
      police cir percent 25 bc 20 ms be 20  ms
   class Best-Effort
      bandwidth percent 5
      random-detect
      random-detect precedence 0 30  ms 100  ms
      queue-limit 100  ms ---→ High Hold-Time since BE is not delay sensitive!
!
interface GigabitEthernet6/2
   description ### Link to the Network Core ###
   ip address 10.159.255.5 255.255.255.252
   no ip directed-broadcast
   ip ospf network point-to-point
   negotiation auto
   service-policy output FOO-CORE -----→ Egress Policy applied!
!
End
```

TIP 10.1 Queue Limit and WRED

The queue limit and WRED thresholds define the maximum time that a packet can spend in the system buffer.

The command *show policy-map interface <interface-name> output class <class-name>* can be used to verify the traffic entering a given class in the egress direction. Various counters are provided and include traffic matches and drops. The following illustration verifies this behavior.

Verification

```
!
12416#show policy-map interface gigabitEthernet 6/2 output class Realtime
  GigabitEthernet6/2
    Service-policy output: FOO-CORE (242)
      Class-map: Realtime (match-any) (8414465/6)
        1115 packets, 115960 bytes -------------------> Hits towards the
       Core
        5 minute offered rate 0bps, drop rate 0bps
        Match: ip dscp 46 (12943090) -------→ Matches based on IP DSCP 46!
        Class of service queue: 23
        Queue-limit: 65536 packets (default)
        Current queue-depth: 0 packets, Maximum queue-depth: 0 packets
        Average queue-depth: 0.000 packets
        Priority
        police:
          cir 25%, burst 250  ms, extended burst 250  ms
          250000000bps, 7812500 limit, 7812500 extended limit
          conformed 1115 packets, 115960 bytes; actions:
            transmit
          exceeded 0 packets, 0 bytes; actions: drop
          conformed 0bps, exceed 0bps
```

Engine 4 and 4+ Line Cards

Now we move on to Engine 4 and Engine 4+ line cards. These series of line cards differ slightly from a configuration perspective compared to their other counterparts, such as the Engine 3 and Engine 5 cards. The difference is that the Engine 4 and Engine 4+ line cards do not support a match criteria based on IP DSCP in the egress direction. Also, more than one classification criterion is not supported on these series of line cards. For instance, the operator can only choose between using IP precedence or MPLS Experimental bits and might not be able to use both together.

Configuration

```
!
class-map match-any Control
  description ### Classification for Control Traffic ###
  match ip precedence 6 7
class-map match-any Realtime
  description ### Classification for Voice Traffic ###
  match ip precedence 5
class-map match-any Best-Effort
  description ### Classification for BE Traffic ###
  match ip precedence 0
class-map match-any Premium
  description ### Classification for Premium Applications ###
  match ip precedence 2 1
class-map match-any Video
  description ### Classification for Video Traffic ###
  match ip precedence 4
!
policy-map FOO-CORE
  class Control
    bandwidth remaining percent 2
  class Video
    bandwidth remaining percent 40
    queue-limit 35  ms
  class Premium
    bandwidth remaining percent 28
    random-detect
    random-detect precedence 1 35  ms 40  ms
    random-detect precedence 2 40  ms 45  ms ---→ Max hold-time is 45ms!
    queue-limit 45  ms
  class Realtime
    priority
  class Best-Effort
    bandwidth remaining percent 5
    random-detect
    random-detect precedence 0 30  ms 100  ms
    queue-limit 100  ms ---→ High Hold-Time since BE is not delay sensitive!
!
interface GigabitEthernet6/4
  description ### Link to the Network Core ###
  ip address 10.159.255.5 255.255.255.252
  no ip directed-broadcast
  ip ospf network point-to-point
  negotiation auto
  service-policy output FOO-CORE -----→ Egress Policy applied!
!
end
```

10.3.6 Core Configurations for the Cisco 12000 Series Routers Using XR

In this section we look at the QoS configuration on the Cisco 12000 routers using IOS-XR. The configurations on the core-facing interfaces are identical to the CRS-1 platforms, and the same configuration can be applied here as well. The following illustration provides insight into this concept.

Configuration

```
!
class-map match-any Control
  match mpls experimental topmost 6 7
  Match precedence 6 7
  Match dscp 48 56
!
class-map match-any Video
  match mpls experimental topmost 4
  Match precedence 4
  Match dscp 32
!
class-map match-any Premium
  match mpls experimental topmost 2 1
  Match precedence 2 1
  Match dscp 16 8
!
class-map match-any Voice
  match mpls experimental topmost 5
  Match precedence 5
  Match dscp 46
!
class-map match-any Best-Effort
  match mpls experimental topmost 0
  Match precedence 0
  Match dscp 0
!
! ======================================
!
policy-map FOO-CORE
  class Voice
    police rate percent 25
      conform-action transmit
      exceed-action drop
    priority
!
class Control
  bandwidth percent 2
```

```
!
class Premium
  random-detect exp 2 40  ms 45  ms
  random-detect exp 1 35  ms 40  ms
  random-detect precedence 2 40  ms 45  ms
  random-detect precedence 1 35  ms 40  ms
  random-detect dscp 16 40  ms 45  ms
  random-detect dscp 8 35  ms 40  ms
  bandwidth percent 28
  queue-limit 45  ms
!
class Video
  bandwidth percent 40
  queue-limit 35  ms
!
class Best-Effort
  random-detect exp 0 30  ms 100  ms
  random-detect precedence 0 30  ms 100  ms
  random-detect dscp 0 30  ms 100  ms
  bandwidth percent 5
  queue-limit 100  ms
! ====================================
!
interface GigabitEthernet 0/1/1/3
  description <Core facing interface>
  service-policy output FOO-CORE
!
end
```

10.3.7 Core Configurations for the Cisco 7200 Series Routers

This section illustrates the configurations on the 7200 platform. The following illustration provides insight into the details. Once again the class map configurations reflect IP DSCP/IP precedence values for classification in the network core. The example uses only IP DSCP values, just to provide diversity in the configuration samples illustrated in this chapter.

Configuration

```
!
class-map match-any Control
  description ### Classification for Control Traffic ###
  match mpls experimental 6 7
```

```
  Match ip dscp 48 56
class-map match-any Realtime
  description ### Classification for Voice Traffic ###
  match mpls experimental 5
  Match ip dscp 46
class-map match-any Premium
  description ### Classification for Premium Applications ###
  match mpls experimental 2 1
  Match ip dscp 16 8
class-map match-any Video
  description ### Classification for Video Traffic ###
  match mpls experimental 4
  Match ip dscp 32
class-map match-any Best-Effort
  description ### Classification for BE Traffic ###
  match any
!
policy-map FOO-CORE
  class Control
    bandwidth percent 2
  class Video ---→ The Video queue does not use WRED!
    bandwidth percent 40
    queue-limit 35  ms
  class Premium
    bandwidth percent 28
    random-detect
    random-detect exponential-weighting-constant 13 -→ Value for GE Link!
    random-detect precedence 1 35  ms 40  ms 1
    random-detect precedence 2 40  ms 45  ms 1---→ Max hold-time is 45ms!
    queue-limit 45  ms
  class Realtime
    priority percent 25
  class Best-Effort
    bandwidth percent 4 ----------→ Reduced from 5% to 4%!
    random-detect
    random-detect exponential-weighting-constant 13
    random-detect precedence 0 30  ms 100  ms 1
    queue-limit 100ms ---→ High Hold-Time since BE is not delay sensitive!
!
interface GigabitEthernet0/3
  description ### Link to Network Core ###
  ip address 10.159.255.6 255.255.255.252
  no ip directed-broadcast
  ip ospf network point-to-point
  duplex auto
  speed auto
  media-type gbic
```

```
   negotiation auto
   service-policy output FOO-CORE ----→ Egress Policy!
!
End
```

10.3.8 Core Configurations for the Cisco 7600 Series Routers

This section illustrates the configurations for the 7600 Series of routers. The following illustration uses an Enhanced OSM card to provide details. The various line cards are not illustrated in this section, since they were addressed in Chapter 8. Moreover, as mentioned earlier in this section, the only difference in QoS configurations for this type of traffic is based on the classification criterion used in the network core, and it is safe to assume that this would be consistent across the various line cards from a configuration standpoint.

Configuration

```
!
class-map match-any Control
   description ### Classification for Control Traffic ###
   match mpls experimental topmost 6 7
   Match ip dscp 48 56
class-map match-any Realtime
   description ### Classification for Voice Traffic ###
   match mpls experimental topmost 5
   Match ip dscp 46
class-map match-any Premium
   description ### Classification for Premium Applications ###
   match mpls experimental topmost 2 1
   Match ip dscp 16 8
class-map match-any Video
   description ### Classification for Video Traffic ###
   match mpls experimental topmost 4
   Match ip dscp 32
class-map match-any Best-Effort
   description ### Classification for BE Traffic ###
   match any
!
!
policy-map FOO-CORE
   class Control
      bandwidth percent 2
   class Video
      bandwidth percent 40
```

```
      queue-limit 4167 packets
   class Premium
      bandwidth percent 28
      random-detect
      random-detect precedence 1 2916 4167
      random-detect precedence 2 4167 5000
      queue-limit 5000 packets
   class Best-Effort
      bandwidth percent 5
      random-detect
      random-detect precedence 0 3333 8333
      queue-limit 8333 packets
   class Realtime
    police cir percent 25
      priority
!
interface GE-WAN4/1
   description ### Link to Network Core ###
   ip address 10.159.240.6 255.255.255.252
   no ip directed-broadcast
   ip ospf network point-to-point
   duplex auto
   speed auto
   media-type gbic
   negotiation auto
   service-policy output FOO-CORE ----→ Egress Policy!
!
End
```

10.3.9 Core Configurations for the Cisco CRS-1 Series Routers

This section illustrates the configurations for the CRS-1 Series of routers using Cisco IOS-XR software. The interface type chosen for the illustration is 10GE SPA. The QoS configuration on all the interfaces for the CRS-1 routers is identical, and the same configuration can be applied to all line-card types.

In the following illustration, the WRED profiles are configured for all three classification criteria: IP precedence, IP DSCP, and MPLS Experimental bits. This is to ensure that early packet drop characteristics apply to all the traffic types.

Configuration

```
!
class-map match-any Control
   match mpls experimental topmost 6 7
```

```
   Match precedence 6 7
   Match dscp 48 56
!
class-map match-any Video
   match mpls experimental topmost 4
   Match precedence 4
   Match dscp 32
!
class-map match-any Premium
   match mpls experimental topmost 2 1
   Match precedence 2 1
   Match dscp 16 8
!
class-map match-any Voice
   match mpls experimental topmost 5
   Match precedence 5
   Match dscp 46
!
class-map match-any Best-Effort
   match mpls experimental topmost 0
   Match precedence 0
   Match dscp 0
!
! ====================================
!
policy-map FOO-CORE
   class Voice
      police rate percent 25
         conform-action transmit
         exceed-action drop
      priority
!
class Control
   bandwidth percent 2
!
class Premium
   random-detect exp 2 40  ms 45  ms
   random-detect exp 1 35  ms 40  ms
   random-detect precedence 2 40  ms 45  ms
   random-detect precedence 1 35  ms 40  ms
   random-detect dscp 16 40  ms 45  ms
   random-detect dscp 8 35  ms 40  ms
   bandwidth percent 28
   queue-limit 45  ms
!
class Video
```

```
   bandwidth percent 40
   queue-limit 35  ms
 !
 class Best-Effort
   random-detect exp 0 30  ms 100  ms
   random-detect precedence 0 30  ms 100  ms
   random-detect dscp 0 30  ms 100  ms
   bandwidth percent 5
   queue-limit 100  ms
 ! ===================================
 !
interface TenGigE 0/0/0/3
  description <Core facing interface>
  service-policy output FOO-CORE
 !
end
```

10.4 Summary

This chapter provided guidelines and implementation-specific details on configuring QoS for MPLS Unlabeled Internet traffic. Once again, information provided in this chapter is intended to help the reader understand the nuances of implementing QoS for this traffic type and build a framework for deployment. The finer details will always need optimization based on a wide variety of requirements, so there cannot be any hard and fast rules for deployment.

CHAPTER 11

Cisco IOS and IOS-XR Quality-of-Service Implementation for Multicast Services

11.1 Overview

In its current form, native multicast and multicast VPN traffic is not label-switched in the network core. Even if the underlying infrastructure uses MPLS for forwarding traffic, multicast traffic is transported as pure IP (or unlabeled) traffic. Therefore it is safe to state that all the principles of implementation discussed in Chapter 10, "Cisco IOS and IOS-XR Quality-of-Service Implementation for IP Internet Services," can be used for this category of traffic, too.

This section elaborates on the configuration templates for each platform type and highlights certain important implementation-specific nuances wherever applicable. Once again, we do not cover all the line cards for each platform, since the key aspect to remember is that marking criterion at the edge and classification in the core are the only differences between implementing QoS for unlabeled traffic (multicast and Internet in the Pure IP form) and label-switched traffic (MPLS VPNs and other traffic that is label switched). The implementation-specific aspects are very similar between Chapter 10 and Chapter 11.

11.2 QoS Implementation for Multicast Services

This section covers implementation and MQC configuration details for the network edge and core. Cisco CRS-1, Cisco 12000, Cisco 7600, and Cisco 7200-based platforms are covered based on our IP NGN topology illustrated in the previous implementation chapters. Multicast VPN services are chosen to illustrate the configurations needed. From a QoS standpoint there is no difference between multicast VPN and native IP multicast services. Multicast VPN services are offered via MPLS Layer3 VPNs, but the traffic flows are still unlabeled and traffic is transported as Pure IP traffic.

Once again, all the configuration templates will follow the QoS framework as proposed in all the implementation chapters starting with Chapter 8. The QoS framework is once again illustrated in Figure 11.1 for the sake of ease in reading.

11.2.1 Edge Configurations for the Cisco 12000 Series Routers

This section focuses on providing the configuration templates for building the needed QoS framework at the edge layer and essentially focuses on the appropriate marking scheme required

		SLA Characteristics							
Service Class	Application	Loss	Delay	Jitter	BW	IP Prec	DSCP	Markdown	Oversub
Control	Routing and Control	☑	☑	-	~2%	6,7	48,56	No	No
Real-time	Voice	☑	☑	☑	~25%	5	46	No	No
Video	IPTV and TelePresence	☑	☑	-	~40%	4	32	No	No
Premium	Streaming video, intranet, and Premium data applications	☑	-	-	~28%	2,1	16,8	Yes 2 → 1 16 → 8	Low
Best-Effort	Broadband users and low-priority data	-	-	-	~5%	0	0	No	Med./High

Figure 11.1: The Six-Class Model

for building a QoS infrastructure for multicast VPN services. Various line-card combinations on the Cisco 12000 are used to illustrate the configurations, only when there is a difference in the QoS implementation that makes a given line card unique in its implementation.

Engine 3 Line Cards

In terms of customer requirements, the customer WIRE-CORP has subscribed to a multicast VPN service to interconnect the video-based infrastructure between various offices via the SP core. The customer has subscribed to the Video class for all multicast traffic, and the subscribed contractual rate is 20 Mbps. Figure 11.2 illustrates this scenario in more detail.

The following configuration illustration highlights the configuration required for classifying all traffic flowing via a given interface/VLAN that is supposed to be streaming video traffic and appropriately marking this traffic within an IP precedence value of 4, which gets mapped to the Video class in the SP network core. Class map video and policy map video are used for classification and marking functions, respectively. The multicast VPN-specific commands are also provided in the illustration for the sake of completeness. However, note that all multicast-specific aspects that are not relevant to the QoS implementation are not covered in this chapter.

The *hw-module slot 6 ip multicast egress-qos enable* command enables egress multicast QoS on the ISE (Engine 3) line cards. Similarly, the command *hw-module slot 6 ip multicast egress-qos no-priority-queue* prevents multicast traffic from being sent to the LLQ/priority queue. In our example, we allocate all multicast traffic to the Video queue. Last, the command *hw-module slot 6 ip multicast hw-accelerate source-table size 16 offset 0* enables fast-path multicast forwarding.

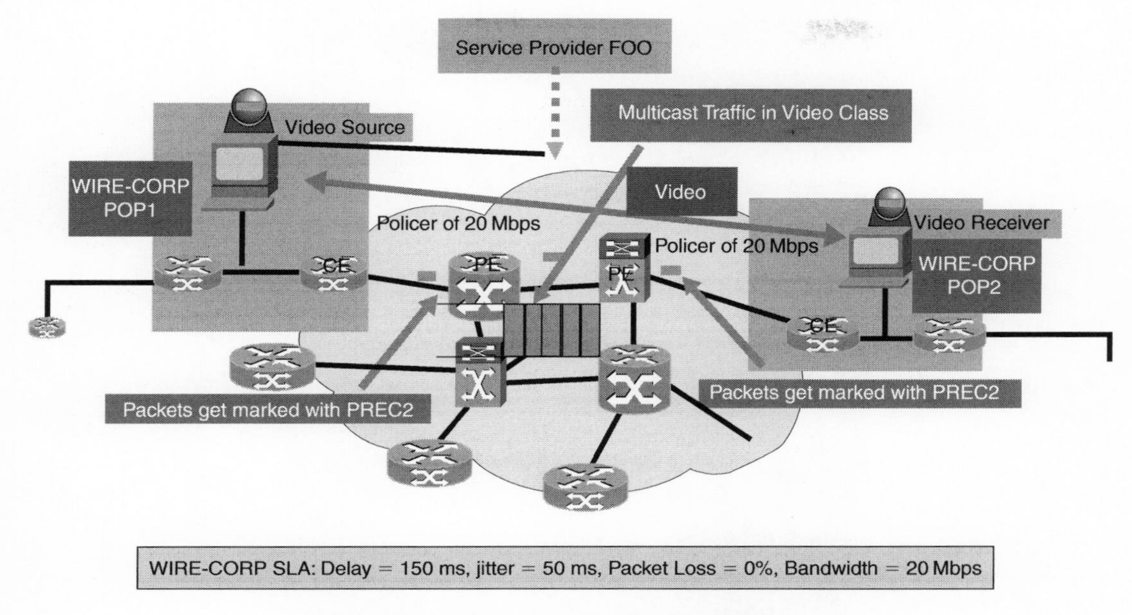

Figure 11.2: Customer Service Requirements

The Fast-Path Multicast Forwarding feature allows the Cisco 12000 router to forward packets in the hardware-based Layer 3 forwarding engine (fast path) on Engine 3 line cards instead of having multicast traffic sent to the line card's CPU for slower path processing. Normally IP packets are switched on a line card's CPU using Multicast Distributed Fast Switching (MDFS). MDFS fast-path forwarding reduces the load on the line card's CPU for slower-path processing. Hardware engine-based multicast forwarding, however, provides even higher-speed switching than MDFS. Because packet forwarding is performed on the line card in the hardware switching engine, higher forwarding rates are possible. Also, more CPU resources are free to perform other features and control-plane processes. The implementation of the Fast-Path Multicast Forwarding feature on Cisco 12000 Series Internet routers is compatible with multicast routing protocols, such as Protocol Independent Multicast Dense Mode (PIM-DM), PIM Sparse Mode (PIM-SM), and source-specific multicast (SSM).

Configuration

```
!
hw-module slot 6 qos interface queues 8 ---→ Enables 8 egress queues!
!
ip vrf WIRECORP-L3VPN
   rd 63333:255
   route-target export 63333:255
   route-target import 63333:255
```

```
    mdt default 225.1.1.1
    mdt data 226.0.2 .0 0.0.0.255 threshold 1
!
interface GigabitEthernet6/3.1000
    description ### MPLS L3VPN Interface ###
    encapsulation dot1Q 1000
    ip vrf forwarding WIRECORP-L3VPN
    ip address 8.8.8.1 255.255.255.252
    no ip directed-broadcast
    ip pim sparse-dense-mode
    service-policy input Video --→ Ingress Service Policy!
!
interface Loopback0
    ip address 10.159.253.1 255.255.255.255
    no ip directed-broadcast
    ip pim sparse-dense-mode
!
!
interface Loopback1000
    description ### mVPN interface for WIRECORP-L3VPN ###
    ip vrf forwarding WIRECORP-L3VPN
    ip address 222.222.222.222 255.255.255.255
    no ip directed-broadcast
    ip pim sparse-mode
!
hw-module slot 6 ip multicast egress-qos enable
hw-module slot 6 ip multicast egress-qos no-priority-queue
hw-module slot 6 ip multicast hw-accelerate source-table size 16 offset 0
!
ip multicast-routing distributed
ip multicast-routing vrf WIRECORP-L3VPN distributed
!
ip pim vrf WIRECORP-L3VPN rp-address 222.222.222.222
!
!
class-map match-any Video
    description ### Matching Any ###
    match any
!
policy-map Video
    class Video

police cir 20480000 bc 128000 be 128000 conform-action set-prec-transmit 4 exceed-action
drop
!
End
```

Verification

```
!
12416#show policy-map interface gigabitEthernet 6/3.1000
  GigabitEthernet6/3.1000
    Service-policy input: Video (432)
      Class-map: Video (match-any) (13255777/1)
        11105 packets, 1110500 bytes ----------------> Hits from the edge!
        5 minute offered rate 12000 bps, drop rate 0 bps
        Match: any (10802354)
      police:
          10240000 bps, 128000 limit, 128000 extended limit
          conformed 100 packets, 256000 bytes; actions:
            set-prec-transmit 4
          exceeded 0 packets, 0 bytes; actions:
            drop
[Output Truncated]
```

The preceding output verifies the classification and marking process at the network edge. In our illustration, all incoming traffic on a given VLAN is marked with IP precedence 4. An account of the number of packets matching this criterion is visible in the output of the *show policy-map interface* command.

Engine 5 Line Cards

When the same scenario is applied on Engine 5 line cards, the following configuration is needed. The only difference in configuration between the Engine 3 and Engine 5 line cards is that Engine 5 cards do not require the explicit configuration of the command *hw-module slot 6 qos interface queues 8*. All the other configurations are identical in nature. The following illustration provides an insight.

Configuration

```
!
ip vrf ACME-L3VPN
   rd 63333:255
   route-target export 63333:255
   route-target import 63333:255
   mdt default 225.1.1.1
   mdt data 226.0.2 .0 0.0.0.255 threshold 1
!
interface GigabitEthernet6/3.1000
   description ### MPLS L3VPN Interface ###
   encapsulation dot1Q 1000
```

```
    ip vrf forwarding ACME-L3VPN
    ip address 8.8.8.1 255.255.255.252
    no ip directed-broadcast
    ip pim sparse-dense-mode
    service-policy input Voice --→ Ingress Service Policy!
!
interface Loopback0
    ip address 10.159.253.1 255.255.255.255
    no ip directed-broadcast
    ip pim sparse-dense-mode
!
!
interface Loopback1000
    description ### mVPN interface for ACME-L3VPN ###
    ip vrf forwarding ACME-L3VPN
    ip address 222.222.222.222 255.255.255.255
    no ip directed-broadcast
    ip pim sparse-mode
!
ip multicast-routing distributed
ip multicast-routing vrf ACME-L3VPN distributed
!
ip pim vrf ACME-L3VPN rp-address 222.222.222.222
!
!
class-map match-any Video
    description ### Matching Any ###
    match any
!
policy-map Video
    class Video
police cir 20480000 bc 128000 be 128000 conform-action set-prec-transmit 4
exceed-action drop
!
End
```

Engine 4 Line Cards

When Engine 4 line cards are deployed on the egress (core facing), although the egress multicast QoS configuration is applied to the egress interface, these engines cannot fulfill the lookup for packet classification, queue selection, and RED profile selection. Irrespective of the egress QoS configuration, all multicast traffic will only enter the default queue. To support multicast traffic to enter into other nondefault queues, Tofab (Rx Cos) using the legacy CLI needs to be configured in the network ingress, wherein the specific CoS identification for multicast traffic is performed in the ingress. The following illustration uses an Engine 3 LC as the ingress interface.

Configuration

```
!
!
cos-queue-group multicast-cos
precedence 4 queue 1 ------ Identifies the precedence value!
queue 1 40
!
rx-cos-slot 6 multicast-table ---→ E3 LC is in Slot 6!
slot-table-cos multicast-table
multicast multicast-cos
!
End
```

11.2.2 Edge Configurations for the Cisco 7200 Series Routers

This section illustrates the QoS configuration template for the 7200 Series routers.

In terms of customer requirements, the customer ACME has subscribed to a multicast VPN service to interconnect the video-based infrastructure between various offices via the SP core. The customer has multiple traffic types, such as voice and data, in addition to multicast-based video and uses an existing marking scheme within the enterprise. As per the existing marking scheme, video traffic is marked DSCP 16. The marking for other traffic types is not important from this chapter's point of view. Figure 11.3 illustrates the flow in more detail.

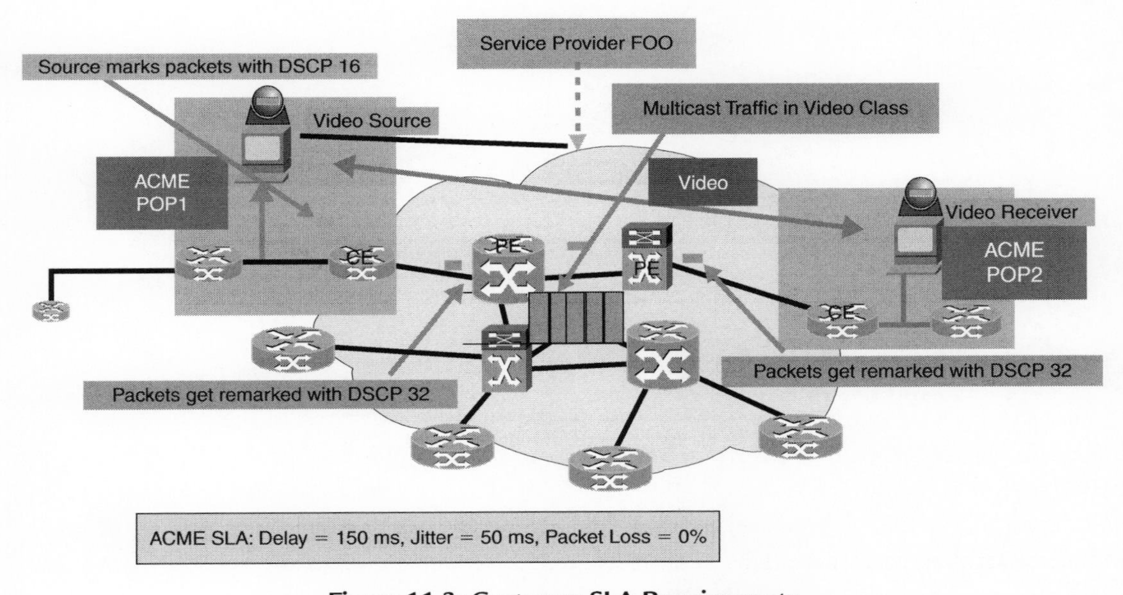

Figure 11.3: Customer SLA Requirements

Class map video and policy map video are used to match and mark traffic as per the SP policy. The policy map marks incoming video traffic as DSCP 32, which corresponds to the video queue. The customer uses a full rate port, and hence no ingress policers are used in the PE routers.

NOTE 11.1: Marking Traffic

Remarking at the PE will result in the customer TOS values being overwritten because the code point for marking is common between the customer and service provider, which is IP TOS.

Configuration

```
!
!
interface GigabitEthernet0/1.1000
   description ### CE Interface to Router 7206C ###
   encapsulation dot1Q 1000
   ip vrf forwarding ACME-L3VPN
   ip address 1.1.1.1 255.255.255.252
   no ip directed-broadcast
   ip pim sparse-dense-mode
   ip ospf network point-to-point
   service-policy input Video ---→ Ingress Service Policy!
!
interface Loopback0
   ip address 10.159.253.3 255.255.255.255
   no ip directed-broadcast
   ip pim sparse-dense-mode
!
interface Loopback1000
   description ### For mVPN ACME-L3VPN ###
   ip vrf forwarding ACME-L3VPN
   ip address 111.111.111.1 255.255.255.255
   no ip directed-broadcast
   ip pim sparse-dense-mode
!
ip vrf ACME-L3VPN
   rd 63333:255
   route-target export 63333:255
   route-target import 63333:255
   mdt default 225.1.1.1
   mdt data 226.0.2.0 0.0.0.255 threshold 1
!
ip multicast-routing
ip multicast-routing vrf ACME-L3VPN
!
```

```
ip pim vrf ACME-L3VPN rp-address 222.222.222.222
!
class-map match-any Video
   description ### Matching DSCP 46 ###
   match ip dscp 16
!
policy-map Video
   class Video
    set dscp 32
!
End
```

Verification

```
7206B#show policy-map interface GigabitEthernet 0/1.1000
 GigabitEthernet0/1.1000
   Service-policy input: Video (176)
    Class-map: Video (match-any) (15940177/1)
    3 packets, 354 bytes ---------------------------------------> Hits!
     5 minute offered rate 0 bps, drop rate 0 bps
     Match: ip dscp 16 (14096434)
      3 packets, 354 bytes
      5 minute rate 0 bps
     QoS Set
      ip dscp 32
       Packets marked 3
```

11.2.3 Edge Configurations for the Cisco 7600 Series Routers

In this section, the edge configurations for the 7600 Series of routers are illustrated. The same scenario used in the previous section (7200) is used here.

Configuration

```
!
interface Vlan1000
   description ### L3VPN Interface to CE 3845B ###
   ip vrf forwarding ACME-L3VPN
   ip address 2.2.2.1 255.255.255.252
   ip pim sparse-dense-mode
   no snmp trap link-status
   service-policy input Video --→ Ingress Service Policy!
!
```

```
ip vrf ACME-L3VPN
   rd 63333:255
   route-target export 63333:255
   route-target import 63333:255
   mdt default 225.1.1.1
   mdt data 226.0.4.0 0.0.0.255 threshold 1
!
ip multicast-routing
ip multicast-routing vrf ACME-L3VPN
!
ip pim vrf ACME-L3VPN rp-address 222.222.222.222
!
class-map match-any Video
   description ### Matching DSCP 46 ###
   match ip dscp 16
!
policy-map Video
   class Video
    set dscp 32
!
End
```

11.2.4 Core Configurations for the Cisco 12000 Series Routers Using IOS

Now that we've seen the various options used for classifying and marking of traffic at the network edge, this section lays emphasis on the required configurations for queuing and scheduling traffic in the network core. In this section we look at the configurations in the network core for supporting multicast traffic. Configurations in the SP network core need to reflect the values that have been used for marking traffic in the network edge. Once again, note that the core configurations for multicast traffic and unlabeled Internet traffic illustrated in Chapter 10 are identical. However, some amount of detail is presented in this chapter for completeness.

Engine 3 and 5 Line Cards

The following configuration includes IP precedence and IP DSCP values within the various class maps in addition to MPLS Experimental bits. This is required to classify and appropriately queue and schedule traffic in the network core. As mentioned earlier in this section, multicast traffic will have no label associations and hence will be routed in the network core rather than being label switched (which is the case for MPLS VPNs), so the IP DSCP/IP precedence values will be used for QoS functionality.

Configuration

```
!
class-map match-any Control
   description ### Classification for Control Traffic ###
   match mpls experimental 6 7
   Match ip dscp 48 56
   Match ip precedence 6 7
class-map match-any Realtime
   description ### Classification for Voice Traffic ###
   match mpls experimental 5
   Match ip dscp 46
   Match ip precedence 5
class-map match-any Premium
   description ### Classification for Premium Applications ###
   match mpls experimental 2 1
   Match ip dscp 16 8
   Match ip precedence 2 1
class-map match-any Video
   description ### Classification for Video Traffic ###
   match mpls experimental 4
   Match ip dscp 32
   Match ip precedence 4
class-map match-any Best-Effort
   description ### Classification for BE Traffic ###
   match any
!
policy-map FOO-CORE
   class Control
     bandwidth percent 2
   class Video ---→ The Video queue does not use WRED!
     bandwidth percent 40
     queue-limit 35 ms
   class Premium
     bandwidth percent 28
     random-detect
     random-detect precedence 1 35 ms 40 ms
     random-detect precedence 2 40 ms 45 ms --- → Max hold-time is 45ms!
     queue-limit 45 ms
   class Realtime
     priority
    police cir percent 25 bc 20 ms be 20 ms
   class Best-Effort
     bandwidth percent 5
     random-detect
     random-detect precedence 0 30 ms 100 ms
```

```
    queue-limit 100 ms ---→ High Hold-Time since BE is not delay sensitive!
!
interface GigabitEthernet6/2
   description ### Link to the Network Core ###
   ip address 10.159.255.5 255.255.255.252
   no ip directed-broadcast
   ip ospf network point-to-point
   negotiation auto
   service-policy output FOO-CORE -----→ Egress Policy applied!
!
End
```

The command *show policy-map interface <interface-name> output class <class-name>* can be used to verify the traffic entering a given class in the egress direction. Various counters are provided that include traffic matches and drops. The following illustration verifies this behavior.

Verification

```
!
12416#show policy-map interface gigabitEthernet 6/2 output class Realtime
   GigabitEthernet6/2
     Service-policy output: FOO-CORE (242)
       Class-map: Realtime (match-any) (8414465/6)
         1115 packets, 115960 bytes -------------------> Hits towards the Core
         5 minute offered rate 0 bps, drop rate 0 bps
         Match: ip dscp 46 (12943090) -------→ Matches based on IP DSCP 46!
         Class of service queue: 23
         Queue-limit: 65536 packets (default)
         Current queue-depth: 0 packets, Maximum queue-depth: 0 packets
         Average queue-depth: 0.000 packets
         Priority
         police:
           cir 25%, burst 250 ms, extended burst 250 ms
           250000000 bps, 7812500 limit, 7812500 extended limit
           conformed 1115 packets, 115960 bytes; actions:
             transmit
           exceeded 0 packets, 0 bytes; actions: drop
           conformed 0 bps, exceed 0 bps
```

Engine 4 and Engine 4+ Line Cards

Now we move on to Engine 4 and Engine 4+ line cards. These series of line cards differ slightly from a configuration perspective compared to their other counterparts such as Engine 3 and Engine 5. The difference is that the Engine 4 and Engine 4+ line cards do not support match criteria based on IP DSCP. Also, more than one classification criterion is not supported on these series of line cards. For instance, the operator can only choose between using IP precedence or MPLS Experimental bits and may not be able to use both together.

Configuration

```
!
class-map match-any Control
   description ### Classification for Control Traffic ###
   match ip precedence 6 7
class-map match-any Realtime
   description ### Classification for Voice Traffic ###
   match ip precedence 5
class-map match-any Best-Effort
   description ### Classification for BE Traffic ###
   match ip precedence 0
class-map match-any Premium
   description ### Classification for Premium Applications ###
   match ip precedence 2 1
class-map match-any Video
   description ### Classification for Video Traffic ###
   match ip precedence 4
!
policy-map FOO-CORE
   class Control
     bandwidth remaining percent 2
   class Video
     bandwidth remaining percent 40
     queue-limit 35 ms
   class Premium
     bandwidth remaining percent 28
     random-detect
     random-detect precedence 1 35 ms 40 ms
     random-detect precedence 2 40 ms 45 ms ---→ Max hold-time is 45ms!
     queue-limit 45 ms
   class Realtime
     priority
   class Best-Effort
     bandwidth remaining percent 5
     random-detect
     random-detect precedence 0 30 ms 100 ms
     queue-limit 100 ms ---→ High Hold-Time since BE is not delay sensitive!
!
interface GigabitEthernet6/4
   description ### Link to the Network Core ###
   ip address 10.159.255.5 255.255.255.252
```

```
  no ip directed-broadcast
  ip ospf network point-to-point
  negotiation auto
  service-policy output FOO-CORE ------→ Egress Policy applied!
 !
end
```

11.2.5 Core Configurations for the Cisco 12000 Series Routers Using XR

In this section, we look at the QoS configuration on the Cisco 12000 Series routers using IOS-XR. The configurations on the core-facing interfaces are identical to the CRS-1 platforms, and the same configuration can be applied here as well. The following illustration provides insight.

Configuration

```
!
class-map match-any Control
   match mpls experimental topmost 6 7
   Match precedence 6 7
   Match dscp 48 56
!
class-map match-any Video
   match mpls experimental topmost 4
   Match precedence 4
   Match dscp 32
!
class-map match-any Premium
   match mpls experimental topmost 2 1
   Match precedence 2 1
   Match dscp 16 8
!
class-map match-any Voice
   match mpls experimental topmost 5
   Match precedence 5
   Match dscp 46
!
class-map match-any Best-Effort
   match mpls experimental topmost 0
   Match precedence 0
   Match dscp 0
!
! ====================================
!
```

```
policy-map FOO-CORE
   class Voice
     police rate percent 25
       conform-action transmit
       exceed-action drop
     priority
  !
  class Control
    bandwidth percent 2
  !
  class Premium
    random-detect exp 2 40 ms 45 ms
    random-detect exp 1 35 ms 40 ms
    random-detect precedence 2 40 ms 45 ms
    random-detect precedence 1 35 ms 40 ms
    random-detect dscp 16 40 ms 45 ms
    random-detect dscp 8 35 ms 40 ms
    bandwidth percent 28
    queue-limit 45 ms
  !
  class Video
    bandwidth percent 40
    queue-limit 35 ms
  !
  class Best-Effort
    random-detect exp 0 30 ms 100 ms
    random-detect precedence 0 30 ms 100 ms
    random-detect dscp 0 30 ms 100 ms
    bandwidth percent 5
    queue-limit 100 ms
! =====================================
!
interface GigabitEthernet 0/1/1/3
  description <Core facing interface>
  service-policy output FOO-CORE
!
end
```

11.2.6 Core Configurations for the Cisco 7200 Series Routers

This section illustrates the configurations on the 7200 platform. The following illustration provides insight into the details. Once again the class map configurations reflect IP DSCP/IP precedence values for classification in the network core. The following example uses only IP DSCP values, just to provide diversity in the configuration samples illustrated in this chapter.

Configuration

```
!
class-map match-any Control
   description ### Classification for Control Traffic ###
   match mpls experimental 6 7
   Match ip dscp 48 56
class-map match-any Realtime
   description ### Classification for Voice Traffic ###
   match mpls experimental 5
   Match ip dscp 46
class-map match-any Premium
   description ### Classification for Premium Applications  ###
   match mpls experimental 2 1
   Match ip dscp 16 8
class-map match-any Video
   description ### Classification for Video Traffic ###
   match mpls experimental 4
   Match ip dscp 32
class-map match-any Best-Effort
   description ### Classification for BE Traffic ###
   match any
!
policy-map FOO-CORE
   class Control
     bandwidth percent 2
   class Video ---→ The Video queue does not use WRED!
     bandwidth percent 40
     queue-limit 35 ms
   class Premium
     bandwidth percent 28
     random-detect
     random-detect exponential-weighting-constant 13 –→ Value for GE Link!
     random-detect precedence 1 35 ms 40 ms 1
     random-detect precedence 2 40 ms 45 ms 1---→ Max hold-time is 45 ms!
     queue-limit 45 ms
   class Realtime
     priority percent 25
   class Best-Effort
     bandwidth percent 4 ---------→ Reduced from 5% to 4%!
     random-detect
     random-detect exponential-weighting-constant 13
     random-detect precedence 0 30 ms 100 ms 1
     queue-limit 100 ms ---→ High Hold-Time since BE is not delay
   sensitive!
!
interface GigabitEthernet0/3
```

```
    description ### Link to Network Core ###
    ip address 10.159.255.6 255.255.255.252
    no ip directed-broadcast
    ip ospf network point-to-point
    duplex auto
    speed auto
    media-type gbic
    negotiation auto
    service-policy output FOO-CORE ----→ Egress Policy!
!
End
```

11.2.7 Core Configurations for the Cisco 7600 Series Routers

This section illustrates the configurations for the 7600 Series of routers. The following illustration uses an Enhanced OSM card to provide the details. The various line cards are not illustrated in this section, since they were addressed in Chapter 8. Moreover, as mentioned earlier in this section, the only difference in QoS configurations for this type of traffic is based on the classification criterion used in the network core, and it is safe to assume that this would be consistent across the various line cards from a configuration standpoint.

Configuration

```
!
class-map match-any Control
   description ### Classification for Control Traffic ###
   match mpls experimental topmost 6 7
   Match ip dscp 48 56
class-map match-any Realtime
   description ### Classification for Voice Traffic ###
   match mpls experimental topmost 5
   Match ip dscp 46
class-map match-any Premium
   description ### Classification for Premium Applications ###
   match mpls experimental topmost 2 1
   Match ip dscp 16 8
class-map match-any Video
   description ### Classification for Video Traffic ###
   match mpls experimental topmost 4
   Match ip dscp 32
class-map match-any Best-Effort
   description ### Classification for BE Traffic ###
```

```
    match any
!
!
policy-map FOO-CORE
    class Control
       bandwidth percent 2
    class Video
       bandwidth percent 40
       queue-limit 4167 packets
    class Premium
       bandwidth percent 28
       random-detect
       random-detect precedence 1 2916 4167
       random-detect precedence 2 4167 5000
       queue-limit 5000 packets
    class Best-Effort
       bandwidth percent 5
       random-detect
       random-detect precedence 0 3333 8333
       queue-limit 8333 packets
    class Realtime
      police cir percent 25
       priority
!
interface GE-WAN4/1
  description ### Link to Network Core ###
    ip address 10.159.240.6 255.255.255.252
    no ip directed-broadcast
    ip ospf network point-to-point
    duplex auto
    speed auto
    media-type gbic
    negotiation auto
    service-policy output FOO-CORE ----→ Egress Policy!
!
End
```

11.2.8 Core Configurations for the Cisco CRS-1 Series Routers

This section illustrates the configurations for the CRS-1 Series of routers using Cisco IOS-XR software. The interface type chosen for the illustration is 10GE SPA. The QoS configuration on all the interfaces for the CRS-1 routers is identical, and the same configuration can be applied to all line-card types.

In this illustration, the WRED profiles are configured for all three classifications criteria: IP precedence, IP DSCP, and MPLS Experimental bits. This is to ensure that early packet drop characteristics apply to all the traffic types.

Configuration

```
!
class-map match-any Control
   match mpls experimental topmost 6 7
   Match precedence 6 7
   Match dscp 48 56
!
class-map match-any Video
   match mpls experimental topmost 4
   Match precedence 4
   Match dscp 32
!
class-map match-any Premium
   match mpls experimental topmost 2 1
   Match precedence 2 1
   Match dscp 16 8
!
class-map match-any Voice
   match mpls experimental topmost 5
   Match precedence 5
   Match dscp 46
!
class-map match-any Best-Effort
   match mpls experimental topmost 0
   Match precedence 0
   Match dscp 0
!
! =====================================
!
policy-map FOO-CORE
   class Voice
      police rate percent 25
         conform-action transmit
         exceed-action drop
      priority
 !
   class Control
      bandwidth percent 2
 !
   class Premium
```

```
      random-detect exp 2 40 ms 45 ms
      random-detect exp 1 35 ms 40 ms
      random-detect precedence 2 40 ms 45 ms
      random-detect precedence 1 35 ms 40 ms
      random-detect dscp 16 40 ms 45 ms
      random-detect dscp 8 35 ms 40 ms
      bandwidth percent 28
      queue-limit 45 ms
 !
   class Video
      bandwidth percent 40
      queue-limit 35 ms
 !
   class Best-Effort
      random-detect exp 0 30 ms 100 ms
      random-detect precedence 0 30 ms 100 ms
      random-detect dscp 0 30 ms 100 ms
      bandwidth percent 5
      queue-limit 100 ms
! ====================================
!
interface TenGigE 0/0/0/3
   description <Core facing interface>
   service-policy output FOO-CORE
!
end
```

11.3 Preserving Customer ToS Values

In certain circumstances, an SP might need to preserve its end-customer ToS values while enforcing per-hop behaviors as per the provider's QoS policy. Looking at the following scenario, where customer ABC, subscribing to a multicast VPN service from SP FOO, needs to preserve its ToS values for appropriate processing within its enterprise boundary. In this situation, it might be evident that the SP needs to remark the IP ToS values at the network edge to enforce the appropriate QoS policy/behavior for the given customer. This is where the conflict occurs, since the customer IP ToS values will get rewritten by default when an ingress "service policy" is configured on the PE routers.

The Cisco 12000 (Engine 3 and Engine 5) and the Cisco CRS-1 platforms support a feature that enables an SP to mark the IP ToS values on the mVPN tunnel and leave the IP ToS markings on the customer's IP "encapsulated" packet intact. This ensures that customer values are preserved and transparent to the SP QoS markings at the provider edge. The configurations for IOS and IOS-XR are shown here.

IOS Configuration

```
!
ip vrf ABC-L3VPN
   rd 63333:255
   route-target export 63333:255
   route-target import 63333:255
   mdt default 225.1.1.1
   mdt data 226.0.2 .0 0.0.0.255 threshold 1
!
class-map match-any Video
   description ### Matching Traffic marked with DSCP EF ###
   match any
!
policy-map Video
   class Video
   police cir 512000 bc 4000 be 4000 conform-action set-ip-dscp-tunnel-
  transmit <dscp value> exceed-action drop --------→ Set DSCP value on the
  Tunnel header!
!
interface GigabitEthernet6/6
   no ip address
   no ip directed-broadcast
   negotiation auto
!
interface GigabitEthernet6/6.1000 ------→ PE-CE interface!
   description ### MPLS L3VPN Interface ###
   encapsulation dot1Q 1000
   ip vrf forwarding ABC-L3VPN
   ip address 8.8.8.1 255.255.255.252
   no ip directed-broadcast
   service-policy input Video-→ Ingress Service Policy applied!
!
end
```

The following configuration marks the DSCP Tunnel header with DSCP 7 for all traffic that conforms to the ingress policer, whereas excess traffic is marked DSCP 6.

IOS-XR Configuration

```
interface Multilink0/8/3/0/1.4 point-to-point
   vrf MVRF_5
   ipv4 address 67.1.5.1 255.255.255.0
   ipv4 verify unicast source reachable-via rx
   service-policy input 2R3C_dual_set <<<<<--------- MVPN Policy attached
  on ingress interface
```

```
  !
policy-map 2R3C_dual_set
   class prec1
     police rate 64 kbps peak-rate 10 mbps
        conform-action set dscp tunnel 7
        exceed-action set dscp tunnel 6
     !
  !
 class prec2
   police rate 64 kbps peak-rate 10 mbps
      conform-action set dscp tunnel 7
      exceed-action set dscp tunnel 6
  !
end
```

11.4 Summary

This chapter provided guidelines and implementation-specific details on configuring QoS for multicast traffic. Once again, information provided in this chapter is intended to help the reader understand the nuances of implementing multicast QoS.

CHAPTER 12

Proof of Concept for Verifying QoS Behavior in Cisco IP NGN Networks

12.1 Overview

Now that we've discussed recommendations for deploying QoS as well as understanding the implementation of QoS for the various services that can exist in an IP NGN infrastructure, the question that arises is: How do we verify whether the deployment of QoS is serving its purpose? In other words, how does an operator know whether the deployed QoS framework is really making a difference to the network and actually protecting critical applications during periods of congestion? We know, and have seen in the preceding chapters, the use of the various *show* commands that are available both in Cisco IOS and XR that present a good amount of detail in terms of verifying system-specific statistics from a QoS standpoint. However, these commands do not have the ability to present details on metrics such as delay and jitter, which are extremely important in verifying and validating service-level agreements that are offered to end customers. Moreover, SPs would like to create a baseline of sorts to equip them for understanding possible outcomes and trends in the network and their relative impact on traffic during a sequence of events such as congestion. To achieve these goals, we need to rely on tools known as *traffic generators* to simulate traffic flows and introduce bottlenecks in the network so that we can create a baseline of traffic behavior and understand the impact of QoS in this whole process.

In this chapter we create a *proof of concept* to verify QoS behavior under various circumstances. We connect a traffic generator to the network to define a series of tests and capture the various outputs, which we also analyze in detail. Note that this chapter does not intend to provide performance metrics for any specific Cisco platform, line card, or software version. Furthermore, naming conventions used in the test illustrations do not reflect any particular platform, standard, or methodology. Therefore, if there is any reference made to these in the illustrations, it is only coincidental. Another critical aspect to note is that the metrics shown in the output do not reflect the actual performance values that might be obtained while deploying a particular Cisco platform. We only intend to demonstrate the process involved in testing QoS and examine the behavior in a network, with and without the deployment of QoS. Therefore it is highly important for the reader to view this chapter as a guideline for validating QoS rather than as a reference with absolute metrics in regard to Cisco platforms.

12.2 Test Setup

To validate the behavior of a network with QoS and without QoS, we use the following setup in a lab and analyze the results in the subsequent sections of this chapter.

The test setup that will be used in the examples uses a traffic generator connected to a Cisco core router, also known as the system under test (SUT), as illustrated in Figure 12.1.

As illustrated in Figure 12.1, the traffic generator (highlighted as Agilant packet generator) is connected to a Core router using three interfaces. The two OC-48 interfaces on the traffic generator are configured as ingress ports, meaning that they would generate traffic toward the core, which is the Gigabit Ethernet interface on the traffic generator. The Gigabit Ethernet interface is configured as the egress interface to simulate the behavior of a link in the network core. This is a simple yet effective way to simulate a network to validate our requirement. Once we have the results, it is easy to determine the PHB in regard to SLAs on a given node in the network core.

The following streams with values are used for the entire chapter, unless otherwise stated:

- One voice stream: 114 Mb using a packet size of 80 bytes.
- One multicast stream: 126 Mb using a packet size of 1500 bytes.
- Four data streams: Varied bandwidth sizes (as we'll see in a moment) using a packet size of 300 bytes each.

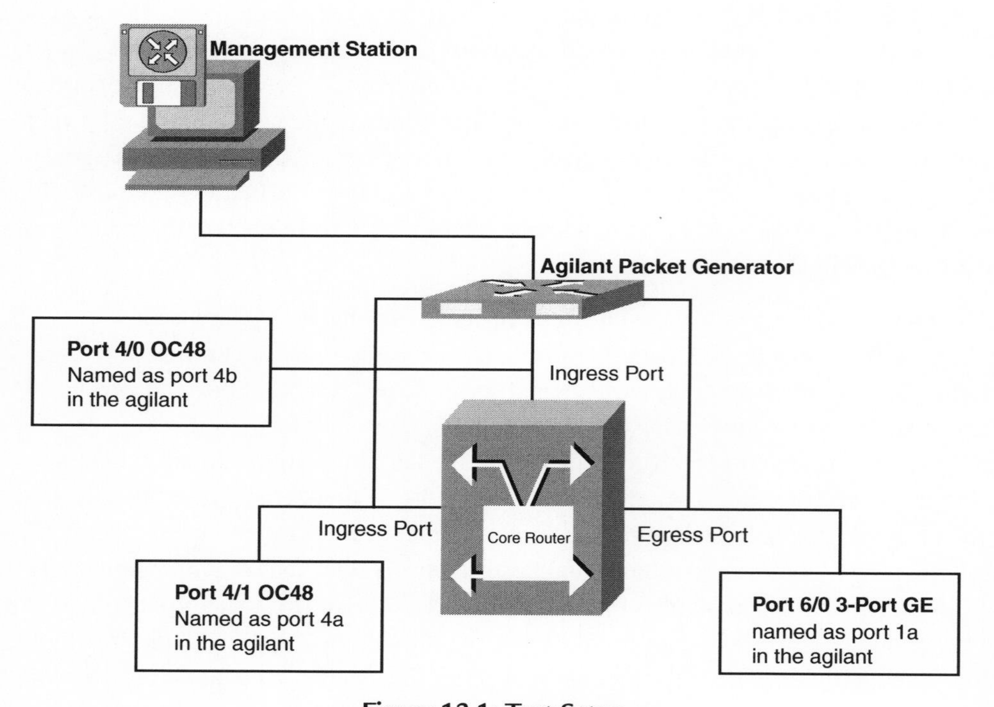

Figure 12.1: Test Setup

For the test, we use the following traffic-to-class mapping as illustrated in Figure 12.2. In total, seven classes are used.

12.3 Test Procedure Without QoS Enabled

We start examining the impact of traffic without any QoS features enabled in the core router. Once we understand the impact due to the lack of QoS being enabled, it is easier to compare the results with the other tests that are about to follow and that are executed with QoS enabled.

As mentioned in the previous section, we use the specified voice and multicast stream. In addition, we use four data streams of 180 Mb each, as illustrated in detail in the following section.

12.3.1 Testing Using Four Data Streams of 180 Mb Each

In this test we start to notice packet drops due to volume of traffic being sent into the SUT. However, two aspects are of significant importance:

- We have an increased latency for voice packets that is in the scale of 14 ms, as seen in Figure 12.3. (We would able to see that this value is significantly higher than the results we would notice in the tests with QoS enabled.)
- All traffic classes, including voice and multicast, have a huge share of drops.

This clearly indicates lack of protection for voice and multicast traffic, which are highly sensitive to packet loss and would have an extremely negative impact on applications. Second, lack of congestion avoidance (WRED) results in traffic being dropped randomly without a preference/priority, which is an expected outcome since an operator does not want all traffic impacted during a period of congestion and would prefer a sequence in the traffic being dropped (lower-priority traffic first and higher next).

Examining Figure 12.3, we notice that the count in the Packets Not Received and Sequence Errors fields are extremely high. The fields are circled. This is an indication of the drop

Class	Precedence	Traffic
Evil traffic	0	All nonidentified off-net traffic (off-net)
On net ···· on net	1	Traffic that stays within the SP network (on-net)
LSP services	2	LSP traffic, SMTP POP FTP DNS telnet SSH WWW HTTPS
SME	3	Enterprise customers, a gold service
Real-Time, nonvoice	4	TV, real-time gaming
Voice	5	RTP VoIP traffic
Network control messages	6-7	BGP and other control messages

Figure 12.2: Classes for Test

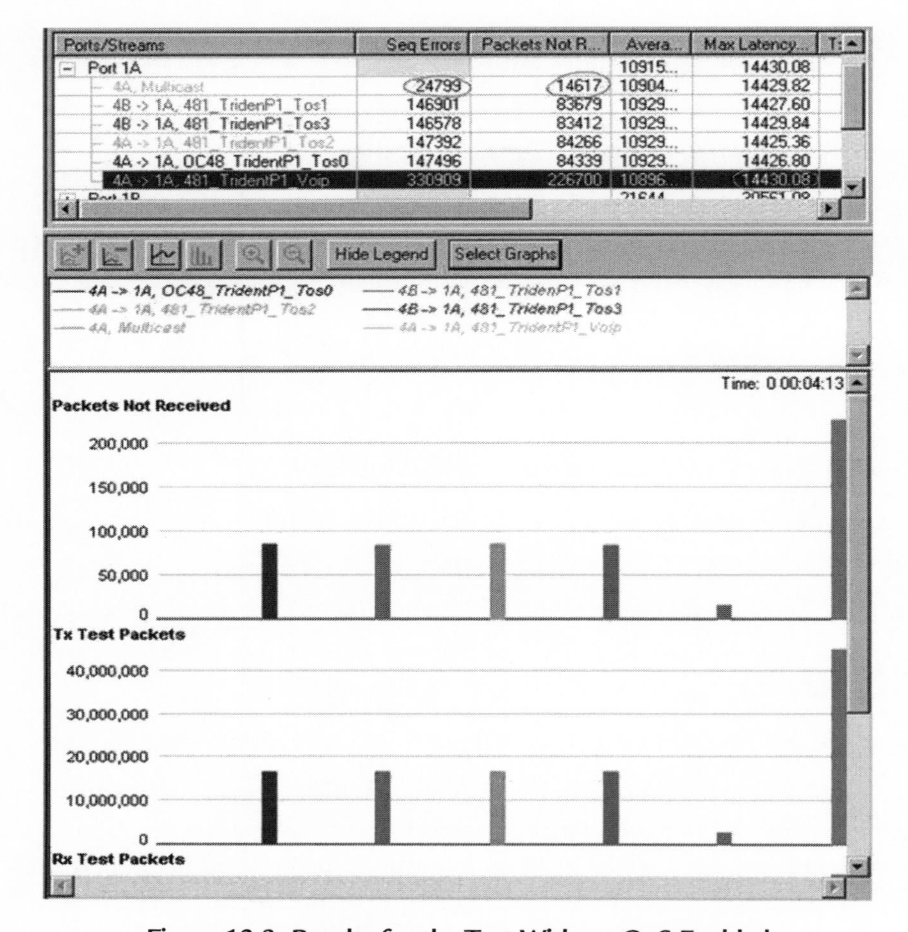

Figure 12.3: Results for the Test Without QoS Enabled

rate for a given class of traffic. Let's look at the illustration in Figure 12.3 to better understand this idea.

12.4 Test Procedure with QoS Enabled

Here we examine the impact on traffic, with QoS enabled in the network. The same set of classes illustrated in Figure 12.4 is used in this case, too. A more elaborate set of classes is used for the tests in this chapter compared to the SP FOO QoS classes used in previous chapters so that we have more variety in the outputs. However, the guidelines for validation are more important and hence this chapter focuses on illustrating that. The illustration is provided again here to provide for easy reference while reading.

Prior to enabling QoS, let's look at some of the requirements of each of the traffic classes and the appropriate treatment they require. Looking at Figure 12.4, we understand that the classes Network Control Messages, Voice, and Real-Time Nonvoice are highly critical, so they will

Class	Precedence	Traffic
Evil traffic	0	All nonidentified off-net traffic (off-net)
On net ···· on net	1	Traffic that stays within the SP network (on-net)
LSP services	2	LSP traffic, SMTP POP FTP DNS telnet SSH WWW HTTPS
SME	3	Enterprise customers, a gold service
Real-Time, nonvoice	4	TV, real-time gaming
Voice	5	RTP VoIP traffic
Network control messages	6-7	BGP and other control messages

Figure 12.4: Classes for Test

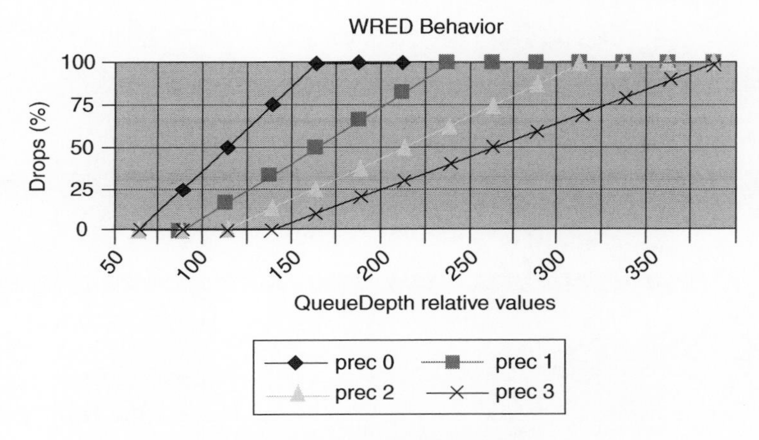

Figure 12.5: WRED Profiles

not be subject to any early drop characteristics such as WRED. The remaining four classes will be subject to WRED in the order of a higher to lower precedence. Therefore, the higher the precedence, the lower the drop rate during congestion.

In effect, it will allow a situation in which Precedence 0 packets will begin to drop during congestion. After that we would also start to drop Precedence 1 if the congestion continues, then Precedence 2 and finally Precedence 3. This concept is illustrated in Figure 12.5. The objective is to also have as low a latency as possible for voice traffic and finally nil drops for voice and multicast traffic.

> **NOTE 12.1: Configurations**
>
> QoS CLI configurations are not illustrated in this chapter since WRED thresholds and other characteristics of defining a QoS policy were detailed in other chapters.

Table 12.1 illustrates the various streams used for each of the test procedures detailed in this section.

Table 12.1: Summary of Test Details

Test	Voice and Multimedia Streams	Data Stream
Test 1	1 × 14 Mb/1 × 126 Mb	4 × 170 Mb
Test 2	1 × 14 Mb/1 × 126 Mb	4 × 180 Mb
Test 3	1 × 14 Mb/1 × 126 Mb	4 × 185 Mb
Test 4	1 × 14 Mb/1 × 126 Mb	4 × 200 Mb

NOTE 12.2: Test Results

The test results in this section are not necessarily a reflection of the true performance of any specific platform. All results should be viewed without any platform-specific reference or bias. For platform-specific performance values, refer to the Cisco CCO documentation.

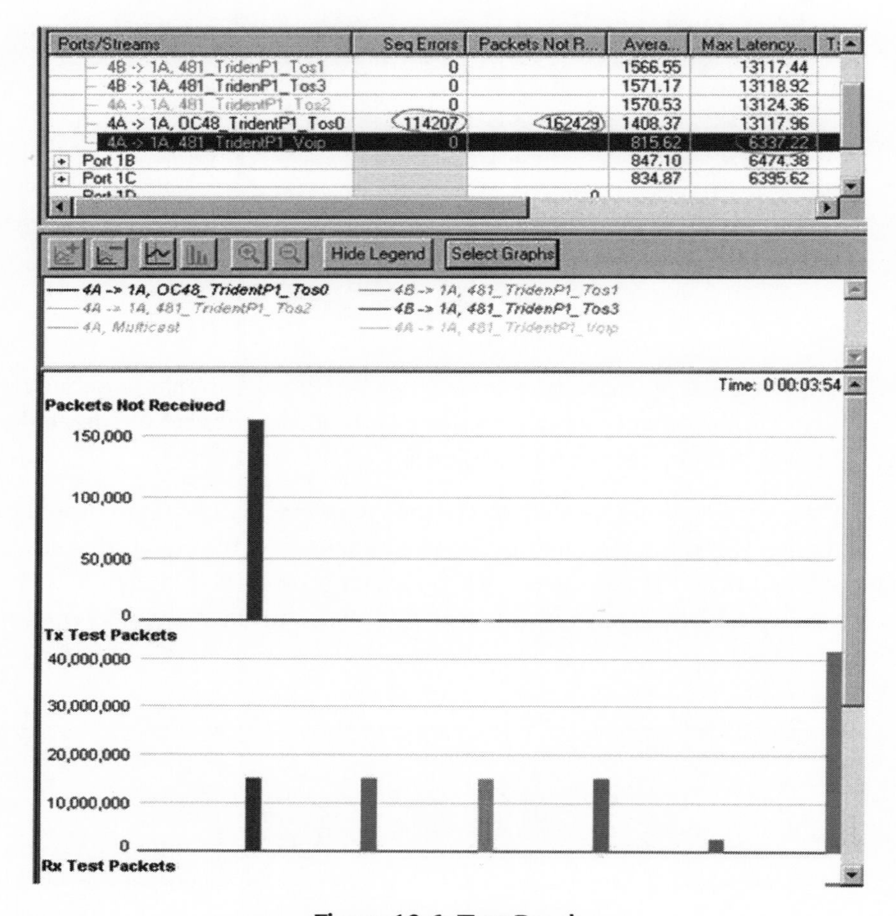

Figure 12.6: Test Result

12.4.1 Test Using Four Data Streams of 170 Mb Each

This test transmits four data streams of 170 Mb in addition to the voice and multicast streams distributed over the two OC-48 ingress interfaces, providing a total bandwidth of 920 Mb. Figure 12.6 shows that the Precedence 0 packets identified by the stream name *OC48_TridentP1_Tos0* in the fifth row begin to drop. The Sequence Errors and Packets Not Received columns circled indicate the number of packets that have dropped and received out of sequence. This is the expected behavior, since the system's congestion avoidance (WRED) mechanism starts to drop packets in the order of lowest to highest in terms of priority. This way higher-priority traffic is affected only after lower-priority counterparts have already been subjected to an aggressive drop rate.

The next two columns to examine are Average Latency, which indicates the average trend in delays for a given class, and Maximum Latency, which indicates the highest delay incurred for the specific class. In this test we can notice that the maximum latency of voice traffic is at 6 ms, as shown in Figure 12.6.

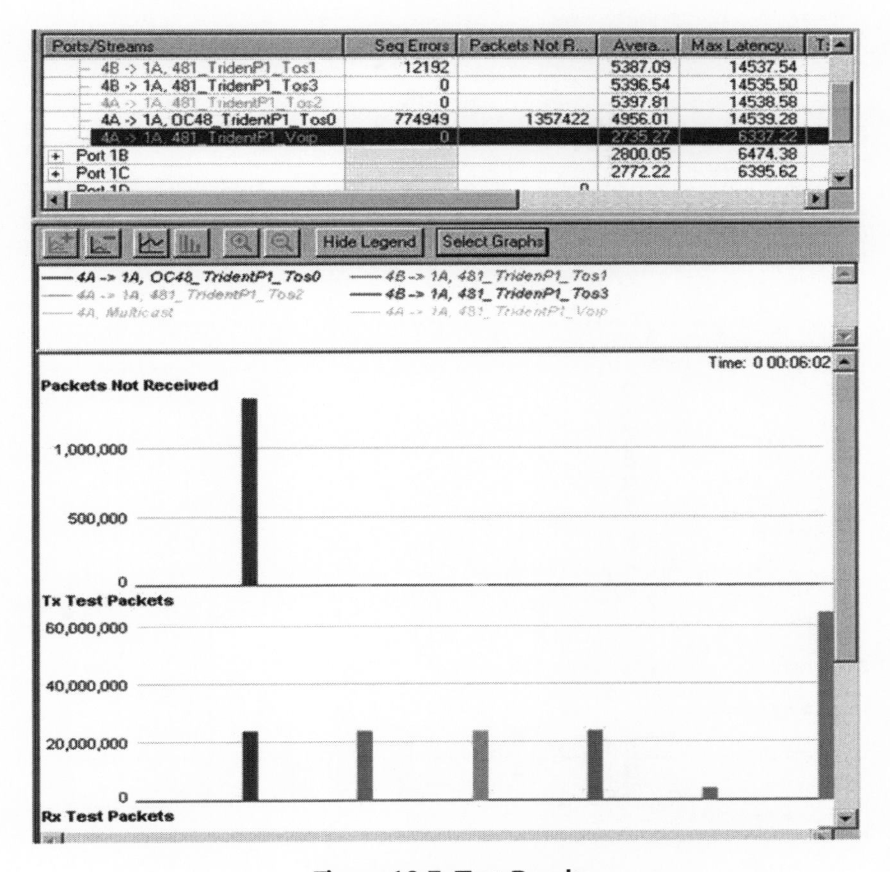

Figure 12.7: Test Result

12.4.2 Test Using Four Data Streams of 180 Mb Each

This test increases the four data streams to 180 Mb in addition to the voice and multicast stream distributed via the two OC-48 ingress interfaces, giving a total bandwidth of 960 Mb. We can see in Figure 12.7 that we start to drop packets from the Precedence 1 class as well. It is to be noted that the stream is not stopped before we start to increase it on the traffic generator. So the difference between the number of drops in Stream 0 and Stream 1 is cumulative. Once again, note that the maximum latency of voice traffic is at 6 ms, and there is no increase in this figure due to the additional congestion incurred.

12.4.3 Test Using Four Data Streams of 185 Mb Each

In this test the four data streams are increased further to 185 Mb, in addition to the voice and multicast stream distributed via the two OC-48 ingress interfaces, giving a total bandwidth of 980 Mb. Figure 12.8 shows that packets from the Precedence 2 class are beginning to be

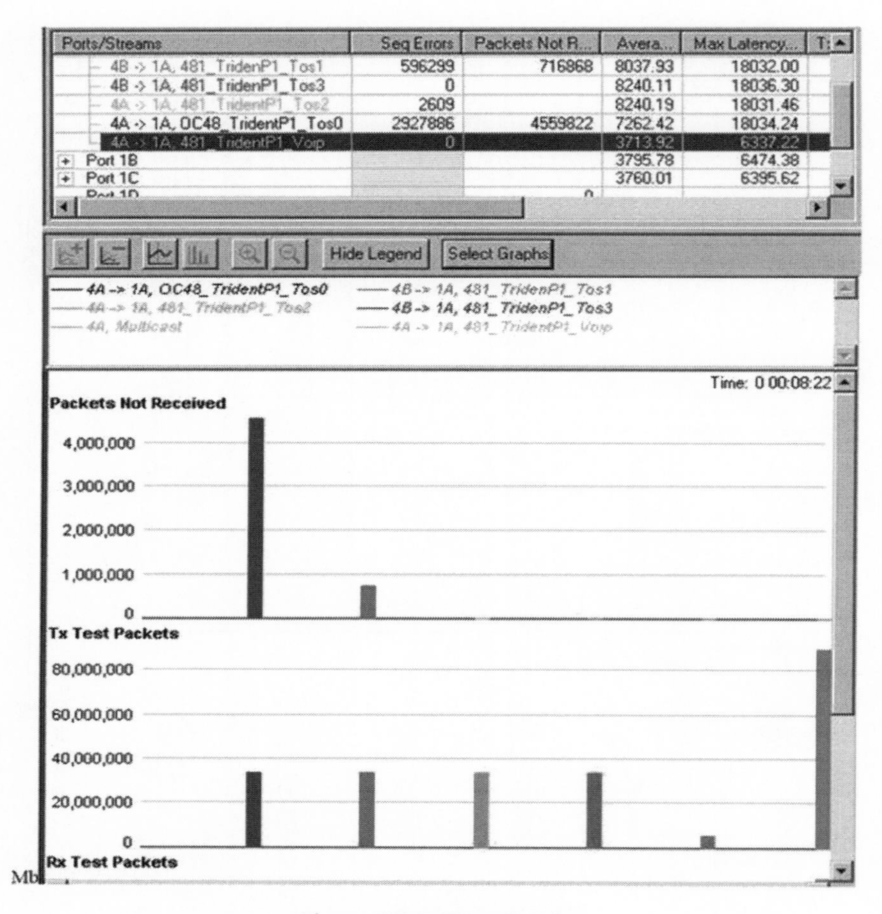

Figure 12.8: Test Result

dropped as well, in addition to Precedence 1 and Precedence 0. VoIP traffic is still subject to the same amount of latency without any increase.

12.4.4 Test Using Four Data Streams of 200 Mb Each

This test increases the four data streams further to 185 Mb, in addition to the voice and multicast stream distributed via the two OC-48 ingress interfaces, giving a total bandwidth of 1040 Mb (excess to 1 Gigabit Ethernet). We can see in Figure 12.9 that we marginally start to drop packets from the Precedence 3 class as well, in addition to Precedence 2, Precedence 1, and Precedence 0. VoIP traffic is still subject to the same amount of latency without any increase. Similarly, multicast traffic has no drops.

12.5 Stopping and Starting the Streams

When the streams are stopped and restarted to generate a graph that has the cleared counters and illustrate the statistics during congestion, it is evident that all the classes have packets that have been dropped, with the exception of VoIP and multicast. This is the primary objective

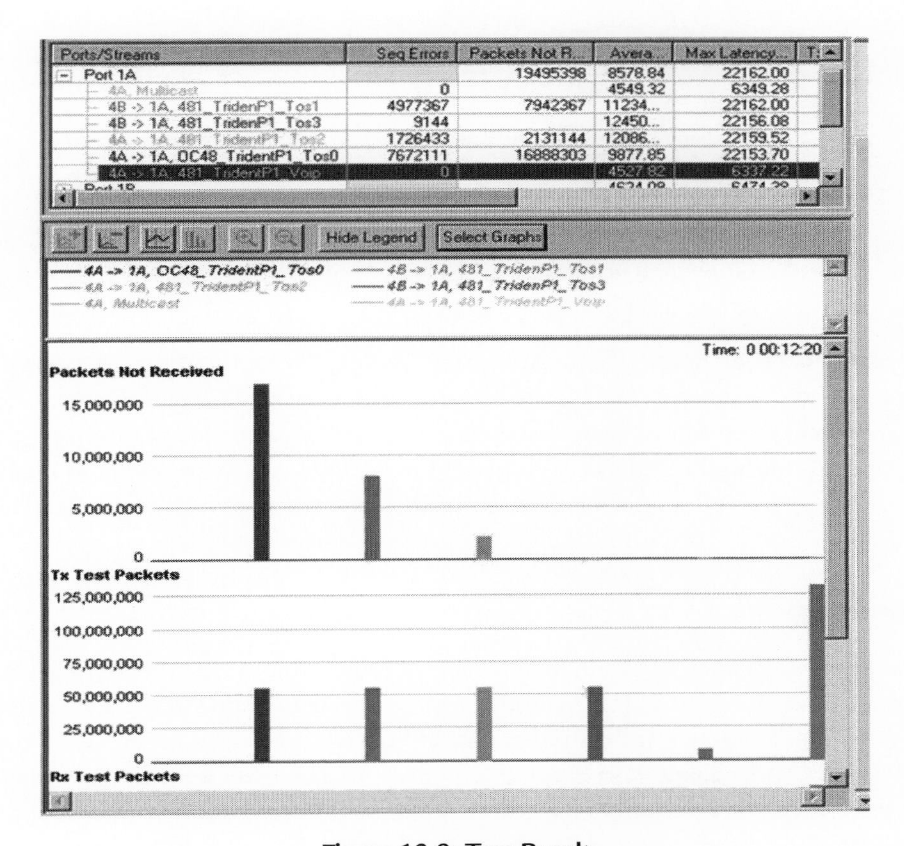

Figure 12.9: Test Result

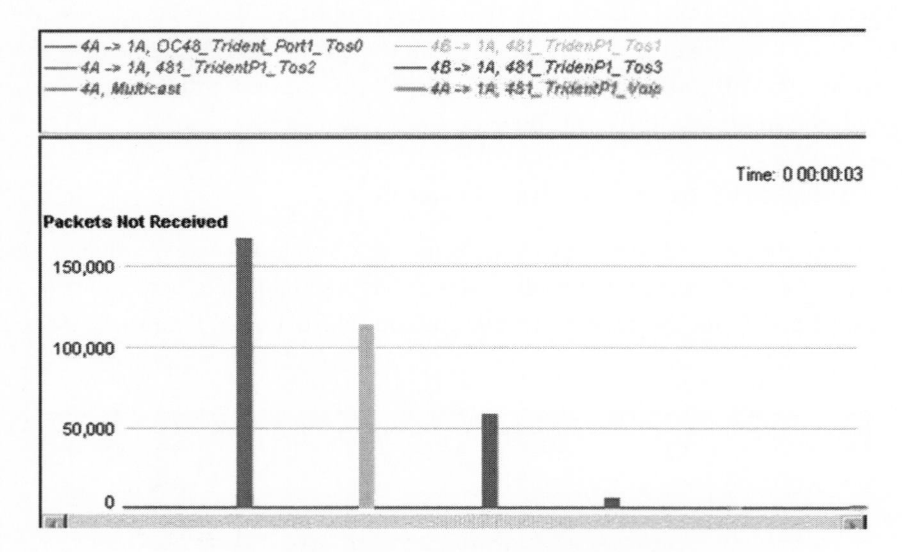

Figure 12.10: Summary of Test Results

of QoS—to protect sensitive and critical traffic during periods of congestion and network instability. This idea is illustrated in Figure 12.10.

Let's look at another illustration, just to summarize and capture our findings on when exactly traffic belonging to the various classes gets dropped. In Figure 12.11, we notice that, depending on the bandwidth of the streams, each class gets dropped. The sequence of drops begins with the lowest-priority traffic (Precedence 0) impacted first, followed by the higher to the highest. In this way, there is no random mechanism of traffic being dropped; instead, a selective choice is followed.

12.6 Summary

In this chapter we did a deep dive into the nuances of understanding how to measure the performance of QoS in regard to various traffic types. This is the most reliable way to gain insight into creating a baseline for various products (services packaged for end customers) that a carrier may offer. The chapter also highlighted the difference that QoS can offer wherein we notice that lack of QoS can result in all traffic types being affected during times of congestion and network stability. As we discussed in the early chapters of this book, QoS does help

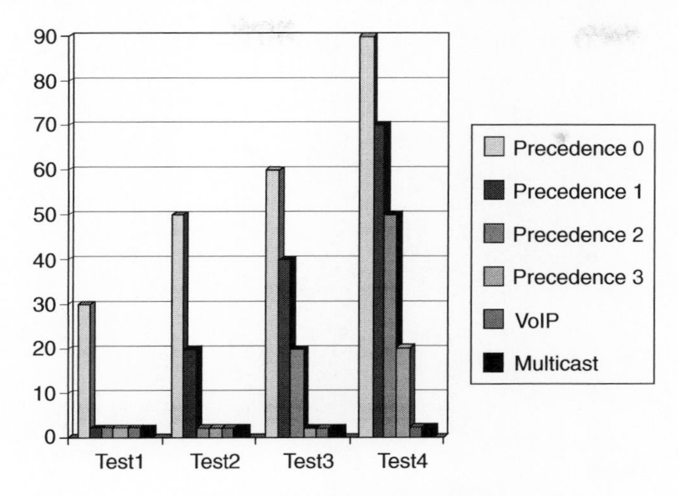

Figure 12.11: Drop Pattern

offer predictable and consistent performance for different traffic types, during both normal operations (times of network stability) as well as times of instability. This ensures that the service levels that a carrier's end customer experiences is consistent and does not take a model of "use when available," which is synonymous with the best-effort approach.

This chapter illustrated a test methodology using third-party tools and software to validate key metrics in a simulated environment, but it is important to note that test criteria and the actual setup of a simulated environment can vary based on the actual needs of a given carrier. For instance, the actual streams used might need to take into account details such as traffic types, mix, MTU sizes, and burstiness, to name a few. This would mean more customization to reflect actual needs. The results for the tests may vary based on the platform and line card used, wherein a certain platform type may offer 10 μs latency for the LLQ whereas another variant may impose 10 ms for packet forwarding. Therefore it is important to factor in these elements during the actual testing.

CHAPTER 13

Performance Monitoring and Measurement

13.1 Overview

This chapter introduces measurement of network performance in the context of an overall service-level agreement (SLA) framework. Performance measurement is a necessary component of service assurance in a service provider operational function.

QoS implementation within a next-generation network (NGN) is a means of enforcing the basic SLA parameters of the following:

- *Delay.* Often also referred to as *latency*, delay is made up of three components: propagation, serialization, and queuing. *Propagation delay* is the time it takes for the physical signal to traverse the path. *Serialization delay* is the time it takes to actually transmit the packet. *Queuing delay* is the time a packet spends in router queues.
- *Jitter.* Jitter is delay variation caused by queue depth variation in router devices or possibly load sharing across different paths with different time characteristics.
- *Packet loss.* The percentage of packets failing to reach the destination. Packet loss has minimal impact on UDP packet streams in general, with the exception of extremely loss-sensitive applications such as IPTV. TCP packet streams can be negatively impacted as the transmit window narrows.
- *Packets out of order.* This parameter is not commonly measured; however, it is important to many emerging applications, such as IPTV.

The SLA parameters may be based on traffic requirements or the premium paid by customers expecting preferential treatment. QoS is a set of technical features that enforces a PHB. This set of PHBs at each element within the traffic path gives the profile for latency, jitter, and packet loss for a given service, end to end.

NOTE 13.1: Out-of-Order Packet Detection

Out-of-order packets are generally a path issue where load balancing is employed. In some instances, a flawed router architecture can also lead to out-of-order packets across a single hop. The method for detection is limited to end-to-end techniques, as discussed later in this chapter.

The concept of an NGN is convergence of services such as voice, video, data, and signaling, with varying delivery requirements on a single network infrastructure, as discussed in Chapter 1. The monitoring, measurement, and reporting of the various services against the expected SLA parameters are essential for the following reasons:

- Troubleshooting faults related to service performance
- Proactive capacity planning to ensure that predictable network performance is maintained over time
- Billing customers
- Answering customer queries on actual versus contracted service performance

SLA monitoring and measurement are a reflection of the QoS framework implemented within a network. The term *measurement* refers to the tools and framework used to collect the raw data associated with SLA performance. *Monitoring* refers to the tools that collate, interpret, and report on the actual performance of the network based on the raw data available from the measurement tools. Note that many service providers implement more than one measurement and monitoring technique, depending on requirements across proactive, formal reporting and reactive fault isolation.

This chapter gives an overview of the more popular options for measuring performance in SP IP networks. Each of the approaches is discussed with emphasis on the tools available for measurement rather than the management platforms used to collate, interpret, and present the data.

13.2 The Importance of Performance Measurement and Monitoring

Chapter 1 explored the evolution of networks toward consolidated infrastructure carrying traffic with varying SLA requirements. In many cases the traffic will include enterprise services for which contracts exist between the SP and the customer, defining performance parameters and penalties when these SLAs are not met. Even though there might be no formal, contractual agreement with the broader user base, such as Internet or wireless users, expectations regarding service can remain and may lead to customers shifting to other providers in the event of dissatisfaction.

This evolution has seen the advent of networks with complex and stringent QoS frameworks to deliver the service SLAs while maintaining efficient use of expensive network resources such as bandwidth and routing devices.

Figure 13.1 shows examples of the SLA requirements that can be expected for end-user service types.

In a converged NGN, the SP may also be carrying traffic that includes mobile 3G, as discussed in Chapter 5. The SLA requirements for 3GPP QoS traffic types for Global Roaming eXchange (GRX) are as shown in Figure 13.2.

In this diagram, the Traffic Handling Priority (THP) and Service Data Unit (SDU) are as defined by the 3GPP standards.

Traffic Type	Maximum Packet Loss	Maximum One-Way Latency	Max. Jitter
VoIP	1%	200 ms	30 ms
Videoconferencing	1%	200 ms	30 ms
IPTV broadcast video	0.001%	250 ms	50 ms

Figure 13.1: Multimedia SLA Requirements

3GPP QoS Information		DiffServ PHB	DSCP	QoS Requirement on GRX				Service Example
Traffic Class	THP			Max Delay	Max Jitter	Packet Loss	SDU Error Ratio	
Conversational	N/A	EF	101110	20 ms	5 ms	0.5%	10^{-6}	VoIP, Video Conferencing
Streaming	N/A	$AF4_1$	100010	40 ms	5 ms	0.5%	10^{-6}	Audio/Video Streaming
Interactive	1	$AF3_1$	011010	250 ms	N/A	0.1%	10^{-8}	Transactional Services
	2	$AF2_1$	010010	300 ms	N/A	0.1%	10^{-8}	Web Browsing
	3	$AF1_1$	001010	350 ms	N/A	0.1%	10^{-8}	Telnet
Background	N/A	BE	000000	400 ms	N/A	0.1%	10^{-8}	Email Download

Figure 13.2: QoS Mapping for 3G Data from GSMA PRD IR.34

These SLA parameters are delivered through the QoS implementation within the network infrastructure. As shown in the examples, these parameters can be very specific per service and must be accurately monitored to ensure that SLAs are met by the QoS framework. Accurate measurement and monitoring are essential for many aspects of the operational life cycle, from reactive network operation through service fulfillment and assurance.

The basic components of operating an NGN are operation, maintenance, fulfillment, and assurance:

- *Operation.* The set of services essential to manage the IP network in an optimal and secure manner. These services provide the day-to-day technical supervision of the network infrastructure to proactively identify faults to be addressed and reactively handle reported faults from network elements.
- *Maintenance.* The set of services to maintain the network and execute operational changes in an efficient, consistent, and transparent manner. This includes all activities for the

execution of proactive and reactive maintenance tasks to ensure that services provided to customers are continuously available and performing to SLA performance levels.

- *Fulfillment.* The set of services to provide requested products and services to network customers in a timely and efficient manner, ensuring the expected level of customer satisfaction. These services provision and activate services and network parameters.
- *Assurance.* This set of services ensures that network quality and service delivery meet the requirements of the service as defined in the SLAs. This process manages the SLAs and reports service performance to the service provider and customer.

NOTE 13.2: Performance Measurement for Network Security Attack Mitigation

With the escalation of security incidents on the Internet and the convergence of services, including Internet, onto a single NGN infrastructure, effective attack detection and response are essential to ensure that SLAs are maintained. Performance measurement can characterize expected, granular network behavior, allowing timely identification of network attacks as part of a cohesive security strategy.

Monitoring and measuring performance span each of these operational categories as follows:

- *Operation.* Proactive fault identification through performance monitoring and measurement. Fault isolation for specific services is based on performance monitoring information.
- *Maintenance.* Performance monitoring provides baseline understanding of network behavior, enabling efficient and proactive capacity planning of expensive transmission resources.
- *Fulfillment.* Prior to connection of a new customer or service with SLA requirements, the impact to the existing link utilization within a given class of service must be understood based on accurate performance monitoring and measurement.
- *Assurance.* Performance monitoring and measurement are the cornerstone of service assurance. The monitoring information is required to prove that SLAs have been met as contractually agreed.

The mechanisms chosen for performance monitoring and measurement must be scalable and granular enough to give the information required in a timely and accurate manner. This must be achieved without significantly impacting performance of the network in terms of bandwidth or network router and switch CPU.

13.3 Performance Measurement Framework

Performance monitoring and measurement in an NGN are essential elements of effective service delivery, as discussed in the previous sections. To achieve a scalable, timely, and accurate outcome, a structured, consistent framework for measurement is required.

This section presents a framework for understanding and comparing the measurement techniques available to the service provider. Note that this framework must be part of a wider process flow, including monitoring, if the output of the measurement is to be appropriately understood and acted on.

Measuring the performance of an IP network can be broken into four basic areas:

- *Sampling method.* Exactly what traffic is measured and how?
- *Collection method.* How is the sampled traffic collected for correlation?
- *Scope of measurement.* What aspects of performance are measured?
- *Perspective of measurement.* Is the perspective from the user service or the network?

Each of these areas has implementation options with associated advantages and disadvantages. Table 13.1 summarizes options within each performance measurement category, giving a

Table 13.1: Performance Measurement Framework Categories

Measurement Category	Category Options	Definition	Advantages	Disadvantages
Sampling	Observed/ passive	Service and end-user network performance is monitored by measuring specific, actual application traffic flows in real time	Most accurate for live application traffic on a specified transmission link	Limited to measuring: - Preconfigured traffic types, which might not be present on the network at all times - Preconfigured traffic patterns, which might not reflect patterns for new or future applications
	Synthetic/ active	Network traffic is generated specifically for the purpose of measuring network performance	Measures performance: - Between any two points in the network - Controllable, on a continuous basis - By traffic class based on IP precedence marking	Only an approximation for performance of live traffic. Requires additional traffic generated in the network CPU load on sender and receiver devices can give false performance data
Collection	Embedded agent	Mechanisms for collecting performance statistics are integrated into the communication device	Gathers metrics that cannot be observed externally; end-to-end monitoring possible	Device performance implications when collection is enabled

Continued

Table 13.1 Continued

Measurement Category	Category Options	Definition	Advantages	Disadvantages
	External probe	Mechanisms for collection of performance statistics are through a purpose-built and dedicated device	No performance impact on network devices; scalable approach as network and services grow	More hardware to administer; observed statistics limited to points of deployment
Scope	Device/link	Performance measurement based on analysis of specific device or device interface	Detailed application performance monitoring of critical network links	Difficult to correlate collected data to get end-to-end view
	End to end/path	Performance measurement based on analysis of parameters across multiple network hops from end to end	Closely reflects end-user experience, enabling accurate troubleshooting, capacity planning; can detect out-of-order packet issues	Detailed knowledge of relevant end-to-end paths is needed; compromise on selection of paths likely
				Difficult to scale in NGN environment
Perspective	User	Measurement based on performance statistics measured at the end-user device	Most accurate measurement of end-user experience	Scale and distribution issues; possibly intrusive on end-user device Compromise on selection of end users likely
	Network	Measurement based on performance statistics measured in network devices	Easier to deploy and nonintrusive to the end user; identifies network performance issue	Approximation of end-user experience only

high-level description of each implementation option and associated advantages and disadvantages of each approach.

Clearly, collecting the data alone is not adequate for a full performance measurement framework. The data produced from the measurement tools must be correlated and presented in a meaningful and timely manner by an appropriate monitoring tool. As previously noted, this chapter focuses on the measurement aspects rather than the monitoring tools. Monitoring tool options are given for each of the measurement techniques explored here; however, further details will not be presented in this chapter.

Subsequent sections discuss a variety of tools and features available to the service provider for implementing performance measurement. We'll compare each of these options with the framework as defined in this section.

13.4 Performance Measurement Options

As previously discussed, *performance measurement* refers to the tools and mechanisms used in a network to measure performance parameters. A variety of options are available to a service provider seeking to monitor performance in the network.

The more popular measurement options are:

- Simple Network Management Protocol (SNMP)
- NetFlow
- IP SLAs
- Network-Based Application Recognition (NBAR)
- Cisco Command-Line Interface (CLI)

Each of these options is explored in the following sections. The options are compared to the performance measurement framework as defined in the previous section, giving details of implementation within an SP network where relevant.

13.5 Simple Network Management Protocol

SNMP was developed in 1988 as a management-enabling protocol running at the application layer. SNMP is a simple, robust, and mature technology that when introduced was actually intended only as an interim solution.

In SNMP, there is generally a collection of devices within a system to be managed and one or more associated systems managing them. A software component called an *agent* runs on each managed device and reports information via SNMP to the managing systems.

SNMP agents offer management data on the managed devices as variables, but the protocol also permits active management tasks, including modifying and applying a new configuration. The managing system can retrieve the information from the agent using the GET, GETNEXT, and GETBULK commands. Additionally, the agent can push data to the managing system using the TRAP or INFORM commands. Management systems can send configuration changes using the SET protocol operation to actively manage a system.

The variables accessible via SNMP are organized in hierarchies called *management information bases* (MIBs). SNMP is part of the Internet network management architecture. This architecture is described in the following sections.

SNMP allows network operators to facilitate the exchange of management information between devices for the following basic goals:

- Manage network performance
- Monitor network activities
- Find and solve network problems

SNMP is a connectionless communication protocol based on User Datagram Protocol (UDP). SNMP agents typically listen on UDP port 161 for information requests, with traps generally sent on port 162.

The components of SNMP network management fall into three broad categories:

- Managed devices (such as a router or switch)
- SNMP agents and MIBs, including remote monitoring
- (RMON) MIBs, which run on managed devices
- SNMP management applications that communicate with agents to get statistics and alerts from the managed devices

An SNMP management application, together with the host it runs on, is commonly referred to as a Network Management System (NMS).

According to the parameters defined in the "Performance Measurement Framework" section, Table 13.2 gives an overview of IP SLA as a measurement tool.

SNMP supports the following performance-monitoring MIBs:

- CISCO-CLASS-BASED-QOS-MIB (MQC)
- CISCO-PORT-QOS-MIB (switches)
- CISCO-CAR-MIB (legacy configuration)

Additionally, SNMP provides access to data generated by the following technologies with the associated MIBs:

- NBAR-CISCO-NBAR-PROTOCOL-DISCOVERY-MIB
- IP SLA-CISCO-RTTMON-MIB
- NetFlow-CISCO-NETFLOW-MIB

Table 13.2: SNMP Performance Measurement Overview

Measurement Category	Category Implementation	Definition
Sampling	Observed/passive	Service and end-user network performance is monitored by measuring specific, actual application traffic flows in real time. *Note:* SNMP allows collection of statistics from IP SLA, which is an active sampling technology.
Collection	Embedded agent	Mechanisms for collection of performance statistics are integrated into the communication device.
Scope	Device/link	Performance measurement based on analysis of a specific device or device interface.
Perspective	Network	Measurement based on performance statistics measured in network devices.

Refer to the relevant sections for NBAR, IP SLA, and NetFlow for information regarding SNMP data access.

13.5.1 SNMP Overview

As specified in Internet RFCs and various best-practices documents, a network management system comprises the following:

- *Network elements.* Hardware devices such as computers, routers, and terminal servers that are connected to form networks.
- *Agents.* Software modules that reside in network elements. They collect and store management information, such as the number of error packets received by a network element.
- *Managed objects.* Characteristics of a network element that can be managed. For example, a list of currently active TCP circuits in a particular host computer is a managed object. Managed objects differ from *variables*, which are particular object instances. Using our example, an object instance is a single active TCP circuit in a particular host computer. Managed objects can be scalar (defining a single object instance) or tabular (defining multiple, related instances).
- *Management information base (MIB).* A collection of managed objects residing in a virtual information store. Collections of related managed objects are defined in specific MIB modules.
- *Syntax notation.* A language used to describe an MIB's managed objects in a machine-independent format. Consistent use of a syntax notation allows various types of computers to share information. Internet management systems use a subset of the International Organization for Standardization (ISO) Open System Interconnection (OSI) Abstract Syntax Notation (ASN.1) to define both the packets exchanged by the management protocol and the objects that are to be managed.
- *Structure of Management Information (SMI).* Defines the rules for describing management information. The SMI is defined using ASN.1.
- *Network management stations (NMSs).* Sometimes called *consoles*, these devices execute management applications that monitor and control network elements. Physically, NMSs are usually engineering workstation-caliber computers with fast CPUs, megapixel color displays, substantial memory, and abundant disk space. At least one NMS must be present in each managed environment.
- *Parties.* Defined in the SNMPv2 standards as logical SNMPv2 entities that can initiate or receive SNMPv2 communication. Each SNMPv2 party comprises a single, unique party identity, a logical network location, a single authentication protocol, and a single privacy protocol. SNMPv2 messages are communicated between two parties. An SNMPv2 entity can define multiple parties, each with different parameters. For example, different parties can use different authentication and/or privacy protocols.

- *Management protocol.* Used to convey management information between agents and NMSs. SNMP is the Internet community's de facto standard management protocol.

The SNMP protocol operates at the application layer (Layer 7) of the OSI model. It specifies five core Protocol Data Units (PDUs) as follows:

- *GET REQUEST.* Used to retrieve a piece of management information.
- *GETNEXT REQUEST*. Used iteratively to retrieve sequences of management information.
- *GET RESPONSE.* Used by the agent to respond with data to *get* and *set* requests from the manager.
- *SET REQUEST*. Used to initialize and make a change to a value of the network element.
- *TRAP*. Used to report an alert or other asynchronous event about a managed subsystem.

In SNMPv1, asynchronous event reports are called *traps,* whereas they are called *notifications* in later versions of SNMP. In SMIv1 MIB modules, traps are defined using the *TRAP-TYPE* macro; in SMIv2 MIB modules, traps are defined using the *NOTIFICATION-TYPE* macro.

Additional PDUs were added in SNMPv2, as follows:

- *GETBULK REQUEST*. A faster iterator used to retrieve sequences of management information.
- *INFORM*. Similar to a trap, but the receiver must respond with an acknowledgment *RESPONSE* message.
- *REPORT*. Definable by an administrative framework.

13.5.2 Management Information Bases

SNMP is a protocol for communicating management information; as such, it does not define which variables a managed system should support. Rather, SNMP relies on an extensible design, whereby the available information is defined by MIBs. MIBs describe the structure of the management data of a device subsystem; they use a hierarchical namespace containing object identifiers (OIDs). Each OID identifies a variable that can be read or set via the SNMP. MIBs use the standard notation as defined by ASN.1.

The MIB hierarchy is typically depicted as a tree with a nameless root, the levels of which are assigned by various organizations, as shown in Figure 13.3.

The top-level MIB OIDs belong to various standards organizations; lower-level OIDs are allocated by associated organizations and vendors. This model permits management across all layers of the OSI reference model, extending into applications such as databases, email, and the Java EE reference model, because MIBs can be defined for all such area-specific information and operations.

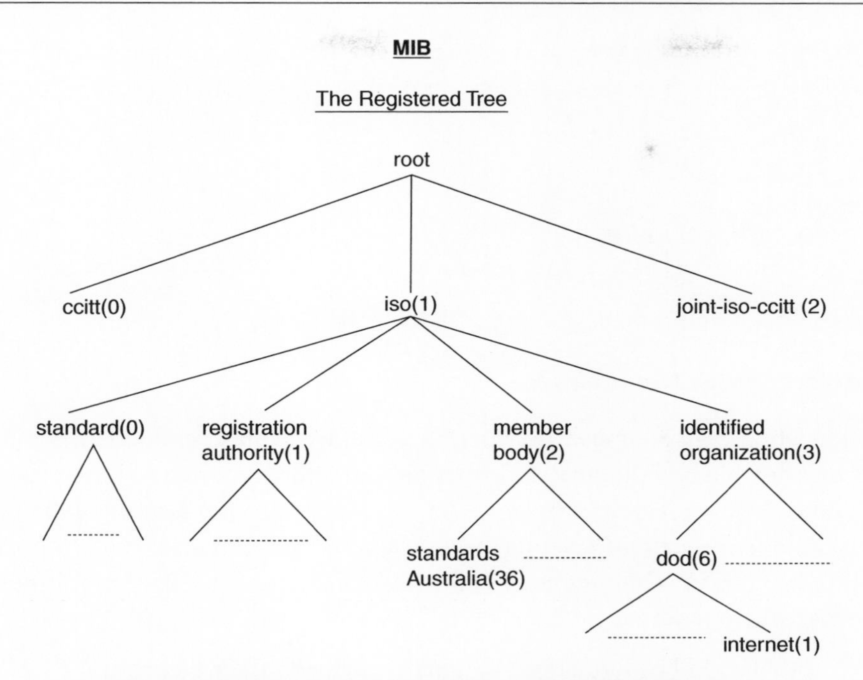

Figure 13.3: SNMP Management Information Base Tree Format

A managed object, which can be referred to as an *MIB object* or simply an *MIB*, is one of any number of specific characteristics of a managed device. Managed objects are made up of one or more object instances (identified by their OIDs), which are essentially variables.

The SNMP standards define two types of managed objects:

- Scalar objects that define a single object instance
- Tabular objects that define multiple related object instances that are grouped in MIB tables

An example of a managed object is *atInput*, which is a scalar object containing a single object instance, the integer value that indicates the total number of input AppleTalk packets on a router interface. The *atinput* object is detailed here:

```
iso (1) . org (3) . dod (6) . internet (1) . private (4) .
enterprises (1) . cisco (9)
 |
 - -- temporary (3)
  |
  + -- tmpdecnet (1)
  |
  + -- tmpxns (2)
  |
  - -- tmpappletalk (3)
  ||
  || -- atInput (1)
```

```
Specific Object Information
Object atInput
OID 1.3.6.1.4.1.9.3.3.1
Type INTEGER
Permission read-only
Status mandatory
MIB OLD-CISCO-APPLETALK-MIB
Description "Total input count of number of AppleTalk packets."
```

An OID uniquely identifies a managed object in the MIB hierarchy.

13.5.3 Abstract Syntax Notation One

In telecommunications and computer networking, Abstract Syntax Notation One (ASN.1) is a standard and flexible notation that describes data structures for representing, encoding, transmitting, and decoding data. It provides a set of formal rules for describing the structure of objects that are independent of machine-specific encoding techniques and is a precise, formal notation that removes ambiguities. This gives a well-known reference for interoperation between vendors where required.

ASN.1 is a joint ISO and ITU-T standard, originally defined in 1984 as part of CCITT X.409:1984. ASN.1 moved to its own standard, X.208, in 1988 due to wide applicability. The substantially revised 1995 version is covered by the X.680 series. An adapted subset of ASN.1, Structure of Management Information (SMI), is specified in SNMP to define sets of related MIB objects; these sets are termed *MIB modules*.

13.5.4 Simple Network Management Protocol Version 1

The SNMPv1 SMI specifies the use of a number of SMI-specific data types, divided into two categories as follows:

- *Simple data types*. Three unique values are the integer data type (a whole number with a sign from –231 to 230), the octet string (from 0 to 65535), and the object ID derived from the set of all object identifiers allocated according to the rules specified in ASN.1.
- *Application-wide data types*. There are seven available in the SNMPv1 SMI: network address, counters, gauges, time ticks, opaques, integers, and unsigned integers.

The SNMPv1 SMI defines highly structured MIB tables that are used to group the instances of a tabular object (that is, an object that contains multiple variables). Tables are composed of zero or more rows that are indexed in a way that allows SNMP to retrieve or alter an entire row with a single *Get, GetNext,* or *Set* command.

13.5.5 Simple Network Management Protocol Version 2

The SNMPv2 SMI is described in RFC-2578. Version 2 has additions and enhancements to the SNMPv1 SMI-specific data types, including additional bit strings, network addresses, and counters.

Bit strings are defined only in SNMPv2 and comprise zero or more named bits that specify a value. Network addresses represent an address from a particular protocol family beyond IPv4. Counters are nonnegative integers that increase until they reach a maximum value and then return to zero. In SNMPv1, a 32-bit counter size is specified. In SNMPv2, 32-bit and 64-bit counters are defined and allowed.

The SNMPv2 SMI also specifies information modules, which define a group of related definitions. Three types of SMI information modules exist:

- *MIB modules* contain definitions of interrelated managed objects.
- *Compliance statements* provide a systematic way to describe a group of managed objects that must be implemented for conformance to a standard.
- *Capability statements* indicate the precise level of support that an agent claims with respect to an MIB group. An NMS can adjust its behavior toward agents according to the capability statements associated with each agent.

13.5.6 Simple Network Management Protocol Version 3

SNMPv3 is defined by RFC-3411–RFC-3418 (also known as STD0062). SNMPv3 added security and remote configuration enhancements to the SNMP implementation standards. SNMPv3 was standardized and introduced in 2004. The IETF has designated SNMPv3 a full Internet standard, the highest maturity level for an RFC.

SNMPv3 provides the following important security features:

- Message integrity to ensure packet is received as it was sent
- Authentication at the management tool to verify that the message is from a valid source
- Encryption of SNMP packets at the source agent

13.5.7 Cisco-Class-Based-QoS-MIB

The Cisco-Class-Based-QoS-MIB is the primary accounting mechanism for QoS configurations based on MQC. The Cisco-Class-Based-QoS-MIB enables read-only access to active MQC configurations for access to statistics, where *active* refers to any configured policy that has been attached to one or more interfaces on a router device.

This MIB does not allow configuration; this must be done through MQC. There will be no *ciscoCBQosMIB* statistics if QoS is not configured or QoS is configured but not via MQC, or if the device is not running IOS or IOS-XR.

The Cisco-Class-Based-QoS-MIB supports the tables as shown in Figure 13.4.

As shown, there are two broad categories in the MIB tables. The first is the configuration information; the second is the actual statistics for the applied configuration. An example of the *cbQosClassMapstats* table use is shown in Figure 13.5.

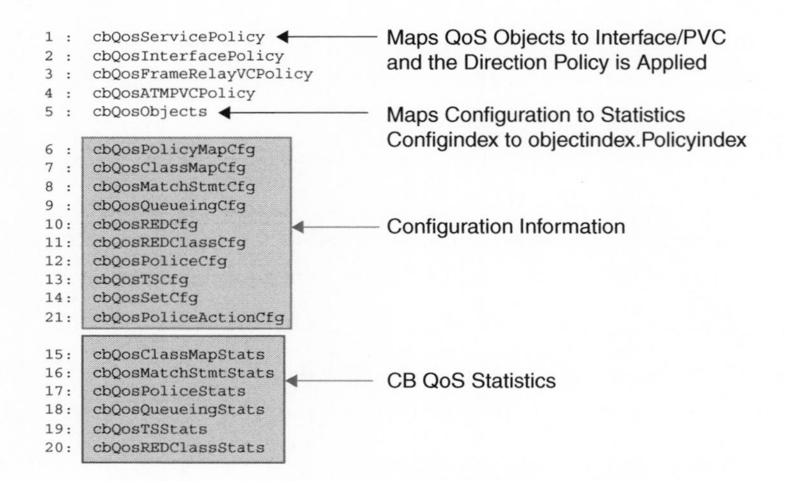

Figure 13.4: CISCO-CLASS-BASED-QoS MIB

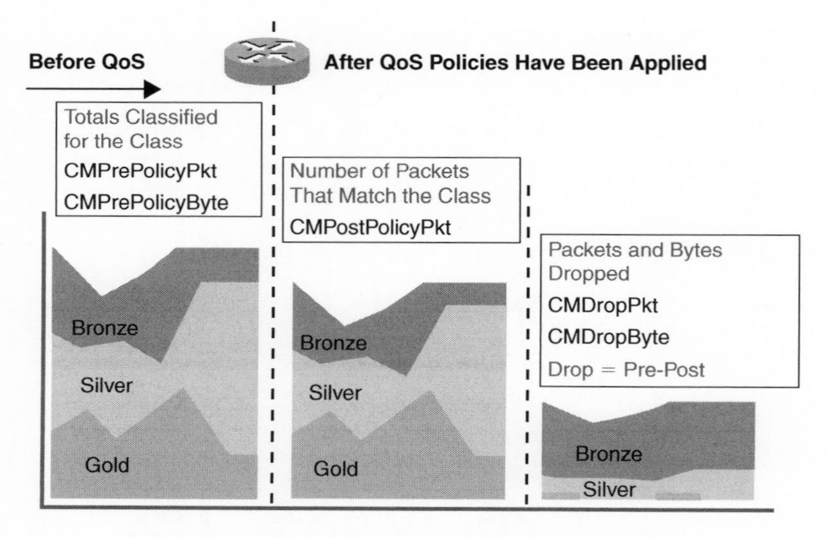

Figure 13.5: CISCO-CLASS-BASED-QoS MIB Tables

Various tables are available for measuring packets accepted on an interface, matched to a given policy, and any that are dropped in the process. With an appropriate tool for collating and interpreting these data, the operator has a powerful method for understanding network behavior.

13.5.8 SNMP Management Platforms

A variety of platforms are available for SNMP. Cisco provides the QoS Policy Manager, IP Solution Center, and CNS Performance Engine. Additionally, partners including Concord eHealth and InfoVista have support for Cisco and other vendor MIBs.

Table 13.3: NetFlow Performance Measurement Overview

Measurement Category	Category Implementation	Definition
Sampling	Observed/passive	Service and end-user network performance is monitored by measuring specific, actual application traffic flows in real time
Collection	Embedded agent	Mechanisms for collection of performance statistics are integrated into the communication device
Scope	Device/link	Performance measurement based on analysis of specific device or device interface
Perspective	Network	Measurement based on performance statistics measured in network devices

13.6 NetFlow

NetFlow was developed and patented by Cisco Systems in 1996. NetFlow has subsequently been implemented by other vendors and is recognized as the *de facto* standard for network traffic measurement in the communications industry.

NetFlow is a flexible, powerful feature that enables network and security monitoring, network planning, traffic analysis, and accounting through the collection of statistics on real data flows in the network. NetFlow is an embedded feature within Cisco IOS.

According to the parameters defined in the "Performance Measurement Framework" section, Table 13.3 gives an overview of IP SLA as a measurement tool.

NetFlow allows performance reporting and operational functions as follows:

- Application and network usage
- Network productivity and utilization of network resources
- The impact of changes to the network
- Network anomaly and security vulnerabilities

Cisco IOS NetFlow enables operators to understand who, what, when, where, and how network traffic is flowing. NetFlow allows network behavior to be baselined and completely understood, giving advantages in change control, troubleshooting, and proactive recognition of anomalies caused by security attacks.

13.6.1 NetFlow Technical Overview

SNMP MIBs were the preferred tool for monitoring traffic use in networks prior to the advent of NetFlow technology. SNMP gives insight into bandwidth usage, including per-class traffic, but the granularity is lacking for more advanced operational functions.

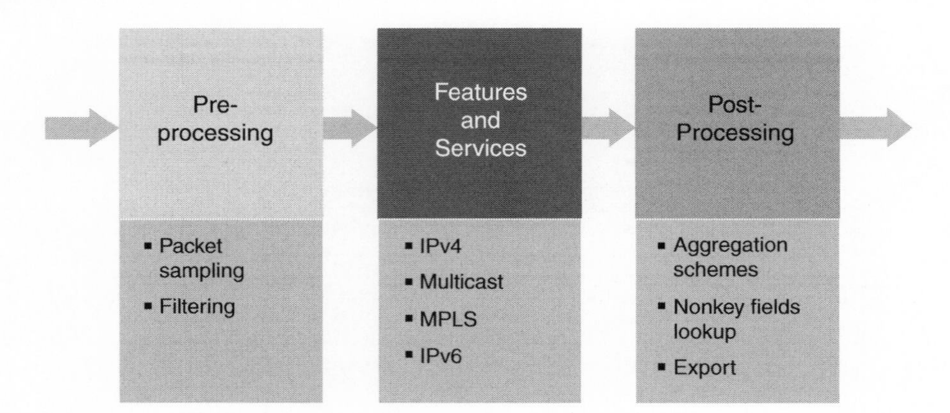

Figure 13.6: NetFlow Processing Order

Traffic is processed in a specific, defined order to ensure consistency and scalability, as shown in Figure 13.6.

The first step is preprocessing in the router. Packets are sampled at the configured or default rate and filtered according to defined criteria, if required. Generally the provider will choose an acceptable sampling rate rather than processing every packet. One hundred percent processing on high-speed routers particularly can cause performance issues.

The next step is categorizing the sampled traffic based on features and services such as IP version and unicast versus multicast.

The final step is the preparation for exporting the data according to the requirements and collector-supported standards.

Figure 13.7 gives an overview of NetFlow operation in an IP network.

Traffic is sampled and categorized as it transits a router with information stored in memory. Parameters shown at left in the figure may be stored as part of a basic IP traffic flow, which is actually defined by seven parameters referred to as *key fields* on Cisco router platforms.

13.6.2 NetFlow Flow Records

NetFlow maintains per-flow data in flow records, including the key fields and nonkey fields, which include value fields and lookup fields. The key and nonkey fields are defined as follows:

- *Key fields.* Key fields define the flow record. The seven key fields that constitute a flow are source IP address, destination IP address, source port, destination port, Layer 3 protocol, ToS, and input interface. An attribute in the packet is used to create a flow record. If the set of key field values is unique, a new flow is created.
- *Nonkey fields.* These include Value fields and a Lookup field, which are not used to define a flow; instead they provide additional information of use to the operator. Value

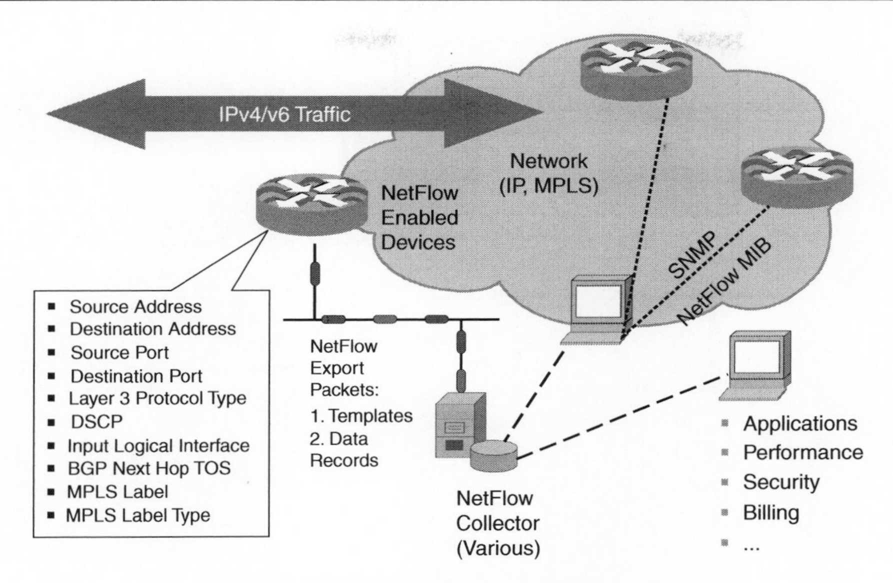

Figure 13.7: NetFlow Architecture

fields are additional fields and counters, such as packet and byte counter and start and stop time stamps. Lookup fields are additional information that are added to the flow, such as next hop address, source/destination AS number, and so on.

> **NOTE 13.3: Traffic Flow on Catalyst Switch/Routers**
>
> Catalyst-based platforms allow flexible definition of traffic flows based on set formats. Refer to the "Catalyst Flow Definition" section later in this chapter for details.

A traditional IP flow with the seven key fields is as shown in Figure 13.8.

NetFlow takes the following three basic steps to identify, store, and export a flow:

1. Inspect a packet's seven key fields and identify the values (for router platforms as previously noted).
2. If the set of key field values is unique, create a flow record or cache entry.
3. Export the flow to the collector. (Prerequisites for export are discussed later in this chapter.)

Figure 13.9 gives an example of two packets transiting a router device.

As shown, two packets are received on the ingress interface of the router device. The first packet is sampled, recognized as a flow, creating a flow record in cache memory. Note that as discussed, although the flow is identified based on the seven key fields, additional information associated with the flow may also be stored in the cached flow record. Likewise, the second packet is sampled and inspected, and an additional flow record is created in cache.

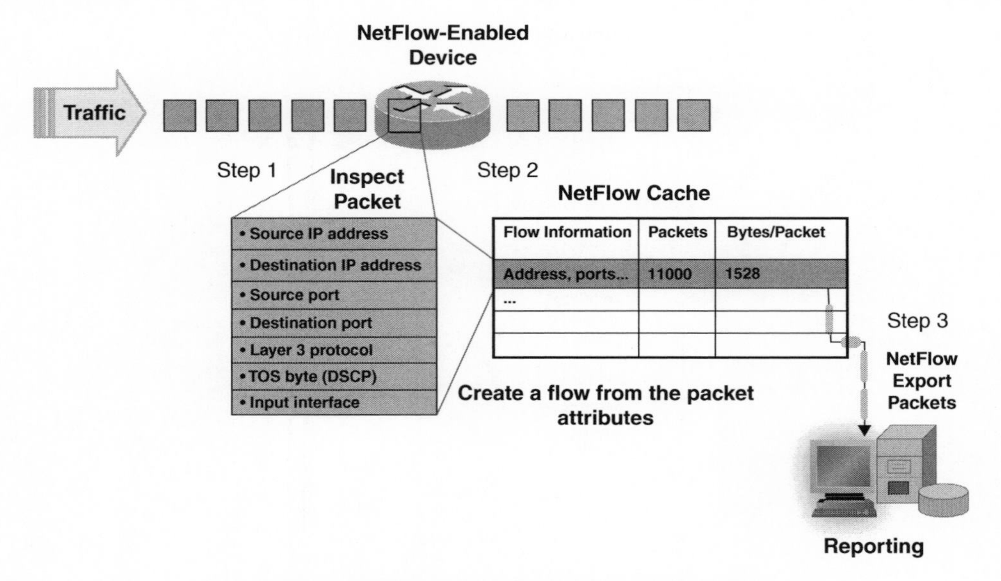

Figure 13.8: NetFlow Operation Overview

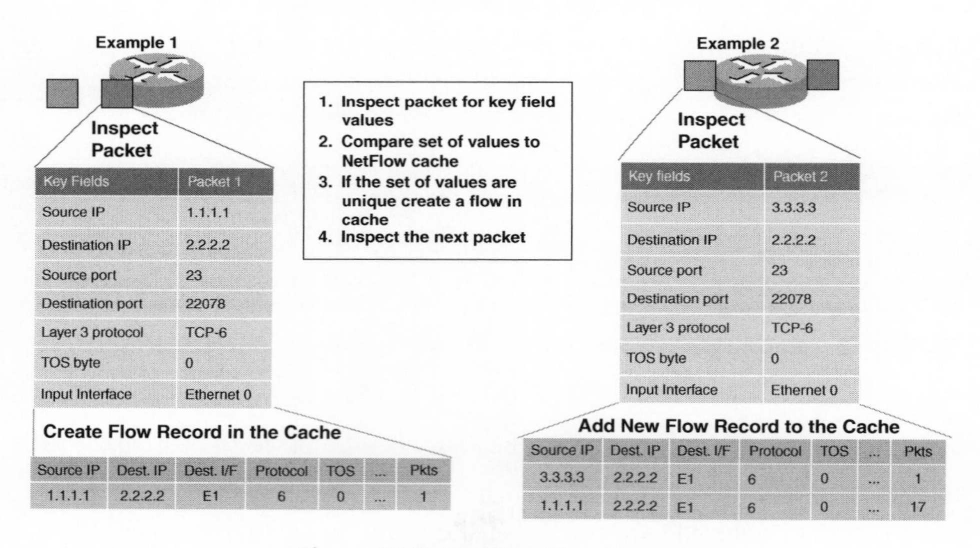

Figure 13.9: NetFlow Flow Record

Figure 13.10 gives a more detailed view of the NetFlow flow record held in cache. The flow entry, expiration criteria, and export process are also identified.

The seven key fields defining a flow are circled. Flows are created and maintained in the cache until expiration of the flow is declared. The criteria for expiration, as shown in the figure, are as follows:

- *Inactive Timer Expired (15 Sec Is Default).* If no packets are received for the user-defined inactive timer period, the flow is declared terminated.

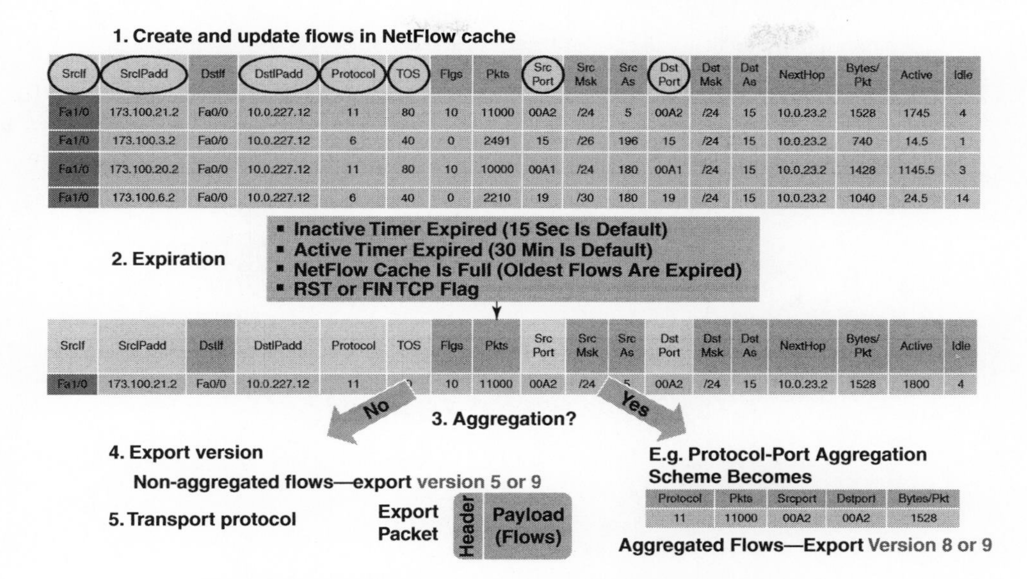

SrcIf	SrcIPadd	DstIf	DstIPadd	Protocol	TOS	Flgs	Pkts	Src Port	Src Msk	Src As	Dst Port	Dst Msk	Dst As	NextHop	Bytes/Pkt	Active	Idle
Fa1/0	173.100.21.2	Fa0/0	10.0.227.12	11	80	10	11000	00A2	/24	5	00A2	/24	15	10.0.23.2	1528	1745	4
Fa1/0	173.100.3.2	Fa0/0	10.0.227.12	6	40	0	2491	15	/26	196	15	/24	15	10.0.23.2	740	14.5	1
Fa1/0	173.100.20.2	Fa0/0	10.0.227.12	11	80	10	10000	00A1	/24	180	00A1	/24	15	10.0.23.2	1428	1145.5	3
Fa1/0	173.100.6.2	Fa0/0	10.0.227.12	6	40	0	2210	19	/30	180	19	/24	15	10.0.23.2	1040	24.5	14

SrcIf	SrcIPadd	DstIf	DstIPadd	Protocol	TOS	Flgs	Pkts	Src Port	Src Msk	Src As	Dst Port	Dst Msk	Dst As	NextHop	Bytes/Pkt	Active	Idle
Fa1/0	173.100.21.2	Fa0/0	10.0.227.12	11	[illegible]	10	11000	00A2	/24	5	00A2	/24	15	10.0.23.2	1528	1800	4

Protocol	Pkts	Srcport	Dstport	Bytes/Pkt
11	11000	00A2	00A2	1528

Figure 13.10: NetFlow Cache Management and Export

- *Active Timer Expired (30 Min Is Default).* If the flow continues beyond the user-defined active timer period, the flow is declared terminated, even if further traffic is flowing.
- *NetFlow Cache Is Full (Oldest Flows Are Expired).* In the event that the cache memory allocated to NetFlow data is exceeded, the flows with the longest active timer will be exported, despite no other criteria for expiration being met.
- *RST or FIN TCP Flag* is received, indicating the flow is terminated.

When the flow is terminated, NetFlow checks the configuration for treatment of the flow record. Depending on the configuration and the data export version, the operator can execute aggregation of flows in a predefined format prior to export, allowing less traffic in the exported data and less processing overhead at the collector and monitoring tool. Alternatively, the flows can be exported without any aggregation of the data. Note that export version 8 only supports aggregation of flows for export. Versions 1 and 5 only support nonaggregated export. Version 9 can be configured for either aggregated or nonaggregated export. Refer to the next section for details on NetFlow export versions.

The data are then formatted according to the appropriate export version, as discussed in the next section, and transported to the collector as configured.

13.6.3 NetFlow Configuration Overview

This section gives basic NetFlow cache configuration examples only. Figure 13.11 shows configuration of NetFlow on Cisco router platforms.

```
Router(config)# interface <slot/port/subinterface>
Router(config-if)# ip flow ingress
Router(config-if)# ip flow egress

Router(config)# ip flow-cache entries <number>
Router(config)# ip flow-cache timeout active <minutes>
Router(config)# ip flow-cache timeout inactive <seconds>

Router(config)# ip flow-export version <version>
[origin as|peer-as|bgp-nexthop]
Router(config)# ip flow-export destination <address> <port>
Router(config)# ip flow-export source <interface>
```

Figure 13.11: NetFlow Basic Configuration

The configuration steps as shown in the figure are:

- *interface <slot/port/subinterface>*. Choose the interface for NetFlow activation.
- *ip flow ingress* and *ip flow egress.* Enable NetFlow on the interface for ingress traffic, egress traffic, or both.
- *ip flow-cache entries <number>*. Define the maximum number of flow entries in the cache. The default varies based on platform; generally 25 percent of the memory in the router is the maximum that can be allocated to the NetFlow cache.
- *ip flow-cache entries timeout active <minutes>*. Define the minutes an active flow will remain in the cache before expiration; 30 minutes is the default.
- *ip flow-cache entries timeout inactive <seconds>*. Define the seconds an inactive flow will remain in the cache before expiration; 15 seconds is the default.
- *ip flow-export version <version>*. Configure the export version (discussed later in this chapter).
- *ip flow-export destination <address> <port>*. Configure the export destination device.
- *ip flow-export source <interface>*. Configure the source interface for exported data packets. Generally a loopback on the router is used.

13.6.4 Catalyst Flow Definition

The Catalyst platform allows a flexible approach to the definition of a flow rather than relying on the seven flow keys used for router platforms. This flexible key approach is referred to as the *flow mask* and has six optional, predefined formats, as shown in Figure 13.12.

The flow keys are as shown in the figure. These keys are used to define a flow in the same way as the seven key fields on the Cisco router platforms. Additional fields are shown as nonkey; hence they will be stored and exported as part of each flow record.

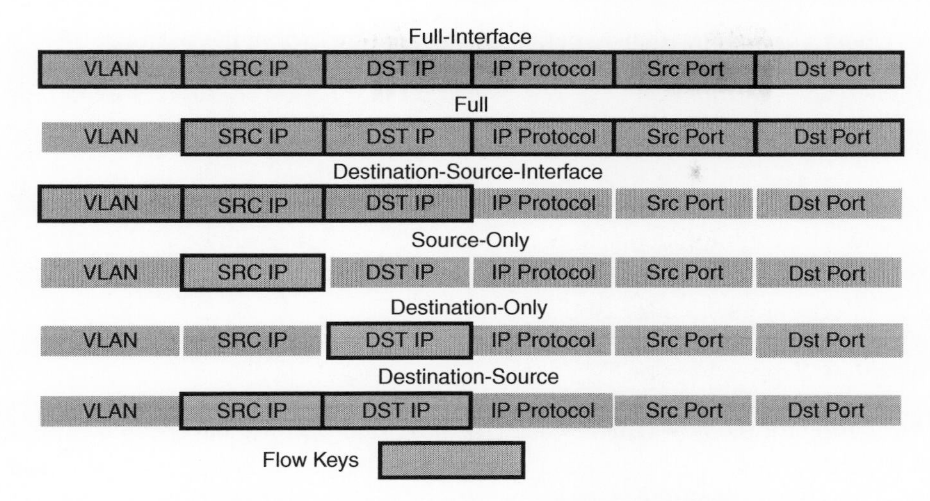

Figure 13.12: Flow Keys on Catalyst Platforms

```
C6500 (config)#mls netflow

C6500 (config)#mls flow ip ?
  destination                          destination flow keyword
  destination-source                   destination-source flow keyword
  full                                 full flow keyword
  interface-destination-source         interface-destination-source flow keyword
  interface-full                       interface full flow keyword
  source                               source only flow keyword
C6500(config)#mls nde sender version ?
  5
  7

C6500(config)#mls nde interface

C6500(config)#mls aging normal 32


C6500(config)#ip flow-export destination 10.66.231.10

C6500(config)#interface g1/1
C6500(config-if)#ip route-cache flow
```

Figure 13.13: NetFlow Configuration on Catalyst Platforms

Figure 13.13 shows configuration of NetFlow on a Catalyst 6500 switch with the PFC/MSFC enhancement.

The configuration steps as shown in the figure are:

- *mls netflow*. Enable NetFlow on the router platform.
- *mls flow ip <options>*. Set the flow mask based on six predefined options.
- *mls nde sender version <5,7>*. Set the Netflow Data Export (NDE) record version on the PFC.
- *mls nde interface*. Populate the interface field in an NDE packet.

- *mls aging normal 32*. Change default hardware timer for aging of flows.
- *ip flow-export destination* *<ip address>*. Set destination address for export data.
- *ip route-cache flow*. Enable NetFlow on selected interface.

After enabling NetFlow on the platform, the user sets the Flow Mask format as defined previously. The final configuration step is enabling the NetFlow caching on the appropriate interface. Note that the flow-mask selection is at a platform configuration level and hence applies to all interfaces enabled for NetFlow.

13.6.5 NetFlow Export Version

NetFlow formatting for the flow data has changed little from the original specifications. What has changed is the format for the aggregation and export of the NetFlow data. The format for the data export defines the capabilities that may be explored at the collector and monitoring tools.

Table 13.4 gives an overview of the NetFlow versions up to the current V9.

Version 5 of the NetFlow export options is by far the most popular and widely deployed, gaining industry acceptance for enterprise and SP operators alike. Version 9 is gaining favor in more contemporary NGN deployments for its flexibility to precisely match operational processes around network planning and security attack detection, becoming of critical importance to multiservice operators.

NetFlow Version 5

As previously mentioned, Version 5 is by far the most widely deployed export version for NetFlow data. Version 5 is a fixed export version that does not allow aggregation of data prior to export.

Figure 13.14 shows the Version 5 data exported to the collector.

The seven key fields defining a unique IP flow are circled. The remaining fields are nonkey and will be stored in cache and included with each flow exported to the collector device.

Table 13.4: NetFlow Export Versions

NetFlow Version	Comments
1	Original specification exporting basic flow information with seven key fields
5	Standard and most commonly adopted, enhanced to include additional nonkey fields
7	Specific to Cisco Catalyst 6500 and 7600 Series switches; similar to Version 5 but does not include AS, interface, TCP flag, and TOS information
8	Choice of 11 aggregation schemes; reduces resource usage
9	Flexible, extensible file export format to enable easier support of additional fields and technologies such as MPLS, multicast, and BGP next hop

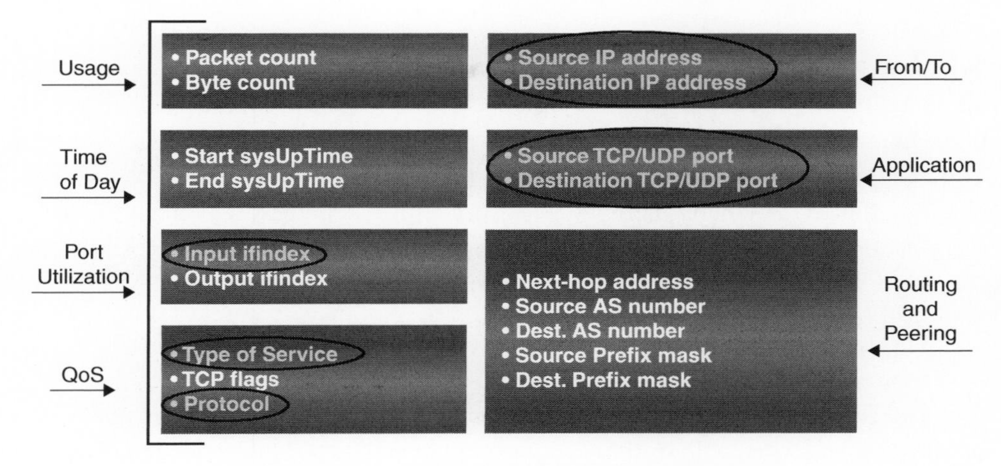

Figure 13.14: NetFlow Export Version 5 Format

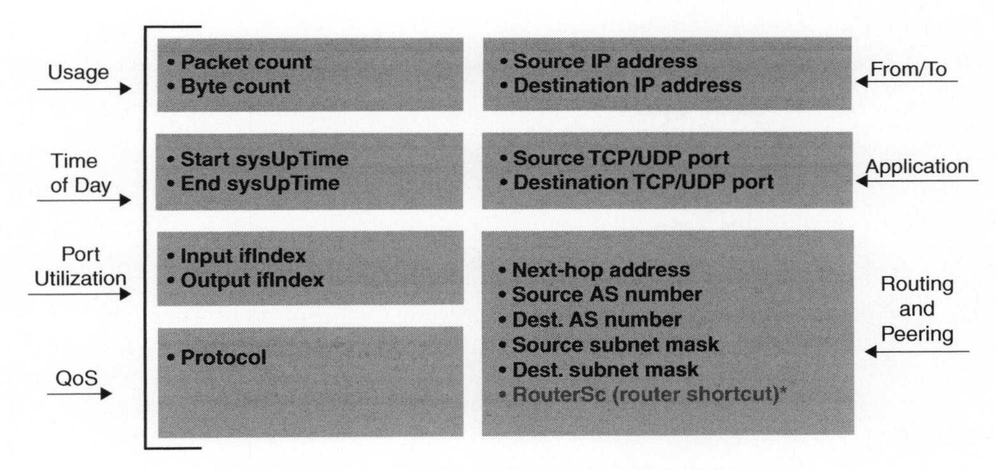

Figure 13.15: NetFlow Export Version 7 Format

NetFlow Version 7

NetFlow Export Version 7 was originally designed for the Catalyst 5000 switches. NetFlow Export Version 7 was supported on the Catalyst 5000 Series NetFlow Feature Card (NFFC), a hardware-based NetFlow engine. Version 7 provides accounting information more appropriate to Ethernet switching environments. Version 7 was subsequently implemented on Catalyst 6500 Series Switches with Sup1 supervisor engines, Multi-Layer Switching (MLS)-enabled sup2 engines, or CEF-capable SUP2 engines.

Figure 13.15 shows the Version 7 data exported to the collector.

Note that a key field that defines an IP flow, namely ToS, is absent from the Version 7 format. The RouteSc field, marked with an asterisk, is not in the Version 5 export format.

NetFlow Version 8

NetFlow Export Version 8 has a format identical to Version 5. Version 8 allows router-based fixed-format aggregation schemes, enabling the NetFlow router to summarize NetFlow data. This aggregation prior to data transport allows reduced NetFlow export data volume, hence reducing export bandwidth requirements, at the expense of additional processing by the NetFlow router. Originally there were five predefined schemes, which have since been expanded to 11 aggregation schemes, allowing greater flexibility for the collector and monitoring tools. The majority of the recently added schemes aggregate based on the ToS byte field. More than one aggregation scheme can be enabled simultaneously on a single NetFlow.

NetFlow Version 9

As service provider and enterprise networks became more sophisticated, requirements evolved for a more flexible and extensible NetFlow export implementation. Designing extensibility in the NetFlow feature allows integration of new technologies and data types without requiring new versions of code. Adding greater flexibility to the flow definition and export data format allows more precise matching of results to business needs with greater efficiency and speed. NetFlow Version 9 was designed to include these new evolving requirements from network operators.

NetFlow Version 9 is an export protocol with no actual changes to the metering process in the router device. Cisco has lodged IETF RFC-3954, "Cisco Systems NetFlow Services Export Version 9," for standardization of this export scheme. Version 9 relies on templates and separate flow records that are sent at regular, configurable intervals. The templates are composed of type and length, with the flow records based on a template ID and value field.

Figure 13.16 gives an overview of the NetFlow Version 9 export packet format.

When configuring NetFlow Version 9, matching ID numbers are the way to associate a given template to the appropriate data records, as shown in the packet format. Each data record within

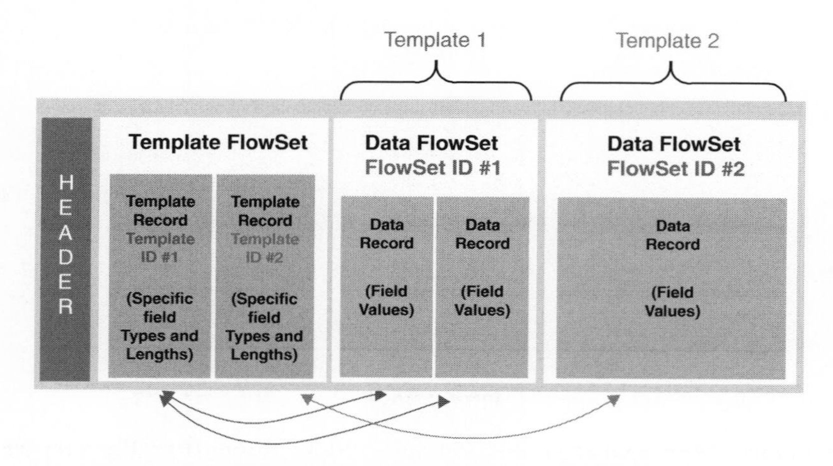

Figure 13.16: NetFlow Export Version 9 Packet Format

a data FlowSet represents one flow. If exported flows have the same configured key fields, they can be contained in the same template record for greater efficiency in bandwidth during export.

The IP header for NetFlow Version 9 follows the same format as prior NetFlow versions from 5 onward to ensure backward compatibility in the collector device.

The exported packets are sent using UDP by default, but reliable transport, such as TCP or Stream Control Transport Protocol (SCTP), can be used where appropriate. UDP, though fast and simple, has no security or mechanism for recognizing and recovering lost packets. SCTP (RFC-4960) allows reliable data transfer, with congestion control and avoidance, multihoming support, and basic security protection against common flood attacks (SYN flood).

13.6.6 Flexible NetFlow

Operators have found the existing fixed export formats, such as 1, 5, 7, and 8, are not flexible and adaptable enough for rapidly evolving network environments, such as in service providers. Each subsequent export version contains new fields, causing incompatibility with previous versions that might be widely deployed and making adoption complicated.

The concept of Flexible NetFlow (FNF) was invented to completely separate the collection and export processes. FNF allows completely customized NetFlow record formats, including key fields, unlike the previous Export versions, based on the following configurable fields:

- *Key.* Choice of flow keys includes IPv4 header, transport (TCP, UDP), routing, flow (direction, sampler), and interface. This allows granularity beyond the traditional seven key fields.
- *Nonkey.* As previously discussed, nonkey fields are not used to define a flow and are exported along with the flow and provide additional information.
- *Counter.* Number of packets and bytes in flow.
- *Timestamp.* Timestamps for first and last packets in flow.

FNF allows an operator to tailor a cache for specific applications in the most accurate possible manner. This gives better scalability as flow records are customized for particular applications, therefore reducing redundant information and the number of flows to monitor.

Figure 13.17 gives an overview of the steps required to configure Flexible NetFlow. The combination of these three steps is referred to as a NetFlow Flow Monitor.

The flow monitor is a flow cache containing user-defined flow records. A configured monitor is applied to an interface, either ingress or egress. Packet sampling is possible per flow monitor for greater granularity at the expense of additional processing overhead.

As shown in the figure, a flow monitor has the following components:

- *Flow record.* Defines what is captured by NetFlow. Either predefined or user-defined templates, which include key and nonkey fields.

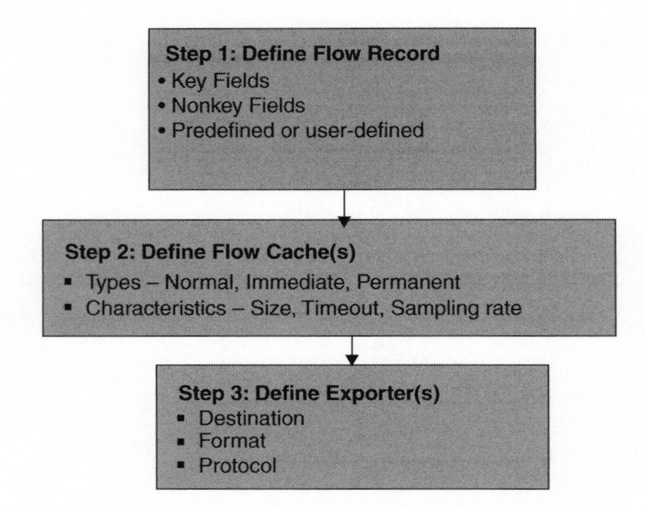

Figure 13.17: Flexible NetFlow Configuration Steps

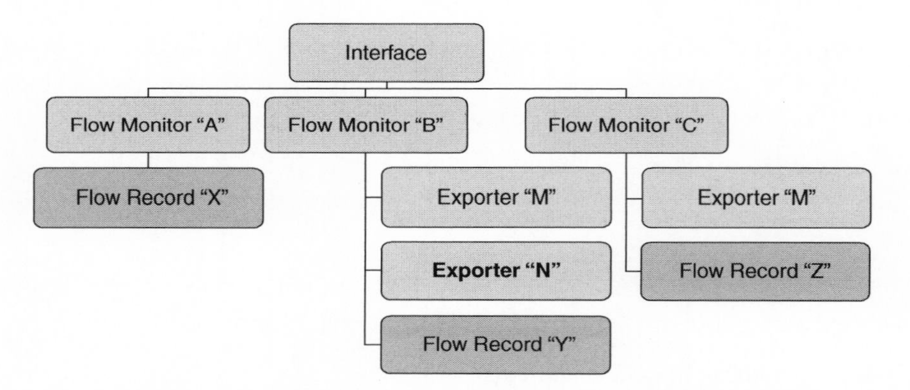

Figure 13.18: NetFlow Flexible Implementation Model

- *Flow cache.* Defines aspects of the cache held in router memory.
- *Flow exporter.* Where NetFlow will be exported to. There may be multiple flow exporters per Flow Monitor for redundancy.

The model adopted for Flexible NetFlow is shown in Figure 13.18.

The rules for implementation as shown in the figure are as follows:

- There will be a single record generated per monitor.
- The user may configure multiple monitors per interface.
- The user may configure multiple exporters per monitor.

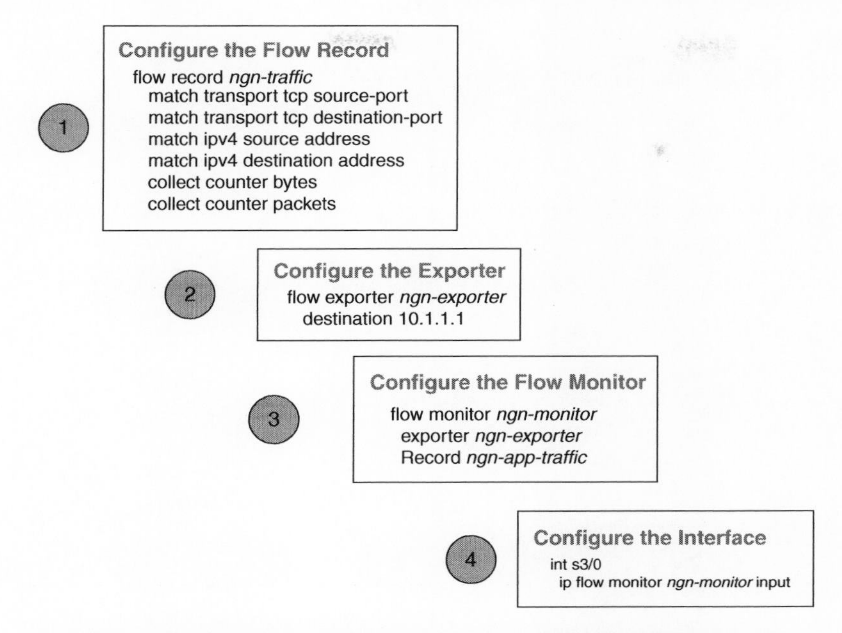

Figure 13.19: NetFlow Flexible Implementation Model Configuration

This scheme gives maximum flexibility to the operator with a simple, modular approach to configuration. Figure 13.19 shows an example of configuration based on the flexible implementation model.

As shown in the figure, the Flow Record is defined including the key fields to be exported. The export target device is then configured. Then a Flow Record, comprised of a configured Flow Record and one or more export destinations, is created. As previously noted, more than one export target can be configured for a single Flow Monitor. When export is required, the data are packetized in the appropriate transport protocol and forwarded toward the export target or targets using IP unicast.

The FNF architecture allows very powerful and specific insight into network performance and characteristics. Figure 13.20 gives an example of the applications FNF enables in an SP network environment.

The example shows two Flow Monitors active on the given router. The first is based on the seven traditional IP flow fields with some additional nonkey fields included in the export to enable traffic analysis. The second is tailored specifically to recognize an SYN flood attack with only required key and nonkey fields configured.

Flexible NetFlow introduces the concept of Normal, Immediate, and Permanent cache types for added flexibility. These cache types are defined as follows:

- *Normal cache.* This option is based on the existing NetFlow implementations, with more granular active and inactive timers down to a 1 second minimum.

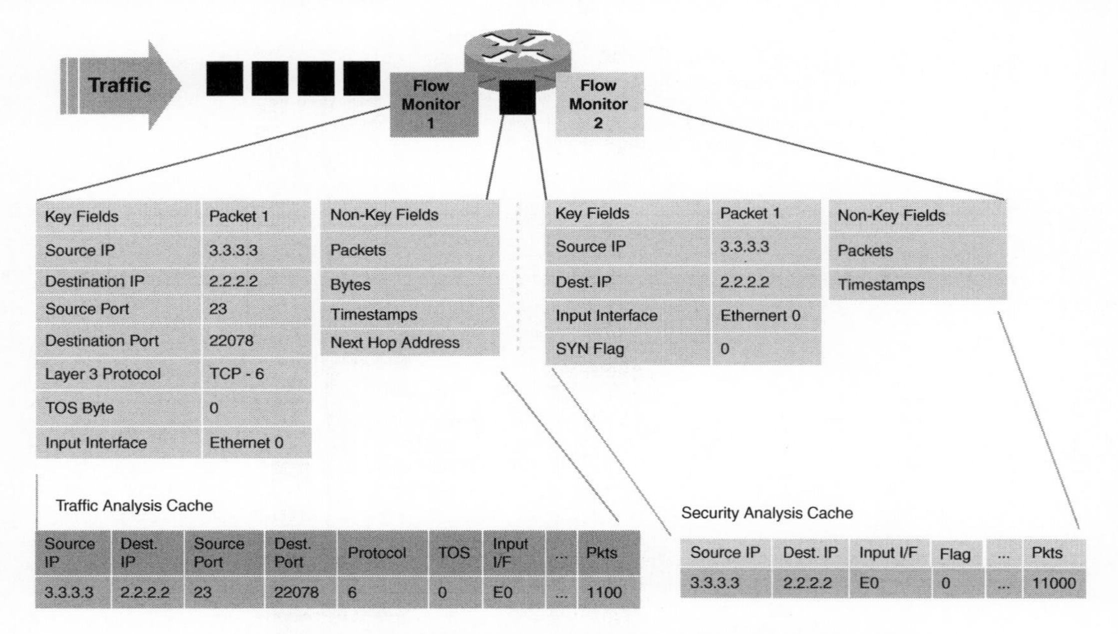

Figure 13.20: Flexible NetFlow Network Application Example

- *Immediate cache.* This option allows flow accounts for a single packet to be exported allowing real-time traffic monitoring, DDoS detection, or when transient flows are required for tasks such as sampling. Note that the Immediate cache option must be used intelligently because it can result in a large amount of export data.
- *Permanent cache.* This option allows tracking of a set of flows without expiration from the cache. The entire cache is periodically exported based on an update timer rather than legacy counters.

13.6.7 NetFlow Monitoring Tools

As previously mentioned, a performance-monitoring tool will collate and interpret the NetFlow data, giving longer trends and more meaningful representation of network characteristics.

Figure 13.21 shows the implementation of NetFlow in a network end to end.

The NetFlow data from the router or switch is saved in the local cache memory. These data may be aggregated prior to export, depending on the export version and configuration chosen by the operator. The exported data are sent to a collector device, where they are filtered and aggregated. The collector may be Cisco supplied, such as the NetFlow collector, RemoteMONitoring (RMON) or Network Analysis Module (NAM, for the 6500/7600 and 2800/3700/3800), a purpose-built partner device, or even some primitive freeware collectors available to operators. Tools will access these data for various operational and billing applications, including security attack assessment, traffic planning, and billing.

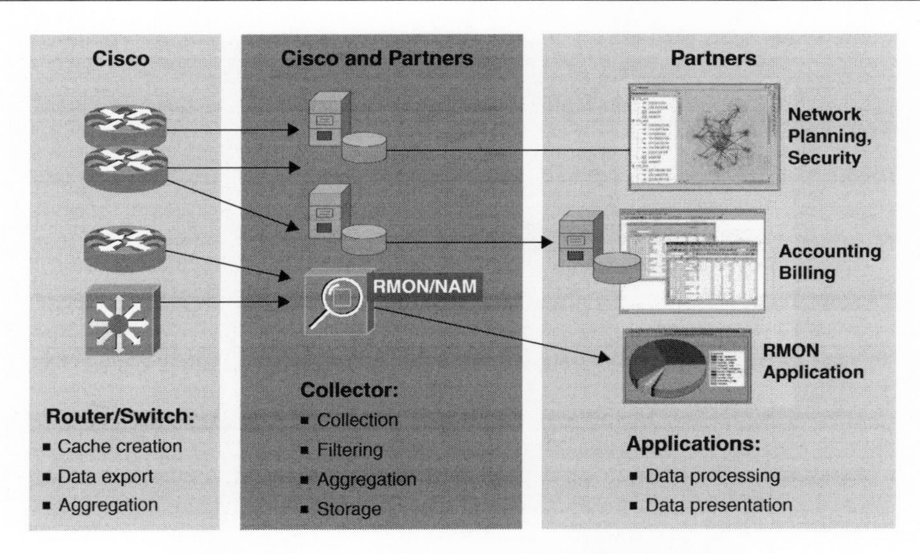

Figure 13.21: NetFlow Network Implementation

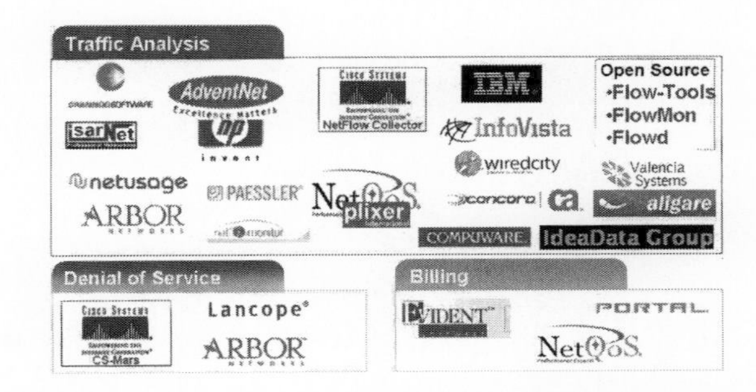

Figure 13.22: NetFlow Third-Party and Cisco Applications

Figure 13.22 shows Cisco and third-party companies that use NetFlow traffic data as the basis for network traffic analysis, security detection monitoring, and billing information.

13.7 IP Service-Level Agreement

Cisco IOS IP Service Level Agreement (IP SLA) is a network performance measurement feature, included in Cisco IOS, that uses the synthetic or active monitoring technique, which generates traffic specifically for the purpose of measurement, as described in the Performance Measurement Framework section.

IP SLA was originally called *RTR* and was renamed SAA in IOS code version 12.0(5)T. The original code base was referred to as *Engine 1*. A new Engine 2 code base rewrite was introduced in 12.2(11)T. Engine 2 code is faster and consumes less memory and is the basis for existing IP SLA implementation in Cisco IOS software. Shortly after the release of Engine 2 code, the CLI commands were changed to IP SLA.

Table 13.5: IP SLA Performance Measurement Overview

Measurement Category	Category Implementation	Definition
Sampling	Synthetic/active	Network traffic is generated specifically for the purpose of measuring network performance
Collection	Embedded agent External probe	Mechanisms for collecting performance statistics are integrated into the communication device Mechanisms for collecting performance statistics are through a purpose-built and dedicated device. *Note:* IP SLA can use a dedicated probe device to offload CPU cycles from the service traffic-forwarding devices
Scope	End to end/path	Performance measurement based on analysis of parameters across multiple network hops from end to end
Perspective	Network	Measurement based on performance statistics measured in network devices

According to the parameters defined in the "Performance Measurement Framework" section, Table 13.5 gives an overview of IP SLA as a measurement tool.

Cisco IOS IP SLAs can be configured to measure performance between multiple points in the network, depending on the measurement requirements.

IP SLA uses a variety of protocols at the network level to generate the traffic for measuring metrics, depending on requirements. There are generic protocols, such as UDP and ICMP, and specific protocols, such as DNS and DHCP, required to measure performance metrics of critical applications servers. Other protocols include HTTP, LDP, H.323, SIP, and specific user-configured UDP and TCP ports.

Time-stamp information embedded in the IP SLA traffic is used to calculate performance metrics, including jitter and latency, and application-specific metrics such as server response time and MOS voice-quality scores. In addition, IP SLA can measure nontime-related parameters such as packet loss, packet sequence, and connectivity.

In summary, the Cisco IOS IP SLA feature is capable of measuring the following performance metrics:

- Delay (round trip and one way)
- Jitter (one way)
- Packet loss (one way)
- Packet sequencing
- Path
- Connectivity

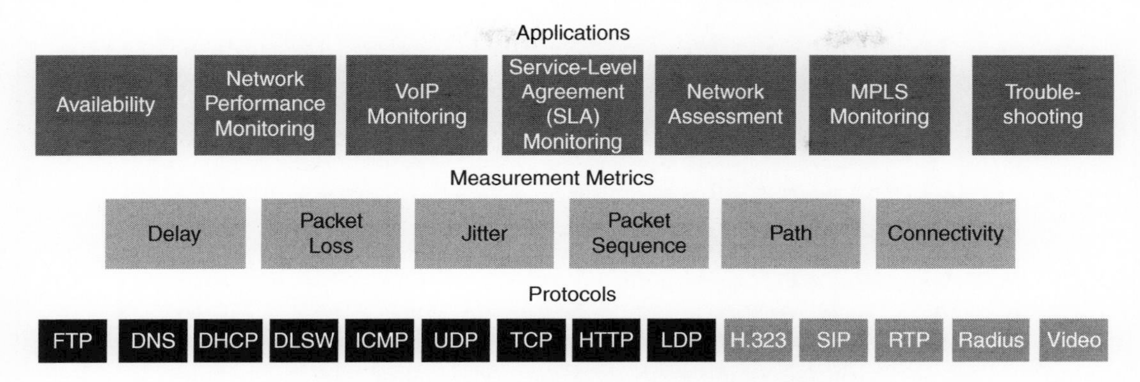

Figure 13.23: IP SLA Implementation Layers

With the appropriate monitoring tools for collating and interpreting the data, IP SLA gives a powerful, flexible tool for managing a network beyond SLA reporting. The following list summarizes the performance applications enabled by IP SLA metrics:

- *Edge-to-edge network availability monitoring.* Verifies connectivity between selected points in the network.
- *Network performance monitoring.* Measures jitter, latency, and packet loss in the network.
- *VoIP monitoring.* IP SLA includes the ability to specifically measure voice services, long regarded as having the strictest SLA requirements prior to the advent of IPTV services.
- *Customer service-level agreement monitoring.* SLA monitoring, measurement, and verification.
- *IP service network health assessment.* Verifies that the network performance is sufficient for new IP services or customer overlay. Monitoring and measurement after service deployment.
- *MPLS monitoring.* MPLS service capabilities were required as IP SLA became increasingly popular in SP networks evolving toward multiservice capabilities.
- *Troubleshooting of network operation.* Accurate and relevant performance reduces troubleshooting time.

Figure 13.23 gives an overview of the protocols generated by IP SLA, the metrics that can be measured, and the performance applications for which these metrics can ultimately be used in the service provider's operational life cycle.

NOTE 13.4: Network Assessment Using IP SLA

IP SLA measurement traffic may be used for capacity planning in a network. Declining latency, jitter, or packet-loss performance for probe traffic injected within a class may indicate that bandwidth parameters are being exceeded in QoS configuration. Note that although IP SLA can be used for capacity planning in this manner, a provider may find that this is a reactive approach in which capacity thresholds become obvious only when exceeded. Passive sampling collections methods, such as NetFlow, are more appropriate because they give statistics on actual service traffic forwarded, allowing a proactive approach to capacity planning.

13.7.1 IP SLA Measurement Architecture

IP SLA operation relies on the concept of a source device to inject the traffic for measurement into the network at appropriate points in the topology. The source may be embedded in a traffic-forwarding router or offloaded to a dedicated router, commonly referred to as a *shadow router*. The source device is responsible for originating probe packets and is the only device that requires configuration for IP SLA to work. Additionally, all the measurement data are stored and polled from the source device.

The source traffic requires a target device for measurements to be made. This target can be any IP device, including a router, switch, or host such as an application server. Some measurement operations require the target to run the IP SLA responder feature (this device must be running Cisco IOS code and does not require specific configuration, as described later in this chapter), such as jitter, for example.

The raw measurement data are then collected by a monitoring management tool for collating, interpreting, and reporting via SNMP or CLI.

Figure 13.24 gives an overview of the IP SLA architecture.

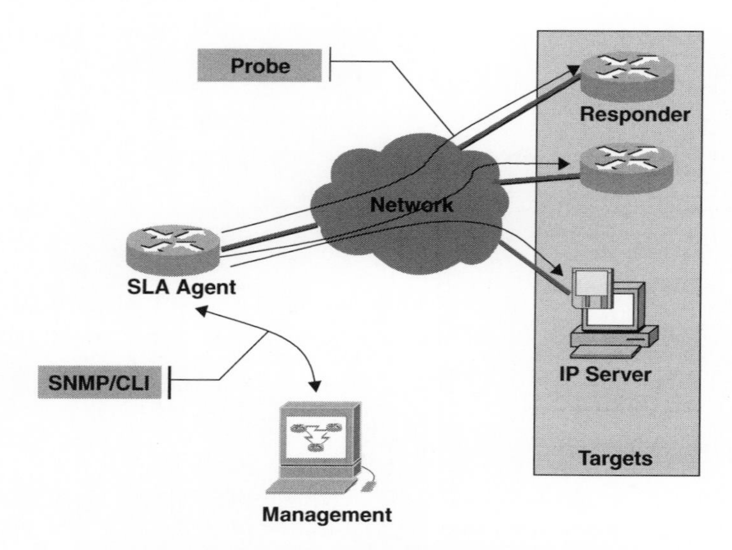

Figure 13.24: IP SLA Architecture Overview

When SNMP is used for collection, traps can be set when predefined thresholds are met or exceeded, as measured by IP SLA. These traps can trigger further analysis automatically if configured by the operator.

13.7.2 IP SLA Measurement Timing

The target for probe traffic can be any IP device in the network depending on the measurement requirements and constraints. Where the target device is a Cisco router, the device can be configured with IP SLA Responder capabilities to enhance the measurement data for latency and jitter where millisecond accuracy is required. This is assuming that the router has the appropriate software version supporting IP SLA Responder functionality.

Figure 13.25 shows the general timing for round-trip measurements using IP SLA. Note that although the figure depicts a router as the target, this might not necessarily be the case; as noted previously, the target device can be any IP-enabled device.

The source router injects the measurement traffic from the egress interface at time TS1 toward the target device. The traffic will reach the target device ingress interface at time TS2. The target device will send the response from the egress interface toward the source at time TS3, which will include some processing time TS3 – TS2, as shown in the figure. The response will reach the source router ingress interface at time TS4, which will then be recognized by the IP SLA software at TS5 after a processing time of TS5 – TS4. The IP SLA source router is programmed to automatically eliminate the processing time to allow greater measurement accuracy.

NOTE 13.5: Probe Traffic Processing Time

The processing time on the source router must be removed from the round-trip time to ensure measurement accuracy. The path taken through the router for data traffic is different from the process-intensive path taken for IP SLA measurement probe traffic. Additionally, the probe traffic may be injected from a shadow router, explained later in this section, which is not in the data path for service traffic; hence inclusion of processing time is irrelevant.

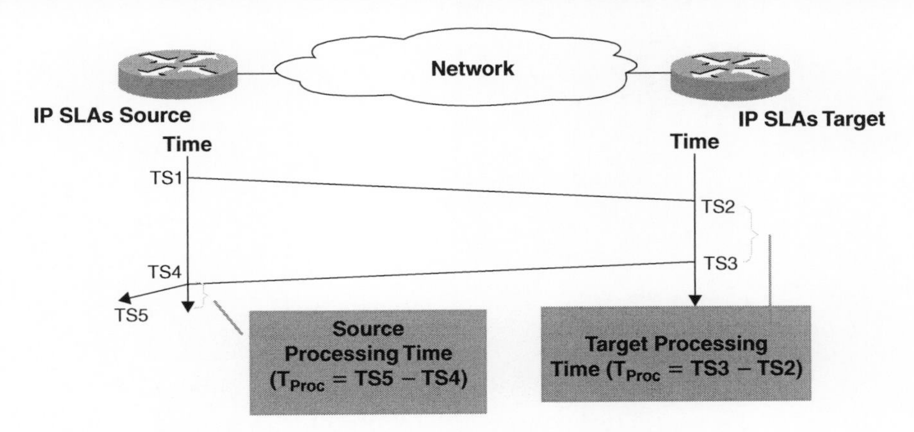

Figure 13.25: IP SLA Measurement Accuracy

The processing time on a target router is variable, depending on probe traffic type, CPU load, queuing/buffering time, and forwarding platform architecture. This can give unpredictable results, with an error proportional to the processing time compared with the total path propagation delay. The points made regarding probe traffic processing time on the source router are equally applicable to the responding router. The greater the processing time with respect to the time taken for traffic to transit the network, the more meaningless the measurement data.

The round-trip delay, without IP SLA Responder enabled on the target router, is:

$$TS5 - TS1 - TProc(Source) = TS4 - TS1$$

The one-way delay without IP SLA Responder enabled is:

$$TS3 - TS1$$

The IP SLA Responder feature can be enabled on the target router for enhanced accuracy. This feature allows the target router to subtract the processing time from the response time stamp.

The target router can be configured as an IP SLA responder by issuing the CLI command *ip sla monitor responder* or by setting *rttMonApplResponder. 0 = 1* with SNMP. This is the only configuration command required on the target Responder, since the IP SLA Sender uses the IP SLA Control Protocol (CP) to communicate with the Responder prior to sending any measurement traffic. The IP SLA CP allows the Responder to understand the type of operation, the port used, and the duration of the test.

Figure 13.26 shows an overview of the IP SLA Control Protocol operation.

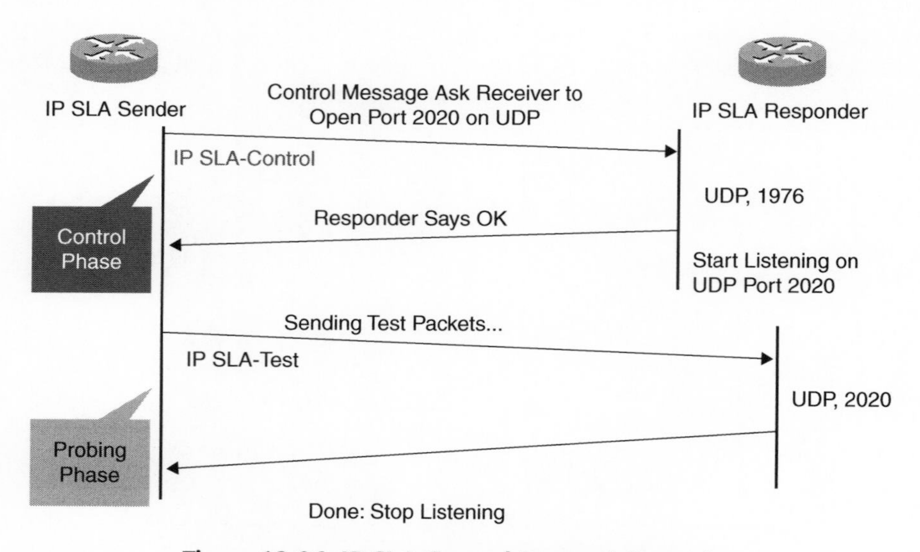

Figure 13.26: IP SLA Control Protocol Operation

Note that the IP SLA CP can be secured using MD5 authentication where security is a concern. In modern multiservice NGNs, security is always a concern, necessitating authentication features such as MD5 wherever possible.

The round-trip delay with IP SLA Responder enabled is:

$$(TS5 - TS1) - T\,Proc(Source) - TProc(Target) = TS4 - TS1 - TProc(Target)$$

The one-way delay with IP SLA Responder enabled is:

$$TS2 - TS1$$

The IP SLA Responder feature allows the target device to take two time stamps:

- When the packet arrives on the ingress interface at interrupt level
- As the packet is sent from the egress interface

Both time stamps are sent in the payload of the reply packet from the Responder to the Sender. Using the ingress interface time stamp from the IP SLA Responder router allows elimination of the processing time at the target device. The time-stamp accuracy is submillisecond (ms) in later versions of Cisco IOS. This feature gives IP SLA a clear advantage over IP probe devices relying on ICMP traffic for network profile and measurement.

13.7.3 IP SLA Operation Types

IP SLA has a variety of operation types that can be used to generate measurement data. The three basic type categories are ICMP, UDP, and Service probes.

Figure 13.27 shows the operations available on the IP SLA Sender using the CLI command.

```
R3(config)#ip sla monitor 1
R3(config)-ip-sla-monitor)#type ?
IP SLAs entry configuration commands:
  dhcp         DHCP Operation
  dns          DNS Query Operation
  echo         Echo Operation
  frame-relay  Frame-Relay Operation
  ftp          FTP Operation
  http         HTTP Operation
  path-echo    Path Discovered Echo Operation
  path-jitter  Path Discovered Jitter Operation
  slm          SLM Operation
  tcp-connect  TCP Connect Operation
  udp-echo     UDP Echo Operation
  voip         Voice Over IP Operation
```

Figure 13.27: IP SLA IOS Type Command

The injected traffic parameters include packet size, packet spacing, protocol type, and DSCP marking. The operation can be scheduled to generate traffic and retrieve performance measurements at specific times with predefined frequency to deliver the expected accuracy. For example, a service provider may include greater granularity of measurement at peak traffic times, when performance issues are more likely.

The measurement data from the Cisco IOS IP SLA operation are stored within the RTTMON MIB or available through the CLI for Network Monitoring Tools to retrieve IP SLA statistics.

Cisco IOS IP SLA may be configured to monitor per QoS class traffic by setting the DiffServ Code Point (DSCP) bits in the probe traffic. A destination router running Cisco IOS Software can be configured as a Cisco IOS IP SLA Responder, which processes measurement packets and provides detailed time-stamp information for greater measurement accuracy, as previously noted.

IP SLA is capable of return-trip or unidirectional measurements for all metrics. As previously mentioned, Cisco IOS IP SLA provides a proactive notification feature with an SNMP trap generated in the event that a preset performance threshold is crossed. Basic SNMP trap types available are round-trip time, average jitter, one-way latency, jitter, packet loss, MOS, and connectivity tests.

Service providers can configure Cisco IOS IP SLA to execute a new operation automatically when the threshold is crossed. For example, when latency exceeds an end-to-end threshold, a secondary operation can be launched to measure hop-by-hop latency, allowing isolation of the offending link or device in the network.

Subsequent sections give an overview of the operation types and deployment scenarios for IP SLA in an SP network.

13.7.4 Internet Control Message Protocol Packet Measurement Options

ICMP has the following measurement operations:

- ICMP Echo
- ICMP PathJitter

The most basic ICMP measurement is ICMP Echo. This test gives round-trip time for ICMP echoes to any IP device capable of responding. Figures 13.28 and 13.29 give configuration and example measurement output for this IP SLA operation.

```
ip sla monitor 1
  type echo protocol ipIcmpEcho 10.1.100.1
  tos 32

  frequency 120
ip sla monitor schedule 1 life forever start-time now
```

Figure 13.28: IP SLA ICMP Echo Measurement Configuration

The configuration steps as shown in the figure are:

- *ip sla monitor <operation-number>*. Used to begin configuration for an IP SLAs operation.
- *type pathEcho protocol ipIcmpEcho {destination-ip-address | destination-hostname} [source-ipaddr {ip-address | hostname}]*. Configure a Cisco IOS IP SLA Internet Control Message Protocol (ICMP) path echo operation, and use the type *pathEcho protocol ipIcmpEcho* command in IP SLA monitor configuration mode.
- *tos <number>*. Service type byte in IPv4 header. Range is from 0–255 with default 0.
- *frequency <seconds>*. Number of seconds between the IP SLA operations. Default is 60 seconds.
- *ip sla monitor schedule operation-number [life {forever | seconds}] [start-time {hh:mm[:ss] [month day | day month] | pending | now | after hh:mm:ss}] [ageout seconds] [recurring]*. Configure the scheduling parameters for a single Cisco IOS IP SLA operation.

The other ICMP measurement operation feature in IP SLA is the ICMP PathJitter option. This feature measures the round-trip delay, packet loss, and jitter hop by hop.

The ICMP PathJitter measurement is executed in two phases: path discovery and per-hop measurement, as shown in Figure 13.30.

The first phase is to discover the hops with a trace route, shown in the figure with a 1 next to the trace-route path. The next step is to evaluate each hop one by one for round-trip time, packet loss, and round-trip jitter, shown in the figure with a 2.

Figure 13.31 shows configuration of the IP SLA PathJitter option.

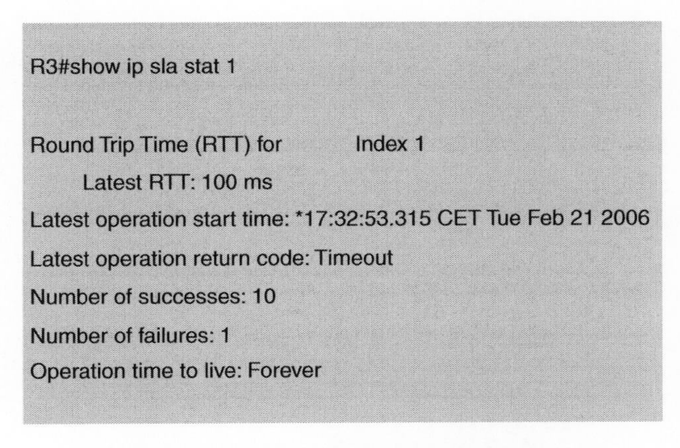

```
R3#show ip sla stat 1

Round Trip Time (RTT) for        Index 1
        Latest RTT: 100 ms
Latest operation start time: *17:32:53.315 CET Tue Feb 21 2006
Latest operation return code: Timeout
Number of successes: 10
Number of failures: 1
Operation time to live: Forever
```

Figure 13.29: IP SLA ICMP Echo Output

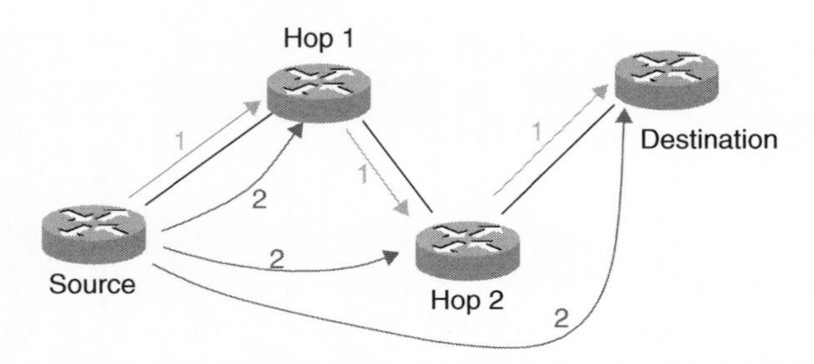

Figure 13.30: IP SLA ICMP PathJitter Operation

```
ip sla monitor 1
      type path-jitter dest-ipaddr 10.52.128.1 [options]
ip sla monitor schedule 1 start-time now
```

Figure 13.31: IP SLA ICMP PathJitter Configuration

The configuration steps as shown in the figure are:

- *ip sla monitor <operation-number>*. Used to begin configuration for an IP SLA operation.
- *type pathJitter dest-ipaddr {destination-ip-address | destination-hostname} [source-ipaddr {ip-address | hostname}] [num-packets packet-number] [interval milliseconds] [targetOnly]*. Configure a Cisco IOS IP SLA Internet Control Message Protocol (ICMP) path jitter operation.
- *ip sla monitor schedule operation-number [life {forever | seconds}] [start-time {hh: mm[:ss] [month day | day month] | pending | now | after hh:mm:ss}] [ageout seconds] [recurring]*. Configure the scheduling parameters for a single Cisco IOS IP SLA operation.

Figure 13.32 shows an example of output results for the IP SLA ICMP PathJitter operation.

When the ICMP measurement method is used, the target device processing time cannot be removed from the overall response time. Hence, depending on the ratio of processing time to overall return-trip response time and the intended use of the measurement results, this monitoring approach could be unacceptably inaccurate.

13.7.5 UDP Packet Measurement Options

UDP has the following measurement operations:

- UDP Echo
- ICMP Jitter

```
sh ip sla mon stat 1 details

---- Path Jitter Statistics ----

Source IP                 - 10.52.132.5
Destination IP            - 10.52.128.1
Number of Echos           - 10
Interval between Echos - 20 ms
Target Only               - Disabled (default)

Hop IP 10.52.132.2:
        RTT:1                  PacketLoss:0           Jitter:0
        MinRTT:1               MaxRTT:2               SumRTT:19      Sum2RTT:37
        MinPosJitter:1         MaxPosJitter:1         SumPos:1       Sum2Pos:1
        MinNegJitter:0         MaxNegJitter:0         SumNeg:0       Sum2Neg:0
        OutOfSequence:0        DiscardedSamples:0
Hop IP 10.52.128.1:
        RTT:1                  PacketLoss:0           Jitter:0
        MinRTT:1               MaxRTT:3               SumRTT:14      Sum2RTT:24
        MinPosJitter:2         MaxPosJitter:2         SumPos:2       Sum2Pos:4
        MinNegJitter:1         MaxNegJitter:1         SumNeg:2       Sum2Neg:2
        OutOfSequence:0        DiscardedSamples:0
```

Figure 13.32: IP SLA ICMP PathJitter Output

```
ip sla monitor 1
  type udp-echo 172.16.6.17
ip sla monitor schedule 1 start-time now
```

Figure 13.33: IP SLA UDP Echo Configuration

The IP SLA UDP Echo operation uses either the well-known UDP Port 7 (echo service) or any other custom port as defined by the operator. IP SLA Responder may be used with this measurement method for more accurate results, allowing processing delays subtracted on both source and destination as previously described. Note that IP SLA Responder is not required.

Figure 13.33 shows an example UDP Echo configuration using IP SLA.

The configuration steps as shown in the figure are:

- *ip sla monitor <operation-number>*. Used to begin configuration for an IP SLA operation.
- *type udpEcho dest-ipaddr {ip-address | hostname} dest-port port-number [source-ipaddr {ip-address | hostname} source-port port-number] [control {enable | disable}]*. Define a Cisco IOS IP SLA User Datagram Protocol (UDP) echo operation.
- *ip sla monitor schedule operation-number [life {forever | seconds}] [start-time {hh:mm[:ss] [month day | day month] | pending | now | after hh:mm:ss}] [ageout seconds] [recurring]*. Configure the scheduling parameters for a single Cisco IOS IP SLA operation.

The associated output for the UDP Echo operation is shown in Figure 13.34.

The UDP Jitter option in IP SLA measures the delay, delay variance (jitter), and packet loss by generating periodic UDP traffic. Measurements can be made unidirectional or round trip. This

```
R3#show ip sla monitor stat 1 details

Round Trip Time (RTT) for Index 1
     Latest RTT: 1 milliseconds
Latest operation start time: *17:42:45.475 CET Tue Feb 21 2006
Latest operation return code: OK
Over thresholds occurred: FALSE
Number  of successes: 1
Number of failures: 3
Operation time to live: 3397 sec
Operational state of entry: Active
Last time this entry was reset: Never
```

Figure 13.34: IP SLA UDP Echo Output

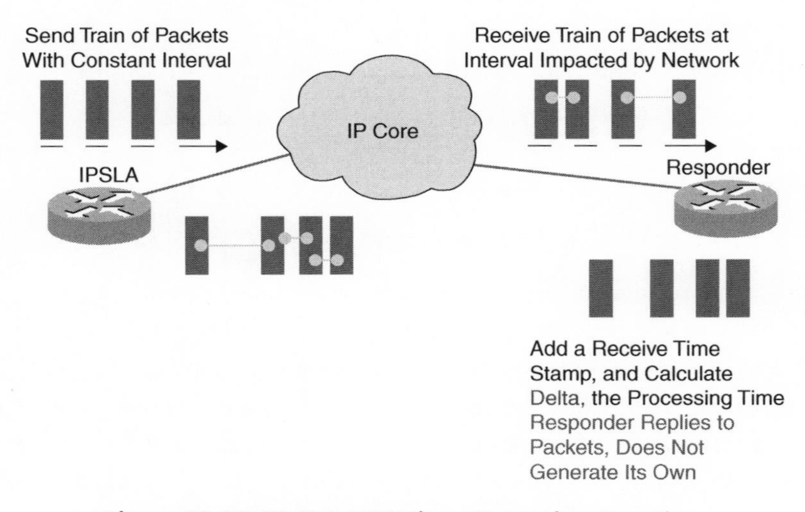

Figure 13.35: IP SLA UDP Jitter Operation Overview

feature can also detect and report out-of-sequence and corrupted packets. This feature must have an IP SLA Responder-enabled router as the target device. This operation can measure MOS and ICPIF scores for VoIP. ToS can be set in the UDP packets to enable specific QoS measurements.

Figure 13.35 gives an overview of the IP SLA UDP jitter operation.

UDP packets are generated from the IP SLA Sender with very precise inter packet timing. This allows a reference for jitter measurement on the received traffic at the source.

Figure 13.36 gives a detailed view of how IP SLA uses the UDP packets for jitter measurement.

The time-stamp information is copied to the replying packets, as described previously. The IP SLA Responder allows processing time to be removed from the final results, allowing accuracy

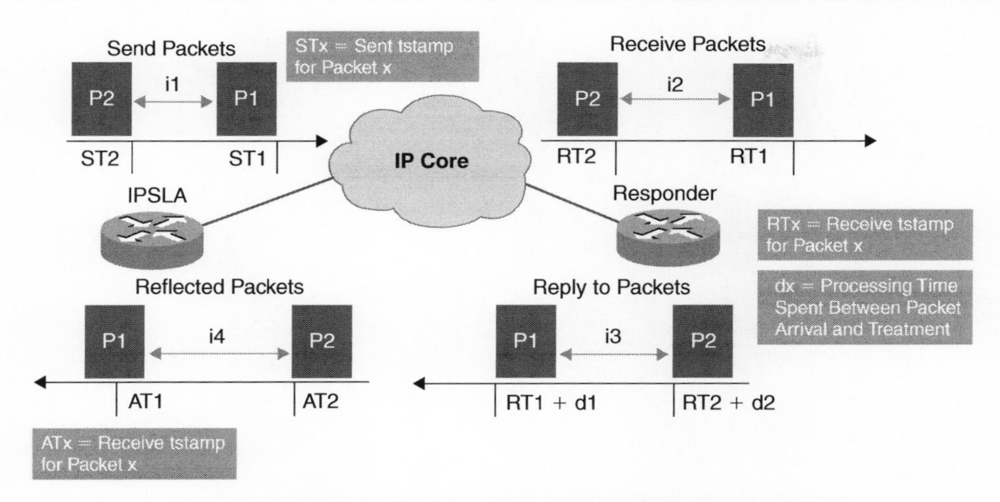

Figure 13.36: UDP Jitter Measurement Detailed Operation

to within 0.1 ms. The returned packet includes time stamps: STx, RTx, ATx, and dx, allowing the source to calculate:

$$\text{JitterSD} = (\text{RT2} - \text{RT1}) - (\text{ST2} - \text{ST1}) = \text{i2} - \text{i1}$$
$$\text{JitterDS} = (\text{AT2} - \text{AT1}) - ((\text{RT2} + \text{d2}) - (\text{RT1} + \text{d1})) = \text{i4} - \text{i3}$$

where JitterSD refers to the jitter from source to destination and JitterDS refers to the jitter from destination to source.

If UDP packets are sent with 10 ms interval, positive jitter means that they have been received with more than 10 ms interval, negative jitter means less than 10 ms interval, and zero jitter means they are received with the same interpacket delay, hence the variance is zero.

For two-way jitter computation, the Sender and Receiver do not require clocks to be synchronized. If one-way jitter measurement is required, the clocks on source and target routers must be synchronized using NTP. If the Sender and Receiver are not synchronized, IP SLA ignores the measurement by filling in 0 s.

The UDP Jitter operation is capable of measuring lost packets and out-of-sequence packets. Each packet sent is sequenced to allow these measurements. Figure 13.37 shows an example of packet-loss measurement using the IP SLA UDP jitter option.

As shown in the figure, the packet and Ack must be received, otherwise the packet will be declared lost.

Figure 13.38 shows configuration of the IP SLA UDP Jitter operation in IOS CLI.

The configuration steps as shown in the figure are:

- *ip sla monitor <operation-number>*. Used to begin configuration for an IP SLA operation.

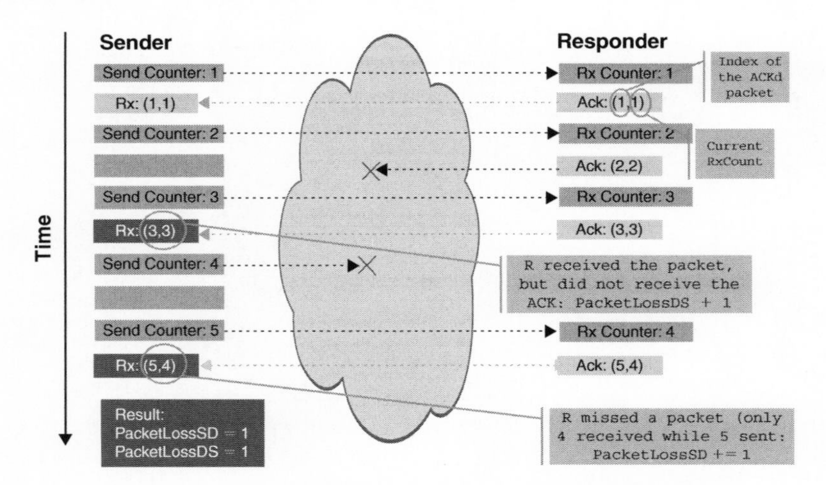

Figure 13.37: IP SLA UDP Jitter Packet-Loss Measurement

```
Source#
    ip sla monitor 5
     type jitter dest-ipaddr 10.52.130.68 dest-port 16384 num-
    packets 1000 interval 20
     tos 0x2E
     request-data-size 200
    ip sla monitor schedule 5 life forever start-time now
    ntp server 10.0.0.2

Target#
    ntp server 10.0.0.2
    ip sla monitor responder
```

Figure 13.38: IP SLA UDP Jitter Configuration

- *type jitter dest-ipaddr {destination-ip-address | destination-hostname} dest-port port-number [source-ipaddr {ip-address | hostname}] [source-port port-number] [control {enable | disable}] [num-packets number-of-packets] [interval interpacket-interval]*. Configure a Cisco IOS IP SLA User Datagram Protocol (UDP) jitter operation.
- *tos <number>*. Set ToS field in IPv4 header.
- *request-data-size <number>*. Size (in bytes) of the protocol data in the payload of the request packet of the operation. The range is from 0 to the maximum of the protocol.
- *ip sla monitor schedule operation-number [life {forever | seconds}] [start-time {hh:mm[:ss] [month day | day month] | pending | now | after hh:mm:ss}] [ageout seconds] [recurring]*. Configure the scheduling parameters for a single Cisco IOS IP SLA operation.
- *ip sla monitor responder*. Enable the Cisco IOS IP SLA Responder for general IP SLAs operations.

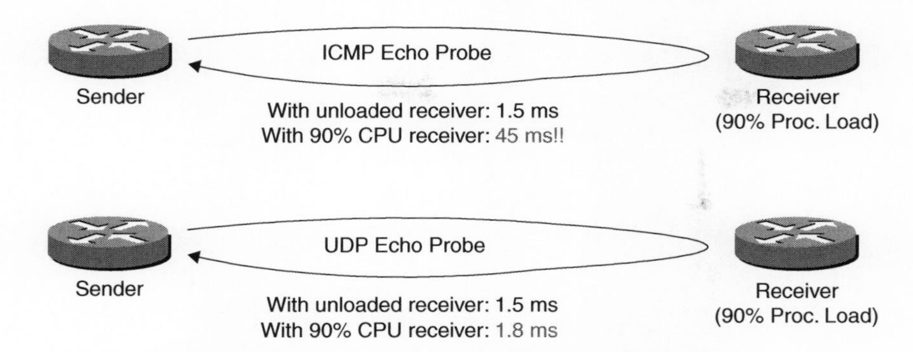

Figure 13.39: IP SLA ICMP Versus UDP Accuracy

13.7.6 ICMP vs. UDP Measurement Accuracy

One point worth noting is the impact of target device CPU load on ICMP Echo-based performance measurement. ICMP Echo replies require the target device to accept the ICMP echo request, process the request, construct a framed reply, queue the reply, and forward it out the appropriate egress interface. In situations where the CPU load on the target device is 90 percent or more, the processor-intensive ICMP Echo reply can lead to high errors in the measurement data.

Figure 13.39 compares ICMP Echo and UDP Echo response when the receiving router CPU is unloaded and 90 percent loaded.

As shown, the ICMP Echo response from the 90 percent loaded target router introduced a 43.5 ms processing overhead, which equates to an error of 2900 percent, rendering the result meaningless. Further adding to the inaccuracy is the likelihood that each time an ICMP Echo reply is received, the error will be significantly different, as tends to be the case when high CPU issues are involved.

The UDP Echo technique yields superior results, as expected. The CPU load is not as much an issue in responding to the UDP Echo type compared with the ICMP Echo response.

13.7.7 Services Connection Measurement

IP SLA has the capability to measure application and TCP connection metrics if required. These include basic TCP connection as well as application-specific performance for DNS, DHCP, DLSw+, FTP, HTTP, and Voice MOS.

The IP SLA TCP Connect Operation measures the time taken by the source to perform a TCP connect operation to the destination device or host. The target device can be any IP host or IP SLA Responder router. This operation is used to simulate Telnet, SSH, and SQL connections for the purpose of measuring response time.

Figure 13.40 gives an overview of the measurement using IP SLA TCP connect.

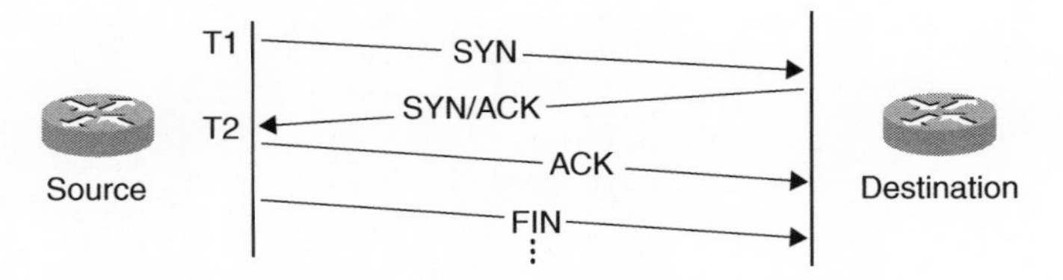

Figure 13.40: IP SLA TCP Connection Measurement

```
ip sla monitor 1
 type tcp-connect 10.100.1.100 9
ip sla schedule 1 start-time now
```

Figure 13.41: IP SLA TCP Connection Configuration

TCP provides communications that need to be established before data can be transferred. TCP connections have three phases:

- Connection establishment
- Data transfer
- Connection termination

To establish a connection, TCP uses a three-way handshake protocol. Before a client can connect to a target server, the server must first bind to a port for connection establishment; this is called a *passive open*. Once the passive open is established, a client may initiate an *active open*.

To establish a connection, the three-way handshake is as follows:

- The active open is performed by the client sending a SYN to the server.
- In response, the server replies with a SYN-ACK.
- Finally, the client sends an ACK back to the server.

Connection termination requires an endpoint to transmit a FIN packet, which the other end acknowledges with an ACK. Therefore, a typical tear-down requires a pair of FIN and ACK segments from each TCP endpoint.

The measured TCP connect time is the difference between sending the initial SYN and receiving the subsequent ACK, shown as T2 – T1 in the figure.

Figure 13.41 shows CLI syntax for enabling the TCP connection measurement feature in IP SLA, followed by the results expected from the type of measurement option shown in Figure 13.42.

The configuration steps as shown in the figure are:

- *ip sla monitor <operation-number>*. Used to begin configuration for an IP SLA operation.

```
Router#sh ip sla monitor statistics 1 detail
Round trip time (RTT) Index 1
    Latest RTT: 1 ms
Latest operation start time: 14:20:26:272 CET Mon Mar 13 2006
Latest operation return code: ok
Over thresholds occurred: False
Number of successes: 24
Number of failures: 0
Operation time to live: Forever
Operational state of entry: Active
Last time this entry was reset: Never
```

Figure 13.42: IP SLA TCP Connection Output

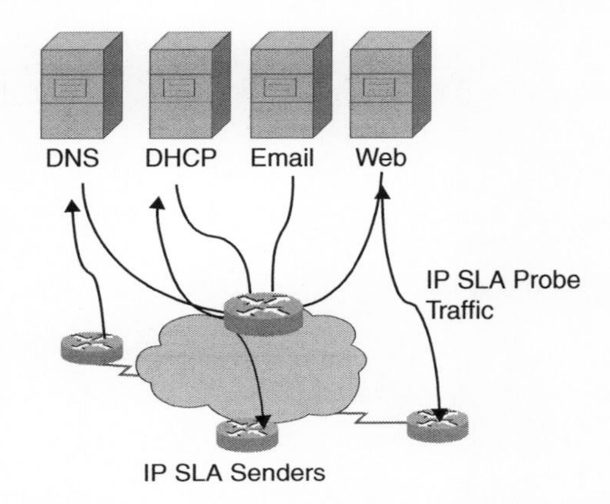

Figure 13.43: IP SLA Service Performance Measurement

- *type tcpConnect dest-ipaddr {destination-ip-address | destination-hostname} dest-port port-number [source-ipaddr {ip-address | hostname} source-port port-number] [control {enable | disable}]*. Define a Cisco IOS IP SLA Transmission Control Protocol (TCP) connection operation.
- *ip sla monitor schedule operation-number [life {forever | seconds}] [start-time {hh:mm[:ss] [month day | day month] | pending | now | after hh:mm:ss}] [ageout seconds] [recurring]*. Configure the scheduling parameters for a single Cisco IOS IP SLA operation.

Beyond the basic ability to ensure TCP connection, IP SLA gives specific measurement of critical applications for the SP, including DNS, DHCP, and HTTP. Figure 13.43 gives an overview of the measurement of these applications using IP SLA.

As shown, strategically placed IP SLA Senders can generate traffic capable of checking performance parameters relevant to each of the applications being measured. Generally the sender will be as close to the end users as possible to ensure that realistic measurements are made, possibly the last-hop router before the users or a strategically placed shadow router. There is more information on this topic later in this chapter.

```
ip sla monitor 1
  type dns target-addr www.cisco.com
      name-server 10.1.1.1
ip sla monitor schedule 1 start-time now
```

Figure 13.44: IP SLA DNS Measurement Configuration

IP SLA DNS Performance Measurement

The IP SLA DNS option measures the time taken between sending a DNS request and receiving the reply. This will give a baseline understanding of DNS performance, which is considered a critical element for Internet-surfing interpretation of speed.

The IP SLA sender queries for an IP address if the configuration specifies a hostname (forward) or queries for a hostname if the configuration specifies an IP address (reverse).

Figure 13.44 shows configuration for DNS performance testing using IP SLA.

The configuration steps as shown in the figure are:

- *ip sla monitor <operation-number>*. Used to begin configuration for an IP SLA operation.
- *type dns target-addr {target-hostname | target-ip-address} name-server ip-address [source-ipaddr {ip-address | hostname} source-port port-number]*. Configure a Cisco IOS IP SLA Domain Name System (DNS) operation.
- *ip sla monitor schedule operation-number [life {forever | seconds}] [start-time {hh: mm[:ss] [month day | day month] | pending | now | after hh:mm:ss}] [ageout seconds] [recurring]*. Configure the scheduling parameters for a single Cisco IOS IP SLA operation.

As shown in the example, the IP address request is for www.cisco.com and is issued to the DNS server 10.1.1.1.

IP SLA DHCP Performance Measurement

The IP SLA DHCP performance option measures the time taken to discover a DHCP Server and obtain an IP address lease. IP SLA releases the IP address immediately after the measurement is complete.

Figure 13.45 shows configuration for DHCP performance testing using IP SLA.

As shown in the example, the IP address request is issued to the DHCP server 10.1.1.1.

IP SLA HTTP Performance Measurement

The IP SLA HTTP performance option measures server responsiveness for DNS request, TCP connection, time to first byte and HTTP transaction time. IP SLA includes support for HTTP

```
ip sla monitor 1
  type dhcp dest 10.1.1.1 [opt 82]
ip sla monitor schedule 1 start-time now
```

Figure 13.45: IP SLA DHCP Measurement Configuration

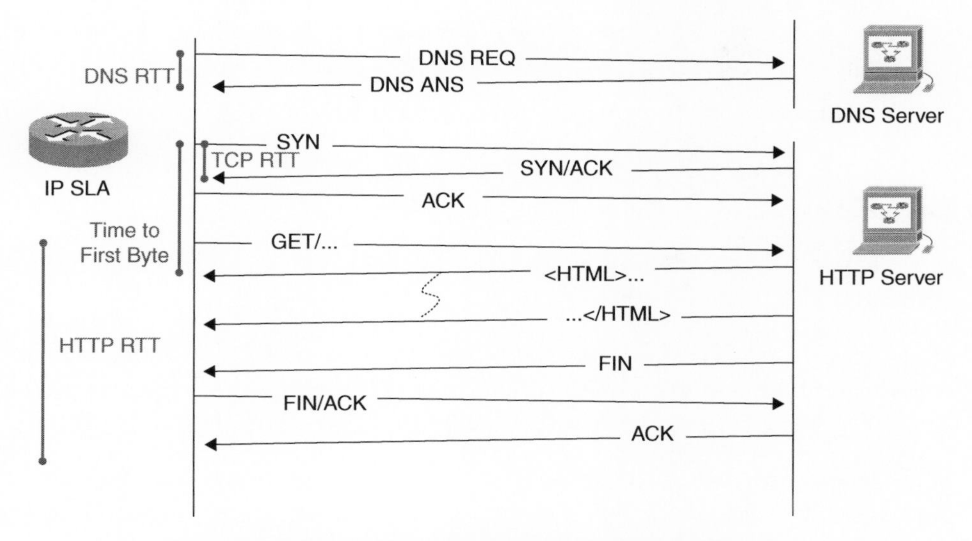

Figure 13.46: IP SLA HTTP Measurement Options

```
ip sla monitor 1
  type http operation get url http://www.cisco.com/go/ipsla
ip sla monitor schedule 1 start-time now
```

Figure 13.47: IP SLA HTTP Measurement Configuration

Proxy servers. In this performance measurement, IP SLA Responder is not required, since the target device is an IP host.

Figure 13.46 shows the operation of the IP SLA HTTP option for measurement of DNS, time to first byte, and HTTP round-trip times.

IP SLA HTTP supports *GET* requests and custom configured *RAW* requests. For the *GET* request, IP SLA will automatically format the request based on the URL specified in the CLI configuration. If the *RAW* option is adopted, the operator must manually configure the entire content of the HTTP request. The IP SLA *RAW* format allows configuration of control fields such as authentication for specific measurements.

Figure 13.47 shows configuration for HTTP performance testing using IP SLA with a basic *GET* request.

```
ip sla monitor 1
 type http operation raw url http://www.cisco.com
       http-raw-request
          GET /lab/index.html HTTP/1.0\r\n
              Authorization: Basic btNpdGT4biNvoZe=\r\n
              \r\n
exit
ip sla monitor schedule 1 start-time now
```

Figure 13.48: IP SLA HTTP Measurement RAW Configuration

The configuration steps as shown in the figure are:

- *ip sla monitor <operation-number>*. Used to begin configuration for an IP SLA operation.
- *type http operation {get | raw} url url [name-server ip-address] [version version-number] [source-ipaddr {ip-address | hostname}] [source-port port-number] [cache {enable | disable}] [proxy proxy-url]*. Configure a Cisco IOS IP SLA HTTP operation.
- *ip sla monitor schedule operation-number [life {forever | seconds}] [start-time {hh:mm[:ss] [month day | day month] | pending | now | after hh:mm:ss}] [ageout seconds] [recurring]*. Configure the scheduling parameters for a single Cisco IOS IP SLA operation.

In this example, the IP SLA sender will automatically generate the *GET* request string after resolving the address using DNS. Additional options with this command are as follows:

- *cache*. Enable or disable download of cached HTTP page.
- *name-server*. Name server.
- *proxy*. Proxy information.
- *source-ipaddr*. Source address.
- *source-port*. Source port.
- *version*. Version number.

The configuration shown in Figure 13.48 gives an example of HTTP RAW implementation using IP SLA.

This example shows inclusion of the authentication string as part of the command issued using HTTP.

IP SLA FTP Performance Measurement

The IP SLA FTP measurement option measures the time to download a file from a selected target server. Clearly, for the most accurate results, larger files are preferred; however, obviously

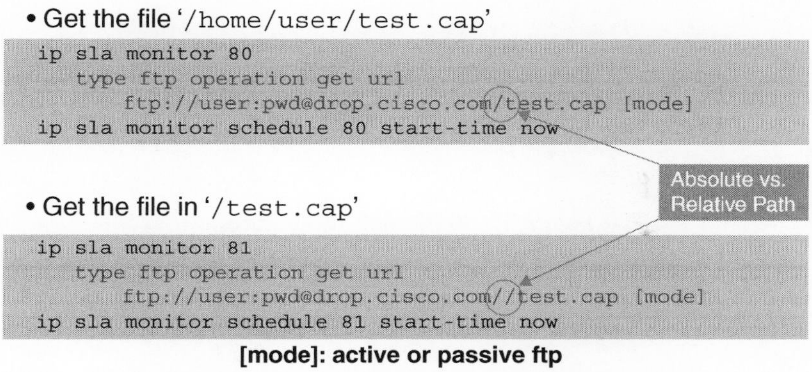

• Get the file '/home/user/test.cap'

```
ip sla monitor 80
   type ftp operation get url
       ftp://user:pwd@drop.cisco.com/test.cap [mode]
ip sla monitor schedule 80 start-time now
```


• Get the file in '/test.cap'

```
ip sla monitor 81
   type ftp operation get url
       ftp://user:pwd@drop.cisco.com//test.cap [mode]
ip sla monitor schedule 81 start-time now
```

[mode]: active or passive ftp

Figure 13.49: IP SLA FTP Measurement Configuration

this requires additional bandwidth for measurement purposes. Active or passive mode of FTP transfer is supported. Given the target device is an IP host, IP SLA Responder is not supported.

Figure 13.49 show configuration options for IP SLA FTP measurement in Cisco IOS.

The configuration steps as shown in the figure are:

- *ip sla monitor <operation-number>*. Used to begin configuration for an IP SLA operation.
- *type ftp operation get url url [source-ipaddr {ip-address | hostname}] [mode {passive | active}*. Configure a Cisco IOS IP SLA File Transfer Protocol (FTP) *GET* operation.
- *ip sla monitor schedule operation-number [life {forever | seconds}] [start-time {hh:mm[:ss] [month day | day month] | pending | now | after hh:mm:ss}] [ageout seconds] [recurring]*. Configure the scheduling parameters for a single Cisco IOS IP SLA operation.

13.7.8 QoS Per-Class Measurement

IP SLA has the capability to mark the ToS field in the IP header. This allows measurement of performance metrics within selected classes. In a multiservice NGN, the performance requirements, which could map to SLA contracts, are generally per class; hence measurement and reporting against each class is essential. Even where SLA contracts are not committed to external customers, the SP will almost certainly still require per-class measurement for operational purposes such as troubleshooting and capacity planning.

Figure 13.50 shows the command-line setting of IP ToS in Cisco IOS for IP SLA.

In IP SLA, the setting of ToS bits is supported for QoS class testing, as previously mentioned. Figure 13.51 gives an example the ToS bit setting.

As shown in the example, if the DSCP is 40, the appropriate ToS will be 160, which is A0 in hexadecimal.

```
ip sla monitor 1
 type jitter dest-ipaddr 10.20.100.1 dest-port 16384 \
        interval 20 num-packets 5000
 tos 0xB0
 frequency 60
 request-data-size 172
ip sla monitor schedule 1 start-time now
```

Figure 13.50: IP SLA ToS Setting

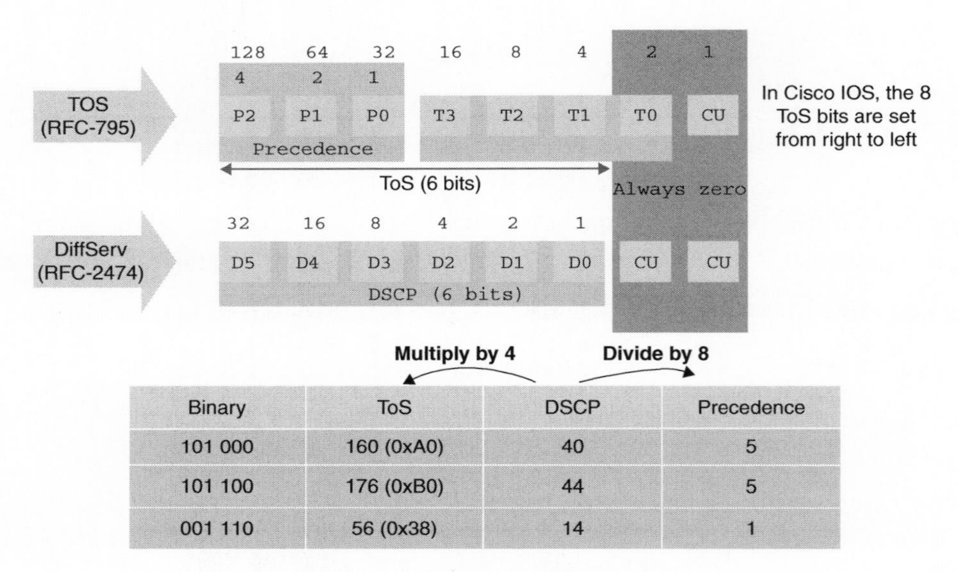

Binary	ToS	DSCP	Precedence
101 000	160 (0xA0)	40	5
101 100	176 (0xB0)	44	5
001 110	56 (0x38)	14	1

Figure 13.51: DSCP-to-ToS Conversion

13.7.9 IP SLA Deployment

IP SLA deployment is an important consideration to a service provider. An SP will have to consider the measurement approach in the context of the following parameters:

- *What services are being offered by the network?* Enterprise services with or without managed CPE, different classes of services, voice, hosting services.
- *What KPIs or SLAs are being committed?* A service provider should never offer any performance metrics without understanding and agreeing with the customer on exactly how they are measured and reported.
- *What KPIs must be measured for operational purposes?* Often the KPIs reported to end customers are a subset of the measurements required for operational purposes such as troubleshooting and capacity planning.
- *The network topology.* The topology will influence the most appropriate measurement deployment strategy.

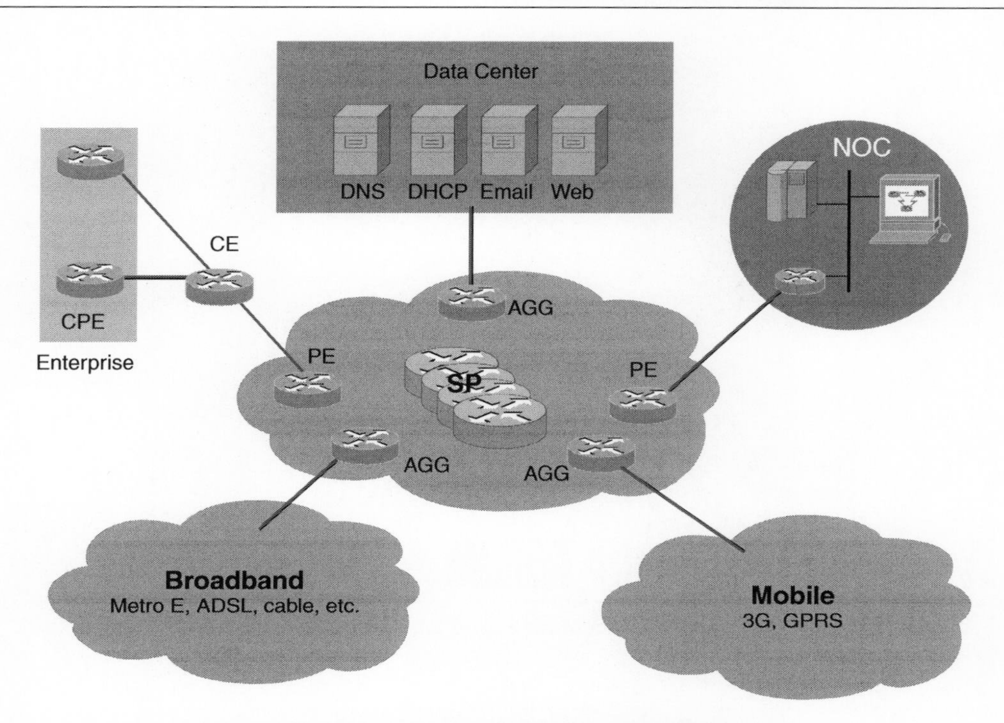

Figure 13.52: Service Provider Reference Architecture

Based on the metrics to be measured for reporting and operational purposes, the SP will have a variety of measurements required for various components of the network.

Figure 13.52 shows the reference architecture for an SP multiservice network.

The following sections give an overview of the deployment options for IP SLA in a service provider network.

13.7.10 IP SLA Services Measurement Scope

Enterprise customers represent the most likely situation in which SPs will be required to offer key performance indicators with associated SLA contracts. As such, measurement of service availability, delay, packet loss, and jitter must be adequate for reporting and operational support.

There are three basic models for connection of enterprise customers:

- *Unmanaged Customer Premises Equipment (CPE).* In this model, the SP is only responsible for network performance up to the PE port facing the CE router. The customer is responsible for the CE and the last-mile transport from the PE to CE.

The unmanaged CPE model is shown in Figure 13.53.

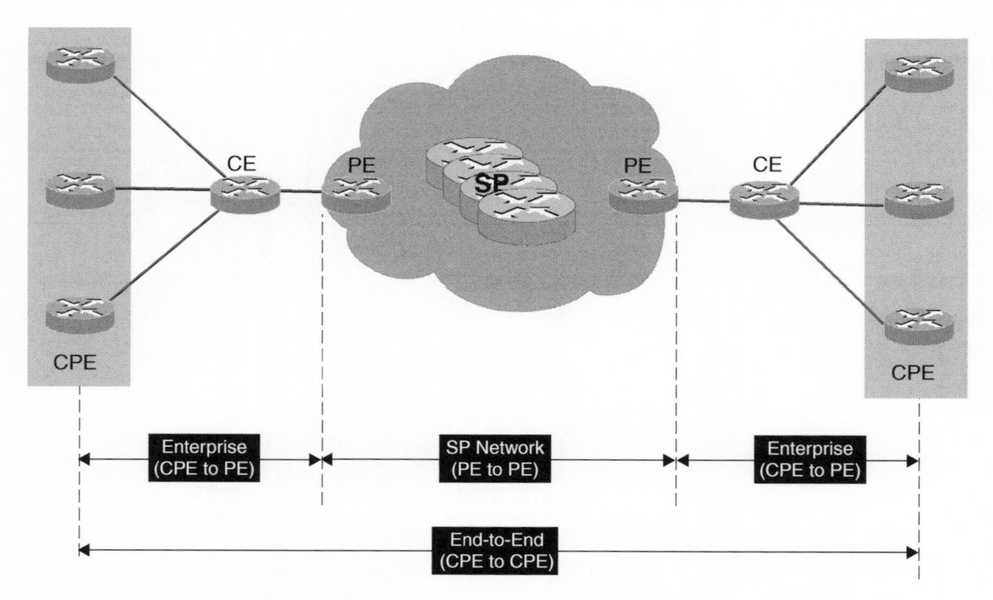

Figure 13.53: Unmanaged CE Architecture

> **NOTE 13.6: Unmanaged CE and Last Mile**
>
> The unmanaged CE and last-mile transport are not a common model for enterprise connectivity. Generally the enterprise customer will prefer models whereby the last-mile transmission is managed as part of the bundled VPN service from the service provider.

- *Managed Customer Premises Equipment (CPE).* In this model, the SP is responsible for network performance up to and including the CE router. This includes the last-mile transport from the PE to the CE.

The managed CPE model is shown in Figure 13.54.

- *Unmanaged Customer Premises Equipment (CPE) managed last mile.* In this model, the SP is responsible for network performance up to the CE port facing the PE router. The provider is therefore responsible for the last-mile transport from the PE to CE.

The unmanaged CPE managed last-mile model is shown in Figure 13.55.

> **NOTE 13.7: Performance Measurement with the Unmanaged CE Architectures**
>
> Performance SLAs in enterprise connectivity models with unmanaged CE should not extend to the CE device. Issues arise in traffic from the CE toward the PE where QoS configuration is the responsibility of the enterprise and therefore out of the control of the SP. Hence SLAs cannot be agreed beyond the SP PE router unless the CE and last mile are managed by the SP.

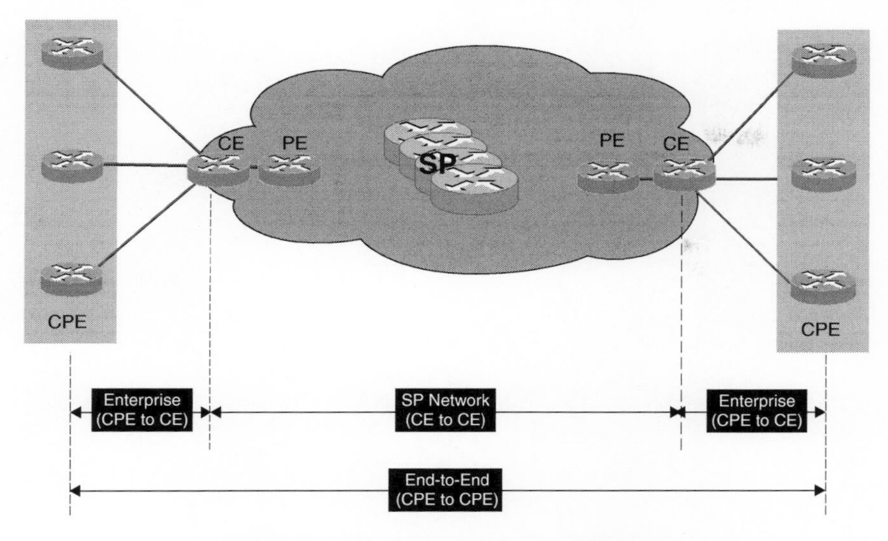

Figure 13.54: Managed CE Architecture

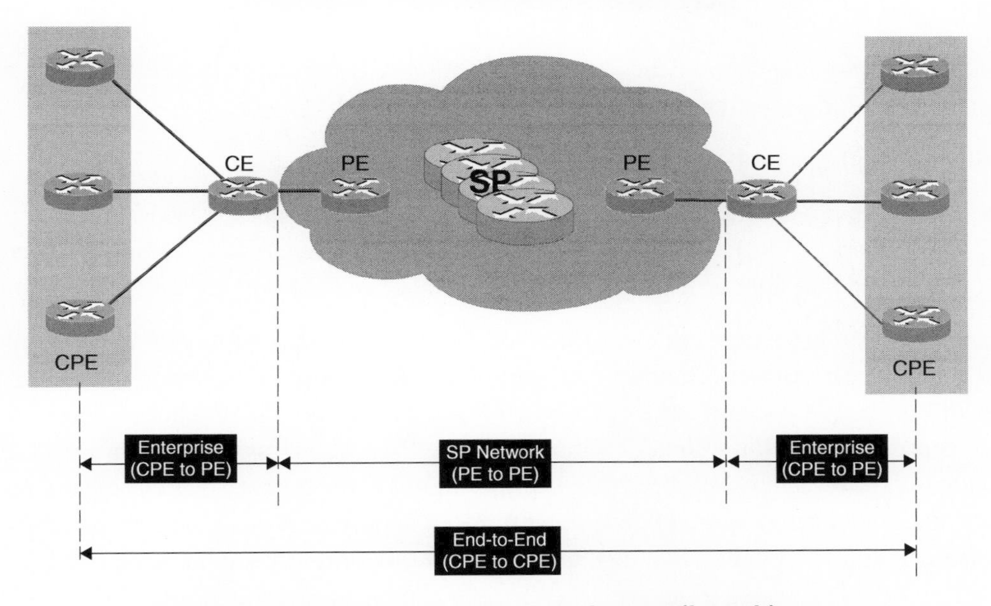

Figure 13.55: Unmanaged CE Managed Last-Mile Architecture

13.7.11 IP SLA Measurement Within the Service Provider Network

There are three basic approaches to deployment within the SP network domain as follows:

- Full mesh
- Partial mesh
- Composite mesh

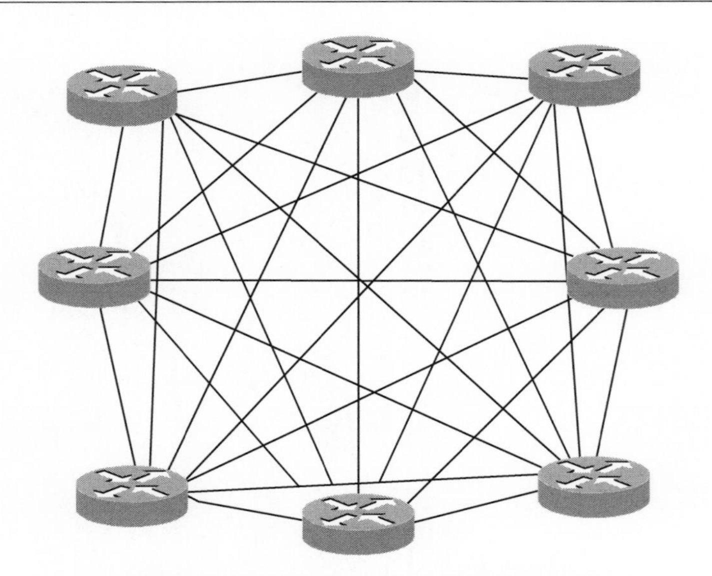

Figure 13.56: IP SLA Full Mesh Deployment

Each of these deployment approaches can span within an SP domain only or extend to CPE connected at enterprise customer sites, for example.

The full mesh deployment is as shown in Figure 13.56.

Full mesh deployment has the obvious benefit of accuracy and relevance. Probe traffic passing through the network can be collated for every possible path that user or service traffic will transit. Measurements can therefore be used for reporting and operational purposes without compromise.

In medium-sized to large network infrastructures, full mesh IP SLA deployment simply cannot scale. The number of routers requiring configuration as IP SLA senders is proportional to the number of PE routers. As with any circuit-based full mesh design, the number of operations required is proportional to the square of the number of PEs, which may be several per POP. The bandwidth generated for probe traffic is proportional to the number of PEs squared and the accuracy and granularity required hence in a full mesh deployment this traffic may become a significant percentage of bandwidth on expensive domestic or international links.

Figure 13.57 shows a partial mesh approach to IP SLA deployment.

Partial mesh deployment is based on strategic selection of paths, PEs, and sites for measurement. For example, critical aggregated core POPs and trunks that are more likely to be congested may be selected for measurement. Depending on the network topology, this approach can dramatically reduce the number of probes and amount of synthetic traffic generated.

Ultimately, any deployment strategy other than full mesh is a calculated compromise. Monitoring results will be an approximation of the overall topology, which could be adequate for reporting but not for operational functions such as troubleshooting.

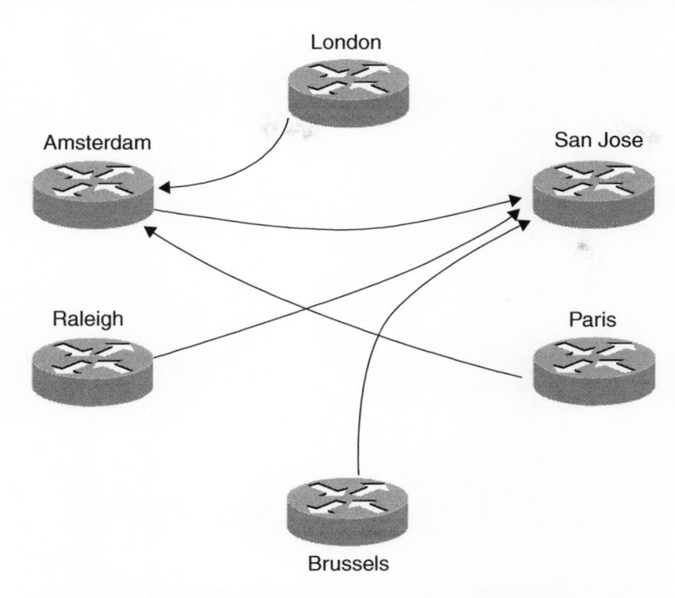

Figure 13.57: IP SLA Partial Mesh Deployment

Another alternative for deployment is referred to as a *composite mesh*, as shown in Figure 13.58.

This deployment scenario is highly dependent on the network topology. In situations in which there are islands of POPs giving regions of network coverage, connected via high-speed trunks to a central region, composite mesh deployment is an option. An example could be where there is a northern region and a southern region aggregated to a regional hub POP, which is then connected with a high-speed trunk. This scenario can allow measurement using IP SLA within each region and across the northern/southern trunk. The results can then be added as required to give an end-to-end view.

This deployment scenario can negate many of the issues of *N*-squared operations associated with full mesh, without the level of compromise required for partial mesh. One disadvantage is that measurement of jitter and MOS is not possible end to end, since this metric can be negative or positive, which is not readily captured using IP SLA; hence adding these parameters is meaningless.

13.7.12 IP SLA Dedicated Probe Router

As previously mentioned, IP SLA can use a forwarding router for the source/agent functionality or a dedicated router, referred to as a *shadow* or *probe router*. The operator may decide to use a dedicated shadow router if the following constraints exist:

- CPU of the alternative traffic-forwarding router is at risk of exceeding an acceptable level should IP SLA agent functionality be enabled.
- A large number of IP SLA operations are required in a meshed, granular architecture for acceptable measurements to be made. An example is a large, multiservice NGN infrastructure.

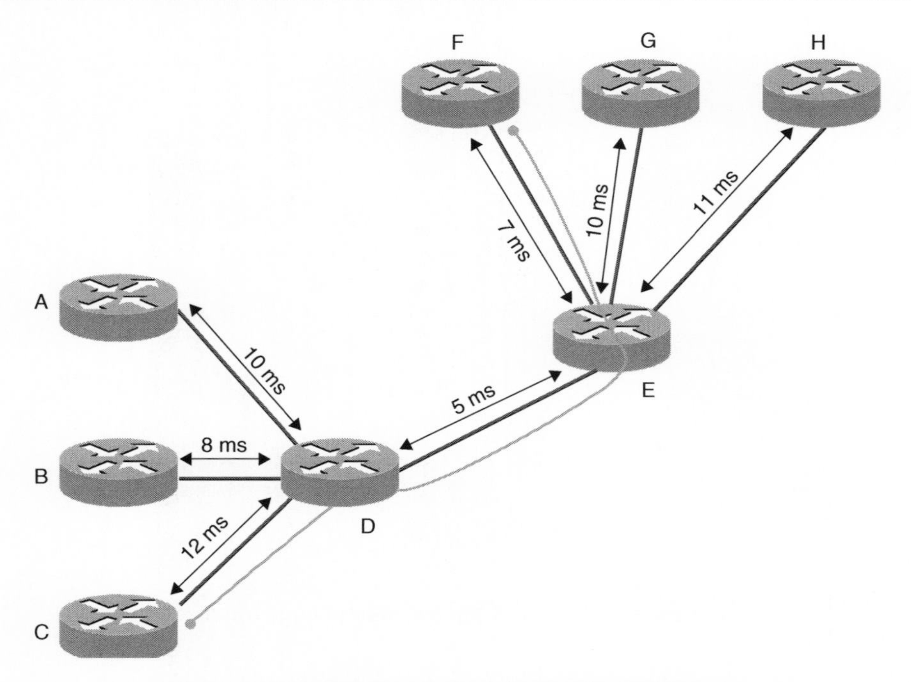

Figure 13.58: IP SLA Composite Mesh Deployment

- The edge router has insufficient memory to maintain IP SLA measurement data and the forwarding table for service traffic.
- Measurement traffic destined for the monitoring tool and the service forwarding traffic plane are separate. The provider may choose to run a separate transport network specifically to manage traffic. Note that a traffic-forwarding router may still be configured to utilize a management transport network specifically for forwarding IP SLA measurement data.
- Reduce change management risk to network availability. In the event of changes being required to the IP SLA configuration, this can be done to a probe router without impact to the service traffic-forwarding devices. One example is in the event of the IP SLA feature being used for fault management where different measurements are enabled, then disabled to facilitate troubleshooting. Were the service forwarding router being used for IP SLA, such changes would not be recommended.
- Reduce features on traffic-forwarding routers to mitigate possible production network outages. Typically the stability of a complex routing device is inversely proportional to the number of features enabled; hence offloading IP SLA features to a dedicated probe device may improve network availability.

Figure 13.59 depicts the placement of an IP SLA shadow router in an SP's network.

Placement of the shadow router is critical to the measurement accuracy of IP SLA. In general, the operator will place the router parallel to the PE device using the same QoS configuration

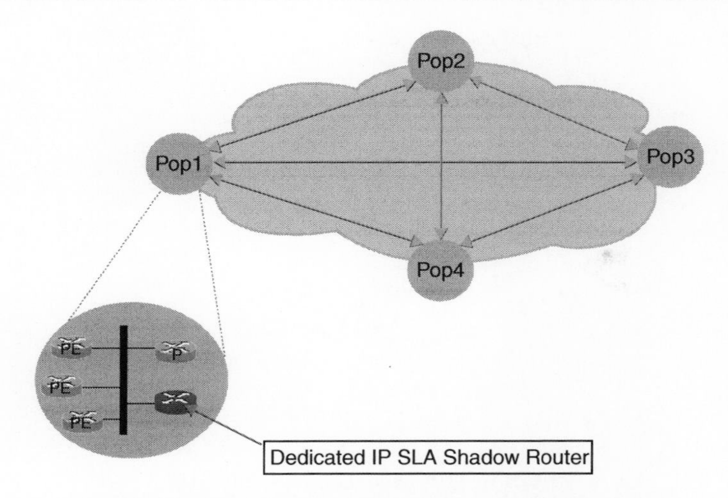

Figure 13.59: IP SLA Shadow Router Example

and connection type to ensure that results are as close to those experienced by the service traffic as possible.

13.7.13 IP SLA for MPLS VPN

For IP SLA to be effective in modern SP networks, it must include the capability to measure metrics within selected VPNs. This is particularly relevant for enterprise services in which SLAs are agreed and contractually committed. As shown in Figure 13.60, if the IP SLA sender is the PE device and is not MPLS VRF aware, the probe traffic will only use the global routing table, making VPN measurement impossible.

The IP SLA operations have been VRF-aware in more recent IOS versions, allowing ICMP Echo, ICMP Path Echo, UDP Echo, and UDP Jitter operations to be executed within a VRF. The command *vrf vrf-name* is included as a CLI option, as shown in Figure 13.61.

An alternative approach is to use an IP SLA shadow router for MPLS VPN measurements. In this case the shadow router can act as a CE to the PE for each of the VRFs requiring measurement. Logical or physical interfaces can be included in the VRF at the PE, as shown in Figure 13.62.

This removes the measurement load from the PE device and negates the requirement for VRF awareness on the IP SLA Sender. If the CPE is managed by the SP and the router is capable of running the feature, the IP SLA source may be the CPE itself. This gives a more accurate measurement from the user perspective if this option is available.

13.8 IP SLA Monitoring Tools

IP SLA is a feature capable of generating the measurement data for performance in an IP network. As previously mentioned, a performance-monitoring tool will collate and interpret the data, giving longer trends and more meaningful representation of network characteristics.

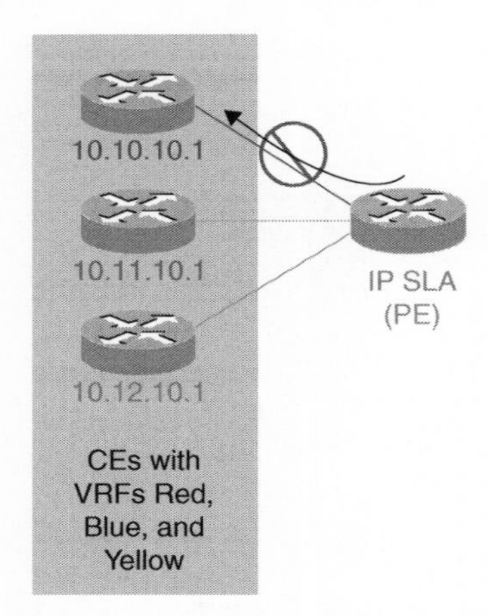

Figure 13.60: IP SLA Measurement for MPLS VPN

```
ip sla monitor 1
 type jitter dest-ipaddr 1.1.1.1 dest-port 80
 vrf blue
ip sla monitor schedule 1 start-time now
```

Figure 13.61: IP SLA MPLS VPN Configuration

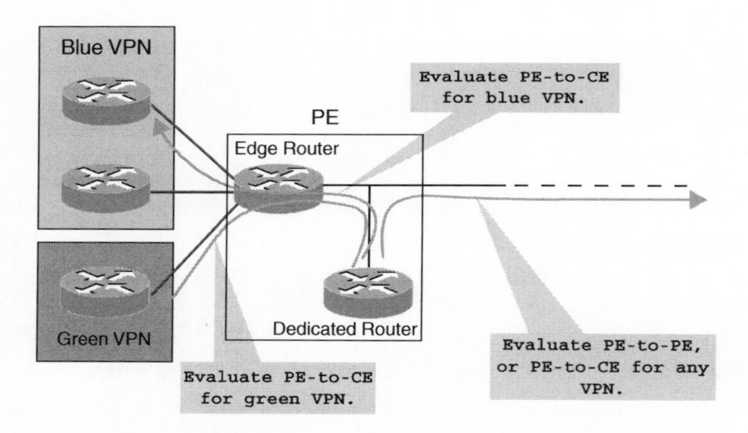

Figure 13.62: IP SLA MPLS VPN Shadow Router Deployment

Figure 13.63 shows third-party companies that use IP SLA measurement data as the basis for network performance monitoring.

Each of the third-party monitoring tools has different features, advantages, and disadvantages, depending on the application in either enterprise or SP networks. In the SP realm, Concord and InfoVista are certainly very popular options due to their scalability and functionality aligning specifically with SP requirements.

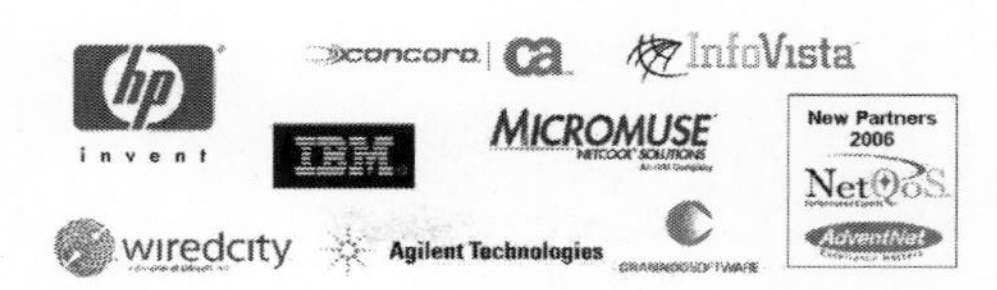

Figure 13.63: IP SLA Third-Party Monitoring Tools

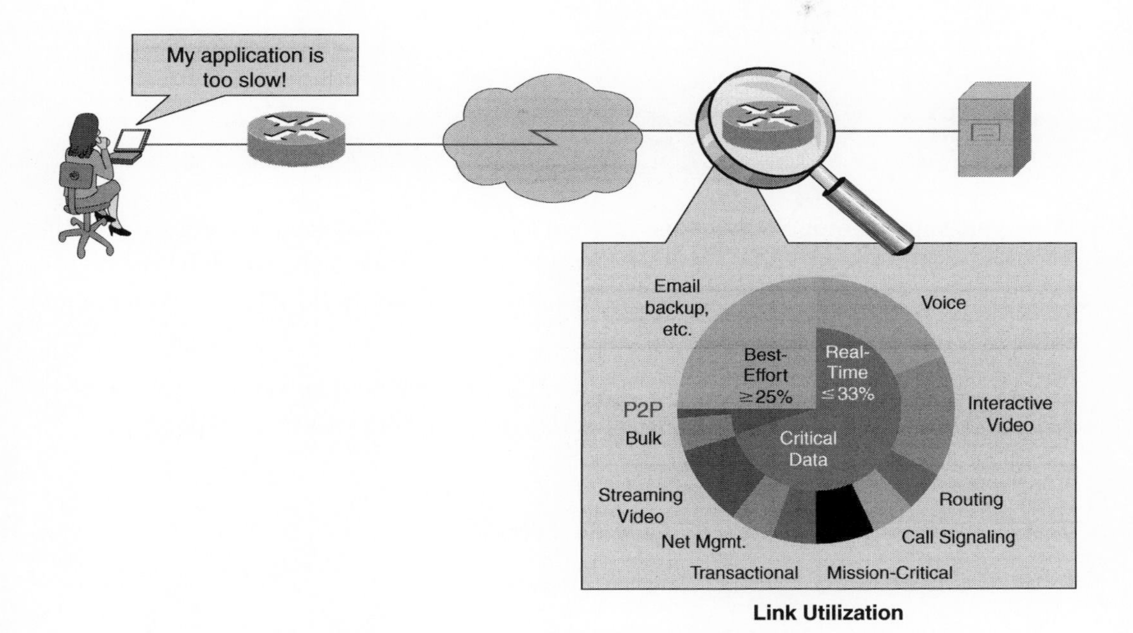

Figure 13.64: NBAR Operation Overview

13.8.1 Network-Based Application Recognition

Network-Based Application Recognition (NBAR) is a feature first available in Cisco IOS Software Release 12.0(5)XE2. NBAR provides specific and granular classification and protocol discovery for traffic transiting an IP router in a network infrastructure. NBAR can specifically recognize a wide variety of applications, such as Web-based and client/server applications—even those that dynamically assign TCP and UDP port numbers, which are generally problematic for identifying and classifying. Figure 13.64 gives an overview of NBAR in a network.

NBAR has the ability to execute protocol analysis in real time, giving some performance-monitoring capabilities particularly useful for network planning and troubleshooting. NBAR is capable of comparing traffic to a wide variety of known protocols and providing information on throughput.

According to the parameters defined in the "Performance Measurement Framework" section, Table 13.6 gives an overview of NBAR as a measurement tool.

Table 13.6: NBAR Performance Measurement Overview

Measurement Category	Category Implementation	Definition
Sampling	Observed/passive	Service and end-user network performance is monitored by measuring specific, actual application traffic flows in real time
Collection	Embedded agent	Mechanisms for collecting performance statistics are integrated into the communication device
Scope	Device/link	Performance measurement based on analysis of specific device or device interface
Perspective	Network	Measurement based on performance statistics measured in network devices

NBAR may be activated for classification through CLI using a class map definition with *match protocol <protocol-name>*, where *protocol-name* is an NBAR-defined protocol. Enabling protocol discovery through CLI using *ip nbar protocol-discovery* in the interface configuration mode will also activate NBAR.

NBAR may also be activated by enabling AutoQoS, a new feature that combines protocol discovery with class-based traffic measurement to automatically generate QoS policies.

NBAR Protocol Support

NBAR is capable of classifying applications as follows:

- Statically assigned TCP and UDP port numbers
- Non-TCP and non-UDP IP protocols
- Dynamic TCP and UDP port numbers assigned during protocol connection establishment
- Classification based on deep packet inspection; NBAR can look deeper into the packet to identify applications
- HTTP traffic by URL, hostname, header fields, or MIME type using regular expressions such as *, ?, [ ], Citrix ICA traffic, RTP payload type classification
- Currently supports more than 90 protocols/applications

Figure 13.65 gives an overview of NBAR packet classification options.

Note that not all protocols are shown in the figure. A more exhaustive list is shown in Figure 13.66.

New applications can be dynamically added by the network operator using a Packet Description Language Module (PDLM). In general, a Cisco IOS code upgrade or reboot is not required to add new PDLMs. Note that PDLMs must be produced by Cisco engineers.

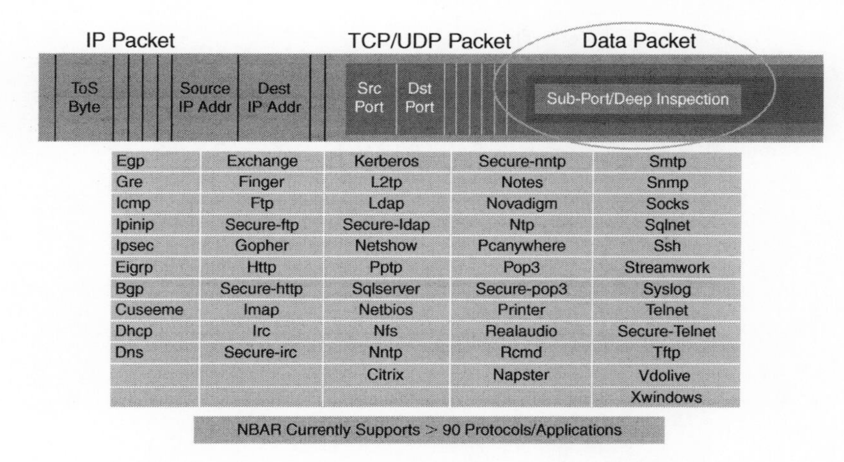

Figure 13.65: NBAR Classification Overview

Enterprise Applications	Security and Tunneling	Network Mail Services	Internet
Citrix ICA	GRE	IMAP	FTP
PCAnywhere	IPINIP	POP3	Gopher
Novadigm	IPsec	Exchange	HTTP
SAP	L2TP	Notes	IRC
Routing Protocols	MS-PPTP	SMTP	Telnet
BGP	SFTP	**Directory**	TFTP
EGP	SHTTP	DHCP/BOOTP	NNTP
EIGRP	SIMAP	Finger	NetBIOS
OSPF	SIRC	DNS	NTP
RIP	SLDAP	Kerberos	Print
Network Management	SNNTP	LDAP	X-Windows
ICMP	SPOP3	**Streaming Media**	**Peer-to-Peer**
SNMP	STELNET	CU-SeeMe	BitTorrent
Syslog	SOCKS	Netshow	Direct Connect
RPC	SSH	Real Audio	eDonkey/eMule
NFS	**Voice**	StreamWorks	FastTrack
SUN-RPC	H.323	VDOLive	Gnutella
Database	RTCP	RTSP	KaZaA
SQL*NET	RTP	MGCP	WinMX
MS SQL Server	SIP	**Signaling**	
	SCCP/Skinny	RSVP	
	Skype		

Figure 13.66: NBAR Protocol Support List

PDLM is the heart of the NBAR engine. The Protocol Description Language (PDL) is part of the Cisco IOS image defining the baseline protocols supported in the code version. The baseline protocols can be viewed using the CLI command *show ip nbar version*. PDLM allows additional protocol support to be downloaded from CCO as required. These can be viewed using the CLI command *show ip nbar pdlm*.

```
router(config-if)#ip nbar protocol-discovery

Router# show ip nbar protocol-discovery [interface interface-spec][stats
{byte-count|bit-rate|packet-count}] [protocol protocol-name| top-n number}]

router# show ip nbar protocol-discovery interface FastEthernet 6/0

  FastEthernet6/0
                    Input                         Output
  Protocol          Packet Count                  Packet Count
                    Byte Count                    Byte Count
                    5 minute bit rate (bps)       5 minute bit rate (bps)
  -----------       -------------------------     -------------------------
  http              316773                        0
                    26340105                      0
                    3000                          0
  pop3              4437                          7367
                    2301891                       339213
                    3000                          0
  snmp              279538                        14644
                    319106191                     673624
                    0                             0
  ftp               8979                          7714
                    906550                        694260
                    0                             0
  ...
  Total             17203819                      151684936
                    19161397327                   50967034611
                    4179000                       6620000
```

Figure 13.67: NBAR Protocol Configuration and Output

There is no proactive notification of new PDLM, so to load a PDLM to a router, connect to the following URL: www.cisco.com/cgi-bin/tablebuild.pl/pdlm

NBAR Packet Classification

After application recognition, the router can invoke specific services as configured by the operator. NBAR is particularly useful with quality-of-service (QoS) classification allowing granular and accurate enforcement. NBAR supports the following QoS features:

- Guaranteed bandwidth with Class-Based Weighted Fair Queuing (CBWFQ)
- Policing and limiting bandwidth
- Marking (ToS or IP DSCP)
- Drop policy with weighted random early detection (WRED)

NBAR Protocol Discovery

NBAR allows protocol discovery per interface, providing real-time statistics on applications per protocol, bidirectional statistics for bit rate (bps), packet counts, and byte counts.

NBAR allows traffic statistics collection for all protocols known to NBAR through PDL or PDLM. NBAR will discover application protocols transiting an interface, either input or output. NBAR can be applied independently of an SP applied through Modular QoS Configuration (MQC).

Figure 13.67 shows configuration of the NBAR protocol discovery and the subsequent output that can be expected.

Table 13.7: NBAR Protocol Discovery MIB Tables

Table	Description	SNMP Access
cnpdSupportedProtocols	List of all supported protocols	Read-only
cnpdAllStats	All NBAR statistics per interface	Read-only
cnpdTopNstats	Top-*N* table statistics	Read-only
cnpdThresholdhistory	History of falling/rising events	Read-only
cnpdStatus	Enable or disable NBAR per interface, including time stamp	Read-write
cnpdTopNconfig	Configure top-*N* table by interface	Read-write
cnpdThresholdconfig	Protocol threshold configuration	Read-write
cnpdNotificationsconfig	Enable traps	Read-write
cnpdMIBNotifications	Rising or falling events	Read-write

SNMP may also be used for accessing NBAR protocol discovery data. The NBAR Protocol Discover MIB will automatically use all PDLMs available to build a statistics table. All protocols will be listed in the SNMP statistics table, with all 0s used to indicate no packets matching a given protocol. SNMP also allows the user to configure and view multiple "top-*N*" statistics tables listing protocols by bandwidth usage. The operator may also configure notifications when defined thresholds are crossed.

Table 13.7 shows supported tables in the NBAR Protocol Discovery MIB, with brief descriptions.

Thresholds may be set on individual protocols on a specific interface or on a selected statistic, regardless of protocol type. Thresholds may also be set for any combination of supported protocols and/or all protocols as required, giving a flexible solution.

Notifications (traps) may be triggered based on these defined thresholds. SNMP notification is generated and sent with a summary of threshold information included in the trap. Hysterisis mechanism stops multiple traps occurring for the same breached threshold within a sample period.

13.8.2 Command-Line Interface

The Cisco CLI may be used for accessing performance data for performance measurement features such as IP SLA, NBAR, and NetFlow. CLI may also be used for accessing QoS performance data directly using selected commands.

In the context of QoS performance, the most relevant command for Cisco router platforms is *show policy-map <interface>*. This command gives detailed information on the number of packets, bytes, and average data rate for a given class defined in the policy map applied to a given interface.

Figure 13.68 gives an example of the output expected from the command.

As shown, each class map in the policy map is listed with the associated match criteria and statistics for packets, bytes, and data rate.

```
#show policy-map interface serial 0/2/1
Serial0/2/1

Service-policy : inner_toPE
 Class-map: ef_toPE (match-any)
 67182 packets, 6559656 bytes
 30 second offered rate 0 bps,
          drop rate 0 bps
Match: ip dscp ef (46)
 67182 packets, 6559656 bytes
 30 second rate 0 bps
 Queueing
  Strict Priority
  Output Queue: Conversation 24
  Bandwidth 50 (kbps) Burst 1250 (Bytes)
 (pkts matched/bytes matched) 28136/1352768
 (total drops/bytes drops) 294/18400
  police:
    cir 50000 bps, bc 1562 bytes
    conformed 57467 packets, 4829248 bytes;
    actions: transmit
    exceeded 8091 packets, 1645920 bytes;
    actions: drop
    conformed 0 bps, exceed 0 bps
Class-map: af4_toPE (match-any)
716176 packets, 29235196 bytes
30 second offered rate 8000 bps,
          drop rate 0 bps
Match: ip dscp cs4 (32) af41 (34)
 715982 packets, 29219676 bytes
 30 second rate 8000 bps
Match: ip dscp af42 (36) af43 (38)
   0 packets, 0 bytes
   30 second rate 0 bps
Match: protocol ntp
    194 packets, 15520 bytes
    30 second rate 0 bps
Queueing
 Output Queue: Conversation 25
 Bandwidth 100 (kbps) Max Threshold 64 (packets)
  (pkts matched/bytes matched) 495810/23671304
  (depth/total drops/no-buffer drops) 0/0/0
Class-map: class-default (match-any)
  24515193 packets, 654530939 bytes
  30 second offered rate 380000 bps,
     drop rate 190000 bps
 Match: any
```

Figure 13.68: Show Policy Map Interface Command

Although the information is significant, in the context of an SP, CLI is relegated to configuration verification and troubleshooting. Typically CLI cannot scale to give meaningful results in the way IP SLA and NetFlow can when coupled with the appropriate monitoring tools.

13.9 Service Provider Deployment Example

Many performance measurement tools have been presented in this chapter. For the SP seeking to deploy a cohesive solution, more than one of these tools will typically be required, particularly with a multiservice network carrying critical services.

This section gives an overview of how a selection of measurement tools may be used for an operational and reporting solution. The tools chosen by the SP will depend largely on the services it offers and any associated SLAs it has with its customers.

An operator must consider two broad requirements for measurement in the network:

- *Reporting.* The network operator must report against SLAs to customers and, in the event of outsourced operations, the SP board. These reports must relate directly to agreed SLAs. Measurements for reporting are generally static, with very few changes.
- *Operational.* The network operator needs accurate and timely measurement of network performance for operational purposes, to ensure effective troubleshooting and proactive fault identification. Examples include security attack identification and capacity planning. Measurements for operational purposes are generally very dynamic, changing frequently, and may be reactive during fault identification and isolation.

This section presents a simple, high-level solution for a medium-sized service provider. The general approach to measurement is described with customer and outsourced operator SLAs defined. Specific monitoring tools and device configurations are not given.

13.9.1 Service Provider NightOwl Requirements

Service Provider NightOwl has the following services supported by the network infrastructure:

- Broadband users accessing data in the Internet
- Enterprise VPN customer with managed CPE and Gold, Silver, Bronze, and Best-Effort traffic classes
- Enterprise VPN customers with unmanaged CPE with only Best-Effort traffic class

NightOwl has a modest network infrastructure as follows:

- The network spans four regions: central, north, south, and east
- Twelve core POP sites with 24 routers partially meshed with high-speed POS interfaces, three core sites in each region
- Thirty-two PE routers for enterprise customer connectivity, both managed and unmanaged, eight PEs in each region
- Forty-four edge routers aggregating broadband users, 20 routers in central, eight in each of the remaining three regions
- Four Internet Gateway routers (IGW) in a single central location for domestic and international peering

13.9.2 NightOwl Service-Level Agreements

The Service Provider NightOwl has decided to outsource network operations for the core IP infrastructure. Hence NightOwl has SLAs with external customers and the chosen operator. NightOwl offers the customer SLAs shown in Table 13.8.

Table 13.8: Customer Service-Level Agreements

Customer Type	Availability	Packet Loss	Latency	Jitter
Broadband user	N/A	N/A	N/A	N/A
Enterprise customer unmanaged CPE: Best Effort	98%	N/A	N/A	N/A
Enterprise customer managed CPE: Gold	99.9%	0.2%	150 ms (Spoke CPE to hub CPE)	30 ms (Spoke CPE to hub CPE)
Enterprise customer managed CPE: Silver	99.5%	0.5%	250 ms (Spoke CPE to hub CPE)	40 ms (Spoke CPE to hub CPE)
Enterprise customer managed CPE: Bronze	99%	1.0%	N/A	N/A

NOTE 13.8: Contractual SLA vs. Customer Expectations

Although broadband users do not have contractual SLAs, this does not preclude expectations of service. Customer experience in terms of network availability, connection time (access to the network, including authentication and address allocation), and browsing/download time (DNS address resolution and download speed) are becoming more stringent in the face of growing competition and proliferation of telecommuting workers. As such, a prudent SP will set standards for and measure network performance parameters, even in the absence of formal SLAs.

Table 13.9 gives details of the reporting scope of measurements for each of the agreed service types and SLAs.

The reporting measurement scope is designed to be meaningful without placing an unnecessary burden on the network in terms of excessive measurement and management traffic. This is a compromise among accuracy, complexity, and network impact.

13.9.3 NightOwl Operator Service-Level Agreements

As previously described, SP NightOwl has outsourced the network infrastructure operations to a specialist operator. The scope of the outsourcing is for all PE and Core routers in the network supporting all services and traffic types. The agreed operator SLAs are shown in Table 13.10.

Note that the SLAs enforced on the operator are well within the SLA figures committed to the customers, as expected. In fact, in the case of broadband and best-effort traffic, SLAs are enforced on the operator despite no contractual commitment to the end user. This is in recognition of the fact that, as previously mentioned, all users have performance expectations, even though no SLAs are agreed.

The reporting scope for operator SLA measurement is as shown in Table 13.11.

The test PEs and broadband edge routers, as defined in the SLA scope, are to be chosen by the SP. The operator will also have operational measurements to assist in troubleshooting and proactive fault identification (see Table 13.12).

Table 13.9: Customer SLA Reporting Measurement Scope

Customer Type	Measurement Scope
Broadband user	N/A
Enterprise customer unmanaged CPE: Best Effort	Where customer has hub/spoke topology: From all customer spoke site attached PEs to all customer hub site attached PEs Where customer has meshed topology: Maximum of three site attached PE(s) chosen from each region, meshed with all other site attached PE(s) (total maximum possible: 12 PEs) Last-mile connection to customer site and customer CPE performance are not measured
Enterprise customer managed CPE: Gold	Where customer has hub/spoke topology: From all customer spoke site CPEs to all customer hub site CPEs Where customer has meshed topology: Maximum of three site CPEs chosen from each region, meshed with all other site CPEs (total maximum possible: 12 CPEs)
Enterprise customer managed CPE: Silver	Where customer has hub/spoke topology: From all customer spoke site CPEs to all customer hub site CPEs Where customer has meshed topology: Maximum of three site CPEs chosen from each region, meshed with all other site CPEs (total maximum possible: 12 CPEs)
Enterprise customer managed CPE: Bronze	Where customer has hub/spoke topology: From all customer spoke site CPEs to all customer hub site CPEs Where customer has meshed topology: Maximum of three site CPEs chosen from each region, meshed with all other site CPEs (total maximum possible: 12 CPEs)

Table 13.10: Core Network Operator Service-Level Agreements

Traffic Type	Availability	Packet Loss	Latency	Jitter
Best Effort	99% (Broadband aggregation to Internet gateway, PE to PE)	2.0% (Broadband aggregation to Internet gateway, PE to PE)	250 ms (Broadband aggregation to Internet gateway, PE to PE)	50 ms (Broadband aggregation to Internet gateway, PE to PE)
Gold	99.99%	0.1%	50 ms (PE to PE)	20 ms (Spoke CPE to hub CPE)
Silver	99.95%	0.25%	80 ms (PE to PE)	30 ms (PE to PE)
Bronze	99.9%	0.5%	100 ms (PE to PE)	50 ms (PE to PE)

Table 13.11: Operator SLA Reporting Measurement Scope

Traffic Type	Measurement Scope
Best Effort	Three enterprise VPN PEs in each region, fully meshed (total: 12 PEs) Four broadband edge routers in each region to two IGW routers in central region
Gold	Three enterprise VPN PEs in each region, fully meshed (total: 12 PEs)
Silver	Three enterprise VPN PEs in each region, fully meshed (total: 12 PEs)
Bronze	Three enterprise VPN PEs in each region, fully meshed (total: 12 PEs)

Table 13.12: Operator SLA Operational Measurement Scope

Traffic Type	Measurement Scope
Security	Traffic profile anomaly security attack detection
Broadband user experience	DHCP performance: Three broadband edge routers per region to central DHCP servers DNS performance: Three broadband edge routers per region to central DNS servers
Capacity planning	Monitoring of bandwidth usage on all trunks between core routers

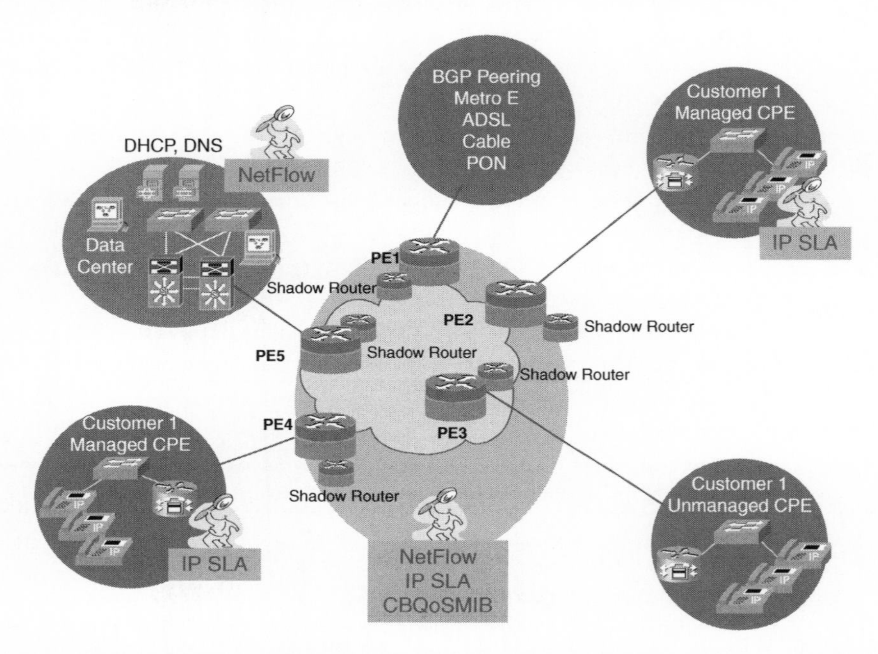

Figure 13.69: Service Provider Performance Measurement Deployment Example

Note that reactive operational measurements triggered as part of fault isolation and troubleshooting are not listed. As shown in the table, the network operator will focus on operational measurements around security, broadband user experience, and capacity planning. These measurements will be used to ensure service integrity without being formally reported to the SP.

13.9.4 Service Provider NightOwl Measurement Solution

The measurement solution chosen by the SP and network operator must meet the requirements for customer SLA reporting, operator SLA reporting, and operational monitoring as defined in the previous section. Figure 13.69 gives an overview of the measurement solution with recommended feature deployment at each network layer.

NOTE 13.9: Network Availability Measurement

Overall network availability will be measured using the trouble-ticketing system run by the network operator. Network availability will be defined as follows: (Total operational minutes – Total unplanned outage minutes)/(Total operational minutes).

All performance measurement tasks for reporting on both customer and operator SLAs will use the IP SLA with an appropriate monitoring tool.

Measurements in the core network for broadband edge routers and enterprise VPN routers will be via shadow routers, to allow for scalable and flexible measurement. Refer to the IP SLA section in this chapter for details. Measurements from the managed CPE will use IP SLA without a shadow router.

IP SLA UDP Jitter operation will be used to measure packet loss, latency, and jitter. All target devices for measurement will have the IP SLA Responder feature enabled to ensure accurate results.

In the case of the NightOwl operator, the out-of-band network management routers will also act as the IP SLA shadow routers, giving a cost-effective solution.

In the core network, the features used for operational measurement are as follows:

- NetFlow
- IP SLA
- CBQoSMIB

NetFlow will be used by an appropriate security monitoring tool, such as Arbor, for security attack detection in the core infrastructure. NetFlow allows the monitoring tool to understand typical network traffic behavior and explore anomalies based on an understanding of security attack profiles.

IP SLA will be used for measuring broadband user experience. IP SLA will periodically test the performance of the DHCP and DNS servers, which are critical to the user experience. After a period of baselining acceptable behavior, the operator can use performance data to recognize issues if there is a complaint regarding poor performance. These data can also be used to justify additional servers or distributed locations for server implementation, should the need arise.

The CBQoSMIB allows an understanding of interface utilization per class that is essential for effective capacity planning. All interfaces in the core network will be measured for traffic per class, which will be trended over time to help the operator understand when upgrades will be required prior to degraded network performance.

13.10 Summary

This chapter gave an overview of the tools available to the service provider for executing performance management in an IP network. The basic performance data access mechanisms of SNMP, NBAR, NetFlow, IP SLA, and CLI were reviewed in the context of performance management.

CHAPTER 14

Summary

14.1 Introduction

As discussed in Chapter 1, many of the traditional services carried on telco networks have evolved to an IP converged protocol for transport. These include voice, private data for enterprises and mobile signaling, voice, and data. This convergence at the network protocol layer has driven providers to embrace convergence of the network infrastructure itself. As discussed, the benefits are enormous, allowing streamlining of CapEx and OpEx.

This convergence capability brings significant opportunities and associated challenges. The opportunity for consolidation of equipment and operational teams far outweighs the technical challenges of scaling, security, and efficient use of equipment and expensive bandwidth. The two most notable aspects of the service providers' CapEx and OpEx are the infrastructure equipment outlay and the ongoing fees for transmission. In general, the cost of the infrastructure can be considered proportional to the transmission bandwidth because additional bandwidth leads to a proportional increase in equipment and line cards required to support that bandwidth. As such, efficient use of bandwidth is important in the reduction of CapEx and OpEx.

A robust QoS implementation is key to meeting the vast requirements of services ranging from mobile network signaling to broadband Internet surfing in the most effective, bandwidth-efficient manner. Hence the appropriate design and deployment of QoS in the network are essential to the service provider seeking the most efficient converged infrastructure implementation.

14.2 The Evolution of IP Routed Networks

Traffic can be generally characterized as a stream of packets of varying duration between a source and a destination. Examples include a voice call, video call, file transfer, or Web access. IP traffic flows using TCP as the Layer 4 protocol can generally adapt to packet losses by reducing the transfer speed. UDP relies on the application to adapt where possible; generally any excessive packet loss, delay, or jitter can be problematic, depending on the application.

The first generation of IP routers had memory and processing power limitations, relegating them to the simple task of forwarding a packet based in the destination address. Routing protocols determining the path of a packet through the network were incapable of understanding congestion, QoS, and other parameters useful in optimizing traffic flows. The concept of recognizing flows or enforcing any type of traffic prioritization was technically unfeasible at this point in history. In the context of requirements for file transfer and email at the time, this was adequate. As IP emerged to become a converged network layer protocol, the best-effort approach to data transport was no longer effective.

ATM was designed to recognize the requirement for some form of differentiated data prioritization. ATM started the trend toward broad categories of traffic treatment to scale the implementation and management of large networks. Overlaying traffic types onto ATM with short duration flows, as typical in the IP world, was difficult, given the lengthy call setup time required. Bursty traffic flows with small IP packets, such as Voice over IP, proved inefficient in an ATM infrastructure. As IP grew in popularity at the edge, the momentum for ATM as a technology declined.

Based on the QoS model adopted for ATM, IP routed networks moved toward distinct categories of traffic priorities for transport across the core. The implementation of QoS varies depending on the number of classes and the infrastructure capabilities. One common aspect of all current implementations is the grouping of traffic into a selection of class categories, as per ATM. This grouping is to allow scaling in the deployment, measurement, and monitoring of traffic. One important additional benefit is simplicity of the deployment, which has advantages in implementation and troubleshooting. The service provider can use the aggregated class model to ensure that the core requires no further QoS configuration changes after the initial deployment.

A properly designed and operated network with a cohesive QoS implementation based on aggregated classes and capacity planning methodology allows traffic with varying delivery requirements to be successfully transported across the network infrastructure. The interpretation of success in this context may be considered as meeting or exceeding the traffic requirements for latency, jitter, and packet loss.

14.3 Compromised Traffic Delivery

If there is a flaw in the existing implementations of QoS, it is lack of flexibility and adaptability specific to traffic flows. A traffic flow is generally defined as the flow between a source and destination device for a specific application. In modern IP networks, the priority of a traffic flow may be determined by the source (for example, a customer paying for a premium service), the destination (for example, a data center server with DNS), or the application (for example, voice or video versus email).

As mentioned, QoS relies on classifying traffic into a selection of classes based on DSCP, IP Prec, or MPLS EXP bits. As such there will be a level of compromise in the delivery of some traffic flows that do not fall directly into one of the predefined classes. For example, a specific interactive service might require SLAs that are not as strict as voice yet are more stringent than the next configured class. The service provider then needs to decide whether to burden the LLQ class with this traffic or to use the next available class, which could lead to poor application performance.

This compromise continues into areas of performance measurement, monitoring, and reporting. Performance tools, such as CBQoSMIB and IP SLA, will give measurement data according to classes rather than actual services traffic. Tools such as NetFlow can give insight into specific flows; however, linking this insight to specific customers is cumbersome.

14.4 Future Directions in the Deployment of QoS

The optimal IP network will recognize individual flows traffic flows and their associated traffic delivery requirements, which can include contracts with priority customers. The network will understand the topology, including bandwidth and link latency, as well as the current state of the network, including utilization, bit errors, and average availability. The network will route traffic based on all these parameters and will react to congestion by terminating individual flows or rejecting new flows rather than potentially compromising all traffic flows. Topology changes will lead to intelligent rerouting of traffic flows only as required rather than a full rebuild of routing tables and impact to all traffic.

This new network will also be capable of understanding SLAs to a point where routing, traffic prioritization, and call admission control decisions will be made based on average SLA parameter goals across a reporting period. For example, if failures in the network have placed a customer SLA contract in jeopardy of failing agreed goals over a reporting period of one month, the network will automatically elevate that customer traffic priority for traffic delivery. This prioritization will include using the highest availability path through the network, ensuring priority of the customer traffic flows over that path and protecting that path from issues such as packet loss due to network reconvergence.

This new approach requires a closer cooperation between the management platform and the routing network elements. The management platform combined with the network infrastructure must understand individual traffic flows in the context of SLA parameters as well as the specific network behavior, including bandwidth, link and device stability and availability, and any changes made over time.

With the advent of highly scalable, microcode and hardware-based ASICS, the potential for very granular and specific traffic treatment exists in the network environment. The inclusion of the Flow Label in IPv6 (explained on the following section) enables granular identification of traffic requirements at the sending device. Coupled with matching monitoring tools, a hybrid solution exists with a classification system for broadband and small and medium-sized business (SMB) and specific flow-based traffic treatment for any critical services such as voice, video, signaling, and premium customers. Deep packet inspection technologies such as

NBAR and Service Control Engines are further enhancing the networks' ability to allow this working model for network operators. Possibly the biggest gap exists in the integration of the management platforms with performance-monitoring tools and the elements of the network infrastructure.

An operating model encompassing accurate reporting, security attack detection and mitigation, fault identification, and capacity planning with accurate traffic treatment around SLA parameters, including packet loss, latency, and jitter, is possible with scalable, deep packet inspection and tools that understand traffic flows. ASIC technology will enable this model to scale in the SP environment.

14.5 The IPv6 Flow Label

RFC-3967 presents the concept of a flow label, intended to simplify the process of state establishment in routing devices. This RFC identifies situations in which the identification of a traditional flow (five-tuple of source address, destination address, ports, and protocol type) within a network may be difficult or impossible as a result of tunneling or encryption.

The IPv6 header is as shown in Figure 14.1.

The 8-bit traffic class field is used to set specific precedence or differentiated services code point (DSCP) values, allowing packets to be marked with different priorities. These values are used in the same manner as the IPv4 ToS or DSCP field.

IPv6 has a 20-bit field known as the *flow label*. The flow label is marked by the source node only. The flow label enables per-flow recognition for differentiation at the IP layer. According to the RFC, the flow label must not be modified by an intermediate node. The FRC recommends a three-tuple identification method using the flow label, the source address, and the destination address fields. This enables efficient IPv6 flow classification, relying only on basic IPv6 header fields in fixed positions within the packet.

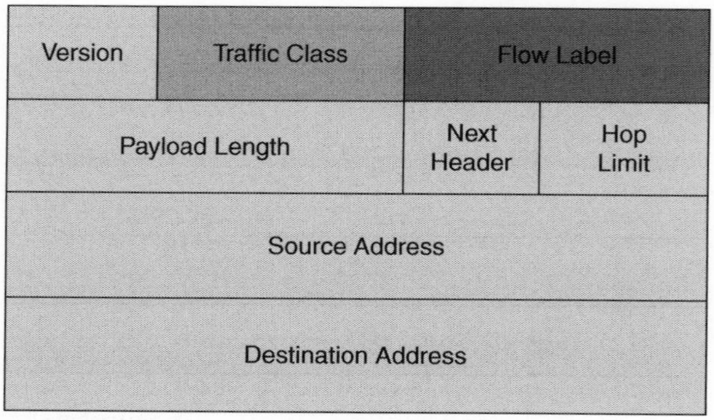

Figure 14.1: IPv6 Header

The key advantage of the three-tuple approach is that transit routers do not require processing of the inner packet to identify a flow, which reduces CPU burden, expensive hardware ASICs, and issues related to tunneling and encryption, as previously identified in the RFC.

This simple and scalable traffic flow classification method will allow effective and granular routing of traffic based on flows rather than simply the destination. More precise recognition and treatment of traffic requirements in terms of latency, delay, jitter, and packet loss will be possible when coupled with hardware capable of storing and processing state tables typical of large SP network nodes.

An interesting consideration for the flow label would be a definition of how the traffic flow needs to be treated to meet application requirements. Requirements such as envelopes for latency, jitter, packet loss, and packet order would enable first-hop and intermediate router nodes to understand and respond to the true requirements of the application. This would allow a flexible approach to new service overlay in constantly changing networks such as SPs operating NGN infrastructures.

14.6 Summary

The advent of the next-generation network carrying multiservice traffic is challenging the existing framework for QoS enforcement. The need for a new approach has evolved and is becoming technically possible with the advent of new technology.

An architecture with a tightly integrated management platform and traffic-forwarding infrastructure would allow a network capable of making decisions on individual traffic flows based on SLA contracts and network profile parameters.

Index

Printed and bound by CPI Group (UK) Ltd, Croydon, CR0 4YY
11/06/2025
01899189-0019